D1559292

Foundations of Casualty Actuarial Science

Casualty Actuarial Society
One Penn Plaza
250 West 34th Street
New York, NY 10119
(212) 560-1018

Copyright 1990 Casualty Actuarial Society
Printed by R&S Financial Printing
ISBN 0-9624762-0-X

PREFACE

This landmark book is the first published, complete text containing the fundamentals of casualty actuarial science as practiced in North America. It is intended as an introduction to casualty actuarial concepts and practices. Its target audiences are members and students of the Casualty Actuarial Society, university and college students, plus insurance and general business professionals with a need for basic knowledge on these topics.

In designing the textbook, the Casualty Actuarial Society concluded that the readership would be best served by having each chapter written by an expert in the topic covered by the chapter. Therefore, each chapter is individually authored and the styles and organization vary somewhat. The chapters reflect the views of the individual authors and the content should not be considered as the official opinion of the Casualty Actuarial Society.

The book would not have been possible, were it not for the dedication of the chapter authors, Steven P. D'Arcy, Robert J. Finger, Charles C. Hewitt, Jr., Charles L. McClenahan, Gary S. Patrik, Matthew Rodermund, Margaret W. Tiller, Gary G. Venter, and Ronald F. Wiser, who produced actual text and met the challenge of deadlines.

The development of this text is not solely attributable to the authors' efforts, however. To the many who have helped along the way, on behalf of the Textbook Steering Committee, I offer sincere thanks. At the risk of overlooking someone's contribution, I would like to thank those who have helped this project to its conclusion.

The genesis of this book was in 1969 with L.H. Longley-Cook, at the time he joined the faculty of Georgia State University. The end product of the effort is this text, *Foundations of Casualty Actuarial Science.* Along the way, the project was furthered through the successive leadership efforts of Charles C. Hewitt Jr., Richard L. Johe, W. James MacGinnittie, C.K. Khury, and Charles L. McClenahan. And, of course, there are those authors, especially Bernard L. Webb, whose efforts produced the predecessor draft chapters, known collectively as *Casualty Contingencies.*

Thanks also go to members of the Textbook Steering Committee, whose organization, planning, leadership, and follow-through brought this book to its publication: Donald T. Bashline, Lisa G. Chanzit, William R. Gillam, Richard A. Lino, and Edward P. Lotkowski. All of the work of the Textbook Steering Committee was done under the aegis of the Vice President—Development Charles A. Bryan to whom the committee owes much for his continued involvement and encouragement.

Each of the chapters was reviewed by an ad hoc panel of experts. The task of each panelist was to read a draft chapter, to note areas requiring editing, and to meet with the author at a group session to discuss the findings. Those unable to attend the meetings spent time on the telephone with authors or corresponded with them. Thanks go to: Nolan E. Asch, Steven D. Basson, Robert A. Bear, Paul J. Braithwaite, Charles A. Bryan, Jerome A. Degerness, James A. Faber, Patricia A. Furst, Robert A. Giambo, Owen M. Gleeson, Anthony J. Grippa, David N. Hafling, Philip E. Heckman, Charles C. Hewitt Jr., John J. Kollar, Howard C. Mahler, John S. McGuinness, Michael A. McMurray, Glenn G. Meyers, Michael J. Miller, Robert A. Miller III, Deborah M. Rosenberg, Alan I. Schwartz, Jane C. Taylor, Michael A. Walters, and Richard G. Woll.

Thanks also go to all those who offered their comments to the authors through special review sessions at meetings of the CAS. Each of the chapters was printed in draft form in the *Forum* and each author held an individual session at a CAS meeting to receive comments from the membership at large. I am unable to name these individuals, but I thank them heartily for their efforts nonetheless.

The penultimate effort on the book was the technical editing done by Alan Kennedy of the American Academy of Actuaries. His skilled hand may appear invisible to the reader, but its presence is much appreciated. And, finally, the actual printing of the text was accomplished through the efforts of the Editorial Committee, chaired by Eugene C. Connell, with Robert F. Lowe serving as editor of Special Publications.

It is the sincere hope of the Textbook Steering Committee that this textbook will serve its purpose well in the years to come. This is the first edition of what must be a living document. Undoubtedly, there will be continuous review, resulting in deletions, additions, and updates. I hope that this edition has started a process which will continue successfully over the years. It is my personal privilege to have been part of this process, at such an auspicious time.

Textbook Steering Committee
November 1989

Irene K. Bass, Chair
Steven D. Basson, Vice-Chair
Donald T. Bashline
Lisa G. Chanzit
William R. Gillam
Edward P. Lotkowski

CONTRIBUTORS

STEPHEN P. D'ARCY, Ph.D., Associate Professor of Finance at the University of Illinois at Urbana-Champaign, has won the Campus Award for Excellence in Undergraduate Teaching. He has served on the Governor's Task Force on Medical Malpractice and published papers on insurance and finance in the *Journal of Risk and Insurance, Proceedings* of the Casualty Actuarial Society, *Journal of Insurance Regulation* and *Journal of Business.* He also co-authored *The Financial Theory of Pricing Property-Liability Insurance Contracts.* He is a Fellow of the Casualty Actuarial Society and a Member of the American Academy of Actuaries.

ROBERT J. FINGER, Principal of the actuarial consulting firm William M. Mercer Meidinger Hansen, Incorporated, has written several papers for the *Proceedings* of the Casualty Actuarial Society and Casualty Actuarial Society *Discussion Paper Program*, including papers on ratemaking, reserving, and tax issues. He is a Fellow of the Casualty Actuarial Society, a Member of the American Academy of Actuaries, a Chartered Property and Casualty Underwriter, and a member of the State Bar of California.

CHARLES C. HEWITT, JR., President and CEO of Metropolitan Reinsurance Company prior to his retirement in 1985, is a past-president of the Casualty Actuarial Society and the author of numerous papers for the *Proceedings* of the Casualty Actuarial Society. Among these papers is "Credibility for Severity," for which he was the first person to be awarded the Dorweiler Prize. He is a Fellow of the Casualty Actuarial Society and a Member of the American Academy of Actuaries.

CHARLES L. MCCLENAHAN, Principal of the actuarial consulting firm William M. Mercer Meidinger Hansen, Incorporated, has written several papers and articles on various casualty actuarial topics. He is a Fellow of the Casualty Actuarial Society, an Associate of the Society of Actuaries and a Member of the American Academy of Actuaries.

GARY PATRIK, Senior Vice President and Actuary of North American Reinsurance Corporation, is the author of various articles for the *Proceedings* of the Casualty Actuarial Society, the Casualty Loss Reserve Seminar, and the IASA Proceedings. He assisted in the writing of *Loss Distributions* by Hogg and Klugman, and is a co-winner of the Michelbacher Prize and the Boleslaw Monic Fund Competition, both in 1980. He is a Fellow of the Casualty Actuarial Society, a Member of the American Academy of Actuaries, a Chartered Property and Casualty Underwriter, and a member of ASTIN.

MATTHEW RODERMUND, Vice President and Actuary of the Munich American Reinsurance Company for twenty years preceding his retirement in 1981, served as editor, from 1974 through 1989, of *The Actuarial Review*, newsletter of the Casualty Actuarial Society. He is a Fellow of the Casualty Actuarial Society and a Member of the American Academy of Actuaries.

MARGARET WILKINSON TILLER, President of Tiller Consulting Group, Inc., an actuarial and environmental risk consulting firm, is the lead author of the RM56 textbook, *Essentials of Risk Financing*, and has authored many articles in actuarial and risk management publications. She is a Fellow of the Casualty Actuarial Society, an Associate of the Society of Actuaries, a Member of the American Academy of Actuaries, a Member of the Conference of Actuaries in Public Practice, a Chartered Property and Casualty Underwriter and holds an Insurance Institute of America diploma of Associate in Risk Management. She is also a member of the International Actuarial Association and the International Association of Consulting Actuaries.

GARY G. VENTER, President of the Workers' Compensation Reinsurance Bureau, has authored numerous papers on credibility, loss distributions, and risk charges for insurance, which have appeared in the *Proceedings* of the Casualty Actuarial Society, *Insurance Mathematics and Economics*, ARCH, the Casualty Actuarial Society call paper program, the Casualty Actuarial Society Forum, Casualty Actuarial Society Syllabus study notes, and the National Council on Compensation Insurance *Digest*. He is a Fellow of the Casualty Actuarial Society, a Member of the American Academy of Actuaries, and a member of ASTIN, AFIR, and the International Actuarial Association.

RONALD M. WISER, Vice President of Progressive Casualty Insurance Company, is the author of several papers including "The Cost of Mixing Reinsurance" and "An Algorithm for Premium Adjustment with Scarce Data" which appeared in the *Proceedings* of the Casualty Actuarial Society. He has received both the Michelbacher and the Dorweiler prizes from the Casualty Actuarial Society. He is a Fellow of the Casualty Actuarial Society, an Associate of the Society of Actuaries, and a Member of the American Academy of Actuaries.

CONTENTS

Chapter 1
INTRODUCTION
by Matthew Rodermund

What It's All About

If it is agreed that an actuary is one who analyzes the current financial implications of future contingent events, then it might also be agreed that actuarial science concerns, first, the realistic perception of such contingent events and, second, the critical study of their current financial implications.

The foregoing definitions of the actuary and of actuarial science apply to all types of actuaries—life, health, pension, and casualty and property—but in different degrees and clothed in different perspectives. The future contingent events for life and pension actuaries involve, mostly, mortality, but life actuaries study the current financial implications of dying, and pension actuaries the financial implications of continued living. For health actuaries, the future contingent events are sickness and disability (with death as the extreme case), and they ponder the current financial implications of the need (by individuals and by the social order) for medical treatment and rehabilitation.

Surely, much can be written about the actuarial science of disciplines other than casualty and property insurance, but this book is about casualty actuarial science; to that discipline we will confine our remarks.

For casualty actuarial science (we will omit the word "property" for convenience, just as we do in the name of the Casualty Actuarial Society), the future contingent events are so widely varied that they cannot be described in a phrase. They may best be characterized by Murphy's Law: If it can happen, it will. The current financial implications of such events defy precise measurement. And classical probability procedures haven't helped much. That is why casualty actuaries must embrace a priori, or even intuitive, probabilities, in addition to experience indications, if they are to get on with their jobs.

The mention of probabilities reminds us to state the obvious, that probability theory (whether classical or Bayesian) forms the basis of actuarial science. If the actuaries hadn't had probability theory, they would have had to invent it. In "An Introduction to Credibility Theory," Laurence H. Longley-Cook (1962) quotes a statement by E. W. Phillips, from *Biometry of the Measurement of Mortality,* which is interesting because in 1935 it forecast as destiny for actuaries what was already rooted into their lives. It also foretold their future concerns:

> The calculus of probability is a fascinating subject, and one which is destined to play a large part in actuarial science; and a day may come when it can truly be said of the actuary that he has fused together the theories of finance and probability.

The Beginnings

It all began with the advent of workmen's (now *workers*) compensation. That statement holds for casualty actuarial science, and it holds for the Casualty Actuarial and Statistical Society of America (CASSA), which later became the Casualty Actuarial Society. The first constitutionally accepted state workmen's compensation law, passed in Wisconsin in 1911, began to excite interest among scattered members of both the Actuarial Society of America (mostly in the East) and the American Institute of Actuaries (mostly in the Midwest). Even before the New York State Workmen's Compensation Act was passed, in 1914, the interested actuaries (plus many people whose interest was not actuarial but either statistical or social or both—including, among the latter, I. M. Rubinow, the founder and first president of CASSA) had realized the need to establish a technically sound basis for this new "social" insurance. Out of this interest came the professional society that we have inherited.

Considerable work in ratemaking for employers liability insurance had been done in the late 1890s; it depended largely on loss ratio comparisons, and these were studied for about eight industrial classifications in each of several regions of the country. In 1909, a conference on workmen's compensation was held (in Atlantic City) at which papers by future charter members of CASSA were among those presented. In his book, *Social Insurance,* published in 1913,

Rubinow included a section on industrial accidents. In 1914, Albert H. Mowbray, who was to be one of the charter members of CASSA, presented to the Actuarial Society of America a paper on the criteria for testing the adequacy of rates for workmen's compensation insurance (1914a). At the same meeting, Harwood E. Ryan, also to be a CASSA charter member, delivered "A Method of Determining Pure Premiums for Workmen's Compensation Insurance" (1914).

On November 7 that same year, CASSA was born.

The new society tackled the workmen's compensation problems directly. Among the first (and it has ever been thus) was the question of how to use relatively scanty experience to make justifiable rates. The second paper in Volume I of the *Proceedings*, by Mowbray (clearly one of the giants at that time), was "How Extensive a Payroll Exposure Is Necessary To Give a Dependable Pure Premium?" (1914b). That paper represented the first formal introduction to the concept of credibility, the concept that the volume of past experience of a risk or class of risks is a considerable factor in the weight, or "credibility," to be given such experience in using it for ratemaking.

It is the concept of credibility that has been the casualty actuaries' most important and most enduring contribution to casualty actuarial science. Any list of the great contributors to casualty actuarial science would also be a list of those who developed and implemented the theories of credibility: Albert H. Mowbray, Albert W. Whitney, G. F. Michelbacher, Winfield W. Greene, Francis S. Perryman, Paul Dorweiler, Thomas O. Carlson, Arthur L. Bailey, Laurence H. Longley-Cook, Robert A. Bailey (Arthur Bailey's son), LeRoy J. Simon, Frank Harwayne, Lester B. Dropkin, Allen L. Mayerson, Charles C. Hewitt Jr., Hans Bühlmann (a Swiss actuary). If we have omitted names of others who have made comparable contributions, we are sorry. The foregoing are the ones who stand out in our memory.

Days To Remember

One of the memorable moments in the development of casualty actuarial science came in 1917, at a meeting of the Actuarial Section of the National Reference Committee on Workmen's Compensation

Insurance. The event is described in Albert Whitney's famous paper, "The Theory of Experience Rating," presented at the May 1918 CASSA meeting. According to Whitney, the committee—Winfield W. Greene, chairman; Albert H. Mowbray; Benedict D. Flynn; George D. Moore; and Joseph H. Woodward; all charter members and future presidents of the Society—was seeking to formulate a plan of experience rating of workmen's compensation risks.

The problem of experience rating, Whitney wrote, "arises out of the necessity of striking a balance between class experience on the one hand and risk experience on the other." Whitney's paper traced and analyzed verbally and mathematically the general line of reasoning pursued by the committee, which apparently had struggled at some length with the problem of the weight to be given risk experience, examining and rejecting many suggestions and assumptions. The committee used the term "credibility" and the notation Z to express this "weight," and sought to quantify it. Then Win Greene suggested that the relatively complicated second term of the denominator of an equation that the committee agreed summed up its thinking (No. 22 in Whitney's exposition) be taken as a constant. The development of his suggestion resulted in

$$Z = \frac{P}{P + K} .$$

Voila!

That formula (where P is exposure and K a constant), which underlies most of the credibility studies since then, has generally been attributed to Albert Whitney, because it first appeared and was analyzed in his paper (referred to above), but apparently it sprang out of the deliberations of the special actuarial committee on workmen's compensation, and, specifically, was one of Win Greene's suggestions.

Casualty actuarial science was born at that moment. The concept of credibility clearly has fascinated the casualty actuarial profession, and, later on, some of the life actuaries, who took it up mainly for group insurance.

In his 1918 paper on the theory of experience rating, Whitney explored the implications of the credibility concept contained in the statement of the Z formula. He recognized, for instance, that reasonable values of *K* would have to be determined by judgment, depending on underlying factors.

Such judgment considerations were treated by Michelbacher in "The Practice of Experience Rating," presented at the same 1918 CASSA meeting as the Whitney paper. It was quite a day for actuarial science. Michelbacher's paper complemented Whitney's, setting forth the development of a practical plan from the theoretical principles discussed by Whitney. In the plan, greater credibility was given to a greater amount of observable data. Workmen's compensation loss experience was divided into two groups—death and permanent total disability losses in one, all other losses in the second. Credibility factors were calculated separately for each group. In later years the losses were divided into three groups—serious, non-serious, and medical.

Whitney had assumed that inherent hazards differed among classifications of risks, and he assumed a knowledge of the distribution of such hazards; but in his mathematical development he, in effect, reversed his assumptions and fell back on Bayes's Rule, which, prior to Laplace's generalization, declared that, a priori, all possible events were equally likely. Whitney's efforts were criticized, but he was aware that the casualty actuaries had practical problems of statistical estimation to attend to—specifically, reliable and marketable ratemaking where classical statistics didn't provide acceptable answers—and he pursued his own line of study.

Among the other practical problems confronting actuaries was finding a way to establish full credibility. The Z formula didn't allow full credibility, but there were many buyers of workmen's compensation insurance who insisted that they should be rated solely on their own experience. How this problem has been resolved over the years, in many lines of insurance, in many kinds of experience and retrospective rating, and in classification rating, is one of the great stories in casualty actuarial science, and is covered in the various chapters of this book.

Retrospective Rating

Albert Whitney, who developed the theory of experience rating, had also shown an early interest in retrospective rating, and he passed along his interest to Paul Dorweiler, his understudy in the National Workmen's Compensation Service Bureau. Retrospective rating, which was explored, described, and refined by Dorweiler in the 1920s, 1930s, and 1940s (Dorweiler 1927, 1933, 1936, 1941), and also by other well-known actuaries in the 1940s, was the next—after experience rating—important contribution to the methodologies of casualty actuarial science by members of the Society.

It was a rating scheme applied on top of experience rating, and it permitted workmen's compensation risks whose estimated premiums were greater than certain specified minimums to limit their final retrospective premiums, depending on losses, to amounts between preselected maximum and minimum percentages of the audited premiums. Obviously, risks whose loss records were better than average could save on their workmen's compensation costs, first prospectively through experience rating, then at policy expiration through retrospective rating. Insurance charges in the retro plan protected the insurance company against the probability that the risk, because of high losses, would exceed the preselected maximum premium; and there was a saving from the excess charge to recognize the probability that, because of low losses, the calculated retrospective premium would be less than the minimum.

Again the credibility concept, in which the measurement of risk is related to the volume of experience, came into play, because the charges and savings were higher for small premium accounts than for large. Originally there were several tabular retrospective rating plans whose maximum and minimum premium percentages were specified for varying sizes of risk, the range between the maximum and minimum percentages being less for small risks than for large. Another plan (Plan D, so-called) was created for risks that preferred to select their own maximums and minimums. Moreover, Plan D made it possible to combine large workmen's compensation and liability insurance risks in a single rating scheme, which applied also on an interstate basis. The table from which insurance companies calculated the excess charges and the savings for Plan D, once called "Table M"—now "The Table of Insurance Charges"—is one of the more esoteric features of the casualty insurance rating scheme.

At any rate, retrospective rating was not widely used in the 1930s and early 1940s. One of the reasons was that large mutual carriers were strongly opposed to it because they had their own dividend schemes to reward better than average risks. The use of retrospective rating expanded during the war years, especially in war-related industries. Although stock companies were the principal writers, the mutuals, which insured many large workmen's compensation risks, became more receptive to the idea. In December 1948, a plan developed by the New York Compensation Insurance Rating Board (accepted by mutual as well as stock companies) was approved by the New York Superintendent of Insurance. Since then retrospective rating has played a major role countrywide in workmen's compensation and liability insurance. And Paul Dorweiler is still considered its actuarial father.

An Actuary To Remember

It would not be proper, in the introduction to a book on casualty actuarial science, to fail to give recognition to the contributions of Arthur L. Bailey. His papers in the *Proceedings*, from 1942 through 1950, give such a solid foundation to casualty actuarial concepts that today they underlie all other sources of basic reading required of those who aspire to the actuarial profession. His 1950 paper, even in its hefty title, "Credibility Procedures—Laplace's Generalization of Bayes' Rule and the Combination of Collateral Knowledge with Observed Data" (1950a), goes to the heart of the casualty actuarial endeavor. Be warned, however, that its technical content is not easy reading.

In addition to his mathematical brilliance—and in spite of it—Arthur Bailey had a way of presenting ideas so lucidly that even lay people could get his message. Some of Bailey's words about the actuary and his work are remarkably simple and direct. For example, in his 1942 paper, "Sampling Theory in Casualty Insurance," he said:

> Thus the losses paid by an insurer never actually reflect the hazard covered, but are always an isolated sample of all possible amounts of losses which might have been incurred. It is this condition, of never being able to determine, even from hindsight, what the exact value of the inherent coverage was, that has brought the actuary into being.

Again, from "Credibility Procedures," Bailey's 1950 paper cited above, speaking of the need for different schedules of credibility for different components, and even for different intervals, of workmen's compensation losses:

> The trained statistician cries, "Absurd! Directly contrary to any of the accepted theories of statistical estimation." The actuaries themselves have to admit that they have gone beyond anything that has been proven mathematically, that all of the values involved are still selected on the basis of judgment, and that the only demonstration they can make is that, in actual practice, it works. Let us not forget, however, that they have made this demonstration many times. It does work!

In a discussion in the *Journal of the American Teachers of Insurance* (1950b), Bailey stated, on the differences in philosophy of the casualty actuary and the classical statistician:

> First, there is the belief of casualty underwriters that they are not devoid of knowledge before they have acquired any statistics. This belief is probably held by operating personnel in all businesses. When a new form of insurance is initiated or a new classification or territory established, there may be a considerable variety in the opinion of individual underwriters as to what the rates should be; but the consensus of opinion invariably produces a rate. This rate soon becomes embedded in the minds of the underwriters as the "right" rate. Later, when statistics as to the actual losses under the new coverage, classification or territory, finally are acquired, the problem is not "what should the rate have been?" but "how much should the existing rate be changed as a result of the factors observed?" In revisions of rates for regular coverages, classes and territories, this is always the question.
>
> The statistical methods, developed by the mathematicians and available in the standard textbooks on statistical procedures, deal with the evaluation of the indications of a group of observations, but under the tacit or implicit assumption that no knowledge existed prior to the making of those particular observations. The credibility procedures, used in the revisions of casualty rates, have been developed by casualty actuaries to give consistent weightings to additional knowledge in its combination with already existing knowledge.

Writing of such clarity does not often appear in our literature. Would that it did, because the casualty actuary needs to relate ever more closely to the public he or she serves.

Tom Carlson, another eminent actuary, in a 1964 presentation to the International Congress of Actuaries, said that Arthur Bailey was "probably the most profound contributor to casualty actuarial theory the United States has produced." Whether or not Arthur Bailey is mentioned specifically in the diverse chapters of this book, it is certain that much of the thought expressed in those chapters will have had its foundation in his contributions.

Credibility and the Private Passenger Car

Roughly ten years after Arthur Bailey's studies, interest grew in the possibility of rating private passenger automobile policies on the basis of individual driving records. In 1959, Robert Bailey and LeRoy Simon presented a paper—"An Actuarial Note on the Credibility of Experience of a Single Private Passenger Car"—that affected actuarial science profoundly, not only in the United States, but also in Europe. In the same year, Frank Harwayne wrote "Merit Rating in Private Passenger Automobile Liability Insurance and the California Driver Record Study," in which he suggested that the negative binomial distribution is preferable to the Poisson as a description of risk distributions by numbers of accidents. Thereupon, Lester Dropkin prepared "Some Considerations on Automobile Rating Systems Utilizing Individual Driving Records" (1959), expanding and developing the advantages of the negative binomial as a tool in rating private passenger cars.

The following year, LeRoy Simon's paper, "The Negative Binomial and Poisson Distributions Compared" (1960), indicated that the Poisson distribution underestimates the probability of the number of accidents that will be experienced by one car or a fleet of cars. It turned out that the negative binomial concept, for all its actuarial brilliance, was an enigma to all but a handful of CAS members; and Harwayne, Dropkin, Simon, and Charlie Hewitt (whose 1960 paper applied the negative binomial to Canadian auto experience) and

Tom Carlson (whose "Negative Binomial Rationale" appeared in 1962) were regarded with awe—and amused toleration.

In the same year as the Simon paper, Dropkin wrote "Automobile Merit Rating and Inverse Probabilities" (1960), in which he developed a general expression for the probability of x accidents in subsequent years, knowing that a specified number of accidents had occurred in a given time period. Inverse probability—a priori probability—was the key, and thus the solution was afforded through Bayes's theorem.

All seven of the papers cited lean heavily on the theories of credibility that had been developed in previous years. To that extent the influence of the credibility concept in casualty actuarial science was again demonstrated. Moreover, in private passenger car rating, exposure and loss frequencies were small compared to those available in workmen's compensation and liability experience rating and classification rating. The utility of the credibility concept was greatly expanded.

A Scientific Oasis

In 1962, a great boon was afforded to members and students of the Casualty Actuarial Society when Laurence H. Longley-Cook presented his monograph, "An Introduction to Credibility Theory." In relatively simple and concise terms, Longley-Cook brought together the essentials of the concept of credibility that had been developed since Whitney. The treatise unraveled a lot of the mystery that had troubled many actuaries who realized how vital the subject was but hadn't taken the time, or lacked the capacity, to pore through the profound and technically challenging writings that had accumulated in the *Proceedings*.

But Longley-Cook had a reassuring word for those who worried that their relative inexpertise in credibility theory might adversely affect their own actuarial skills:

> It is perhaps necessary to stress that credibility procedures are not a substitute for informed judgment, but an aid thereto. Of necessity so many practical considerations must enter into any actuarial work that the student cannot substitute

the blind application of a credibility formula for the careful consideration of all aspects of an actuarial problem.

Closing the Credibility Gap

We have seen that the concept of credibility was used in casualty actuarial ratemaking procedures for both commercial and personal insurance. But the theoretical justification for such use differed considerably from the basic tenets of classical statistical theory. Quoting Arthur Bailey again (1950a):

> There have been rare instances of rebellion against this [classical statistical] philosophy by practical statisticians who have insisted that they actually had a considerable store of knowledge apart from the specific observations being analyzed. Philosophers have recently discussed the credibilities to be given to various elements of knowledge, thus undermining the accepted philosophy of the statisticians. However, it appears to be only in the actuarial field that there has been an organized revolt against discarding all prior knowledge when an estimate is to be made using newly acquired data.

Allen L. Mayerson, in his 1964 paper, "A Bayesian View of Credibility," bridged this gap between casualty actuarial practice and statistical theory. He pointed, first, to outstanding books by Savage in 1954, Schlaifer in 1959, and Raiffa and Schlaifer in 1961, which in effect rebelled against the classical approach and saluted a trend toward the use of prior knowledge for statistical inference. And he referred to advances that had been made in probability and stochastic processes. Those advances resulted in mathematical techniques that lend themselves to the solution of actuarial problems—techniques that can more easily be used by actuaries. In his paper, Mayerson's purpose was "to attempt to continue the work started 15 years ago by Bailey, and, using modern probability concepts, try to develop a theory of credibility which will bridge the gap that now separates the actuarial from the statistical world." And "to summarize the Bayesian point of view, to show its relevance to credibility theory, and to express credibility concepts in terms which are meaningful to a mathematical statistician."

Mayerson proceeded to do exactly what he promised. In the conclusion of a review of this paper in the 1965 *PCAS*, Charles C. Hewitt Jr. said:

> This is one of the most significant papers presented to this Society in many years and, happily, should produce much controversy and further thought in this important area. European actuaries have outstripped us in the classical "theory of risk." Professor Mayerson has distilled the essence of American achievement in the areas of credibility and the Bayesian approach.

Credibility and Severity

Neither Mayerson nor Hewitt was totally satisfied. The credibility studies of Albert Whitney and Arthur Bailey had involved the distribution of the number of claims alone, ignoring the distribution of claim amounts. Bailey had said (1950a):

> In casualty insurance, the inherent hazard of an insured, or of a classification of insureds, is the product of an inherent frequency of loss occurrence and an inherent average amount of loss. . . . At the present time there is little or no knowledge as to the correlation between frequencies of loss and average loss amounts in casualty insurance. It is the hope of this writer that someone with a knowledge of the statistical behavior of [such] products will undertake the development of the appropriate procedure.

Of course Mayerson and Hewitt were aware that Francis Perryman, as far back as 1932, had developed a formula for full credibility of the pure premium (the pure premium is the product of the claim frequency and the average claim amount), and that in 1962 Longley-Cook had developed the same formula in slightly different form. But Perryman and Longley-Cook had assumed that both the claim frequency and the average claim cost are normally distributed. Mayerson and Hewitt believed that such an assumption is not necessary, that credibility tables can be derived from actual data. So they accepted Bailey's challenge. In 1968 Mayerson, with the collaboration of Donald A. Jones and Newton L. Bowers Jr., fellow professors of mathematics at the University of Michigan, presented "On the Credibility of the Pure Premium," and in 1970 Hewitt presented "Credibility for Severity."

Mayerson et al developed formulas that indicated that the number of claims required for full credibility of the pure premium is considerably more than the number required for full credibility of the claim frequency. The paper "attempted to supply a basis for more accurate and scientific credibility tables. . . . If losses by size data were available for various coverages, both countrywide and state, it would be possible to calculate the full credibility point for each coverage and state."

Hewitt's paper brought to attention the enormous contribution that Hans Bühlmann had made to basic credibility theory (1967). In addition, Hewitt employed a clever analogy to a casualty insurance situation by using the roll of two dice to indicate frequency and two six-slot spinners to indicate severity. With those he was able to apply credibility concepts to combinations of frequency, severity, and their product—pure premium. The paper concluded that, as expected, "Credibility is greatest when severity is ignored entirely (as has been the case in the past)." When the sizes of claims are introduced, a degree of credibility is obtained by limiting the values at which losses enter the rating; but as the limits are increased and more of the value of the individual claims enters the rating, the credibility decreases. It reaches a fixed value when all loss amounts are included.

Reserves

The concept of credibility is fundamental to all aspects of casualty actuarial science. In ratemaking, the credibility of loss experience is of course basic; but the experience includes reserves for unpaid losses, and in the 1970s and 1980s the credibility of the reserves alone became a matter of increasing concern. Such concern was directed only partly at the effect of the reserves on the reasonableness of the rates; it was also directed quite pointedly at the effect of the reserves on the financial position of the company issuing the rates.

Here the practitioner of casualty actuarial science walks a fine line indeed. His competence is questioned by the marketplace if it believes he sets the reserves so high that rates are unaffordable; by his own production department if rates are seen as unsalable; by his CEO if profits are unreachable; by the IRS if taxes turn out to be negligible. On the other hand, the actuary's competence is also questioned if his CEO, or his own auditors, or the state auditors, believe the reserves are too low to discharge future contingent liabilities. The actuary's lot is not a happy one.

Happy or not, he must evaluate the credibility of the development of losses and of all the available ancillary information that affects the reserves. He will draw on whatever casualty actuarial science he has mastered. Of course, his knowledge of Bayesian principles and other actuarial techniques is not his only tool in the reserving process. Mastery of casualty actuarial science implies not only familiarity, but also limited expertise, in economics, finance, demographics, engineering, law, medicine, ecology, what else—it sounds frightening. But if he is indeed one who analyzes the current financial implications of future contingent events, he can't afford to be solely a mathematician.

Reinsurance

It was the 1960s before casualty actuaries became involved in reinsurance, and it was the 1970s before reinsurance companies in large numbers decided it was useful to have casualty actuaries around. But the services that actuaries have rendered in reinsurance have been more visible in financial areas than in underwriting and rating. The sharp inflation in the United States in the 1970s caused reinsurance managers serious concern about their reserves. In excess of loss reinsurance (which predominates in the casualty business), most of the losses are big ones and of types that take a long time to settle. Inflation made any book of casualty excess of loss reserves suspect, and actuaries were brought in to employ whatever scientific methods they had available to establish adequate reserves.

Unfortunately, in many instances the actuarial calculations suggested such large increases in reserves that their use would have seriously threatened the policyholders surplus of the reinsurers. That in turn would have brought low ratings by A.M. Best, the financial watchdog of the industry. Reinsurers with low ratings from Best cannot compete in the marketplace. The result was that actuarially produced reserves were not always accepted by management. Many reinsurance operations failed during the late 1970s and early 1980s. Those that survived were aided considerably by large investment earnings from the high interest rates that accompanied the inflation. The companies that used the reserves their actuaries recommended showed huge underwriting losses, but investment earnings kept them in business.

Casualty actuarial science has not been employed to any great extent (at least until recently) in reinsurance rating. In 1952, long before actuaries became part of the reinsurance picture, L.H. Longley-Cook prepared for the CAS *Proceedings* "A Statistical Study of Large Fire Losses with Application to a Problem in Catastrophe Insurance." Catastrophe reinsurance in property lines is usually on an excess of loss basis, but covers losses by wind (tornado, hurricane) as well as losses by fire. Longley-Cook's paper was not applicable to wind losses, but it should have been useful to fire underwriters at the time, because it gave them a guide to determining a premium for a broad cover when the premium for some other cover (a lower layer, for example) had been established.

The principal reason that actuarial science has had little impact in pricing reinsurance contracts is that the pricing process usually consists of a bargaining session between the reinsurance underwriter and the client. All the participants are generally well-informed, they are favored with a high degree of integrity, and their negotiations are conducted in a spirit of free and open competition. In a paper presented in 1972, "Actuarial Applications in Catastrophe Reinsurance," LeRoy Simon suggested that "One of the important contributions that the actuary can make to the reinsurance field is the maintenance of logical consistency among the various alternatives that may be considered at different stages of the negotiation process." He mentioned contract modifications that might be discussed, such as altering the retention, changing the thickness of the layer, or subdividing the layer. In his paper he set up mathematical models that implied the actuarial relationships among such alternatives.

Another notable contribution to actuarial science in reinsurance was the 1977 paper by Robert S. Miccolis, "On the Theory of Increased Limits and Excess of Loss Pricing." Like Simon, Miccolis created a mathematical model that he hoped would be helpful in making pricing judgments or evaluating such judgments. Sometimes the *evaluation* of reinsurance pricing judgments is as close as the actuary gets to the nitty-gritty of the reinsurance business.

Pro rata reinsurance has little need for actuarial input, principally because the main element of judgment concerns the commission rate, and that usually turns out to be a compromise of the difference between the expense loadings of the client and those of the reinsurer. Frequently the parties agree to a sliding-scale commission rate, which is inversely related to loss ratio. Actuarial expertise is not customarily needed for such an agreement.

Actuaries also get involved in deep financial analyses of ceding companies, as well as of reinsurers. Here, elements of ruin theory come into play, an area in which European actuaries have specialized. In periods of high inflation, especially, mathematical analyses of the risks involved in various underwriting and financial commitments are vital for the well-being, not only of the insurers and reinsurers, but also of the general public, which relies on their services.

Nevertheless, in spite of the limited efforts that actuaries can make in the reinsurance business, it's the uncertainties of the business that are fascinating, that stir the imagination to greater exploration. Whether or not new discoveries are to be made, it's a fun game.

Classifications—and Politics

In the 1980s, the problems of reserving have almost dwarfed the problems of ratemaking. Company actuaries and board and bureau actuaries today have a good idea how to produce rates for primary coverages, assuming the possession of experience of some degree of credibility. But, aside from the reserving, a new factor, one that actuaries used not to worry about unduly, has entered ratemaking considerations: classification distinctions. Actuaries used to take it for granted that fairness in ratemaking demanded homogeneous classifications with similar risk characteristics. It seemed reasonable, for example, that since women as a class live longer than men, their life insurance rates should be lower, their annuity rates higher. If young unmarried female drivers under a certain age have significantly better accident records than unmarried males of the same age, then the automobile insurance rates for the young women should be lower. If the mistakes of surgeons and obstetricians and anesthetists cause more physical disability than those of internists and dermatologists, higher malpractice insurance premiums for the more serious offenders are reasonable.

Today the casualty actuarial scientist must add considerations of politics and sociology to the areas of necessary knowledge we have mentioned. Yet, such considerations are really not new. Many years ago, life insurance actuaries agreed that black men and women would not be rated higher than whites, even though mortality studies clearly showed lower longevity for black people as a class. Politically, rating according to experience indications, in this situation, was not feasible. Underwriters and actuaries eventually recognized that the different mortality indications resulted probably from economic conditions, so that the indicated experience distinctions were not really related to color, but rather to relative affluence. Presumably, mortality for whites is also affected by relative affluence. Thus, although the decision not to differentiate between blacks and whites was political, it actually reflected an inability to classify all lives according to more realistic guidelines.

Many of the classification problems in life and automobile insurance are now political and social. Apparently some feminists are willing to pay higher insurance costs in order to eliminate what they regard as sexist discrimination. For actuaries, the resolution of the argument simply involves combining classifications that they had formerly regarded as independently ratable. The inherent factors that truly cause the female experience to be different from the male are not easily classifiable. Actuaries have been unable to set up new risk classifications that could be equally applicable to women and men.

The political-social dilemma for actuaries (principally for life and health actuaries) has been sharply exemplified in the epidemic of acquired immunodeficiency syndrome (AIDS). The natural inclination is to establish a separate classification for those who are found to have the AIDS virus. For many reasons, however, some politicians and segments of the public have resisted insurance company use of the AIDS blood test. Actuarial science, in what looks like an actuarial problem, has not been a strong factor.

The problems in malpractice and other liability lines are not only political, but also legal and economic and social. Here the solutions are not as easy as for the female-male issue. Society needs the protection from liability losses that insurance once afforded but no longer affords willingly—at least in some areas of coverage. The necessary resolution of this troubling situation will come probably from the combined efforts of government, industry (insurance and other), and the legal and medical professions. For our purposes, the important fact is that casualty actuarial science must henceforth include political and social realities in its already widening scope.

The Need in Other Fields

The ever-widening scope of casualty actuarial science requires that its rationales be part of the equipment of any individual organization or institution whose successful operation depends on a realistic evaluation of "future contingent events." Clearly, no insurance organization can afford to be unaware of the concept of credibility, and the same should be true of the growing profession of risk management, now that risk retention legislation is on the scene. Dependence on data that does not necessarily indicate what its compilers claim for it is one of the hazards of risk management, as it is of insurance. A little research would surely uncover instances of failure—or near failure—of a venture mainly because of a careless evaluation of future contingent events. For example, a more cautious evaluation of future events in the oil industry might have spared the Continental Illinois Bank its troubles in 1984 by limiting its lending ventures.

Actuarial techniques are being applied in the investment business to a greater extent than ever before. The employment of actuaries by investment houses for the analysis of companies as investment prospects is becoming more common. And although governmental institutions in their regulatory capacity may only infrequently apply scientific techniques, most regulators, in the exercise of their oversight responsibilities, certainly are aware that the techniques exist.

Is That All It Is?

The opening paragraphs of this introduction are headed "What It's All About." Readers who have come this far may conclude from what they've read that casualty actuarial science is the study and application of the theory of credibility, and that's all. Is it all? One might ask, what about the theory of probability? Probability, of course, is part of classical statistical theory, and the record shows that classical statistical theory alone has not provided the tools necessary adequately to measure risk in any line of insurance, including life. Bayes, and then Laplace, added a different dimension to the classical theory. Out of that dimension came the basis for the theory of credibility.

Insurance is a risk business, which is required to price its product before it knows what its costs will be. The theory of credibility has made the most significant contribution to quantifying the risk aspects of the insurance product, and thus qualifies as the dominant factor in casualty actuarial science.

How about the theory of risk? European actuaries, and many professors of mathematics and statistics in the United States, have been studying and writing about the theory of risk for years; but only recently have American actuaries actively pursued it. The Casualty Actuarial Society established a Committee on Theory of Risk in 1977; and the committee has been presenting risk theoretic issues in forums and panel discussions, recommending readings on risk theory for the *Syllabus*, and compiling a bibliography. So far, relatively few papers on issues in risk theory have been presented to the Society. Although risk theory, by definition, connotes the idea of insurance, its students have not, to any great extent, offered ideas — actuarial or otherwise — for implementing its principles. It seems as though, in a practical sense, risk theory still stands on the shoulders of the theory of credibility.

Casualty actuarial science may also be thought to include the development of the methodologies of classification rating, experience rating, retrospective rating, and other rating schemes; but in our opinion the fundamentals of ratemaking stem from the theory of credibility, and the methodologies are a matter of applying the agreed-upon principles to the data at hand. We point to the various tables used in rating—credibility tables for classification rating, tables of primary and excess losses, and other implements of experience and retrospective rating, such as D ratios, K values, B values, W values, Table M; their creation is a skilled actuarial function, but we're not sure it is properly includible as a basic aspect of casualty actuarial science. Rather, it is an operation that puts to practical use the theoretical concepts of actuarial science.

Closing Thoughts

Thus, casualty actuarial science has come a long way from its tentative beginnings in workmen's compensation insurance in 1914. Not only has the technology expanded, but the need for the technology has expanded. It is hoped this textbook will contribute to the comprehension of actuarial science by members and students of the Casualty Actuarial Society, and by outsiders who are being drawn into the actuarial world whether they planned it or not.

Quotations from the presidential address of Francis S. Perryman in 1939 are appropriate to close an introduction to this casualty actuarial science textbook. The first was used by Laurence H. Longley-Cook at the conclusion of his monograph on credibility theory in 1962; and the second was quoted by Dudley M. Pruitt at the end of his monumental paper, "The First Fifty Years," in 1964. We unhesitatingly re-use them here, because more than twenty-five years later we find Mr. Perryman's words to be even wiser and more prescient than the Messrs. Longley-Cook and Pruitt probably imagined:

> . . . the business finds itself with still a large number of problems on its hands, many of which we know the actuary will eventually have to solve. Let him, therefore—the casualty actuary about whom I have been talking—continue to grapple with these problems, knowing full well that he has an enormous advantage in the possession of a scientific mind and of scientific methods; with these he will, on his merits, be called on to play a larger and most responsible part in the business of casualty insurance (1939:294).

His (the actuary's) will be the privilege of using his knowledge and experience, his actuarial tools and methods, so as to solve our modern social problems, our problems of living together in harmony and cooperativeness; for this is sure, that such problems will be solved and they can be dealt with only by scientific methods that are in essence those we use and know as our actuarial ones (1939:296).

References

Bailey, Arthur L. 1942. Sampling theory in casualty insurance. *PCAS* 29:50.

—-. 1950a. Credibility procedures—Laplace's generalization of Bayes' rule and the combination of collateral knowledge with observed data. *PCAS* 37:7.

—-. 1950b. *Journal of the American Teachers of Insurance*. 17:24.

Bailey, Robert A., and Simon, LeRoy J. 1959. An actuarial note on the credibility of experience of a single private passenger car. *PCAS* 46:159.

Bühlmann, Hans. 1967. Experience rating and credibility. *ASTIN Bulletin* 4:199.

Carlson, T. O. 1962. Negative binomial rationale. *PCAS* 49:177.

—-. 1964. Observations on casualty insurance rate making theory in the United States. *Transactions of the 17th International Congress of Actuaries* 541.

Dorweiler, Paul. 1927. Observations on making rates for excess compensation insurance. *PCAS* 13:154; also *PCAS* 20 (1933), *PCAS* 23 (1936), and *PCAS* 28 (1941).

Dropkin, Lester B. 1959. Some considerations on automobile rating systems utilizing individual driving records. *PCAS* 46:165.

—-. 1960. Automobile merit rating and inverse probabilities. *PCAS* 47:37.

Harwayne, Frank. 1959. Merit rating in private passenger automobile liability insurance and the California driver record study. *PCAS* 46:189.

Hewitt, Charles C., Jr. 1960. The negative binomial applied to the Canadian merit rating plan for individual automobile risks. *PCAS* 47:55.

—-. 1965. Discussion on Mayerson's A Bayesian view of credibility. *PCAS* 52:127

—-. 1970. Credibility for severity. *PCAS* 57:148.

Longley-Cook, L. H. 1952. A statistical study of large fire losses with application to a problem in catastrophe reinsurance. *PCAS* 39:77.

—-. 1962. An introduction to credibility theory. *PCAS* 49:195.

Mayerson, Allen L. 1964. A Bayesian view of credibility. *PCAS* 51:85.

Mayerson, Allen L., Jones, Donald A., and Bowers, Newton L., Jr. 1968. On the credibility of the pure premium. *PCAS* 55:175.

Michelbacher, G. F. 1918. The practice of experience rating. *PCAS* 4:293.

Miccolis, Robert S. 1977. On the theory of increased limits and excess of loss pricing. *PCAS* 64:27.

Mowbray, Albert H. 1914a. Criteria for testing the adequacy of rates for workmen's compensation insurance. *TASA* 15:89.

—-. 1914b. How extensive a payroll exposure is necessary to give a dependable pure premium? *PCAS* 1:24.

Perryman, Francis S. 1932. Some notes on credibility. *PCAS* 19:65.

—-. 1939. "The Casualty Actuary" (Presidential Address). *PCAS* 25:294, 296.

Phillips, E. W. 1935. *Biometry of the measurement of mortality.* Privately published.

Pruitt, Dudley M. 1964. The first fifty years. *PCAS* 51:179.

Raiffa, Howard, and Schlaifer, Robert. 1961. *Applied statistical decision theory.* Cambridge: Harvard University Press.

Rubinow, I. M. 1913. *Social insurance.* New York: Henry Holt & Co.

Ryan, H. E. 1914. A method of determining pure premiums for workmen's compensation insurance. *TASA* 15:364.

Savage, Leonard J. 1954. *The foundations of statistics.* New York: John Wiley & Sons.

Schlaifer, Robert. 1959. *Probability and statistics for business decisions.* New York: McGraw-Hill.

Simon, LeRoy J. 1960. The negative binomial and Poisson distributions compared. *PCAS* 47:20.

—-. 1972. Actuarial applications in catastrophe reinsurance. *PCAS* 59:196.

Whitney, Albert W. 1918. The theory of experience rating. *PCAS* 4:274.

Chapter 2
RATEMAKING
by Charles L. McClenahan

Introduction

The Concept of Manual Ratemaking

From the earliest days of marine insurance, premium charges have been based upon specific characteristics of the individual risk being priced. Lloyd's of London based early hull rates in part upon the design and protection of each specific ship, and the classification assigned to each vessel was written down in a book or **manual** for use by the individual underwriters. Eighteenth century dwelling fire insurance rates in the U.S. were based upon roof type and basic construction. While these early rate manuals were meant to provide general guidance to the underwriters in setting the specific rates, rather than the actual rates to be charged, they contained many of the elements associated with present-day property and liability rate manuals including recognition of differing loss costs between classifications, expense provision, and provision for adverse deviation and profit.

One of the most persistent misconceptions associated with property and liability insurance is the level of accuracy which actuaries are believed to achieve in the assessment of individual loss propensity. Over the years, as the doctrine of *caveat emptor* has been eroded and insurance risks have become increasingly complex, rate manuals have evolved to the point that, for many lines of insurance, they provide the exact premium to be charged for providing a specific coverage to a specific risk for a specific period. It is important, however, not to confuse the level of precision inherent in the rate manual with the level of accuracy. The latter will be judged in the cold light of actual loss experience. No matter how refined the classification and rating process may become, manual rates are still **estimates of average costs** based upon a combination of statistical methods and professional judgment.

This chapter will deal with the basic actuarial methods and assumptions underlying the development of manual rates. While a complete treatment of the subject might well fill several books, the key elements will be covered to such an extent that the reader of this chapter will gain an understanding of the basic actuarial concepts and techniques involved in the review and analysis of manual rates for property and liability coverages.

Basic Terminology

While ratemaking is neither pure science nor pure art, both the scientific and artistic elements of the subject demand the use of precise language. Property and casualty insurance is a complicated business which can be best represented and understood in a technical financial context. Many of the misconceptions about property and liability insurance can be directly attributed to either the failure to use precise terminology, or the failure to understand the terminology in precise terms. This section will introduce some definitions of some of the more important terms used by casualty actuaries.

Exposure

The basic rating unit underlying an insurance premium is called an **exposure.**The unit of exposure will vary based upon the characteristics of the insurance coverage involved. For automobile insurance, one automobile insured for a period of twelve months is a car year. A single policy providing coverage on three automobiles for a six month term would involve 1.5 car years. The most commonly used exposure statistics are **written exposures,** those units of exposures on policies written during the period in question, **earned exposures,** the exposure units actually exposed to loss during the period, and **in-force exposures,** the exposure units exposed to loss at a given point in time. In order to illustrate these three statistics, consider the following four twelve-month, single-car automobile policies:

Effective Date	Written Exposure 1987	Written Exposure 1988	Earned Exposure 1987	Earned Exposure 1988	In-Force Exposure 1/1/88
1/1/87	1.00	0.00	1.00	0.00	0.00
4/1/87	1.00	0.00	0.75	0.25	1.00
7/1/87	1.00	0.00	0.50	0.50	1.00
10/1/87	1.00	0.00	0.25	0.75	1.00
Total	4.00	0.00	2.50	1.50	3.00

Note that the in-force exposure counts a full car year for each twelve-month policy in force as of 1/1/88, regardless of the length of the remaining term.

The specific exposure unit used for a given type of insurance depends upon several factors, including reasonableness, ease of determination, responsiveness to change, and historical practice.

Reasonableness—it is obvious that the exposure unit should be a reasonable measure of the exposure to loss. While every exposure unit definition compromises this principle to some degree—for example a 1988 Rolls Royce and a 1978 Chevrolet might each represent a car year exposure—the selected measure should directly relate to loss potential to the extent possible.

Ease of Determination—the most reasonable and responsive exposure definition is of no use if it cannot be accurately determined. While the most appropriate exposure for products liability insurance might be the number of products currently in use, this number would generally be impossible to determine. If an exposure base is not subject to determination, then an insurer can never be assured of receiving the proper premium for the actual exposure.

Responsiveness to Change—an exposure unit which reflects changes in the exposure to loss is preferable to one which does not. The exposure unit for workers' compensation insurance, which provides benefits which are keyed to average wagelevels, is payroll. This is obviously preferable to number of employees, for example, as the payroll will change with the prevailing wage levels.

Historical Practice—where a significant body of historical exposure data is available, any change in the exposure base could render the prior history unusable. Since ratemaking generally depends upon the review of past statistical indications, exposure bases are rarely changed once they have been established.

Claim

A **claim** is a demand for payment by an insured or by an allegedly injured third party under the terms and conditions of an insurance contract. The individual making the claim is the **claimant**, and there can be multiple claimants within a single claim. Claim statistics are key elements in the ratemaking process. Generally, insurers maintain claim data based upon **accident date**—the date of the occurrence which gave rise to the claim, and **report date**—the date the insurer receives notice of the claim. Claim data can then be aggregated based upon these dates. For example, the total of all claims with accident dates during 1988 is the accident year 1988 claim count.

Frequency

Because the number of claims is directly related to the number of exposures, actuaries express claim incidence in terms of **frequency** per exposure unit.

$$F_k = \frac{kC}{E} \tag{1}$$

Where:
F_k = frequency per k exposure units
K = scale factor
C = claim count
E = exposure units

For example, if we earned 32,458 car years of exposure during 1988 and we incur 814 claims with 1988 accident dates, then the 1988 accident year claim frequency per 1,000 earned exposures is 25.08, calculated as follows:

$$F_{1000} = \frac{1000(814)}{32,458} = 25.08$$

Where the context is established by either data or previous exposition it might be appropriate to refer to this simply as the **frequency**. In general, however, the need for precision would require that the more specific language **accident year frequency per 1,000 earned car years** be used.

Losses and Loss Adjustment Expenses

Amounts paid or payable to claimants under the terms of insurance policies are referred to as **losses. Paid losses** are those losses for a particular period which have actually been paid to claimants. Where there is an expectation that a payment will be made in the future, a claim will have an associated **case reserve** representing the estimated amount of that payment. The sum of all paid losses and case reserves for a specific accident year at a specific point in time is known as the **accident year case-incurred losses.** The term **case-incurred** is used to distinguish this statistic from **ultimate incurred losses** which include losses which have not yet been reported to the insurance company as of the case-incurred evaluation date.

Over time, as more losses are paid and more information becomes available about unpaid claims, accident year case-incurred losses will tend to approach their ultimate value. Generally, because of the reporting of additional claims which were not included in earlier evaluations, accident year case-incurred losses tend to increase over time. In order to keep track of the individual evaluations of case-incurred losses for an accident year, actuaries use the concept of the **accident year age.** The accident year age is generally expressed in months. By convention, the accident year is age 12 months at the end of the last day of the accident year. Therefore, the 1987 accident year evaluated as of 6/30/88 would be referred to as the age 18 evaluation of the 1987 accident year.

Figure 1 represents a graphical interpretation of a typical case-incurred loss development pattern—in this case for automobile liability.

Case—Incurred Loss Development
Auto Liability

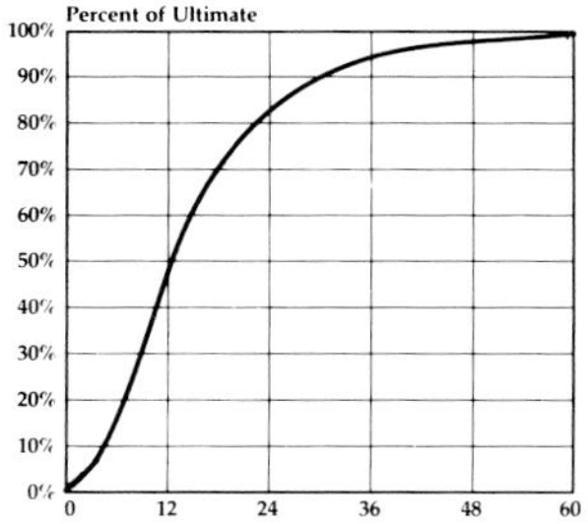

Accident Year Age in Months

Figure 1

Insurance company expenses associated with the settlement of claims, as distinguished from the marketing, investment, or general administrative operations, are referred to as **loss adjustment expenses**. Those loss adjustment expenses which can be directly related to a specific claim are called **allocated loss adjustment expenses** and those which cannot are called **unallocated loss adjustment expenses.**

Severity

Average loss per claim is called **severity**. Severities can be on a **pure loss** basis, excluding all loss adjustment expenses, or they can include allocated or total loss adjustment expenses. The loss component can be paid, case-incurred or projected ultimate and the claims component can be reported, paid, closed, or projected ultimate. This profusion of available options again requires that the actuary be precise in the references to the components. Note the differences between **accident year case-incurred loss severity per reported claim and report year paid loss and allocated severity per closed claim**. However the loss and claim components are defined, the formula for severity is simply:

$$S = \frac{L}{C} \tag{2}$$

Where: S = severity
L = losses
C = claim count

Pure Premium

Another important statistic is the average loss per unit of exposure or the **pure premium**. The reader will by now appreciate the need for precise component definition either in terminology or through context, so the various options will not be recited. The formula for the pure premium is:

$$P = \frac{L}{E} \tag{3}$$

Where: P = pure premium
L = losses
E = exposure units

Note that the pure premium can also be expressed as:

$$P = \frac{C}{E} \times \frac{L}{C}$$

Where: C = claim count

Or, where frequency is per unit of exposure:

$$P = F_1 \times S \tag{4}$$

In other words, **pure premium equals the product of frequency per unit of exposure and severity.**

Expense, Profit and Contingencies

In order to determine the price for a specific insurance coverage, appropriate provisions must be made for expenses (other than any loss adjustment expenses included in the pure premium) and profit. The profit provision is generally termed the (underwriting) **profit and contingencies** provision reflecting the fact that profits, if any, will be based upon actual results and not expectations or projections. For the purposes of this discussion we will distinguish between **fixed**

expenses per unit of exposure, which do not depend upon premium, and **variable expenses** which vary directly with price.

This treatment gives rise to the following formula for the **rate per unit of exposure:**

$$R = \frac{P + F}{1\text{-}V\text{-}Q} \tag{5}$$

Where:
R = rate per unit of exposure
P = pure premium
F = fixed expense per exposure
V = variable expense factor
Q = profit and contingencies factor

As an example, assume the following:

Loss and loss adjustment expense pure premium	\$75.00
Fixed expense per exposure	\$12.50
Variable expense factor	17.50%
Profit and contingencies factor	5.00%

The appropriate rate for this example would be calculated as follows:

$$\text{Rate} = \frac{\$75.00 + \$12.50}{1\text{-}.175\text{-}.050} = \$112.90$$

The individual components of the rate would therefore be as follows:

Pure premium	\$75.00
Fixed expenses	12.50
Variable expenses (\$112.90 × .175)	19.76
Profit and contingencies (\$112.90 × .050)	5.64
Total	\$112.90

Premium

Application of the rate(s) to the individual exposures to be covered by an insurance policy produces the **premium** for that policy. If, in the above example, the unit of exposure is a commercial vehicle and we are rating a policy for 15 commercial vehicles, the premium would be calculated as follows:

$$\$112.90 \times 15 = \$1{,}693.50$$

Premium, like exposure, can be either **written, earned, or in-force**. If the policy in question was written for a twelve month term on 7/1/87 then that policy would have contributed the following amounts as of 12/31/87:

Calendar year 1987 written premium	$1,693.50
Calendar year 1987 earned premium	846.75
12/31/87 premium in-force	$1,693.50

Loss Ratio

Probably the single most widely-used statistic in the analysis of insurance losses is the **loss ratio** or losses divided by premium. Again the need for precision cannot be overemphasized. There is a great difference between a loss ratio based upon paid losses as of accident year age 12 and written premium (termed an **age 12 accident year written-paid pure loss ratio**) and one which is based upon ultimate incurred loss and loss adjustment expenses and earned premium **(ultimate accident year earned-incurred loss and loss adjustment expense ratio)** although either can be properly referred to as a loss ratio.

The Goal of the Manual Ratemaking Process

Broadly stated, the goal of the ratemaking process is to determine rates which will, when applied to the exposures underlying the risks being written, provide sufficient funds to pay expected losses and expenses; maintain an adequate margin for adverse deviation; and produce a reasonable return on (any) funds provided by investors. In addition, manual rates are generally subject to regulatory review and, while detailed discussion of regulatory requirements is beyond the scope of this text, this review is often based upon the regulatory standard that *"rates shall not be inadequate, excessive, or unfairly discriminatory between risks of like kind and quality."*

Internally, there will generally be a review of the competitiveness of the rate levels in the marketplace. While the actuary may be directly involved in both internal and external discussions relating to these reviews, it is the actuary's primary responsibility to recommend rates which can be reasonably expected to be adequate over the period in which they are to be used.

Adequately pricing a line of insurance involves substantial judgment. While actuaries are trained in mathematics and statistics, the actuarial process underlying manual ratemaking also requires substantial understanding of the underwriting, economic, social, and political factors which have in the past impacted the insurance results and will impact those results in the future.

Structure of the Rating Plan

Up to this point the discussion of manual rates has related to the concept of an identified unit of exposure. In practice, manual rates are based upon a number of factors in addition to the basic exposure unit. For example, the elements involved in the rating of a single private passenger automobile insurance policy might include the following:

Age of insured(s)
Sex of insured(s)
Marital status of insured(s)
Prior driving record of insured(s)
Annual mileage driven
Primary use of vehicle(s)
Make and model of vehicle(s)
Age of vehicle(s)
Garaging location of vehicle(s)

The structure of the various elements involved in the manual rating of a specific risk is known as the **rating plan**. Various specific elements are often referred to as **classifications, sub-classifications,** or **rating factors.** Rating plans serve to allow the manual rating process to reflect identified differences in loss propensity. Failing to reflect such factors can result in two separate situations. Where a known positive characteristic, i.e. a characteristic tending to be associated with reduced loss propensity, is not reflected in the rating plan, the rate applied to risks possessing that positive characteristic will be too high. This would encourage the insuring of these risks to the partial or total exclusion of risks not possessing the positive characteristic, a practice referred to as **skimming the cream.** On the other hand, the failure to reflect a known negative characteristic will result in the application of a rate which is too low. If other companies are reflecting the negative factor in their rating plans, the result will be a tendency towards insuring risks possessing the negative characteristic, a situation known as **adverse selection.**

Risk characteristics underlying a manual rating plan can be broadly identified as those generally impacting frequency and those generally impacting severity. Prior driving record is an example of a factor which has been demonstrated to correlate with frequency. Individuals with recent automobile accidents and traffic violations have, **as a class,** higher frequencies of future claims than do those individuals with no recent accidents or violations. Individuals driving high-powered sports cars have, **as a class,** higher frequencies than those driving family sedans. Annual mileage driven has an obvious impact on frequency.

On the severity side, some vehicles tend to be more susceptible to damage in collisions than do other vehicles. Repair parts for a Rolls Royce costs more than do those for a Chevrolet. A late model automobile is more valuable than a ten-year-old "clunker" and will therefore, **on average,** have a higher associated severity.

The above examples deal with private passenger automobile insurance, but other lines have identifiable risk characteristics as well. In commercial fire insurance, restaurants generally have a higher frequency than do clothing stores. The presence or absence of a sprinkler system will impact severity as will the value of the building and contents being insured. Workers' compensation statistics detail higher frequencies for manufacturing employees than for clerical workers. For every type of property and casualty insurance, there are identifiable factors which impact upon frequency and severity of losses.

The subject of risk classification will be discussed in detail in chapter 5. In addition, the reflection of specific individual risk differences, as opposed to class differences, will be treated in chapter 3. For the purposes of this chapter, it is sufficient to be aware of the existence of and need for rating plans reflecting identifiable risk classification differences.

The Ratemaking Process

In this section we will deal with the basic techniques used by casualty actuaries in the development of manual rates. The reader must bear in mind that this discussion will be general in nature—a complete discussion of the elements involved in a single complex line of insurance might require several hundred pages. Nevertheless, the key elements of manual ratemaking will be addressed to such an extent that a good understanding of the actuarial process of manual ratemaking should result.

Basic Manual Ratemaking Methods

There are two basic approaches to addressing the problem of manual ratemaking: the **pure premium method** and the **loss ratio method.** We will examine the mathematics underlying each method and then develop a relationship between the two.

Pure Premium Method

The pure premium method develops indicated rates—those rates which are expected to provide for the expected losses and expenses and provide the expected profit—based upon formula (5).

$$R = \frac{P+F}{1\text{-}V\text{-}Q} \tag{5}$$

Where:
R = (indicated) rate per unit of exposure
P = pure premium
F = fixed expense per exposure
V = variable expense factor
Q = profit and contingencies factor

The pure premium used in the formula is based upon **experience losses,** which are trended projected ultimate losses (or losses and loss adjustment expenses) for the experience period under review, and the exposures earned during the experience period. The methods underlying the trending and projection of the losses will be discussed later in this chapter.

Loss Ratio Method

The loss ratio method develops indicated **rate changes** rather than indicated rates. Indicated rates are determined by application of an adjustment factor, the ratio of the **experience loss ratio** to a **target loss ratio,** to the current rates. The experience loss ratio is the ratio of the experience losses to the **on-level earned premium**—the earned premium which would have resulted for the experience period had the current rates been in effect for the entire period. In mathematical terms the loss ratio method works as follows:

$$R = AR_0 \tag{6}$$

Where: R = indicated rate
R_0 = current rate
A = adjustment factor
= W/T
W = experience loss ratio
T = target loss ratio

Looking first at the target loss ratio:

$$T = \frac{1\text{-}V\text{-}Q}{1+G} \tag{7}$$

Where: V = premium-related expense factor
Q = profit and contingencies factor
G = ratio of non-premium-related expenses to losses

And then the experience loss ratio:

$$W = \frac{L}{ER_0} \tag{8}$$

Where:

L = experience losses
E = experience period earned exposure
R_0 = current rate

Using (6), (7), and (8) we can see:

$$A = \frac{L/(ER_0)}{(1\text{-}V\text{-}Q)/(1+G)}$$

$$= \frac{L(1+G)}{ER_0(1\text{-}V\text{-}Q)} \qquad (9)$$

and, substituting (9) into (6):

$$R = \frac{L(1+G)}{E(1\text{-}V\text{-}Q)} \qquad (10)$$

Relationship Between Pure Premium and Loss Ratio Methods

It has been emphasized in this chapter that manual rates are estimates. Nevertheless, they generally represent **precise** estimates based upon reasonable and consistent assumptions. This being the case, we should be able to demonstrate that the pure premium and loss ratio methods will produce identical rates when applied to identical data and using consistent assumptions. This demonstration is quite simple. It starts with formula (10), the formula for the indicated rate under the loss ratio method:

$$R = \frac{L(1+G)}{E(1\text{-}V\text{-}Q)} \qquad (10)$$

Now, the loss ratio method uses experience losses while the pure premium method is based upon experience pure premium. The relationship between the two comes from (3):

$$P = \frac{L}{E} \qquad (3)$$

which can be expressed as

$$L = EP$$

Also, the loss ratio method relates non-premium-related expenses to losses while the pure premium method uses exposures as the base for these expenses. The relationship can be expressed as follows:

$$G = \frac{EF}{L}$$

$$= \frac{F}{P}$$

Substituting for L and G in formula (10) produces the following:

$$R = \frac{EP[1 + (F/P)]}{E(1\text{-}V\text{-}Q)}$$

Or:

$$R = \frac{P + F}{1\text{-}V\text{-}Q} \qquad (5)$$

This is the formula for the indicated rate under the pure premium method. The equivalence of the two methods is therefore demonstrated.

Selection of Appropriate Method

Because the two methods can be expected to produce identical results when consistently applied to a common set of data, the question arises as to which approach is the more appropriate for any given situation. Having dealt with the mathematical aspects of the two methods, let us now look at some of the practical differences.

Pure Premium Method	Loss Ratio Method
Based on exposure	Based on premium
Does not require existing rates	Requires existing rates
Does not use on-level premium	Uses on-level premium
Produces indicated rates	Produces indicated rate changes

Noting the above differences, the following guidelines would seem to be reasonable:

Pure premium method requires well-defined, responsive exposures. The pure premium method is based on losses per unit exposure. Where the exposure unit is not available or is not reasonably consistent between risks, as in the case of commercial fire insurance, the pure premium method cannot be used.

Loss ratio method cannot be used for a new line. Because the loss ratio method produces indicated rate changes, its use requires an established rate and premium history. Where manual rates are required for a new line of business, and assuming there are relevant loss statistics available, the pure premium method must be used. Of course, if no statistical data are available, then neither method can be used.

Pure premium method is preferable where on-level premium is difficult to calculate. In some instances, such as commercial lines where individual risk rating adjustments are made to individual policies, it is difficult to determine the on-level earned premium required for the loss ratio method. Where this is the case it is more appropriate to use the pure premium method if possible.

Need for Common Basis

Whichever ratemaking method is selected, the actuary needs to make certain that the experience losses are on a basis consistent with the exposures and premiums being used. This requires that adjustments be made for observed changes in the data. This section will deal with some of the more common sources of change in the underlying data and will discuss methods for dealing with those changes.

Selection of Experience Period

Determination of the loss experience period to be used in the manual ratemaking process involves a combination of statistical and judgmental elements. There is a natural preference for using the most recent incurred loss experience available since it is generally most representative of the current situation. However, this experience will also contain a higher proportion of unpaid losses than will more mature periods and is therefore more subject to loss development projection errors. Where the business involved is subject to catastrophe losses, as in the case of windstorm coverage in hurricane-prone areas, the experience period must be representative of the average catastrophe incidence. Finally, the experience period must contain sufficient loss experience that the resulting indications will have statistical significance or **credibility.**

Reinsurance

Ceded reinsurance, which is discussed in depth in chapter 6, serves to reduce an insurer's exposure to large losses, either individual or in the aggregate, in exchange for a reinsurance premium. While there may be instances in which a reinsurance program represents such a significant transfer of risk that separate and distinct provision for the reinsurance premium is appropriate, such cases are beyond the scope of this chapter. In general, the analysis of manual rates is based upon direct, that is before reflection of reinsurance, premium and loss data. Where reinsurance costs are significant they are often treated as a separate element of the expense provision.

Differences in Coverage

Wherever possible, major coverages within a line of insurance are generally treated separately. For example, liability experience under homeowners policies is often reviewed separately from the property experience. Auto collision data is usually analyzed separately by deductible. Professional liability policies written on a claims-made basis are generally not combined with those written on an occurrence basis for ratemaking purposes. Note that unless the mix has been consistent over the entire experience period these separations will require the segregation of premium and exposure data as well as the loss experience.

Treatment of Increased Limits

Liability coverage rate manuals generally provide rates for a basic limit of liability along with **increased limits factors** to be applied to these base rates where higher limits are desired. As will be seen in a later section, these increased limits factors tend to change over time. In addition there will be a general movement toward the purchase of higher limits as inflation erodes purchasing power. For these reasons premiums and losses used in the manual ratemaking process should be adjusted to a basic limits basis.

On-Level Premium—Adjusting for Prior Rate Changes

Where, as is the general case, the experience period extends over several years there have typically been changes in manual rate levels between the beginning of the experience period and the date as of which the rates are being reviewed. If the actuary is using the loss ratio method in the development of the indicated rate level changes, the earned premium underlying the loss ratio calculations must be on a current rate level basis.

Where the capability exists, the best method for bringing past premiums to an on-level basis is to re-rate each policy using current rates. Doing this manually is generally far too time-consuming to be practical, but where sufficient detail is available in the computer files and if rating software is available, the resulting on-level premiums will be quite accurate. This method is referred to as the **extension of exposures** technique.

When extension of exposures cannot be used, an alternative, called the **parallelogram method,** is available. This method adjusts calendar year earned premiums to current rate levels based upon simple geometric relationships and an underlying assumption that exposure is uniformly distributed over time.

As an example, assume that the experience period in question consists of the three years 1985, 1986, and 1987. Further assume that each policy has a twelve month term. Finally, assume that rate increases have been taken as follows:

+ 17.8% effective 7/1/82
+ 12.5% effective 7/1/84
+ 10.0% effective 7/1/86

Because we are dealing with twelve-month policies, all of the premium earned during the earliest year of the experience period—1985—was written at either the 7/1/82 rate level or the 7/1/84 rate level. If we assign the 7/1/82 rate level a relative value of 1.000, then the 7/1/84 rate level has a relative value of 1.125 and the 7/1/86 rate level has a relative value of (1.125)(1.100) = 1.2375.

Figure 2 provides a representation of these data under the parallelogram method. The x-axis represents the date on which a policy is effective, and the y-axis represents the portion of exposure earned.

Development of On-Level Premium

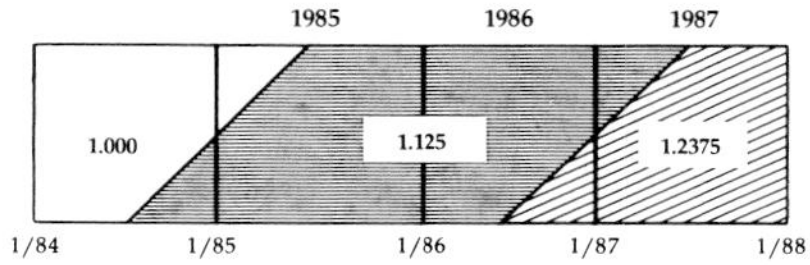

Figure 2

Each calendar year of earned premium can now be viewed as a unit square one year wide and 100% of exposure high. Figure 3 illustrates this treatment of the 1985 year.

On-Level Premium Factor

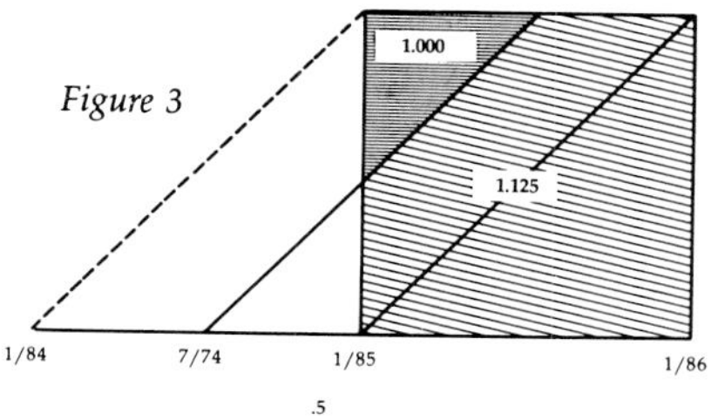

Figure 3

As shown in Figure 4, we can now use simple geometry to determine the portions of 1985 earned exposure written at the 1.000 and 1.125 relative levels.

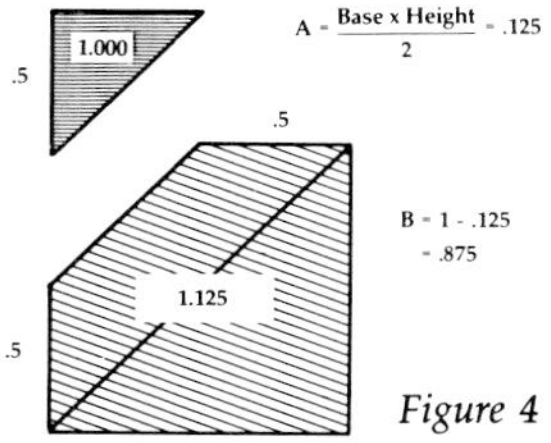

Figure 4

According to the parallelogram model, .125 of the 1985 earned exposure arises from policies written at the 1.000 relative level and

.875 of the exposure was written at a relative level of 1.125. The average 1985 relative earned rate level is therefore [(.125)(1.000) + (.875)(1.125)] = 1.1094. Since the current relative average rate level is 1.2375, the 1985 calendar year earned premium must be multiplied by (1.2375/1.1094) = 1.1155 to reflect current rate levels. The 1.1155 is referred to as the 1985 **on-level factor.**

We can repeat this process for the 1986 and 1987 years to generate the following:

Calendar Year	Portion of Earned at Relative Level			On-Level Factor
	1.000	1.125	1.2375	
1985	.125	.875	.000	1.1155
1986	.000	.875	.125	1.0864
1987	.000	.125	.875	1.0115

These on-level factors are then applied to the calendar year earned premiums to generate approximate on-level earned premiums. For example:

Calendar Year	Calendar Year Earned Premium	On-Level Factor	Approximate On-Level Earned Premium
1985	$1,926,981	1.1155	$2,149,547
1986	2,299,865	1.0864	2,498,573
1987	2,562,996	1.0115	2,592,470
Total	$6,789,842		$7,240,590

As noted earlier, the parallelogram method is based upon an assumption that exposures are written uniformly over the calendar period. In cases where material changes in exposure level have occurred over the period, or where there is a non-uniform pattern to the written exposures, the parallelogram method may not produce a reasonable approximation of on-level earned premium. While a discussion of adjustments to the simple model underlying the parallelogram method is beyond the scope of this chapter, Miller and Davis (1976) have proposed an alternative model which reflects actual exposure patterns.

Trended, Projected Ultimate Losses

We are now ready to discuss the methodology underlying the development of the trended, projected ultimate losses. This element represents the most significant part of any ratemaking analysis and requires both statistical expertise and actuarial judgment. Whether the pure premium method or the loss ratio method is being used, the accuracy with which losses are projected will determine the adequacy of the resulting manual rates.

Inclusion of Loss Adjustment Expenses

The actuary must determine whether to make projections on a pure loss basis, or whether to include allocated loss adjustment expenses with losses. Unallocated loss adjustment data are rarely available in sufficient detail for inclusion with losses and allocated loss adjustment expenses, and are generally treated as part of the expense provision—frequently as a ratio to loss and allocated loss adjustment expenses.

While the decision whether to include allocated loss expense data with losses is generally made based upon data availability, there is one situation in which it is essential that the allocated loss adjustment expenses be combined with the losses. Some liability policies contain limits of liability which apply to both losses and allocated loss adjustment expenses. Where manual rates are being developed for such policies, allocated loss adjustment expenses should be treated as losses.

Projection to Ultimate—the Loss Development Method

A significant portion of the entirety of casualty actuarial literature produced in this century deals with the methods and techniques for projecting unpaid, and often unreported, losses to their ultimate settlement values. Even a casual treatment of the subject is beyond the scope of this chapter. Nevertheless, the general concepts discussed in this section will be based upon the use of projected ultimate losses and claim counts. A thorough understanding of the issues involved in manual ratemaking requires that the context of the problem be clear. At least one technique for projection to ultimate is needed and we will use the most common—the **loss development method**.

The loss development method is based upon the assumption that claims move from unreported to reported-and-unpaid to paid in a pattern which is sufficiently consistent that past experience can be used to predict future development. Claim counts, or losses, are arrayed by accident year (or report year or on some other basis) and accident year age. The resulting data form a triangle of known values. As an example, consider the following accident year reported claim count development data:

Accident Year	Age 12	Age 24	Age 36	Age 48	Age 60	Age 72
1982	1,804	2,173	2,374	2,416	2,416	2,416
1983	1,935	2,379	2,424	2,552	2,552	
1984	2,103	2,384	2,514	2,646		
1985	2,169	2,580	2,722			
1986	2,346	2,783				
1987	2,337					

Remembering the concept of accident year age it can be seen, for example, that as of 12/31/85 there were 2,424 claims reported for accidents occurring during 1983. By 12/31/86 this number had developed to 2,552. Horizontal movement to the right represents **development,** vertical movement downward represents **change in exposure level,** and positive-sloped diagonals represent **evaluation dates.** The lower diagonal represents the latest available evaluation—in this case 12/31/87.

Accident Year	Age 12	Age 24	Age 36	Age 48	Age 60	Age 72
1982						2,416
1983					2,552	
1984				2,646		
1985			2,722			
1986		2,783				
1987	2,337					

The next step in the process is to reflect the development history arithmetically. This involves the division of each evaluation subsequent to the first by the immediately preceding evaluation. The resulting ratio is called an **age-to-age development factor** or, sometimes, a **link ratio.** For example, the **accident year 1982 12-24 reported claim count development factor** from our example is 2,173/1,804 = 1.2045.

Accident Year	Age 12	Age 24	Age 36	Age 48	Age 60	Age 72
1982	1,804	2,173	2,374	2,416	2,416	2,416
1983	1,935	2,379	2,424	2,552	2,552	
1984	2,103	2,384	2,514	2,646		
1985	2,169	2,580	2,722			
1986	2,346	2,783				
1987	2,337					

2,173/1,804 = 1.2045

We can now produce a second data triangle consisting of age-to-age development factors.

Accident Year	12-24	24-36	36-48	48-60	60-72
1982	1.2045	1.0925	1.0177	1.0000	1.0000
1983	1.2295	1.0189	1.0528	1.0000	
1984	1.1336	1.0545	1.0525		
1985	1.1895	1.0550			
1986	1.1863				

Based upon the observed development factors, age-to-age factors are selected and successively multiplied to generate **age-to-ultimate factors.** These age-to-ultimate factors are then applied to the latest diagonal of the development data to yield projected ultimate values.

Accident Year	Accident Year Age	Selected Age-to-Age Factor	Age-to-Ultimate Factor	Reported Claims 12/31/87	Projected Ultimate Claims
1982	72	—	1.0000	2,416	2,416
1983	60	1.0000	1.0000	2,552	2,552
1984	48	1.0000	1.0000	2,646	2,646
1985	36	1.0450	1.0450	2,722	2,844
1986	24	1.0550	1.1025	2,783	3,068
1987	12	1.1900	1.3120	2,337	3,066

An identical process can be applied to either paid or case-incurred losses. Generally, case-incurred values are used, especially where the development period extends over several years. Note that losses tend to take longer to develop fully than do reported claims. This is due to the **settlement lag**—the period between loss reporting and loss payment—which affects losses but not reported claims and represents additional development potential beyond the **reporting lag**—the period between loss occurrence and loss reporting—which affects both claims and losses.

An example of the loss development method applied to case-incurred loss and allocated loss adjustment expense data is contained in the Appendix to this chapter.

In some instances, most notably where premiums are subject to audit adjustments, as is often true for workers' compensation insurance, premium data requires projection to ultimate in order that the premium being used in the ratemaking calculations properly reflects the actual exposure level which gave rise to the ultimate losses. One method for handling this situation is to aggregate data on a **policy year,** rather than an accident year, basis. Policy year data is based upon the year in which the policy giving rise to exposures, premiums, claims and losses is effective. Another method involves the projection of written premium to ultimate and the recalculation of earned premium, referred to as **exposure year earned premium,** based upon the projected ultimate written premium. In either case, the projection techniques involved are similar to the loss development method.

Identification of Trends

Once claims and losses have been projected to an ultimate basis it is necessary to adjust the data for any underlying trends which are expected to produce changes in indications between the experience period and the period during which the manual rates will be in effect. For example, if rates are being reviewed as of 12/31/87 based upon 1985 accident year data and the new rates are expected to go into effect on 7/1/88, the projected ultimate losses for the 1985 accident year are representative of loss exposure as of approximately 7/1/85 and the indicated rates must cover loss exposure as of approximately 7/1/89. (This is based upon the assumption that the revised rates will be in effect for 12 months, from 7/1/88 through 6/30/89. Assuming a one-year policy term, the average policy will therefore run from 1/1/89 through 12/31/89 and the midpoint of loss occurrence under that policy will be 7/1/89.) To the extent that there are identifiable trends in the loss data, the impact of those trends must be reflected over the 48 months between the midpoint of the experience period and the average exposure date to which the rates will apply.

The most obvious trend affecting the ratemaking data is the trend in severity. Monetary inflation, increases in jury awards, and increases in medical expenses are examples of factors which cause upward trends in loss severities. Frequency is also subject to trend. Court decisions may open new grounds for litigation which would increase liability frequencies. Legal and social pressures might reduce the incidence of driving under the influence of alcohol, thus reducing automobile insurance frequencies. In workers' compensation an amendment in the governing law can cause changes in both severity and frequency of loss.

Some exposure bases also exhibit identifiable trends. Workers' compensation uses payroll as an exposure base and products liability coverage might be based upon dollars of sales. Both of these exposures will reflect some degree of trend. Automobile physical damage rates are based upon the value of the automobiles being insured. As automobile prices increase, the physical damage premiums will reflect the change, even though no rate change has been made. When using the loss ratio method for ratemaking it is important that the effect of such trends on premium be properly reflected.

While frequency and severity trends are often analyzed separately, it is sometimes preferable to look at trends in the pure premium, thus combining the impacts of frequency and severity.

Reflection of Trends

Actuaries generally approach the problem of how to reflect observed trends by fitting an appropriate curve to the observed data.

The most important word in the preceding sentence is **appropriate.** Consider the following hypothetical projected accident year severity data:

Accident Year	Projected Severity
1980	$ 309
1981	532
1982	763
1983	996
1984	1,225
1985	1,444
1986	1,647
1987	1,828

It so happens that the third-degree polynomial $y = -x^3 + 10x^2 + 200x + 100$ produces a perfect fit to the above data where x is defined as the accident year minus 1979. Figure 5 shows the result of this fit graphically.

Severity Trend
Third Degree Polynomial Fit

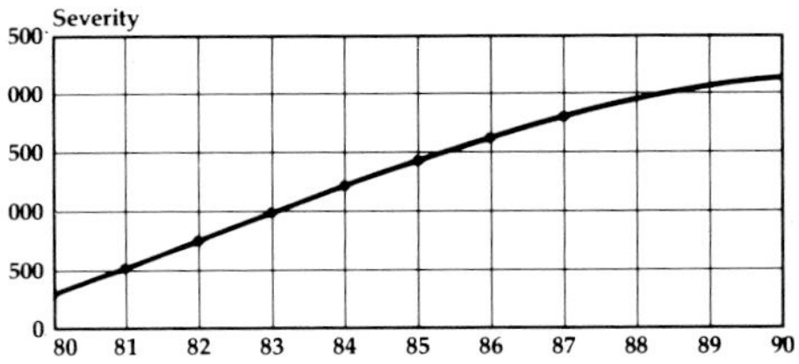

Accident Year

Figure 5

Based upon the strength of the fit one might be tempted to use the third-degree polynomial to project future severity changes. But is a third-degree polynomial really appropriate for a severity trend model?

If we extend the x axis out through accident year 1998 we see the following results. Viewed in this manner it is apparent that, regardless of how well it might fit our observations, the third-degree polynomial model is not one which is reasonable for projection of severity changes.

Severity Trend
Third Degree Polynomial Fit

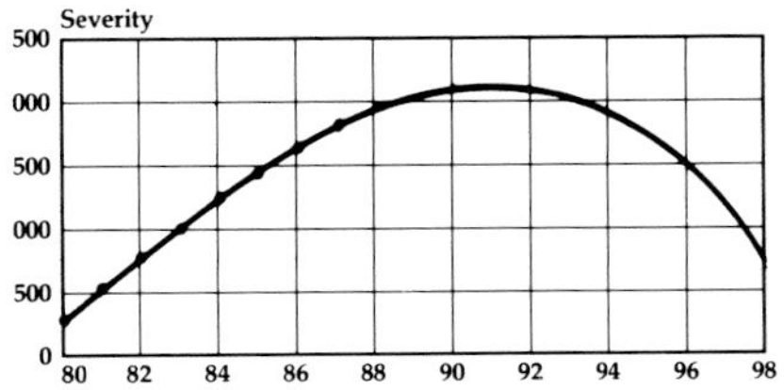

Accident Year

Figure 6

While other appropriate models are available, most of the trending models used by casualty actuaries in ratemaking take one of two forms:

Linear	y	$=$	$ax + b$, or
Exponential	y	$=$	be^{ax}

Note that the exponential model can be expressed as:

$$ln(y) = ax + ln(b)$$

Or, with the substitutions $y' = ln(y)$ and $b' = ln(b)$:

$$y' = ax + b'$$

Since either model can therefore be expressed in terms of a linear function, the standard first-degree least-squares regression method can be applied to the observed data to determine the trend model. Note that the linear model will produce a model in which the projection will increase by a constant amount (a) for each unit change in x. The exponential model will produce a constant rate of change of $e^a - 1$, with each value being e^a times the prior value. Drawing an analogy to the mathematics of finance, the linear model is analogous to simple interest while the exponential model is analogous to compound interest.

While either linear or exponential models can be used to reflect increasing trends, where the observed trend is decreasing the use of a linear model will produce negative values at some point in the future. The use of a linear model over an extended period in such cases is generally inappropriate since frequency, severity, pure premium, and exposure must all be greater than or equal to zero.

Exhibits IV, V, VII, and VIII of the Appendix to this chapter provide examples of the application of both linear and exponential trend models using both loss ratio and pure premium methods.

Effects of Limits on Severity Trend

Where the loss experience under review involves the application of limits of liability, it is important that the effects of those limits on severity trend be properly reflected. In order to understand the interaction between limits and severity trend, consider the hypothetical situation in which individual losses can occur for any amount between $1 and $90,000. Assume that insurance coverage against these losses is available at four limits of liability: $10,000 per occurrence, $25,000 per occurrence, $50,000 per occurrence, and $100,000 per occurrence. Note that since losses can only be as great as $90,000, the $100,000 limit coverage is basically unlimited.

In order to analyze the operation of severity trend on the various limits, it will be necessary to look at losses by layer of liability. The following chart illustrates this layering for four different loss amounts.

	Distribution of Loss Amount by Layer			
Loss Amount	First $10,000	$15,000 excess of $10,000	$25,000 excess of $25,000	$50,000 excess of $50,000
$ 5,000	$ 5,000			
20,000	10,000	10,000		
40,000	10,000	15,000	15,000	
70,000	10,000	15,000	25,000	20,000
Total	$35,000	$40,000	$40,000	$20,000

The total line represents the distribution of the $135,000 of losses by layer, assuming that one claim of each amount occurred. Consider now the effect of a constant 10% increase in each claim amount.

	Distribution of Loss Amount by Layer			
Loss Amount	First $10,000	$15,000 excess of $10,000	$25,000 excess of $25,000	$50,000 excess of $50,000
$ 5,500	$ 5,500			
22,000	10,000	12,000		
44,000	10,000	15,000	19,000	
77,000	10,000	15,000	25,000	27,000
Total	$35,500	$42,000	$44,000	$27,000
Increase	1.43%	5.00%	10.00%	35.00%

While the total losses have increased by 10% from \$135,000 to \$148,500, the rate of increase is not constant across the layers. This is due to the fact that the larger claims have already saturated the lower layers, thus reducing the impact of severity increases on these layers. Figure 7 provides a graphical representation of this effect by claim size for each of the four layers.

Effect of 10% Severity Trend by Layer

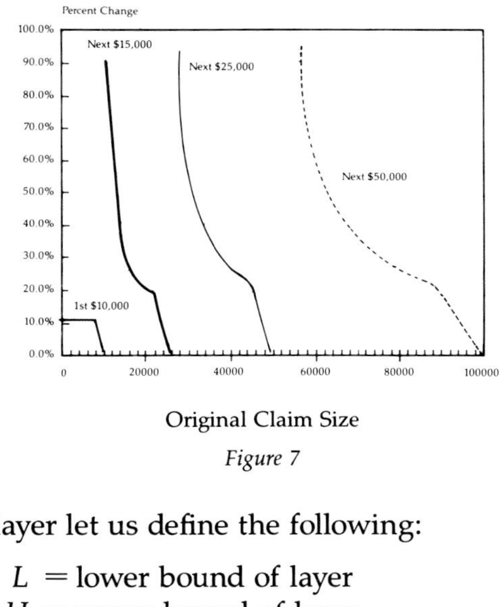

Original Claim Size

Figure 7

For each layer let us define the following:

L = lower bound of layer
U = upper bound of layer
X = unlimited loss size (before trend)
T = severity increase rate (e.g. 10% = 0.1)

The impact of the severity increase on any given layer can be expressed as:

Original Loss Size	**Rate of Increase in Layer**
$X < \frac{L}{(1+T)}$	Undefined
$\frac{L}{(1+T)} < X < \frac{U}{(1+T)}$	$\frac{(1+T)(X)-L}{X-L} - 1 = \frac{TX}{X-L}$
$\frac{U}{(1+T)} < X < U$	$\frac{U-L}{X-L} - 1 = \frac{U-X}{X-L}$
$U < X$	0

The four-loss distribution used in the illustration of the impact of policy limit on severity trend is not realistic for most liability lines. In general we see frequency decreasing as loss size increases. If we assume a loss distribution as shown in Figure 8, then the impact of a 10% severity increase on each limit will be as shown in Figure 9.

Theoretical Claim Distribution

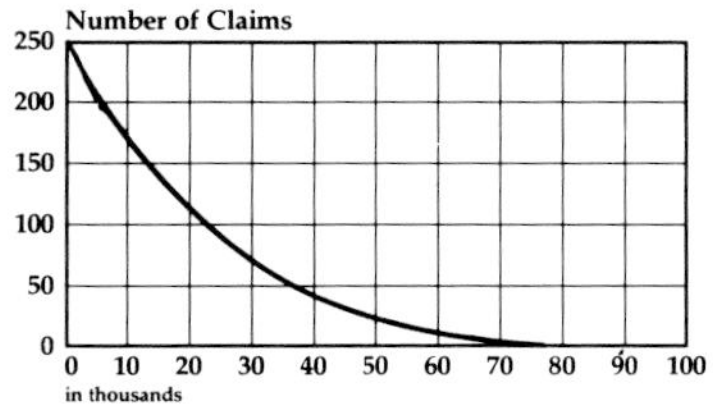

Original Claim Size

Figure 8

Effect of 10% Severity Trend by Limit

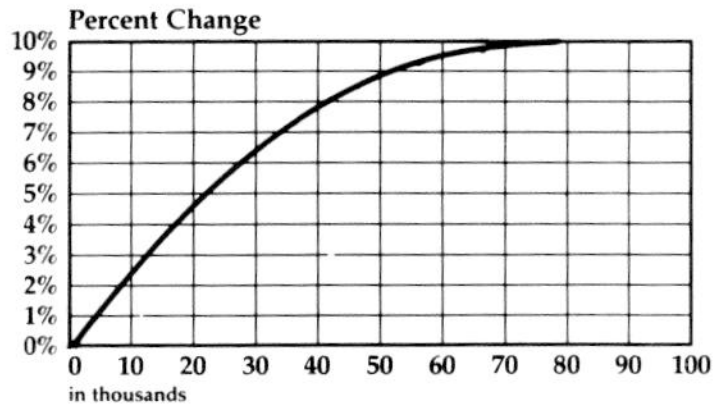

Policy Limit

Figure 9

Where severity trend has been analyzed based upon unlimited loss data or loss data including limits higher than the basic level, the resulting indicated severity trend must be adjusted before it is applied to basic limits losses. Because such adjustment will require knowledge of the underlying size-of-loss distribution, it is generally preferable to use basic limits data in the severity trend analysis.

Trend Based Upon External Data

Where sufficient loss or claim experience to produce reliable trend indications is not available, the actuary might supplement or supplant the available experience with external data. Insurance trade associations, statistical bureaus, and the U.S. Government produce insurance and general economic data regularly. While the appropriate source for the data will, of course, depend upon the specific ratemaking situation, Masterson (1968) provides a good general reference on the subject. Lommele and Sturgis (1974) provide an interesting example of the application of economic data to the problem of forecasting workers' compensation insurance results.

Trend and Loss Development—The "Overlap Fallacy"

It has occasionally been suggested that there is a double-counting of severity trend in the ratemaking process where both loss development factors—which reflect severity changes as development on unpaid claims—and severity trend factors are applied to losses. Cook dealt with this subject in detail, and with elegance, in a 1970 paper. In order to properly understand the relationship between loss development and trend factors, assume a situation in which the experience period is the 1986 accident year and indicated rates are expected to be in effect from 7/1/87 through 6/30/88. Now consider a single claim with accident date 7/1/86 and which will settle on 12/31/88. If a similar claim should occur during the effective period of the indicated rates, say on 7/1/88, we would expect an equivalent settlement lag and would project that the 7/1/88 claim would settle on 12/31/90. Figure 10 illustrates the hypothetical situation graphically.

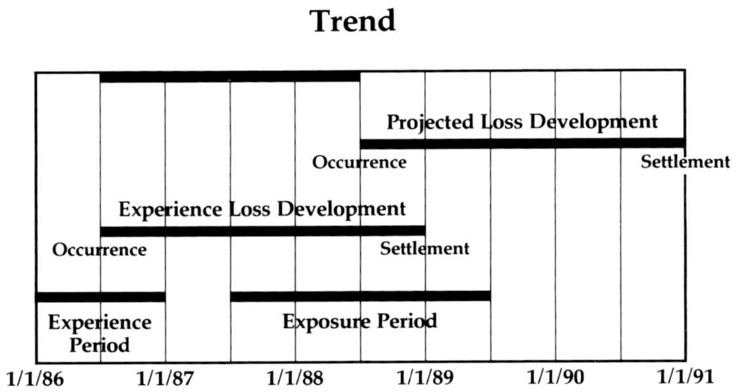

Figure 10

Note that the ratemaking problem, as respects this single hypothetical claim, is to project the ultimate settlement value as of 12/31/90 based upon the single observed claim which occurred on 7/1/86—a total projection period of 54 months. The loss development factor will reflect the underlying severity trend during the 30 months between occurrence on 7/1/88 and settlement on 12/31/90. The trend factor will reflect the severity trend between the midpoint of the experience period (7/1/86) and the midpoint of the exposure period (7/1/88), which accounts for the remaining 24 months of the projection period. Note that while both trend and loss development factors do reflect underlying severity trends, there is no overlap between the two, and both are required.

Trended Projected Ultimate Losses

The application of loss development and trending techniques to the underlying loss data produces the trended projected ultimate losses which are the experience losses underlying the application of either the pure premium or the loss ratio methods to produce the indicated rates or rate changes.

Expense Provisions

While a detailed discussion of the reflection of expenses in the ratemaking process is beyond the scope of this chapter, the need for continuity requires at least a limited treatment at this point. For purposes of illustration of the general concepts involved in the reflection of expense provisions in manual rates, assume both that the loss ratio method is being used to develop base rate indications for a line of business, and that allocated loss adjustment expenses are being combined with the experience losses. Suppose that for the latest year the line of business produced the following results on a direct basis:

Written premium	$11,540,000
Earned premium	10,832,000
Incurred loss and allocated loss adjustment expense	7,538,000
Incurred unallocated loss adjustment expenses	484,000
Commissions	1,731,000
Taxes, licenses & fees	260,000
Other acquisition expenses	646,000
General expenses	737,000
Total loss and expense	$11,396,000

Since our losses and expenses exceeded the earned premium by $564,000 for the year it may be appropriate that we review the adequacy of the underlying rates. Since we are using the loss ratio method we need to develop a target loss ratio. Referring back to formula (7):

$$T = \frac{1\text{-}V\text{-}Q}{1+G} \tag{7}$$

Where: T = target loss ratio
V = premium-related expense factor
Q = profit and contingencies factor
G = ratio of non-premium-related expenses to losses

In order to develop the target loss ratio we therefore need factors for premium-related and for non-premium-related expenses and a profit and contingencies factor. Deferring the discussion of profit and contingencies provisions to the next section, we will look at the expense factors.

Traditional application of the loss ratio method assumes that only the loss adjustment expenses are non-premium-related. Using this approach we can determine the value for G in formula (7) by dividing the unallocated loss adjustment expenses of $484,000 by the loss and allocated loss expense of $7,538,000. G is therefore (484/7538) = .0642.

The determination of V in formula (7) is then simply the ratio of the other expenses to premiums. But which premiums—written or earned? Since commissions and premium taxes are generally paid based upon direct written premium, it would seem appropriate to use written premium in the denominator for these expenses. Other acquisition expenses are expended to produce premium, so it might be appropriate to relate those to written premium as well. But the general expenses of the insurance operation involve functions unrelated to the production of premium which could not be immediately eliminated if the company were to cease writing business. For this reason the general expenses are usually related to earned premium.

Based upon the above, we now calculate V as follows:

Ratio of commissions to written	(1,731/11,540)	.1500
Ratio of taxes, licenses & fees to written	(260/11,540)	.0225
Ratio of other acquisition to written	(646/11/540)	.0560
Ratio of general to earned	(737/10,832)	.0680
Total premium-related expense factor		.2965

If, for the moment, we assume that the profit and contingencies factor is zero, we can apply formula (7) and determine our target loss ratio:

$$T = \frac{1\text{-}.2965\text{-}0}{1 + .0642} = .6611$$

Profit and Contingencies

While generally among the smaller of the elements in any calculation of indicated manual rates, the profit and contingencies provision represents the essence of insurance in that it is designed to reflect the basic elements of risk and rewards associated with the transaction of the insurance business. While a complete discussion of the topic of appropriate provisions for profit and contingencies are beyond the scope of this chapter, the reader should be aware that there is a distinction between the profit portion, which will generally be based upon some target rate of return, and the contingencies portion, which addresses the potential for adverse deviation.

Sources of Insurance Profit

Highly simplified, the property and casualty insurance operation involves the collection of premium from insureds, the investment of the funds collected, and the payment of expenses and insured losses. If the premiums collected exceed the expenses and losses paid, the insurer makes what is called an **underwriting profit;** if not, there is an **underwriting loss.** In addition, the insurer will generally make an **investment profit** arising out of the investment of funds between premium collection and payment of expenses and losses. In this simplified context, the insurer might be viewed as a leveraged investment operation, with underwriting profits or losses being analogous to negative or positive interest expenses on borrowed funds.

Profit Provisions in Manual Rates

Until the mid 1960s insurance rates would typically include a profit and contingencies provision of approximately 5% of premium. While this practice was rooted more in tradition than in financial analysis, it must be understood that the practice existed in an environment in which property insurance represented a much greater portion of the insurance business than it does today, and in which inflation and interest rates were generally low. In that environment investment income tended to be viewed as a gratuity rather than the major source of income it has become. The 5% provision produced sufficient underwriting profits to support the growth of the industry, and it was not generally viewed as being excessive.

The growth of the liability lines, increased inflation, and higher interest rates resulted in investment profits which dwarfed the underwriting profits. Not only did this change the way insurance management viewed its financial results and plans, but also it focused regulatory attention on the overall rate of return for insurers, rather than on the underwriting results. This regulatory involvement generally took the form of downward adjustments to the traditional 5% profit and contingencies provision to reflect investment income on funds supplied by policyholders. In some jurisdictions, the allowed profit provisions for certain lines became negative.

One of the major problems inherent in the development of a general methodology for the reflection of profit in manual rates is that premium may not be the proper benchmark against which profits should be assessed. Going back to our leveraged investment operation analogy, the specific inclusion of a profit provision based upon premium is the analog to the measurement of profit against borrowed funds—the more you borrow, the more you should earn. If, on the other hand, premiums are viewed in the traditional way, as sales, premium-based profit provisions make more sense.

Unfortunately, the obvious alternative to basing profits on premiums—using return-on-equity as the benchmark—has its own disadvantages. From a regulatory standpoint it both rewards highly leveraged operations and discourages entry to the market, both of which run contrary to regulatory desires. In addition, where rates are made by industry or state rating bureaus, the rates cannot be expected to produce equal return on equity for each company using them.

Risk Elements

A portion of the profit and contingencies provision represents a provision for adverse deviation or a **risk loading.** There are two separate and distinct risk elements inherent in the ratemaking function.

These are generally termed **parameter risk** and **process risk.** Parameter risk is simply the risk associated with the selection of the parameters underlying the applicable model of the process. Selecting the wrong loss development factors, resulting in erroneous experience losses, is an example of parameter risk. Process risk, in contrast, is the risk associated with the projection of future contingencies which are inherently variable. Even if we properly evaluate the mean frequency and the mean severity, the actual observed results will generally vary from the underlying means.

From a financial standpoint it is important to understand that the primary protection against adverse deviation is provided by the surplus (equity) of the insurer. If manual rates alone were required to produce sufficient funds to adequately protect the policyholders and claimants from sustaining any economic loss arising out of the policy period in which the rates were in effect, most property and casualty coverages would be unaffordable. It is more proper to view the profit and contingencies provision as providing sufficient funds to offset the economic costs associated with the net borrowings from the insurer's surplus required to offset the adverse deviations.

One method for determination of an appropriate profit and contingencies provision is the *ruin theory* approach. This method involves the development of a probabilistic model of the insurance operation and then, generally through Monte Carlo simulation, determining the probability of ruin (insolvency) over a fixed period of time. A maximum acceptable probability of ruin is then determined and the rate level assumption underlying the model is adjusted to the minimum rate level producing a ruin probability less than or equal to the acceptable level. The difference between the resultant adjusted rate level assumption and the rate level assumption with no risk margin is then used as the profit and contingencies provision.

Overall Rate Indications

The determination of the overall average indicated rate change will be made on the basis of the experience losses, expense provisions, profit and contingencies provisions and, in the case of the loss ratio method, on-level earned premium. As will be seen, the development of the overall rate change indication is generally only the beginning of the manual ratemaking process, not the end.

For illustrative purposes, assume that the loss ratio method is being applied to the following data:

(1) Experience loss and allocated—accident years 1985-87	$23,163,751
(2) On-level earned premium—calendar years 1985-87	31,811,448
(3) Experience loss and allocated ratio [(1)/(2)]	.7282
(4) Target loss and allocated ratio	.6611

The rate change indication follows directly:

(5) Indicated overall rate level change [(3)/(4)]-1.0 = .1014

Credibility Considerations

The concept of credibility, the weight to be assigned to an indication relative to one or more alternative indications, is the topic of chapter 7. For the purposes of this chapter, it is only necessary to understand that a statistical indication I_1 has an associated credibility z, between 0 and 1, relative to some other indication I_2. The resulting **credibility-weighted indication** $I_{1,2}$ is determined by the formula:

$$I_{1,2} = z(I_1) + (1\text{-}z)(I_2)$$

If, for example, the credibility associated with our overall rate level indication of + 7.28% is .85, and we have an alternative indication, from some source, of + 4.50%, the credibility-weighted indication would be 6.86%, determined as follows:

$$(.85)(.0728) + (.15)(.0450) = .0686$$

In the application of credibility weighting, the actuary must be careful to use only reasonable alternative indications. The complement of credibility (1-z) should be applied to an indication which can be expected to reflect consistent trends in the same general way as the underlying data. For example, where statewide indicated rate changes are less than fully credible, regional or countrywide indications might be a reasonable alternative indication.

Classification Rates

If rate manuals contained a single rate for a given state, the overall rate change indication would be all that was required. But a rate manual will generally contain rates based upon individual classification and sub-classification. In addition, where geographical location of the risk is an important factor, rates may also be shown by rating territory. While classification ratemaking will be discussed in chapter 5, the basics of the process will be illustrated in this section.

Base Rates

In order to facilitate the process of individual rate determination, especially where rates are computer-generated, classification and territorial rates are generally related to some base rate. The advantages to this system are apparent when one considers that there may be as many as 200 classifications for as many as 50 territories in a private passenger automobile rate manual for a given state. Determination of 250 classification and territorial relativities is obviously less time-consuming, and more reasonable from a statistical standpoint, than is the determination of 10,000 classification and territorial rates.

Indicated Classification Relativities

The relationship between the rate for a given classification (or territory) to the base rate is the classification (or territorial) **relativity.** The determination of indicated classification relativities is similar to the process used in the overall rate level analysis. If the pure premium method is used, the pure premium for the classification is divided by the pure premium for the base classification to generate the indicated relativity.

If the loss ratio method is used, the on-level earned premium for each classification must be adjusted to the base classification level before the experience loss ratios are calculated. Consider the following three-class situation:

(1) Class	(2) Current Relativity to Class 1	(3) On-Level Earned Premium	(4) Class 1 On-Level Earned (3)/(2)	(5) Experience Loss and Allocated	(6) Loss and Allocated Ratio (5)/(4)	(7) Indicated Relativity to Class 1
1	1.0000	$14,370,968	$14,370,968	$11,003,868	0.7657	1.0000
2	1.4500	9,438,017	6,508,977	6,541,840	1.0050	1.3125
3	1.8000	8,002,463	4,445,813	5,618,043	1.2636	1.6503
Total		$31,811,448	$25,325,758	$23,163,751		

In practice, the resulting indicated relativities are generally credibility-weighted with the existing relativities. This protects the relativities for smaller classifications against short-term fluctuations in experience.

Correction for Off-Balance

Assume that the existing base rate is $160. If we have determined that we need a 10.14% increase overall, the indicated base rate is (1.1014)($160) = $176.22. The indicated rate changes by classification are therefore:

Class 1: [(176.22)(1.0000)/(160)(1.0000)]-1 = +.1014
Class 2: [(176.22)(1.3125)/(160)(1.4500)]-1 = −.0031
Class 3: [(176.22)(1.6503)/(160)(1.8000)]-1 = +.0098

Applying these indicated classification rate changes to the on-level earned premium we get the following:

Class 1: $14,370,968 × 1.1014 = $15,828,184
Class 2: 9,438,017 × 0.9969 = 9,408,759
Class 3: 8,002,463 × 1.0098 = 8,080,887

The on-level earned premium at these base rates and classification relativities would be $15,828,184 + $9,408,759 + $8,080,887 = $33,317,830. This represents only a 4.74% increase over the $31,811,448 on-level earned premium at the current rate levels. The difference between this and the 10.14% overall indication is the **off-balance.** The off-balance exists because the indicated classification relativities produce an average classification relativity different from the average classification relativity underlying the current rates. In this case, the Class 1 relativity is unchanged while the relativities for the other two classes are decreased.

We correct for this off-balance by increasing the indicated base rate by an off-balance factor of 1.1014/1.0474 = 1.0516. The corrected indicated base rate is then (1.0516)($176.22) = $185.31. This will produce the following corrected indicated rate changes by classification:

Class 1:	[(185.31)(1.0000)/(160)(1.0000)]-1 =	+.1582
Class 2:	[(185.31)(1.3125)/(160)(1.4500)]-1 =	+.0484
Class 3:	[(185.31)(1.6503)/(160)(1.8000)]-1 =	+.0619

Applying these corrected indicated classification rate changes to the on-level earned premium, we get the following:

Class 1:	$14,370,968 ×	1.1582 =	$16,644,455
Class 2:	9,438,017 ×	1.0484 =	9,894,817
Class 3:	8,002,463 ×	1.0619 =	8,497,815

The resulting on-level premium aggregates to $35,037,087 or 10.14% more than the current on-level earned. The corrected base rate of $185.31, in conjunction with the revised classification relativities, now provides the overall level of rate increase indicated.

The Appendix to this chapter contains a more complex example involving both classification and territorial relativities.

Limitation of Rate Changes

Occasionally, due to regulatory requirements or marketing considerations, it is necessary that individual rate changes be limited to a maximum increase or decrease. In the above example, assume that it has been determined that no classification rate may increase or decrease by more than 12.5%. Since the Class 1 rate change indicated is 15.82%, it needs to be limited to 12.50%, or a revised rate of ($160)(1.1250) = $180.00.

Reducing the Class 1 rate to $180.00 has two effects. First, it reduces the indicated on-level earned premium for Class 1 from $16,644,455 to $16,167,339, a reduction of $477,116. If we are to make up for this loss by increasing the rates for the remaining classes, we need an increase of \$477,116/(\$9,408,759 + \$8,080,887) or .0273 in Class 2 and Class 3 rates. The second effect of the limitation arises because Class 1 is the base rate. Since the base rate is being reduced, the class relativities must be increased by a factor of 1.1582/1.1250 = 1.0295 to compensate for the change. The factor necessary to correct for the off-balance due to the limitation is therefore (1.0273)(1.0295) = 1.0576. The resulting class relativities are:

Class 2:	(1.3125)(1.0576) = 1.3881
Class 3:	(1.6503)(1.0576) = 1.7454

The calculations of the resulting increases by classification and overall increase in on-level premium are left as exercises for the reader.

Increased Limits

The final topic to be addressed in this chapter is increased-limits ratemaking. While the level of attention to the development of rates for increased limits is sometimes less than that given the development of basic limits rates, the number of increased limits factors which exceed 2.000 should serve to focus attention on this important element of manual ratemaking. In an earlier discussion we saw how the severity trend in excess layers increases as the lower bound of the layer increases. This effect alone is sufficient to produce a general upward movement in increased limits factors. When combined with the effects of our increased litigiousness as a society, the need for regular review of increased limits rate adequacy should be apparent. In this section we will provide brief descriptions of three methods available for the review of increased limits experience.

Trending Individual Losses

This method involves the application of severity trend to a body of individual loss data. Generally, closed claim data are used in order to avoid the problems associated with projecting loss development on individual claims. In order to apply the method, an annual severity trend factor is first determined. This trend factor is then applied to each closed claim for the period from date of closure to the applicable effective period for the indicated increased limits factors. The resulting distribution of trended closed claims is then used to determine the appropriate increased limits factors.

Note that the application of this method requires the use of unlimited losses as the projection base. Since insurers are frequently unaware of the unlimited loss amounts associated with closed claims, this method is often based upon special data surveys.

Loss Development by Layer

Another method which can be used to analyze increased limits experience is to look at loss development patterns by layer. This process involves segregating case-incurred loss data by policy limit and loss layer and then tracking the observed loss development factors in each layer. Generally, the sparsity of data in the upper limits precludes the use of this method.

Fitted Size-of-Loss Distribution

The third method is related to the individual loss trending method. In this method, a theoretical size-of-loss distribution is fitted to existing individual loss data. The resulting distribution can then be used to examine the effects of severity trend on various limits and as a basis for the increased limits factors.

Summary

While this chapter has covered most of what could be considered the basics of manual ratemaking, every line of insurance will have characteristics requiring specialized treatment. For each method illustrated in this chapter, there are situations in which its application would be clearly inappropriate. There is no substitute for informed judgment arising out of a thorough understanding of the characteristics of the insurance coverage being priced. The actuary who becomes a slave to ratemaking methodology rather than a student of the business will, at some point, be led astray.

References

Cook, C. F. 1970. Trend and loss development factors. PCAS 57:1.

Lommele, J. A., and Sturgis, R. W. 1974. An econometric model of workers' compensation. PCAS 61:170.

Masterson, N. E. 1968. Economic factors in liability and property insurance claim costs, 1935-1967. PCAS 55:61.

Miller, D. L., and Davis, G. E. 1976. A refined model for premium adjustment. PCAS 63:117.

Ratemaking
Questions for Discussion

The Concept of Manual Ratemaking

What is the major difference between the pricing of a manufactured item and property and liability ratemaking? What other services or products are similar to insurance as far as pricing is concerned?

Basic Terminology

What might be the appropriate exposure base for an insurance product providing coverage against window breakage?

Which of the following would generally be considered as a part of unallocated loss adjustment expenses?

a) Outside legal expenses on a specific claim
b) Salary of the Claims Vice President
c) Costs associated with printing the rate manual

Some lines of insurance, for example automobile collision, are characterized as **high frequency-low severity** while others, such as professional liability are **low frequency-high severity** lines. Which type would generally be expected to exhibit the lower variability of pure premium?

A certain insurer paid losses during a year equal to 10% of the premiums written during the same year. Assuming that expenses amounted to 25% of written premiums, what can be determined about the adequacy of the insurer's rates? What type of loss ratio is the 10%? Is there a more meaningful alternative?

The Goal of the Ratemaking Process

Which of the following are generally reviewed as part of the actuary's primary responsibility in ratemaking?

a) Pure premium
b) Affordability of coverage
c) Desired level of profit
d) What the competition is charging

e) Changes in applicable tax law
f) Anticipated marketing expenses
g) Relationship between price and demand for coverage

Structure of the Rating Plan

Consider an insurer providing guarantees of individual student loans to undergraduates. What elements might be considered in the rating plan? What might be the result of failure to reflect each element?

Basic Manual Ratemaking Methods

For each of the following, discuss the relative merits of the pure premium and loss ratio methods:

Coverage	Exposure Base
Auto Liability	Car Year
Homeowners	Dwelling Year
Products Liability	Annual Sales

Need for Common Basis

Over the last five years an insurer's loss experience on Florida mobile-homeowners has been better than expected. The Marketing Department has requested that rates be reduced to generate additional business. What consideration might the actuary give to the the level of hurricane activity over the past five years? Over the past 100 years?

Given the following rate change history for a level book of 12-month term policies uniformly distributed throughout the experience period, what is the appropriate on-level factor to apply to the 1988 earned premium in order to produce earned premium at the 10/1/88 rate level? [1.1382]

10/1/86	+ 10%
10/1/87	+ 15%
10/1/88	+ 10%

Trended, Projected Ultimate Losses

Over the past five years a company has experienced exposure growth of 10%, 50%, 25%, 10% and 5% during the first, second, third, fourth and fifth years respectively. Assuming the growth occurred uniformly throughout each year, what impact would the changes in the growth rates be expected to have on the age-to-age development factors?

A company has been very successful writing professional liability insurance for college professors with a $10,000 per claim policy limit. Frequency has been stable and net severity has been increasing at less than 3% per year and now stands at $8,200 per claim. As a result of the good experience, the company has decided to increase the policy limit to $100,000 per claim. How might the pricing actuary project the severity trend for the revised product?

Inflation, which has been running at between 4% and 6% per year, suddenly increases to 15% per year and is expected to remain at that higher level. What impact might this have on indicated severity trend factors? What impact might it have on expected loss development factors? Is it double-counting to reflect both?

Expense Provisions

Given the following, calculate the target loss ratio assuming a 5% profit and contingencies factor. [.5833]

Written premium	$1,000,000
Earned premium	900,000
Incurred losses and allocated loss expenses	500,000
Incurred unallocated loss expenses	40,000
Commissions paid	200,000
Premium taxes paid	20,000
Other acquisition expenses	50,000
General expenses	45,000

Profit and Contingencies

You are the actuary for a rating bureau and have been charged with the responsibility for the recommendation of rates for use by each of the bureau members, regardless of size or financial condition. How might you reflect the profit and contingencies loading in the rates? What problems or opportunities might your selection of method create for individual bureau members?

Overall Rate Indication

Your company writes 100% of the market for a certain insurance coverage yet the experience base is so small that it cannot be considered to be fully (100%) credible. What options might be available in developing a credibility—weighted indication?

Classification and Territorial Rates

In a given jurisdiction, rates are not allowed to increase by more than 25% for any given classification. Your indicated rate increase for a classification which represents 60% of total premium volume is 45%. The president of your company wants you to produce rates which are adequate, on average, for the entire jurisdiction. Your major competitor does not provide coverage for risks in your largest classification. How might you treat the off-balance resulting from the 25% capping of rate increases?

Increased Limits

Although your company has never paid a claim greater than $1,000,000, you are concerned about the rate adequacy of your $2,000,000 limit policy. How might you estimate the appropriate additional charge for the $1,000,000 excess of your $1,000,000 basic limit?

Appendix

This appendix contains a complete, though simplified, example of a manual rate analysis of private passenger automobile bodily injury. The data are totally fictitious but are meant to be reasonably representative of actual data which might be observed in practice. The appendix consists of 16 sheets which are meant to provide an example of the exhibits that might accompany a rate filing with a regulatory body. Following is a brief description of each of these sheets.

Sheet 1 is meant to represent the existing rate manual, effective 7/1/86, for the coverage under review. The manual contains basic limits rates for each of three classifications within each of three territories, along with a single increased limits factor to adjust the rates for basic limits of $20,000 per person, $40,000 per occurrence (20/40) upward to limits of $100,000 per person, $300,000 per occurrence (100/300). Territorial and classification rates are keyed to a base rate of $160 for Territory 2, Class 1.

Sheet 2 demonstrates the computation of the on-level earned premium based upon the extension of exposures technique. The experience period is the three years 1985–1987 and the earned exposures, by class and territory, for each of those years are multiplied by the appropriate current rate to yield the on-level earned.

Sheet 3 shows the projection of ultimate loss and allocated loss adjustment expense for accident years 1982–1987, using the case-incurred loss development method.

Sheet 4 contains the projected ultimate claim counts for accident years 1982–1987, based upon the reported count development method.

Sheet 5 details the calculation of the severity trend factor based upon the projected incurred losses and ultimate claims for accident years 1982–1987. The trend factor is based upon a linear least-squares fit.

Sheet 6 addresses the frequency trend factor based upon the earned exposures and projected ultimate claims for accident years 1982–1987, based upon an exponential least-squares fit.

Sheet 7 contains the calculation of the target loss and allocated loss expense ratio. Note that there is no specific provision for profit and contingencies in this example, the assumption being that the investment profits will be sufficient.

Sheet 8 presents the calculation of the indicated statewide rate level change, using the loss ratio method.

Sheet 9 contains projections of trended projected ultimate losses and allocated loss expenses by accident year, classification, and territory for accident years 1985–1987.

Sheet 10 demonstrates the calculation of indicated classification and territorial pure premiums and pure premium relativities.

Sheet 11 shows the calculation of credibility-weighted classification relativities and the selection of relativities to be used.

Sheet 12 shows the calculation of credibility-weighted territorial relativities and the selection of relativities to be used.

Sheet 13 details the correction for off-balance resulting from the selected classification and territorial relativities.

Sheet 14 shows the development of the revised basic limits rates and the calculation of the resulting statewide rate level change.

Sheet 15 describes the calculation of the revised 100/300 increased limits factor using the individual trended loss approach.

Sheet 16 is the proposed rate manual to be effective 7/1/88.

Appendix
Sheet 1

EXAMPLE AUTO INSURANCE COMPANY

Rate Manual—7/1/86

Private Passenger Auto Bodily Injury
20/40 Basic Limits

Territory	Class 1 Adult Drivers, No Youthful Operators	Class 2 Family with Youthful Drivers Not Principal Op.	Class 3 Youthful Owners or Principal Operators
1—Central City	$224	$325	$403
2—Midway Valley	160	232	288
3—Remainder of State	136	197	245

Increased Limits

Limit	Factor
100/300	1.300

Appendix
Sheet 2

EXHIBIT I

EXAMPLE AUTO INSURANCE COMPANY

Private Passenger Auto Bodily Injury
Basic Limits

Development of Indicated Statewide Rate Level Change

A. Earned Premium at Current Rate Level

	Class 1	Class 2	Class 3	Total
Earned Exposures:				
1985 Territory 1	7,807	3,877	1,553	13,237
Territory 2	11,659	4,976	3,930	20,565
Territory 3	5,760	2,639	3,030	11,429
Total	25,226	11,492	8,513	45,231
1986 Territory 1	8,539	4,181	1,697	14,417
Territory 2	12,957	5,442	4,262	22,661
Territory 3	5,834	2,614	3,057	11,505
Total	27,330	12,237	9,016	48,583
1987 Territory 1	9,366	4,551	1,870	15,787
Territory 2	14,284	5,939	4,669	24,892
Territory 3	5,961	2,591	3,036	11,588
Total	29,611	13,081	9,575	52,267
Current Rate Level:				
Territory 1	$224	$325	$403	
Territory 2	$160	$232	$288	
Territory 3	$136	$197	$245	
On-Level Earned Premium:				
1985 Territory 1	$1,748,768	$1,260,025	$ 625,859	$ 3,634,652
Territory 2	1,865,440	1,154,432	1,131,840	4,151,712
Territory 3	783,360	519,883	742,350	2,045,593
Total	$4,397,568	$2,934,340	$2,500,049	$ 9,831,957
1986 Territory 1	$1,912,736	$1,358,825	$ 683,891	$ 3,955,452
Territory 2	2,073,120	1,262,544	1,227,456	4,563,120
Territory 3	793,424	514,958	748,965	2,057,347
Total	$4,779,280	$3,136,327	$2,660,312	$10,575,919
1987 Territory 1	$2,097,984	$1,479,075	$ 753,610	$ 4,330,669
Territory 2	2,285,440	1,377,848	1,344,672	5,007,960
Territory 3	810,696	510,427	743,820	2,064,943
Total	$5,194,120	$3,367,350	$2,842,102	$11,403,572

Appendix
Sheet 3

EXHIBIT II

EXAMPLE AUTO INSURANCE COMPANY

Private Passenger Auto Bodily Injury
Basic Limits

Development of Indicated Statewide Rate Level Change

B. Projected Ultimate Accident Year Loss and Allocated Loss Expense

Acc Year	Cumulative Basic Limits Case-Incurred Loss and Allocated Loss Expense					
	Age 12	Age 24	Age 36	Age 48	Age 60	Age 72
1982	$2,116,135	$3,128,695	$3,543,445	$3,707,375	$3,854,220	$3,928,805
1983	2,315,920	3,527,197	3,992,805	4,182,133	4,338,765	
1984	2,743,657	4,051,950	4,593,472	4,797,194		
1985	3,130,262	4,589,430	5,230,437			
1986	3,625,418	5,380,617				
1987	3,919,522					

Acc Year	Incremental Loss Development Factors					
	12-24	24-36	36-48	48-60	60-72	72-Ultimate
1982	1.4785	1.1326	1.0463	1.0396	1.0194	
1983	1.5230	1.1320	1.0474	1.0375		
1984	1.4768	1.1336	1.0444			
1985	1.4661	1.1397				
1986	1.4841					
Selected	1.4800	1.1350	1.0450	1.0385	1.0200	1.0000
Ultimate	1.8595	1.2564	1.1070	1.0593	1.0200	1.0000

Accident Year	Loss & Allocated 12/31/87	Ultimate Factor	Projected Ultimate Loss & Allocated
1982	$3,928,805	1.0000	$3,928,805
1983	4,338,765	1.0200	4,425,540
1984	4,797,194	1.0593	5,081,668
1985	5,230,437	1.1070	5,790,094
1986	5,380,617	1.2564	6,760,207
1987	3,919,522	1.8595	7,288,351

Appendix
Sheet 4

EXHIBIT III

EXAMPLE AUTO INSURANCE COMPANY

Private Passenger Auto Bodily Injury
Basic Limits

Development of Indicated Statewide Rate Level Change

C. Projected Ultimate Accident Year Claim Counts

Acc Year	Cumulative Reported Claims					
	Age 12	Age 24	Age 36	Age 48	Age 60	Age 72
1982	1,804	2,173	2,374	2,416	2,416	2,416
1983	1,935	2,379	2,424	2,552	2,552	
1984	2,103	2,384	2,514	2,646		
1985	2,169	2,580	2,722			
1986	2,346	2,783				
1987	2,337					

Acc Year	Incremental Claim Development Factors					
	12-24	24-36	36-48	48-60	60-72	72-Ultimate
1982	1.2045	1.0925	1.0177	1.0000	1.0000	
1983	1.2295	1.0189	1.0528	1.0000		
1984	1.1336	1.0545	1.0525			
1985	1.1895	1.0550				
1986	1.1863					
Selected	1.1900	1.0550	1.0450	1.0000	1.0000	1.0000
Ultimate	1.3120	1.1025	1.0450	1.0000	1.0000	1.0000

Accident Year	Reported Claims 12/31/87	Ultimate Factor	Projected Ultimate Claims
1982	2,416	1.0000	2,416
1983	2,552	1.0000	2,552
1984	2,646	1.0000	2,646
1985	2,722	1.0450	2,844
1986	2,783	1.1025	3,068
1987	2,337	1.3120	3,066

Appendix
Sheet 5

EXHIBIT IV

EXAMPLE AUTO INSURANCE COMPANY

Private Passenger Auto Bodily Injury
Basic Limits
Development of Indicated Statewide Rate Level Change

D. Development of Severity Trend Factor—Basic Limits

Accident Year	Projected Loss & Allocated (Exh II)	Projected Ultimate Claims (Exh III)	Projected Ultimate Average Severity	Linear Least-Squares Fit [1]
1982	$3,928,805	2,416	$1,626	$1,605.90
1983	4,425,540	2,552	1,734	1,756.67
1984	5,081,668	2,646	1,921	1,907.44
1985	5,790,094	2,844	2,036	2,058.21
1986	6,760,207	3,068	2,203	2,208.98
1987	7,288,351	3,066	2,377	2,359.75

Annual Severity Trend Factor (1987/1986 Least-Squares) 1.0683

[1] $y = mx + b$ where: x = Accident Year—1981
$m = 150.77$
$b = 1455.13$

Severity Trend
Private Passenger B.I.—Basic Limits

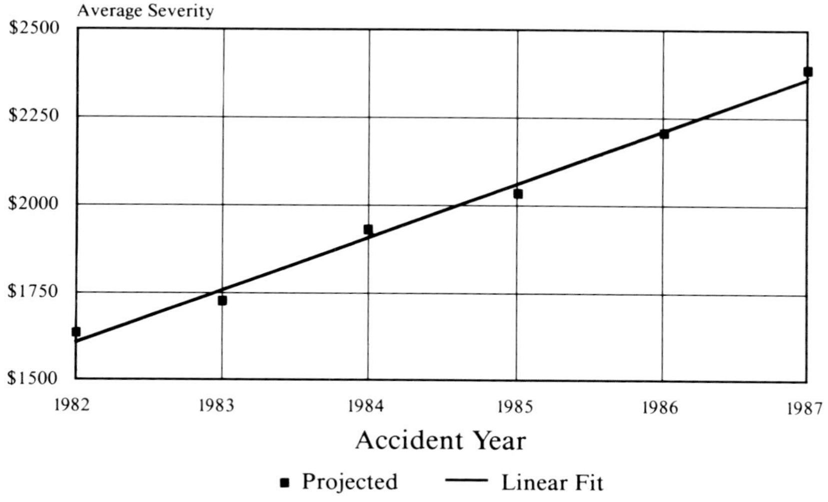

Appendix
Sheet 6

EXHIBIT V

EXAMPLE AUTO INSURANCE COMPANY

Private Passenger Auto Bodily Injury
Basic Limits

Development of Indicated Statewide Rate Level Change

E. Development of Frequency Trend Factor

Accident Year	Projected Ultimate Claims (Exh III)	Earned Exposures	Projected Ultimate Frequency	Exponential Least-Squares Fit [2]
1982	2,416	37,846	0.0638	0.0647
1983	2,552	39,771	0.0642	0.0638
1984	2,646	42,135	0.0628	0.0630
1985	2,844	45,231	0.0629	0.0621
1986	3,068	48,583	0.0613	0.0621
1987	3,066	52,267	0.0587	0.0605

Annual Frequency Trend Factor (1987/1986 Least-Squares) 0.9867

[2] $y = ae^{bx}$ where: x = Accident Year—1981
a = .065562
b = .013417

Frequency Trend
Private Passenger B.I.

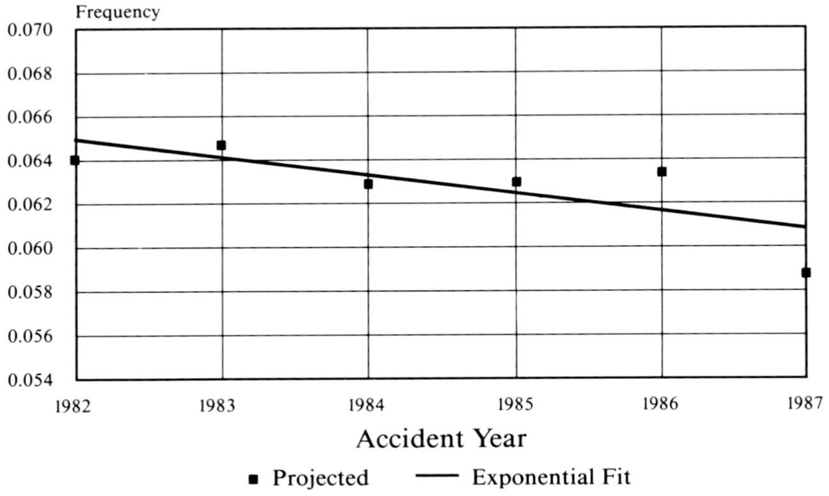

Appendix
Sheet 7

EXHIBIT VI

EXAMPLE AUTO INSURANCE COMPANY

Private Passenger Auto Bodily Injury
Basic Limits

Development of Indicated Statewide Rate Level Change

F. Development of Target Loss & Allocated Loss Expense Ratio

(1)	Commissions as % of Premium	15.00%
(2)	Taxes, Licenses, Fees as % of Premium	2.25%
(3)	Other Acquisition Expense as % of Premium	5.60%
(4)	General Expense as % of Premium	6.80%
(5)	Premium-Based Expense [(1) + (2) + (3) + (4)]	29.65%
(6)	Unallocated Loss Expense as % of Loss & Allocated Loss Expense	6.42%
(7)	Target Loss and Allocated Loss Expense Ratio [1.0 − (5)] / [1.0 + (6)]	66.11%

Appendix
Sheet 8

EXHIBIT VII

EXAMPLE AUTO INSURANCE COMPANY

Private Passenger Auto Bodily Injury
Basic Limits

Development of Indicated Statewide Rate Level Change

G. Development of Statewide Indication

[1] Accident Year	[2] Projected Loss & Allocated (Exh II)	[3] Midpoint Experience Period	[4] Years to 7/1/89	Trend Factor to 7/1/89 [5] Severity 1.0683[4] (Exh IV)	Trend Factor to 7/1/89 [6] Frequency .9867[4] (Exh V)
1985	$5,790,094	7/1/85	4.0	1.3025	0.9479
1986	6,760,207	7/1/86	3.0	1.2192	0.9606
1987	7,288,351	7/1/87	2.0	1.1413	0.9735

[7] Accident Year	[8] Trended Loss & Allocated [2] × [5] × [6]	[9] On-Level Earned Premium (Exh I)	[10] Trended On-Level Loss & Allocated Ratio [8]/[9]	[11] Target Loss & Allocated Ratio (Exh VI)	[12] Indicated Statewide Rate Level Change {([10]/[11]) + 1.000}
1985	$7,148,680	$9,831,957	72.71%		
1986	7,917,308	10,575,919	74.86		
1987	8,097,763	11,403,572	71.01		
Total	$23,163,751	$31,811,448	72.82%	66.11%	10.14%

Appendix
Sheet 9

EXHIBIT VIII

EXAMPLE AUTO INSURANCE COMPANY

Private Passenger Auto Bodily Injury
Basic Limits

Development of Indicated Rate Level Change by Class and Territory

H. Development of Trended Loss & Allocated by Class and Territory

Terr	Class	Acc Year	[1] Loss & Allocated 12/31/87	[2] Ultimate Factor (Exh II)	[3] Severity Trend to 7/1/89 (Exh VII)	[4] Frequency Trend to 7/1/89 (Exh VII)	[5] Trended Projected Loss & Allocated [1]×[2]× [3]×[4]
1	1	1985	$ 986,617	1.1070	1.3025	0.9479	$1,348,455
1	1	1986	982,778	1.2564	1.2192	0.9606	1,446,109
1	1	1987	797,650	1.8595	1.1413	0.9735	1,647,951
1	2	1985	680,769	1.1070	1.3025	0.9479	930,438
1	2	1986	703,406	1.2564	1.2192	0.9606	1,035,027
1	2	1987	456,899	1.8595	1.1413	0.9735	943.957
1	3	1985	325,397	1.1070	1.3025	0.9479	444,735
1	3	1986	343,738	1.2564	1.2192	0.9606	505,793
1	3	1987	252,790	1.8595	1.1413	0.9735	522,266
2	1	1985	1,062,395	1.1070	1.3025	0.9479	1,452,024
2	1	1986	1,170,978	1.2564	1.2192	0.9606	1,723,035
2	1	1987	848,551	1.8595	1.1413	0.9735	1,753,113
2	2	1985	597,044	1.1070	1.3025	0.9479	816,008
2	2	1986	575,004	1.2564	1.2192	0.9606	846,090
2	2	1987	449,123	1.8595	1.1413	0.9735	927,892
2	3	1985	557,332	1.1070	1.3025	0.9479	761,731
2	3	1986	650,645	1.2564	1.2192	0.9606	957,391
2	3	1987	469,963	1.8595	1.1413	0.9735	970,947
3	1	1985	401,622	1.1070	1.3025	0.9479	548,915
3	1	1986	394,358	1.2564	1.2192	0.9606	580,278
3	1	1987	243,943	1.8595	1.1413	0.9735	503,988
3	2	1985	252,439	1.1070	1.3025	0.9479	345,020
3	2	1986	228,313	1.2564	1.2192	0.9606	335,951
3	2	1987	174,954	1.8595	1.1413	0.9735	361,456
3	3	1985	366,822	1.1070	1.3025	0.9479	501,353
3	3	1986	331,397	1.2564	1.2192	0.9606	487,634
3	3	1987	225,649	1.8595	1.1413	0.9735	466,193

Appendix
Sheet 10

EXHIBIT IX

EXAMPLE AUTO INSURANCE COMPANY

Private Passenger Auto Bodily Injury
Basic Limits

Development of Indicated Rate Level Change by Class and Territory

I. Development of Trended Pure Premium by Class and Territory

Terr	Class	Acc Year	[1] Trended Projected Loss & Allocated (Exh VIII)	[2] Earned Exposure (Exh I)	[3] Trended Pure Premium [1]/[2]	[4] Relativity to Class 1	[5] Relativity to Terr 2
1	1	1985	$1,348,455	7,807	$172.72	1.0000	1.3869
1	1	1986	1,446,109	8,539	169.35	1.0000	1.2735
1	1	1987	1,647,951	9,366	175.95	1.0000	1.4336
1	2	1985	930,438	3,877	239.99	1.3894	1.4634
1	2	1986	1,035,027	4,181	247.55	1.4618	1.5923
1	2	1987	943,957	4,551	207.42	1.1788	1.3276
1	3	1985	444,735	1,553	286.37	1.6580	1.4775
1	3	1986	505,793	1,697	298.05	1.7599	1.3268
1	3	1987	522,266	1,870	279.29	1.5873	1.3430
2	1	1985	1,452,024	11,659	124.54	1.0000	1.0000
2	1	1986	1,723,035	12,957	132.98	1.0000	1.0000
2	1	1987	1,753,113	14,284	122.73	1.0000	1.0000
2	2	1985	816,008	4,976	163.99	1.3167	1.0000
2	2	1986	846,090	5,442	155.47	1.1691	1.0000
2	2	1987	927,892	5,939	156.24	1.2730	1.0000
2	3	1985	761,731	3,930	193.82	1.5563	1.0000
2	3	1986	957,391	4,262	224.63	1.6892	1.0000
2	3	1987	970,947	4,669	207.96	1.6944	1.0000
3	1	1985	548,915	5,760	95.30	1.0000	0.7652
3	1	1986	580,278	5,834	99.46	1.0000	0.7480
3	1	1987	503,988	5,961	84.55	1.0000	0.6889
3	2	1985	345,020	2,639	130.74	1.3719	0.7972
3	2	1986	335,951	2,614	128.52	1.2921	0.8266
3	2	1987	361,456	2,591	139.50	1.6500	0.8929
3	3	1985	501,353	3,030	165.46	1.7363	0.8537
3	3	1986	487,634	3,057	159.51	1.6037	0.7101
3	3	1987	466,193	3,036	153.56	1.8162	0.7384

Appendix
Sheet 11

EXHIBIT X

EXAMPLE AUTO INSURANCE COMPANY

Private Passenger Auto Bodily Injury
Basic Limits

Development of Indicated Rate Level Change by Class and Territory

J. Development of Indicated Class Relativity to Class 1

Class	Terr	Acc Year	[1] Earned Exposure (Exh IX)	[2] Relativity to Class 1 (Exh IX)	[3] Weighted Relativity [1] × [2]
2	1	1985	3,877	1.3894	5,386.70
	1	1986	4,181	1.4618	6,111.79
	1	1987	4,551	1.1788	5,364.72
	2	1985	4,976	1.3167	6,551.90
	2	1986	5,442	1.1691	6,362.24
	2	1987	5,939	1.2730	7,560.35
	3	1985	2,639	1.3719	3,620.44
	3	1986	2,614	1.2921	3,377.55
	3	1987	2,591	1.6500	4,275.15
	Total	Total	36,810	1.3206	48,610.84

Current Class 2 Relativity	1.4500
Credibility = [Exposure/ (Exposure + 25,000)]	0.5955
Credibility Weighted Indication	1.3729
Selected Relativity	1.3700

Class	Terr	Acc Year	[1] Earned Exposure (Exh IX)	[2] Relativity to Class 1 (Exh IX)	[3] Weighted Relativity [1] × [2]
3	1	1985	1,553	1.6580	2,574.87
	1	1986	1,697	1.7599	2,986.55
	1	1987	1,870	1.5873	2,968.25
	2	1985	3,930	1.5563	6,116.26
	2	1986	4,262	1.6892	7,199.37
	2	1987	4,669	1.6944	7,911.15
	3	1985	3,030	1.7363	5,260.99
	3	1986	3,057	1.6037	4,902.51
	3	1987	3,036	1.8162	5,513.98
	Total	Total	27,104	1.6763	45,433.94

Current Class 3 Relativity	1.8000
Credibility = [Exposure/ (Exposure + 25,000)]	0.5202
Credibility Weighted Indication	1.7356
Selected Relativity	1.7400

Appendix
Sheet 12

EXHIBIT XI

EXAMPLE AUTO INSURANCE COMPANY

Private Passenger Auto Bodily Injury
Basic Limits

Development of Indicated Rate Level Change by Class and Territory

K. Development of Indicated Territorial Relativity to Territory 2

Terr	Class	Acc Year	[1] Earned Exposure (Exh IX)	[2] Relativity to Terr 2 (Exh IX)	[3] Weighted Relativity [1] × [2]
1	1	1985	7,807	1.3869	10,827.53
	1	1986	8,539	1.2735	10,874.42
	1	1987	9,366	1.4336	13,427.10
	2	1985	3,877	1.4635	5,673.99
	2	1986	4,181	1.5923	6,657.41
	2	1987	4,551	1.3276	6,041.91
	3	1985	1,553	1.4775	2,294.56
	3	1986	1,697	1.3268	2,251.58
	3	1987	1,870	1.3430	2,511.41
	Total	Total	43,441	1.3941	60,559.89

Current Territory 1 Relativity	1.4000
Credibility = [Exposure/ (Exposure + 25,000)]	0.6347
Credibility Weighted Indication	1.3962
Selected Relativity	1.4000

Terr	Class	Acc Year	[1] Earned Exposure (Exh IX)	[2] Relativity to Terr 2 (Exh IX)	[3] Weighted Relativity [1] × [2]
3	1	1985	5,760	0.7652	4,407.55
	1	1986	5,834	0.7480	4,363.83
	1	1987	5,961	0.6889	4,106.53
	2	1985	2,639	0.7972	2,103.81
	2	1986	2,614	0.8266	2,160.73
	2	1987	2,591	0.8929	2,313.50
	3	1985	3,030	0.8537	2,586.71
	3	1986	3,057	0.7101	2,170.78
	3	1987	3,036	0.7384	2,241.78
	Total	Total	34,522	0.7663	26,455.23

Current Territory 3 Relativity	0.8500
Credibility = [Exposure/ (Exposure + 25,000)]	0.5800
Credibility Weighted Indication	0.8015
Selected Relativity	0.8000

Appendix
Sheet 13

EXHIBIT XII

EXAMPLE AUTO INSURANCE COMPANY

Private Passenger Auto Bodily Injury
Basic Limits

Development of Indicated Rate Level Change by Class and Territory

L. Adjustment of Base Rate Level Change for Class and Territory Off-Balance

Terr	Class	Acc Year	[1] On-Level Earned Premium (Exh I)	[2] Current Class Relativity (Exh X)	[3] Current Territorial Relativity (Exh XI)	[4] Current Relativity to Terr 2 Class 1 [2]×[3]
1	1	1987	$ 2,097,984	1.0000	1.4000	1.4000
1	2	1987	1,479,075	1.4500	1.4000	2.0300
1	3	1987	753,610	1.8000	1.4000	2.5200
2	1	1987	2,285,440	1.0000	1.0000	1.0000
2	2	1987	1,377,848	1.4500	1.0000	1.4500
2	3	1987	1,344,672	1.8000	1.0000	1.8000
3	1	1987	810,696	1.0000	0.8500	0.8500
3	2	1987	510,427	1.4500	0.8500	1.2325
3	3	1987	743,820	1.8000	0.8500	1.5300
		Total	$11,403,572			

Terr	Class	Acc Year	[5] Proposed Class Relativity (Exh X)	[6] Proposed Territorial Relativity (Exh XI)	[7] Proposed Relativity to Terr 2 Class 1 [5]×[6]	[8] Effect of Relativity Changes [7]/[4]−1	[9] Premium Effect [1]×[8]
1	1	1987	1.0000	1.4000	1.4000	0.00%	$0
1	2	1987	1.3700	1.4000	1.9180	−5.52	($81,604)
1	3	1987	1.7400	1.4000	2.4360	−3.33	($25,120)
2	1	1987	1.0000	1.0000	1.0000	0.00	$0
2	2	1987	1.3700	1.0000	1.3700	−5.52	($76,019)
2	3	1987	1.7400	1.0000	1.7400	−3.33	($44,822)
3	1	1987	1.0000	0.8000	0.8000	−5.88	($47,688)
3	2	1987	1.3700	0.8000	1.0960	−11.08	($56,530)
3	3	1987	1.7400	0.8000	1.3920	−9.02	($67,090)
		Total				−3.50%	($398,873)

Indicated Statewide Rate Change (Exhibit VII)	10.14%
Indicated Base Rate Change (1.1014/.9650)-1	14.13%
Current Class 1 Territory 2 Rate	$160
Indicated Class 1 Territory 2 Rate	$183

Appendix
Sheet 14

EXHIBIT XIII

EXAMPLE AUTO INSURANCE COMPANY

Private Passenger Auto Bodily Injury
Basic Limits

Development of Indicated Rate Level Change by Class and Territory

M. Development of Basic Limits Rates by Class and Territory

[1] Class	[2] Territory	[3] Class Relativity (Exh X)	[4] Territorial Relativity (Exh XI)	[5] Base Rate (Exh XII)	[6] Class & Territory Rate [3]×[4]×[5]
1	1	1.0000	1.4000	$183	$256
	2	1.0000	1.0000	183	183
	3	1.0000	0.8000	183	146
2	1	1.3700	1.4000	183	351
	2	1.3700	1.0000	183	251
	3	1.3700	0.8000	183	201
3	1	1.7400	1.4000	183	446
	2	1.7400	1.0000	183	318
	3	1.7400	0.8000	183	255

[1] Class	[2] Territory	[7] 1987 Earned Exposures (Exh I)	[8] New Level Earned Premium [6]×[7]	[9] Current Level 1987 Earned Premium (Exh I)	[10] Statewide Rate Level Change ([8]/[9]) − 1
1	1	9,366	$ 2,397,696	$ 2,097,984	
	2	14,284	2,613,972	2,285,440	
	3	5,961	870,306	810,696	
2	1	4,551	1,597,401	1,479,075	
	2	5,939	1,490,689	1,377,848	
	3	2,591	520,791	510,427	
3	1	1,870	834,020	753,610	
	2	4,669	1,484,742	1,344,672	
	3	3,036	774,180	743,820	
Total	Total	52,267	$12,583,797	$11,403,572	10.35%

Appendix
Sheet 15

EXHIBIT XIV

EXAMPLE AUTO INSURANCE COMPANY

Private Passenger Auto Bodily Injury
Basic Limits

Development of Indicated 100/300 Increased Limits Factor

	Claim	Distribution of Trended Losses [a]		
Unlimited Loss Amount	**Count**	**Unlimited**	**20/40**	**100/300**
\$ 1—\$ 20,000	4,249	\$17,706,594	\$17,706,594	\$17,706,594
20,001— 30,000	244	5,842,632	5,340,562	5,842,632
30,001— 40,000	150	5,102,257	3,884,463	5,102,257
40,001— 50,000	107	4,819,591	2,902,869	4,819,591
50,001— 60,000	54	2,910,399	1,436,150	2,910,399
60,001— 70,000	25	1,641,237	743,278	1,641,237
70,001— 80,000	21	1,587,230	611,920	1,587,230
80,001— 90,000	20	1,660,283	588,525	1,660,283
90,001— 100,000	13	1,268,376	368,077	1,268,376
100,001— 200,000	6	681,544	193,968	660,723
200,001— 500,000	16	4,354,732	439,906	2,031,077
	4,905	\$47,574,875	\$34,216,312	\$45,230,399

[1]	Indicated 100/300 Factor (\$45,230,399/\$34,216,312)	1.3219
[2]	100/300 Factor Indicated as of 12/31/85	1.2683
[3]	Annual Trend [(1.3219/1.2683) + (1/2)] − 1.0000	2.09%
[4]	Projected 7/1/89 100/300 Factor [1] × {(1 + [3]) + 1.5}	1.3636
[5]	Selected 100/300 Factor	1.3500

[a] Based upon unlimited claims closed from 1975 through 1987 trended to 12/31/87 at an annual rate of 8.5%.

Appendix
Sheet 16

EXAMPLE AUTO INSURANCE COMPANY

Rate Manual—7/1/88

Private Passenger Auto Bodily Injury
20/40 Basic Limits

Territory	Class 1 Adult Drivers, No Youthful Operators	Class 2 Family with Youthful Drivers Not Principal Op.	Class 3 Youthful Owners or Principal Operators
1—Central City	$256	$351	$446
2—Midway Valley	183	251	318
3—Remainder of State	146	201	255

Increased Limits

Limit	Factor
100/300	1.35

Chapter 3
INDIVIDUAL RISK RATING
by Margaret Wilkinson Tiller

Introduction

Manual ratemaking determines what rates should be charged average members of groups of entities for specified coverage and entity characteristics. Individual risk rating supplements manual rates by modifying the group rates in whole or in part to reflect an individual entity's experience.

If all entities in all rating groups were truly homogeneous, differences in experience among entities would be fortuitous. While homogeneity is the goal of manual ratemaking, it is not usually possible to achieve. In addition, some entities are large enough that their experience is, to some extent, "credible." Individual risk rating is appropriate when there is a combination of non-homogeneous rating groups and entities with credible experience.

This chapter discusses individual risk rating in general terms and provides examples from both traditional (insurance) and non-traditional risk financing mechanisms. The latter include risk retention groups, pools, and individual entities retaining risk. In this chapter it is assumed that the manual rates are properly determined, unless otherwise noted.

Goals of Individual Risk Rating

For an insurer, the primary goal of individual risk rating is to price the coverage provided more accurately than if rates were based only on manual rates. Non-traditional risk financing mechanisms also may use individual risk rating techniques, to allocate costs.

For groups of entities, such as pools or risk retention groups, the primary goals of individual risk rating (sometimes referred to as cost allocation) are to allocate costs to participants more accurately and to

---

"Individual Risk Rating" Copyright © 1989 by Margaret Wilkinson Tiller

motivate participation in risk control programs. These are also the goals of individual risk rating for individual entities retaining ("self-insuring") all or part of their risks and allocating the associated costs to departments or other units. Individual entities purchasing insurance may similarly wish to allocate the insurance costs to their departments or other units. For individual entities in either situation, the units to which the costs are being allocated take the role of participants or "insureds." Some entities may participate in individual risk rating systems as both allocator and allocatee.

The motivation to participate in risk control programs is a secondary goal of insurers using individual risk rating. Other goals of insurers and other entities using individual risk rating are to balance appropriately risk sharing and risk bearing and to provide information to design or modify risk control programs. For individual entities, the allocation of costs to units allows for more accurate pricing of products and services.

Attributes of Good Individual Risk Rating Systems

Good individual risk rating systems have the following attributes:

- serve the needs of the organization using them,
- appropriately balance risk sharing and risk bearing,
- are not subject to internal or external manipulation,
- are simple to administer,
- are easy to understand, and
- do not subject the affected entities to large fluctuations in costs from one year to the next due to unusual or catastrophic experience.

Some of these attributes may overlap. As practical considerations may override one or more of these attributes, all are listed.

Prior to designing any individual risk rating system, the organization designing it should determine what its needs are. These needs may simply be the goals listed above, or the entity may have different needs that override traditional cost allocation goals. For example, a corporation offering a new product may wish to allocate its product liability insurance costs for the new product to existing products to keep the cost of the new product down until it becomes popular.

An individual risk rating system should appropriately balance risk sharing and risk bearing. The costs for small entities whose experience is not at all credible should be determined solely based on risk sharing. Large entities whose experience is completely credible might have their costs solely based on risk bearing. Entities between these extremes should have their costs based on a weighting of risk sharing and risk bearing.

Individual risk rating systems should not be subject to internal or external manipulation. Manipulation is internal if the entity to which costs are being allocated can influence the cost allocation. An example is the entity to which costs are being allocated setting the case reserves used in the individual risk rating calculation. Manipulation is external if some agency other than the entity to which costs are being allocated can influence the cost allocation. An example is a marketing manager who can override the pricing results of the individual risk rating calculation without additional information.

As a practical consideration, individual risk rating systems should be simple to administer. If a system proves very complicated to administer, it might not be applied. A system that is simple to administer is also more likely to be easy to understand. Understanding is important particularly in those situations in which participation in risk control programs is one of the goals: the easier a system is to understand, the better will be the motivation to participate, assuming the system is appropriately designed.

A good individual risk rating system does not subject the affected entities to large fluctuations in costs from one year to the next due to unusual experience. An individual risk rating system should reflect an entity's experience only to the extent that it is credible. Unusual experience is not credible because it is not a true reflection of the entity's underlying exposure to loss. An individual risk rating system that reasonably balances risk sharing and risk bearing usually has this attribute of moderating the effect of unusual cost fluctuations. However, a system could have this attribute without reasonably balancing risk sharing and risk bearing.

Overview of Individual Risk Rating

There are two basic types of individual risk rating systems: prospective and retrospective. Prospective systems use past experience to determine costs for the future. Retrospective systems use the actual experience of the period to determine the final costs for that period.

Retrospective systems are more responsive to experience changes than prospective systems. This is an advantage when a primary goal is to motivate participation in risk control programs. This responsiveness also means that retrospective systems result in less stable costs from one time period to the next than do prospective systems. The final cost using a retrospective system is not known until many years after the subject period.

While different systems use different formulae, all individual risk rating systems weight experience and exposure. The weight assigned to the experience component is a reflection of the credibility of the entity's experience as a valid predictor of future costs.

There are practical considerations that affect individual risk rating systems. It may be appropriate to use alternative exposure bases and data if those desired are not readily available. Additionally, if one of the goals is to motivate participation in risk control programs and the results of the individual risk rating calculation do not make a material difference to the entity to which costs are being allocated, there will probably be no such motivation.

For individual entities allocating risk financing costs to units, several additional factors influence how effectively an individual risk rating system will meet its goals. These include variations in tax rates and systems, the ability of units to purchase their own insurance, and whether and how unit managers get the benefits or penalties of the costs allocated to their units.

Terminology

The insurance industry is notorious for using words in different ways, even within the same company. It is important to understand in every situation how terms are used, as different usage could produce different results. Some basic terms used in this chapter are discussed below.

Claims and Occurrences

A "claim" is a demand by an individual or other entity to recover for loss. An "occurrence" is a series of incidents happening over a specified, short period of time that collectively result in personal injury or property damage. Note that one occurrence may have multiple claims associated with it. Examples are a hurricane which takes place over several days and generates many claims and an automobile accident in which several people, each of whom files a claim, are injured.

In this chapter "claim" and "occurrence" are used as defined above. Different rating plans may use these terms differently. For example, "claim" is often used when "occurrence" is meant. Additionally, some entities count the different components of a claim as separate claims. For example, a general liability claim with both bodily injury and property damage may be counted as two claims.

"Claim" is often used also to refer to "loss." "Claim" and "occurrence" are indicator words: they indicate either presence or absence and not amount.

Many individual risk rating systems limit the losses used in the experience portion of the calculation. These limits are usually applied to each occurrence. Some formulae for the credibility used in the individual risk rating calculation rely on the number of occurrences.

Loss, ALAE, and ULAE

"Loss" refers to the amount associated with a claim. This is the amount a claim is worth, not the request for payment. For liability, "loss" includes bodily injury, property damage, and personal damage.

For workers' compensation, "loss" includes medical, indemnity, and rehabilitation benefits.

Allocated loss adjustment expenses (ALAE) are attorneys' fees, investigative fees, etc., associated with settling a particular claim. Unallocated loss adjustment expenses (ULAE) are expenses associated with adjusting claims which are not allocated to settlement of a particular claim.

For an insurer, ALAE are usually costs such as outside legal counsel, investigators, expert witnesses, and court costs, and ULAE are usually the costs of the claim department, including office space, salaries and benefits, supplies, etc. However, some insurers use no outside resources to settle claims (and have no ALAE) while other insurers keep time and expense records for the claim department and charge the costs to claims as ALAE (and have no ULAE). Similar situations can occur with non-traditional risk financing mechanisms.

"Loss" sometimes refers to loss only and sometimes to loss and ALAE. Different individual risk rating systems treat losses, ALAE, and ULAE differently. And the same system used by different entities may produce different results if ALAE and ULAE are defined differently.

Time Periods

An accident period is the period in which an occurrence occurs, regardless of when any policies covering it are written, when the occurrence is reported, or when the associated claims are closed and losses and ALAE are paid. A policy period is the period during which an occurrence occurs for policies written during a specified time, regardless of when the associated claims are reported or are closed and losses and ALAE paid.

Exhibit 1 illustrates the accident period and policy period concepts for policies written to cover accidents occurring during the policy period (referred to as an occurrence-basis policy). The accident years are represented by vertical lines, the policy years by 45 degree lines. Note that accident year 1981 contains accidents (occurrences)

Exhibit 1

Accident Year/Policy Year Illustration for Occurrence Policies

Combined

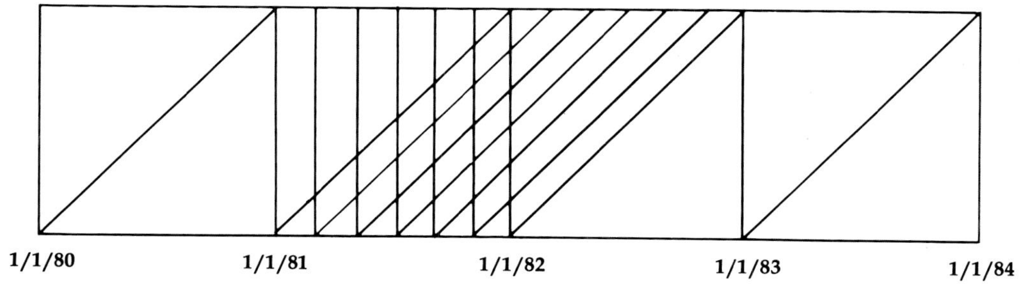

Accident Year

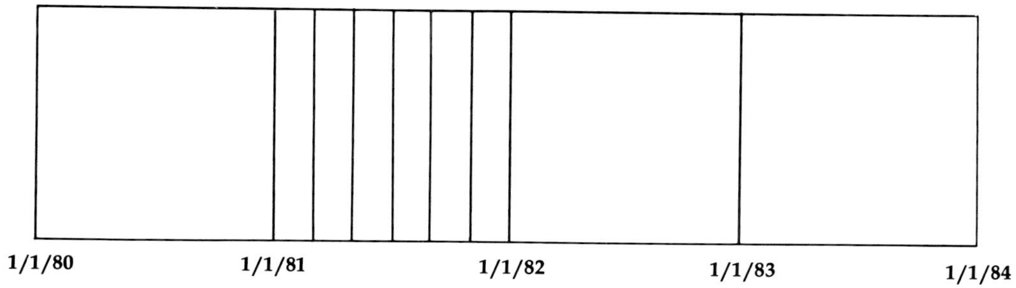

Accident Year 1981 contains accidents associated with policies written in 1980 and 1981.

Policy Year

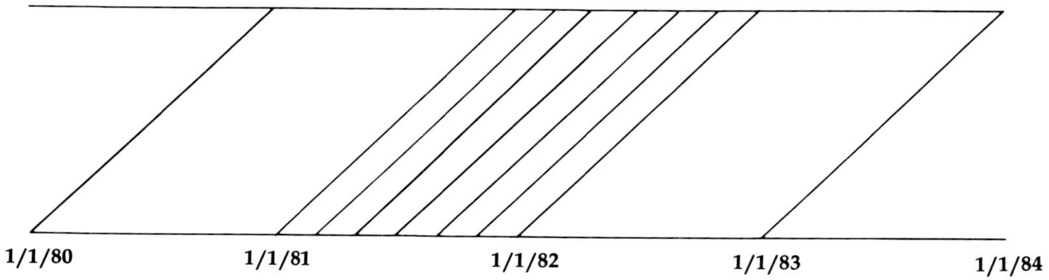

Policy year 1981 contains some accidents that occur in 1981 and some that occur in 1982.

associated with policies written in 1980 and 1981, and policy year 1981 contains some accidents that occur in 1981 and some that occur in 1982. A policy written December 31, 1981, will have almost all accidents associated with it occurring in 1982. For any one entity with an occurrence-basis policy, the policy period is the same as the accident period.

Not all policies are written to cover accidents occurring during the policy period. Two other options are "claims-made" and "claims-paid." Claims-made policies cover occurrences (or claims, depending on policy definitions) first reported during the policy period, regardless of the occurrence date or when the associated losses and ALAE are paid, provided that the occurrence date is after the retroactive date. Claims-paid policies cover the losses (or losses and ALAE, depending on policy definitions) paid during the policy period, regardless of the associated occurrence or claim report dates if these dates are after the appropriate retroactive dates. Retroactive dates are used to prevent duplicate coverage in converting from occurrence-basis policies to claims-made or claims-paid. If an entity changes from occurrence-basis to claims-made to claims-paid, two retroactive dates, one for occurrences and one for reporting, will be necessary.

There are many coverage questions that arise with claims-made and claims-paid policies because of poor coverage wording. The two main questions are:

- Is the coverage for claims or for occurrences?
- How is the report (or payment) date defined?

Non-traditional risk financing mechanisms also have these time-period concepts. For example, individual entities retaining risk may decide to fund during each fiscal year only for those occurrences reported during the fiscal year.

The time-period concepts are important in individual risk rating because the first step in designing or understanding such a system is to know what costs are involved. This depends on the coverage provided or the funding basis, both of which are a function of the time period under consideration.

Loss Components

Paid losses are losses that have been paid. Outstanding losses, or case reserves, are estimates by the claim examiner of the remaining amount required to settle particular claims, based on the knowledge about those claims at a particular date. Case reserving involves many subjective judgments, so different examiners may set reserves on the same claim at different amounts.

Case reserves, when added to the payments on open claims, do not necessarily reflect the ultimate settlement amount. Case reserves are based on knowledge at a particular point in time. In general, additional information about a claim tends to reveal that the cost of the claim is higher than previously thought, rather than lower. This means that there is usually an upward development of the payments on open claims plus case reserves on a given group of claims. The difference between the current total of payments on open claims plus case reserves and the ultimate settlement value for a given group of claims is called "case reserve development." Note that occurrence-basis and claims-made coverage need a reserve to reflect case reserve development to estimate ultimate costs.

Occurrence-basis coverage will also need a reserve to reflect unreported occurrences to estimate ultimate costs. Claims-made coverage will need a reserve to reflect unreported claims if coverage is provided for occurrences reported during a particular period, since all claims associated with an occurrence may not be reported at the same time. The unreported occurrences/claims reserve is the true "IBNR" (incurred but not reported) reserve. The term "IBNR" is sometimes used to refer to the true unreported occurrences/claims reserve and the case reserve development (see below).

"Reported losses" refers to the sum of payments plus case reserves. "Unreported losses" refers to the case reserve development plus unreported occurrences/claims reserve. "Incurred losses" refers to the sum of reported and unreported losses. Note that unreported losses and incurred losses contain different items for occurrence and claims-made coverage and may contain different items for different types of claims-made coverage. "Ultimate losses" refers to an estimate of "incurred losses."

"Case reserves" are sometimes used when "reported losses" are meant. Many entities refer to "reported losses" as "incurred losses" and to "unreported losses" as "IBNR." The result is confusion, with incurred losses plus incurred but not reported losses equaling incurred losses.

Exhibit 2

Loss Terminology Illustration

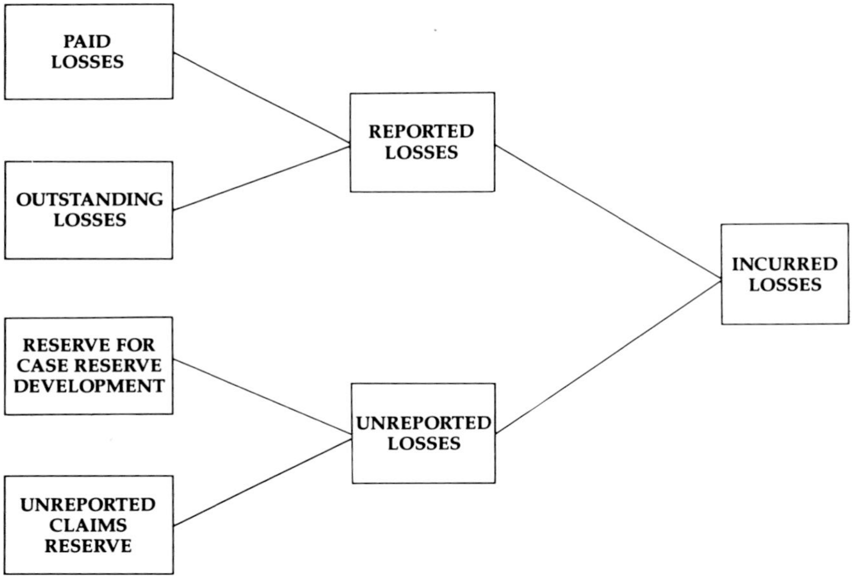

Exhibit 2 illustrates the loss component terminology used in this chapter. These terms also apply to ALAE. Different rating plans sometimes treat losses and ALAE together, sometimes separately, and sometimes as a mixture. An example of the last is treating paid losses and paid ALAE separately, but setting case reserves for losses and ALAE combined or for losses only. The treatment of ALAE in this chapter is specified in each situation in which it appears.

To design, understand, or use an individual risk rating system properly, loss component terminology for the system and the data available to be used by the system must be well-defined.

Frequency and Severity

Two other terms that have different usage in different situations and that arise in conjunction with individual risk rating systems are "frequency" and "severity." Frequency is the number of claims (or occurrences) per exposure unit. "Frequency" is sometimes incorrectly used to refer to the number of claims or occurrences. Frequency is a relative, not an absolute, measure.

Severity is the average loss per claim (or per occurrence). Note that "loss" may include or exclude ALAE.

What is to be Allocated

The second task in designing or understanding an individual risk rating system (after determining goals) is to determine what is to be allocated. For traditional insurance, the answer often is all costs. These include losses, ALAE, ULAE, reinsurance premium, risk control costs, overhead, taxes, miscellaneous expenses, and profit associated with insurance policies of the type being written (e.g., occurrence).

Non-traditional risk financing mechanisms and individual entities allocating risk financing costs back to units also may want to allocate all costs associated with the risk financing program. Those costs may include different items, such as excess insurance premium and a risk margin (money for adverse loss and ALAE experience), and exclude others, such as taxes and profit. Non-traditional risk financing mechanisms and individual entities allocating costs back to units and even some insurers may want to allocate only some subset of costs, such as losses, ALAE, and ULAE, with other costs treated in a different manner.

Note that part of the determination of what is to be allocated involves determining the basis on which policies are written or on which funding occurs. This is necessary so that the various components subject to the allocation are appropriately tabulated and adjusted.

Prospective Systems

There are three basic types of prospective individual risk rating systems: schedule rating, experience rating, and some types of composite rating. Schedule rating takes into consideration characteristics that are expected to affect loss and ALAE experience but that are not reflected in that experience. Experience rating uses an entity's actual experience to modify manual rates (determined by the entity's rating group). Composite rating simplifies the premium calculation for large, complex entities and, in some instances, allows the entities' experience to affect the premium developed from manual rates or to determine the rates regardless of rating group.

Schedule Rating

Schedule rating is the only individual risk rating system that does not directly reflect an entity's claim experience; in theory, it recognizes characteristics that are expected to have a material effect on an entity's experience but that are not actually reflected in that experience. These characteristics could result from recent changes in exposure (such as the addition of a swimming pool in an apartment complex) or risk control programs (such as the recent implementation of a new program). Schedule rating is also used for entities that are too small to qualify for experience rating or composite rating.

Schedule rating systems usually take the form of percentage credits and debits. These credits and debits are sometimes applied before and sometimes after experience rating. There may be a limit to the total debit or credit that an entity can receive.

Note that schedule credits and debits apply only to those characteristics which should affect an entity's loss and ALAE experience. If a characteristic is listed which should not affect a particular entity's loss and ALAE experience, there should be no adjustment to the manual rates for that characteristic for that entity.

Also note that the application of schedule credits and debits may take considerable underwriting judgment. A schedule rating system that is based on objective criteria will result in more consistent treatment of affected entities than a system that relies on subjective evaluation. This is illustrated by the two examples of schedule rating that follow.

Insurance Services Office (ISO) Commercial General Liability Experience and Schedule Rating Plan: Schedule Rating

This section discusses the ISO General Liability Schedule Rating Plan, as revised in July 1988.

For eligible entities, the manual rates may be modified according to the table below in addition to any experience rating modification. The maximum schedule rating modification is 25% up or down.

ISO General Liability Schedule Rating Table

A.	Location	
	(i) Exposure Inside Premises	− 5% to + 5%
	(ii) Exposure Outside Premises	− 5% to + 5%
B.	Premises — Condition, Care	− 10% to + 10%
C.	Equipment — Type, Condition, Care	− 10% to + 10%
D.	Classification Peculiarities	− 10% to + 10%
E.	Employees — Selection, Training, Supervision, Experience	− 6% to + 6%
F.	Cooperation	
	(i) Medical Facilities	− 2% to + 2%
	(ii) Safety Program	− 2% to + 2%

This plan relies heavily on subjective evaluation. For example:

- What is it about the condition and care of the premises that results in a credit of 10%, 9%, etc.?
- Will different underwriters give identical schedule credits and debits in identical situations?
- Will the same underwriter give identical schedule credits and debits in identical situations?

Roller Skating Rink Risk Retention Group Schedule Rating Plan

This schedule rating plan is similar to one developed for a roller skating rink risk retention group offering general liability coverage. All participating entities are eligible. There is no explicit maximum schedule rating modification. The maximum schedule credit is that inherent in the plan (40%). Note that only credits are given. The manual rates are based on experience for rinks in which none of the characteristics in the schedule rating plan were present.

The general credit list is as follows:

A.	Floor supervision	+ 10%
B.	Premises	+ 5%
C.	Rental Skates	+ 5%
D.	Management	+ 5%
E.	Incident Report	+ 10%
F.	First Aid	+ 5%
	Total	+ 40%

Details of the floor supervision credit follow:

Rink must meet or exceed industry safety standard of one floor supervisor per 200 skaters at all times.

Rink has a written policy or procedure which includes:

- a distinctive uniform or vest for floor supervisors;
- a provision that floor supervisors must be paid employees, owners, or family members of owners;

- a provision that floor supervisors must be at least 18 years of age; and
- a written training program for floor supervisors.

The floor supervisor training program must include the following provisions at a minimum:

- Floor guards should inspect the floor continually for foreign objects.
- During special numbers or events, floor guards should keep unqualified skaters off the floor.
- Floor guards should follow a written policy regarding unruly skaters.
- Floor guards should follow detailed, written instructions in case of an accident, including:
  - not moving the injured skater,
  - diverting skaters from the injured skater,
  - notifying management of an incident, and
  - a procedure for obtaining emergency medical/police/fire assistance.

Floor supervisor training must include a minimum of one safety meeting per calendar quarter.

Floor supervisor training must be recorded and verified by the employee.

ALL OF THE ABOVE MUST BE PRESENT TO EARN THE 10% CREDIT. NO PARTIAL CREDIT WILL BE GIVEN.

The other credits similarly rely on objective criteria that can be verified by audit and/or surprise inspections. All credits encourage activities that should favorably affect loss and ALAE experience. Note that credit is given for activities which a rink has just begun, regardless of its actions in the past.

Because the manual premium is based on experience for rinks in which none of the characteristics in the schedule rating plan were present, there should be no "off-balance," i.e., the premium collected should cover the expected costs. If the manual premium used data for rinks which did have some of the characteristics in the schedule rating plan, the manual rates would need to be corrected for the off-balance resulting from a schedule rating plan that only gives credits.

Experience Rating

All individual risk rating systems are a form of experience rating because they reflect an entity's actual experience or characteristics that should affect the entity's experience. However, the term "experience rating" has come to mean a particular type of prospective system, discussed in this section.

Experience rating is used when the past, with appropriate adjustments, is predictive of the future. Actual losses, and sometimes ALAE, for a prior period are compared to expected losses (and ALAE). The weighting of the actual and expected experience results in the cost to the subject entity for the current period.

To have an "apples to apples" comparison, several different combinations of experience and exposure can be used, including the following:

- actual paid losses (and ALAE) at a particular date and the expected paid losses (and ALAE) at that date, both for the experience period;
- reported losses (and ALAE) at a particular date and the expected reported losses (and ALAE) at that date, both for the experience period;
- projected ultimate losses (and ALAE) and expected ultimate losses, both for the experience period; and
- projected ultimate losses (and ALAE) for the experience period adjusted to the current exposure and dollar levels and

expected ultimate losses for the current period at the current dollar and exposure levels.

Projected ultimate losses are the expected ultimate settlement value of all subject claims/occurrences. Projected ultimate ALAE are the expected ultimate ALAE costs of all subject claims/occurrences. The expected losses (and ALAE) are based on past or current exposure, as appropriate. The adjustments to current dollar and exposure levels should reflect such items as:

- economic and social inflation;
- changes in the number, size, and type of entities; and
- changes in policy limits.

Social inflation includes such items as changes in litigiousness, judicial decisions, and legislation which directly or indirectly affect the cost of settling claims.

The three components of experience, exposure, and credibility (the weighting factor) and some additional considerations are discussed below.

Experience

The experience component should be related to the exposure component, as detailed above, and to the basis on which policies are written or funding occurs. If the policy to be rated is written on an occurrence basis, any of the four combinations listed above for accidents occurring in the experience period could be used. If the policy to be rated is written on a claims-paid basis, the two best combinations are those using paid losses or projected ultimate losses adjusted to current exposure and dollar levels, both for payments made during the experience period. If the costs to be allocated include ALAE, ALAE usually should be included with losses in the calculation.

The length of the experience rating period usually ranges from two to five years. The shorter the period, the more responsive the plan will be to changes that truly affect loss (and ALAE) experience, such as changes in the risk control program, and the more subject to unusual fluctuations in loss (and ALAE) experience. Conversely, a longer period will result in less responsiveness to changes and to unusual or catastrophic occurrences.

To reduce the effect of unusual or catastrophic occurrences, many experience rating plans place per occurrence limits on the losses (and ALAE) used in the experience rating calculation. These limits sometimes apply to losses only, with ALAE unlimited or treated in a different manner, and sometimes to losses and ALAE combined. Note that if actual losses (and ALAE) are limited, the expected losses (and ALAE) must also be limited, to maintain an "apples to apples" comparison. If losses (and ALAE) are limited, the cost of expected losses (and ALAE) above the per occurrence limit must be accounted for in some manner. Annual or other period aggregate limits may also be used.

If projected ultimate losses are to be used in the experience rating calculation, they can be developed in a number of ways similar to those used to develop projected ultimate losses used to determine manual rates. Projected ultimate losses are often based on paid or reported losses at a particular date.

For the last experience combination listed above, projected ultimate losses are adjusted to current exposure and dollar levels. Dollar-level adjustments should include both economic and social inflation.

Exposure adjustments include both converting the experience period to the current period (e.g., dividing by three to go from a three-year experience period to a one-year current period) and adjusting for changes in the magnitude of the exposure. Both can be accomplished at once by dividing the projected ultimate losses for the experience period, adjusted to current dollar level, by the exposure for the experience period, adjusted to current dollar level if appropriate, and applying this "rate" to the exposure for the current period.

Exposure

The expected losses are a function of the past or current exposure, as appropriate. The exposure component should be related to the experience component, as detailed above. For the first three combinations listed above, past exposure is used; for the last combination, current exposure is used.

Expected losses are usually estimated as the product of an expected loss rate and the exposure base. The expected loss rate can be based on the manual rates for the prior or current period, adjusted to the appropriate dollar level. For example, to develop expected loss rates for a prior period, the current expected loss rate could be adjusted to the prior period's dollar level, or the prior period's expected loss rates could be used directly. The former approach is usually better if there have been no underlying changes in the nature of the exposure because the current expected loss rate is based on more recent information than the prior period's loss rates.

The exposure base used should reflect the underlying risk of loss and ALAE. It is not always possible to use the theoretically optimal exposure base. In practice, insurers and non-traditional risk financing mechanisms often use whatever exposure base insurers use in their premium calculations.

For general liability, exposure bases often used are sales, payroll, total operating expenditures, and square footage, adjusted for any underlying differences. For workers' compensation the exposure base is usually payroll adjusted for differences in payroll type (e.g., a coal miner is expected to have more losses and ALAE per payroll dollar than a secretary, even though both are employed by the same entity). For property, exposure bases often used include actual cash value, stated amount, or replacement cost.

Non-traditional risk financing mechanisms may use different exposure bases for different costs. For example, for a public entity workers' compensation pool, the exposure base for all administrative costs may be full-time-equivalent employees while the exposure base for losses and ALAE is payroll, with both full-time-equivalent employees and payroll adjusted for differences in payroll type. The use of two exposure bases may be the result of different payroll scales being used by different participants.

Individual entities allocating risk financing costs to units may also use different exposure bases for different costs. And some costs, such as the cost of a policy that applies only to one unit, may be allocated without using the experience rating plan.

Credibility

The actual (experience) and expected (exposure) components of the experience rating calculation are weighted to produce the costs the entity under consideration will pay. The weight assigned to the experience component is called "credibility," and commonly denoted by "Z." The weight assigned to the exposure component is $1 - Z$. This is also called the credibility complement. Credibility reflects the degree of belief that the entity's experience is a valid predictor of future costs. The credibility selected should consider the validity of the component to which the credibility complement is being applied.

Credibility has three criteria that must be met:

1. Credibility must not be less than zero or greater than one.
2. Credibility should increase as the size of risk increases, all else being equal.
3. The percentage change for any loss of a given size should decrease as the size of risk increases.

These criteria can also be shown as mathematical relationships. Using Z for credibility and E for size of risk:

1. $0 < Z < 1$
2. $\dfrac{dZ}{dE} > 0$
3. $\dfrac{d}{dE}\left(\dfrac{Z}{E}\right) < 0$

Exhibit 3

General Credibility Illustration

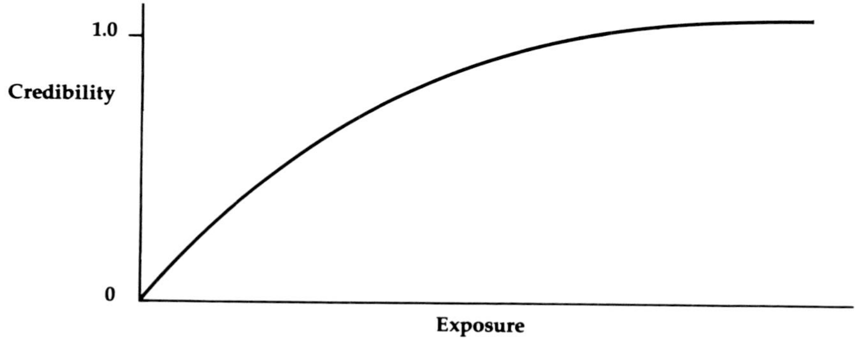

These three criteria are met if credibility follows the curve shown in Exhibit 3. Note that size of risk is represented in the diagram by exposure. Size of risk can also be based on expected losses or expected number of claims. Chapter 7 contains a detailed discussion of credibility.

Other Considerations

Experience rating plans may be designed so that there is a minimum or maximum premium change. These are often based on the prior year's premium adjusted for changes in exposure. For example, the maximum premium change from one year to the next may be the change indicated by any exposure changes plus or minus 25%. This means that if there is an increase of 15% because of an increase in exposure, the total increase possible after application of the experience rating plan is 40% (15% + 25%).

The premium collected under experience rating plans may not equal the expected premium in total. This means that the plan has an "off-balance." If this can be anticipated and does not reflect a true difference between experience-rated and non-experience-rated risks, the experience rating plan can include, as a last step, multiplication by a factor to correct for this off-balance. Alternatively, the manual rates can include an off-balance correction. This latter approach affects non-experience-rated entities also.

ISO Commercial General Liability Experience and Schedule Rating Plan: Experience Rating

The ISO Commercial General Liability Experience Rating Plan, as revised in July 1988, is illustrated in Exhibits 4 and 5. This example is used throughout the following discussion of the plan.

This plan may be used for occurrence and claims-made general liability coverages, with a few exceptions, for those entities meeting the eligibility criteria specified in the plan. The coverage in the example is premises/operations and products/completed operations for policy period 1/1–12/31/88, written on a third-year claims-made basis.

The experience is represented by the projected ultimate losses and ALAE for the experience period. The exposure is represented by the expected losses and ALAE for the experience period. Both the projected ultimate losses and ALAE, and expected losses and ALAE, are limited to a $25,000 per occurrence basic limit, which applies to losses only, and by a maximum single limit per occurrence (MSL), which applies to the basic limits losses and unlimited ALAE.

The experience period is the three policy periods completed at least six months prior to the rating date. If three policy periods are not available, one or two may be used. Occurrences and premiums associated with tail coverage on claims-made policies are excluded. In the example, the three policy periods are 1/1–12/31/84, 1/1–12/31/85, and 1/1–12/31/86. The older two were written on an

Exhibit 4

ISO Experience Rating Sample Calculation

Basic Calculation

Coverage:	Premises/Operations and Products/Completed Operations
Policy Being Rated:	1/1–12/31/88 Third-Year Claims-Made
Experience Period:	1/1–12/31/84 Occurrence 1/1–12/31/85 Occurrence 1/1–12/31/86 First-Year Claims-Made

I.	Experience Component:	
	A. Reported Losses and ALAE at 9/30/87 Limited by Basic Limits and MSL	44,300
	B. Expected Unreported Losses and ALAE at 9/30/87 Limited by Basic Limits and MSL (See Exhibit 5)	12,381
	C. Projected Ultimate Losses and ALAE Limited by Basic Limits and MSL [(A) + (B)]	56,681
	D. Total Basic Limits Premium Subject to Experience Rating (See Exhibit 5)	138,965
	E. Actual Loss and ALAE Ratio [(C) / (D)]	0.408
II.	Exposure Component: Expected Loss and ALAE Ratio	0.469
III.	Credibility:	0.580
IV.	Experience (Credit)/Debit: {[(I.E) − (II) / (II) × (III)]}	− 7.6%

Notes: MSL is the maximum single limit per occurrence, applied to basic limits losses and unlimited ALAE. It is based on the total basic limits premium subject to experience rating (subject premium).

The adjusted expected loss ratio and credibility are supplied by ISO. Credibility is based on the total basic limits premium subject to experience rating.

Exhibit 5

ISO Experience Rating Sample Calculation

Expected Unreported Losses and ALAE at 9/30/87 and Subject Premium

Policy Period	Coverage	Current Basic Limits Premium	Policy Adjustment Factors Table 1	Policy Adjustment Factors Table 2	Detrend Factors	Subject Premium	Adjusted Expected Loss & ALAE Ratio	Expected Percentage B/L Losses & ALAE Unreported at 9/30/87	Expected B/L Losses & ALAE Unreported at 9/30/87
(1)	(2)	(3)	(4)	(5)	(6)	(7)	(8)	(9)	(10)
1/1–12/31/84	Prem/Ops	47,500	1.06	1.00	0.724	36,453	0.469	10.7%	1,829
	Products	15,500	1.16	1.00	0.735	13,215	0.469	48.6%	3,012
1/1–12/31/85	Prem/Ops	47,500	1.06	1.00	0.785	39,525	0.469	19.4%	3,596
	Products	15,500	1.16	1.00	0.794	14,276	0.469	58.9%	3,944
1/1–12/31/86	Prem/Ops	47,500	1.06	0.67	0.851	28,708	0.469	0.0%	0
	Products	15,500	1.16	0.44	0.858	6,788	0.469	0.0%	0
Total						138,965			12,381

Notes: (3) is for the 1/1–12/31/88 third-year claims-made policy

(4) adjusts premium up to an occurrence level

(5) adjusts for experience period being claims-made, reflecting claims-made year

(6) adjusts current premium by the reciprocal of the loss trend

(7) = (3) × (4) × (5) × (6)

(8) and (10) also reflect MSL

(10) = (7) × (8) × (9)

Advisory values for (4), (5), (6), (8), and (9) are supplied by ISO

MSL is the maximum single limit per occurrence, applied to basic limits losses and unlimited ALAE. It is based on the total basic limits premium subject to experience rating (subject premium), the credibility, and the adjusted expected loss and ALAE ratio, so as to produce a maximum allowable "swing" in experience modification of 0.30 due to a single occurrence.

occurrence basis; the most recent on a first-year claims-made basis. The evaluation date is 9/30/87.

The projected ultimate losses and ALAE limited by basic limits and MSL for the experience period are the sum of the reported losses and ALAE at 9/30/87 and the expected unreported losses and ALAE at 9/30/87, both limited by basic limits and the MSL. The experience component is the actual loss and ALAE ratio, the projected ultimate losses and ALAE limited by basic limits and MSL divided by the subject premium (the total basic limits premium subject to experience rating).

The exposure base is premium. The exposure component is the expected loss ratio adjusted for the various limits. The actual and expected loss ratios are compared using a credibility factor to arrive at the experience credit (percentage reduction in premium) or debit (percentage increase in premium). This plan has no minimums, maximums, or explicit off-balance correction.

Exhibit 4 shows the basic calculation. Exhibit 5 shows the calculation of the expected unreported losses and ALAE at 9/30/87 and subject premium. The expected unreported losses and ALAE at 9/30/87 are the product of the subject premium, adjusted expected loss and ALAE ratio, and expected percentage losses and ALAE unreported at 9/30/87. These three quantities reflect the effect of basic limits losses and the MSL.

Note that there is no adjustment for unreported losses and ALAE for the claims-made policies, even though there may be case reserve development. This results in a probable understatement of the actual loss and ALAE ratio and a resulting probable overstatement of any credits or understatement of any debits, if case reserve development is greater than zero.

The subject premium for each year of the experience period is the product of the current basic limits premium (which is a third-year claims-made premium), two policy adjustment factors, and a detrend factor. The Table 1 policy adjustment factors adjust premium to an occurrence level. The Table 2 policy adjustment factors adjust premium to the respective policy type (occurrence or claims-made) for each year of the experience period. Table 2 factors also eliminate premium related to midi-tail coverage. Midi-tail coverage is the coverage associated with the limited automatic extended reporting period.

In 1/1–12/31/86 in the example, the third-year claims-made premium is adjusted up to an occurrence basis by the Table 1 factor and down to a first-year claims-made basis (excluding the midi-tail) by the Table 2 factor because the experience for the 1/1–12/31/86 period is first-year claims-made. The detrend factors, which are applied to current premium, actually adjust for loss trends since the policy period. In other words, the detrend factor is the reciprocal of the loss trend. The loss trend is normally applied to losses. For the alternate "Appendix B" determination of subject premiums, both the loss trend and exposure trend are included in the detrend factors. These factors do not adjust for changes in coverage, such as changes in exclusions.

Note that there is an implicit assumption that exposure for the past is the same as the current exposure, except for changes in dollar value. This assumption is not reasonable if there has been growth or decline in the underlying exposure. If this is the case, an alternate calculation ("Appendix B") should be used to derive subject premium.

The calculation performed to determine the experience credit/(debit) is as follows:

$$CD = \frac{ALR - AELR}{AELR} \times Z$$

where $AELR$ = Adjusted Expected Loss and ALAE Ratio
ALR = Actual Loss and ALAE Ratio
Z = Credibility
CD = (Credit)/Debit

This can be rearranged to a more familiar form:

$$M = \frac{[A \times Z] + [E \times (1 - Z)]}{E}$$

where E = Expected Losses and ALAE Limited by Basic Limits and MSL
A = Actual Losses and ALAE Limited by Basic Limits and MSL
Z = Credibility
M = Modification Factor

E and A are calculated as follows:

$$E = \text{Subject Premium} \times AELR$$

and

$$A = \text{Projected Ultimate Losses and ALAE Limited by Basic Limits and MSL}$$

Note that

$$M = 1 + CD$$

For the example:

$CD = -7.6\%$ from Exhibit 4
$E = 65{,}175$
$A = 56{,}681$
$Z = 0.580$
$M = 0.924 = 1 + (-0.076)$

The plan does not specify whether the experience credit or debit is applied to total limits premium or only to the basic limits premium. This plan has special rules for treating non-standard expense allowances, deductibles, and experience periods with no claims.

Workers' Compensation Pool Experience Rating Plan

The experience rating plan of a workers' compensation pool for fire districts in one state is illustrated in Exhibits 6 through 8. This example is used throughout the following discussion of the plan.

This plan is used for occurrence workers' compensation coverage written on a guaranteed cost basis for all entities participating in the pool. Pool participation has been constant since the pool's inception and is not expected to change for 7/1/88–89, the policy period in question. All policies renew 7/1.

The costs to be allocated using a weighting of experience and exposure are the expected losses and ALAE for 7/1/88–89, discounted for anticipated investment income. The estimated discounted expected expenses other than ALAE for 7/1/88–89 are distributed to participants on the basis of the expected full-time-equivalent (FTE) personnel for 7/1/88–89.

The experience is represented by reported losses and ALAE at 6/30/87 for the experience period, adjusted for changes in FTE personnel. The exposure base is expected FTE employees for the 7/1/88–89 period. The reported losses and ALAE at 6/30/87 are limited to $25,000 per occurrence. The experience period is the latest three complete policy periods, i.e., 7/1/84–85, 7/1/85–86, and 7/1/86–87. Credibility is based on FTE employees for the experience period.

FTE personnel are used rather than payroll as an exposure base, for the credibility base, and to allocate estimated discounted expenses for 7/1/88–89. FTE personnel is a better exposure base than payroll in this instance because of the presence in some of the districts of volunteer firefighters and pay scale discrepancies between districts. Volunteer firefighters are covered by workers' compensation law. The nature of workers' compensation claims for firefighters (many minor cost claims and a few large cost claims) and the pay-scale discrepancies indicate that some costs and credibility are more closely related to FTE personnel than payroll.

The plan has a built-in minimum: the estimated discounted administrative expenses for 7/1/88–89, as allocated based on expected FTE personnel for 7/1/88–89. The plan also has a maximum for each participant: 25% above the prior year's contribution (for 7/1/87–88 in this example), adjusted for any increase in total recommended contribution but not for any decrease (a 30% increase in this example, from $853,000 to $1,109,000). The total increase allowable in this example is 62.5% ((1.300 $\times$ 1.250) − 1.000).

Exhibit 6

Workers' Compensation Pool Experience Rating Sample Calculation

Premium Determination

Fire District	Minimum Premium	Maximum Premium	*A*	*E*	*Z*	Premium for 7/1/88–89 Unadjusted	Adjusted #1	Adjusted #2
(1)	(2)	(3)	(4)	(5)	(6)	(7)	(8)	(9)
A	93,384	372,825	290,914	280,491	0.59	380,075	376,698	372,825
B	1,494	8,634	821	4,487	0.00	5,980	5,927	5,958
C	18,810	93,623	15,286	56,497	0.12	70,319	69,694	70,063
D	8,409	53,402	6,163	25,257	0.00	33,666	33,367	33,544
E	28,546	171,593	172,188	85,742	0.25	136,014	134,805	135,518
F	38,615	222,414	128,716	115,985	0.33	158,778	157,368	158,200
G	166	1,599	0	499	0.00	664	659	662
H	6,805	41,251	44,007	20,439	0.00	27,243	27,001	27,144
I	13,167	72,625	10,922	39,548	0.09	50,228	49,782	50,045
J	52,999	270,257	121,658	159,188	0.39	197,500	195,745	196,780
K	4,868	28,141	37,010	14,623	0.00	19,491	19,318	19,420
L	1,715	9,593	145	5,151	0.00	6,866	6,805	6,841
M	2,987	15,670	4,105	8,973	0.00	11,960	11,854	11,917
N	5,034	24,623	65	15,121	0.00	20,156	19,977	20,082
Total	277,000	1,386,250	832,000	832,000		1,118,941	1,109,000	1,109,000

Notes: (2) = (6) of Exhibit 8

(3) = (8) of Exhibit 8

(4) = (7) of Exhibit 7

(5) = (3) of Exhibit 8

(6) = (5) of Exhibit 8

(7) = (2) + (4) × (6) + (5) × [1.00 − (6)]

(8) = [(7) × 1,109,000] ÷ Total (7). 1,109,000 is the recommended contribution for 7/1/88–89

(9) = (8), adjusted for maximum premiums with amount over maximum premiums reallocated based on (8)

Exhibit 7

Workers' Compensation Pool Experience Rating Sample Calculation

Determination of A

Fire District	Reported Limited Losses & ALAE at 6/30/87	FTE Personnel 7/1/84–87	Raw Annual Loss & ALAE Rate [(2)/(3)]	FTE Personnel 7/1/88–89	A Unadjusted [(4) × (5)]	A Adjusted
(1)	(2)	(3)	(4)	(5)	(6)	(7)
A	350,240	463.3	755.97	168.8	127,607	290,914
B	1,000	7.5	133.33	2.7	360	821
C	15,126	76.7	197.21	34.0	6,705	15,286
D	8,892	50.0	177.84	15.2	2,703	6,163
E	193,214	132.0	1463.74	51.6	75,529	172,188
F	147,865	182.8	808.89	69.8	56,460	128,716
G	0	1.6	0.00	0.3	0	0
H	56,654	36.1	1569.36	12.3	19,303	44,007
I	13,809	68.6	201.30	23.8	4,791	10,922
J	130,682	234.6	557.04	95.8	53,365	121,658
K	47,965	26.0	1844.81	8.8	16,234	37,010
L	185	9.0	20.56	3.1	64	145
M	4,768	14.3	333.43	5.4	1,801	4,105
N	63	20.0	3.15	9.1	29	65
Total/Avg.	970,463	1322.5	733.81	500.7	364,951	832,000

Note: (7) = 832,000 × [(6) / Total (6)]. 832,000 is the discounted expected losses and ALAE for 7/1/88–89.

Workers' Compensation Pool Experience Rating Sample Calculation

Determination of E, Z, Minimum Premium, and Maximum Premium

Fire District	FTE Personnel 7/1/88–89	*E*	FTE Personnel 7/1/84–87	Credibility (*Z*)	Estimated Discounted Admin. Costs 7/1/88–89	Contribution 7/1/87–88	Maximum Premium 7/1/88–89
(1)	(2)	(3)	(4)	(5)	(6)	(7)	(8)
A	168.8	280,491	463.3	0.59	93,384	229,410	372,825
B	2.7	4,487	7.5	0.00	1,494	5,313	8,634
C	34.0	56,497	76.7	0.12	18,810	57,609	93,623
D	15.2	25,257	50.0	0.00	8,409	32,860	53,402
E	51.6	85,742	132.0	0.25	28,546	105,586	171,593
F	69.8	115,985	182.8	0.33	38,615	136,858	222,414
G	0.3	499	1.6	0.00	166	984	1,599
H	12.3	20,439	36.1	0.00	6,805	25,383	41,251
I	23.8	39,548	68.6	0.09	13,167	44,688	72,625
J	95.8	159,188	234.6	0.39	52,999	166,297	270,257
K	8.8	14,623	26.0	0.00	4,868	17,316	28,141
L	3.1	5,151	9.0	0.00	1,715	5,903	9,593
M	5.4	8,973	14.3	0.00	2,987	9,642	15,670
N	9.1	15,121	20.0	0.00	5,034	15,151	24,623
Total	500.7	832,000	1,322.5		277,000	853,000	1,386,250

Notes: (3) is distributed based on (2). 832,000 is the discounted expected losses and ALAE for 7/1/88–89.

(5) is determined based on (4) as follows:

FTE Personnel Years	Credibility
60 or less	0.00
60–1,199	$\left[\dfrac{\text{FTE personnel years}-60}{1{,}140}\right]^{1/2}$
1,200 or more	1.00

(6) is distributed based on (2). This is the minimum premium.

(8) = (7) × (1,109,000/853,000) × 1.25. 1,109,000 is the total recommended contribution for 7/1/88–89.

Because pool participation has been and is expected to remain constant, it is possible to calculate the exact off-balance and adjust accordingly so that the total dollars collected are the total recommended contribution for the group. The allocation of the off-balance to districts may need several iterations, depending on the effect of the minimums and maximums.

Exhibit 6 shows the premium determination. Exhibit 7 shows the determination of A, the discounted expected losses and ALAE for 7/1/88–89 allocated based on experience. Exhibit 8 shows the determination of E (the discounted expected losses and ALAE for 7/1/88–89 allocated based on exposure), Z (credibility), minimum premium, and maximum premium.

The premium before adjustment for off-balance, minimums, and maximums is determined as follows:

$$\text{Unadjusted Premium} = \text{Minimum Premium} + \{(A \times Z) + [E \times (1.000 - Z)]\}.$$

The unadjusted premium for the example is shown in column (7) of Exhibit 6. Column (8) of Exhibit 6 shows the premium adjusted for the off-balance. Column (9) of Exhibit 6 shows the premium adjusted for maximum premiums combined with an additional off-balance calculation. Note that in the example, no participant's premium was lower than the applicable minimum. Any amounts under minimum premiums would have to be reallocated similarly to the reallocation of the amounts over maximum premiums.

A is the discounted expected losses and ALAE for 7/1/88–89 allocated based on experience (calculated in Exhibit 7). The reported losses and ALAE at 6/30/87 for accident period 7/1/84–87 are limited to $25,000 per occurrence. The ratio of these to FTE personnel for 7/1/84–87 results in the raw annual loss and ALAE rate. The raw annual loss and ALAE rate is applied to the expected FTE personnel for 7/1/88–89 to obtain unadjusted A's. The unadjusted A's are adjusted so that the desired total of $832,000 of discounted expected losses and ALAE for 7/1/88–89 would be collected if all participants had credibilities of 1.00.

E is the discounted expected losses and ALAE for 7/1/88–89 allocated based on exposure. The E's are calculated in Exhibit 8 by distributing the $832,000 in proportion to the expected FTE personnel for 7/1/88–89. This is what would be collected if all participants had credibility of 0.00. The credibilities (Z) are based on FTE personnel for 7/1/84-87 and the formula in Exhibit 8. The minimum and maximum premiums are also calculated in Exhibit 8.

National Council on Compensation Insurance (NCCI) Experience Rating Plan

The NCCI experience rating plan has the unique characteristic of dividing the losses for each claim into a primary portion and an excess portion. The expected and actual primary portions are compared using one credibility factor, and the expected and actual excess portions are compared using another credibility factor. The credibility factor applied to the actual primary losses is higher than that applied to the actual excess losses. The formulae for splitting the expected and actual losses and determining the primary and excess credibility factors are discussed in more detail in Chapter 7. A brief summary of the plan is shown below.

The calculation to determine the experience modification is as follows:

$$M = \frac{A_p + C + (A_e \times w)}{E_p + C + (E_e \times w)}$$

where

M = Experience Modification Factor
A_p = Actual Primary Losses
E_p = Expected Primary Losses
A_e = Actual Excess Losses
E_e = Expected Excess Losses
C = Stabilizing Value
w = Excess Losses Weighting Factor

This formula is also sometimes expressed as follows:

$$M = \frac{A_p + [w \times A_e] + [(1 - w) \times E_e] + B}{E + B}$$

where B is a different stabilizing value than C. B is a function of w and C.

Note that $M = 1 + CD$, where CD is the experience rating (credit)/debit.

The experience period is the three complete policy periods at the time the calculation is made. The actual losses are the reported losses evaluated at 18, 30, and 42 months from the beginning of the policy (accident) years.

The expected losses are the actual payroll for the experience period years multiplied by the manual expected loss rates for the prospective period. The expected loss rates reflect the losses expected to be reported at the 18, 30, and 42 month evaluations of the latest three available policy periods.

w and C (and, hence, B) result from the specific credibility formulae.

Composite Rating

Composite rating is an administrative tool to facilitate the rating of large, complex risks upon audit. Instead of rating different coverages using different exposure bases, all applicable coverages are rated using one, composite, exposure base.

The composite rate to be applied to the composite exposure base is determined at the beginning of the policy period under consideration based on historical exposures. Estimated exposures are used if exact exposures are not available. This composite rate is used to determine the deposit premium based on the estimated composite exposure base and the final premium based on the audited composite exposure base. The composite rate may be based on manual rates to which the appropriate experience modification factors have been applied or on the entity's experience. The remainder of this section

Exhibit 9
Page 1 of 2

ISO Composite Rating Plan Loss-Rated Risks Example

Types of Losses Covered: General Liability, Automobile Liability, Automobile Physical Damage, Glass, and Theft

Experience Period: Five years beginning between six and five and one-half years prior to the date the composite rate is to be effective. As few as three years, beginning between four and three and one-half years prior to the date the composite rate is to be effectitve, may be used if that is all that is available.

Experience: For each type of loss, calculate by accident year and in total the adjusted projected ultimate losses and ALAE as follows:

Reported Limited Losses & ALAE At Latest Evaluation Date	×	Loss & ALAE Development Factor	×	Conversion Factor From Claims-Made to Occurrence	×	Loss & ALAE Trend Factors to Current Year	×	Factors to Reflect Other Changes

Adjusted Composite Exposure for Experience Period: For the experience period, calculate the adjusted composite exposure as follows:

Composite Exposure for Exper. Period	×	Exposure Trend Factors	×	Factors to Reflect Other Changes

Exhibit 9
Page 2 of 2

Adjusted Premium for Experience Period:	For each type of loss, calculate the loss premium as follows:

$$\text{Adjusted Projected Ultimate Losses \& ALAE} \times \text{Conversion Factor From Occurrence to Claims-Made} \div \text{Expected Loss \& ALAE Ratio}$$

Total these to get the total adjusted premium for the experience period.

Composite Rate:	The composite rate is calculated as follows:

$$\text{Adjusted Premium for Exper. Period} \div \text{Adjusted Composite Exposure for Exper. Period}$$

Final Premium:	The final premium is calculated as follows:

$$\text{Audited Exposure for Policy Period} \times \text{Composite Rate}$$

Notes:	Various per occurrence limits apply to reported losses and ALAE.

For automobile physical damage, exclude ALAE.

The following are provided by ISO on an advisory basis:

- loss and ALAE development factors,
- conversion factors from occurrence to claims-made,
- loss & ALAE trend factors,
- exposure trend factors,
- conversion factors from claims-made to occurrence, and
- expected loss and ALAE ratios.

discusses the latter case, using the loss rating portion of the ISO Composite Rating Plan for Automobile Physical Damage, Automobile Liability, General Liability, Glass and Theft Insurance (revised October 1988) as an example.

Exhibit 9 shows the basic formulae for the ISO Composite Rating Plan loss-rated risks example. Eligibility for loss rating is based on the reported losses and ALAE at the latest evaluation date, limited to various per occurrence limits, for the same period of time as the experience period to be used in the calculation. Different eligibility requirements apply for different combinations of coverage and limits. The premium charged is based solely on the entity's experience, adjusted for differences in coverage type (occurrence or claims-made year), trends in losses and ALAE and exposure, and other factors which may affect the appropriateness of the composite rate. The entity's experience has an implicit 100% credibility.

The composite rate is the adjusted premium for the experience period divided by the adjusted composite exposure base for the experience period. The adjusted premium for the experience period is the sum of the adjusted projected ultimate losses and ALAE, converted from occurrence to claims-made basis if appropriate, divided by the expected loss and ALAE ratio, for each type of loss. The adjusted composite exposure base for the experience period is the composite exposure base for the experience period, adjusted by exposure trend factors. The projected ultimate losses and ALAE are the reported losses and ALAE at latest evaluation date developed to ultimate, converted from claims-made to occurrence if appropriate, trended to the year for which the composite rate is being calculated, and adjusted for other changes if appropriate.

The reported losses and ALAE used in the calculation are subject to various per occurrence limits. The plan has special rules for treating non-standard expense allowances, deductibles, and limits larger than those used in the composite rating calculation. The deposit premium is not subject to experience rating since it is based solely on the entity's experience under the limits used in the calculation. The final premium may be subject to retrospective rating. Both deposit and final premiums may be subject to schedule rating.

Retrospective Rating

While experience rating and some forms of composite rating assume that the past, with appropriate adjustments, is predictive of the future, retrospective rating uses the experience during the period to determine the costs for the period. This approach makes costs based on retrospective rating plans more responsive to changes in experience and more subject to unusual fluctuations in experience than is the case with experience rating or composite rating plans. However, retrospective rating is very similar to prospective experience rating in many ways.

As with experience rating, actual losses, and sometimes ALAE, are compared to expected losses (and ALAE), although in this case they are both for the current period. To have an "apples to apples" comparison, several different experience and exposure combinations can be used, including the following:

- actual paid losses (and ALAE) at a particular date and the expected paid losses (and ALAE) at that date, both for the experience period;
- reported losses (and ALAE) at a particular date and the expected reported losses (and ALAE) at that date, both for the experience period; and
- projected ultimate losses (and ALAE) and expected losses, both for the experience period.

These are the same as the first three combinations listed for experience rating.

As with experience rating, the experience component should be related to the exposure component and to the basis on which policies are written or funding occurs. If the costs to be allocated include ALAE, ALAE should be included with losses in the calculation.

The length of the retrospective rating period is usually one or three years. As with experience rating, the shorter the period, the more responsive the plan will be to changes that truly affect loss and ALAE experience, such as changes in the risk control program, and the more subject to unusual fluctuations in loss and ALAE experience. Conversely, a longer period will result in less responsiveness to changes and to unusual or catastrophic occurrences.

Retrospective rating plans may also limit losses (and ALAE) per occurrence and in aggregate to reduce the effect of unusual or catastrophic occurrences, as may experience rating plans.

If projected ultimate losses are to be used in the retrospective rating calculation, they can be developed in a number of ways similar to those used to develop projected ultimate losses used to determine manual rates. Projected ultimate losses are often based on paid or reported losses at a particular date.

The expected losses are a function of the current exposure. The exposure component should be related to the experience component, as detailed above. As for experience rating, expected losses are usually a product of an expected loss rate and the exposure base.

As is also true for experience rating, the exposure base used should reflect the underlying risk of loss and ALAE. It is not always possible to use the theoretically optimal exposure base. In practice, insurers and non-traditional risk financing mechanisms often use whatever exposure base insurers use in their premium calculations.

Credibility has the same function and is used in the same way for retrospective rating as for experience rating. Retrospective rating plans also may have minimum or maximum premium charges and need to be corrected for off-balance, as with experience rating plans.

Retrospective rating plans require a deposit premium at the beginning of the policy period. The deposit premium is an estimate of the ultimate premium for the policy period and may be determined using an experience rating plan. Retrospective premium adjustments are made periodically after the end of the policy period for a predetermined number of adjustments or until the insurer and insured agree to end the adjustments.

Two examples of retrospective rating plans are discussed below.

NCCI Retrospective Rating Plan

The NCCI Retrospective Rating Plan applies to workers' compensation and employers' liability for eligible insureds. An insured must elect to participate in the plan, and the insurer must agree.

The basic formulae are shown in Exhibit 10. Losses, some ALAE for workers' compensation, and all ALAE for employer's liability are the subject of the allocation. Some aircraft-related claims are excluded and the costs of some accidents involving more than one person are limited. All other costs are collected as a function of the losses, exposure (as represented by the standard premium), or, for taxes only, the retrospective premium before taxes. All policies are written on an occurrence basis.

The deposit premium collected at the beginning of the period is the experience-rated premium. Retrospective adjustments are made using claim data at 18, 30, 42,. . . months after the beginning of the policy period, if it is a one-year retrospective period, until insurer and insured agree there will be no more. For a three-year retrospective period, the claim data are evaluated at 42, 54, 66,. . . months after the beginning of the policy period.

There is no direct application of credibility in this plan. For losses under any applicable limits, the experience is given implicit credibility of 1.000. Losses over any applicable limits are given zero credibility, and money for them is collected based on exposure, as represented by standard premium and the applicable excess loss factor.

The plan allows for selection of minimum and maximum retrospective premiums. Costs above the maximum less those below the minimum are collected from or credited to the insured based on exposure, as represented by standard premium. Various minimum and maximum retrospective premium combinations are possible (including no minimum or maximum). The choice of minimum and maximum premiums affects the basic premium. The basic premium includes the expenses of the guaranteed cost premium and an insurance charge which reflects the minimum and maximum premiums, so that the average retrospective rating premium is expected to equal the guaranteed cost premium.

The general retrospective rating formula calculates retrospective premium as the sum of basic premium and converted losses, both multiplied by the tax multiplier. The basic premium, which is a function of the standard premium (exposure), provides for the following costs:

- insurer expenses such as acquiring and servicing the insured's account;
- risk control services, premium audit, and general administration of the insurance;
- loss adjustment expenses in excess of those provided for by the loss conversion factor;
- a net charge for limiting the retrospective premium between the minimum and maximum retrospective premiums; and
- an allowance for the insurer's possible profit or for contingencies.

The converted losses are the reported limited losses at the evaluation date multiplied by the loss conversion factor. The loss conversion factor covers the ULAE and ALAE not included with the losses. The tax multiplier covers licenses, fees, assessments, and taxes which the insurer must pay on the premium it collects.

There are two additional elements the insured may elect if the insurer agrees: a loss limitation resulting in an excess loss premium and a retrospective development premium. Both these premiums are subject to the tax multiplier. The retrospective rating formula with these elective premium elements is also shown in Exhibit 10.

Exhibit 10
Page 1 of 2

NCCI Retrospective Rating Plan Example

Experience Period: One or Three Years

Deposit Premium: Experience-Rated Premium

Retrospective Adjustments: Uses claim data at 18, 30, 42,. . . months from the beginning of a one-year policy period and claim data at 42, 54, 66,. . . months from the beginning of a three-year policy period.

Retrospective Rating Formula:

$$\text{Retro. Premium} = \text{Basic Premium} + \text{Converted Losses} \times \text{Tax Multiplier}$$

$$\text{Basic Premium} = \text{Standard Premium} \times \text{Basic Premium Factor}$$

Standard Premium = Manual Premium modified for experience rating, loss constants, and minimum premium excluding premium discount and expense constants.

$$\text{Converted Losses} = \text{Reported Limited Losses at Eval. Date} \times \text{Loss Conversion Factor}$$

Reported limited losses include: interest on judgments; expenses incurred in obtaining third party recoveries, and ALAE for employer's liability claims; exclude some aircraft-related claims; and have limits on some accidents involving more than one person.

Exhibit 10
Page 2 of 2

Retrospective Rating Formula With Elective Premium Elements:

Retro. Premium = Basic Premium + Converted Losses + Excess Loss Premium + Retro. Devel. Premium × Tax Multiplier

Excess Loss Premium = Standard Premium × Excess Loss Premium Factor × Loss Conversion Factor

Retro. Devel. Premium = Standard Premium × Retro. Devel. Factor × Loss Conversion Factor

Converted losses are calculated as above, but reported limited losses now also have a per accident limit.

Minimum and Maximum Retrospective Premiums:

Minimum Retro. Premium = Standard Premium × Minimum Retro. Premium Factor

Maximum Retro. Premium = Standard Premium × Maximum Retro. Premium Factor

Note: The following are provided by NCCI:

- Basic Premium Factor
- Excess Loss Premium Factor
- Loss Conversion Factor
- Maximum Retrospective Premium Factor
- Minimum Retrospective Premium Factor
- Retrospective Development Factor
- Tax Multiplier

If the loss limitation is accepted, the reported limited losses at any evaluation are further limited to an agreed-upon amount per accident. The cost of losses above this amount and related ALAE and ULAE are collected through the excess loss premium. It is a function of standard premium (exposure).

Because reported limited losses tend to develop over time upwards to the ultimate limited losses, the first retrospective adjustment is likely to result in the insurer returning premium to the insured. Successive retrospective adjustments will probably result in most of, if not all of or more than, this amount being returned by the insured to the insurer. To smooth out these back-and-forth payments, some insureds opt to use the retrospective development premium, which attempts to offset this process. The retrospective development premium is a function of standard premium (exposure). It is used only for the first three retrospective adjustments and decreases over time.

Note that there does not seem to be any part of the formula that recovers for the cost of the excluded aircraft-related claims and amounts above limits on accidents involving more than one person. There is also an overlap of the excess loss premium and basic premium. The excess loss premium collects for losses and related expenses above the per accident limit; the basic premium collects for losses and related expenses above the maximum limit, some of which are the result of losses above the per accident limit. This overlap is currently compensated for by a tabular deduction from the excess loss premium. This deduction is dependent on the size of risk and the loss ratio associated with the maximum limit in the specific plan.

Automobile Physical Damage Insurance Retrospective Allocation to Units by Single Entity

Exhibit 11 illustrates the retrospective allocation of automobile physical damage insurance premium to units by a single entity. The coverage is actual cash value, written on an occurrence basis for one year.

Exhibit 11

Automobile Physical Damage Insurance Retrospective Allocation to Units by Single Entity Example

Deposit Premium

Unit	Expected Number of Vehicle Years	Expected Cost of Insurance Allocated Based on Exposure
(1)	(2)	(3)
A	500	50,000
B	1,000	100,000
C	750	75,000
D	500	50,000
E	2,500	250,000
Total	5,250	525,000

Note: (3) is allocated based on (2). (3) is the deposit premium.

Retrospective Premium

Unit	Actual Number of Vehicle Years	Actual Cost of Insurance Allocated Based on Exposure	Reported Losses & ALAE at 18 Months	Actual Cost of Insurance Allocated Based on Experience	Credibility	Retro. Premium
(1)	(2)	(3)	(4)	(5)	(6)	(7)
A	525	48,659	35,000	52,778	0.25	49,688
B	1,050	97,317	60,000	90,476	0.25	95,607
C	600	55,610	60,000	90,476	0.25	64,326
D	500	46,341	30,000	45,238	0.25	46,066
E	2,450	227,073	130,000	196,032	0.25	219,313
Total	5,125	475,000	315,000	475,000		475,000

Notes: (3) is allocated based on (2)
(5) is allocated based on (4)
(7) = (3) × [1.00 − (6)] + [(5) × (6)]

The deposit premium collected from the units at the beginning of the period is based on the expected cost of insurance, allocated to each unit based on exposure as represented by the expected number of vehicles. There is no distinction for different types of vehicles. This is reasonable if each unit has the same expected cost per vehicle.

There is one retrospective adjustment, made using data at 18 months after the beginning of the policy year. Only one adjustment is made because automobile physical damage claims are reported and settled very quickly and the actual exposure is known shortly after the year ends. The actual cost of the insurance is allocated based on audited exposure (actual number of vehicles) and on reported losses and ALAE. These two allocations are weighted using credibility. Losses and ALAE are unlimited because the cost of any one occurrence is limited by the actual cash value of the vehicle in the accident plus any ALAE, which should be small. All experience is given a credibility of 0.25 regardless of the exposure size to make the plan easier for the unit managers to understand.

The plan has no minimum and maximum retrospective premiums. The plan has no off-balance correction, as none is needed because the credibility factors are the same for all units.

Designing an Individual Risk Rating System

To design an individual risk rating system such as those previously discussed, the following steps should be taken:

1. Determine the goals for the system.
2. Determine what is to be allocated.
3. Determine what kinds of exposure and experience data are available.
4. Decide whether the system will be prospective, retrospective, or a combination.

5. If the system is to be prospective, decide if it will be a schedule rating system, an experience rating system, a composite rating system, or a combination.
6. Design the schedule rating portion of the system.
7. Determine the experience component separately for each remaining portion of the system.
   a. Determine the type of experience to be used.
   b. Determine the experience period.
   c. Decide if there will be any per occurrence or aggregate limits.
8. Determine the exposure component separately for each remaining portion of the system.
   a. Determine the type of exposure to be used.
   b. Determine the exposure period.
9. Determine the credibility component separately for each remaining portion of the system.
10. Consider any other desired plan features such as a minimum or maximum premium charge.
11. Estimate if the system has an off-balance. If so, correct it if indicated.
12. Review the system and determine if it meets the stated goals and attributes of a good individual risk rating system. If not, make changes to the system.
13. Run sample calculations to see if the system functions as expected. If not, make any indicated changes.
14. Collect necessary data and put the system into use.
15. Review the plan at least every three years to be certain that it meets current needs. Needs can change or the situation may change so that the system no longer performs as expected. An example of the latter is that a per occurrence limit selected

three years ago may no longer be reasonable because of economic and social inflation.

Summary

Individual risk rating systems supplement the manual rates by modifying the group rates to reflect an individual entity's experience. They can be used by an insurer for all its insureds in one line of coverage, by risk sharing pools to allocate costs among a fixed group of members, or by an individual entity to allocate risk financing costs among its divisions.

Individual risk rating systems should be tailored to the needs of the specific situation in which they will be used. This produces systems with widely varying design, but all should follow the general principles and structures outlined in this chapter.

Bibliography

Ammeter, H. 1962. Experience rating — a new application of the collective theory of risk. *ASTIN Bulletin* 2:261

Dorweiler, P. 1934. A survey of risk credibility in experience rating. *PCAS* 21:1. Reprinted in *PCAS* 58:90

Fitzgibbon, W. J., Jr. 1985. Reserving for retrospective returns. *PCAS* 52:203. See also discussions by Hope, F. J., *PCAS* 53:185, and Uhthoff, D. R., *PCAS* 53:187

Foster, R. B. 1954. The boiler and machinery premium adjustment rating plan. *PCAS* 41:135

Harwayne, F. 1976. Accident limitations for retrospective rating. *PCAS* 63:1. See also discussions by Bradley, D. R., *PCAS* 64:93; Finger, R. J., *PCAS* 63:32; and Taylor, F. and Lattanzio, F., *PCAS* 64:96

Hewitt, C. C. 1967. Loss ratio distribution — a model. *PCAS* 64:70. See also discussion by Hachemeister, C. A., *PCAS* 54:89

Kulp, C. A., and Hall, J. W. 1968. *Casualty insurance*, Chapter 22. New York: The Ronald Press Company

Insurance Services Office. 1985. *Commercial fire rating schedule*

- - -. 1988. *Composite rating plan for automobile physical damage, automobile liability, general liability, glass and theft insurance*

- - -. 1988. *Commercial general liability experience and schedule rating plan*

- - -. 1987. *Retrospective rating plan for automobile, general liability, glass and theft*

Lee, Y. S. 1988. The mathematics of excess loss coverages and retrospective rating — a graphical approach. *PCAS* 75:49

Loimaranta, K. 1977. On the calculation of variances and credibilities by experience rating. *ASTIN Bulletin* 9:203

McClure, R. D. 1972 An actuarial note on experience rating nuclear property insurance. *PCAS* 59:150. See also discussion by Hurley, R. L., *PCAS* 60:105

Meyers, G. 1980. An analysis of retrospective rating. *PCAS* 67:110. See also discussion by Fiebrink, M. E., *PCAS* 68:113, and Golz, J. F., *1980 Discussion Paper Program.* Casualty Actuarial Society

National Council on Compensation Insurance. 1984. *Experience rating plan*

- - -. 1984. *Retrospective rating plan manual for workers' compensation and employers' liability insurance*

Perryman, F. S. 1937. Experience rating plan credibilities. *PCAS* 24:60. Also *PCAS* 58:143

Skurnick, D. 1974. The California table L. *PCAS* 61:177. See also discussions by Harwayne, F., *PCAS* 62:16 and Snader, R., *PCAS* 62:24

Snader, R. H. 1980. Fundamentals of individual risk rating and related topics. Casualty Actuarial Society

Stafford, J. R. 1981a. *Workers' compensation and employers' liability experience rating.* Palatine, Illinois: J & M Publications

- - -. 1981b. *Retrospective rating.* Palatine, Illinois: J & M Publications

Stanard, J. N. 1980. Experience rates as estimators: a simulation of their bias and variance, including discussion by Robertson, J. P. *1980 Discussion Paper Program.* Casualty Actuarial Society.

Surety Association of America. 1976. *Experience rating plan — financial institutions*

Taylor, G. C. 1974. Experience rating with credibility adjustment of the manual premium. *ASTIN Bulletin* 7:323

Uhthoff, D. R. 1959. The compensation experience rating plan — a current review. *PCAS* 46:285. See also discussions by Marshall, R. M., *PCAS* 47:191; Johnson, R. A., *PCAS* 47:198; and Allen, E. S., *PCAS* 47:200

Valerius, Nels. 1942. Risk distributions underlying insurance charges in the retrospective rating plan. *PCAS* 29:96

Webb, B. L., Launie, J. J., Rokes, W. P., and Baglini, N. A. 1981. *Insurance company operations.* II(10). American Institute of Property and Liability Underwriters

Chapter 4
LOSS RESERVING
by Ronald F. Wiser

Introduction

One of the major challenges to the casualty actuary is the estimation of the necessary financial provision for the unpaid liabilities of an insurer to claimants.

The practical approaches devised by actuaries who have worked on providing these estimates include a wide range of techniques that have not yet been formulated into a precise science. The intent of this chapter is to provide insight into the techniques used by practicing actuaries in estimating claim liabilities. Many papers that begin the task of formulating a rigorous basis for these techniques can be found in the bibliography.

A large number of numerical examples demonstrate the computations. The accompanying discussions are focused on interpreting the numerical computations. The computations are only one means used by the practicing actuary to arrive at an opinion about an insurer's estimated liability. Experience and judgment are still the most important components of the actuary's opinion. There is no single formula that will provide reserve estimates.

Throughout this chapter, the term "insurer" is meant to represent any risk bearer for property and casualty exposures, whether an insurance company, a reciprocal exchange, a self-insured entity, a pool, a trust, an association, or other form of organization.

Loss reserving is the term used to denote the actuarial process of estimating the needed amount of loss reserves. A loss reserve is a provision for an insurer's liability for claims.

Accounting Concepts

In order to understand the necessity for the loss reserving process, it is helpful to have a conceptual understanding of the basic accounting principles applicable to insurers. A general reference on accounting principles is Davidson, et al [1982].

The accounting process produces two important statements, the balance sheet and the income statement, that document the financial position and performance of a firm, respectively. The reliability and usefulness of both of these statements are dependent on the accuracy of loss reserves. Most insurers need to prepare these statements under rules promulgated by generally accepted accounting procedures (GAAP).

The Balance Sheet

The balance sheet reports on the financial position of the firm at a specific point in time. It shows the levels of assets and liabilities, and the status of the shareholders' equity, or surplus, for the insurer. The reporting follows the simple equation:

$$\text{Assets} = \text{Liabilities} + \text{Owners' Equity}$$

An asset is any economic resource that is held by the firm. An asset could be cash, stocks and bonds, real estate, or agents' receivables, for example.

Liabilities are claims on the resources of the firm, to satisfy obligations of the firm. Liabilities could be mortgages, bank debt, bonds issued, premiums received from clients but not yet earned, or benefits payable on behalf of clients due to contractual obligations, for example.

Owners' equity is the owners' claim on the assets of the firm. The owners' claim is always subordinate to all other liabilities of the firm. It is actually the balancing item in the equation above. Owners' equity is generally called the surplus of the insurer. For mutual insurers, the policyholders are the owners and the surplus belongs to them.

When liabilities exceed assets, the value of the owners' equity is negative, and the firm is insolvent. Another way to write the equation of financial position is then given by:

$$\text{Owners' Equity} = \text{Assets} - \text{Liabilities}$$

Through common usage the term "loss reserve" has come to denote the property and casualty company's provision for its liability for claims by or against policyholders. Loss reserving is the process of estimating the amount of the company's liabilities for such claims ("losses") which the company has contracted to settle for its policyholders.

Loss reserving is an actuarial function because it involves the current financial evaluation of future contingent events. These contingencies apply to obligations that have already been assumed by the company through an insurance contract. They are:

1) Future developments on claims already reported, and,
2) Claims to be reported in the future, based on events that have already occurred.

A total loss reserve for an insurer is composed of five elements:

1) Case reserves assigned to specific claims,
2) A provision for future development on known claims,
3) A provision for claims that re-open after they have been closed,
4) A provision for claims that have occurred but have not yet been reported to the insurer, and
5) A provision for claims that have been reported to the insurer but have not yet been recorded.

The Income Statement

The income statement measures changes in owners' equity during a stated period of time. Owners' equity can be subdivided into the capital contributed by the owners and any earnings of the firm from past periods retained in the firm. Thus,

$$\text{Owners' Equity} = \text{Contributed Capital} + \text{Retained Earnings}$$

The income statement measures the firm's performance in the period ended as follows:

Income = Revenue − Expense

Revenue measures the inflow of assets from providing products or services. An insurer's revenue also includes the investment income earned on assets it holds. Expense measures the outflow of assets that are consumed in providing the firm's products or services.

Income may be either used to increase owners' equity in the firm (i.e. increase retained earnings) or distributed to owners as dividends. This can be written as

Income = Change in Retained Earnings +
Dividends to Owners

This series of equations then defines the relationship between the balance sheet and the income statement. This relationship can be obtained by chaining together the basic accounting equations above.

Income = Change in Retained Earnings +
Dividends to Owners;

but,

Retained Earnings = Owners' Equity −
Contributed Capital;

and,

Owners' Equity = Assets − Liabilities.

thus,

Retained Earnings = Assets − Liabilities −
Contributed Capital;

and,

Income = Change in Assets − Change in Liabilities −
Change in Contributed Capital +
Dividends to Owners.

This formula demonstrates the relationship between the balance sheet and the income statement of a firm. In particular, note that any change in a liability account, such as loss reserves, has a direct impact on insurer's income.

The Definition of Liabilities

An obligation satisfies the accounting definition of a liability if it possesses three essential characteristics (Davidson et al, 386-387):

1) The obligation involves a probable future sacrifice of resources at a specified or determinable date;
2) The firm has little or no discretion to avoid the transfer; and
3) The transaction or event giving rise to the obligation has already occurred.

A claim liability of a property and casualty insurer satisfies the second and third characteristics above. The first requirement is not generally satisfied in property and casualty claim situations. For instance, in a workers' compensation claim, payments must be made periodically at specified times, often weekly. However, in a third-party liability situation it is not possible to specify the date on which settlement will be made.

A loss reserve is a contingent liability in the sense that each specific claim under adjustment depends on some future contingent event to determine the extent of the insurer's liability. Two tests are proposed by the accounting literature to determine if a contingent liability should be recognized on the company's balance sheet. These are:

1) Information at the time of preparation of the financial reports indicates that it is likely that a liability has been incurred, and
2) the amount of the liability can be reasonably estimated.

Clearly, an insurer's loss reserves satisfy both these conditions.

Cash versus Accrual Basis of Accounting

The balance sheet and income statement may be prepared under different accounting bases—cash or accrual (Davidson et al, 80-84).

The cash basis recognizes revenues when they are received, and expenses are reported in the period expenditures are made. For very simple businesses such as professional services, the cash basis may be adequate. However, for most businesses the cash basis of accounting does an unsatisfactory job of matching revenues with associated expenses.

The accrual basis of accounting recognizes revenue as it is earned. Likewise, costs are reported as expenses in the same period as the revenues giving rise to those costs are recognized. This results in an income statement that more appropriately matches costs with appropriate revenues.

For the property and casualty operation, this results in recognition of earned premium, rather than written premiums, as revenue. Earned premium is generally calculated through the use of a liability account termed the unearned premium reserve. Thus,

$$\begin{aligned}\text{Earned Premium} = {} & \text{Written Premium} + \\ & \text{Beginning Unearned Premium Reserve} - \\ & \text{Ending Unearned Premium Reserve}\end{aligned}$$

Earned premium is an income statement item, hence it relates to a specific time period. Unearned premium is a balance sheet account, hence can be calculated as of a specific date. In this case, the unearned premiums as of the beginning and end dates of the earnings period are calculated.

The unearned premium reserve is that portion of the written premium that has not been exposed to loss. These are funds that have been received from the policyholders, but for which services have not yet been provided. For the property and casualty company, the service is indemnity for financial losses due to exposure over a period of time to the chance of loss from the perils insured against. Thus, unearned premium reserves are liabilities of the company to policyholders.

Generally the amount of the unearned premium is easy to calculate. Most property and casualty policies are for a fixed term, say six months or one year, and the premium revenues can be considered as earned pro-rata over the policy term. A company may calculate its unearned premium liability on a daily pro-rata basis, or monthly. For daily pro-rata calculations, a $1000 policy written on January 1, would require an unearned premium reserve of $657.53 after 125 days of coverage had elapsed on April 15.

Similarly, policyholder benefits are expenses incurred by the firm, which must be matched to the revenues earned on the policies. It would clearly be inappropriate to count only paid losses and paid loss adjustment expense as expenses. This is due to the long delays between the time period for which insurance protection is afforded under the policy, and the actual liquidation of the obligations assumed under the terms of the policies.

The expenses incurred for policy benefits can be computed through use of the "loss reserve" liability account. The formula is:

$$\text{Incurred Losses} = \text{Paid Losses} + \text{Ending Claim Liability} - \text{Beginning Claim Liability.}$$

Unlike most businesses, the property and casualty business is characterized by positive net cash flows. This results because premiums for the protection are generally received at the beginning of the policy period. Also, there are various delays until the actual liquidation of policy benefits. The measurement and financial quantification of these delays is the result of the loss reserve estimation process.

Finally, insurers that are regulated by the states will actually have to keep accrual accounting books on a "statutory" basis that satisfies state insurance laws. The statutory accounting standards differ from GAAP standards in several ways. Among them,

1) Acquisition costs must be expensed when the policy is written.

2) Certain assets are not recognized.

3) Bonds are valued at amortized value, not market value.

Claim Department Reserving Activity

A look at the structure of a typical loss reserve case inventory will aid in understanding the processes at work when we observe loss development. For the moment, let us consider loss development as simply the change in the amount of a loss reserve inventory in a specified period of time. While in the aggregate we may only be able to observe the increase in total dollars of loss reserve (e.g., given only Annual Statement data), the change in total case reserve inventory is the result of a number of natural transition processes that can be found in any reserve inventory. An understanding of this structure will allow the loss reserve analyst to investigate reasons for observed development patterns (Degerness 1983).

The accompanying table tracks the types of activity that may occur in a loss reserve inventory during any one time period. Initially, there are 1,015 claims that are open and in the process of adjustment by the insurer's claim department. Losses will enter either as new claims (line 2), reopened claims (line 3), or zero reserves (line 4). A reopened claim is one that has previously been closed, but requires a pending claim file, because of further adjusting activity. This must be distinguished from a closed claim that simply requires an additional payment after closure, i.e. a prematurely closed claim (included in line 15). Such a claim is not reopened because no further adjusting effort is expected to be necessary after the single payment.

A particular type of new claim that should be distinguished from others is the precautionary reserve claim or zero reserve claim. This is used to establish a file as a means of monitoring a potential liability situation. No dollar value, or a nominal amount, is put up on the claim file because there is not yet a strong enough fact situation that a liability of the company exists. However, there is potential for liability and the situation must be closely monitored by the company. The use of these precautionary files is most often found on excess or reinsurance losses. When the primary carrier is another company, there may be very little information in the file initially established, other than the mandatory notice required by the excess policy wording.

Many companies also use a "fast track" claim category (line 14). This is simply a claim that is paid without a claim file ever being established. This procedure is often used on small property claims, such as auto physical damage or homeowners.

Case Reserve Activity

	Counts	Amounts
1. Beginning Outstanding	1,015	$5,673,633
2. New Reserves	80	270,850
3. Reopened Reserves	29	84,472
4. Zero Reserves	2	0
5. Reserve Increases	28	163,995
6. Subtotal: Increases (2 + 3 + 4 + 5)	139	$ 519,317
7. Reserve Decreases	81	(57,433)
8. Closed with Payment	30	(713,281)
9. Closed without Payment	71	(147,291)
10. Subtotal: Decreases (7 + 8 + 9)	182	($ 918,005)
11. Total Reserve Change (Counts 2 + 3 + 4 − 8 − 9) (Amounts: 6 + 10)	10	($ 398,688)
12. Final Payments	30	793,180
13. Partial payments	82	60,514
14. Fast Track Payments	8	29,281
15. All Other	51	32,943
16. Total Payments (12 + 13 + 14 + 15)	171	$ 915,918
17. Salvage/Subrogation	28	(3,269)
18. Incurred Loss (11 + 16 + 17)		513,961
19. Ending Outstanding (1 + 11)	1,025	$5,274,945

Once a claim has entered the inventory, it is managed by a claim adjuster until closure of the file or settlement. For reserve analysis purposes, we record only the financial changes that result from the claim adjusters activities.

Referring to the above, we have categorized the types of financial actions we are interested in recording. Reserve increases (line 5) or decreases (line 7) are changes in open claim file valuations, and the file remains open after the change in valuation. These changes in reserve valuation may be accompanied by a loss or expense payment.

Note that partial payments may be split into payments with and without incurred effect for the file. A payment may have no incurred effect if the remaining reserve is reduced by the amount of the payment. Recall the basic accounting formula for incurred losses:

$$\text{Incurred Loss} = \text{Paid Loss} + \text{Ending Loss Reserve} - \text{Beginning Loss Reserve.}$$

Thus if the claim adjuster reduces the case reserve by the amount of payment, there is no incurred loss effect. Often, automated claim systems will reduce the case reserve by the amount of the payment. This requires the adjuster to take specific reserve action only if he intends to change his total valuation of the claim file.

One of the most important statistics to monitor for any claim inventory is the number of claim closings (lines 8 and 9). Note the distinction between claims closed without payment and those closed with some payment of loss or expense. In terms of simple monitoring of reserve activity, the rate of claim closings should be carefully watched. Often, a change in the closing rate can lead the analyst to discover an important operational change in claims administration.

The incurred effect of reserve closings can be calculated from the same accounting formula:

$$\text{Incurred Loss} = \text{Paid Loss} - \text{Beginning Reserve.}$$

Note that the ending reserve on a closed claim is zero, hence the formula simplifies as above. For our example, for the 101 closing payments (30 closed with payment, 71 without payment) we can calculate that:

$$\text{Incurred Loss} = \$793{,}180 - \$713{,}281 - \$147{,}291$$

$$\text{Incurred Loss} = (\$67{,}392).$$

Note that for this period, there is actually a savings on claims closed. This can often be the case, especially for lines of business that generate a high proportion of claims closed with no payment. If we only consider claims that close with payment, there is no savings:

$$\text{Incurred Loss} = \$793{,}180 - \$713{,}281 = \$79{,}899$$

In addition to claim payments associated with reserve files, we also can have payments to which no currently open files are attached. Fast Track payments have been mentioned above. There are also other miscellaneous payments, including payments on files already closed.

Note that almost all of the 82 partial claim payments on line 13 are associated with reserve decreases on line 7. This may be a result of the automatic decrease of case reserves to offset the amount of partial payments.

Once a file is closed with regard to the insurer's obligation to the policyholder, it may still be pursued for recoveries from third parties of some part of the indemnity amount. Thus, the assumption of the obligation to defend and settle a policyholder's claim usually carries with it the assumption of the policyholder's right to recovery of the amount of damages. This right of recovery is called subrogation. An example of subrogation involves the payment of a collision claim by an insurer. If a third party was responsible for the damage, the insurer making the collision coverage payment to its insured has the right to recover the amount of damages from the responsible party.

In addition to subrogation situations, the payment of first party benefits is usually accompanied by the insurer's taking of title to the damaged property. This property can often be disposed of for a partial recovery of the amount paid to the policyholder for adjustment of the loss, and is called salvage. An example of a common salvage situation involves an automobile accident in which the insured's vehicle is a total loss. The insurer reimburses the insured for the value of the vehicle and takes title to the vehicle. The auto is then disposed of for any scrap value and the proceeds reduce the amount of loss.

Note that both of these activities serve to reduce the insurer's net payout. Then the total amount paid in the period is

$$\text{Paid loss} = \$915{,}918 - \$3{,}269 = \$912{,}649$$

An Actuarial Model of Loss Development

Both the accounting model and the claims model of the reserving process deal with aggregates over a certain time period. Further, the claim department is concerned with individual file actions. An actuarial model can be constructed that supplies a structure behind the aggregate financial descriptions of claims activity.

This can serve as a conceptual starting point for the analysis of reserves from the actuary's viewpoint.

The basic mathematical form of an actuarial loss development model is outlined below. However the rest of this chapter will document existing practices of loss reserve development as opposed to a theoretical development of the modeling approach.

Let $v(x)$ be the amount of loss arising from instant x, i.e. $v(x)$ can be thought of as the loss density. Then the amount of ultimate loss in the time period (a,b) can be calculated as

$$\int_a^b v(x)\, dx.$$

All observations of loss reserve situations are observations of various aggregate amounts, hence the form of $v(x)$ cannot be observed directly.

Since most observations of the loss amounts are at periods short of ultimate development, we need to recognize the development of loss statistics over time. This can be done by introducing a development function $D(t)$, where D is a continuous function with

$$D(t) = 0, \text{ for } t < 0,$$

$$D(t) = 1, \text{ for } t > T,$$

where loss development continues for a duration of T.

Then aggregate losses from period (a,b) developed through time c are given by

$$\int_a^b \int_0^c v(x)D(x+t)\, dt\, dx$$

The actuarial model requires that a proper form and parameters for the functions v and D be found that fit the observed aggregate calendar period loss data.

For instance if $v(x) = k$, a constant volume of losses, then

$$\int_a^b \int_0^c v(x)D(x+t)\, dt\, dx = k\int_a^b \int_0^c D(x+t)\, dtdx$$

If the aggregate data yields the following set observations,

1) Case reserves on accidents occurring in the third quarter of 1987

   a) increased 77.3% from September 30, 1987 to December 31, 1987;

   b) increased 35.5% from December 31, 1987 to March 31, 1987;

   c) increased 18.1% from March 31, 1988 to June 30, 1988 etc.

2) Case reserves on accidents occurring in the fourth quarter of 1987

   a) increased 99.4% from December 31, 1987 to March 31, 1988;

b) increased 33.6% from March 31, 1988 to June 30, 1988;

c) increased 22.3% from June 30, 1988 to September 30, 1988;

and so forth for quarters through the end of 1988, then one can set up the following set of equations for third quarter 1987:

$$(1.773) \int_0^{.25} \int_0^{.25} v(x)D(x+t)\, dt\, dx$$

$$= \int_0^{.25} \int_0^{.5} v(x)D(x+t)\, dtdx$$

$$(1.355) \int_0^{.25} \int_0^{.5} v(x)D(x+t)\, dt\, dx$$

$$= \int_0^{.25} \int_0^{.75} v(x)D(x+t)\, dt\, dx$$

etc . . .

Similarly, we have the following equations for fourth quarter 1987:

$$(1.994) \int_{.25}^{.50} \int_0^{.25} v(x)D(x+t)\, dt\, dx$$

$$= \int_{.25}^{.50} \int_0^{.50} v(x)D(x+t)\, dtdx$$

$$(1.336) \int_{.25}^{.50} \int_0^{.5} v(x)D(x+t)\, dt\, dx$$

$$= \int_{.25}^{.50} \int_{0}^{.75} v(x)D(x + t)\, dtdx$$

etc . . .

From the form of these equations it is clear that the rate of growth $v(x)$ in the underlying incurred losses is embedded in the observed loss development factors. The impact of growth on loss development is extremely important. Generally, in a growing book of business, loss development factors will be less than in a steady state situation. Likewise, in a declining volume of losses, loss development factors will be higher than steady state factors. The benefit of the actuarial model of loss development is the capability to factor out growth effects and measure the underlying "true" loss development (Simon 1970).

These equations can be solved for the best fit set of parameters for the data and the chosen form of the development function $D(t)$. The appropriate functions that represent loss development patterns are just starting to be explored by actuaries (McClenahan 1988; Philbrick 1986).

Loss Reserving Definitions

Loss reserve estimation is approached by the actuary from a much different perspective than that of the claim adjuster. The loss reserve model reviewed above is very close to the claims operations view of the financial aggregate loss reserves. The analyst should understand the claims and accounting perspectives of the total loss reserve, but will most often deal with issues inherent in the actuarial approach to the loss reserve aggregate. The principles under which the actuary performs the reserve estimation process have been adopted by the CAS Board.

First it is essential to define basic loss reserve terminology that can be used to standardize discussions of the loss reserve estimation process.

Loss reserve estimation procedures can only be properly applied to grouped data. A loss reserve inventory should deal with claim files arising from a time period with an explicit beginning and ending date. The start and end dates must relate to one of the distinctive dates in the life of a claim file. This could be the date of reporting, the date of loss, the date of policy inception, or the date of claim closing. The dates specified must be unambiguous and characteristic of an important event in the life of a claim.

The reserve inventory will also often be specified in terms of claims arising from a specific geographic location, as well as specified policy coverages. This aspect is important to considerations of homogeneity and credibility.

Accounting Date

A loss reserve is an estimate of the liability for unpaid claims as of a given date, called the accounting date. An accounting date may be any date. However it is generally a date for which a financial statement is prepared. This is most often a month end, quarter end, or year end.

Valuation Date

A loss reserve inventory as of a fixed accounting date may be evaluated at a date different than the accounting date. The valuation date of a reserve liability is the date as of which the evaluation of the reserve liability is made. Thus we need to evaluate reserve liabilities as of the close of a financial period. The valuation and accounting date would be identical. However for monitoring the accuracy of our evaluations we do a quarterly hindsight evaluation of the year end. These quarterly valuation dates would be different than the year end accounting of the inventory we are evaluating. As a further example, it is common in liability rate studies to evaluate the latest accident year loss reserves aged three months after the close of the year.

Since the loss reserve liability is always an estimate, and the amount of the estimate will change as of successive valuation dates, we should establish some conventional terminology to discuss the results of the loss reserve process.

The **required loss reserve** as of a given accounting date is the amount that must ultimately be paid to settle all claim liabilities. The value of the required loss reserve can only be known when all claims have been finally settled. Thus, the required loss reserve as of a given accounting date is a fixed number that does not change at different valuation dates. However, the value of the required loss reserve is generally unknown for an extremely long period of time.

The **indicated loss reserve** is the result of the actuarial analysis of a reserve inventory as of a given accounting date conducted as of a certain valuation date. This indicated loss reserve is the analyst's opinion of the amount of the required loss reserve. This estimate will change with successive valuation dates and will converge to the required loss reserve as the time between valuation date and the accounting date of the inventory increases.

The **carried loss reserve** is the amount of unpaid claim liability shown on external or internal financial statements. The carried loss reserve for any subgroup of business is the result of the method of generating carried reserves used by the reporting entity for financial reporting reasons.

The **loss reserve margin** is the difference between the carried reserve and the required reserve. Since the required reserve is an unknown quantity we only have an indicated margin. The indicated loss reserve margin is defined to be the carried loss reserve minus the indicated loss reserve. One should not generally expect the margin to be zero, since for any subset of an entity's business it is unlikely that the carried loss reserve will be identical to either the indicated or required loss reserve. Even further, when the loss reserve is split into components the carried reserve for any component will most often not be identical to the indicated loss reserve.

The **loss reserve** can be considered to consist of two major subdivisions, the reserve for known claims and the reserve for unknown claims. Each of these major divisions can then be further broken into subdivisions. Known claims are those claims for which the entity has actually recorded some liability on its books at some point in time. Thus a known claim may have been considered closed at one point, but later need to be reopened for further adjustment.

The **reserve for known claims** may be considered to consist of case reserves, a reserve for future development on case reserves, and a reserve for reopened claims. Note that the total required reserve for known reserves is estimated by the indicated reserve for known claims. The indicated reserve for known claims is the sum of the carried case reserves for known claims, the indicated provision for future development on known claims, and the indicated provision for reopened claims.

The **case reserve** is defined as the sum of the values assigned to specific claims by the entity's case reserving procedure. Most often a claims file is valued by an estimate placed on the file by the claims examiner. The term adjusters' estimates is used to refer to the aggregate of the estimates made by claims personnel on individual claims, based on the facts of those particular claims. Formula reserves may be placed on reported cases. Formula reserves are reserves established by formulas for groups or classes of claims. The formulas may be based on any of a number of factors such as coverage, state, age, limits, severity of injury, or other variables.

The **total reserve** for unreported claims consists of a reserve for claims incurred but not recorded (IBNR). This reserve can be further subdivided into a reserve for claims incurred but not yet reported to the company, and a reserve for those claims reported to the company but not yet recorded on the company's books. This reserve may sometimes be referred to as a pipeline reserve. This distinction is important under claims made coverages, when the pipeline reserve is the only IBNR reserve needed. Most data used for estimation measures the lags from the time a loss is incurred to the time the claim is recorded on the insurer's books and records. If such data is used for the estimation process, then the estimated liability for both "pipeline claims in transit" and unreported claims will result.

Development is defined as the difference, on successive valuation dates, between observed values of certain fundamental quantities that may be used in the loss reserve estimation process. These changes can be changes in paid and carried amounts. Development on reported claims as of two valuation dates consists of the additional paid on case reserves plus the change in case reserves from the first valuation date. Recall that this is also the definition of incurred loss in a calendar period.

Thus,

Development in the period from x to $x + y$ on Known Cases as of $x - w$ =

(Paid in the period from x to $x + y$ on Known Cases as of $x - w$) +

(Change in Carried Reserves in the period from x to $x + y$ on Known Cases as of $x - w$)

Often, we may speak of development on a case reserve inventory as of a certain date. Another type of development relates to IBNR claims. The development of IBNR claims is often referred to as **emergence of IBNR**. In reviewing the development on the prior year end reserve, it is useful to divide the total development into its case development and IBNR emergence components.

The **loss adjustment expense reserve** for a particular exposure period is the amount required to cover all future expenses required to investigate and settle claims incurred in the exposure period. This covers claims yet to be reported as well as claims already known.

Loss adjustment reserves may be charged to specific claims or may be general claims expense not directly attributable to any one file. This distinction lead to separate consideration of allocated loss adjustment expense and unallocated loss adjustment expense.

Allocated loss adjustment expenses are those expenses such as attorneys' fees and legal expense which are incurred with and are assigned to specific claims. **Unallocated loss adjustment expenses** are all other claim adjustment expenses, such as salaries, heat, light and rent, which are associated with the claim adjustment function but are not readily assignable to specific claims.

Data Availability and Organization

The availability of proper data is essential to the task of estimating loss and loss adjustment expense reserve needs. The actuary is responsible for informing management of the need for sufficiently detailed and quality data to obtain reliable reserve estimates. Some general considerations regarding data sources have been established by the CAS Statement of Principles on Loss Reserving.

The data should first be grouped into homogeneous categories. Homogeneity can be an issue across any of grouping of data. The first choice of the analyst must be the criteria along which homogeneity must be attained. These criteria could be locations, coverages, limits or layers, classes, organizational units, among others.

Data must be presented that clearly displays development of losses by accident period, policy period, or report period, to enable the actuary to project the ultimate level of losses.

The effectiveness of the method depends very much on the organization of the historical data. Suppose that the paid losses for a line of business totalled $71,273,000 in 1988. This is the sort of information one might be able to obtain from simple accounting exhibits. It would be more useful to know the composition of this paid amount according to some "aging" criterion. Thus, we would be interested in the information that $11,346,000 of this paid amount relates to occurrences with 1988 date of loss. Similarly, we would want to know that $16,567,000 of the 1988 payments relate to losses with 1987 dates of loss, and so forth. Thus the 1988 paid loss amount contains more information if we can split it into components by year loss. By date of loss occurrence, we would find:

	(000 omitted)
Paid on 1988 losses:	$11,346
Paid on 1987 losses:	16,567
Paid on 1986 losses:	19,935
Paid on 1985 losses:	11,956
Paid on 1984 losses:	5,985
Paid on 1983 losses:	3,210
Paid on 1982 losses:	2,274
Total paid loss in 1988	$71,273

Since we now know that $11,346,000 was paid on 1988 losses during the year 1988, we would like to know the comparable amount paid on 1987 losses during 1987. We can find that a total of $73,972,000 was paid in 1987 on this line of business, and that $17,001,000 is for losses that occurred during 1987. Further, the full 1987 paid amount can be split into amounts (in thousands) paid on accidents from different years as was done for 1988 payments:

	(000 omitted)
Paid on 1987 losses:	$17,001
Paid on 1986 losses:	22,343
Paid on 1985 losses:	13,036
Paid on 1984 losses:	9,098
Paid on 1983 losses:	6,235
Paid on 1982 losses:	4,693
Paid on 1981 losses:	1,566
Total paid loss in 1987	$73,972

Comparison of these amounts by loss year for several calendar years would quickly become awkward. This calls for a more useful method of data organization that facilitates the comparisons we want to make between the accident year components of calendar year paid amounts.

One of the most common ways to organize such data is the loss development triangle. For a given accident year, which is the year the claim occurred, all payments on claims from that accident year are displayed in the same column. Each row indicates a subsequent year of payments on claims of that accident year.

For instance, the payments in thousands, on accident years 1982 through 1988 can be displayed as follows:

Developed Months	Accident Years 1982	1983	1984	1985	1986	1987	1988
12	$22,603	$22,054	$20,166	$19,297	$20,555	$17,001	$11,346
24	17,461	21,916	18,981	18,058	22,343	16,567	
36	14,237	14,767	12,172	13,036	19,935		
48	9,813	13,104	9,098	11,956			
60	7,143	6,235	5,985				
72	4,693	3,211					
84	2,274						

Now we see that the loss payments of the 1988 calendar year appear on the lowest diagonal of the triangle. Similarly, the 1987 calendar year payments appear on the second lowest diagonal. This data organization greatly facilitates comparison of the development history expected of an accident year. For instance, it is immediately apparent that payments on an accident year during the second annual period of payment seem to be roughly equivalent to the amount paid in the first 12 months of payment.

While this arrangement shows the amount paid in each 12 month period, it is often convenient to accumulate the payments on a given loss year. This would result in the following triangle of cumulative loss payments:

Developed Months	Accident Years 1982	1983	1984	1985	1986	1987	1988
12	$22,603	$22,054	$20,166	$19,297	$20,555	$17,001	$11,346
24	40,064	43,970	39,147	37,355	42,898	33,568	
36	54,301	58,737	51,319	50,391	62,832		
48	64,114	71,841	60,417	62,347			
60	71,257	78,076	66,402				
72	75,950	81,287					
84	78,224						

Review of the data is conveniently done in this triangular format. This array of data follows the development of a given fixed grouping of claims until all claims reach their ultimate settlement amounts. Some of the possible data arrays that may be inspected are presented in the Exploratory Data Analysis section below.

Berquist and Sherman (1977) give some rules for relevant data to be used for reserve analysis.

1. Data may be provided by accident year, report year, policy year, underwriting year, or calendar year (in descending order of preference), by development year.

2. The number of years of development should be great enough so that further developments will be negligible. (See the discussion of tail factors below).

3. Allocated loss expenses should be included with losses or shown separately; and clearly labelled as such.

Reserve Estimation Strategy

The overall approach to a reserve valuation problem can be broken into four phases;

1) **Review of the data** to identify its key characteristics and possible anomalies. Balancing of data to other verified sources should be undertaken at this point.

2) Application of appropriate **reserve estimation techniques**.

3) **Evaluation** of the conflicting results of the various reserve methods used, with an attempt to reconcile or explain the bases for different projections. At this point the proposed reserving ultimates are evaluated in contexts outside their original frame of analysis.

4) Prepare projections of **reserve development** that can be monitored over the subsequent calendar periods. Deviations of actual from projected developments of counts or amounts is one of the most useful diagnostic tools in evaluating accuracy of reserve estimates.

Within this broad overall context, there are numerous specific concerns of the analyst:

1) Understanding trends and changes affecting the data base. A review of the available data before the application of the reserve methods should take place to identify any trends or abrupt changes that may be evident from the data itself. A number of possible influences could be evident:

   a) underwriting policies or procedures can change over the time frame included in a reserve review. Usually some accompanying fact situations can be documented such as changes in classes written, geographic areas, or changes in key underwriting personnel.

   b) claims adjusting changes can be the result of expansion or consolidation of offices, or changes in claims department management. Changes in claims office procedures or automated claim support and payment systems can change claim development history.

   c) accounting changes may be apparent from the data. A very common cause is a change in computerized accounting routines.

   d) the legal/social environment can change abruptly. This is especially a possibility if the data are concentrated from one state.

2) Subdivide or combine data as necessary to achieve the largest possible block of homogeneous data.

3) In a block of data it is necessary to understand the key provisions of the underlying contracts. Endorsements that may affect loss development, such as reporting endorsements allowing later reporting of claims may require a further separation of the data. The deductible and limit profiles of the business may have changed over the time span. Both can have a dramatic effect on loss development. Likewise reinsurance contracts can impact loss development, so that the reinsurance history of a

block of business needs to be documented to allow the analyst to interpret the development history.

4) Homogeneity of data is necessary in order to draw valid conclusions about the likely future loss development outcomes. While a block of data may be considered heterogeneous in terms of locations or other descriptors, we are only interested in homogeneity of behavior from the aspect of loss development.

5) Credibility of the data requires a volume of data that will allow a stable history of development patterns to be determined. The amount of data needed to give credibility to indicated results will often depend on the average and the variability of loss size.

6) It is necessary to be able to identify the expected development patterns of the business. This is useful if the data are sparse, and recourse to external development patterns is necessary. Books of business with very different development patterns should not be combined for loss reserve studies. Issues of homogeneity and credibility for loss reserving should most often be thought of in terms of their impact on loss on development patterns.

7) The existence of a block of reserves discounted for interest in a book of business adds additional complexities. The discounted case reserves should be isolated and evaluated separately. This includes discounting for mortality as well as interest rates. Hence any pension reserves, as in workers compensation, should be separately identified by data coding. The evaluation of the reserve should be made taking these discounted case reserves into consideration.

8) Groupings of data should be made of business with similar frequency and severity characteristics. Clearly, a high frequency, low severity could easily mask the development of a low frequency, high severity line. The two should be separated before the loss reserve analysis is performed.

9) There is widely different frequency of reopened claims by line of insurance. In some lines like physical damage, the potential for reopens can almost be ignored. In other cases, like workers compensation, the analyst must isolate the reopened claim data and evaluate this liability explicitly. One key issue in reopened claim liabilities is that the exposure base for reopened claims is the past inventory of all closed claims, and not the current volume of business.

10) Credibility and homogeneity of data from even the same line of business is greatly enhanced if the policy limits or layers of loss are very similar. For example, loss development data on General Liability excess reinsurance may not be very stable or useful if not grouped by underlying limits and layer widths. Similarly, history on book of basic limits auto liability business is of little value in evaluating a new book with $1 million limits. Aggregate limits of liability or even large losses that are capped at policy limits are very important facts for the loss reserve analyst to take into account in his analysis.

11) The potential for recoveries from salvage or subrogation, or even large deductibles is extremely important. Most often these recovery potentials should be estimated separately from the gross data, before recoveries. This requires appropriate data coding be set up.

12) Members of pools and associations often get results reported in bulk without appropriate loss or record dates. This data must be isolated from internal company records and a separate evaluation of loss reserve liabilities made.

13) Changes in company operations can be the source of some of most important impacts on loss development patterns. A complete history of all company actions that the loss reserve actuary feels could have had a significant impact on reserve history should be kept as part of the analysis discussion.

14) External changes in state laws or judicial precedents must be evaluated and commented on. Occasionally, a high impact change like the introduction of no-fault auto insurance clearly changes the business environment. However, even less noticeable changes, such as administrative rulings allowing cash settlements for workers compensation indemnity cases will have a significant impact on the loss reserve actuary's ultimate estimated liabilities.

Exploratory Data Analysis

Before the actuary begins his attempts to project immature loss data to ultimate loss estimates, it is important to review the data. The objective of this review is to understand the data in terms of

1) rate of development,
2) smoothness of development,
3) presence of large losses,
4) volume of data.

Review of the data will allow the analyst to form conclusions about:

1) appropriate projection methodologies,
2) anomalies in the data,
3) appropriate questions to ask management concerning issues that manifest themselves in the data, that will further the analyst's understanding of the book of business that generated the data.

Some of the more common data displays that should be reviewed by the actuary follow.

Cumulative Incurred Losses: An incurred loss triangle contains the history of combined paid losses and case reserves. The example below is an "accident year triangle", a history of losses incurred organized with losses from the same year of loss in the same column. A review of the incurred loss triangle points to a fluctuating level of losses since 1982. Note that the dip in losses reported on the 1985 accident year as of 12 months did not result in less loss reported through 48 months of development. This should alert the analyst to search for possible processing slowdowns at year end 1985, or major fluctuations in case reserve adequacy. In light of this, the analyst must consider how to interpret the low level of 1988 accident year incurred losses. Clearly, some measure of exposure is called for—whether earned exposures, earned premiums, or even policies in force. This will help determine whether a level of ultimate incurred losses proportional to the low reported 1988 incurred is reasonable. The situation with loss processing as well as case reserve adequacy needs to be probed in order to decide on the proper 1988 accident year reserve.

	Accident Years						
Developed Months	**1982**	**1983**	**1984**	**1985**	**1986**	**1987**	**1988**
12	$58,641	$63,732	$51,779	$40,143	$55,665	$43,401	$28,800
24	74,804	79,512	68,175	67,978	80,296	57,547	
36	77,323	83,680	69,802	75,144	87,961		
48	77,890	85,366	69,694	77,947			
60	80,728	88,152	70,041				
72	82,280	87,413					
84	82,372						

Cumulative Paid Losses: A paid loss triangle contains the history of paid losses. Small variations in paid loss as of 12 months can be seen to be indicative of very large differences in ultimate accident year losses. The low reported incurred on 1985 accident year is also paralleled by a lower paid loss amount on the 1985 accident year. The 20% drop from 1984 to 1985 incurred losses seen above produces only a 5% drop in paid claims from 1984 to 1985 accident years, as of the initial reporting. The large 1988 drop in payment indicates a much more severe change in claims environment than the 1985 drop of 5%. The analyst would look for evidence of lower 1988 exposure levels to explain the reported losses.

Developed Months	Accident Years 1982	1983	1984	1985	1986	1987	1988
12	$22,603	$22,054	$20,166	$19,297	$20,555	$17,001	$11,346
24	40,064	43,970	39,147	37,355	42,898	33,568	
36	54,301	58,737	51,319	50,391	62,832		
48	64,114	71,841	60,417	62,347			
60	71,257	78,076	66,402				
72	75,950	81,287					
84	78,224						

Incremental Incurred Losses: This triangle shows the incremental incurred losses in each successive 12 month period. It is useful for the analyst to gauge the reasonability of yearly aggregate loss accumulations on an accident year. Note the "speedup" of incurred losses in 12 to 24 months aging of the 1985 accident year (calendar year 1986), when incurred losses increased $27,835,000. It appears that the second annual development on the 1986 accident year of $24,632,000 is also unusually large when compared to accident years 1984 and prior. Thus, the analyst must suspect that processing problems were also apparent in the organization at year end 1986. Questions to key managers in Claims and Underwriting should help the analyst gather information to confirm this suspicion. This triangle also shows directly the amount of development on the oldest development periods.

Developed Months	Accident Years 1982	1983	1984	1985	1986	1987	1988
12	$58,641	$63,732	$51,779	$40,143	$55,665	$43,401	$28,800
24	16,163	5,779	16,396	27,835	24,632	14,147	
36	2,519	4,168	1,627	7,166	7,665		
48	567	1,686	(107)	2,803			
60	2,838	2,786	347				
72	1,552	(739)					
84	92						

Incremental Paid Losses: This triangle shows the incremental paid losses in each successive 12 month period. We see immediately that payments during the second annual development period on an accident year are roughly equal to the amount paid in the first annual development period. Thus, we form an expectation that any reasonable projected development to ultimate must yield at least $10-12 million projected paid losses during the 12 to 24 month development on 1988 accident year.

	Accident Years						
Developed Months	**1982**	**1983**	**1984**	**1985**	**1986**	**1987**	**1988**
12	$22,603	$22,054	$20,166	$19,297	$20,555	$17,001	$11,346
24	17,461	21,916	18,981	18,058	22,343	16,567	
36	14,237	14,767	12,172	13,036	19,935		
48	9,813	13,104	9,098	11,956			
60	7,143	6,235	5,985				
72	4,693	3,211					
84	2,274						

Paid Claims as a Percent of Incurred Claims: This triangle divides paid losses at each development by reported losses as at the same development age. This statistic tests the consistency of development of paid and reported losses. It also may give warning of case reserve inadequacies. This statistic clearly flags the 1985 accident year as being inconsistent with history. The high ratio indicates that the case reserve portion of the 1985 accident year incurred losses as of year end 1985 was much weaker than historically. One benefit of this statistic is that it appears concurrent with the analysis, and does not rely on hindsight. The crucial 1988 year looks normal with regard to case reserves.

	Accident Years						
Developed Months	**1982**	**1983**	**1984**	**1985**	**1986**	**1987**	**1988**
12	38.5%	34.6%	38.9%	48.1%	36.9%	39.2%	39.4%
24	53.6	55.3	57.4	55.0	53.4	58.3	
36	70.2	70.2	73.5	67.1	71.4		
48	82.3	84.2	86.7	80.0			
60	88.3	88.6	94.8				
72	92.3	93.0					
84	95.0						

Reported Claim Counts: Claim count history is extremely important in any loss reserve analysis. This triangle simply displays all reported claims by annual development period. We can conclude that essentially all claims are reported within 24 months on this line. The 1988 accident year does have a much lower level of reported claims than prior accident years. A radical change in volume such as 1988 accident year displays should alert us to consider the "Simon Effect" on our loss development patterns (see Simon 1970).

	Accident Years						
Developed Months	**1982**	**1983**	**1984**	**1985**	**1986**	**1987**	**1988**
12	32,751	33,736	27,067	24,928	25,229	17,632	15,609
24	41,201	39,528	32,740	29,796	31,930	21,801	
36	41,618	39,926	33,084	30,074	32,281		
48	41,755	40,044	33,183	30,169			
60	41,773	40,072	33,209				
72	41,774	40,072					
84	41,774						

Closed Paid Claim Counts: The cumulative claims closed with payment are displayed. Note that this is not all closed claims. See claims closed with no payment below. The processing problem at the end of 1985 and 1986 again appears in this statistic, which suggests the need to understand possible changes in company operations that occurred during 1985-1986. The closing counts for 1987 and 1988 support the hypothesis of reduced exposures.

	Accident Years						
Developed Months	**1982**	**1983**	**1984**	**1985**	**1986**	**1987**	**1988**
12	23,355	22,662	18,951	16,631	17,381	12,666	10,592
24	31,940	30,294	25,197	22,894	24,581	16,669	
36	33,288	31,588	26,214	23,806	25,765		
48	33,860	32,129	26,582	24,229			
60	34,091	32,323	26,777				
72	34,247	32,433					
84	34,294						

No-claim Counts: Claims may also be closed without any payment. The claims closed with no payment could easily account for over half or more of all claims reported for some lines such as such as medical malpractice. This display does not show any unusual patterns.

	Accident Years						
Developed Months	**1982**	**1983**	**1984**	**1985**	**1986**	**1987**	**1988**
12	2,646	3,142	2,752	2,343	2,238	1,749	1,246
24	6,285	6,529	5,366	4,744	4,666	3,458	
36	6,935	7,053	5,840	5,132	5,375		
48	7,240	7,308	6,050	5,400			
60	7,353	7,411	6,185				
72	7,393	7,465					
84	7,412						

Closed as Percent of Reported Claim Counts: Total closed claims can be related to claims reported. This is a monitor on closing activities. We can see a very steady performance of this ratio as of 12 and 24 months of development for accident years 1982 to 1987. Note the slightly lower closing ratio on the 1988 accident year. This should be explored with the claims department. On a property line this could be the result of a catastrophe in December, but in a liability line it indicates potential processing problems.

	Accident Years						
Developed Months	**1982**	**1983**	**1984**	**1985**	**1986**	**1987**	**1988**
12	79.4%	76.5%	80.2%	76.1%	77.8%	81.8%	75.8%
24	92.8	93.2	93.4	92.8	91.6	92.3	
36	96.6	96.8	96.9	96.2	96.5		
48	98.4	98.5	98.3	98.2			
60	99.2	99.2	99.3				
72	99.7	99.6					
84	99.8						

Open Claim Counts: This triangle displays open claims, i.e. claims reported less all claims closed. Note that there were almost 2,000 fewer claims reported on the 1988 accident year than on the 1987 accident in the initial 12 months of reporting. However, at the end of 1988, there are almost 500 more claims open on the 1988 accident year than the 3,217 claims open on the 1987 accident year at the end of 1987. This could be the result of some very significant changes in the organization.

	Accident Years						
Developed Months	**1982**	**1983**	**1984**	**1985**	**1986**	**1987**	**1988**
12	6,750	7,932	5,364	5,954	5,610	3,217	3,771
24	2,976	2,705	2,177	2,158	2,683	1,674	
36	1,395	1,285	1,030	1,136	1,141		
48	655	607	551	540			
60	329	338	247				
72	134	174					
84	68						

Average Open Claim Amount: This triangle tracks the average amount reserved on open claims. Note the 1988 average open case reserve has dropped from the prior year's level. This should be investigated with the claim department. Combined with the greater number of 1988 open reserves, a processing problem should be suspected. Note that the 1985 accident year showed a similar drop in its open reserve account.

	Accident Years						
Developed Months	**1982**	**1983**	**1984**	**1985**	**1986**	**1987**	**1988**
12	$ 5,339	$ 5,254	$ 5,894	$ 3,501	$ 6,258	$ 8,206	$4,629
24	11,671	13,137	13,334	14,190	13,941	14,324	
36	16,499	19,405	17,939	21,798	22,026		
48	21,029	22,285	16,832	28,896			
60	28,782	29,820	14,722				
72	47,240	35,209					
84	60,722						

Increase in Average Open Claim: This triangle charts the annual increase in average open reserve between accident periods as of each development age. This is useful for determining if case reserves are keeping up with reasonable inflationary increases. The 1985-86 increases at 12 months of development average out to a 6.1% annual increase during the two years. Since the first column has no logical entry it can be used to report the multi-year average growth in case reserve.

		Accident Years					
Developed Months	Average	1983	1984	1985	1986	1987	1988
12	97.6%	98.4%	112.2%	59.4%	178.7%	131.1%	56.4%
24	104.2	112.6	101.5	106.4	98.2	102.7	
36	107.5	117.6	92.4	121.5	101.0		
48	111.2	106.0	75.5	171.7			
60	71.5	103.6	49.4				
72	74.5	74.5					

Average Closed Claim: This triangle shows paid losses divided by closed with payment counts. Note that these average are very regular with no reversals across accident years, until 1988 as of 12 months.

		Accident Years					
Developed Months	1982	1983	1984	1985	1986	1987	1988
12	$ 968	$ 973	$1,064	$1,160	$1,183	$1,342	$1,071
24	1,254	1,451	1,554	1,632	1,745	2,014	
36	1,631	1,859	1,958	2,117	2,439		
48	1,894	2,236	2,273	2,573			
60	2,090	2,415	2,480				
72	2,218	2,506					
84	2,281						

Increase in Average Closed Claim: This triangle shows the annual increase in average paid claim amount between accident years as of identical development periods. The first column is also used to display the multi-year average increase in closed claim values. It is useful to compare the annual increases in open case reserves to these increases in closed claim amounts. This allows the actuary to evaluate if the claim department reserves are keeping pace with inflationary increases in settlements. The analyst might suspect that a serious backlog in paid claims for the 1988 accident years.

		Accident Years					
Developed Months	**Average**	**1983**	**1984**	**1985**	**1986**	**1987**	**1988**
12	101.7%	100.6%	109.3%	109.0%	101.9%	113.5%	79.8%
24	109.9	115.7	107.0	105.0	107.0	115.4	
36	110.6	114.0	105.3	108.1	115.2		
48	110.8	118.1	101.6	113.2			
60	108.9	115.6	102.7				
72	113.0	113.0					

Closed Claims as a Percent of Open Claims: The rate of claim closure is one of the most important indicators of the condition of the claim department. This statistic shows some deterioration in claims performance in calendar year 1987. Only 78% of the 1986 inventory and 60% of the 1985 inventory was closed during the 1987 calendar year. Some level of recovery is evident during calendar year 1988 on the 1986 and 1985 inventories. However, the analyst might surmise that the closing activity on the 1987 inventory may have slipped in order to allow the catch up activity on the older inventories. These indications of processing problems should be probed with questions for claims management.

			Accident Years			
Developed Months	**1982**	**1983**	**1984**	**1985**	**1986**	**1987**
24	80.4%	80.3%	80.3%	80.1%	78.2%	77.3%
36	67.1	67.2	68.5	60.2	70.6	
48	62.8	61.9	56.1	60.8		
60	52.5	48.9	59.9			
72	59.6	48.5				
84	49.3					

Loss Reserve Estimation Methodologies

Aggregate versus Structural Reserving Methodologies

While there are many methods for the projection of reserves to ultimate values, these methods fall into two very simple groups; aggregate methods and structural methods.

An aggregate reserve method is one which simply projects the growth behavior of a reserve inventory, without taking advantage of any particular knowledge of the structure of the processes within the inventory. Most simple and frequently used reserve methods fall in this category. An aggregate reserve method takes little advantage of the fact that we are estimating loss reserve requirements. The methods can be equally well used to project ultimate values of any growth process. Some examples might be the ultimate response rate to a direct mail campaign, or the loan defaults in a loan portfolio.

A structural reserve method is one which uses some particular aspect of the dynamics of the insurance or loss reserving process to obtain ultimate incurred loss estimates. These methods model some aspect of the loss reserve process, and generally are more complex than aggregate methods. One example is the reserve method due to Fisher and Lange that estimates claim counts and closure patterns and values of a reserve inventory (Fisher and Lange (1973)). Other examples of structural methods are given in Finger (1976), McClenahan (1975), and Taylor (1977). Each structural method seems to model only part of the reserve process. No universal model has emerged.

In actuarial practice, detailed models of loss reserve development are seldom used to actually establish reserves. Most reserve estimation work is done using aggregate reserve methods supplemented with the experience of the reserve analyst.

Aggregate Reserving Methodologies

Triangular Methods

One of the most common methods used to estimate ultimate loss levels consists of tracking the history of a group of claims with similar definitional groupings. The data for this purpose are arranged in a triangular loss format as discussed above. An undeveloped loss year is "completed" to its expected ultimate payout, based on the assumption that each loss year will be completed in some fashion "analogous" to prior years. The assumptions the actuary makes about the relationship of past patterns on future ones defines the nature of this "analogy". For instance, suppose we have a triangular display of cumulative paid losses as described above.

Developed Months	Accident Years 1982	1983	1984	1985	1986	1987	1988
12	$22,603	$22,054	$20,166	$19,297	$20,555	$17,001	$11,346
24	40,064	43,970	39,147	37,355	42,898	33,568	
36	54,301	58,737	51,319	50,391	62,832		
48	64,114	71,841	60,417	62,347			
60	71,257	78,076	66,402				
72	75,950	81,287					
84	78,224						

A review of the data in the first row "as of 12 months" indicates that some rather extreme fluctuations in loss volumes seem to have taken place over the last seven years. This should be checked out by a review of the historical claim count triangles, and also earned exposure history, or earned premiums at a uniform exposure level as a proxy. These concerns are discussed above under the data exploration topics.

Our concern is that these shifts in volume of losses make it difficult to reach any conclusion about this development. Thus we would like to "normalize" the development history by removing this volume effect. This is accomplished by studying the aging effect within each accident year as follows.

Developed Months	Accident Years 1982	1983	1984	1985	1986	1987
12-24	1.773	1.994	1.941	1.936	2.087	1.974
24-36	1.355	1.336	1.311	1.349	1.465	
36-48	1.181	1.223	1.177	1.237		
48-60	1.111	1.087	1.099			
60-72	1.066	1.041				
72-84	1.030					

This triangular display represents the historical development of each accident year. For instance, the development from 12 to 24 months on accident year 1984 is an increase in paid losses of 97.4% ($33,568 / $17,001). Now the range of variation is considerably reduced. One can see that 12-24 month development seems to vary from a low of 1.773 to 2.087. The high 1986 development of 2.087 seems to be outside a reasonable range of development factors observed in recent time periods. If we can predict the next 12-24 month development that we expect to see take place during 1987, we would be able to forecast the 1988 accident year paid losses at 24 months of development.

Thus our next task should consist of predicting the 1988 accident year 12-24 month paid loss development factor. One common technique is to inspect several averages of the age-to-age factors. The averages should provide a guide in selecting the next calendar period's development on that accident year.

Paid Loss Development Factors

	Developed Months					
Accident Year	12–24	24–36	36–48	48–60	60–72	72–84
1982	1.773	1.355	1.181	1.111	1.066	1.030
1983	1.994	1.336	1.223	1.087	1.041	
1984	1.941	1.311	1.177	1.099		
1985	1.936	1.349	1.237			
1986	2.087	1.465				
1987	1.974					
Average	1.951	1.363	1.205	1.099	1.053	1.03
Avg Last 3	1.999	1.375	1.213	1.099	1.053	1.03
Avg Last 4	1.985	1.365	1.213	1.099	1.053	1.03
Avg Exc Hi & Lo	1.961	1.347	1.202	1.087	1.053	1.03
Weighted Average	1.948	1.364	1.205	1.099	1.053	1.03
Harmonic Mean	1.948	1.362	1.204	1.099	1.053	1.03

There is a practically unlimited number of ways to average the historical development factors. The key point to remember is that these averages are only guides to selection of the next reasonable development, based on all information the loss reserve actuary has developed from his reviews with management as well as the historical loss development.

Let's review the averages displayed above. The "average" line is simply the arithmetic average of all historical loss development factors at that stage of development. Similarly, the "Avg Last 3" and "Avg Last 4" are simple arithmetic averages of the latest 3 and latest 4 development factors at a given point of development. The "Avg Excluding Hi & Lo" are the arithmetic average of the developments other than the highest and lowest. The "Weighted Average" is weighted by amount of incurred loss. The harmonic mean is the n'th root of the n historical development factors.

Notice that we are generally interested in examining the averages of the latest few development periods. Hence we calculate averages of the latest three or four factors. An alternative display of averages that allow us to inspect the behavior of the averages as more historical points are added is often useful. Like many actuarial procedures, the analyst is asked to make a judgement of the most appropriate trade-off between stability (i.e., more development periods in the average computation) and responsiveness (i.e., only include the latest few development periods in the average).

The familiar triangular format also becomes a convenient way to inspect the addition of more development points in the averages.

Arithmetic Average of. . .

Developed Months	Latest	Last 2	Last 3	Last 4	Last 5	Last 6
12-24	1.974	2.031	1.999	1.985	1.986	1.951
24-36	1.465	1.407	1.375	1.365	1.363	
36-48	1.237	1.207	1.213	1.205		
48-60	1.099	1.093	1.099			
60-72	1.041	1.053				
72-84	1.030					

Inspection of such past historical trends allows the analyst to complete the lower triangle by filling it in with his projections of future development factors. For instance, let's assume the analyst chose the following development patterns along the right diagonal as the most likely over the next 12 months.

Developed Months	Accident Years 1982	1983	1984	1985	1986	1987	1988
12-24	1.773	1.994	1.941	1.936	2.087	1.974	2.000
24-36	1.355	1.336	1.311	1.349	1.465	1.350	
36-48	1.181	1.223	1.177	1.237	1.270		
48-60	1.111	1.087	1.099	1.085			
60-72	1.066	1.041	1.060				
72-84	1.030	1.018					
84-Ult	1.010						

The selected expected developments for the 1989 calendar period are shown below the actual historical developments for each accident year. Note that often the selected developments are not identical to any of the selected averages. For instance the 12 to 24 month expected development is 2.000. Notice that the historical 12 to 24 month developments have been trending upwards since 1982 with exception of the 1986 year. Review of this history with claims and systems manager indicates that a new claim processing system was installed in 1986 that necessitated a longer installation period than anticipated. Thus the analyst views the 1986 development as an anomaly. This is supported by the recovery of the 1987 development to a value that seems to fit in with the trend of increasing developments. It is extremely important to realize that once the suspected anomalous development pattern on 1986 accident year has been identified, further information must be sought about company operations that may have caused this anomaly. This information can in most cases not be acquired through further study of the numbers, but requires the actuary to gather additional information, often of a qualitative nature.

The search for an explanation of recent unusual historical developments is critical to the reserve estimate, because the analyst must decide whether the situation causing the abnormal loss development is still a factor that can affect future developments. In this case the new claim processing system has been in place since the end of 1986, and the 1987 year was closed with a return to more normal paid loss development patterns in the 1988 calendar year. This leads the analyst to discount the 1986 development from 12 to 24 months as a nonrecurring situation. In turn the analyst does not wish to use the averages for two reasons:

1. the data show a clear trend, making averaging inappropriate;
2. the unusual 1986 development should not be included in any average.

Contrast this situation to the following. Suppose the analyst had determined that the unusual development was due to several large losses that required large payments in 1987. This is clearly a situation that could happen again in any particular year, absent any changes in policy limit profiles or reinsurance retentions, and should receive some weight in future scenarios. In this situation, the averages with the 1986 accident year development from 12 to 24 months should be used as a guide to the 1989 calendar year paid development on the 1988 accident year.

The choice of the next projected development of 24 to 36 months is difficult because of the unusually high development of 146% on the 1986 reported paid losses from 24 to 36 months. At this point the analyst must regard the 1986 accident year as very unusual. A note should be made to inspect the projected ultimate on this accident year very carefully once development factors have been selected.

Investigation of events in 1988 indicates that several large case payments were evident on 1986 accident year cases, but this was on classes of business no longer written by the company. Accordingly the 1986 development cannot be used again in the choice of the next calendar year's development on the 1987 accident year.

Developed Months	Accident Years 1982	1983	1984	1985	1986	1987	1988
12-24	1.773	1.994	1.941	1.936	2.087	1.974	2.000
24-36	1.355	1.336	1.311	1.349	1.465	1.350	1.350
36-48	1.181	1.223	1.177	1.237	1.270	1.290	
48-60	1.111	1.087	1.099	1.085	1.100		
60-72	1.066	1.041	1.060	1.060			
72-84	1.030	1.018	1.018				
84-Ult	1.053						

Once the development factors for calendar year 1989 have been chosen, for accident years 1983 through 1988, the analyst must forecast development for the 1990 calendar year. The 1990 calendar year developments are not necessarily the same as the 1989 calendar year forecast development factors. For instance, the developments from 36 to 48 months have shown a distinct trend upward in our history. The analyst chooses to believe that this trend will continue in the development observed in 1989 and 1990 calendar years. This is a critical assumption that will add a significant amount to the estimated loss reserve liabilities of the insurer. This assumption needs to be highlighted in a report on the reserve analysis. The situation causing the trending developments should be discussed with the claims department and an understanding of claim settlement practices that may be causing this trended development sought. Subsequent reserve analyses should retest this trended development assumption. The analyst should monitor whether actual 1987 and 1988 calendar year developments prove to follow the assumed pattern.

Note the projected 1990 calendar year development on the 1986 accident year is higher than the similar 48 to 60 month development selected for the 1985 accident year. This selection reflects the analyst's finding that the 1986 accident year contained more hazardous classes than the preceding years. These classes were assumed to account for the higher development on the 1986 accident year from 24 to 36 months. While the selected factor of 1.100 is only slightly higher than the "normal" selected development of 1.085 at this age, the analyst feels some recognition must be given to the past behavior of this more hazardous business mix. Since there are no data older than 1986 in this business, the higher selected factor on 1986 is an example of a judgement based on the analyst's experience.

In a report on the loss reserve analysis, the analyst should disclose his assumptions that the 1986 year will reflect a more severe development pattern due to information he has learned about its more severe business mix.

In reviewing the assumptions, the analyst now desires a more consistent opinion on the 1986 accident year. That is, although the development of 1.270 from 36 to 48 months is trended, it should probably be even higher to reflect the business mix of the 1986 accident year. The amount of the adjustment is in question. The analyst finds that the 24 to 36 month development on 1986 at 1.465 is higher than the selected average development based on the observed developments of 1982–85 of 1.350. It is also assumed that this differential of 1.0852 (the relativity of the observed 1.465 to the "projected" 1.350) should dampen back to unity with the passage of time. The analyst decides to reflect this dampening effect by taking the square root of the differential with the passage of each year. Thus, the differential for the 36 to 48 month development should be the square root of 1.0852 or 1.042. This results in a development from 36 to 48 months of 1.323, given by 1.27 multiplied by 1.042. Again, this method of dampening the observed differential in 1986 accident year development is driven more by the analyst's experience than a set mathematical formula.

	Accident Years						
Developed Months	**1982**	**1983**	**1984**	**1985**	**1986**	**1987**	**1988**
12-24	1.773	1.994	1.941	1.936	2.087	1.974	2.000
24-36	1.355	1.336	1.311	1.349	1.465	1.350	1.350
36-48	1.181	1.223	1.177	1.237	1.320	1.290	1.310
48-60	1.111	1.087	1.099	1.095	1.100	1.085	1.085
60-72	1.066	1.041	1.060	1.060	1.060	1.060	1.060
72-84	1.030	1.030	1.018	1.018	1.018	1.018	1.018
84-Ult	1.053	1.053	1.053	1.053	1.053	1.053	1.053
Dev to Ult	1.053	1.085	1.136	1.244	1.650	2.147	4.361

In the above triangle all development factors have been chosen for future periods. This is a forecast of the paid loss development to be expected on these accident years in calendar years 1989 and forward. As can be seen from the process of selection of development factors the analyst should:

1. be able to recognize normal levels of random fluctuation in developments,

2. recognize aberrations in development patterns and be able to isolate their causes, and determine if they are ongoing or one time changes in development,

3. recognize trends in loss development patterns.

The analyst was also required to make a projection of paid loss from 84 months of age to ultimate settlement. Generally, the historical data should extend back a enough to make the projected development to ultimate, or tail factor as it is often called, very small. The selection of a tail factor is made difficult by two factors:

1. there is generally little relevant data available,

2. the tail factor affects all accident years reserve needs, thus has a disproportionate leverage on the total reserve need.

In this case, the analyst selects a tail factor of 5.3% additional development after 84 months of age, based on a subjective judgement and a review of cases over seven year old that were settled in the last calendar year.

This triangle can be then transformed into its dollar equivalents, by successively multiplying the selected development factors by the last actual report of incurred losses.

Developed Months	Accident Years 1982	1983	1984	1985	1986	1987	1988
12	$22,603	$22,054	$20,166	$19,297	$ 20,555	$17,001	$11,346
24	40,064	43,970	39,147	37,355	42,898	33,568	**22,692**
36	54,301	58,737	51,319	50,391	62,832	**45,317**	**30,634**
48	64,114	71,841	60,417	62,347	**82,938**	**58,458**	**40,131**
60	71,257	78,076	66,402	**68,270**	**91,232**	**63,427**	**43,542**
72	75,950	81,287	**70,386**	**72,366**	**96,706**	**67,233**	**46,154**
84	78,224	**83,726**	**71,653**	**73,669**	**98,447**	**68,443**	**46,985**
Ultimate	**$82,372**	**$88,163**	**$75,451**	**$77,573**	**$103,664**	**$72,070**	**$49,475**
Pd to Date	$78,224	$81,287	$66,402	$62,347	$ 62,832	$33,568	$11,346
Reserve	$ 4,148	$ 6,876	$ 9,049	$15,226	$ 40,832	$38,502	$38,129
						Total Reserve	$152,762

This particular analysis of the paid loss data indicates that a reserve of about $153 million is necessary to provide for unpaid loss reserve liabilities from accident years 1982 through 1988.

While an estimate is available for a reserve need for this book of business, we can note at least two deficiencies in our knowledge at this point. First, we have not made any use of other available information, such as claim counts or case reserve values. Second, we have no means of evaluating prospectively the confidence we should have in this single forecast of the future. Both of these concerns can be addressed by alternative forecasts of ultimate loss reserve need using other information available to us.

A triangular development analysis can also be developed using paid losses plus case reserves. Case reserves could be either adjuster determined or set by use of average values. Assume incurred losses as presented below.

Developed Months	Accident Years 1982	1983	1984	1985	1986	1987	1988
12	$58,641	$63,732	$51,779	$40,143	$55,665	$43,401	$28,800
24	74,804	79,512	68,175	67,978	80,296	57,547	
36	77,323	83,680	69,802	75,144	87,961		
48	77,890	85,366	69,694	77,947			
60	80,728	88,152	70,041				
72	82,280	87,413					
84	82,372						

Age to age development factors may be calculated for this data.

Developed Months	Accident Years 1982	1983	1984	1985	1986	1987
12-24	1.276	1.248	1.317	1.693	1.443	1.326
24-36	1.034	1.052	1.024	1.105	1.095	
36-48	1.007	1.020	0.998	1.037		
48-60	1.036	1.033	1.005			
60-72	1.019	0.992				
72-84	1.001					

Use the triangular format to inspect the addition of more development points in the averages.

Developed Months	Arithmetic Average of... Latest	Last 2	Last 3	Last 4	Last 5	Last 6
12-24	1.326	1.384	1.487	1.445	1.405	1.384
24-36	1.095	1.100	1.075	1.069	1.062	
36-48	1.037	1.018	1.019	1.016		
48-60	1.005	1.019	1.025			
60-72	0.992	1.005				
72-84	1.001					

Assume the analyst chose the following development patterns along the right diagonal as the most likely over the next 12 months.

Developed Months	Accident Years 1982	1983	1984	1985	1986	1987	1988
12-24	1.276	1.248	1.317	1.693	1.443	1.326	1.350
24-36	1.034	1.052	1.024	1.105	1.095	1.095	
36-48	1.007	1.020	0.998	1.037	1.020		
48-60	1.036	1.033	1.005	1.020			
60-72	1.019	0.992	1.000				
72-84	1.001	1.000					
84-Ult	1.001						

Now complete the selections of all other development factors as below.

Developed Months	Accident Years 1982	1983	1984	1985	1986	1987	1988
12-24	1.276	1.248	1.317	1.693	1.443	1.326	1.350
24-36	1.034	1.052	1.024	1.105	1.095	1.095	1.095
36-48	1.007	1.020	0.998	1.037	1.020	1.020	1.020
48-60	1.036	1.033	1.005	1.020	1.020	1.020	1.020
60-72	1.019	0.992	1.000	1.000	1.000	1.000	1.000
72-84	1.001	1.000	1.000	1.000	1.000	1.000	1.000
84-Ult	1.010	1.010	1.010	1.010	1.010	1.010	1.010
Dev to Ult	1.001	1.010	1.010	1.030	1.051	1.151	1.553

Based on factors chosen above the complete projection of incurred losses by accident year may be completed.

Developed Months	Accident Years 1982	1983	1984	1985	1986	1987	1988
12	$58,641	$63,732	$51,799	$40,143	$55,665	$43,401	$28,800
24	74,804	79,512	68,175	67,978	80,296	57,547	**38,880**
36	77,323	83,680	69,802	75,144	87,961	**63,014**	**42,574**
48	77,890	85,366	69,694	77,947	**89,720**	**64,275**	**43,426**
60	80,278	88,152	70,041	**79,506**	**91,515**	**65,560**	**44,294**
72	82,280	87,413	**70,041**	**79,509**	**91,515**	**65,560**	**44,294**
84	82,372	**87,413**	**70,041**	**79,509**	**91,515**	**65,560**	**44,294**
Ultimate	**$83,196**	**$87,413**	**$70,741**	**$80,301**	**$92,430**	**$66,216**	**$44,737**
Pd to Date	$78,224	$81,287	$66,402	$62,347	$62,832	$33,568	$11,346
Reserve	$ 4,972	$ 7,000	$ 4,339	$17,954	$29,598	$32,648	$33,391
							Total Reserve $129,902

This particular analysis of the incurred loss data indicates that a reserve of about $130 million is necessary to provide for unpaid loss and loss adjustment expenses from accident years 1982 through 1988. This is substantially different from the $153 million reserve estimate obtained through a paid loss projection. Any difference in estimates clearly raises questions that need to be investigated by the analyst in an attempt to reconcile the reserve estimate using two sets of loss data.

The pattern of claim reporting should be reviewed in the same fashion. Reported claims are shown below.

Developed Months	Accident Years 1982	1983	1984	1985	1986	1987	1988
12	32,751	33,736	27,067	24,928	25,229	17,632	15,609
24	41,201	39,528	32,740	29,796	31,930	21,801	
36	41,618	39,926	33,084	30,074	32,281		
48	41,755	40,044	33,183	30,169			
60	41,773	40,072	33,209				
72	41,774	40,072					
84	41,774						

Age to age development factors may be calculated for this data.

Developed Months	Accident Years 1982	1983	1984	1985	1986	1987
12-24	1.258	1.172	1.210	1.195	1.266	1.236
24-36	1.010	1.010	1.011	1.009	1.011	
36-48	1.003	1.003	1.003	1.003		
48-60	1.000	1.001	1.001			
60-72	1.000	1.000				
72-84	1.000					

Use the triangular format as a convenient way to inspect the addition of more development points in the averages.

Developed Months	Arithmetic Average of... Latest	Last 2	Last 3	Last 4	Last 5	Last 6
12-24	1.236	1.251	1.232	1.227	1.216	1.223
24-36	1.011	1.010	1.010	1.010	1.010	
36-48	1.003	1.003	1.003	1.003		
48-60	1.001	1.001	1.001			
60-72	1.000	1.000				
72-84	1.000					

Assume the analyst chose the following development patterns as the most likely characterizations of development of total claims on those accident years to their ultimate reported level.

Developed Months	Accident Years 1982	1983	1984	1985	1986	1987	1988
12-24	1.258	1.172	1.210	1.195	1.266	1.236	1.200
24-36	1.010	1.010	1.011	1.009	1.011	1.012	1.012
36-48	1.003	1.003	1.003	1.003	1.003	1.003	1.003
48-60	1.000	1.001	1.001	1.001	1.001	1.001	1.001
60-72	1.000	1.000	1.000	1.000	1.000	1.000	1.000
72-84	1.000	1.000	1.000	1.000	1.000	1.000	1.000
84-Ult	1.000	1.000	1.000	1.000	1.000	1.000	1.000
Dev to Ult	1.000	1.000	1.000	1.001	1.004	1.016	1.219

Based on factors chosen above, the complete projection of incurred loss counts by accident year may be completed.

Developed Months	Accident Years 1982	1983	1984	1985	1986	1987	1988
12	32,751	33,736	27,067	24,928	25,229	17,632	15,609
24	41,201	39,528	32,740	29,796	31,930	21,801	**18,731**
36	41,618	39,926	33,084	30,074	32,281	**22,063**	**18,956**
48	41,755	40,044	33,183	30,169	**32,378**	**22,129**	**19,012**
60	41,773	40,072	33,209	**30,199**	**32,410**	**22,151**	**19,031**
72	41,774	40,072	**33,209**	**30,199**	**32,410**	**22,151**	**19,031**
84	41,774	**40,072**	**33,209**	**30,199**	**32,410**	**22,151**	**19,031**
Ultimate	**41,774**	**40,072**	**33,209**	**30,199**	**32,410**	**22,151**	**19,031**
Reported	41,774	40,072	33,209	30,169	32,281	21,801	15,609
Unreported	0	0	0	30	129	350	3,422

Total Unreported 3,932

This analysis implies about 3,900 claims remain to be reported. By itself, this analysis is useful as an indicator of true IBNR reporting. However the projected ultimate claims may also be used to reduce the paid and incurred triangles to an average basis. Note that these incurred counts include those claims closed without loss payment.

It is possible to project the net claim count after claims closed without payment are excluded. Let the following triangle represent the history of claims reported that are closed with no loss payment.

Developed Months	Accident Years 1982	1983	1984	1985	1986	1987	1988
12	2,646	3,142	2,752	2,343	2,238	1,749	1,246
24	6,285	6,529	5,366	4,744	4,666	3,458	
36	6,935	7,053	5,840	5,132	5,375		
48	7,240	7,308	6,050	5,400			
60	7,353	7,411	6,185				
72	7,393	7,465					
84	7,412						

As a percent of total reported claims, these no-claims show the following relationships. Note that for this line, it appears about 18% of the claims reported will be closed with no indemnity payment.

Developed Months	Accident Years 1982	1983	1984	1985	1986	1987	1988
12	8.1%	9.3%	10.2%	9.4%	8.9%	9.9%	8.0%
24	15.3	16.5	16.4	15.9	14.6	15.9	
36	16.7	17.7	17.7	17.1	16.7		
48	17.3	18.2	18.2	17.9			
60	17.6	18.5	18.6				
72	17.7	18.6					
84	17.7						

This triangular display may be completed to obtain an ultimate estimate of the percent of reported claims closed with no indemnity payment, or alternatively, the reported claims could be reduced for the claims closed with no indemnity.

Developed Months	Accident Years 1982	1983	1984	1985	1986	1987	1988
12	30,105	30,594	24,315	22,585	22,991	15,883	14,363
24	34,916	32,999	27,374	25,052	27,264	18,343	
36	34,683	32,873	27,244	24,942	26,906		
48	34,515	32,736	27,133	24,769			
60	34,420	32,661	27,024				
72	34,381	32,607					
84	34,362						

Age to age development factors may be calculated for these data representing claims reported net of claims closed without payment.

Developed Months	Accident Years 1982	1983	1984	1985	1986	1987
12-24	1.160	1.079	1.126	1.109	1.186	1.155
24-36	0.993	0.996	0.995	0.996	0.987	
36-48	0.995	0.996	0.996	0.993		
48-60	0.997	0.998	0.996			
60-72	0.999	0.998				
72-84	0.999					

Use the triangular format as a convenient way to inspect the addition of more development points in the averages.

Developed Months	Arithmetic Average of... Latest	Last 2	Last 3	Last 4	Last 5	Last 6
12-24	1.155	1.170	1.150	1.144	1.131	1.136
24-36	0.987	0.991	0.993	0.993	0.993	
36-48	0.993	0.994	0.995	0.995		
48-60	0.996	0.997	0.997			
60-72	0.998	0.999				
72-84	0.999					

Assume the analyst chose the following development patterns as the most likely to ultimate settlement.

Developed Months	Accident Years 1982	1983	1984	1985	1986	1987	1988
12-24	1.160	1.079	1.126	1.109	1.186	1.155	1.120
24-36	0.993	0.996	0.995	0.996	0.987	0.996	0.996
36-48	0.995	0.996	0.996	0.993	0.994	0.994	0.994
48-60	0.997	0.998	0.996	0.996	0.996	0.996	0.996
60-72	0.999	0.998	0.998	0.998	0.998	0.998	0.998
72-84	0.999	0.999	0.999	0.999	0.999	0.999	0.999
84-Ult	0.999	0.999	0.999	0.999	0.999	0.999	0.999
Dev to Ult	0.999	0.998	0.996	0.992	0.986	0.982	1.100

Based on factors chosen above, the complete projection of net incurred loss counts by accident year may be obtained.

Developed Months	Accident Years 1982	1983	1984	1985	1986	1987	1988
12	30,105	30,594	24,315	22,585	22,991	15,883	14,363
24	34,916	32.999	27,374	25,052	27,264	18,343	**16,087**
36	34,683	32,873	27,244	24,942	26,906	**18,270**	**16,022**
48	34,515	32,736	27,133	24,769	**26,744**	**18,160**	**15,926**
60	34,420	32,661	27,024	**24,670**	**26,637**	**18,087**	**15,862**
72	34,381	32,607	**25,970**	**24,620**	**26,584**	**18,051**	**15,831**
84	34,362	**32,574**	**26,943**	**24,596**	**26,558**	**18,033**	**15,815**
Ultimate	**34,328**	**32,542**	**26,916**	**24,571**	**26,531**	**18,015**	**15,799**

A history of average paid claim accounts can be obtained by dividing the paid amounts by the number of paid and closed claims.

Developed Months	Accident Years 1982	1983	1984	1985	1986	1987	1988
12	$ 968	$ 973	$1,064	$1,160	$1,183	$1,342	$1,071
24	1,254	1,451	1,554	1,632	1,745	2,014	
36	1,631	1,859	1,958	2,117	2,439		
48	1,894	2,236	2,273	2,573			
60	2,090	2,415	2,480				
72	2,218	2,506					
84	2,281						

Note that these average paid amounts will represent both average closing payment, plus any amounts paid on claims before closure. In some lines, such as worker's compensation, these interim payments can be substantial. In those cases, this technique may not be as useful as for lines that close with a single payment.

Developed Months	Accident Years 1982	1983	1984	1985	1986	1987
12-24	1.296	1.491	1.460	1.406	1.476	1.500
24-36	1.300	1.281	1.260	1.300	1.397	
36-48	1.161	1.203	1.161	1.216		
48-60	1.104	1.080	1.091			
60-72	1.061	1.038				
72-84	1.029					

Use the triangular format as a convenient way to inspect the addition of more development points in the averages.

Developed Months	Arithmetic Average of... Latest	Last 2	Last 3	Last 4	Last 5	Last 6
12-24	1.500	1.488	1.461	1.461	1.467	1.438
24-36	1.397	1.347	1.318	1.309	1.307	
36-48	1.216	1.188	1.193	1.185		
48-60	1.091	1.086	1.092			
60-72	1.038	1.050				
72-84	1.029					

Assume the analyst chose the following development patterns below. Note that the 12-24 factor on the 1988 year has been chosen to be quite high to compensate for the low average amount of $1,071 paid during 1988.

Developed Months	Accident Years 1982	1983	1984	1985	1986	1987	1988
12-24	1.296	1.491	1.460	1.406	1.476	1.500	1.600
24-36	1.300	1.281	1.260	1.297	1.397	1.400	1.400
36-48	1.161	1.203	1.161	1.216	1.200	1.200	1.200
48-60	1.104	1.080	1.091	1.090	1.090	1.090	1.090
60-72	1.061	1.038	1.045	1.045	1.045	1.045	1.045
72-84	1.029	1.020	1.020	1.020	1.020	1.020	1.020
84-Ult	1.010	1.010	1.010	1.010	1.010	1.010	1.010
Dev to Ult	1.010	1.030	1.077	1.173	1.408	1.971	3.154

Based on factors chosen above the complete projection of average paid loss by accident year may be completed.

				Accident Years			
Developed Months	**1982**	**1983**	**1984**	**1985**	**1986**	**1987**	**1988**
12	$ 968	$ 973	$ 1,064	$ 1,160	$ 1,183	$ 1,342	$ 1,071
24	1,254	1,451	1,554	1,632	1,745	2,014	**1,714**
36	1,631	1,859	1,958	2,117	2,439	**2,819**	**2,399**
48	1,894	2,236	2,273	2,573	**2,926**	**3,383**	**2,879**
60	2,090	2,415	2,480	**2,805**	**3,190**	**3,688**	**3,138**
72	2,218	22,506	**2,591**	**2,931**	**3,333**	**3,854**	**3,279**
84	2,281	**2,556**	**2,643**	**2,990**	**3,400**	**3,931**	**3,345**
Ultimate	**$ 2,304**	**$ 2,582**	**$ 2,670**	**$ 3,020**	**$ 3,434**	**$ 3,970**	**$ 3,378**
Counts	34,328	32,542	26,916	24,571	26,531	18,015	15,799
Ultimate	$79,085	$84,023	$71,857	$74,194	$91,107	$71,520	$53,369
Pd to Date	$78,224	$81,287	$66,402	$62,347	$62,832	$33,568	$11,346
Reserve	$ 860	$ 2,736	$ 5,455	$11,847	$28,275	$37,952	$42,023
						Total Reserve	$125,593

The 1988 average paid claim at ultimate appears to be completely unreasonable at $3,378 per claim, compared to past values projected. A review of annual increases in the ultimate average paid amount follows:

	1982	**1983**	**1984**	**1985**	**1986**	**1987**	**1988**
Ultimate	$ 2,304	$ 2,582	$ 2,670	$ 3,020	$ 3,434	$ 3,970	$ 3,378
Annual Increase		12.1%	3.4%	13.1%	13.7%	15.6%	− 14.9%

This indicates that a 12% increase from the 1987 value might be more in line with past experience. Using this increase yields an average payment of $4,446 per claim closed.

Ultimate	$ 2,304	$ 2,582	$ 2,670	$ 3,020	$ 3,434	$ 3,970	$ 4,446
Counts	34,328	32,542	26,916	24,571	26,531	18,015	15,799
Ultimate	$79,085	$84,023	$71,857	$74,194	$91,107	$71,520	$70,242
Pd to Date	$78,224	$81,287	$66,402	$62,347	$62,832	$33,568	$11,346
Reserve	$ 860	$ 2,736	$ 5,455	$11,847	$28,275	$37,952	$58,896
						Total Reserve	$146,021

The resulting reserve estimate based on average paid data has allowed us to correct for an obvious aberration in paid claims. This aberration was not noticable from the aggregate paid or incurred histories. This provides an example of the necessity of using several methods in investigating reserve needs.

A similar projection can be made of the average amount of loss incurred per reported claim closed.

Developed Months	1982	1983	1984	1985	1986	1987	1988
12	$1,948	$2,083	$2,130	$1,777	$2,421	$2,733	$2,005
24	2,142	2,409	2,490	2,713	2,945	3,137	
36	2,229	2,546	2,562	3,013	3,269		
48	2,257	2,608	2,569	3,147			
60	2,345	2,699	2,592				
72	2,393	2,681					
84	2,397						

Age to age historical development factors may be calculated for these data.

Developed Months	1982	1983	1984	1985	1986	1987
12-24	1.100	1.157	1.169	1.527	1.216	1.148
24-36	1.041	1.056	1.029	1.110	1.110	
36-48	1.012	1.024	1.003	1.045		
48-60	1.039	1.035	1.009			
60-72	1.020	0.993				
72-84	1.002					

Use the triangular format as a convenient way to inspect the addition of more development points in the averages.

	Arithmetic Average of...					
Developed Months	Latest	Last 2	Last 3	Last 4	Last 5	Last 6
12-24	1.148	1.182	1.297	1.265	1.243	1.220
24-36	1.110	1.110	1.083	1.076	1.069	
36-48	1.045	1.024	1.024	1.021		
48-60	1.009	1.022	1.028			
60-72	0.993	1.007				
72-84	1.002					

Assume the analyst chose the following development patterns as the most likely outcome.

Developed Months	Accident Years						
	1982	1983	1984	1985	1986	1987	1988
12-24	1.100	1.157	1.169	1.527	1.216	1.148	1.300
24-36	1.041	1.056	1.029	1.110	1.110	1.100	1.100
36-48	1.012	1.024	1.003	1.045	1.025	1.025	1.025
48-60	1.039	1.035	1.009	1.025	1.025	1.025	1.025
60-72	1.020	0.993	1.000	1.000	1.000	1.000	1.000
72-84	1.002	1.003	1.003	1.003	1.003	1.003	1.003
84-Ult	1.000	1.000	1.000	1.000	1.000	1.000	1.000
Dev to Ult	1.000	1.003	1.003	1.028	1.054	1.159	1.507

Based on factors chosen above, the complete projection of average incurred losses by accident year may be completed.

Developed Months	1982	1983	1984	1985	1986	1987	1988
12	$ 1,948	$ 2,083	$ 2,130	$ 1,777	$ 2,421	$ 2,733	$ 2,005
24	2,142	2,409	2,490	2,713	2,945	3,137	**2,607**
36	2,229	2,546	2,562	3,013	3,269	**3,451**	**2,867**
48	2,257	2,608	2,569	3,147	**3,351**	**3,537**	**2,939**
60	2,345	2,699	2,592	**3,226**	**3,435**	**3,626**	**3,012**
72	2,393	2,681	**2,592**	**3,226**	**3,435**	**3,626**	**3,012**
84	2,397	**2,689**	**2,600**	**3,235**	**3,445**	**3,637**	**3,022**
Ultimate	**2,397**	**2,689**	**2,600**	**3,235**	**3,445**	**3,637**	**3,022**
Counts	34,328	32,542	26,916	24,571	26,531	18,015	15,799
Ultimate	$82,290	$87,500	$69,970	$79,496	$91,400	$65,514	$47,738
Paid to Date	$78,224	$81,287	$66,402	$62,347	$62,832	$33,568	$11,346
Reserve	$ 4,066	$ 6,213	$ 3,568	$17,149	$28,568	$31,946	$36,392
						Total Reserve	$127,902

The ultimate reserve estimate resulting from this average incurred history indicates a reserve of $128 million is needed. Hoewever, the same problem noted with the 1988 paid claim averages is noted here. The 1988 average ultimate incurred claim of $3,022 does not look realistic based on the steady increases of average incurred losses since 1982.

	1982	1983	1984	1985	1986	1987	1988
Ultimate	$2,397	$2,689	$2,600	$3,235	$3,445	$3,637	$3,022
Annual Increase		12.2%	− 3.3%	24.4%	6.5%	5.6%	− 16.9%

Since the average incurred amounts have been increasing at an average rate of 8.7% from 1982 to 1987, this would imply an average incurred of $3,637 multiplied by 1.087 or $3,953. With 15,799 claims at ultimate settlement, the total incurred for 1988 will be $62,453,447, or almost $15 million dollars higher than our original projection. This implies a reserve of $143 million is required to provide for the ultimate disposition of all claims.

The triangular loss development factor methods applied to the four different loss statistics above yields the following different sets of ultimate accident year incurred losses.

	Accident Years						
Method	**1982**	**1983**	**1984**	**1985**	**1986**	**1987**	**1988**
Paid	$82,372	$88,163	$75,451	$77,573	$103,664	$72,070	$49,475
Incurred	$83,196	$87,413	$70,741	$80,301	$92,430	$66,216	$44,737
Avg Paid	$79,085	$84,023	$71,857	$74,194	$91,107	$71,520	$70,242
Avg Inc'd	$82,290	$87,500	$69,970	$79,496	$91,400	$65,514	$62,453

Note that there is substantial variation from method to method. The analyst must still choose his point estimate in some fashion. This choice will be dependent on the supporting information the analyst has developed concerning the company's operations as well as further statistical tests discussed below. However, at this point there is strong reason to suspect that both the aggregate paid an incurred loss projection methods has substantially underestimated the 1988 ultimate loss amounts.

Reserve Development Methods

The triangular methods have used either paid or incurred data, exclusively, but have not made any use of historical relationships between paid amounts and case reserved amounts. The reserve development method attempts to analyze the adequacy of case reserves based on the history of payments against those case reserves. In order to be able to interpret the procedure in terms of payments on case reserves, we present the following report year paid and reserve data. Report year data are organized by year of report to the company, as opposed to year of loss for accident year. This array freezes the inventory of loss to study only those cases actually reported to a company during a calendar year. Thus, there can be no late reported claims on a report year compilation. This method is discussed in Marker and Mohl (1980) and Mohl (1987).

Case Loss Reserve by Report Year

Developed Months	1982	1983	1984	1985	1986	1987	1988
12	$46,770	$53,422	$41,802	$40,334	$47,500	$42,219	$30,416
24	31,944	36,588	28,899	28,266	35,455	27,221	
36	18,832	21,214	15,798	18,312	22,225		
48	9,559	11,345	95,600	8,724			
60	4,999	8,049	5,403				
72	2,821	3,701					
84	1,693						

Incremental Paid by Report Year

Developed Months	1982	1983	1984	1985	1986	1987	1988
12	$30,001	$29,421	$26,601	$24,981	$27,595	$25,886	$15,220
24	16,021	18,081	17,078	15,251	18,196	17,700	
36	14,144	16,904	13,169	12,665	17,687		
48	8,238	10,811	7,522	9,465			
60	5,923	4,942	4,739				
72	3,119	2,930					
84	1,145						

The fundamental idea of the reserve development method of reserve evaluation is to track the development of a case reserve amount into subsequent paid losses and remaining reserves. For instance, the $42,219 in reserves from report year 1987 cases has developed into $17,700 of paid loss during 1988, with $27,221 remaining in reserve as of the end of 1988. We are then interested in the amount we expect to be paid on the $27,221 reserve during the next 12 months. The entire liquidation pattern of the report year reserves can then be charted and used to evaluate the ultimate liquidation value of the report year case reserves.

Consider the following ratios of amounts paid on the prior calendar period's open reserves:

Paid on Reserve Ratio by Report Year

Developed Months	1982	1983	1984	1985	1986	1987
12-24	0.340	0.338	0.409	0.378	0.383	0.420
24-36	0.442	0.462	0.454	0.448	0.500	
36-48	0.438	0.514	0.473	0.519		
48-60	0.621	0.440	0.495			
60-72	0.636	0.364				
72-84	0.392					

Likewise, we can create the array of ratios of remaining in reserve compared to the open reserve of the prior calendar period.

Remaining in Reserve Ratio by Report Year

Developed Months	1982	1983	1984	1985	1986	1987
12-24	0.683	0.685	0.691	0.701	0.746	0.645
24-36	0.590	0.580	0.547	0.648	0.627	
36-48	0.508	0.535	6.051	0.476		
48-60	0.523	0.709	0.057			
60-72	0.564	0.460				
72-84	0.600					

Note that the sum of these two ratios, gives a history of the amount developed on prior calendar period's open reserves.

Incurred Loss Development by Report Year

Developed Months	1982	1983	1984	1985	1986	1987
12-24	1.023	1.023	1.100	1.079	1.130	1.065
24-36	1.032	1.042	1.001	1.096	1.126	
36-48	0.945	1.049	6.524	0.995		
48-60	1.144	1.149	0.551			
60-72	1.200	0.824				
72-84	0.992					

In order to complete the projection of ultimate reserve outcomes both the Paid on Reserve and the Remaining Reserve on Reserve developments must be projected.

Use the triangular format as a convenient way to inspect the averages of Paid on Reserve Ratios.

Developed Months	Arithmetic Average of. . .					
	Latest	Last 2	Last 3	Last 4	Last 5	Last 6
12-24	0.420	0.402	0.394	0.398	0.386	0.378
24-36	0.500	0.474	0.467	0.466	0.461	
36-48	0.519	0.496	0.502	0.486		
48-60	0.495	0.467	0.519			
60-72	0.364	0.500				
72-84	0.392					

The following development patterns were chosen as the most likely to occur for paid on open reserve amounts.

Developed Months	Report Years						
	1982	1983	1984	1985	1986	1987	1988
12-24	0.340	0.338	0.409	0.378	0.383	0.420	0.420
24-36	0.442	0.462	0.454	0.448	0.500	0.500	0.500
36-48	0.438	0.514	0.473	0.519	0.500	0.500	0.500
48-60	0.621	0.440	0.495	0.500	0.500	0.500	0.500
60-72	0.636	0.364	0.500	0.500	0.500	0.500	0.500
72-84	0.392	0.400	0.400	0.400	0.400	0.400	0.400
84-Ult	1.000	1.000	1.000	1.000	1.000	1.000	1.000

The same exercise must carried out for the remaining on reserve

Developed Months	Report Years					
	1982	1983	1984	1985	1986	1987
12-24	0.683	0.685	0.691	0.701	0.746	0.645
24-36	0.590	0.580	0.547	0.648	0.627	
36-48	0.508	0.535	6.051	0.476		
48-60	0.523	0.709	0.057			
60-72	0.564	0.460				
72-84	0.600					

Use the triangular format as a convenient way to inspect the addition of more development points in the averages.

Arithmetic Average of. . .

Developed Months	Latest	Last 2	Last 3	Last 4	Last 5	Last 6
12-24	0.645	0.696	0.697	0.696	0.694	0.692
24-36	0.627	0.637	0.607	0.600	0.598	
36-48	0.476	3.264	2.354	1.893		
48-60	0.057	0.383	0.430			
60-72	0.460	0.512				
72-84	0.600					

The following development patterns were chosen as the most likely for reserves remaining open related to prior open reserve amount.

Report Years

Developed Months	1982	1983	1984	1985	1986	1987	1988
12-24	0.683	0.685	0.691	0.701	0.746	0.645	0.690
24-36	0.590	0.580	0.547	0.648	0.627	0.635	0.635
36-48	0.508	0.535	6.051	0.476	0.530	0.530	0.530
48-60	0.523	0.709	0.057	0.600	0.600	0.600	0.600
60-72	0.564	0.460	0.500	0.500	0.500	0.500	0.500
72-84	0.600	0.600	0.600	0.600	0.600	0.600	0.600
84-Ult	0.000	0.000	0.000	0.000	0.000	0.000	0.000

Note that this statistic is the amount remaining on reserve so that the 84 month to ultimate development must be zero. Thus selection of tail factors is not an issue in this reserve projection methodology.

Once development factor scenarios have been constructed, it is necessary to complete the settlement projections in their dollar terms. An example using the 1986 report year is the most direct illustration of the completion technique involved.

There is $22.2 million of case reserves outstanding on the 1986 report year as of the end of 1988. The completed development factors indicate that 53% of this reserve will remain in reserve, while 50% of the reserve will be paid out, for a total adverse development of 3% on the 1986 report year cases during 1988.

We can complete the projection of remaining reserves, by using the relationships as above.

Developed Months	Case Loss Reserves by Report Years 1982	1983	1984	1985	1986	1987	1988
12	$46,649	$53,415	$41,793	$40,328	$47,471	$42,122	$29,490
24	31,939	36,568	28,986	28,248	35,406	27,097	**20,348**
36	18,827	21,014	15,907	18,243	22,200	**17,207**	**12,921**
48	9,552	11,235	9,577	8,698	**11,766**	**9,119**	**6,848**
60	4,991	8,043	5,376	**5,219**	**7,060**	**5,472**	**4,109**
72	2,799	3,656	**2,688**	**2,609**	**3,530**	**2,736**	**2,054**
84	1,685	**2,194**	**1,613**	**1,566**	**2,118**	**1,642**	**1,233**
Ultimate	**0**	**0**	**0**	**0**	**0**	**0**	**0**

Based on the amounts remaining in reserve, annual paid amounts by report period can be derived simply by using the selected paid on reserve factors. For instance, on the $22,200,000 of reserves open at the end of 1988 on 1986 reported claims, 50% will be paid out in 1989. This is $11.1 million of paid claims.

Developed Months	Paid Losses by Report Year 1982	1983	1984	1985	1986	1987	1988
12	$30,001	$29,421	$26,601	$24,981	$27,595	$25,886	$15,220
24	16,021	18,081	17,078	15,251	18,196	17,700	**12,386**
36	14,144	16,904	13,169	12,665	17,687	**13,549**	**10,174**
48	8,238	10,811	7,522	9,465	**11,100**	**8,603**	**6,461**
60	5,923	4,942	4,739	**4,349**	**5,883**	**4,560**	**3,424**
72	3,119	2,930	**2,688**	**2,609**	**3,530**	**2,736**	**2,054**
84	1,145	**1,462**	**1,075**	**1,044**	**1,412**	**1,094**	**822**
Ultimate	$ 1,685	$ 2,194	$ 1,613	$ 1,566	$ 2,118	$ 1,642	$ 1,233

Thus the incremental paid loss projections accumulate to paid losses by report years as below.

Developed Months	Paid Losses by Report Years 1982	1983	1984	1985	1986	1987	1988
12	$30,001	$29,421	$26,601	$24,981	$27,595	$25,886	$15,220
24	46,022	47,502	43,679	40,232	45,791	43,586	**27,606**
36	60,166	64,406	56,848	52,897	63,478	**57,135**	**37,780**
48	68,404	75,217	64,370	62,362	**74,578**	**65,738**	**44,240**
60	74,327	80,159	69,109	**66,711**	**80,461**	**70,298**	**47,664**
72	77,446	83,089	**71,797**	**69,320**	**83,991**	**73,033**	**49,719**
84	78,591	**84,551**	**72,872**	**70,364**	**85,403**	**74,128**	**50,541**
Ultimate	$80,276	$86,745	$74,485	$71,930	$87,521	$75,769	$51,773
Reserve:							
Required	$ 1,685	$ 3,656	$ 5,376	$ 9,568	$24,043	$32,183	$36,553
Carried	$ 1,685	$ 3,656	$ 5,376	$ 8,698	$22,200	$27,097	$29,490
Additional Case Reserve Need							
	$ 0	$ 0	$ 0	$ 870	$ 1,843	$ 5,086	$ 7,063
							$14,862
Reported Case Adequacy							
	100.0%	100.0%	100.0%	90.9%	92.3%	84.2%	80.7%

This analysis indicates a case reserving pattern with case reserves deficient 20% in the first 12 months, 15% at age 12 to 24 months, 7-8% at age 24 to 48 months. After 48 months we expect case reserves to be adequate. Note that report year analysis can only evaluate case reserve adequacy. The IBNR liability for this line would require additional analysis.

While the reserve development method is simplest to interpret on report year data, it may also be used on accident period data on an accident year basis. New claims will enter the claim inventory so that the interpretation of paid on open reserve history is made more difficult. In order to apply the method to accident period data one must be able to assume that IBNR claim activity is related consistently to claims already reported. This assumption is a reasonable one for most lines of business that have the bulk of their claims reported in the first accident period to serve as a stable base for IBNR projections.

Assume we take the accident year paid and incurred triangles that were presented above.

Remaining Case Reserve by Accident Year

Developed Months	1982	1983	1984	1985	1986	1987	1988
12	$36,038	$41,679	$31,613	$20,846	$35,110	$26,400	$17,454
24	34,740	35,542	29,028	30,623	37,399	23,980	
36	23,022	24,943	18,483	24,753	25,129		
48	13,776	13,525	9,277	15,600			
60	9,471	10,076	3,639				
72	6,330	6,126					
84	4,148						

Incremental Paid by Accident Year

Developed Months	1982	1983	1984	1985	1986	1987	1988
12	$22,603	$22,054	$20,166	$19,297	$20,555	$17,001	$11,346
24	17,461	21,916	18,981	18,058	22,343	16,567	
36	14,237	14,767	12,172	13,036	19,935		
48	9,813	13,104	9,098	11,956			
60	7,143	6,235	5,985				
72	4,693	3,211					
84	2,274						

Consider the following ratios of paid on open reserves.

Paid on Reserve Ratio by Accident Year

Developed Months	1982	1983	1984	1985	1986	1987
12-24	0.485	0.526	0.600	0.866	0.636	0.628
24-36	0.410	0.415	0.419	0.426	0.533	
36-48	0.426	0.525	0.492	0.483		
48-60	0.519	0.461	0.645			
60-72	0.495	0.319				
72-84	0.359					

Likewise, we can create the array of ratios of remaining in reserve.

Remaining in Reserve Ratio by Accident Year

Developed Months	1982	1983	1984	1985	1986	1987
12-24	0.964	0.853	0.918	1.469	1.065	0.908
24-36	0.663	0.702	0.637	0.808	0.672	
36-48	0.598	0.542	0.502	0.630		
48-60	0.687	0.745	0.392			
60-72	0.668	0.608				
72-84	0.655					

Note that the sum of these two ratios, gives a history of the amount developed on reserves, now including IBNR claims.

Accident Years

Developed Months	1982	1983	1984	1985	1986	1987
12-24	1.449	1.379	1.519	2.335	1.702	1.536
24-36	1.073	1.117	1.056	1.234	1.205	
36-48	1.025	1.068	0.994	1.113		
48-60	1.206	1.206	1.037			
60-72	1.164	0.927				
72-84	1.015					

In order to complete the projection of ultimate reserve outcomes both the paid on reserve and the remaining reserve on reserve developments must be projected.

Use the triangular format as a convenient way to inspect the addition of more development points in the averages.

Arithmetic Average of. . .

Developed Months	Latest	Last 2	Last 3	Last 4	Last 5	Last 6
12-24	0.628	0.632	0.710	0.683	0.651	0.623
24-36	0.533	0.479	0.459	0.448	0.441	
36-48	0.483	0.488	0.500	0.482		
48-60	0.645	0.553	0.542			
60-72	0.319	0.407				
72-84	0.359					

Assume the analyst chose the following development patterns along the right diagonal as the most likely to be paid as percent of reserve over the next 12 month periods.

Developed Months	Accident Years						
	1982	1983	1984	1985	1986	1987	1988
12-24	0.485	0.526	0.600	0.866	0.636	0.628	0.600
24-36	0.410	0.415	0.419	0.426	0.533	0.460	0.460
36-48	0.426	0.525	0.492	0.483	0.495	0.495	0.495
48-60	0.519	0.461	0.645	0.500	0.500	0.500	0.500
60-72	0.495	0.319	0.510	0.510	0.510	0.510	0.510
72-84	0.359	0.430	0.430	0.430	0.430	0.430	0.430
84-Ult	1.010	1.010	1.010	1.010	1.010	1.010	1.010

The same exercise must be carried out for the remaining reserve on reserve ratios on an accident year basis.

Developed Months	Accident Years					
	1982	1983	1984	1985	1986	1987
12-24	0.964	0.853	0.918	1.469	1.065	0.908
24-36	0.663	0.702	0.637	0.808	0.672	
36-48	0.598	0.542	0.502	0.630		
48-60	0.687	0.745	0.392			
60-72	0.668	0.608				
72-84	0.655					

Use the triangular format as a convenient way to inspect the addition of more development points in the averages.

Developed Months	Arithmetic Average of...					
	Latest	Last 2	Last 3	Last 4	Last 5	Last 6
12-24	0.908	0.987	1.148	1.090	1.043	1.030
24-36	0.672	0.740	0.706	0.705	0.696	
36-48	0.630	0.566	0.558	0.568		
48-60	0.392	0.569	0.608			
60-72	0.608	0.638				
72-84	0.655					

Assume the analyst chose the following development patterns of reserves as ratio to prior accident period reserves.

Developed Months	Accident Years						
	1982	1983	1984	1985	1986	1987	1988
12-24	0.964	0.853	0.918	1.469	1.065	0.908	1.000
24-36	0.663	0.702	0.637	0.808	0.672	0.750	0.750
36-48	0.598	0.542	0.502	0.630	0.600	0.600	0.600
48-60	0.687	0.745	0.392	0.600	0.600	0.600	0.600
60-72	0.668	0.608	0.650	0.650	0.650	0.650	0.650
72-84	0.655	0.655	0.655	0.655	0.655	0.655	0.655
84-Ult	0.000	0.000	0.000	0.000	0.000	0.000	0.000

We can complete the projection of remaining reserves

Developed Months	Case Loss Reserves by Accident Year						
	1982	1983	1984	1985	1986	1987	1988
12	$36,038	$41,679	$31,613	$20,846	$35,110	$26,400	$17,454
24	31,939	36,568	28,986	28,248	35,406	27,097	**17,454**
36	18,827	21,014	15,907	18,243	22,200	**20,323**	**13,091**
48	9,552	11,235	9,577	8,698	**13,320**	**12,194**	**7,854**
60	4,991	8,043	5,376	**5,219**	**7,992**	**7,316**	**4,713**
72	2,799	3,656	**3,494**	**3,392**	**5,195**	**4,756**	**3,063**
84	1,685	**2,395**	**2,289**	**2,222**	**3,403**	**3,115**	**2,006**
Ultimate	**$ 0**	**$ 0**	**$ 0**	**$ 0**	**$ 0**	**$ 0**	**$ 0**

Based on the amounts remaining in reserve, annual paid amounts by accident period can be derived simply by using the selected paid on reserve factors.

Developed Months	Paid Losses by Accident Year						
	1982	1983	1984	1985	1986	1987	1988
12	$22,603	$22,054	$20,166	$19,297	$20,555	$17,001	$11,346
24	15,879	18,080	17,078	15,251	18,196	17,697	**10,473**
36	14,117	16,904	13,169	12,665	17,687	**12,465**	**8,029**
48	8,241	10,811	7,522	9,465	**10,989**	**10,060**	**6,480**
60	5,935	4,942	4,739	**4,349**	**6,660**	**6,097**	**3,927**
72	3,172	2,930	**2,742**	**2,662**	**4,076**	**3,731**	**2,403**
84	1,097	**1,572**	**1,503**	**1,459**	**2,234**	**2,045**	**1,317**
Ultimate	**$ 1,702**	**$ 2,419**	**$ 2,312**	**$ 2,244**	**$ 3,437**	**$ 3,146**	**$ 2,026**

Thus the incremental paid loss projections can be accumulated to yield ultimate payment estimates by accident year.

	Paid Losses by Accident Year						
Developed Months	**1982**	**1983**	**1984**	**1985**	**1986**	**1987**	**1988**
12	$22,603	$22,054	$20,166	$19,297	$20,555	$17,001	$11,346
24	38,482	40,134	37,244	34,548	38,751	34,698	**21,819**
36	52,599	57,038	50,413	47,213	56,438	**47,163**	**29,848**
48	60,840	67,849	57,935	56,678	**67,427**	**57,223**	**36,327**
60	66,775	72,791	62,674	**61,027**	**74,087**	**63,319**	**40,255**
72	69,947	75,721	**65,416**	**63,688**	**78,163**	**67,051**	**42,658**
84	71,044	**77,293**	**66,918**	**65,147**	**80,397**	**69,095**	**43,975**
Ultimate	**$72,746**	**$79,711**	**$69,230**	**$67,391**	**$83,833**	**$72,241**	**$46,002**
Reserve Required	$ 1,702	$ 3,991	$ 6,556	$10,713	$27,395	$37,543	$34,656
							Total $122,556

This analysis results in a total indicated reserve requirement of $123 million. Note this estimate is closest to the $130 million estimate based on the method that used aggregate incurred historical data.

Budgeted IBNR

There are many cases where historical case incurred amounts are reported over a long time period (10 years or longer) and very little of the incurred loss is reported in the first two to three years. Most excess lines of insurance, as well as reinsurance lines fit into this category. In addition, many lines such as contract bond surety may report faster than excess lines, but are subject to very large occasional losses. This behavior makes it inappropriate to use reported losses as the sole base for projecting ultimate losses.

The Budgeted IBNR technique smooths out the projected ultimates by relying on smoothed development factors and expected losses to project future incurred development (Bornhuetter and Ferguson (1972)). Assume we have the following incurred loss data as follows, by accident year.

Developed Months	Accident Years						
	1982	1983	1984	1985	1986	1987	1988
12	$58,641	$63,732	$51,779	$40,143	$55,665	$43,401	$28,800
24	74,804	79,512	68,175	67,978	80,296	57,547	
36	77,323	83,680	69,802	75,144	87,961		
48	77,890	85,366	69,694	77,947			
60	80,728	88,152	70,041				
72	82,280	87,413					
84	82,372						

Derive the history of development factors at successive ages.

Developed Months	Accident Years					
	1982	1983	1984	1985	1986	1987
12-24	1.276	1.248	1.317	1.693	1.443	1.326
24-36	1.034	1.052	1.024	1.105	1.095	
36-48	1.007	1.020	0.998	1.037		
48-60	1.036	1.033	1.005			
60-72	1.019	0.992				
72-84	1.001					

Use the triangular format as a convenient way to inspect the addition of more development points in the averages.

Developed Months	Arithmetic Average of. . .					
	Latest	Last 2	Last 3	Last 4	Last 5	Last 6
12-24	1.326	1.384	1.487	1.445	1.405	1.384
24-36	1.095	1.100	1.075	1.069	1.062	
36-48	1.037	1.018	1.019	1.016		
48-60	1.005	1.019	1.025			
60-72	0.992	1.005				
72-84	1.001					

Assume the analyst chose the following development patterns of incurred loss amounts for future development periods.

Developed Months	Accident Years 1982	1983	1984	1985	1986	1987	1988
12-24	1.276	1.248	1.317	1.693	1.443	1.326	1.400
24-36	1.034	1.052	1.024	1.105	1.095	1.070	1.070
36-48	1.007	1.020	0.998	1.037	1.020	1.020	1.020
48-60	1.036	1.033	1.005	1.020	1.020	1.020	1.020
60-72	1.019	0.992	1.000	1.000	1.000	1.000	1.000
72-84	1.001	1.000	1.000	1.000	1.000	1.000	1.000
84-Ult	1.010	1.010	1.010	1.010	1.010	1.010	1.010

These development factors for one period can be multiplied together to produce age to ultimate factors.

Developed Months	Age to Ultimate Factors 1982	1983	1984	1985	1986	1987	1988
12-Ult	1.419	1.385	1.366	2.000	1.660	1.491	1.574
24-Ult	1.112	1.110	1.038	1.181	1.151	1.124	1.124
36-Ult	1.076	1.055	1.013	1.069	1.051	1.051	1.051
48-Ult	1.068	1.034	1.015	1.030	1.030	1.030	1.030
60-Ult	1.031	1.002	1.010	1.010	1.010	1.010	1.010
72-Ult	1.011	1.010	1.010	1.010	1.010	1.010	1.010
84-Ult	1.010	1.010	1.010	1.010	1.010	1.010	1.010

These age to ultimate factors can be interpreted to mean that an accident year is 99% reported as of 60 months, since the development from 60 months to ultimate is given by a factor of 1.010. Likewise, as of 12 months the 1988 accident year is expected to be 63.5% reported in incurred amounts, given by 1/1.574. This implies that 36.5% of the ultimate incurred loss for 1986 remains to be reported as of the end of 1988.

Clearly, if one had an estimate for 1988 accident year ultimate losses, one should set a reserve amount equal to 36.5% of this estimate as the appropriate reserve as of 12/31/88. The Budgeted IBNR technique is the use of this estimated reserve as the appropriate reserve. The problem has been reduced to the estimate of ultimate incurred losses. One ready candidate is the earned premium for the accident year times the expected loss ratio, or the pricing assumption ultimate incurred loss amount.

If the earned premiums and expected loss ratios for each year are given below we can apply this method to our incurred losses.

Budgeted IBNR Method

Accident Years

Developed Months	**1982**	**1983**	**1984**	**1985**	**1986**	**1987**	**1988**
1) Earned Premium							
	$101,946	$112,068	$89,796	$101,930	$117,327	$84,051	$56,787
2) Reported Loss Ratio							
	80.8%	78.0%	78.0%	76.5%	75.0%	68.5%	50.7%
3) Expected Loss Ratio							
	80.0%	80.0%	80.0%	78.0%	78.0%	78.0%	78.0%
4) Expected Ultimate							
(3) × (1)	$81,557	$89,655	$71,837	$79,506	$91,515	$65,560	$44,294
5) Development to Ultimate							
	1.010	1.010	1.010	1.030	1.051	1.124	1.574
6) Remaining Development							
1.0 - 1/(6)	1.0%	1.0%	1.0%	2.9%	4.8%	11.1%	36.5%
7) Remaining Reserve							
(6) × (4)	$807	$888	$711	$2,331	$4,425	$7,251	$16,155
							Total $32,568
8) Developed to Date							
	$82,372	$87,413	$70,041	$77,947	$87,961	$57,547	$28,800
9) Ultimate Estimate							
(7) + (8)	$83,180	$88,301	$70,752	$80,277	$92,386	$64,799	$44,955
10) Ultimate Loss Ratio							
(9) / (1)	81.6%	78.8%	78.8%	78.8%	78.7%	77.1%	79.2%
11) Paid Claims							
	$78,224	$81,287	$66,402	$62,347	$62,832	$33,568	$11,346
12) Reserve							
(9) - (11)	$4,955	$7,014	$4,350	$17,930	$29,553	$31,231	$33,609
							Total $128,643

A simple analysis shows that this reserve method is related to the incurred loss development method above. Let $d(a,n)$ be the n to ultimate development factor for accident year a. Let $U(a)$ be an estimate of ultimate incurred losses for period a, and $I(a,n)$ be the amount of reported incurred losses due to period a at time n. Then the new revised ultimate $U'(a)$ is given by $U'(a) = I(a,n) + U(a) \times [1 - 1/d(a,n)]$.

This can be written

$$U'(a) = [I(a,n) \times d(a,n)]/d(a,n) + U(a) \times [1 - 1/d(a,n)].$$

But $I(a,n) \times d(a,n)$ is simply the development factor projection ultimate for period a. Hence the revised ultimate is simply a weighted average of the ultimate estimate $U(a)$ with the development factor projection for period a, where the ultimate estimate $U(a)$ is given weight $[1 - 1/d(a,n)]$. Note that at very early developments, when the development factor $d(a,n)$ is very large, the bulk of the weight is given the initial ultimate estimate $U(a)$. Thus, this method acts as a smoothing of very long-tailed or unstable loss development lines.

Loss Adjustment Expenses

An extremely important part of the loss reserve evaluation process is the evaluation of loss adjustment expense liabilities. One approach could be to combine loss adjustment expenses with losses and estimate the total liability. Generally, this approach will not be desirable because the two loss development patterns will be quite different. Thus combining loss adjustment expense with losses is often similar to combining two non-homogeneous lines of business. Different analyses of loss and loss adjustment expense are also necessary to allow for monitoring of actual loss and adjustment expenses versus projected developments of each separate component.

Loss adjustment expenses need always to be split into their allocated and unallocated components. While allocated loss adjustment expenses could be combined with their associated losses this is not possible for unallocated loss adjustment expenses.

Allocated Loss Adjustment Expenses

The allocated loss adjustment expenses can often be further split into subcategories. The most important subcategory is legal fees or defense costs. It will often be conducive to obtaining better estimates of loss adjustment expense to develop legal expense separate from all other allocated expense items.

Case reserve estimates sometimes are not established for loss adjustment expenses. This means that the actuary only has paid allocated loss adjustment expenses to work with. The allocated expense reserve is established on a bulk basis by actuarial estimates, or may be spread to cases by some formula approach. In either case, allocated paid amounts are the only meaningful history available for the analysis.

A common analysis procedure is to compare the allocated expenses paid to the paid losses on the same claims, and follow the development of the relationship of paid allocated expense to paid loss over time.

Assume the same paid loss history from our previous example.

	Accident Years						
Developed Months	**1982**	**1983**	**1984**	**1985**	**1986**	**1987**	**1988**
12	$22,603	$22,054	$20,166	$19,297	$20,555	$17,001	$11,346
24	40,064	43,970	39,147	37,355	42,898	33,568	
36	54,301	58,737	51,319	50,391	62,832		
48	64,114	71,841	60,417	62,347			
60	71,257	78,076	66,402				
72	75,950	81,287					
84	78,224						

We also have available the history of paid allocated loss expense by accident year.

Developed Months	Accident Years 1982	1983	1984	1985	1986	1987	1988
12	$ 554	$ 485	$ 446	$ 405	$ 388	$357	$ 216
24	1,110	1,244	1,104	953	1,025	843	
36	2,118	2,256	1,981	1,809	2,161		
48	3,231	3,578	2,973	2,905			
60	4,211	4,567	3,785				
72	4,170	5,202					
84	5,429						

The relationship of paid allocated loss expense to paid loss is then derived as follows for this history.

Developed Months	Accident Years 1982	1983	1984	1985	1986	1987	1988
12	2.45%	2.20%	2.21%	2.10%	1.89%	2.10%	1.90%
24	2.77	2.83	2.82	2.55	2.39	2.51	
36	3.90	3.84	3.86	3.59	3.44		
48	5.04	4.98	4.92	4.66			
60	5.91	5.85	5.70				
72	5.49	6.40					
84	6.94						

Age to age development factors applying to the ratios of paid allocated loss adjustment expense are given below. We are trying to estimate the ultimate ratio of loss adjustment expense to loss. Once the ultimate ratio is chosen it can be applied to the estimate of ultimate losses to obtain an estimate of ultimate loss adjustment expense. It often helps to think of these ratios of paid allocated expense to paid loss as the cost to settle $100 of loss.

Allocated Cost to Settle $100 of Loss

Developed Months	Accident Years 1982	1983	1984	1985	1986	1987	1988
12	$2.45	$2.20	$2.21	$2.10	$1.89	$2.10	$1.90
24	2.77	2.83	2.82	2.55	2.39	2.51	
36	3.90	3.84	3.86	3.59	3.44		
48	5.04	4.98	4.92	4.66			
60	5.91	5.85	5.70				
72	5.49	6.40					
84	6.94						

The development triangle of these expense amounts is given by

Developed Months	1982	1983	1984	1985	1986	1987
12-24	1.131	1.286	1.276	1.214	1.265	1.195
24-36	1.408	1.357	1.369	1.408	1.439	
36-48	1.292	1.297	1.275	1.298		
48-60	1.173	1.175	1.159			
60-72	0.929	1.094				
72-84	1.264					

We can select development factors expected for future periods by inspecting the behavior of the historical developments and their averages.

Arithmetic Average of. . .

Developed Months	Latest	Last 2	Last 3	Last 4	Last 5	Last 6
12-24	1.195	1.230	1.225	1.238	1.247	1.228
24-36	1.439	1.424	1.405	1.393	1.396	
36-48	1.298	1.286	1.290	1.290		
48-60	1.159	1.167	1.169			
60-72	1.094	1.011				
72-84	1.264					

Assume the analyst chose the following development patterns along the right diagonal as the most likely over the next 12 months.

Developed Months	1982	1983	1984	1985	1986	1987	1988
12-24	1.131	1.286	1.276	1.214	1.265	1.195	1.300
24-36	1.408	1.357	1.369	1.408	1.439	1.400	1.400
36-48	1.292	1.297	1.275	1.298	1.295	1.295	1.295
48-60	1.173	1.175	1.159	1.160	1.160	1.160	1.160
60-72	0.929	1.094	1.025	1.025	1.025	1.025	1.025
72-84	1.264	1.010	1.010	1.010	1.010	1.010	1.010
84-Ult	1.010	1.010	1.010	1.010	1.010	1.010	1.010
DevtoUlt	1.010	1.020	1.046	1.213	1.571	2.199	2.859

Based on factors chosen above the complete projection of paid allocated loss adjustment expense per $100 of loss by accident year may be projected to an ultimate basis.

	Accident Years						
Developed Months	1982	1983	1984	1985	1986	1987	1988
12	2.45%	2.20%	2.21%	2.10%	1.89%	2.10%	1.90%
24	2.77	2.83	2.82	2.55	2.39	2.51	**2.47**
36	3.90	3.84	3.86	3.59	3.44	**3.51**	**3.46**
48	5.04	4.98	4.92	4.66	**4.45**	**4.55**	**4.48**
60	5.91	5.85	5.70	**5.41**	**5.17**	**5.28**	**5.19**
72	5.49	6.40	**5.84**	**5.54**	**5.30**	**5.41**	**5.32**
84	6.94	**6.46**	**5.90**	**5.60**	**5.35**	**5.46**	**5.38**
Ultimate	**7.01**	**6.53**	**5.96**	**5.65**	**5.40**	**5.52**	**5.43**
Ultimate Loss	$78,487	$83,842	$73,849	$73,771	$97,708	$67,190	$79,071

Allocated Expenses: Based on Ultimate Loss

	1982	1983	1984	1985	1986	1987	1988
Ultimate	$ 5,501	$ 5,474	$ 4,401	$ 4,170	$ 5,279	$ 3,709	$ 4,295
Paid	$ 5,429	$ 5,202	$ 3,785	$ 2,905	$ 2,161	$ 843	$ 216
Reserve	$ 73	$ 271	$ 616	$ 1,264	$ 3,118	$ 2,866	$ 4,079
							Total $12,287

This analysis indicates a reserve need of $12.3 million for allocated loss adjustment expenses.

Many variations of this approach are of course possible. In addition, it is possible to simply develop the paid allocated loss expense history in its own right to obtain ultimate estimates. This approach does have the drawback that the estimate is not related to ultimate level of losses, hence it could produce widely varying results in allocated expense paid per $100 of claim paid. The premise of the analysis above is that the relationship of allocated expense to loss dollars is usually fairly stable. This premise must be validated by the analyst in his discussion with the insurer's management.

Variations on the above method include developing the additive increments to the allocated expense to loss ratios in place of the multiplication development of these ratios. If the ratios are very small at early maturities, the additive approach seems to be more stable. In addition, the ratios of incremental allocated loss adjustment expense to incremental paid loss could be developed. Finally, it is sometimes useful to develop an average paid allocated loss expense amount per paid claim count. Clearly, the methods chosen will depend heavily on a review of the data and its characteristics, as well as an understanding of the insurer's operating characteristics with regard to handling of defense and other allocated claim expenses.

Unallocated Loss Adjustment Expenses

In addition to those loss adjustment expense items that are directly involved in the defense of a claim, an insuring entity also has the responsibility to manage each case to conclusion. This requires the recognition of the accrued liability for the general expenses of maintaining a claims department and its attendant rent, utilities, and salary costs. The estimation of the amount of accrued liability is difficult without some detailed expense study available.

Unallocated loss adjustment expenses are recorded on the Annual Statement, however they are simply calendar period claim department expenses. If they are split to lines of business it is usually through an internal expense allocation procedure. The New York Insurance Department's Regulation 30 gives a detailed set of instructions for allocating expenses back to lines of business for the purposes of preparing the Insurance Expense Exhibit. Some combination of claim counts is probably most often used to allocate the unallocated loss adjustment expense to line of business. Some mixture of the following bases is probably most commonly used: number of claims incurred during the year, claims closed during the year, numbers of claims remaining open during the year, number of days claims are open, or number of payment or reserve transactions during the year. Ideally, standard costs could be assigned to each of these, or similar transactions, and total claim department costs allocated in accordance to the distribution of standard costs. The analyst should understand the methods used to allocate these bulk expense items to lines of business or geographic regions before he begins the numerical analysis.

Once unallocated loss expense payments have been assigned to lines of business, we can begin to estimate the reserve. The most common procedure is to estimate the amount of loss adjustment expense that is needed per $100 of claims payments.

Suppose the following history of unallocated loss expense payments exists for the line of business we are reviewing, by calendar year of payment.

Calendar Years						
1982	**1983**	**1984**	**1985**	**1986**	**1987**	**1988**
$12,345	$13,826	$15,486	$17,344	$19,425	$21,756	$24,367

Compare these paid expenses to the paid losses for these same calendar years.

Calendar Years							
1982	**1983**	**1984**	**1985**	**1986**	**1987**	**1988**	**Total**
$91,955	$100,576	$111,530	$130,708	$145,889	$164,051	$171,397	$916,106

Comparing the paid loss adjustment expenses to paid losses for each calendar year results in the following costs per $100 of paid loss

Calendar Years							
1982	**1983**	**1984**	**1985**	**1986**	**1987**	**1988**	**Average**
$13.43	$13.75	$13.88	$13.27	$13.32	$13.26	$14.22	$13.59

These amounts average about \$13.59 in unallocated loss adjustment expense per \$100 of paid loss. However, the amounts paid per paid loss amount comes from a mixture of new and pending claims. The common approach to estimating the liability for unallocated loss adjustment expense requires an assumption concerning the amount of unallocated loss adjustment expense paid on setup of a new claim. One procedure simply assumes that 50% of the total unallocated loss adjustment expense is paid at the outset of the claim. However, it is preferable to review with the claim department the extent of unallocated loss adjustment expense incurred on the establishment of a claim. Assume that this review indicates that 40% of unallocated loss expense is paid to set up an initial claim. Then the estimated liability for unallocated loss adjustment expense is given by

$$.1359 \times \text{IBNR Reserve} + .1359 \times (1 - .40) \times \text{Case Reserve}$$

If the IBNR reserve required is \$90 million and the case reserves total \$320 million, then the total ultimate amount of allocated claim expense liability is,

$$.1359 \times \$90{,}000{,}000 + .1359 \times .60 \times \$320{,}000{,}000$$

which totals \$38,323,800. Note that the reserve amount needed is higher than the amount paid in any one calendar year.

Evaluation of Ultimate Loss Estimates

The application of any particular reserve method to a given body of data will yield a set of estimated ultimate losses. However, each method applied will result in a different set of ultimate losses and an associated reserve estimate. The actuary must still decide on either a best estimate reserve, or a range of possible reserve estimates, or both. Of course, for financial statement purposes, a point estimate of loss reserve requirements must be supplied for the balance sheet.

While a substantial amount of judgement has been an element of the selection and application of each reserving method, the selection of a final reserve estimate is most often a subject of the actuary's experience and judgement. In this section we will present a number of practical tests that will allow one to test a set of estimated ultimate losses for reasonability.

It is important to evaluate the results of each reserving method by attempting to diagnose the reasons the methods vary. The explanation must be the result of the actuary's analysis and experience. The attempt to reconcile a number of different estimates is extremely difficult, but often yields important new insights.

The analysis conducted on the data presented above yielded six different estimates of ultimate losses by accident year. These estimates are the result of different methodologies that are sensitive to different aspects of the reserve development process. This is to be expected, since each method uses only a limited amount of data about the loss development process.

Estimated Ultimate Losses by Accident Year and Method

	Accident Years						
Method	**1982**	**1983**	**1984**	**1985**	**1986**	**1987**	**1988**
Paid	$82,372	$88,163	$75,451	$77,573	$103,664	$72,670	$49,475
Incurred	$83,196	$87,413	$70,741	$80,301	$92,430	$66,216	$44,737
Avg Paid	$79,085	$84,023	$71,857	$74,194	$91,107	$71,520	$70,242
Avg Inc'd	$82,290	$87,500	$69,970	$79,496	$91,400	$65,514	$62,453
Budgeted IBNR	$83,180	$88,308	$70,752	$80,277	$92,386	$64,799	$44,955
Reserve Dev	$72,746	$79,711	$69,230	$67,391	$83,833	$72,241	$46,002

Method	**Required Reserve in $1,000's**
Paid	$152,762
Incurred	$129,902
Average Paid	$146,021
Average Inc'd	$142,617
Budgeted IBNR	$128,643
Reserve Development	$122,556

Suppose the analyst initially selects the following ultimates as candidates for his selections.

Developed Months	Accident Years 1982	1983	1984	1985	1986	1987	1988
Selected	$82,372	$88,287	$70,741	$80,301	$92,430	$66,216	$44,737

The initial selection of these ultimate loss estimates should be tested for reasonability by comparing them to various loss development history displays.

Comparing these selected ultimates to paid history yields the following display of paid as a percent of ultimate.

Paid Losses as % of Ultimate Losses

Developed Months	Accident Years 1982	1983	1984	1985	1986	1987	1988
12	27.4%	25.0%	28.5%	24.0%	22.2%	25.7%	25.4%
24	48.6	49.8	55.3	46.5	46.4	50.7	
36	65.9	66.5	72.5	62.8	68.0		
48	77.8	81.4	85.4	77.6			
60	86.5	88.4	93.9				
72	92.2	92.1					
84	95.0						
Ultimate	$82,372	$88,287	$70,741	$80,301	$92,430	$66,216	$44,737

A similar review of the ultimates with respect to incurred losses is also useful.

Incurred Losses as % of Ultimate Losses

Developed Months	Accident Years 1982	1983	1984	1985	1986	1987	1988
12	71.2%	72.2%	73.2%	50.0%	60.2%	65.5%	64.4%
24	90.8	90.1	96.4	84.7	86.9	86.9	
36	93.9	94.8	98.7	93.6	95.2		
48	94.6	96.7	98.5	97.1			
60	98.0	99.8	99.0				
72	99.9	99.0					
84	100.0						
Ultimate	$82,372	$88,287	$70,741	$80,301	$92,430	$66,216	$44,737

A similar review of the ultimates with respect to carried case reserves is also useful. This display of course is merely the difference between the previous two displays.

Case Reserves as % of Ultimate

Accident Years

Developed Months	1982	1983	1984	1985	1986	1987	1988
12	43.8%	47.2%	44.7%	26.0%	38.0%	39.9%	39.0%
24	42.2	40.3	41.0	38.1	40.5	36.2	
36	27.9	28.3	26.1	30.8	27.2		
48	16.7	15.3	13.1	19.4			
60	11.5	11.4	5.1				
72	7.7	6.9					
84	5.0						
Ultimate	$82,372	$88,287	$70,741	$80,301	$92,430	$66,216	$44,737

Based on the selected ultimates, the required reserve is the difference between the incurred losses and the ultimate. This required reserve is also a "hindsight" test of the selected ultimate.

Required Reserves as % of Ultimate Losses

Accident Years

Developed Months	1982	1983	1984	1985	1986	1987	1988
12	72.6%	75.0%	71.5%	76.0%	77.8%	74.3%	74.6%
24	51.4	50.2	44.7	53.5	53.6	49.3	
36	34.1	33.5	27.5	37.2	32.0		
48	22.2	18.6	14.6	22.4			
60	13.5	11.6	6.1				
72	7.8	7.9					
84	5.0						
Ultimate	$82,372	$88,287	$70,741	$80,301	$92,430	$66,216	$44,737

It is also useful in some cases to review the ratio of the required reserve to the carried case reserve, as this ratio can be very stable for some lines.

	Required Reserves as % of Carried Reserves						
	Accident Years						
Developed Months	**1982**	**1983**	**1984**	**1985**	**1986**	**1987**	**1988**
12	165.9%	158.9%	160.0%	292.6%	204.6%	186.4%	191.3%
24	121.8	124.7	108.8	140.2	132.4	136.1	
36	121.8	118.5	105.1	120.8	117.8		
48	132.5	121.6	111.3	115.1			
60	117.4	101.3	119.2				
72	101.5	114.3					
84	100.0						
Ultimate	$82,372	$88,287	$70,741	$80,301	$92,430	$66,216	$44,737

Review of these statistics indicates that the paid ratios on the 1987 and 1988 ultimates are somewhat high, at 50.7% and 25.4% of ultimate, respectively. However the comparison to 1985 and 1986 is difficult because of the anomalous behavior of these two years.

Once ultimates have been selected, it is extremely important for the analyst to be able to derive projections of the upcoming periods loss development aggregates. These predictions can be monitored over the next period—month, quarter, or year. If actual loss statistics, such as paid losses, case reserves, IBNR counts, and CWP's actually come in close to the forecast development amount, the analyst can have more confidence in his analysis and understanding of the reserve situation.

For example, based on the incurred loss development method estimate of ultimate losses of $44,737,000 on the 1988 accident year, we should expect to see emergence of incurred losses amounting to $10,080,000 during 1989 on the 1988 accident year. These expected loss emergence forecasts come directly from the diagonal of the incurred loss triangle used by the analyst to develop his ultimate estimates.

The forecast incurred loss expected in calendar year 1989 is (in $1,000's):

			Accident Years				
1982	1983	1984	1985	1986	1987	1988	Total
$0	$0	$0	$1,559	$1,759	$5,467	$10,080	$18,865

This indicates a total of $18,865,000 of incurred loss should emerge during 1989 based on the analyst's selection of loss development factors. The benefit of monitoring the near term forecast is clear. The accuracy of the ultimate estimate on accident year 1988 will take several more years to ascertain. The development projection for the next calendar year is available and its accuracy can be measured in only one year.

Miscellaneous Topics

Reserve Discounting

In establishing the liabilities for losses and loss adjustment expenses, it is often necessary to recognize the time value of money. Recall that in all of the loss reserve estimation procedures reviewed above, we have not taken interest into account.

In discounting the loss reserve liability for the time value of money, we need a payout schedule for the liability amount. If the liability estimate is given by the paid loss development estimate as below, we have an undiscounted liability of $130,221,000. The payout pattern can be deduced from the completed triangle established by the selection of paid loss development factors.

The paid loss projection is given as follows:

Developed Months	Accident Years 1982	1983	1984	1985	1986	1987	1988
12	$22,603	$22,054	$20,166	$20,555	$20,555	$17,001	$11,346
24	40,064	43,970	39,147	37,355	42,898	33,568	**22,692**
36	54,301	58,737	51,319	50,391	62,832	**45,317**	**30,634**
48	64,114	71,841	60,417	62,347	**82,829**	**58,458**	**40,131**
60	71,257	78,076	66,402	**68,270**	**91,112**	**63,427**	**43,542**
72	75,950	81,287	**70,386**	**72,366**	**96,579**	**67,233**	**46,154**
84	78,224	**83,726**	**71,653**	**73,669**	**98,317**	**68,443**	**46,985**
Ultimate	**$79,006**	**$84,563**	**$72,369**	**$74,405**	**$99,301**	**$69,128**	**$47,455**

which yields the following forecast of paid amounts by calendar year and accident year.

Paid on Accident Year

Calendar Year	Accident Years 1982	1983	1984	1985	1986	1987	1988
1989	$782	$2,439	$3,984	$5,923	$19,997	$11,749	$11,346
1990	0	837	1,267	4,096	8,283	13,142	7,942
1991	0	0	717	1,303	5,467	4,969	9,497
1992	0	0	0	737	1,738	3,806	3,411
1993	0	0	0	0	983	1,210	2,613
1994	0	0	0	0	0	684	831
1995	0	0	0	0	0	0	470

This results in the following payout pattern for the 12/31/88 liability for loss reserves.

Calendar Discount

Discounted Year	Payout	Rate	Payout
1989	$56,220	96.7%	$54,365
1990	35,567	90.3	32,117
1991	21,951	84.4	18,527
1992	9,692	78.9	7,647
1993	4,806	73.8	3,547
1994	1,515	68.9	1,044
1995	470	64.4	303
Total	$130,221		$117,550

Discounting this payout pattern for 7% interest assuming payment in the midpoint of the calendar year results in a discount of almost $13 million, or 10% of the undiscounted amount.

Reserve Estimate Ranges

Throughout our analyses, we have focused on obtaining point estimates of the loss reserve liability. However, we have also found that it is extremely difficult to obtain one single estimate of the loss reserve liability. Each method results in a different answer. Further, to the extent that we are dealing with the estimation of the mean of a stochastic process, the actual result will almost always differ from the estimate.

Clearly, a range of results and a statement of our confidence that the observed reserve liability at final development will be within the stated range is preferable for this sort of process. However, the insurer's balance sheets will continue to require the analyst to supply a point estimate of the reserve liability.

Working with risk theoretical concepts, it is possible to develop a model of the reserve inventory, in terms of frequency and severities. This model can be used to develop confidence intervals for the development of the reserve. The development of such a risk theory model is outside the scope of this chapter. However, work along these lines has been done (see Hayne [1988]).

References

Berquist, J.R., and Sherman, R.E. 1977. Loss reserve adequacy testing: a comprehehsive, systematic approach. *PCAS/64*: 123-185

Bornheutter, R.L., and Ferguson, R.E. 1972. The actuary and IBNR. *PCAS/59*: 181-195

Davidson, S., Stickney, C., and Weil, R. 1982. *Financial Accounting: An Introduction to Concepts, Methods, and Uses.* New York: The Dryden Press

Degerness, J. 1983. Recognition of claim department impact on reserving. *1983 Casualty Loss Reserve Seminar Transcript:* 610-617

Finger, R.J. 1986. Modeling loss reserve development. *PCAS/63*: 90-106

Fisher W., and Lange, J. 1973. Loss reserve testing: a report year approach. *PCAS/60*: 189-207

Hayne, R.M. 1988. Application of collective risk theory to estimate variability in loss reserves. *1988 CAS Discussion Paper Program:* 275-300

Marker, J.O., and Mohl, F.J. 1980. Rating claims-made insurance policies. *1980 CAS Discussion Paper Program:* 265-304

McClenahan, C.L. 1975. A mathematical model for loss reserve analysis. *PCAS/26*: 134-153

---1988. Liabilities for extended reporting endorsements guarantees under claims-made policies. *1988 Discussion Paper Program:* 345-364

Mohl, F.J. 1987. Reserving for claims-made policies. *1987 Casualty Loss Reserve Seminar Transcript:* 384-402

Philbrick, S.W. 1986. Reserve review of a reinsurance company. *1986 Discussion Paper Program:* 147-162

Simon, L.J. 1970. Distortion in IBNR factors. *PCAS/57*: 64

Taylor, G.D. 1977. Separation of inflation and other effects from the distribution of non-life insurance claim delays. *ASTIN Bulletin:/9*: 217-230.

Chapter 5
RISK CLASSIFICATION
by Robert J. Finger

Introduction

Risk classification involves concepts similar to those in ratemaking (Chapter 1) and individual risk rating (Chapter 2). Actuaries use risk classification primarily in ratemaking when there is not sufficient information to estimate a price for a given individual. In order to derive a price, individuals that are expected to have the same costs are grouped together. The actuary then calculates a price for the group and assumes that the price is applicable to all members of the group. This, in simple terms, is the substance of risk classification.

For purposes of this chapter, we define risk classification as the formulation of different premiums for the same coverage based on group characteristics. These characteristics are called rating variables. For automobile insurance, examples are geography and driver characteristics. Rating variations due to individual claim experience, as well as those due to limits of coverage and deductibles, will not be considered here as part of the classification problem.

Premiums should vary if the underlying costs vary. Costs may vary among groups for all of the elements of insurance cost and income: losses, expenses, investment income, and risk. For losses, as an example, groups may have varying accident frequency or varying average claim costs. Expenses may also differ among groups; in some lines, such as boiler and machinery, inspection expense is a major portion of the premium. Investment income may vary among groups; for example, some insureds may be sued more quickly (emergency physicians versus obstetricians) or claims may be settled more quickly. Finally, risk, defined as variation from the expected, may vary among different types of insureds. For example, more heterogeneous groups are subject to more adverse selection and, hence, more risk. In the remainder of this chapter, the term "costs" will refer to all of the above considerations.

In this chapter, we shall first consider the interaction between classifications and other rating mechanisms, such as exposure bases, marketing, underwriting, and individual risk rating. We shall then review the various criteria (actuarial, operational, social, and legal) for selecting rating variables. We then turn to historical examples of classification systems. Next, we examine measures of classification efficiency. Finally, we shall briefly review problems in and approaches to estimating class relativities. Readers interested in greater detail than provided in this chapter are referred to studies by the Stanford Research Institute (1976) and SRI International (1979).

Relationship To Other Rating Mechanisms

The classification process must be considered within the overall context of marketing, underwriting, and rating. The overall goal is to price an insured properly for a given coverage. This may be accomplished in different ways. Risk classification is one step in a process that makes significant pricing decisions in many ways.

Exposure Base

An important consideration is the exposure base. For personal automobile insurance, the exposure base is an insured car-year. For workers' compensation, exposure can be total payroll, hours worked, or limited payroll (i.e., payroll up to some limit for a given time period). Manual premiums are calculated as the exposure times a rate. For example, if payroll is $1 million and the rate is $5 per $100 of payroll, manual premium is $50,000.

Exposure bases should be as closely proportional to costs as possible. For example, consider workers' compensation, which has both medical and indemnity benefits. If a worker is injured, the worker's medical costs are paid and the worker receives indemnity payments for time lost from work. Indemnity benefits typically are calculated as two-thirds of wages, subject to a maximum equal to the statewide average wage. For example, assume the maximum benefit is $400 per week. If the worker's wages are $600 or more, the worker receives $400; if the wages are $450, the worker receives $300. The most appropriate exposure base would be hours worked for medical benefits, and limited payroll (limited to $600 per week per employee) for indemnity benefits. These exposure bases would be proportional to costs, assuming that all workers have the same accident frequency per hour worked and that average claim size is a function of wages. (It may be argued that accident frequency, the duration of indemnity benefits, or the total amount of medical expense is related to wages. If so, total payroll could be more accurate than hours worked or limited payroll.)

If all employers pay the same wages, or have proportionately the same number of workers at different wage levels, total payroll is an adequate exposure base. If one employer pays higher wages than another, however, total payroll is not as accurate an exposure base as the combination of hours worked and limited payroll. Because accident frequency or severity varies among different insureds, some element of cost variance remains to be rated by a classification system or other means.

Individual Risk Rating

As mentioned above, the goal in all pricing is to evaluate properly the potential costs. When the individual insured is large enough to have credible claims experience, that claims data can be used to modify the rate that would have been charged by a classification plan alone. If the classification plan is relatively simple, the credibility of the individual claim experience will be greater; if the classification plan is more accurate, the individual risk claim experience will have less credibility.

Schedule rating is often part of individual risk rating plans. Underwriters apply judgment to select credits or debits for various items on a schedule. These items are not quantifiable or not includable in a classification or experience rating plan. Schedule rating has the potential for predicting costs more accurately.

Marketing and Underwriting

Insurers may use different strategies for pricing business. As will be pointed out below, many factors that are related to cost potential cannot be objectively defined and rated. Instead of pricing these factors, insurers may adjust their marketing and underwriting practices to account for them.

Two common strategies are: (1) adjust price according to individual cost potential, and (2) accept an individual only if the existing price structure is adequate. (For more detail, see Glendenning and Holtom (1977) and Launie et al. (1976)). The former is more common where premiums are higher. With a larger account, more expense dollars, and more meaningful claims history, an underwriter may feel more comfortable in formulating an individual price.

An alternative to the second strategy is to have several different rate structures within the same insurance group. Due to rate laws, this often requires several different insurance companies. For example, one company in a group may charge standard rates; one charge 20% more; another charges 10% less than standard rates; and a fourth company charges 25% less than standard rates. Using all available information, the underwriter makes a judgment about which rate level is the most appropriate.

In the above case, the underwriter is working with an existing classification plan. Each rate level, presumably, has the level of class detail that can be supported by objective rating variables. The underwriter assesses all other relevant information, including difficult-to-quantify data, to fix the charged rate.

In practice, most insurers consider a certain number of insureds to be uninsurable. This can happen when the number of potential insureds with certain characteristics is so small that cost experience will not be credible. Along the same line, the insureds within any given group may be thought to be too heterogeneous. That is, there may be a greater risk in writing certain individuals because the cost may be much higher than the average (or measured) cost for the group. In both cases, the individual insureds are difficult to rate properly because there is not enough experience with analogous types of insureds.

Notwithstanding the above situation, insurers compete on price for larger individual risks and classes of business. An important consideration is the ability and propensity of insureds to shop for the best price. The more insureds shop, the more an insurer must refine its classification plan. Insurers also vary in their ability to select lower-cost insureds within a classification through underwriting. More successful insurers are said to be "skimming the cream".

When an insurer receives a disproportionate number of higher-cost insureds, relative to its classification plan, it is being adversely selected against. If the adverse selection continues, the insurer must either lose money, change its underwriting criteria, or increase its premiums. Such premium increases may induce the insurer's lower-cost insureds to move to another insurer, creating more adverse selection and producing a need for further premium increases. The insurer can become insolvent, unless it can adequately price its book of business.

In summary, premiums for the same coverage can vary among insureds because of exposure bases, individual risk rating plans, and marketing or underwriting approaches. Classification plans are one aspect, integrated with these others, of accurately pricing individual insureds.

Criteria For Selecting Rating Variables

Criteria for selecting variables may be summarized into the following categories: actuarial, operational, social, and legal. Following this discussion, we describe the ramifications of restricting the use of rating variables.

Actuarial Criteria

Actuarial criteria may also be called "statistical" criteria. They include accuracy, homogeneity, credibility, and reliability. Foremost is accuracy. Rating variables should be related to costs. If costs do not differ for different values of a rating variable, the usual methods for estimating rate relativities will produce the same relativity. In that case, the use of a variable adds to administrative expense, and possibly consumer confusion, but does not affect premiums. As an example, most insurers charge the same automobile insurance premiums for drivers between the ages of 30 and 50, not varying the premium by age. Presumably costs do not vary much by age, or cost variances are due to other identifiable factors. As a practical matter, insurers may gather and maintain cost information on a more detailed basis than the pricing structure; data are maintained so that premium differences may be introduced if there actually prove to be cost differences.

Accuracy is important for at least two reasons: the market mechanism and fairness. In a market economy, insurers that price their products more accurately can be more successful. Suppose, for example, that the cost (including a reasonable profit) of insuring Group A is $100 and the cost of insuring Group B is $200. If an insurer charges both groups $150, it is likely to be undersold in Group A by another insurer. The first insurer will tend to insure more people in Group B and, consequently, to lose money. Thus, when insurers can identify costs more accurately, they can compete more successfully. Greater accuracy generally requires more rating variables and a more detailed classification system.

Another reason for the importance of accuracy is fairness. In the example above, it would be fair for Group A members to pay $100 and Group B members to pay $200, because these are the costs of the goods and services provided to them. (Of course, if there are subgroups within Group A whose costs are $50, $150, and $250, it would be fairer to charge those costs to those subgroups). This concept is often called "actuarial fairness" and it is based on the workings of a market economy.

The second actuarial criterion is homogeneity. This means that all members of a group that receive the same rate or premium should have similar expected costs. As a practical matter, it is difficult to know if all group members do have similar costs. The reason for grouping is the lack of credibility of individual experience. Consequently, for many rating groups, subdivisions of the group may not have much more credibility than individual insureds.

The third actuarial criterion, alluded to above, is credibility. A rating group should be large enough to measure costs with sufficient accuracy. There will always be the desire to estimate costs for smaller groups or subdivisions, even down to the individual insured level. Random fluctuations in claims experience may make this difficult, however. There is an inherent trade-off between theoretical accuracy (i.e., the existence of premiums for smaller and smaller groups) and practical accuracy (i.e., consistent premiums over time).

The fourth actuarial criterion is reliability or predictive stability. Based on a given set of loss data, the apparent cost of different groups may be different. The differences, however, may be due to random fluctuations (analogous to the problem discussed under credibility, above). In addition, the cost differences may change over time. For example, historical cost differences between genders may diminish or disappear as societal roles change. Technology may also change relative cost differences.

In summary, actuarial classification criteria are used in an attempt to group individual insureds into groups that: (1) are relatively homogeneous (all group members have similar costs), (2) are sufficiently large to estimate relative cost differences (credibility), and (3) maintain stable mean costs over time (reliability).

Operational Criteria

Actuarial criteria must be tempered by practical or operational considerations. The most important consideration is that the rating variables have an objective definition. There should be little ambiguity, class definitions should be mutually exclusive and exhaustive, and the opportunity for administrative error should be minimized. For example, automobile insurance underwriters often talk of "maturity" and "responsibility" as important criteria for youthful drivers. These are difficult to define objectively and to apply consistently. The actual rating variables, age, gender, and marital status, may be proxies for the underlying sources of cost variation. Maturity might be a more accurate variable, but it is not practical.

Another important practical consideration is administrative expense. The cost of obtaining and verifying information may exceed the value of the additional accuracy. For example, driving mileage may be a very good indicator of cost. It is probably too expensive to obtain and verify, however. Assume that drivers driving under 7,500 miles per year cost 20% less than those who drive 7,501 to 12,000 miles, who in turn cost 20% less than those who drive more than 12,000 miles. Assume also that the middle group costs $100 per year and that it costs $20 per driver to obtain, process, and verify annual mileage data. In a system utilizing mileage, drivers driving under 7,500 would pay $100 (their previous cost of $80 plus $20 for the additional expense), the middle group would pay $120 and the highest cost group, $145. Nobody would pay less than before! Although this example may be extreme, it demonstrates that added expense to classify may not serve insureds (or insurers) any better than not classifying.

Another practical consideration, alluded to above, is verifiability. If insureds know that they can pay lower premiums by lying, some percentage of them will do so. The effect is to cause honest insureds to pay more than they should, to make up for the dishonest insureds that pay less than they should. There are practical trade-offs among verifiability, administrative expense, and accuracy. Few rating variables are free from manipulation by insureds. Insureds supply most insurance rating information and insurers verify it only to a limited extent. At some point, the expense saved by relying upon unverified information is outweighed by its inaccuracy. In practice, variables are added, at a tolerable cost, as long as they result in improved overall accuracy.

There are several other practical considerations in selecting rating variables. The variables should be intuitively related to costs. Age, in life insurance, is intuitively related (i.e., older people are more likely to die). Age in automobile insurance is less so. Younger operators may tend to be more reckless and older operators may tend to be less observant, but the correlation between age and these factors is less precise than with mortality. Intuitive relationships also improve acceptability, which will be discussed below.

When faced with the cost-verifiability issue, it is often better to use measures that are available for another purpose. If the variable is used only for insurance rating, it is more likely to be manipulated and it may be more difficult to verify. Payroll and sales records, for example, are kept for other purposes, such as taxation. These may be manipulated for those purposes, as well as insurance purposes, but such manipulation may be discouraged by the risk of criminal penalties or adverse relations with suppliers or bankers.

Still another practical consideration is the avoidance of extreme discontinuities. If Group A's rate is $100 and Group B's rate is $300, a Group B insured may obtain a significant premium reduction by qualifying for Group A rates. Thus the incentive to cheat and the expense to verify will be higher if there are fewer classes,with larger differences in premiums. It may be difficult in practice, however, to construct gradual changes in rates because there may be very small numbers of very high-cost insureds. Thus, for credibility purposes, there may be fewer classes, with widely differing rates.

Social Criteria

So far in this section we have discussed the actuarial goals of classification and some of the operational difficulties. Another limitation on classification is "social acceptability" or social considerations. A number of key issues, such as "causality," "controllability," and "affordability" have been the subject of public debate. We shall now briefly describe some of the public concerns.

Privacy is an important concern. People often are reluctant to disclose personal information. This affects accuracy of classification, verifiability, and administrative cost. In automobile insurance, for example, a psychological or behavioral profile might be strongly correlated with claims cost. (It might also be expensive to obtain.) Many people might resist this intrusiveness, however. Although Insurer A might achieve a more accurate rating system by using a psychological profile, the company might not obtain a sufficient amount of business. Insureds may choose to pay more to avoid disclosing personal information.

"Causality" implies an intuitive relationship to insurance costs. Assume there is some rating variable, X, which divides insureds into Groups A, B, C, etc. The rating variable is correlated with costs if the mean costs for the various groups are significantly different. There may be other variables for which there are similar correlations. The "real" reason for the differences in costs may be some entirely different variable or combination of variables. Nevertheless, X is correlated to the cost of providing insurance. X may be a proxy for the "real" cost difference.

"Causality" implies a closer relationship to costs than correlation. (See, for example, the study by the Massachusetts Division of Insurance (1978), p.22.) Mileage in automobile insurance might be considered a causal variable; the more miles a driver drives, the higher the cost of insurance should be (other things being equal). Loss costs can be divided into claim frequency and average claim cost. "Causal" variables, then, could be considered to be directly related to claim frequency or average claim cost. Automobile mileage, presumably, is proportional to claim frequency. Proximity to fire protection, in fire insurance, may be inversely proportional to the average claim cost.

Unfortunately, however, the categorization of variables as "causal" or "non-causal" is ambiguous. With automobile insurance, for example, where and when one drives may be more relevant to costs than mileage. Driving in a large city, with more vehicles, more intersections, and more distractions is probably more hazardous than driving in rural areas. Driving at night or when tired or drunk may be more hazardous than driving in daytime or when fully rested or sober. From an actuarial point of view, correlated variables provide more accurate premiums and are thus more desirable in a competitive market place. Eliminating correlated non-causal variables may produce a less accurate rating system and cause certain market corrections. Those will be discussed later.

"Controllability" may be a desirable rating-variable characteristic. A controllable variable is one which is under the control of the insured. If the insured moderates behavior in a certain way, premiums will be reduced. For example, by installing burglar alarms, the insured reduces claims cost potential and should receive some discount. The use of controllable rating variables encourages accident prevention.

From a practical viewpoint, there may not be very many useful controllable variables. The make and model of automobile in physical damage insurance is controllable. Geographical location is controllable in a broad sense, but not very useful in making day-to-day or short-term decisions. Moving a warehouse or petroleum refinery is not practical; nevertheless, the decision to locate a structure is controllable and insurance costs may be a factor in the decision. Driver-training course credits for automobile insurance are also controllable, but most people may qualify for them, reducing the effect of this variable on rate variations.

Controllable variables may increase administrative costs. If the insured has control over premium costs, the insured can manipulate the rating system and insurers may require verification. As with "causality", "controllability" is a useful concept but there is a shortage of usable rating variables that apply.

Another social consideration is "affordability". In the context of risk classification, it usually arises where classification schemes are more refined, with the attendant spreading of rates. Thus, high rates are often seen as causing affordability problems (even if, for example, the high rate is generated by a youthful operator driving a Corvette in New York City). Another example is the correlation of incomes and insurance rates. In automobile insurance, rates are often highest in urban areas, where, allegedly, most poor people live. In reality, wealthy people also live in urban areas; youthful drivers that can afford any car or a high-priced car probably are not poor. Thus both high rates, per se, and higher rates for lower-income groups pose an affordability concern.

Another aspect of the affordability issue is the necessity of insurance. Many states require automobile liability insurance. Most mortgagors require property insurance. Of course, owning a car or a house is optional. Still another aspect of affordability is availability. If rates are arbitrarily leveled or reduced below cost, the market may not voluntarily provide coverage. Thus rates may be "affordable" but insurers may be very reluctant to insure people at those rates.

Except for the affordability issue, these social issues are based on accuracy arguments. The basic limitations on accuracy are the competitiveness of the insurance industry and the credibility of the cost information. These factors are related in some cases. As long as the insurance industry is competitive, there are incentives (profitability, solvency) to price individual insureds accurately. These incentives may be minimal, however, for small groups of heterogeneous insureds. Restrictions on competition are unlikely to produce a more accurate rating system. The ramifications of restrictions will be discussed after a brief review of legal considerations.

Legal Criteria

We have now considered actuarial, practical, and social considerations. We now turn to the legal context of risk classifications. The following discussion is necessarily brief, but it provides an overview. The circumstances of each particular case (e.g., rating variable, line of insurance, state statutes, and constitutions), will determine its outcome. The following is based on general concepts and principles.

Risk classification may be affected by constitutions (state and federal), statutes, and regulations. Generally, constitutions govern statutes and statutes govern regulations. Constitutions are usually very general, statutes are more specific, and regulations may be the most specific.

Both federal and state constitutions may apply to a risk classification situation. There must, however, be a specific phrase or section that is applicable. The federal constitution is quite broad and vague. The "equal protection clause" ("EPC") might be applicable. Other clauses probably are not. State constitutions are often more specific. Gender discrimination, for example, is specifically mentioned in several state constitutions.

The federal equal protection clause, in the 14th Amendment to the Constitution, reads: "No State shall make or enforce any law which shall . . . deny to any person within its jurisdiction the equal protection of the laws." This points to two requirements: (1) state or governmental action and (2) unequal treatment. "State action" generally means that the state has acted, either on its own or by officially sanctioning the conduct of private individuals. Purely private discrimination is usually not actionable under the EPC. With insurance, the requisite state action is probably the promulgation of rates; the mere approval of or acquiescence in rates probably is not state action. If rates are not regulated at all, rating classifications are probably exempt from the EPC.

Unequal treatment is also a requirement under the EPC. Arguably, basing premium differences on demonstrable cost differences is not unequal treatment.

Because of the requirement of governmental action, constitutional challenges to insurance rating classifications are unlikely to succeed. Statutes, however, can impose restrictions on insurers. In this case, it is the insurers who will try to invoke constitutional provisions to invalidate the statutes. Several other clauses of the U.S. Constitution, such as "due process," "takings", and "contracts" may be applicable. As a general rule, however, courts have been very deferential towards legislatures in their regulation of businesses. Most likely, any statutory restriction on rating variables would be constitutional.

Finally, regulations issued by state insurance departments may affect classifications. Under a constitutional theory (known as the "delegation doctrine") only the legislature may promulgate substantive law; the executive branch merely carries out the will of the legislature. Although states vary considerably, broad discretionary grants of power to executive agencies may be found unconstitutional. Thus insurance commissioners may only be able to act within guidelines provided by legislatures.

In summary, constitutional provisions, statutes, and insurance department regulations all potentially may affect the freedom of insurers to select and use rating variables. As this brief discussion indicates, constitutional provisions are probably not applicable; statutes are practically invulnerable; and regulations may or may not be subject to challenge by insurers.

Ramifications Of Restrictions

Legislatures may abolish the use of certain rating variables or rate variations may be restricted. The consequence will be similar for each, although more extreme for abolition. The discussion below deals with abolition. Insurers can react in three ways: pricing, marketing, and underwriting. In pricing, they can try to find replacement variables. As stated above, there may not be many variables that are suitable, given the above actuarial, operational, and social criteria. Insurers do have incentives to create better variables; they thus may consider the current ones to be the best available. If no replacement variables are found, rates will be levelled and subsidies created. For example, if Group A's cost is $50 and Group B's cost is $150, but the distinction between them cannot be used in rating, both groups may pay $100. Group A would be overcharged by $50 and Group B would be subsidized by $50.

The effect of abolishing rating variables in a competitive market is to create availability problems, unless there are suitable replacement variables. Insurers may withdraw from marketing the coverage to certain groups or refuse to insure them. This will produce, most likely, a larger residual market. Residual markets, such as assigned risk plans in automobile insurance, exist to provide insurance to those not voluntarily insured. Abolition of variables may also affect insurer profitability and solvency. If an insurer, in the above example, has a large percentage of Group B business, it will need to raise its rates or else it will be unprofitable. If it raises its rates, it may drive more of its better business to competitors who have lower rates; this will further increase its costs and require a further rate increase. Eventually, solvency may be threatened.

Abolition of rating variables has social consequences, as well. To some extent, abolition will create subsidies. Insurers may voluntarily insure underpriced groups. Otherwise, residual markets will expand;

since most residual markets are subsidized by the voluntary market, subsidies will be created. Such subsidies, deriving from legislation, are a tax-in-kind. Certain insureds pay more for insurance than they otherwise would have, while others pay less. There is a redistribution of income from the disfavored group to the favored group.

In addition to the subsidies, abolition of rating variables can reduce accident prevention incentives. That is, to the extent accurate pricing promotes accident prevention, less accurate pricing reduces it.

Thus the abolition of rating variables probably will reduce the accuracy of the rating system, which either creates subsidies or else produces availability problems. In either case, accident prevention incentives are reduced.

Examples Of Classification Systems

So far in this chapter, we have discussed the general principles for developing classification systems. In this section, specific systems, with particular emphasis on automobile insurance, will be discussed. To be concrete, some assumptions will be made that may not be widely accepted within either the actuarial profession or the insurance industry. The objective is not to specify all of the relevant factors and only relevant factors, but to present an approach that a knowledgeable actuary may follow. Risk classification is a difficult subject area. In theory, not enough is known about either the underlying causes of loss or the variations in costs between insureds. In practice, there is never enough data for formulating and testing hypotheses. More research needs to be done.

Forces Affecting Classification Systems

Classification systems vary over time. Automobile liability originally had only one classification. By World War II there were three classes (adult, youthful operator, and business use). These became refined into nine classes by subdividing the youthful class and adding more use categories. In 1965, the National Bureau of Casualty Underwriters (a rating bureau, the predecessor to today's Insurance Services Office) introduced a plan which had 260 classifications. In 1970, the number of classes was reduced to 217. Most of the classifications were for youthful operators.

Many forces, chiefly those related to competition, influence classification plans. Generally, the more competitive the marketplace, the more classifications there will be. Assume one insurer charges the same rate, $100, to Groups A and B, but their costs are different, $50 for A and $150 for B. Another insurer could charge Group A $50 and still be profitable. Thus, to the extent insurers can actually identify cost differences, they will tend to make price differentials. Not to do so affects their profitability and, ultimately, their solvency.

Classification systems may also become more refined as coverage becomes more expensive. From the buyer's side, shopping for favorable prices is encouraged when coverage is more expensive. From the insurer's side, more expense dollars may be available to classify and underwrite; in addition, the cost of making mistakes, or of not having as refined a system, is higher when premiums are higher. For example, towing coverage may be priced the same for all automobiles, even though older cars may be more likely to break down and towing costs may be higher in rural areas; at a low premium (e.g. $10 per year), it may not be cost effective to have rate differentials.

Classification systems usually are more refined for larger markets. Considering the credibility of available cost data, more classifications can be supported by larger amounts of insured exposure.

Finally, classification systems have probably become more refined as information technology has progressed. More information can be handled more cost-effectively today than in the past. Let us now turn to automobile insurance classifications.

Automobile Liability Insurance Classifications

Automobile liability insurance classifications can be categorized into the following types of variables: (1) age-gender-marital status, (2) use, (3) geography, and (4) others. Classification plans vary significantly among insurers. (See SRI 1976.) Certain types of factors are widely used; many factors are used by only a few insurers.

Age-gender-marital status primarily distinguishes among youthful operators, although most insurers have a separate class for drivers over 65. Youthful operators generally are those under 25, although most insurers separate single males under 30. Some insurers have separate classes for each age; some group ages, such as 17 to 20 and 21 to 24. Most insurers distinguish between single male principal operators (using the automobile 50% or more) and occasional operators. Many insurers distinguish between single and married female operators, and between principal and other operators for females and married males.

Use categories typically are: pleasure, drive to work (sometimes over or under a given number of miles, one-way, such as 10), business, and farm. Added to this may be annual driving mileage over or under a given amount (such as 7,500). Use categories may vary between adult and youthful operators.

Geographical territories are commonly used in classification plans. Contiguous areas, often delineated by city or county boundaries, are the most common. Some insurers use zip codes, sometimes combining adjacent areas or using some other criteria (such as population density). Territories are the same for all age-gender-marital status classes and all use classes. Territories sometimes vary by coverage. For example, there may be fewer claims for uninsured motorist coverage, so there are fewer separate rating territories.

Several other rating variables are in common use. These include good student and driver training discounts for youthful operators; multiple-car discounts; accident and violation surcharges, and sports car surcharges.

In addition to the above variables, several other variables are used for automobile physical damage insurance. These generally relate to the value of the automobile, its crashworthiness, and its age. Most insurers use the make and model of the car; various makes and models are combined into a series of different rate groups.

Cost Variation in Automobile Insurance

Above are the classification variables that are commonly used in automobile insurance. Some are "causal"-type variables; others are correlated to costs. Below, we will discuss potential reasons for cost differences. Some of these are incorporated into rating variables, while others are used only in underwriting (i.e., risk selection or rejection).

Cost differences can be classified into four broad categories: (1) use of the automobile, (2) driving ability, (3) interaction with the claims mechanism, and (4) the extent of damages. In many of these areas, the available evidence is more subjective than objective. What is presented is thought to be relevant to costs, even though concrete data may be elusive.

Different uses of the automobile contribute to varying cost potential. More driving should produce more exposure to liability and collision claims. Driving conditions (time of day, traffic density, weather) are also important. Automobile theft is a significant factor for comprehensive coverage, therefore location of the car in higher crime neighborhoods is relevant for that coverage.

Mileage may be used directly in rating, although commonly the only distinctions are annual mileage over or under a given amount and mileage to work. Indirectly, mileage may be correlated with multiple-car discounts and some age-gender-marital status classifications. For example, over 65 drivers may drive less or under more favorable conditions; females may drive less than males; married males may drive less than single males. Driving conditions are taken into account, at least indirectly, in geographical territories. The territory is usually defined by the principal garage, which may differ, of course, from where the car is usually operated. Driving conditions are considered more directly in the use variables.

Cost differences may be due to differences in driving ability, arising from familiarity with the driving conditions, experience and training, reaction time, eyesight and hearing, concentration, condition of the automobile, and driving style. Some classification variables are related indirectly to these cost differences. For example, youthful operators have less familiarity and less experience; over-65 drivers may have poorer eyesight or hearing; discounts for driver training are available. Admittedly, individual performance varies greatly within the given rating classes.

Cost differences may also arise from interactions with the claims mechanism. Some people are more claims-conscious than others. This affects the physical damage, personal injury protection, and medical payments coverages for the insured. Geographical differences may be more apparent for liability coverages. Some people may be treated more or less sympathetically by a jury. Some people may press dishonest claims. Some people may be more cooperative in submitting claims or in helping to defend claims. Most of these differences are quite subjective and difficult to quantify in a rating variable. Where higher costs can be discerned, it is more likely that insurers would refuse to insure an individual, rather than try to determine an accurate rate.

Finally, cost differences may result from the extent of damages, given that an accident has occurred. Crashworthiness of the automobile is an obvious rating variable. The same type of accident may produce \$100 of damage in one car and \$1000 of damage in another. The speed with which a car is driven will also affect damages. The use of safety devices, such as air bags or seat belts, will affect costs. Physical impairments may produce higher loss costs. Some of these differences may only be relevant to certain coverages.

To some extent, existing rating variables consider these differences in costs. Sports cars are often surcharged, presumably because they are driven at higher speeds, are prone to greater damage, cause greater damage, or are more prone to trigger lawsuits.

In summary, a variety of factors have been presented that affect claims costs. Some of these are more objective and lend themselves more readily to becoming rating variables. Many factors, however, are quite subjective, very difficult to measure, and almost infeasible as rating variables; underwriters tend to use these factors to decline coverage or assign to a higher-rated company in the group.

To conclude this section, we briefly mention other lines of business. Most lines of business use geographical rating. Workers' compensation classes are mostly based on occupations or industries. There are some 600 different classes used by the National Council on Compensation Insurance in one or more states. Medical malpractice classes are based on specialties, with particular attention to the type of surgery performed, if any. Boiler and machinery rates vary by type of object, because inspection costs are a significant element of the premium. Products liability classes are defined by the type of product. Premises liability is defined by the character of the operation or activity. Homeowners and dwelling fire rating variables include the number of units in the structure and the age and type of the structure. Fire insurance rates are based on the type of construction, type of occupancy, protection features, and special exposure to loss.

Measures Of Efficiency

The quantitative description of the accuracy of classification systems has concerned actuaries for many years. Recently, however, public debate on risk classification has encouraged new research and analysis. This section defines "efficiency" as a measure of a classification system's accuracy.

The reason for classification systems is the variability in costs from one insured to another. The key to measuring efficiency is understanding this variability. Costs vary because claim frequency varies and because claim sizes vary. A perfect classification system would produce the same variability as the insured population. Conversely, a classification system that has less variability than the insured population cannot be perfect, because two insureds may receive the same rate when their costs are actually different.

A complicating factor is the fortuitous nature of insurance. Costs are unknown. When measurements are made of cost variability, it is after certain events have already happened. The same events probably will not happen again. It is uncertain whether the actual events that occurred are representative of what will occur in the future. The future may have more or less variability than the past.

Most existing measures of classification efficiency use the statistical measure of variance. Other measures are possible, including the average deviation and the average absolute deviation. Variance has the advantage of being widely used in many types of statistical applications (e.g., regression analysis and analysis of variance). This section will use variance concepts as an operational measure of efficiency, but other measures could be used.

Likewise, there are many possible formulas for efficiency. The measure most commonly used compares the variance explained by the classification system to the total variance underlying the insured population. (See SRI 1976 and Woll 1979.) If the classification system were perfect, the efficiency would be 100%. If the classifications had no predictive value (i.e., were random with respect to potential costs), the efficiency would be 0%.

This formula requires the calculation of two items: (1) the variance of the classification system and (2) the variance of the insured population. The former is relatively easy to calculate; the latter is unknowable. Each will be discussed in turn.

To determine the variability of the class plan, one needs the class relativities and the percentage of exposures by class. It is assumed that the relativities are the expected values of actual cost differences; if not, the latter should be used instead.

Although formulated in terms of "variance", efficiency can be measured by other numerical calculations. For simplicity, in this chapter we use the concept of the coefficient of variation, or CV, which is the standard deviation divided by the mean. The square of the CV can be used to measure efficiency, as proposed above, in terms of variance. (It is assumed that both the class plan costs and the underlying population costs have the same mean; if not, adjustments can be made.)

For a numerical example, see the table below.

Relativity	Percentage of Exposures	Mean (Extension)	Deviation From Mean	Deviation Squared	Variance (Extension)
.5	.10	.05	1.0	1.00	.1000
1.0	.40	.40	0.5	0.25	.1000
1.5	.30	.45	0.0	0.00	.0000
2.0	.10	.20	0.5	0.25	.0250
3.0	.05	.15	1.5	2.25	.1125
5.0	.05	.25	3.5	12.25	.6125
Total	1.00	1.50			.9500

The coefficient of variation is the standard deviation (.975) divided by the mean (1.5), or 0.65. This numerical example points out several truisms. First, high efficiencies necessarily require extreme rates. Almost two-thirds of the variance is due to the highest cost 5% of insureds. Second, the key to designing highly efficient systems is to find variables that can isolate the highest and lowest cost individuals. Many insured populations seem to have a coefficient of variation of about 1.0. [See SRI (1976).] If this is true for the numerical example above, the efficiency would be about 42% ($.65^2$).

The basic difficulty in computing efficiency is determining the variability of the insured population. Because costs depend upon fortuitous events, the variability is unknowable. It is possible to apply concepts of risk theory, however, to develop some plausible estimates.

The basic types of variability that should be considered are:

- inherent variability in expected accident frequency,
- inherent variability in expected claim size,
- variability in frequency and claim size for an individual insured over time, and
- variability in the actual frequency and claim size, given the expected values.

The list could go on, but it already contains enough substance to challenge the mathematically sophisticated. Few practical applications have involved variability in claim sizes. Most published research includes only expected and actual claim frequency. Woll (1979) has mentioned changing individual frequency over time. (Woll refers to this as the individual's exposure to loss, which he treats as a stochastic process.) Woll's approach can also be extended to pure premiums.

The underlying variability will be measured from actual claim experience. Any such measurement, of course, will only be accurate if the actual data derives from a suitable situation. It is subject to random fluctuations, since the actual data are the result of random processes.

To provide a framework for the measurement, Woll (1979) defines X as the actual number of claims; M, as the distribution of expected frequency for the individual insureds; and P, as the distribution of the individual insured's frequency over time. He derives the following formula:

$$\mathrm{Var}(X) = \mathrm{Var}(M) + \mathrm{E}(M) + \mathrm{E}(Var(P))$$

What is required is Var(*M*), the underlying variability in expected claim frequency (or pure premium). Woll gives four formulas for calculating Var(*M*). These are illustrated in Exhibit I:

EXHIBIT I

NUMBER OF DRIVERS WITH X_i CLAIMS

	First Period Count				First Period	
Second Period Count	**0**	**1**	**2**	**Total**	**Count**	**Frequency**
0	753	135	55	943	245	.2598
1	38	11	4	53	19	.3585
2	2	1	1	4	3	.7500
Total Drivers	793	147	60	1000	267	.2670
Claim Count (second)	42	13	6	61		
(1) Frequency *a(j)*	.0530	.0884	.1000	.0610 = E(*X*) (second)		
(2) Deviation	−.267	.733	1.733			
Deviation Squared	.0713	.5373	3.0033			
(3) Variance (Extension)	.0565	.0790	.1802	.3157 = Var(*X*) (first)		
(4) Frequency ratio	4.377 = *t*					

Notes:

(1) Count ÷ drivers.
(2) Count–overall frequency (.2670) (first period).
(3) Sum over first period counts (percentage of drivers times deviation squared).
(4) First period (.2670) to second period (.0610).

In the above Exhibit, 1000 drivers are observed over two periods. They are categorized by the number of claims in the first and second periods. The first formula was used by SRI and assumes no variation in loss costs over time. This formula almost certainly overestimates the underlying variance, because individual insured frequency varies over time. Data do not need to be grouped for the two different periods, in order to make this calculation.

The next two formulas use the frequency of first period loss-free insureds in the second period. They depend upon linearity in the distribution of insured frequency. The second uses the difference in frequency between insureds with zero and one prior accidents. The third multiplies the claim-free discount by the variance of the observed frequency. The fourth is due to Woll and is the most accurate. $a(j)$ is the claim frequency for insureds with j prior claims. r_j is the percentage of insureds with j prior claims. Note that $E(M) = E(X)$. t is the ratio of claim frequency for the first period to the second period. The first three formulas could use data from either the first period or the second period, as long as consistency is maintained.

$$
\begin{aligned}
(1)\ \mathrm{Var}(M) &= \mathrm{Var}(X) - \mathrm{E}(X) \\
&= .3157 - .2670 \\
&= .0487 \\
\mathrm{E}(M) &= .267 \\
\mathrm{CV}(M) &= .827 \\
(2)\ \mathrm{Var}(M) &= [\mathrm{E}(M)]^2 \frac{a(1) - a(0)}{a(0)} \\
&= .267^2 \frac{(.0884) - (.0530)}{.0530} \\
&= .0476 \\
\mathrm{E}(M) &= .267 \\
\mathrm{CV}(M) &= .817 \\
(3)\ \mathrm{Var}(M) &= \frac{[1 - a(0)]}{\mathrm{E}(X)} \mathrm{Var}(X) \\
&= \frac{[1 - .053]}{.061} .3157 \\
&= .0414 \\
\mathrm{CV}(M) &= .762 \\
(4)\ \mathrm{Var}(M) &= \sum_{j=0} j \, \frac{r_j\, a(j)}{t} - \mathrm{E}(X)^2 \\
&= 1(.147) \frac{(.0884)}{4.377} + 2(.060) \frac{(1000)}{4.377} - .06 \\
&= .0020 \\
\mathrm{E}(M) &= .061 \\
\mathrm{CV}(M) &= .731
\end{aligned}
$$

Other formulas are certainly available. These formulas can be used to estimate heterogeneity of individual classes as well as the overall population. Since these data were limited to two claims, actual data will probably produce higher CV's.

The claim-free discount is a measure of heterogeneity within a class. It can be estimated by taking one minus the ratio of: (1) the frequency of period one claim-free insureds in period two to (2) the overall frequency in period two. If there were no difference in the period two frequencies, frequency would be purely fortuitous within the class and no claim-free discount would be indicated. If the indicated claim-free discount is large, it indicates that claim experience is very meaningful and insureds without claims are significantly different in cost potential.

Measures of efficiency, even if they can be calculated with accuracy and consistency, do not provide a complete answer. The cost of the classification process itself is ignored, for example. Operational and social criteria also may be important. The availability of a feasible, more accurate system is unknown. Efficiency may be low in any given case, but no better system may be available at a reasonable cost. If efficiency is lower, however, it is an indication that there is greater potential to introduce better variables.

What are the implications of efficiency measures for the design of classification systems? To produce a higher efficiency there must be a higher percentage of insureds at more extreme relativities. This is necessary to produce a higher variance or CV. This process, however, runs counter to much public criticism of the insurance industry. Higher rates mean less affordability. In addition, greater efficiency can be produced by any variable that can accurately refine the classification system. Thus, the preference for causal variables is irrelevant to increased efficiency; correlated variables can be just as efficient if they can distinguish cost potential. Similarly, controllable variables are useless unless they can produce greater efficiency. Indeed, controllability and causality are irrelevant; what is important to efficiency is being correlated with costs.

Risk classification efficiency can be approached from another point of view. Insurers have economic incentives to accurately classify insureds. The classification system should be as good as the market allows. In other words, if a group is too small to have credible experience or poses too great a risk (in that there is too much variability in costs within the group), the group may not be very accurately rated. If the group is large and relatively homogeneous, insurers have an incentive to properly classify and rate it.

In summary, existing efficiency measures are a comparison to an abstract ideal. Although they provide an indication of potential improvement, they do not provide useful information about what specific, practical, cost-effective variables might be utilized.

Estimating Class Relativities

In this final section, we begin by describing two general methods of calculating class relativities: a loss ratio approach and a pure premium approach. We then discuss several actuarial problems involved in estimating classification relativities. These include: 1) whether relativities should be additive or multiplicative, 2) how to obtain more and more reliable data, and 3) how to select the appropriate credibility complement for groups with less than fully credible data. This topic was also discussed earlier.

Insurers typically use relativities for classification variables, rather than pure rates, because they are used in different contexts. For example, relativities between classes are likely to be the same from state to state, even though the absolute value of the rate may be quite different. For example, State A may have double the medical malpractice costs of State B. The relativity in costs between general surgeons and general practitioners (with no surgery), however, may be about 5 to 1 in both states.

Data and Approaches

The usual data used for determining class relativities is earned premium or exposure and incurred losses. Severity and frequency may also be considered in selecting relativities, as will be discussed later. In addition, claim counts are often used to determine credibility. Both premium and claim data must be coded with the required classification detail. Policy year or calendar-accident year data can be used; the latter may require special steps to calculate earned premiums or exposures.

When earned premium is used, the method is usually a "loss ratio" method; when earned exposures are used, the method is usually a "pure premium" approach. The loss ratio method can produce equivalent results if "earned premiums at current rates" are calculated. The most accurate approaches require that premium or exposure data be available down to the level of the variables under review. That is, if class and territorial relativities are going to be adjusted, premium or exposure for every combination of class and territory is needed. In some lines of insurance, there are several independent sets of rating variables. In automobile physical damage, for example, there are separate relativities for class (driver and use), territory, age and make of automobile, and coverage (e.g., deductibles). Indeed, there may be separate relativities within the class structure (e.g., for driver training discounts or use). It would be most accurate to simultaneously adjust each set of relativities.

There are advantages and disadvantages of using the loss ratio and pure premium methods. The loss ratio method may be applicable when there is less detailed data available or when there are many different sets of relativities; earned premiums will reflect the various charges made for different classes, territories, and coverages. If earned premiums correspond to historical rate levels, however, it may be difficult to make adjustments for intervening changes in rate relativities. The pure premium approach is usually more accurate, because it requires more information. It also has the advantage of producing frequency and severity relativities, as well as pure premium relativities; the loss ratio method only produces loss ratio and severity relativities. Severity relativities, however, will not be meaningful if the underlying coverage is not consistent (e.g., there are differing deductibles or insured limits).

Loss Ratio Approach

Exhibit II illustrates a loss ratio approach for territorial rates.

EXHIBIT II

TERRITORIAL RELATIVITIES — LOSS RATIO APPROACH

Territory	(1) Earned Premium	(2) Incurred Losses	(3) Claim Count	(4) Severity	(5) Loss Ratio	(6) Indicated Adjustment
A	1,559,200	1,037,495	676	1,535	66.5%	0.987
B	505,438	346,122	242	1,430	68.5%	1.016
C	362,700	252,909	223	1,134	69.7%	1.034
Total	2,427,338	1,636,526	1141	1434	67.4%	

Territory	(7) Credibility	(8) Credible Adjustment	(9) Extension	(10) Balanced Adjustment	(11) Extension
A	0.790	0.990	1,543,106	0.992	1,547,377
B	0.473	1.007	509,192	1.010	510,602
C	0.454	1.016	368,339	1.018	369,358
Total		1.003	2,420,638		2,427,337

	Year 1		Year 2			
Territory	(12) Premium	(13) Base Rate	(14) Premium	(15) Base Rate	(16) Experience Relativity	(17) New Relativity
A	790,000	100	769,200	120	1.000	1.000
B	256,500	60	248,938	70	0.592	0.602
C	135,450	45	227,250	50	0.429	0.440
Total	1,181,950		1,245,388			

Notes:

(4) = (2)/(3)
(5) = (2)/(1)
(6) = (5)/TOTAL (5)
(7) = SQRT (3)/1,082
(8) = ((6)–1)(7) + 1
(9) = (1)(8)
(10) = (8)TOTAL (8)
(11) = (1)(10)
(16) = [(12)(13)/(13–A) + (14)(15)/(15–A)] / [(12) + (14)]
(17) = (16)(10)/ [(16–A)(10–A)]

The given state has three territories. It is assumed that the overall statewide level change has been determined independently. Thus, adjustments of territorial rates must balance each other. The first step is to compare loss ratios. If a territory's loss ratio has been higher than the overall average, its relative rate should be increased. The "indicated adjustment" is the ratio of individual territory loss ratio to the statewide average loss ratio.

In many cases, the rates for a given territory may not be entirely credible. The most common practice is to reduce deviations from the existing rates by a credibility factor. In effect, the credibility complement is the existing rate relativity. After application of the credibility factor, the adjustments may not balance. Thus a separate step is necessary to keep the changes balanced. New relativities are calculated as the old relativity times the balanced adjustment factor. Exhibit III shows the same process for classification rates.

EXHIBIT III
CLASS RELATIVITIES — LOSS RATIO APPROACH

Class	(1) Earned Premium	(2) Incurred Losses	(3) Claim Count	(4) Severity	(5) Loss Ratio	(6) Indicated Adjustment
1	377,500	259,800	361	720	68.8%	1.021
2	129,600	89,820	114	788	69.3%	1.028
3	212,413	128,601	199	646	60.5%	0.898
4	319,850	206,800	278	744	64.7%	0.959
5	321,775	217,170	278	781	67.5%	1.001
6	195,475	153,125	231	663	78.3%	1.162
7	249,075	158,130	246	643	63.5%	0.942
8	280,550	181,320	308	589	64.6%	0.959
9	341,100	241,760	410	590	70.9%	1.051
Total	2,427,338	1,636,526	2,425	675	67.4%	

Class	(7) Credibility	(8) Credible Adjustment	(9) Extension	(10) Balanced Adjustment	(11) Extension
1	0.578	1.012	382,030	1.011	381,685
2	0.325	1.009	130,776	1.008	130,658
3	0.429	0.956	203,120	0.955	202,937
4	0.507	0.979	313,200	0.978	312,917
5	0.507	1.001	321,946	1.000	321,655
6	0.462	1.075	210,096	1.074	209,906
7	0.477	0.972	242,146	0.971	241,927
8	0.534	0.978	274,355	0.977	274,107
9	0.616	1.032	351,863	1.031	351,545
Total		0.999	2,429,532		2,427,338

TERRITORIAL RELATIVITIES — LOSS RATIO APPROACH

	(12)	(13)	(14)	(15)	(16)	(17)
	Year 1		Year 2		Experience	New
Class	Premium	Relativity	Premium	Relativity	Relativity	Relativity
1	186,000	1.00	191,500	1.00	1.000	1.000
2	63,000	0.90	66,600	0.90	0.900	0.914
3	102,300	1.10	110,113	1.15	1.126	1.084
4	156,000	1.50	163,850	1.45	1.474	1.453
5	150,300	1.80	171,475	1.90	1.853	1.867
6	97,600	1.60	97,875	1.50	1.550	1.677
7	127,000	2.00	122,075	1.90	1.951	1.909
8	136,250	2.50	144,300	2.60	2.551	2.512
9	163,500	3.00	177,600	3.20	3.104	3.224
Total	1,181,950		1,245,388			

Notes:

(4) = (2)/(3)
(5) = (2)/(1)
(6) = (5)/TOTAL (5)
(7) = SQRT (3)/1,082
(8) = ((6)–1)(7) + 1
(9) = (1)(8)
(10) = (8)TOTAL (8)
(11) = (1)(10)
(16) = [(12)(13)/(13–A) + (14)(15)/(15–A)] / [(12) + (14)]
(17) = (16)(10)/ [(16–A)(10–A)]

Pure Premium Approach

Exhibit IV shows the same process for territorial rates using a pure premium approach.

EXHIBIT IV

TERRITORIAL RELATIVITIES — PURE PREMIUM APPROACH FIRST ITERATION

Territory	(1) Earned Exposures	(2) Base Exposures	(3) Incurred Losses	(4) Claim Count	(5) Frequency	(6) Severity	(7) Pure Premium
A	9,000	14,423	1,037,495	676	4.7%	1,535	71.94
B	5,500	4,538	346,122	242	5.3%	1,428	76.28
C	5,000	3,182	252,909	223	7.0%	1,135	79.49
Total	19,500	22,142	1,636,526	1,141	5.2%		73.91

Territory	(8) Indicated Adjustment	(9) Current Relativity	(10) New Relativity
A	0.973	1.000	1.000
B	1.032	0.583	0.619
C	1.076	0.417	0.460

Notes:

(2) Based on current rating factors
(5) = (4)/(2)
(6) = (3)/(4)
(7) = (3)/(2)
(8) = (7)/TOTAL (7)
(10) = (8)(9)

Exhibit V shows the same process for class rates.

EXHIBIT V

CLASS RELATIVITIES — PURE PREMIUM APPROACH FIRST ITERATION

Class	(1) Earned Exposures	(2) Base Exposures	(3) Incurred Losses	(4) Claim Count	(5) Frequency	(6) Severity	(7) Pure Premium
1	4,250	3,439	259,800	361	10.5%	720	75.55
2	2,050	1,168	89,820	114	9.8%	788	76.89
3	2,125	1,977	128,601	199	10.1%	646	65.03
4	3,000	2,839	206,800	278	9.8%	744	72.84
5	2,575	2,969	217,170	278	9.4%	781	73.15
6	1,775	1,708	153,125	231	13.5%	663	89.66
7	1,425	2,213	158,130	246	11.1%	643	71.47
8	1,150	2,613	181,320	308	11.8%	589	69.39
9	1,150	3,216	241,760	410	12.7%	590	75.17
Total	19,500	22,142	1,636,526	2,425	11.0%		73.91

Class	(8) Indicated Adjustment	(9) Current Relativity	(10) New Relativity
1	1.022	1.000	1.000
2	1.040	0.900	0.916
3	0.880	1.150	0.990
4	0.986	1.450	1.398
5	0.990	1.900	1.840
6	1.213	1.500	1.780
7	0.967	1.900	1.797
8	0.939	2.600	2.388
9	1.017	3.200	3.184

Notes:

(2) Based on current rating factors
(5) = (4)/(2)
(6) = (3)/(4)
(7) = (3)/(2)
(8) = (7)/TOTAL (7)
(10) = (8)(9)

It should be noted that "base exposures" are used on this exhibit in place of earned exposures. "Base exposures" are calculated using the current rate relativities for all relevant rating variables. If Territory B has a relativity of .58 and Class 2 has a relativity of .9, a Territory B-Class 2 insured would generate .58 times .9 = .52 base exposures. The base is Territory A-Class 1. If the current relativities were exactly balanced with the loss experience, the pure premiums, using base exposures, would all be the same.

The reason for using base exposures instead of actual exposures is to correct for varying exposure levels in the non-reviewed relativities. For example, Territory A and Territory B may differ in the distribution of insureds by class. Another advantage is the recalculation of base exposures on an iterative basis. Other techniques, such as that described by Bailey (1963) provide similar results. The iterative approach proceeds as follows. An initial estimate of territorial relativities is performed. The adjusted relativities are used to recalculate base exposures for a class relativity analysis. The adjusted relativities produced by the class relativity analysis are then used to recalculate base exposures for a territorial relativity analysis. Eventually, the iterations should converge to the most accurate representation of the historical experience.

Exhibits VI and VII show the final iterations.

EXHIBIT VI
TERRITORIAL RELATIVITIES — PURE PREMIUM APPROACH
FINAL ITERATION

Territory	(1) Earned Exposures	(2) Base Exposures	(3) Incurred Losses	(4) Claim Count	(5) Frequency	(6) Severity	(7) Pure Premium
A	9,000	13,936	1,037,495	676	4.9%	1,535	74.45
B	5,500	4,649	346,122	242	5.2%	1,428	74.45
C	5,000	3,397	252,909	223	6.6%	1,135	74.45
Total	19,500	21,983	1,636,526	1141	5.2%		74.45

Territory	(8) Indicated Adjustment	(9) Current Relativity	(10) New Relativity
A	1.000	1.000	1.000
B	1.000	0.601	0.601
C	1.000	0.459	0.459

Notes:

(2) Based on current rating factors
(5) = (4)/(2)
(6) = (3)/(4)
(7) = (3)/(2)
(8) = (7)/TOTAL (7)
(10) = (8)(9)

EXHIBIT VII

CLASS RELATIVITIES — PURE PREMIUM APPROACH FINAL ITERATION

Class	(1) Earned Exposures	(2) Base Exposures	(3) Incurred Losses	(4) Claim Count	(5) Frequency	(6) Severity	(7) Pure Premium
1	4,250	3,490	259,800	361	10.3%	720	74.44
2	2,050	1,206	89,820	114	9.4%	788	74.46
3	2,125	1,728	128,601	199	11.5%	646	74.44
4	3,000	2,778	206,800	278	10.0%	744	74.45
5	2,575	2,917	217,170	278	9.5%	781	74.46
6	1,775	2,057	153,125	231	11.2%	663	74.45
7	1,425	2,124	158,130	246	11.6%	643	74.44
8	1,150	2,436	181,320	308	12.6%	589	74.44
9	1,150	3,248	241,760	410	12.6%	590	74.44
Total	19,500	21,983	1,636,526	2,425	11.0%		74.45

Class	(8) Indicated Adjustment	(9) Current Relativity	(10) New Relativity
1	1.000	1.000	1.000
2	1.000	0.900	0.900
3	1.000	0.990	0.990
4	1.000	1.375	1.375
5	1.000	1.800	1.800
6	1.000	1.750	1.750
7	1.000	1.800	1.800
8	1.000	2.400	2.400
9	1.000	3.200	3.200

Notes:

(2) Based on current rating factors
(5) = (4)/(2)
(6) = (3)/(4)
(7) = (3)/(2)
(8) = (7)/TOTAL (7)
(10) = (8)(9)

As an example, the loss ratio method produced a 1.453 relativity for class 4 (down from an experience period average of 1.474); the pure premium method, first iteration, produced 1.398 (down from 1.45). The final iteration produced 1.375.

Additive or Multiplicative

The above examples used multiplicative relativities. In many, though not most, situations additive relativities are used. For example, a third level of classification could be used in addition to the above territory and class splits. The third level might correspond to automobile use, good-student discount, or driver training discounts.

Philosophically, are the third level differentials additive (i.e., a function of the base rates for a given territory) or multiplicative (i.e., a function of the specific age-gender-marital status and use differentials)? For example, is a good-student discount worth 20% of the base (i.e., adult) rate (additive) or 10% of the actual rate (multiplicative)? The actual rate may be 360% of the base for a 17-year-old male principal operator (multiplicative good student discount equals 36% of base rate) or 150% for a 20-year-old female (multiplicative good student discount equals 15% of base rate). Does "good student" status reduce costs equally for all insureds (additive) or does it affect costs proportionally (multiplicative)?

Unequal Exposure in Underlying Variables

Regardless of which form is chosen for the relativities, estimation is not necessarily straightforward. Certain subdivisions of a rating variable may have a disproportionate share of another rating variable; that is, two rating variables may be highly correlated with each other. For example, assume Group A costs twice Group B and Group X costs twice Group Y. Also assume that AX occurs 40% of the time, AY 10%, BX 10%, and BY 40%. See Exhibit VIII.

EXHIBIT VIII
UNEQUAL EXPOSURE SAMPLE

I. Exposure

	A	B	Total
X	40	10	50
Y	10	40	50
Total	50	50	100

II. Pure Premium

	A	B
X	4	2
Y	2	1

III. Costs

	A	B	Total	Exposures	Relativity
X	160	20	180	50	3.0
Y	20	40	60	50	1.0
Total	180	60	240	100	
Exposures	50	50			
Relativity	3.0	1.0			

The empirical cost for X is 3.6, and for Y, 1.2. Thus the empirical relativity is 3.0, when we know the actual cost is only double. This has happened because disproportionate exposure is concentrated in higher and lower cost groups. In determining the relative cost of X and Y, one may expect half of the exposure to be in Group A and half in Group B. Instead, 80% of X's exposure is in high-cost Group A and 80% of Y's exposure is in low-cost Group B. Thus X looks relatively higher in cost than it actually is. Various methods can be used to adjust for unequal distributions of underlying exposures. The iterative method discussed above is one.

Credibility Considerations

Another estimation problem concerns the credibility of the data. Since competition encourages insurers to refine their classification systems, refinement will generally continue to the point where the credibility of the data becomes minimal.

In the context of classification, credibility involves the assessment of the relative meaningfulness of a group's cost versus the meaningfulness of the credibility complement's cost. Assume for example, that the task is to estimate the cost of Group A. If Group A has a large body of data, that experience alone may be sufficient for estimating its cost. As Group A becomes smaller, at some point it will be useful to compare Group A's empirical costs to the cost of some other group. This other group is the credibility complement. Group A's empirical cost may be twice the cost of the complement. Since Group A has less data or less reliable data, the actuary may decide that Group A's true cost is only 60% higher than the complement.

Thus, two credibility related problems emerge: (1) how to obtain more data or more reliable data, and (2) what is the most appropriate credibility complement? Each of these matters can be discussed at length. The purpose here is to provide an overview.

Obtaining more or more reliable data can be done in several ways. Most obviously, more years of data or, possibly, data from several states (or countrywide) can be used. Of course, the threshold question is whether the broader base actually applies. Has there been a change over time? Do countrywide indications apply in each state?

Another method is to give more weight to more stable phenomena. For example, relativities can be based primarily on frequency (by looking only at claim counts or by limiting the size of claims), instead of pure premiums. Partial pure premiums can be calculated. For example, property damage liability costs may be more stable than bodily injury liability; workers' compensation medical costs may be more stable than deaths or permanent disabilities. In determining relativities, more emphasis (credibility) is given to the more stable phenomena.

The choice of credibility complement may be more difficult than obtaining more or more reliable data. It may not be clear which group is most nearly the same as the group in question. National or regional data may be applicable. Related industry group data may be applicable. In most of these cases, adjustments must be made because the level of costs can be quite different for the complement. Often, the percentage change in the complement is considered, rather then the actual value. As a last resort, the complement may be based on the prior year's analysis; this, in effect, takes more years of data into account.

Exhibit IX illustrates some of the credibility issues:

EXHIBIT IX

CLASS RATING EXAMPLE

Current Relativity = 8.4

Rating Group		Years	Exposures	Relativities to Group 1: Frequency	Severity	Pure Premium
I.	**Raw Data**					
	A	79-88	420	4.2	1.15	4.9
		81-88	340	4.6	1.18	5.4
		84-88	193	4.6	1.10	5.1
		86-88	93	4.7	1.36	6.3
	B	79-88	846	5.1	1.16	5.9
		81-88	635	5.6	1.22	6.9
		84-88	304	5.2	1.07	5.6
		86-88	147	6.0	1.26	7.6
	C	79-88	293	5.9	1.93	11.3
		81-88	233	6.1	1.98	12.1
		84-88	133	4.8	1.72	8.3
		86-88	69	4.5	1.69	7.6
II.	**Conclusions**					
	A			4.8	1.25	6.0
	B			5.6	1.25	7.0
	C			6.0	1.33	8.0

The problem is choosing rate relativities for a group of surgical specialties. At the current time, all specialties shown on Exhibit IX are being charged 8.4 times the base. Data is grouped for various combinations of accident years (all groups ending with 1988). Relativities to the base are shown for claim frequency, severity, and pure premium. The severity relativity for all surgery classifications is about 1.25.

The frequencies seem to be different for the different groups, although Groups B and C could possibly have the same frequency.

The severities are much different for Group C, although the number of claims is relatively small (17 for the 10-year period).

Selected relativities were based on judgment rather than a formal credibility formula. Essentially, claim frequency was given high-credibility. The overall severity for surgeons (1.25) was used for Groups A and B, although actual data is not much different. The severity for Group C reflects a small upward adjustment to the overall surgeons' relativity (about 15% credibility). The selected pure premium relativities were rounded.

Summary

Risk classification involves the formulation of different premiums for the same coverage based on group characteristics. That is, the task is to price an individual insured, but the available claim data for that individual is insufficient for the purpose. The recourse is to measure group costs and assume that the individual belongs to a certain group. The grouping process may proceed in several dimensions (e.g., class, territory, use).

Premiums should vary because underlying costs vary. Costs may vary due to different claim frequency or average claim size, different administrative expense requirements, different investment income potential, or differing assessments of risk. Risk classification proceeds by identifying variables that distinguish these costs among different insureds. In addition to classification variables, premiums can also vary due to the choice of different exposure bases, individual risk rating methods, and marketing or underwriting strategies.

Various criteria, actuarial, operational, social, and legal, have been suggested for formulating classification variables. Actuarial criteria attempt most accurately to group individual insureds into groups that (1) are relatively homogeneous, (2) are sufficientlylarge to estimate relative cost differences (credibility), and (3) maintain stable mean costs over time (reliability).

Operational criteria include objective definitions, reasonable administrative expense, and verifiability. Social criteria include privacy, causality, controllability, and affordability.

A competitive market tends to produce more refined classifications and accurate premiums. Competition may be limited, however, when the premium volume for a group is small or where there is significant heterogeneity in costs within the group. Most of the social criteria are based on concepts of accuracy. The abolition of certain rating variables likely will reduce rating accuracy, as well as create subsidies or availability problems. The inaccuracy in the current rating systems is primarily determined by the level of competition and the statistical difficulty of rating small groups of insureds.

The absolute efficiency of current classification systems can be estimated, but the estimates depend upon some measurement of the variability in costs among all insureds (which can never be observed directly). Knowing the absolute efficiency, however, is not particularly useful in determining which specific rating variables would be better than current ones.

References

Abraham, Kenneth S. 1985. Efficiency and fairness in insurance risk classification. *Va. Law Review* 71:, 403.

American Academy of Actuaries. 1982. Brief as Amicus Curiae, *Norris v. Arizona Governing Committee.*

American Academy of Actuaries, Committee on Risk Classification. 1980. *Risk classification statement of principles.*

American Academy of Actuaries. 1977. *Report of Academy Task Force on Risk Classification.*

Bailey, Robert A. 1963. Insurance rates with minimum bias. *PCAS* 50.

Butler, Patrick, Butler, Twiss, and Williams, Laurie L. 1988. Sex-divided mileage, accident, and insurance cost data show that auto insurers overcharge most women. *Journal of Insurance Regulation* 6:, 243.

Glendenning, G. William, and Holtom, Robert B. 1977. *Personal lines underwriting.* Malvern, Pa:, Ins. Institute of America.

Holtom, Robert B. 1979. *Restraints on underwriting: risk selection, discrimination and the law.* Cincinnati:, The National Underwriter Co.

Launie, J.J., Lee, J. Finley, and Baglini, Norman A. 1976. *Principles of property and liability underwriting.* Malvern, Pa:, Insurance Institute of America.

Kimball, Spencer L. 1979. Reverse sex discrimination: *Manhart. American Bar Foundation Research Journal.* 83.

Massachusetts Division of Insurance. 1978. *Automobile insurance risk classification: equity and accuracy.*

Meyers, Glenn G. 1984. Empirical Bayesian credibility for workers' compensation classification ratemaking. *PCAS* 71.

National Association of Insurance Commissioners, D-3 Advisory Committee. 1978. *Report of the Rates and Rating Procedures Task Force.*

Skurnick, David. 1974. Revising classification structure using survey data. *PCAS* 61.

SRI International. 1979. *Choice of a regulatory environment for automobile insurance* (Final report).

Stanford Research Institute. 1976. *The role of risk classification in property and casualty insurance: a study of the risk assessment process.*

Wallace, Frances K. 1984. Unisex automobile rating: the Michigan experience. *Journal of Insurance Regulation* 3(2):, 127.

Walters, Michael A. 1981. Risk classification standards. *PCAS* 68.

Woll, Richard G. 1979. A study of risk assessment. *PCAS* 66.

Chapter 6
REINSURANCE
by Gary Patrik

Introduction

This introduction is only a brief review of basic reinsurance concepts and terminology. The interested reader will find more extensive discussions in some of the general reinsurance texts listed in the Bibliography.

What is reinsurance?

Reinsurance is a form of insurance. A reinsurance contract is legally an insurance contract; the reinsurer agrees to indemnify the cedant insurer for a specified share of certain types of insurance claims paid by the cedant for a single insurance policy or a designated set of policies. The terminology used is that the reinsurer assumes the liability ceded. The cession, or share of losses to be paid by the reinsurer, may be defined to be a percentage share or may be defined on some other basis.

The nature and purpose of insurance is to reduce the financial impact upon individuals and corporations from the potential occurrence of specific kinds of contingent events. An insurance company sells many policies which for fixed or bounded (e.g., retro-rated plans) prices guarantee the policyholders that the insurer will indemnify them for part of their financial losses arising from these events. This pooling of liabilities allows the insurer's total losses to be more predictable than is the case for each individual insured. Insurance enables individuals and corporations to perform tasks and manufacture products which might be too risky for one entity. This increases competition and efficiency in a capitalistic marketplace.

The nature and purpose of reinsurance is to reduce the financial impact upon insurance companies from insurance claims, thus further enhancing competition and efficiency in the marketplace. The cession of shares of liability spreads risk further throughout the insurance system. Just as an individual may purchase an insurance policy from an insurer, an insurance company may purchase fairly comprehensive reinsurance from a single reinsurer or from a collection of reinsurers. And a reinsurer may reduce its assumed reinsurance risk by purchasing reinsurance coverages from many other reinsurers, both domestic and worldwide; such a cession of assumed reinsurance liability is called a retrocession.

Reinsurers write business either directly via their own employed account executives or via reinsurance intermediaries. These intermediaries function similarly to brokers in the primary insurance market. It is estimated that more than half of U.S. reinsurance is placed via intermediaries (Webb et al 1984).

The form and wording of reinsurance contracts are not as closely regulated as insurance contracts and there is no rate regulation of reinsurance between private companies. Reinsurance contracts are often manuscript contracts setting forth the unique agreement between the two parties. Because of the many special cases and exceptions in reinsurance, it is difficult to make correct generalizations. Consequently, as you read this chapter, you should often supply for yourself the phrases "It is generally true that. . ." and "Usually. . ." whenever they are not stated.

This heterogeneity of contract wording also means that whenever you are accumulating, analyzing, and comparing various reinsurance data, you must be careful that the reinsurance coverages producing the data are reasonably similar. We will be encountering this problem throughout this chapter.

The functions of reinsurance

Reinsurance does not change the basic nature of an insurance coverage; on a long-term basis, it cannot be expected to make bad business good. But it does provide certain direct assistance to the cedant:

Capacity

With reinsurance, the cedant can write larger policy limits. By ceding shares of all policies or of just larger policies, the net retained loss exposure per individual policy or in total can be kept in line with the cedant's surplus. Thus, smaller insurers can compete with larger insurers, and policies beyond the capacity of any single insurer can be written.

Stabilization

Reinsurance can help stabilize the cedant's underwriting and financial results over time and help protect the cedant's surplus against shocks due to especially large, fortuitous losses. Reinsurance can be written so that the cedant keeps smaller, predictable losses, but shares larger, infrequent losses. It can also be written to provide protection against a larger than predicted accumulation of claims, either from one catastrophic event or from many. Thus the financial effects of large losses or large accumulations of loss are spread out over many years. This decreases the cedant's probability of financial ruin.

Financial results management

Reinsurance can alter the timing of income, enhance statutory and/or GAAP surplus, and improve various financial ratios by which insurers are judged. We will see this as we discuss the effects of various covers below.

Management advice

Many professional reinsurers have the knowledge and ability to provide an informal consulting service for their cedants. This service can include underwriting, marketing, pricing, claims handling, loss prevention, reserving, actuarial, investment, and personnel advice and assistance. Enlightened self-interest forces the reinsurer to critically review the cedant's operation and thus be in a position to offer advice. The reinsurer probably has more expertise in the pricing of high limits policies and in the handling of large and rare claims. Also, through contact with many similar cedant companies, the reinsurer may be able to provide an overview of general trends. Reinsurance intermediaries may also provide some of these same services for their clients.

The forms of reinsurance

Facultative certificates

A facultative certificate reinsures just one primary insured. Its main function is to provide additional capacity. It is used to cover part of certain large, especially hazardous, or unusual exposures to limit their potential impact upon the cedant's net results or to protect the cedant's ongoing treaty results. The reinsurer underwrites and accepts each certificate individually; it is very similar to primary insurance individual risk underwriting. Because facultative reinsurance usually covers the more hazardous or unusual exposures, the reinsurer must be careful of antiselection within and among classes of insureds.

Most property certificate coverage is written on a proportional basis; that is, the reinsurer reimburses a fixed percentage of each specified type of claim on the subject policy. Most casualty certificate coverage is written on an excess basis; that is, the reinsurer reimburses a share (up to some limit) of the part of each specified type of claim on the subject policy which lies above some fixed retention (attachment point).

Facultative automatic agreements or programs

A facultative automatic agreement reinsures many homogeneous policies. Its main function is to provide additional capacity, but also, because it covers many policies, it provides some degree of stabilization. It may be thought of as a collection of individual facultative certificates underwritten simultaneously. It may cover on either a proportional or excess basis. It is usually written for new or special programs marketed by the cedant, and the reinsurer works closely with the cedant to design the primary underwriting and pricing guidelines. For example, a facultative automatic agreement may cover a 90% share of the cedant's personal umbrella business, in which case the reinsurer will almost certainly provide expert advice and will monitor the cedant's underwriting and pricing very closely.

Facultative automatic agreements are usually written on a fixed cost basis, without the retrospective premium adjustments or variable ceding commissions which sometimes exist for treaties (as we shall see below).

There exist some non-obligatory agreements where either the cedant may not be required to cede or the reinsurer may not be required to assume every single policy of a certain type.

Treaty proportional covers

A treaty reinsures a certain part of the loss exposure for a set of insurance policies for a specified coverage period. The set of policies (called "subject" policies) are those of a specified type written during the term of the treaty, but may also include those policies of the same type in force at inception. The subject exposure is usually defined by Annual Statement line of business or some subsets thereof. A treaty covers those claims incurred during its term, but may also cover those claims incurred after treaty termination upon policies in force at termination (run-off exposure). Because a treaty involves a close sharing of much insurance exposure, it can create a close working relationship between the parties; the expertise and services of the reinsurer or intermediary are available to the cedant. This is especially true for treaties written by a direct reinsurer (no intermediary involved) or where there is a strong reinsurer leading a brokered (intermediary) treaty.

A quota-share treaty reinsures a fixed percentage of each subject policy. Its main function is financial results management, but it may also provide some capacity. The reinsurer usually receives the same share of premium as of losses, but allows the cedant to keep a ceding commission commensurate with the primary production and handling costs (underwriting, claims, etc.). Quota-share treaties usually assume in-force exposure at inception. The ceding commission on the ceded unearned premium reserve shifts statutory surplus from the reinsurer to the cedant. Another method of financial results management is the use of a quota-share treaty covering exposure net of all other reinsurance in order to cede enough premium to protect the cedant's net-premium-to-surplus ratio.

For quota-share treaties, the ceding commission often varies within some range inversely to the loss ratio. This allows the cedant to retain better-than-expected profits but protects the reinsurer somewhat from worse-than-expected losses. You should be aware that the term quota share is sometimes misused when the cover is a proportional share of an excess layer; this is more appropriately classified as excess coverage.

A surplus-share treaty also reinsures a fixed percentage of each subject policy, but the share varies by policy according to the relationship between the limit of the policy and the cedant's net retention under the treaty. Its main function is capacity, but it also provides some stabilization. A surplus-share treaty also may assume in-force exposure at inception and return unearned premium at termination, thus providing some financial results management. It is used for property coverage and only rarely used for casualty.

Treaty excess covers

An excess treaty reinsures, up to a limit, a share of the part of loss in excess of some specified cedant retention (attachment point of the treaty). Its main functions are capacity and stabilization. An excess treaty usually covers exposure earned during its in-force term on a losses-occurring or on a claims-made basis, but run-off exposure may be negotiated. The definition of "loss" is important.

For a per-risk excess treaty, a loss is defined to be the sum of all claims arising from one covered loss event or occurrence for a single subject policy. Per-risk excess is used for property exposures to provide protection net of facultative coverage and possibly also net of proportional treaties. It is used for casualty less often than per-occurrence coverage.

For a per-occurrence excess treaty, a loss is defined to be the sum of all claims arising from one covered loss event or occurrence for all subject policies. Per-occurrence excess is used for casualty covers to protect a cedant all the way up from working layers through clash layers.

A working layer per-occurrence excess treaty covers an excess layer for which a number of losses are expected each year. This significant expected frequency of loss creates some stability of the aggregate reinsured loss; so working layers are often retrospectively-rated, with the final reinsurance premium partially determined by the loss experience on the contract.

A higher exposed layer per-occurrence excess treaty attaches above the working layer(s), but within some policy limits. A clash layer usually attaches above policy limits and is only exposed by extra-contractual-obligations or excess-of-policy-limit damages (if covered), by catastrophic workers' compensation accidents and by the "clash" of claims arising from one loss event involving multiple coverages or policies. These higher layer treaties are almost always priced on a fixed cost basis.

A per-occurrence excess treaty used for property exposure is called a catastrophe cover. It is used to protect the net position of the cedant against the accumulation of claims arising from a single large natural event. It is usually stipulated that two or more insureds must be involved before coverage attaches. The cover is usually 90% to 95% of layers excess of the maximum retention the cedant can absorb or over which the reinsurance coverage is affordable.

For an aggregate excess treaty, a loss is the accumulation of all subject losses during a specified time period, usually one year. It usually covers the net retention of the cedant, either property or casualty or both. It protects net results, providing very strong stabilization. Claims arising from natural catastrophes are often excluded from coverage.

Nontraditional covers

These are almost always treaties whose main, and sometimes only, purpose is financial results management. The reinsurer's risk is reduced by various contractual conditions. And the reinsurer's expected margin (profit and expense) is reduced to reflect this.

A financial proportional cover almost always has a ceding commission which varies within some range inversely to the subject loss ratio. The ceded loss share may also decrease somewhat if the loss ratio exceeds some maximum, or the loss share may be fixed at some percentage less than the premium share. The treaty may also have some kind of funding mechanism wherein the aggregate limit of coverage is based upon the fund (net cash position less margin of the reinsurer) plus, of course, some risk layer, at least at the beginning of the contract.

A loss portfolio transfer is a cession of some part of the loss liability of the cedant as of a specified accounting date. It may be a cession of the total liability or, more usually, some aggregate excess layer. It is almost always subject to an aggregate limit, and may have sublimits upon payment timing. The cedant's retention may be stated in terms of dollars and/or time. A loss portfolio transfer may be a pure risk cover, but usually it is essentially a present-value funding of liabilities. It may include profit commissions to be paid to the cedant if the actual loss experience is better than originally anticipated.

A funded aggregate excess cover is, as one might suspect, an aggregate excess treaty for which the losses are essentially funded. It is analogous to a funded loss portfolio transfer except that it covers future occurring losses. In addition to financial results management, it may provide strong stabilization.

A reinsurance program

There is no such thing as a typical reinsurance program. Every company is in a unique situation regarding loss exposure, financial solidity, management culture, future plans, and marketing opportunities. Thus each company needs a unique reinsurance program, a combination of ceded reinsurance covers tailor-made for that company.

Nevertheless, Table 6.1.1 displays a reinsurance program for a medium-sized insurance company that we might regard as being typical:

Table 6.1.1 **A Reinsurance Program For A Medium-Sized Company**

Lines of Business	Type of Reinsurance
A. Fire and Allied Lines HO Section I SMP Section I	1. Proportional facultative certificates to bring each individual policy's net exposure down to $1,000,000
	2. Surplus share of 4 lines not to exceed $800,000; maximum cedant retention of $200,000
	3. Per risk excess working layer $100,000 excess of $100,000
	4. Catastrophe covers: a) 95% of $3,000,000 excess of $2,000,000 b) 95% of $5,000,000 excess of $5,000,000 c) 95% of $5,000,000 excess of $10,000,000 d) 95% of $5,000,000 excess of $15,000,000
B. Casualty Lines excluding Medical Malpractice and Umbrella	1. Facultative certificates for primary per policy coverage excess of $1,000,000
	2. Working layer excess: $300,000 excess of $200,000
	3. Higher exposed layer excess: $500,000 excess of $500,000
	4. Clash layers: a) $4,000,000 excess of $1,000,000 b) $5,000,000 excess of $5,000,000 c) $10,000,000 excess of $10,000,000
C. Personal Umbrellas	1. 90% share facultative automatic program

If the company writes surety, fidelity, marine, medical malpractice or other special business, other similar reinsurance covers would be purchased. If the company is entering a new market (e.g., a new territory or type of business), it may purchase quota share coverage to lessen the financial impact of the new premium volume (and commissions thereon) and to obtain the reinsurer's assistance; or it may want a facultative automatic program for an even closer working relationship with a reinsurer. If the company is exiting from a market, it may purchase a loss portfolio transfer to cover the run-off of loss payments.

The cost of reinsurance to the cedant

The reinsurer's margin

The reinsurer charges a margin over and above ceded loss expectation, commissions and brokerage fees (to the intermediary, if any). It is usually stated as a percentage of the reinsurance premium and is theoretically based upon the reinsurer's expenses, the degree of risk transfer and the magnitude of capacity and financial support, but it is practically influenced by competition in the reinsurance market. The actual resulting margin can differ greatly from that anticipated because of the stochasticity of the loss liability and cash flow transferred.

Brokerage fee

An intermediary charges a brokerage fee for placing the reinsurance coverage and for any other services performed on behalf of the cedant. Although this fee is paid by the reinsurer, it of course enters into the total reinsurance price. Offsetting this cost is the fact that reinsurers writing brokerage business usually have lower internal expenses because they don't maintain separate marketing staffs. The fee is usually a fixed percentage of gross reinsurance premium ceded, but may vary according to specified criteria.

Lost investment income

By transferring premium funds (net of ceding commission) to the intermediary, if any, who then passes on premium—also net of brokerage fee—to the reinsurer, the cedant naturally loses the use of those funds until returned as loss payments or as profit commissions. And the reinsurer theoretically keeps a margin and the intermediary, if any, keeps a fee. On the surface, this loss of investable assets may be diminished if the reinsurer agrees to allow the cedant to withhold funds and keep an account of the funds withheld. But of course the reinsurer will charge a higher margin for this. The actual lost investment income depends upon the actual cash flow on the cover; as with (1), this may be highly stochastic.

Additional cedant expenses

The cedant incurs various expenses for ceding reinsurance. These include the cost of negotiation, the cost of a financial analysis of the reinsurer, accounting and reporting costs, etc.. If an intermediary is involved, the fee covers some of these services to the cedant. In general, facultative is more expensive than treaty because of individual policy negotiation, accounting and loss cessions.

Reciprocity

In order to cede reinsurance, the cedant might be required to assume some liability from the reinsurer. If this assumption is unprofitable, the loss should be considered in the cost of the cession. Reciprocity is not prevalent within the U.S.

Balancing costs and benefits

In balancing the costs and benefits of a reinsurance cover or of a whole reinsurance program, the cedant should consider more than the direct loss coverage benefit and functions. Another major consideration is the reinsurer's financial solidity: will the reinsurer be around to pay late-settled claims many years from now? Also important may be the reinsurer's or intermediary's services, including underwriting, marketing, pricing, claims handling, loss prevention, reserving, actuarial, investments and personnel advice and assistance.

Reinsurance Pricing

General considerations

In general, reinsurance pricing is more uncertain than primary pricing. Coverage terms can be highly individualized, especially for treaties. These terms determine the coverage period, definition of "loss", commission arrangements, premium and loss payment timing, etc. It is often difficult and sometimes impossible to get meaningful and credible loss experience relevant to the cover being evaluated. Often the data are not as they first seem, so one must continually ask questions in order to discover their true nature. Because of these problems of coverage definition and of the meaning of loss and exposure statistics, the degree of risk relative to premium volume is usually much greater for reinsurance business.

Additional risk arises from the low claim frequency and high severity nature of many reinsurance coverages, from the lengthy time delays between the occurrence, reporting, and settlement of covered loss events, and also from the leveraged effect of inflation upon excess claims. In general, the lower the expected loss frequency, the higher the variance of results relative to expectation, and thus the higher the risk level. Also, IBNR emergence and case reserve development are severe problems for casualty excess business. Development beyond 10 years can be large, highly variant, and extremely difficult to evaluate as we shall discuss in the section on "Reinsurance and Loss Reserving." Concomitant is the increased uncertainty for asset-liability matching, because of the very long tail and extreme variability of the distribution of loss payments over time. Future predictability is decreased by greater uncertainty affecting loss severity inflation above excess cover attachment points. All these elements create a situation where the variance (and higher moments) of the loss process and its estimation are much more important relative to the expected value than is the case for primary coverage. For some reinsurance covers, the higher moments (or at least the underwriter/actuary's beliefs regarding fluctuation potential) determine the price.

There are many ways to price reinsurance covers. For any given situation, there is no one right way. In this section, we will discuss a few reasonable methods which illustrate certain differences from ordinary primary pricing. In general, our pricing methods will begin simple and become more complex as the situation demands and as we ask more questions. In many real situations, you might want to get a quick first evaluation via the simplest methods; indeed, if you judge the situation to be either fairly predictable by these methods, or if you judge the risk to be fairly small, you may decide to stop there. If not, you may want to pursue your analysis and pricing along the lines presented here. As in most actuarial work, you should try as many reasonable methods as time permits (and reconcile the answers, if possible).

In this spirit, please note that the pricing formula and the use of the Pareto and lognormal distributions in this chapter are for illustrative purposes. The pricing formula a reinsurance actuary would use depends upon the reinsurer's pricing philosophy and information availability. The probability models should be selected to describe the real situation as best as possible given all the real statistical and analytical cost constraints; Hogg and Klugman (1984) and Patrik (1980) discuss model selection and parameter estimation.

A reinsurance pricing formula

A discussion of the pricing formula to be used in this chapter will illustrate certain differences from primary pricing. Formula 6.2.1 states the minimally acceptable reinsurance premium in terms of reinsurance loss cost, external expenses, internal expenses and target economic return.

Formula 6.2.1 A Reinsurance Pricing Formula

$$RP = \frac{RLC}{(1 - CR - BF)\ (1 - IXL)\ (1 - TER)}$$

where RP = reinsurance premium (gross)

RLC = reinsurance loss cost (reinsurer's expected aggregate loss, undiscounted or discounted)

CR	=	reinsurance ceding commission rate
BF	=	reinsurance brokerage fee (if any)
IXL	=	reinsurer's internal expense loading (as a percent of premium net of CR and BF)
TER	=	reinsurer's target economic return (as a percent of pure risk premium, net of CR, BF and IXL)

The reinsurance loss cost may be undiscounted or discounted according to the reinsurer's philosophy. The reinsurance ceding commission rate and brokerage fee are specified in each particular contract; they are almost always stated as percentages of the reinsurance gross premium RP. On excess coverage, often there is no ceding commission; this is very different from primary coverage where commissions almost always exist. And of course, the existence of a brokerage fee depends upon the existence of a broker (intermediary).

The reinsurer's internal expenses are conveniently stated as a loading to reinsurance premium less external expenses for at least three reasons:

1) This is the reinsurer's actual cash income (unless there are funds withheld).

2) It is relatively easy to account for external expenses by reinsurance line of business. Within line, the reinsurer's underwriting and claims handling effort, and thus expenses, should be similar for each contract, varying only by claims and "risk" volume.

3) Internal expenses by contract should not depend upon the existence or absence of commissions or brokerage expenses; thus the loading should be independent of these.

Finally, the reinsurer's target economic return, or profit and risk charge, is properly related to the loss potential on each contract, and should be appropriately stated in relation to the loss expectation. If the reinsurer chooses not to discount losses, then this TER is a target underwriting return on pure risk premium. A discussion of how to select TERs for various contracts or lines of business is well beyond the scope of this chapter. However, there is extensive actuarial literature on this topic; see especially Bühlmann (1970), Beard et al (1984), and, generally, *The ASTIN Bulletin*.

Let us consider an example. If \$100,000 is the *RLC* on a contract and the reinsurer believes that $TER = 20\%$ is appropriate to compensate for the uncertainty and risk level for the coverage, then the pure risk premium would be $\$100{,}000/(.8) = \$125{,}000$. This is the amount of cash income the reinsurer believes is necessary, net of *all* expenses, to cover the loss potential on the contract. If the reinsurer's internal expense loading is 10% for this type of reinsurance business, then the reinsurer believes that a reasonable reinsurance premium net of external expenses would be $\$125{,}000/(.9) = \$138{,}889$. If the ceding commission and brokerage fee combined were 30%, then it would be loaded onto this to determine a fair reinsurance gross premium as $\$138{,}889/(.7) = \$198{,}413$.

We will be using this formula throughout this chapter.

Facultative certificates

Since a facultative certificate covers a share of a single insurance policy or set of policies covering a single insured, the individual insured can be underwritten and priced. The exposure of the individual insured can be evaluated and manual rates and rating factors can be used. However, since most facultative certificates are written on larger or more hazardous exposures, manual rates and rating factors may not exist or must often be modified. Thus, individual loss experience and a great deal of underwriting judgment are important.

To the extent that actuaries are involved with facultative certificate business, they can be useful in the following ways:

1. Be sure that the facultative underwriters are provided with and know how to use the most current and accurate manual rates and rating factors, e.g., increased limits factors, loss development factors, trend factors, actuarial opinions on rate adequacy by exposure type and by territory (state), etc.

2. Work with the underwriters to design and maintain good pricing methodologies, perhaps in the form of interactive computer programs.

3. Work with the underwriters to design and maintain good portfolio monitoring systems for meaningful categories of their business, both for relative price level and for the monitoring of loss experience.

4. Work with the underwriters to evaluate and determine which lines of business and which exposure layers to concentrate upon as market conditions change.

In contemplating any form of facultative coverage, the underwriter first evaluates the exposure to decide if the risk is acceptable, and then evaluates the rate used by the cedant to decide if it is adequate. The underwriter also determines if the ceding commission fairly covers the cedant's expenses, but does not put the cedant into a significantly more advantageous situation than the reinsurer.

Property certificate coverage on a proportional share basis usually needs little further actuarial assistance. However, the actuary should be involved in the corporate discussion and evaluation of catastrophe accumulation potential.

Evaluating and pricing property certificate coverage on an excess basis is more difficult. There exists very little reliable published information on the rating of property excess coverage. Some underwriters use so-called Lloyds Scales; these are tables of excess loss factors determining the average excess loss as part of the total according to the relationship of excess attachment point to the MPL (maximum possible loss). The MPL, sometimes also called "amount subject", is a very conservative estimate by the individual underwriter of the maximum loss possible on the policy. It includes the maximum full value of contiguous buildings together with contents and also reflects maximum time element (e.g., business interruption) coverage. The actuarial basis for the Lloyds Scales, if any, is lost in the murky remembrance of post-war (World War II) London. There seem to be no published, actuarially sound tables for rating property per-risk excess coverage.

One actuarially sound concept for developing a table of property per-risk excess rating factors would be to express the excess loss cost for coverage above an attachment point up to the MPL as a percentage of the total loss cost. The curve would depend upon the class of business (its severity potential) and upon the size of the MPL, and also upon the relative size of the PML (probable maximum loss). The PML is a less conservative estimate of the largest loss, assuming for example, that the sprinkler system works, that the contents are normal, etc. The difference between MPL and PML is illustrated by considering an office building: the MPL is the total value; the definition of PML varies from underwriter to underwriter, but is usually thought to be three to five floors. The MPL and PML affect the shape of the loss cost curve because one expects, for example, very different loss severity distributions for an insured with a $100,000 MPL and PML versus an insured with a $10,000,000 MPL and $5,000,000 PML. This is illustrated by the accompanying Graph 6.2.2.

Appropriate risk loadings could be incorporated into the table or could be recommended as additional loading factors.

Graph 6.2.2 Example of Claim Severity Cumulative Distribution Function

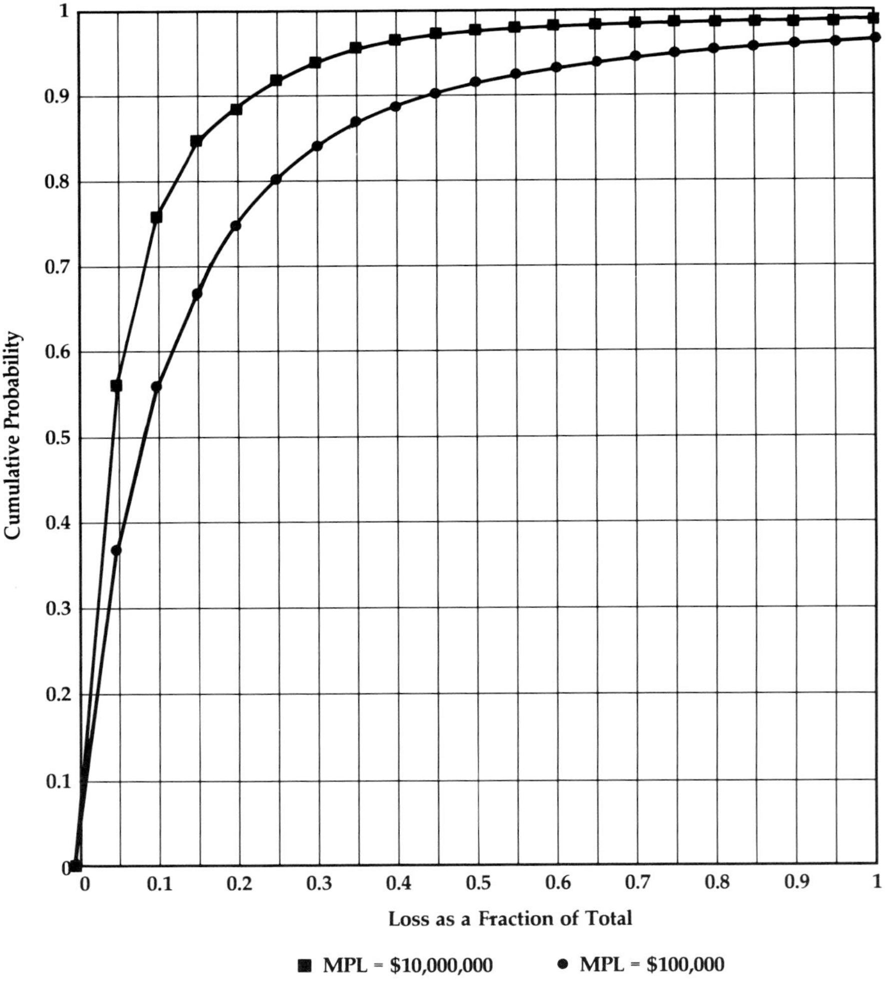

An appropriate pricing formula for an excess cover could use Formula 6.2.1 with RLC defined as follows:

Formula 6.2.3 Reinsurance Expected Loss Cost

$$RLC = \frac{ELCF \times PP \times PPLR}{RCF}$$

where $ELCF$ = excess loss cost factor (from the table; as a percent of total loss cost)

PP = primary company premium

$PPLR$ = primary company permissible loss ratio (including any loss adjustment expenses covered as part of loss).

RCF = rate correction factor (for adequacy of primary rate)

The reinsurance premium can be translated into a reinsurance rate by dividing it by the primary premium PP. If the reinsurer wishes to reflect the investment income to be earned on the contract, then the ELCF would include an appropriate loss discount factor. To maintain consistent terminology with casualty pricing where investment income is more likely to be reflected, we continue to use the term "target economic return" in Formula 6-2 instead of simply "risk and profit loading".

For example, suppose we have the following situation:

Example 6.2.4

Facts:

1. Primary total premium = \$100,000.
2. MPL = PML = \$10,000,000.
3. Attachment point = \$1,000,000.
4. Reinsurance limit = \$4,000,000.

5. $PPLR = 65\%$

6. $CR = 30\%$

7. $BF = 0\%$ (no broker)

8. $IXL = 15\%$

Suppose that for this class of business and for this layer ($4 million excess of $1 million), we (the reinsurer) want to price to a TER of 10%. Also suppose that we believe that the cedant's rate is inadequate by 5%. Thus you can verify that the reinsurer believes the total expected loss cost is:

9. $(PP) \times (PPLR) / RCF = \$100{,}000 \times (.65)/(.95) = \$68{,}421$

Now assume that we believe that the loss severity, including loss adjustment expense, for this class of business and this MPL, is given by a censored (at MPL) Pareto distribution of the following form:

Formula 6.2.5 Censored Pareto Model

$$1 - F(x) = \text{Prob}[X > x] = \begin{cases} (b/(b + x))^q & \text{for } x < 1 \\ O & \text{for } x \geq 1 \end{cases}$$

where the loss size X is expressed as a percent of MPL.

(Properties of the Pareto are outlined in Appendix 6.5A.)

Suppose that the parameters are given by $b = .1$ and $q = 2$.

Obviously, this belief should be based upon as thorough an analysis and modeling of claims data and coverage as possible. Also, please note that the Pareto is used here only for convenience. A more accurate loss severity model may be different (see Hogg and Klugman, 1984).

You can now verify the following facts:

10. $\text{Prob}[X = 1] = [b/(b + 1)]^q = .0083$
(probability of a loss, if it occurs, hitting the MPL)

11. $E[X;c] = [b/(q - 1)]\{1 - [b/(b + c)]^{q-1}\}$
(expected loss cost up to any censor $c \leq 1$)
(See Appendix (6.5A)).

12. $E[X;1] = .0909$ (as a percent of MPL)
(Thus, if a loss occurs, its average size is $909,000)

13. $E[X - .1)\ (.1,.5)] =$
$[b/(q - 1)]\{[b/(b + .1)]^{q-1} - [b/(b + .5)]^{q-1}\}$
$= .0333$ (as a percent of MPL)
(per-occurrence expected loss cost in the reinsured layer)

14. $ELCF = (13)/(12) = .0333/.0909 = .3663$

15. $RLC = (14) \times (9) =$ $25,063

16. $RP =$ $46,803

17. $RR = .468$
(reinsurance rate)

In addition, you can also verify the following facts:

18. $E[N(\text{excess})] = (68{,}241/909{,}000)\text{Prob}[X > .1] = .0188$
(expected number of claims excess of $1,000,000)

19. $E[X(\text{excess})] = (15)/(18) =$ $1,333,138
(expected excess claim size in the layer)

20. The reinsurance gross premium for the layer
$5 million excess of $5 million, with a 15% TER,
is $11,310.

Quite often the pricing situation is much more complicated, with multiple locations and coverages. The underwriter/pricer generally determines a price for each location and each coverage, and then adds them to obtain the total premium.

Instead of working directly with an estimated underlying loss severity distribution like this Pareto, the ELCF (14) might be obtained from a table. Better yet, a pricing procedure such as this can be programmed into an interactive computer package for the underwriters. The package would contain all the appropriate rates and rating factors or underlying loss severity models and parameters to be called upon by the user. It would ask most of the relevant questions of the user and would document the decision trail for each submission seriously contemplated by the underwriter.

For facultative certificate property coverage as with any reinsurance business segment, the pricing cycle is very severe. This is mainly due to naive capital flowing into the market because of easy access, but also due to the short-term nature of most peoples' memories. Thus it is very important to monitor the results closely. Renewal pricing and rate competition in the marketplace should be watched monthly; perhaps summaries derived from the aforementioned pricing system would be appropriate. Quarterly updates of underwriting results by accident year in appropriate business segment detail are very important.

Evaluating and pricing facultative certificate casualty covers is even trickier, due mainly to the uncertainty arising from delayed loss reporting and settlement. Because of this increased uncertainty, the actuary's role can be more important in pricing and monitoring the results.

As with property excess, a cover may be exposure rated via manual rates and increased limits factors, together with exposure evaluation and underwriting judgement. The same Formula 6.2.3 may be used to determine RLC except that the ELCF will be based upon increased limits loss cost tables and the RCF may be determined both by facts and by judgments regarding the cedant's basic limits rate level and increased limits factors.

Since most companies use Insurance Services Office (ISO) increased limits factors for casualty pricing (especially for commercial lines), it is very important that the actuaries very closely monitor ISO factors and understand their meaning.

Most increased limits factors, including those published by ISO, have no provision for allocated loss adjustment expense (ALAE) outside of the basic limit. ALAE is usually covered on an excess basis per claim either 1) proportional to the indemnity loss share of the excess cover vis-a-vis the total, or 2) by adding the ALAE to the indemnity loss before applying the attachment point and limit. Thus ELCFs based upon increased limits factors must be adjusted to cover the reinsurer's share of ALAE.

Since policies subject to facultative coverage are larger than usual, experience rating often comes into play. The simplest method of experience rating is to first experience rate the basic limit or the whole layer up to the proposed excess attachment point, if it is not too high, to get an experience-based loss cost. This experience-based loss cost may be used together with the reinsurer's ELCF table to determine the reinsurance expected loss, which may then be discounted to the RLC.

For a buffer layer of coverage where the likelihood of loss penetration is significant, it might be possible to obtain some indication directly from a careful analysis of the large loss experience of the insured. To see this let us consider the following example:

Example 6.2.7

Facts:

1. Pricing for 1990 policy period
2. General liability premises/operations exposure
3. Policy limit = \$1,000,000, no aggregate
4. Estimated 1990 total limits premium = \$275,000
5. Estimated 1990 basic limits premium (\$25,000 limit) = \$100,000
6. *PPLR* = 70% (excluding unallocated loss adjustment expense from the loss cost)
7. Attachment point = \$250,000
8. Reinsurance limit = \$750,000
9. ALAE covered pro rata
10. *CR* = 20%

11. $BF = 5\%$

12. $IXL = 15\%$

13. Have exposure and loss experience for policy years 1984 through 1988, consisting of exposures, basic and total limits premiums, current evaluation of basic limits losses and a detailed history for each known claim larger than $25,000

Suppose that for this class of business and for this layer ($750,000 excess of $250,000), we (the reinsurer) want to price to an undiscounted TER of 10%. Suppose that the cedant's basic limits premium was determined from a standard experience and schedule rating plan which we believe to be adequate. Also suppose that the cedant uses the appropriate ISO increased limits factors which we believe to be adequate, and which include the ISO risk loading but no ALAE provision for the layer. Suppose the ISO increased limits factors for this exposure are as follows:

Table 6.2.8 (Fictitious) ISO Increased Limits Factors

(1) Policy Limit	(2) Published Factor	(3) Factor without risk load
$ 100,000	1.65	1.5405
250,000	2.10	1.9077
1,000,000	2.75	2.4264

Suppose that the cedant is offering us a manual difference excess premium of $65,000 calculated by:

14. Manual difference excess premium
$= (\$100{,}000)(2.75 - 2.10) = \$65{,}000$

This is the simplest technical price determination possible. Some reinsurers stop here. However, let us continue onward. Suppose that, based upon a study of the relationship of ALAE to claim size for this type of exposure, we believe that an appropriate loading for pro rata ALAE is 10% of indemnity loss cost for this layer. Then if we believe the ISO increased limits factors to be adequate for this exposure, the reinsurance expected loss cost, RLC, could be calculated as follows (with PP = basic limits premium):

15. $RLC = (ELCF) \times (PP) \times (PPLR) \,/\, RCF$
$= [(2.4264\text{-}1.9077)(1.10)][(\$100{,}000)(.70)/(1.00)]$
$= [(0.5187)(1.10)](\$70{,}000)$
$= (0.5706)(\$70{,}000) = \$39{,}942$

ELCF is basic limits expected loss cost

Then the reinsurance premium can be calculated via Formula. You can verify that this premium is:

16. $$\text{Reinsurance premium 1} = \frac{\$39{,}942}{(.75)(.85)(.90)} = \$69{,}616$$

Please note that the assumption that ISO increased limits factors appropriately describe the claim severity potential for this insured is a very crucial assumption. Since facultatively-reinsured exposures are often more hazardous, the underwriter may believe that often the claim severity distribution is more dangerous. The actuary or underwriter designing a facultative certificate pricing procedure may wish to adjust ISO claim severity curves accordingly, or allow the certificate pricer to do so on a case-by-case basis.

Now suppose that we are willing to price to a discounted loss basis. Suppose that we have an estimated expected loss payout pattern for this type of exposure and this layer. And suppose that the corresponding discount factor, using current U.S. Treasury rates (risk-free) timed to the payout pattern and reflecting the implications of the current tax law, is .80. Assume that with the reflection of investment income in the pricing, we wish to increase the TER to 20%. Then you can check that the new RLC and price are:

17. RLC = (.80)($39,942) = $31,954

18. Reinsurance premium 2 = $62,654

In this case, the offered $65,000 premium looks adequate. And the pricing endeavor usually stops here. But what about the large loss experience? Suppose that for accident years 1984-1988, there are three claims known as of June 30, 1989 whose indemnity values are greater than $25,000, none of which are larger than $250,000. Can we use any of the large loss information on this insured to price the cover, or at least to help form an opinion as to the adequacy of the exposure rate premium? If the underwriter wants an answer to this question, what can the actuary say? Let us investigate one possible method for incorporating the excess experience into the pricing consideration.

Advanced Topic 6.2.9

Assume that we believe that the ISO claim severity distribution is reasonably accurate for this insured's large loss exposure and that the ISO distribution can be used to compute probabilities of loss for points above $25,000 and also to compute severity moments. We will use the reported claim frequency excess of $25,000 to judge the relative adequacy of the indicated premiums for the layer $750,000 excess $250,000.

Let us use the fact that there are three reported losses in excess of $25,000 to test the hypothesis that $65,000 is an adequate reinsurance premium with respect to discounted loss cost. To do this, we first calculate what the $65,000 premium implies about reinsurance expected loss cost, claim count, and severity. Assume for convenience that the ISO claim severity distribution is a Pareto of the form in Formula 6.2.5 or Appendix 6.5A with parameters $b = 10{,}000$ and $q = 1.1$ (this is consistent with Table 6.2.8 with a 50% loading for ALAE in the basic limit rate).

You can verify the following facts (using the Example 6.2.7 Facts and a 20% TER):

1. If the reinsurance premium with respect to discounted losses $=$ $65,000, then the discounted expected loss cost $=$ $33,150, and with a discount factor of 0.8, we can calculate the undiscounted expected loss cost $=$ $41,438.

2. $E[X250; 750] = \$329{,}934$
(expected indemnity claim severity in the excess layer \$750,000 excess \$250,000 where X250 notates the excess claim size for claims strictly greater than \$250,000—see Appendix 6.5A, item 10)

3. $E[N250] = 0.1142$
(expected number of claims in excess of \$250,000 —don't forget the 1.10 ALAE loading in (1))

4. $\text{Prob}[X > 250{,}000 \mid X > 25{,}000] = 0.1102$
(Use Formula 6.2.4 or Appendix 6.5A, item 9)

5. $E[N25] = 1.0363$
(expected number of claims in excess of \$25,000)

Now we want to determine what this expectation of 1.0363 claims in excess of \$25,000 in 1990 per \$100,000 of basic limits premium implies for the number of reported claims for accident years 1984-1988 as of June 30, 1989. We need to deflate this 1.0363 claim frequency back to 1984-1988 level and also convert it to an expectation for reported claims.

Suppose that we believe, based upon ISO and other industry information, that the large loss severity trend from 1984 to 1990 is about 13% per annum and the ground-up frequency trend is 1% per annum. (For simplicity, assume constant trends.) And suppose that we believe, based upon the claim severity model, that the severity and frequency trends translate into an 11.9% frequency trend excess of \$25,000. (Note: This can be seen by deflating the Pareto parameter **b** by 13% per annum back for four years and measuring the exponential effect on the probability $\text{Prob}[X > 25{,}000]$. Combine this exponentially smoothed annual change with the 1% ground-up frequency trend to get the 11.9% frequency trend excess of \$25,000.)

Also, suppose that we expect that, based upon reinsurance data for this type of business, claims will be reported over time in a pattern defined by a lognormal distribution with mean 3 and coefficient of variation 1.311 ($\mu = 0.6$, $\sigma = 1$ in the usual parameterization—see

Appendix 6.5B), with time measured from the midpoint of the accident year. Note that this means that 5% of the claims are expected to be reported beyond 10 years after the beginning of the accident year. Suppose that for this cedant, for this insured, we expect claim emergence above $25,000 to be no different from the reinsurance portfolio information. Then the lognormal report lags (percent reported as of each evaluation age) may be used to un-develop the ultimate claims. Note that the basic limits premiums are adjusted to 1990 rate level:

Table 6.2.10 An Implied 1990 Excess Claim Frequency Deflated and Un-developed to 6/30/89 Level

(1) Year	(2) Adjusted BL Prem	(3) Deflated Claim Freq (in $000's)	(4) Expected Report Lag	(5) Expected No. Claims
1984	75	0.5278	.844	0.334
1985	80	0.5906	.784	0.370
1986	85	0.6609	.691	0.388
1987	90	0.7396	.537	0.357
1988	95	0.8276	.274	0.215
Total	425			1.664

If we make the further assumption that the reported claims vary according to a Poisson distribution, a not-too-absurd assumption which is discussed further in Example 6.3.21, then the reported claims for each year will be distributed Poisson with parameter equal to the number in column 5. And the total will be Poisson with parameter 1.664. In this case you can verify the following probability:

6. $\text{Prob}[RN25 \geq 3 \mid E[RN25] = 1.664] = 0.2333$
   where $RN25$ is the number of claims reported excess of $25,000 for accident years 1984-1988 as of 6/30/89.

Is $RN25 = 3$ significant? If $65,000 is an adequate premium, then, under our modeling assumptions, there is a 23% chance of seeing three or more claims. The underwriter must now ponder this, together with all our other knowledge of the particular insured's exposure and general rate adequacy/inadequacy for this class of business in order to make a decision. And don't forget the importance of the assumption that the ISO claim severity distribution is appropriate. We might accept the $65,000 premium offered or we may require at least $71,500 (adjusting the offered manual difference $65,000 to cover ALAE pro rata).

A more sophisticated actuary or underwriter might pursue a Bayesian approach, perhaps setting up a gamma/Poisson a priori claim count model and using the three reported claims to conditionalize the model to a posterior distribution. Or a credibility approach may be taken, weighing the expected 1.664 reported claims with the three actually reported. You can use the ideas in the Credibility chapter to pursue this.

As with property excess, it is clear that the exposure rating methods can be programmed into an interactive computer package for underwriters. It is also clear that the procedure used to calculate the Poisson parameter 1.664 above could be programmed into the package, and that a table of probabilities corresponding to different reported claim levels could be generated so that the underwriter could determine the significance of the number of reported large claims. And a Bayesian or credibility procedure could be programmed. Also, as with property coverage, it is very important to monitor relative rate level and results in appropriate business segment detail. The actuarial evaluations and opinions regarding future case reserve development and IBNR emergence should be very important to the underwriters.

Facultative automatic programs

These large multi-insured programs are very similar to treaties. One difference, however, is that the reinsurance premium for a facultative automatic excess cover is usually computed on a policy-by-policy basis using agreed-upon excess rates, instead of as a rate times total subject premium as is usually the case for treaties. Thus the reinsurance premium may be more responsive to the individual exposures ceded to the reinsurer. The risk of anti-selection against the reinsurer on a non-obligatory contract should be evaluated by the underwriter.

The pricing of these agreements is the same or similar to the pricing of excess treaties.

Reinsurance treaties in general

Since a treaty covers a share of an indeterminate (at the beginning) set of insurance policies, insureds are rarely individually underwritten and priced by the reinsurer. Instead, the reinsurance underwriter/pricer considers the whole set (book of business) of subject policies. To do this, the reinsurer evaluates first the management of the potential cedant. What is their management philosophy and ability? Are they honest, fair-dealing? Do they know what they are doing? Is the company financially solid? What are their business plans? Why do they want reinsurance? Why do they need reinsurance?

Once the reinsurer is satisfied that this is a company and these are people we would like to deal with on a long-term basis, we can then evaluate their underwriting, primary pricing, marketing, and claims handling ability. Since individual insureds are not usually underwritten by the reinsurer, we must be satisfied with the cedant's underwriting expertise and pricing for the exposure we may assume. For any treaty, we must understand the cedant's insurance exposures, rate level, and limits sold. Many reinsurers will send a team of marketing and underwriting people to perform a pre-quote audit, and will also send claims people to review the company's claims handling and reserving practices.

The reinsurer (or the lead reinsurer on a multi-reinsurer brokered treaty) also reviews the structure of the cedant's reinsurance program; that is, how all the reinsurance contracts, facultative and treaty, fit together to provide benefits to the cedant. Lastly, the reinsurer evaluates the particular reinsurance treaties and suggested rates if offered, or we create a program and rates to offer to the cedant company.

Actuaries can provide extremely useful, and often necessary, technical support for treaty business. They can perform the four functions listed at the beginning of the *Facultative Certificates* section (p. 287). They can also get involved in the technical evaluation and pricing of individual large and/or difficult treaties. Experience rating is much more important for treaties, so the actuarial tools of data analysis and loss modeling can be critical to a reinsurer's ability to write difficult exposures, especially casualty exposures where long-tail loss development and IBNR are critical factors.

Proportional treaties

A traditional quota-share treaty covers a share of the cedant's net retention after all other reinsurance covers. The cedant's historical experience net of all other reinsurance must be evaluated. If the cedant's other reinsurance covers have been approximately the same for many years, then Schedules O and P of the cedant's Annual Statement may be used for this evaluation. If the other covers have changed significantly so that the remaining net exposure to be covered differs from the cedant's past net, then the reinsurer must request historical data which can be recast to the proper net exposure. The underwriter/actuary must be careful that the evaluation includes an adequate provision for reported case reserve development and IBNR.

The reinsurer's evaluation of the cedant's net historical experience should not only consider averages, but should reflect the effects of the underwriting/pricing cycle and of random fluctuations. And this history should be adjusted to the future coverage period by the reinsurer's estimates of relative rate level (including the underwriting cycle).

Proportional treaties often have contingent or sliding-scale ceding commissions. In each case, the reinsurer pays the cedant a provisional commission on the reinsurance gross written premium as it is transferred to the reinsurer. At suitable dates (often quarterly), the cumulative experience on the treaty (usually from the beginning if there is a deficit carryforward, or over some period such as three years) is reviewed. If it is profitable, the reinsurer pays the cedant an additional commission; if it is unprofitable, the cedant returns some of the provisional commission to the reinsurer. An example should clarify this.

Example 6.2.11

Facts:

1. 25% quota share on various property lines
2. Cumulative subject written premium = \$44,000,000
3. Cumulative subject earned premium = \$40,000,000
4. Provisional commission = 35%
5. Commission slides 0.5% for each loss ratio 1%
6. Minimum commission = 30%
7. Reinsurer provisional expense and profit margin = 10% (at 55% loss ratio)
8. Cumulative subject incurred loss = \$26,400,000

You can verify the following facts:

9. Subject loss ratio = 66%
10. Indicated cumulative reinsurance commission = 35% + 0.5*(55% − 66%) = 29.5%
11. Cumulative commission adjustment = −5% (minimum)
12. Cumulative reinsurance written premium = \$11,000,000
13. Cumulative reinsurance earned premium = \$10,000,000
14. Cumulative return commission (to reinsurer) = \$500,000 (5% of earned premium; some part may have already been adjusted at previous evaluation dates)

To properly evaluate the historical results on this treaty, the reinsurer must be sure that appropriate loss development is accounted for, and, if the reinsurer wishes to evaluate the bottomline result, then appropriate investment income must be assigned. Also, the reinsurer must consider the long-term required economic return (RER) for this type of treaty and this type of exposure. For each type of cover, each type of exposure, the RER is some fraction of the reinsurer's TER defined earlier. The fraction may be less than one if the reinsurer is willing to be satisfied with a long-term return lower than the pricing formula target.

A simplified evaluation formula parallels the pricing Formula 6.2.1 we saw earlier:

Formula 6.2.12 Evaluation Formula For Existing Contracts

Question: Is $AER \geq RER$? (Evaluation formula)

where

RER = required economic return (on pure premium)

AER = actual economic return (on pure premium)

$$= \frac{(1-CR-BF)\times(1-IXL)\times(1+UPRF)\times REP-DF\times RIL}{(1-CR-BF)\times(1-IXL)\times REP}$$

$UPRF$ = unearned premium reserve factor = $0.5 \times \text{UPRR} \times \text{UPIF}$ (half-year's interest)

$UPRR$ = average ratio of unearned premium reserve to earned premium (for each year)

$UPIF$ = unearned premium reserve investment return factor

REP = reinsurer earned premium (gross)

DF = loss discount factor

RIL = reinsurer incurred loss

CR, BF and IXL as defined in Formula 6.2.1

Suppose that with respect to a conservative risk-free interest rate, the cash flow for this type of contract (or for this contract in particular, if the cash flow is known) allows a loss discount factor of .96 on losses and a 7% short-term investment rate on unearned premium reserve balances held (on average one-half year) by the reinsurer.

Suppose that *UPRR* = 40% for the contract in Example 6.2.11, and the reinsurer needs *IXL* = 10%.

You can verify that, with respect to the minimum 30% commission, the actual economic return on pure premium has been:

15. *AER* = 0.83%

The reinsurer's required economic return should be based upon the degree of risk transferred and upon the statutory surplus relief arising from the ceding commission on the unearned premium reserve. The surplus effect arises from the fact that the cedant's unearned premium liability decreases by the amount of gross unearned premium ceded, while assets decrease only by the amount of the cash transfer, premium net of provisional commission. Since the subject unearned premium is currently $4,000,000, you can verify that the current surplus relief is:

16. Cedant's surplus relief = $350,000.
    (From (1) and (4))

This is, in effect, a statutory surplus loan; which is why a reinsurer will charge an increment on top of the usual risk margin. Suppose in this case, that the reinsurer wants a 7% return on the surplus loan. To keep this simple, suppose that the unearned premium reserve has been constant over time, so that the surplus relief has been constant. From an assumption that UPRR = 40%, you can verify the following facts:

17. One-year reinsurance earned premium = $2,500,000
    (From (12) and (13))

18. One-year required surplus loan return = $24,500
    (From (16))

19. Surplus loan return stated as a return on earned risk pure premium (with provisional *CR* = 35% and *IXL* = 10%) = 1.68%

Suppose the reinsurer needs a minimum 5% risk *RER* (with respect to risk pure premium) for this treaty plus the 1.68% surplus loan return for a total *RER* of 6.68%. Then the 0.83% *AER* might prompt the reinsurer to consider nonrenewal unless the future profitability looks better or the minimum ceding commission can be negotiated downward. You can verify the following:

20. If the loss ratio were 65% ($CR = 30\%$), then the reinsurer's 5% margin on gross ceded premium translates into a 2.35% *AER*.

21. If the loss ratio were 55%, then the reinsurer's 10% margin on gross ceded premium translates into a 11.14% *AER*, thus exceeding the 6.68% *RER*.

The evaluation of a (true ground-up net retention) quota share on casualty exposure would be similar except that the reinsurer would have to be very careful about loss development. And because of the additional uncertainty arising from loss development, most likely the reinsurer's *RER* would be higher.

A property surplus-share treaty is somewhat more difficult to evaluate. Since the reinsurer does not provide coverage for small insureds, and covers larger insureds in proportion to their size above some fixed retention, the reinsurer must be more concerned with the cedant's pricing of larger insureds. An example should clarify this.

Example 6.2.13

Facts:

1. Four line first surplus not to exceed \$800,000

2. Maximum cedant retention = \$200,000

Then the following statements are true:

3. Maximum reinsurance limit per policy = \$800,000

4. For a policy with limit $\leq$ \$200,000, the reinsurer receives no premium and pays no losses.

5. For a policy with limit = \$500,000, the reinsurer receives 60% of the policy's premium less ceding commission and brokerage fee and pays 60% of the policy's losses.

6. For a policy with limit = \$1,000,000, the reinsurer receives 80% of the policy's premium less ceding commission and brokerage fee and pays 80% of the policy's losses.
7. For a policy with limit = \$2,000,000, the reinsurer receives 40% of the policy's premium less ceding commission and brokerage fee and pays 40% of the policy's losses.

It is easy to see that, given this complicated proportional structure depending upon the limit of each policy, the premium and loss accounting for a surplus-share treaty is somewhat complex. Despite this, surplus-share treaties are popular because they provide more large loss protection than a quota share and are much easier for the reinsurer to evaluate and price (usually only the ceding commission and slide is the subject of negotiations) than an excess treaty.

A surplus-share treaty is generally riskier than a simple quota share. So the reinsurer will charge a correspondingly higher margin for risk assumption.

Working cover excess treaties

A working cover is an excess layer where losses are expected. The reinsurer will consider the cedant's policy limits distribution by line of business and will want to examine the historical gross large loss experience in order to determine the types of losses generated by the exposure and to study the development patterns. As we discussed for facultative certificates, an excess cover is usually riskier than a proportional cover. So the reinsurer will be more mindful of the predictive error and fluctuation potential, and will charge a higher margin for assuming this risk.

If losses are covered per-occurrence, then the reinsurer is exposed by policy limits below the attachment point because of the "clash" of losses on different policies or coverages arising from the same occurrence. If ALAE is added to individual claims in order to determine the reinsurer's excess share, then losses from some policy limits below the attachment point will bleed into the excess layer.

The reinsurance premium is usually specified by a reinsurance rate times subject premium. However, for liability coverage, it may be on an increased limits premium collected basis as it often is for facultative automatic programs. Here the total reinsurance premum is the sum of the individually-calculated reinsurance premiums for each policy, as we saw for the premium offered in Example (6.2.7) item 14.

In either case, ideally the reinsurance pricing consists of both an exposure rating and an experience rating, together with a reconciliation of the two rates. The exposure rating differs from facultative certificate pricing in that the reinsurer deals with broad classes of business instead of individual insureds. The reinsurer considers manual rate relativities to bureau rates and/or to other companies writing the same exposure, and evaluates the cedant's experience and schedule rating plans and pricing abilities. The increased limits factors used by the cedant for liability coverages are especially important. The same Formulas 6.2.1 and 6.2.3 can be used, except that the rate correction factor RCF now adjusts for both basic limits and increased limits (in)adequacy. If the coverage is per-occurrence, the reinsurer must load the manual difference rate for the clash exposure. If the coverage includes ALAE, the reinsurer must adjust the manual increased limits factors to account for this additional exposure.

The reinsurer must adjust the historical experience to the estimated level of the proposed coverage period by trend factors for the losses and rate on-level factors for the premiums. This is opposite to the backwards deflation in the facultative Example 6.2.7 we saw earlier. Working cover treaties are often large enough so that many of the risk parameters can be determined either directly from the exposure and loss history or by a credibility weighting of the history with more general information.

For working covers, the provisional reinsurance premium is often subject to retrospective rating, with the final premium over certain coverage periods, such as three years, being adjusted within bounds according to the actual loss experience. A simple example should clarify this.

Example 6.2.14

Facts:

1. Proposed attachment point = \$300,000
2. Proposed reinsurance limit = \$700,000
3. Coverage is per-occurrence
4. Coverage is on an accident year basis (losses occurring on or after the effective date up through the termination date)
5. ALAE is added to indemnity for each claim before the portion excess of the attachment point is calculated and the limit applied
6. Subject exposure is all liability and workers compensation for a medium-sized primary company
7. The cedant wants a proposal for a three-year retrospective rated treaty incepting Jan. 1, 1990
8. $CR = 0\%$
9. $BF = 0\%$
10. Estimated 1990 subject premium = \$100,000,000
11. Possible reinsurance premium range to \$10,000,000
12. An underwriting review has been performed
13. A claims review has been performed
14. We have Annual Statements and Annual Reports for the last five years; a more detailed breakdown of premiums, deviations from bureau manual rates, limits profiles, increased limits fac-tors, basic limits premiums, total subject premiums and basic and total subject losses as of June 30, 1989 by subline for the last five years plus predictions for 1990; a detailed history for each known claim larger than \$25,000 occurring in the last ten years.

15. We have the names of contact people at the ceding company; in particular, an actuary to talk with.

The exposure consists of private passenger and commercial automobile liability, premises/operations general liability with incidental products coverage, homeowners and SMP section II, and workers' compensation. The cedant writes limits up to $10,000,000, but purchases facultative reinsurance for coverage in excess of $1,000,000. The cedant also purchases facultative coverage above $300,000 for any difficult exposures on the reinsurer's exclusion list, and a 90% facultative automatic cover for his umbrella programs.

Before getting into the complications arising from a retrospective rating plan, let us first consider how to go about determining a flat (i.e., fixed) rate.

Note 6.2.15 Burning Cost

A traditional excess rating methodology prevalent among reinsurers is the "burning cost" method. To compute a burning-cost rate, the underwriter divides the sum of known losses in the excess layer occurring over some time period, usually five years, by the cedant's subject premium for the same time period. To get a rate, this ratio is then multiplied by a selected loss development factor, perhaps multiplied by some selected trend factor, loaded by some "free cover" factor and divided by a permissible loss ratio of the form $(1 - CR - BF - IXL - TER)$. Clearly, a problem with this summary approach is that it does not allow you to carefully take into account underlying exposure changes, rate changes, policy limits changes, true excess IBNR emergence and development, true excess claim frequency growth and severity growth, and the excess aggregate loss fluctuation potential. I would argue that burning-cost rating is not very informative even for property excess covers for which it was designed. Unfortunately, it has been misapplied to the pricing of casualty covers. For more on this topic, see Ferguson (1978) and Patrik's review. Recently, the term "burning cost" has sometimes been used to include more legitimate actuarial experience rating methods.

Let us return to the example. For a full discussion of the pricing of casualty working covers, see Patrik and John (1980). We will only sketch an outline of the procedure and add a few improvements developed since then.

STEP 1: The first step is to reconcile with the cedant's audited financial reports, as best as possible, all the exposure and loss data received from the cedant. This is an ongoing process as we ask for and receive more data.

STEP 2: The second step is to segregate the main types of underlying exposure for separate consideration. In this case, we might want to consider the following breakdown:

Table 6.2.16 Exposure Categories

Private passenger automobile

Commercial automobile

Premises/operations

Homeowners Section II

Special Multi-Peril Section II

Workers compensation

Umbrella

These categories can or must be further broken down as desirable or feasible. If we can, it is desirable to split the underlying exposure at least according to applicable increased limits table and by policy limit.

STEP 3: The next step is to perform an exposure rating. This is best done by estimating the aggregate excess loss cost for 1990 based upon the estimated 1990 exposure and general pricing information. The overall exposure loss cost would be the sum of the exposure loss costs for the individual exposure categories. The exposure loss cost for each category would be determined as in Example 6.2.7, item 15.

For example, suppose that the company writes commercial automobile light exposure and the following policy limits distribution is estimated for 1990 for a group of states with the same 10/20 basic limit and the same increased limits tables and, for simplicity, adequate basic rates:

Table 6.2.17 Commercial Automobile Liability

(1) Policy Limit	(2) Estimated Total Subject Premium	(3) Cedant's Inc. Limits Factor	(4) Adequate ELCF
\$ 100,000	\$ 3,000,000	2.10	NA
\$ 300,000	2,000,000	2.40	.0346
\$ 500,000	2,000,000	2.51	.1070
\$ 750,000	1,000,000	2.60	.1449
\$1,000,000 or more	2,000,000	2.66	.1526
Total	\$10,000,000	2.38	

The Adequate ELCFs are stated as fractions of 10/20 basic limits losses including all ALAE; but they allocate to the layer \$700,000 excess of \$300,000 the expected loss plus ALAE per accident arising from each policy limit. The reinsurer has tables of Adequate ELCFs for each type of coverage, attachment point and rate jurisdiction or has an exposure rating computer program to compute them. These are based upon claim severity distributions, as are the increased limits factors.

Assuming that the cedant's permissible loss ratio (expected loss and ALAE to premium) for this business is 65%, you can verify:

16. Manual difference risk pure premium = \$234,040
(From Table 6.2.17, columns 2 and 3: remember that the subject premium is for coverage up to a \$1,000,000 limit)

Suppose we believe that the basic limits loss costs implied by the basic limits premiums and permissible loss ratio are adequate. You can then verify:

17. Expected loss based upon the ELCFs = \$184,964
(From Table 6.2.17, columns 2 and 4)

Note that this is not yet loaded for clash exposure or for risk.

An even better way of estimating an exposure loss cost is to break the estimation down to an estimate of the number of excess claims and an estimate of their sizes. For example, suppose we believe that the indemnity loss distribution is Pareto with $b = 25{,}000$ and $q = 2$ and that the distribution of the sum of indemnity loss and ALAE per claim is Pareto with $b = 30{,}000$ and $q = 2$. Please note that these parameters are selected simply to make the computations easier for you to check; *a* more appropriate current q value is between 1 and 1.2. For convenience, let us continue to use the term "claim" here, although the cover is per-occurrence.

You can verify the entries in Table 6.2.18, where the Table 6.2.17 implied excess loss costs are assumed and we simplistically assume that the effect of adding ALAE to each claim increases the effective policy limit by 20% (along with the parameter change):

Table 6.2.18 Excess Expected Loss, Claim Severity and Count

(1) Policy Limit	(2) Effective Policy Limit	(3) Expected Loss Cost	(4) Expected Claim Severity	(5) Expected Claim Count (3)/(4)
100	120	$ 0	$ 0	0
300	360	18,742	50,769	.3692
500	600	55,418	157,143	.3527
750	900	36,225	212,903	.1701
1,000	1,000	74,579	224,272	.3325
Total		$184,964	$151,053	1.2245

Now we have exposure-determined estimates of excess expected claim count and severity. Why this added complication? The answer is that with a few mild assumptions regarding second (and perhaps third) moments for the claim count and claim amount distributions, we can use a standard risk theoretic model to estimate the distribution of the excess aggregate loss, the loss the reinsurer will cover. This standard model writes the aggregate loss naturally as the sum of the individual claims (i.e., events) as follows:

Formula 6.2.19 Aggregate Loss

$$L = X(1) + X(2) + \ldots + X(N)$$

where L = rv (random variable) for aggregate loss
N = rv for number of claims (occurrences, events)
$X(i)$ = rv for the dollar size of the ith claim

Here N and $X(i)$ refer to the excess number of claims and the excess amount of the ith excess claim respectively. The model relates the distributions of L, N and the $X(i)$'s. In particular, under reasonable assumptions, the kth moment of L is completely determined by the first k moments of N and the $X(i)$'s. The model is outlined in Appendix 6.5C. Here we will only discuss its usage.

Underlying Table 6.2.18 is an assumption that the claim severities follow a censored (at policy limits) Pareto distribution. With this model, or with any other reasonable and tested model, we can easily add another column to the table consisting of the individual claim variance for each policy limit. Likewise, if we assume that the total ground-up claim count follows either a Poisson or a negative binomial distribution, then so do the excess claim counts. So a column of claim count variance for each policy limit can be added.

We can assemble these moments into estimates of the variance of the aggregate loss L for each policy limit. For this case where the parameters for N and the $X(i)$'s are assumed to be known, the L's are independent and their variances can be added to estimate the overall variance for the excess losses arising from this commercial automobile exposure category. Likewise, third and higher moments can be handled. For the more interesting and realistic case where the parameters themselves are uncertain, the L's are no longer independent from the point of view of the observer/actuary, so the second and higher moments do not add. This is covered thoroughly in Patrik and John (1980).

From the first, second, and third moments of L, we can get a pretty good idea of its distribution, and riskiness. If you are really ambitious, you can verify the following:

18. Assuming that the excess claim counts are Poisson, then for the case with known parameters, the standard deviation of the excess aggregate loss arising from the Table 6.2.18 exposure is approximately $185,000.

The estimation of excess exposure for other categories would be similar. For workers' compensation, for example, excess loss cost factor differences would be weighted by estimated subject premium by hazard group, by major state grouping, or you could estimate the underlying claim severity distributions by state by hazard group.

We assemble our estimates of the excess claim count, claim severity, and aggregate excess loss from each exposure category and perform the appropriate additions to get total expectations and higher moments. The total expectations should be loaded for clash exposure arising from more than one policy or coverage for the same occurrence. If we assume that, based upon the cedant's book of business, the loading should be 5%, I would prefer to increase the claim count (and thus aggregate) expectation by 5%. This has the effect of increasing the variance of aggregate excess loss by approximately 5% (see Appendix 6.5C, item 3).

STEP 4: For a working cover such as this, the next step is an experience rating. Since we have a detailed reserving and payment history for each claim over $25,000 for the past ten years (14), we should work with these data. As with the earlier facultative example, we would use the data for each exposure category to evaluate claim count and claim severity in excess of an attachment point lower than the proposed $300,000. For example, if the ground-up claim severity inflation has been less than 13% per annum for the last ten years (and into 1990), then we can evaluate a $100,000 attachment point. The preferred method is to inflate the individual claim values to a common 1990 level and work from there. (See Patrik and John 1980).

Suppose we now have ten-year development triangles for excess of $100,000 inflated claim counts and average sizes for the Commercial Automobile category we were exposure rating. A very delicate issue in the trending is that of policy limits. If a 1980 claim on a policy with limit less than $100,000 inflates to above $100,000, would the policy limit sold in 1990 be greater than $100,000, so to allow this excess claim? Of course, the counter-argument is that policy limits are not increasing as rapidly as claim severity inflation. If possible, information on the cedant's policy limits distributions over time should be obtained; otherwise, Solomon-like judgment must be displayed by the underwriter/actuary.

The excess claim counts can be developed by the usual methods, or better methods if you can manage (see the section "Reinsurance Loss Reserving," p. 335). Claim development statistics from the reinsurer's book of similarly exposed treaties can also be used, and credibility methods can balance the answers. You can be sure that a ten-year triangle is not enough for most excess claims development, so a tail factor for the cedant's experience must be obtained from your broader excess claims IBNR statistics. Excess claim severity development can be studied in total by accident year, by report year, etc., using various actuarial methods, or individual claims can be analyzed judgementally.

Besides the usual development triangles, a fairly good exhibit for examining excess development, making judgments and explaining them to yourself and to underwriters and marketing people is displayed in Exhibit 6.2.20.

This type of format allows you to see if your purely technical answers make sense, especially for claim severity. Sections A and B of Exhibit 6.2.20 have no actuarial estimates at all, except for the adjusted on-level subject pure premiums in column 2. Displayed are the actual closed and known excess claim count and average size growth over the past one-and-one-half years.

The actuarial estimates are concentrated in Section C, columns (5), (6) and (7). The reasonableness of these estimates may be judged in comparison with the facts to date. Try various reasonable estimates on for size. The mean frequency and severity estimates derived from these are displayed in columns (12) and (10) respectively. If we use the estimates which exclude the last two accident years of data, we have a mean frequency of 1.266 per $1,000,000 of subject earned

Exhibit 6.2.20 Commercial Automobile Liability

Section A: Closed Claims (Trended) $400,000 Excess $100,000

(1) Year	(2) Adj Subject Earned Prem (1,000's)	(3) Claim Count at 12/31/87	(4) Average Severity 12/31/87	(5) Claim Count at 12/31/88	(6) Average Severity 12/31/88	(7) Claim Count at 6/30/89	(8) Average Severity 6/30/89	(9) Aggregate (7) × (8) 6/30/89	(10) Claim Freq (7)/(2) × 1,000
1979	$ 8,165	10	$ 74,401	12	$ 79,447	13	$ 81,158	$1,055,059	1,592
1980	8,521	7	52,237	8	56,559	8	56,559	452,472	0.939
1981	8,852	12	87,912	13	91,472	14	100,747	1,410,461	1.582
1982	9,650	4	146,114	4	146,114	5	152,280	761,400	0.518
1983	10,423	8	91,562	10	103,700	10	103,700	1,037,004	0.959
1984	11,200	3	51,128	3	51,128	4	43,475	173,899	0.357
1985	9,523	3	78,155	4	75,386	6	89,522	537,134	0.630
1986	9,822	4	59,554	6	79,707	7	76,414	534,899	0.713
1987	10,023	1	30,000	7	50,117	7	50,117	350,822	0.698
1988	9,927	0	0	0	0	2	$ 91,200	182,400	0.201
Total	$96,106	52	$ 79,570	67	$ 82,096	76	$ 85,468	$6,495,551	0.791
Excludes last 2 Yrs	$76,156	51	$ 80,542	60	$ 85,827	67	$ 88,990	$5,962,329	0.880

Exhibit 6.2.20 Commercial Automobile Liability (continued)

Section B: Reported Claims (Trended) $400,000 Excess $100,000

(1) Year	(2) Adj Subject Earned Prem (1,000's)	(3) Claim Count at 12/31/87	(4) Average Severity 12/31/87	(5) Claim Count at 12/31/88	(6) Average Severity 12/31/88	(7) Claim Count at 6/30/89	(8) Average Severity 6/30/89	(9) Aggregate (7) × (8) 6/30/89	(10) Claim Freq (7)/(2) × 1,000
1979	$ 8,165	13	$ 78,391	13	$ 80,259	13	$ 81,158	$1,055,059	1,592
1980	8,521	8	64,025	8	56,559	9	63,139	568,247	1.056
1981	8,852	15	82,561	18	89,704	17	98,851	1,680,460	1.920
1982	9,650	6	117,410	7	141,633	7	143,905	1,007,336	0.725
1983	10,423	14	89,182	12	99,143	13	100,940	1,312,225	1.247
1984	11.200	6	62,772	7	59,128	7	59,128	413,897	0.625
1985	9,523	5	70,610	10	65,614	12	82,261	987,134	1.260
1986	9,822	6	69,703	9	65,471	9	72,767	654,901	0.916
1987	10,023	2	60,000	10	54,582	11	53,711	590,819	1.097
1988	9,927	0	0	1	$ 60,000	3	$ 70,800	212,400	0.302
Total	$96,106	75	$ 79,875	95	$ 79,639	101	$ 83,985	$8,482,480	1.051
Excludes last 2 Yrs	$76,156	73	$ 80,419	84	$ 82,856	87	$ 88,267	$7,679,261	1.142

Exhibit 6.2.20 Commercial Automobile Liability (continued)

Section C: Predictions for Claims (Trended) $400,000 Excess $100,000

(1) Year	(2) Adj Subject Earned Prem (1,000's)	(3) Open Claims 6/30/89	(4) Open Aver Size 6/30/89	(5) Open Aver Size EST. ULT.	(6) IBNR Claim Count 6/30/89	(7) IBNR Aver Size 6/30/89	(8) IBNR Aggregate (6) × (7)	(9) Total Aggregate	(10) Total Aver Size	(11) Loss Cost Rate (9)/(2)	(12) Total Claim Freq
1979	$ 8,165	0	$ 0	$100,000	0.00	$100,000	$ 0	$ 1,055,059	$ 81,158	12.92%	1.592
1980	8,521	1	115,775	100,000	0.09	100,000	9,091	561,563	61,772	6.59%	1.067
1981	8,852	3	90,000	100,000	0.53	100,000	52,577	1,763,038	100,597	19.92%	1.980
1982	9,650	2	122,968	100,000	0.45	100,000	44,681	1,006,081	135,102	10.43%	0.772
1983	10,423	3	91,740	100,000	1.44	100,000	144,444	1,481,448	102,562	14.21%	1.386
1984	11,200	3	79,999	100,000	1.09	100,000	109,249	583,148	72,060	5.21%	0.723
1985	9,523	6	75,000	100,000	2.69	100,000	268,788	1,405,923	95,720	14.76%	1.542
1986	9,822	2	60,001	100,000	3.11	100,000	311,306	1,046,205	86,370	10.65%	1.233
1987	10,023	4	59,999	100,000	6.63	100,000	662,821	1,413,642	80,192	14.10%	1.759
1988	9,927	1	300,000	100,000	4.09	100,000	409,220	691,620	97,518	6.97%	0.714
Total	$96,106	25	$ 79,477	$100,000	20.12	$100,000	$2,012,176	$11,007,727	$ 90,881	11.45%	1.260
									Std Dev =	4.29%	0.428
Excludes last 2 Yrs	$76,156	20	$ 85,847	$100,000	9.40	$100,000	$ 940,136	$ 8,902,465	$ 92,348	11.59%	1.266
									Std Dev =	4.41%	0.401

pure premium and a mean severity of $92,348 in the layer $400,000 excess of $100,000. This frequency translates into 8.229 claims excess of $100,000 for $6,500,000 of estimated subject pure premium ($10,000,000 * .65) for 1990.

You can verify the following exposure-rating values using the same Pareto claim severity model used in Table 6.2.18:

19. $\text{Prob}[X > 300{,}000 \mid X > 100{,}000\,] = 0.1479$
    $\text{Prob}[(X + \text{ALAE}) > 300{,}000 \mid (X + \text{ALAE}) > 100{,}000] = 0.1552$
    (See Appendix 6.5A, item 9 with $q = 2$, $b = 25{,}000$ or 30,000)

20. Expected claim count excess $100,000 = 7.8898 if ALAE is added to each claim, or 5.9277 (more difficult) otherwise.

    (Remember $E[N300] = 1.2245$ in Table 6.2.18)

21. Expected claim severity excess $100,000 and up to $500,000 = $98,113 if *ALAE* is added to each claim, or $95,238 otherwise. (See Appendix 6.5A, items 8 and 10)

If the Exhibit 6.2.20 experience includes ALAE added to claims, then the experience claim count estimate of 8.229 is incredibly close to the exposure expectation of 7.8898. Likewise, the experience claim severity estimate of $92,348 is remarkably close to the exposure expectation of $98,113.

Patrik (1980), Hogg and Klugman (1984), and Patrik and John (1980) discuss methods for estimating Pareto or other model parameters directly from the excess claims severity data, and the testing of those estimates. This may be useful for translating the experience summarized in Exhibit 6.2.20 into an RLC for the layer $700,000 excess of $300,000 or for any other excess layer.

If the various answers differ but cannot be further reconciled, final answers for excess $100,000 and excess $300,000 claim count and severity can be based upon a credibility balancing of the separate estimates. However, all these differences should not be ignored, but should indeed be included in your estimates of parameter (and model) uncertainty, thus giving rise to more realistic measures of variances, etc. and to risk.

As with the Step 3 exposure rating, these credibility balanced exposure/experience rating estimates are assembled into totals for expectations and variances, and perhaps higher moments. Any other overall adjustments are made, such as for clash exposure.

STEP 5: The last step is specifying the cover terms, and explaining and negotiating. Suppose our totals come out too high with respect to (11). Suppose that the estimated 1990 expected excess aggregate loss is \$10,000,000 with estimated standard deviation (including all of our uncertainty) of \$5,000,000. You can verify that if the distribution of the excess aggregate loss is assumed to be lognormal (a simplistic assumption), then:

22. The lognormal parameters are $\mu = 16.0065$, $\sigma = 0.4724$

23. Prob[$L >$ \$10,000,000] $= 0.41$

24. Prob[$L >$ \$15,000,000] $= 0.14$

25. Prob[$L >$ \$20,000,000] $= 0.04$

Suppose that, based upon both the excess loss data and upon data for similarly exposed contracts, the reinsurer believes that a loss discount factor of .80 is reasonable and the reinsurer needs $IXL = 10\%$ for this cover. If the reinsurer believes that, based both upon the above probabilities (23) through (25) and upon general considerations for this type of exposure, we need $TER = 15\%$, then you can verify that the reinsurer determines a flat premium of (remember, $CR = BF = 0$):

26. Reinsurance premium = \$10,460,000 (rounded)

Suppose that the cedant believes that the excess loss potential is significantly less than our estimate. And they want either a flat rate no higher than 8% of subject premium or a retrospectively-rated treaty with a maximum 10% rate. It's time again for us (the reinsurer) to sharpen our pencils.

The best bet is to recommend that the attachment point be increased to $350,000 or $400,000. Attachment points should naturally increase over time in an inflationary environment. Many cedants have trouble accepting this fact, and the marketing of indexed attachment point contracts in the U.S. market in the late 1970s was an attempt to enforce unobtrusively a status-quo balance between the cedant and reinsurer. However, this reasonable idea turned out to be impractical in the U.S. reinsurance market because it complicated the accounting of claims and because of anti-selection against the reinsurers who sold the idea (the best cedants found fixed attachment point excess coverage).

If you are ambitious, you can verify that for the exposure in Table 6.2.17 (and Pareto $b = 30{,}000$, $q = 2$):

27. Expected claim count excess of $350,000 = 0.9231

28. Expected claim severity excess of $350,000 = $142,775

29. Expected aggregate loss excess of $350,000 = $131,793

Compare these results to Table 6.2.18. For other exposure categories the effects will be similar. Suppose that for a cover of $650,000 excess of $350,000 the reinsurer believes that the expected aggregate loss is $7,000,000 with a standard deviation of $4,000,000.

You can verify that analogously to (22) through (25):

30. The lognormal (simplistic model) parameters are $\mu = 15.6201$, $\sigma = 0.5316$.

31. Prob[$L >$ $10,000,000] = 0.17

32. Prob[$L >$ $15,000,000] = 0.04

33. Prob[$L >$ $20,000,000] = 0.01

In this case the reinsurer might offer a retrospectively-rated treaty of the following form:

34. Provisional rate = 7%

35. Rate = reinsurer's aggregate loss (including an IBNR provision) divided by subject premium
+ 0.5% (reinsurer's margin).

36. Minimum rate = 5%

37. Maximum rate = 10%

38. Profit and deficit carryforward (into successive coverage periods)

The reinsurer would select the minimum and maximum rates so that the overall contract were balanced with respect to potential profit/loss and risk/return.

You can verify, using Formula 6.2.12:

39. If L = \$7,000,000, then AER = 21%
40. If L = \$10,000,000, then AER = 16%
41. If L = \$15,000,000, then AER = −26%

You might recognize that Formula 6.2.12 should be modified slightly for retrospective-rated contracts since, if the aggregate loss is large, the additional premium is only transferred to the reinsurer as the losses are reported and is thus not available for investment from the beginning. This could be handled by modifying the discount factor; this would lower the calculated *AERs* in items 39 through 41. Also, these contracts often have a retrospective-rating period of three years; so the reinsurance loss expectation may be more than three times \$7,000,000 because of inflation and subject exposure growth, and the standard deviation might actually be less than three times \$4,000,000. You need to make intelligent, consistent modelling assumptions.

As with facultative covers, it is clear that much of the above can and should be programmed into an interactive computer package for the underwriters and actuaries. And it is also extremely important to monitor the results of large treaties and groups of treaties. The monitoring of the pricing experience and the monitoring of the loss development and IBNR experience on the reinsurer's books and the reconciliation of both is important.

Higher exposed layer and clash layer excess treaties

Since losses are not "expected" for higher exposed and clash layers, historical loss data is sparse. And yet the layers have loss potential, or else the cedant wouldn't buy reinsurance. Prices for these covers are usually set by market conditions. The actuarial prices are largely determined by the risk loadings, and may or may not be close to the market-determined prices.

Where there is policy limits exposure, an exposure rate may be determined in the same manner as for a working cover. An experience rate may be determined by experience rating the working layers below and using these working cover rates as bases for estimating the higher exposed layer rate. The higher the layer, the greater the relative significance of the workers' compensation exposure, if any, and the clash exposure.

For pure clash layer pricing, the reinsurer should keep experience statistics on all clash covers combined to see how often and to what degree these covers are penetrated, and to see if the historical market-determined rates have been reasonable overall. The rates for various clash layers should bear reasonable relationships to each other, depending upon the underlying exposures and the distance of the attachment points from the policy limits sold. Underwriters sometimes view the market rates with regard to a notion of payback— the premium should cover one loss every m years for some selected m— but this is technical nonsense.

Property catastrophe treaties

The price for a windstorm catastrophe treaty should depend upon the attachment point, upon the cedant's accumulation of property exposure in storm-prone localities, and upon the cedant's net position on each policy after all other reinsurance. Historical experience—large losses and exposure—should be adjusted to the level of the contemplated coverage period. Changes in the cedant's non-catastrophe net retentions may have a great effect upon the catastrophe exposure excess of a given attachment point. That is, a reinsurance program can be very tricky: a small change here can have a big effect there.

The actuary can be very useful in estimating the reinsurer's total accumulated exposure to catastrophe shock losses. For each windstorm-prone locality, reinsurance exposure from every property contract should be estimated. For each contract, this would be based upon the cedant's exposed policy limits and the reinsurance coverage. Thus the reinsurer can see where too much catastrophe potential is accumulated and can better structure its own catastrophe retrocessional program. The same can be done for earthquake exposure.

Various people are working on catastrophe simulation computer programs which estimate loss distributions based upon an insurer's geographic exposure distribution. It may be possible that such programs can be modified for reinsurance use.

Aggregate excess treaties

Aggregate excess treaties are sometimes called stop-loss covers. They may be used to protect the cedant's net loss ratio. For example, suppose the cedant's expected loss ratio is 65% of net earned premium. A stop-loss cover might cover 50% of all net loss payments in excess of a 75% loss ratio up to a 90% loss ratio (the loss ratios are with respect to subject premium net of all other reinsurance coverage). The exposure subject to the treaty could be all or part of the cedant's net exposure.

In a sense, this is the ultimate reinsurance cover for protecting the cedant's net position if all else fails. Because of the magnitude of the risk transfer, you can guess that these covers are quite expensive, and often not available unless written on a nontraditional basis, as we shall see.

Another form of aggregate excess treaty provides coverage over an aggregate deductible on an excess layer. This is more interesting, so we will illustrate this alternative. The concepts for pricing a net stop loss cover are similar.

Example 6.2.21

Facts:

1. The facts are the same as in Example 6.2.14 except that the

cedant wants to retain the first \$10,000,000 of payments for the layer \$700,000 excess of \$300,000.

The cedant might want a \$10,000,000 deductible to avoid trading dollars with the reinsurer for fairly certain loss payments. Keeping the premium for the deductible, the cedant also keeps the investment income.

We (the reinsurer) would have to perform the same analysis we did in Example 6.2.14, except we would now be much more careful in our estimation of the distribution of excess aggregate loss. As we noted before, the best way to build up this distribution is from individual excess claim counts and amounts in Formula 6.2.19. But now, instead of simply estimating the first two or three moments, we may want to use more exact methods such as simulation, or the methods espoused by Phillip Heckman and Glenn Meyers (1983), by Harry Panjer (1981), or by Gary Venter (1983). For most low (excess) frequency cases, there is a positive probability, $\text{Prob}[L = 0] > 0$, a cluster point at 0, that must be accounted for. The Panjer method is especially good for the low frequency case, and has the advantage of being fairly easily explainable to non-mathematicians. We would also be very careful to account for our model and parameter uncertainty, in order to get a proper spread for the aggregate loss distribution.

Suppose we have done all our homework and now have a rigorous estimate of the distribution of aggregate loss in the layer \$700,000 excess of \$300,000 together with an analytic representation of our model and parameter uncertainty. For simplicity, suppose that once again we believe that this can be described by a lognormal with mean \$10,000,000 and standard deviation \$5,000,000. For the degree of accuracy we need here, this is now probably not a good model; we use it here only for convenience.

Remembering item 23 under Example 6.2.14, we have:

2. $\text{Prob}[L > \$10{,}000{,}000] = 0.41$

So even though the deductible is set at the reinsurer's expectation, there is significant probability of loss and thus there should be a substantial expectation in excess of the deductible. For notational convenience, define the reinsurer's loss excess of \$10,000,000, L^e10 in terms of the excess aggregate loss L as follows:

Formula 6.2.22 Reinsurer's Aggregate Excess Loss

$$L10 = \begin{cases} 0 & \text{if } L \leq \$10{,}000{,}000 \\ L - \$10{,}000{,}000 & \text{if } L > \$10{,}000{,}000 \end{cases}$$

Note that this is different from the similar notation used earlier for the number of excess claims and the excess claim size.

You can verify the following (using Appendix 6.5B):

3. $\text{Prob}[L^e10 > \$5{,}000{,}000] = 0.14$
   (See Example 6.2.14, item 24)

4. $\text{Prob}[L^e10 > \$10{,}000{,}000] = 0.04$
   (See Example 6.2.14, item 25)

5. $E[L^e10] = \$1{,}867{,}000$
   (See Appendix 6.5C, item 6)

6. Standard deviation of $L^e10 = \$3{,}688{,}000$

For an unlimited cover, the risk transfer (if measured by 6) overwhelms the expectation of \$1,867,000, so the reinsurer must charge a substantial margin. The cedant will probably be reluctant to pay so large a premium and the reinsurer may be reluctant to assume so great a risk. To cut down the risk transfer and the price, the reinsurer would want an aggregate limit. Suppose the aggregate limit is \$5,000,000. You can verify the following:

7. $E[L^e10;5] = \$1{,}252{,}500$
   (expectation of L^e10 in the layer \$0 to \$5,000,000)
   (See Appendix 6.5C, item 7)

8. Standard deviation of $L^e10;5 = \$1{,}884{,}000$

The aggregate limit of \$5,000,000 may be acceptable to the cedant if they believe an excess aggregate loss of \$15,000,000 is impossible. Remember that our lognormal says that the probability of exceeding \$15,000,000 is about 14%.

Along with our evaluation of the incurred excess aggregate loss distribution, we would more carefully estimate the excess loss payout distribution. Suppose that for each value of $L^e 10;5$, we estimate a discount factor $DF(L^e 10;5)$ based upon the expected payout pattern of $L^e 10;5$, available U.S. Treasury instruments, the effect of taxes, and the risk that the payout may be different from expected.

Suppose we need $IXL = 10\%$ for this limited cover, and $TER = 10\%$ on an undiscounted basis and $TER = 30\%$ on a discounted basis, where an average discount factor is $E[DF(L^e 10;5)] = .60$. Remembering that $CR = BF = 0$, you can use Formula 6.2.1 to verify the following rounded premiums:

9. Reinsurance premium 1 (undiscounted) = \$1,546,300
10. Reinsurance premium 2 (discounted) = \$1,193,000

The cedant may object to paying such a large premium for a pure risk cover - where we believe the chance of the aggregate losses reaching the reinsurer is only 41%, and the chance of a complete \$5,000,000 loss is 14%. So a cover with a long-term funding mechanism and decreased risk transfer (thus lower reinsurance margin) may be more desirable. We will discuss these types of covers in the next section.

Nontraditional reinsurance covers

The simplest example of a reinsurance cover which might be classified as nontraditional is a financial quota share. The Example 6.2.11 quota share could be modified in various ways to emphasize the financial aspects of the cover and diminish the risk transfer, thus diminishing the reinsurer's margin. For example:

Example 6.2.23

Facts: Same as Example 6.2.11 except for:

1. Commission slides 1% with each loss ratio 1%
2. Minimum commission = 20%
3. Reinsurance aggregate limit = 90% of reinsurance premium

4. Premium and loss payments quarterly

5. Penalty negative commission if canceled in a deficit position by cedant

6. Reinsurer expense and profit margin = 2% (at a 63% loss ratio)

The cedant still gets surplus relief from the commission on the ceded unearned premium reserve, and still decreases their premium-to-surplus ratio. You can see the drop in the reinsurer's margin from 10% in Example 6.2.11; the 2% here is just for illustration. The reinsurer's margin is meant to cover the surplus loan as before, plus a small charge for absorbing premium volume, which thus indirectly utilizes further surplus (the reinsurer's surplus is thus not available to support other business). It also covers the reinsurer's expenses plus a small risk charge. If casualty exposure were covered, the reinsurer would credit the cedant with most of the investment income earned on the contract's cash balance according to some specified formula. As long as the contract is in a profitable position, this would be returned to the cedant as an additional commission upon cancellation or sooner.

Assuming $IXL = 2\%$ for this case, you can verify the following, with the other facts remaining as in Example 6.2.11 (loss ratio = 66%, loss discount factor = .96):

7. Actual economic return (AER) = 6.32%
   (Use Formula 6.2.12 with $CR = 32\%$)

8. AER at a 78% loss ratio = 5.89%

9. AER at an 82.81% loss ratio = 0%

10. AER at a 90% loss ratio = −8.80%

When most insurance people think of nontraditional reinsurance, they think of loss portfolio transfers. A cedant may cede all or part of its liability as of a specified accounting date; this may be for a line of business or territory no longer written, or for other reasons. Usually, the reinsurance premium is essentially the present value of the transferred estimated liability, plus reinsurer's expense, surplus use, and risk charges. And the cedant can take reinsurance credit for the liability ceded, thus offsetting all or part of the loss reserve previously set up. For a U.S. cedant, this induces a surplus benefit with respect to statutory accounting.

An example may clarify this. Suppose the cedant in Example 6.2.14 has been told by its domiciliary insurance department that it should increase loss reserves as of December 31, 1989 for the subject exposure by 20%. With insurance department approval, the cedant wishes to purchase a loss portfolio cover for this additional liability. Suppose the cedant would like to minimize the statutory surplus effect as much as possible. Suppose we have the following situation:

Example 6.2.24

Facts: Cedant as in Example 6.2.14, plus:

1. Carried loss reserve 12/31/89 = $150,000,000
2. Required additional reserve = $30,000,000

Suppose that, based upon a thorough analysis of the cedant's financial reports, historical exposure, historical reinsurance program, net loss development, and payout distributions by line and in aggregate, we determine that the additional $30,000,000 could easily be funded by a $15,000,000 payment. To get to this point, besides evaluating the adequacy of the cedant's loss reserves, we would pay careful attention to the historical loss payout patterns and their fluctuations. Has the recent exposure changed in such a way to cause a significant change in future loss payout? Have there been major changes in the cedant's claim department or claims processing? A common analytical technique is to study ratios of cumulative loss payout for each accident year divided by ultimate estimates for each category of exposure.

A simplified example is displayed in Table 6.2.25.

TABLE 6.2.25
Private Passenger Automobile Liability (Fictitious Example)
Cumulative Paid Loss a Ratio of Ultimate Loss

Accident Year	Est Ult Loss	Evaluation Year (End of): 1	2	3	4	5
1984	$ 6,000,000	0.500	0.650	0.800	0.950	1.000
1985	7,000,000	0.400	0.550	0.700	0.900	
1986	8,000,000	0.630	0.700	0.750		
1987	9,000,000	0.350	0.550			
1988	10,000,000	0.400				
1 Weighted Average		0.450	0.610	0.748	0.923	1.000
2 3-yr Wtd Average		0.451	0.600	0.748	0.923	1.000
3 Maximum		0.630	0.700	0.800	0.950	1.000
4 Minimum		0.350	0.550	0.700	0.900	1.000
5 Trimmed Average		0.433	0.600	0.750	0.923	1.000
6 Selected "Mean"		0.450	0.610	0.748	0.923	1.000
7 Selected Extreme		0.630	0.700	0.800	0.950	1.000

Scenario 1: Mean Payout

Accident Year	Est Liability as % of Total	Percent of Liability to be Paid in Year: 1989	1990	1991	1992	1993
1984	0.0	0.0	0.0	0.0	0.0	0.0
1985	7.7	100.0	0.0	0.0	0.0	0.0
1986	25.2	69.5	30.5	0.0	0.0	0.0
1987	39.0	35.3	45.0	19.7	0.0	0.0
1988	55.0	29.1	25.0	31.9	14.0	0.0

Accident Year	Estimated Liability	Amount to be Paid in Year: 1989	1990	1991	1992	1993
1984	$ 0	$ 0	$ 0	$ 0	$ 0	$0
1985	538,462	538,462	0	0	0	0
1986	2,019,048	1,403,663	615,384	0	0	0
1987	3,510,000	1,238,571	1,579,121	692,308	0	0
1988	5,502,500	1,602,500	1,376,190	1,754,579	769,231	0
Total	$11,570,009	$4,783,196	$3,570,696	$2,446,886	$769,231	$0

This table also displays the "mean" dollar payout prediction by calendar year. We would also want to determine maximal extremes based upon extreme values for the ultimate incurred loss by accident year and upon faster than expected payout. The payout predictions from all the covered liabilities would be assembled. If a lower risk, lower margin treaty were contemplated, greater care would be taken with the loss discounting: the reinsurer might consider pricing the payout stream via the use of an immunizing asset portfolio. The bond maturities would be selected to allow adequate margin for the stochastic nature of the payout.

To zero-out the surplus effect on the cedant, we would look for an attachment point where the cash payment for the loss portfolio transfer would approximately match the resulting loss reserve takedown. For example, suppose a reinsurance premium of \$35,000,000 is sufficient for a cover of \$65,000,000 excess of \$115,000,000. This transaction would not change the cedant's beginning surplus (before reserving the additional \$30,000,000).

Another example of a nontraditional reinsurance treaty is a funded aggregate excess cover. Let us transform Example 6.2.21 into such a cover.

Example 6.2.26

Facts: Same as Example 6.2.21 except for:

1. Aggregate limit of \$5,000,000
2. Cedant desires a low cost funding cover.

Recall that the reinsurer's loss expectation is $E[L^e 10;5] =$ \$1,252,500 with a standard deviation of \$1,884,000 and a (discounted) reinsurance premium of \$1,193,000 (Example 6.2.21, items 7, 8 and 10). One possible structure for a funded cover would be that the reinsurer takes an initial premium of \$2,000,000, deducts an expense and profit margin (*IXL* and *TER* combined) of perhaps only 5%, instead of the 40% previously, and allocates 90% of the investment income to the "loss fund". The aggregate limit might be equal to the fund plus \$1,000,000 up to a maximum of \$5,000,000, and loss payments might be made only annually, to allow the fund to grow as large as possible. As with the quota share in Example 6.2.23, there probably would be a penalty negative commission if the cedant cancelled in a deficit position.

Recalling that $\text{Prob}[L^e 10 > 0]$ is estimated to be 41% and the likelihood of a total loss in one year is estimated to be 14% (Example

6.2.21, items 2 and 3), we would expect the fund to build to $5,000,000 fairly rapidly, at which time the cedant and reinsurer could decide to increase the limit. Please note that the aggregate excess attachment point of $10,000,000 should be adjusted appropriately each coverage year to reflect aggregate loss inflation.

Conclusion of the reinsurance pricing section

We have seen some examples of how standard actuarial methods and some not-so-standard actuarial methods apply to reinsurance pricing. We must remember that there is no one right way to price reinsurance. But there are many wrong ways. Common actuarial methods should be used only to the extent they make sense. To avoid major blunders, an underwriter/actuary must always understand as well as possible the underlying primary insurance exposure and must always be aware of the differences between the reinsurance cover contemplated and that primary exposure. The differences usually involve much less specificity of information, longer report and settlement timing delays, and often much smaller frequency together with much larger severity, all inducing a distinctly higher risk situation. But with this goes a glorious opportunity for actuaries and other technically sophisticated people to fully use their theoretical mathematical and stochastic modeling abilities and their statistical data analytical abilities.

In the next section, we will see how reinsurance loss reserving differs from primary insurance loss reserving, and we will discuss some simple methods for dealing with these differences.

Reinsurance Loss Reserving

General considerations

For a reinsurance company, the loss reserve is usually the largest uncertain number in the statement of the company's financial condition. To estimate a loss reserve properly, we must study the run-off of the past business of the company. As a result of this process, we should not only be able to estimate a loss reserve as of a certain point in time, but we should also be able to estimate historical loss ratios, loss reporting patterns, and loss settlement patterns by year, by line and by type of business in enough detail to know whether or not a particular contract or business segment is unprofitable, and if so, when. This information should also be applicable to future pricing and decision-making. The goal is to deliver good management information regarding the company's historical contract portfolio, and also deliver some indications of where the company may be going.

Reinsurance loss reserving has many of the same problems as primary insurance loss reserving, and many of the same methods can be used. But there are also various technical problems which make reinsurance loss reserving somewhat more difficult. First we will survey some of these problems and then examine various techniques for handling them.

Reinsurance loss reserving problems

There seem to be seven major technical problems which make reinsurance loss reserving somewhat more difficult than loss reserving for a primary company. These technical problems are:

Problem 6.3.1. Claim report lags to reinsurers are generally longer, especially for casualty excess losses.

The claim report lag, the time from date of accident until first report to the reinsurer, is exacerbated by the longer reporting pipeline — a claim reported to the cedant must first be perceived as being reportable to the reinsurer, then must filter through the cedant's report system to its reinsurance accounting department, then may journey through an intermediary to the reinsurer, then must be booked and finally appear upon the reinsurer's claim system. The report lag may also be lengthened by an undervaluation of serious claims by the cedant—for a long time, an ultimately serious claim may be valued below the reinsurance reporting threshold. This is not an indictment of primary company claims staffs, but simply an observation that a claims person, faced with insufficient and possibly conflicting information about a potentially serious claim, may tend to reserve to probable "expectation". While this "expectation" may be sufficent for most claims with a certain probable fact pattern, it is those few which blow up above this average which will ultimately be covered by the reinsurer. Thus these larger claims generally are reported later to the reinsurer than are the smaller claims the cedant carries net.

Also, certain kinds of mass tort claims—such as for asbestosis-related injuries—may have really extreme delays in discovery or in reporting to the cedant, and may have the dates of loss specified by a court. If these claims are heavily reinsured, their extreme report lags have a big impact on the reinsurer's experience. Just as we saw these time delays adding greatly to the uncertainty in reinsurance pricing, they also add greatly to the uncertainty in reinsurance loss reserving.

Problem 6.3.2. There is a persistent upward development of most claim reserves.

Economic and social inflation cause this development. It may also be caused by a tendency of claims people to reserve at average values, as noted in Problem 6.3.1. Also, there seems to be a tendency to under-reserve allocated loss adjustment expenses. Thus, early on, the available information may indicate that a claim will pierce the reinsurance retention, but not yet indicate the ultimate severity.

Problem 6.3.3. Claims reporting patterns differ greatly by reinsurance line, by type of contract and specific contract terms, by cedant, and possibly by intermediary.

The exposure assumed by a reinsurance company can be extremely heterogeneous. This is a problem because most loss reserving methods require the existence of large homogeneous bodies of data.

The estimation methods depend upon the working of the so-called law of large numbers; that is, future development en masse will duplicate past development because of the sheer volume of data with similar underlying exposure. Reinsurers do not have this theoretical luxury, since many reinsurance contracts are unique, and even when there exist larger aggregates of similar exposure, loss frequency may be so low and report lags so long that there is extreme fluctuation in historical loss data. Thus, normal actuarial loss development methods may not work very well.

As we discussed in "Reinsurance Pricing," a reinsurer knows much less about the specific exposures being covered than does a primary carrier. Also, the heterogeneity of reinsurance coverages and specific contract terms creates a situation where the actuary never has enough information and finds it difficult to comprehend what is being covered and the true exposure to loss. This is especially true for a reinsurer writing small shares of brokered business.

Problem 6.3.4. Because of the heterogeneity stated in Problem 6.3.3, it is difficult to use industry statistics.

Every two years, the Reinsurance Association of America (RAA) publishes a summary of casualty excess reinsurance loss development statistics. These statistics give a very concrete demonstration of the long report and development lags encountered by reinsurers. However, as is noted by the RAA, the heterogeneity of the exposure and reporting differences by company must be considered when using the statistics for particular loss reserving situations.

Likewise, for any two reinsurers, Annual Statement Schedules O and P by-line exposure and loss development are essentially incomparable. The reason for this is that Annual Statement lines of business do not provide a good breakdown of reinsurance exposure into reasonably homogeneous exposure categories useful for loss reserving; proper categorization follows the pricing categories we have already seen, and will vary by reinsurance company according to the types of business in which the company specializes. This is a problem because many people who are not expert in reinsurance insist upon evaluating a reinsurer's loss reserves according to Schedule O and P statistics. For an actuary examining a reinsurer for the purpose of loss reserving, an appropriate exposure categorization for the particular company may not be as apparent or as easily accomplished as for a primary company.

Likewise, ISO by-line loss development statistics are not directly applicable to reinsurance loss development without significant adjustments which may greatly increase the indicated growth. This is so because for excess coverage, the lag in reserving or reporting claims grows with the attachment point (see Pinto and Gogol 1987), and also because primary company direct statistics do not reflect the additional delays noted in Problem 6.3.1 (see Reinsurance Association of America 1989).

Problem 6.3.5. The reports the reinsurer receives may be lacking certain information.

Most proportional covers require only summary claims information; often the data are not even split by accident year or by coverage year, but are reported by calendar year or by underwriting year. An underwriting year is akin to policy year — all premiums and losses for a contract are assigned to the effective or renewal date of the contract. Calendar year or underwriting year statistics are not sufficient for evaluating loss liabilities by accident year, so various interpretations and adjustments must be made.

Even when there is individual claims reporting, such as on excess covers, there often is insufficient information for the reinsurer's claims people to properly evaluate each claim without exerting great effort in pursuing information from the cedant. This is why it is desirable to have a professional reinsurance claims staff even though the cedant is handling the claims. Also, reinsurance claims people are more accustomed to handling large claims with catastrophic injuries. Thus they are able to advise the cedant's staff (especially in the rehabilitation of seriously injured parties), and sometimes reduce the ultimate payments.

For loss reserving, it is useful to have an exposure measure against which to compare loss estimates. One possible measure is reinsurance premium by year by Annual Statement line. On most contracts, losses may be coded correctly by Annual Statement line. But very often the reinsurance premium is assigned to line according to a percentage-breakdown estimate made at the beginning of the contract and based upon the by-line distribution of subject premium.

To the degree that these percentages do not accurately reflect the reinsurer's loss exposure by Annual Statement line, any by-line comparisons of premiums and losses may be distorted. This adds to the difficulties noted in Problem 6.3.4.

For most treaties, premiums and losses are reported quarterly in arrears; they may not be reported (and paid) until some time in the following quarter. Thus there is an added IBNR exposure for both premiums and losses. The actuary must remember that the latest-year premiums may be incomplete, so they may not be a good measure of latest-year exposure.

Problem 6.3.6. Because of the heterogeneity in coverage and reporting requirements, reinsurers often have data coding and EDP systems problems.

All reinsurers have management information systems problems. The business has grown in size and complexity faster, and expectations regarding the necessary level of data detail have also grown faster, than the ability of reinsurers' data systems to handle and produce the reports requested by marketing, underwriting, claims, accounting, and actuarial staffs. This problem may be endemic to the insurance business, but it is even more true for reinsurance.

Problem 6.3.7. The size of an adequate loss reserve is greater for a reinsurer.

This is not a purely technical problem; it is more a management problem, and many reinsurance companies have stumbled over it. All the above problems act to increase the size of an adequate loss reserve and also make it more uncertain. It is difficult for the actuary to overcome the disbelief on the part of management and marketing people and convince them to allocate adequate resources for loss liabilities. Eventually, claims emerging on old exposure overwhelms this disbelief, at least for those who listen. A cynic might say that many reinsurance managers change jobs often enough to stay ahead of their IBNR. Start-up operations in particular have this problem — if there is no concrete run-off experience to point to, why believe a "doom-saying" actuary.

These seven problems imply that uncertainty in measurement and its accompanying financial risk are large factors in reinsurance loss reserving. This has become an even more important item because the U.S. Tax Reform Act of 1986 requires discounting of loss reserves for income-tax purposes. This discounting eliminates the implicit margin for adverse deviation which had been built into insurance loss reserves simply by not discounting previously. Insurers have lost this implicit risk buffer. Since this buffer now flows into profits and thus is taxed sooner, assets decrease. This clearly increases insurance companies' risk level. The effect on reinsurers is greater.

Components of a Reinsurer's Loss Reserve

The general components of a reinsurer's statutory undiscounted loss reserve are as follows:

1. Case reserves reported by the ceding companies

These may be individual case reports or may be reported in bulk, depending upon the loss reporting requirements of each individual contract. Most excess contracts require individual case reports, while most proportional contracts allow summary loss reporting.

2. Reinsurer additional reserves on individual claims

The reinsurer's claims department usually reviews individual case reserve reports and specifies additional case reserves (ACR) on individual claims as necessary. Additional case reserves may vary considerably by contract and by cedant.

3. Actuarial estimate of future development on (1) and (2)

The future development on known case reserves in total is sometimes known is IBNER, Incurred (and reported) But Not Enough Reserved.

4. Actuarial estimate of pure IBNR

Most actuaries would prefer that separate estimates be made for (3) and for (4), the estimate of pure IBNR, Incurred But Not Reported.

However, because of limitations in their data systems, in practice most reinsurers combine the estimates of (3) and (4). Depending upon the reinsurer's mix of business, these together may amount to more than half the total loss reserve.

Unless otherwise noted, the term IBNR in this chapter stands for the sum of IBNER and pure IBNR.

5. Risk load

The last component of a loss reserve should be the risk loading or adverse-deviation loading necessary to keep the reserve at a suitably conservative level, so as not to allow uncertain income to flow into profits too quickly. Many loss reserving professionals prefer to build this into the reserve implicitly by employing conservative assumptions and methodologies. Many actuaries would prefer to see it estimated and accounted for explicitly. Because of the long-tailed nature of much of their exposure and its heterogeneity and the uncertainty of their statistics, this component is theoretically more important for reinsurers.

The above items (1) through (5) refer to undiscounted statutory loss reserves. Not considered is a loss reserve component for the offset arising from future investment income. Even when we must estimate this for tax purposes and record it on our financial statements, most actuaries would prefer to account for it separately from the undiscounted statutory loss reserve. See the chapter on loss reserving for more discussion on this.

A General Procedure

The steps involved in a reinsurance loss reserving methodology are as follows:

1. Partition the reinsurance portfolio into reasonably homogeneous exposure groups.
2. Analyze the historical development patterns. If possible, consider individual case reserve development and the emergence of IBNR claims separately.

3. Estimate the future development. If possible, estimate the bulk reserves for IBNER and pure IBNR separately.

4. Monitor and test the predictions, at least by calendar-quarter.

Let us now proceed to discuss the first step in some detail.

Exposure groups

It is obviously important to segregate the contracts and loss exposure into categories of business on the basis of loss development potential. Combining loss data from nonhomogeneous exposures into large aggregates can increase measurement error rather than decrease it.

Reasonably homogeneous exposure categories for reinsurance loss reserving have been discussed in the actuarial literature and follow closely the categories used for pricing.

Table 6.3.10 lists various important variables for partitioning a reinsurance portfolio. All affect the pattern of claim report lags to the reinsurer and the development of individual case amounts. The listing is meant to be in approximate priority order.

Table 6.3.10 Partitioning The Reinsurance Portfolio Into Reasonably Homogeneous Exposure Groups

Important variables:

1. Type of contract: facultative, treaty

2. Line of business: property, casualty, bonding, ocean marine, etc.

3. Type of reinsurance cover: quota share, surplus share, excess per-risk, excess per-occurrence, aggregate excess, catastrophe, loss portfolio transfer, etc.

4. Layer: primary, working, higher excess, clash

5. Contract Terms: flat-rated, retro-rated, sunset clause, share of loss adjustment expense, claims-made or occurrence coverage, etc.

6. Type of Cedant: small, large, or E&S company
7. Annual Statement line of business
8. Intermediary

Obviously, a partition by all eight variables would split a portfolio into numerous pieces, many with too little credibility. However, after partitioning by the first three variables, it may be desirable to recognise the effects of various of the other variables. For example, for Treaty Casualty Excess business, certain reinsurers have found that the type of cedant company (6) is an important indicator of report lag.

Since each reinsurer's portfolio is unique and extremely heterogeneous, in order to determine a suitable partition of exposure for reserving and results analysis, we must depend greatly upon the knowledge and expertise of the people writing and underwriting the exposures, the people examining individual claim reports, and the people processing data from the cedants. Their knowledge, together with elementary data analysis (look at simple loss development statistics), point the actuary toward the most important variables.

One possible first-cut partition of assumed reinsurance exposure is shown in Table 6.3.11, remembering that there is no such thing as a "typical" reinsurance company.

Table 6.3.11 Example Of Major Exposure Groups For A Reinsurance Company

Treaty Casualty Excess
Treaty Casualty Proportional
Treaty Property Excess
Treaty Property Proportional
Treaty Property Catastrophe
Facultative Casualty
Facultative Property
Surety Excess
Surety Proportional
Fidelity Excess
Fidelity Proportional

Ocean Marine Treaty
Ocean Marine Facultative
Nontraditional Reinsurance
Miscellaneous Special Contracts, Pools and Associations

Within these major categories, the exposure should be further refined. For example, Treaty Casualty Excess exposure may be further segregated by type of retention (per-occurrence excess vs aggregate excess), by type of cedant company (small vs large vs E&S carriers), by layer of coverage (working vs higher and clash layers) and by Annual Statement line (automobile liability, general liability, workers compensation, medical professional liability). Each of these categories would be expected to have distinctly different lags for claims reported to the reinsurer.

Categories for Treaty Casualty Proportional business would be similar. As we have discussed, some contracts classified as proportional are not shares of first dollar primary layers, but rather shares of higher excess layers; thus, whether the exposure is ground-up or excess may be an important variable.

Loss reserving categories for Facultative Casualty would certainly separate out automatic primary programs (pro rata share of ground-up exposure) and automatic nonprimary programs; the certificate exposure might be split into buffer versus umbrella, if possible, and then further by Annual Statement line.

Likewise for property and other exposures, the loss reserving categories should correspond closely to the pricing categories.

It is convenient to determine the methodologies to be used for the historical analyses and estimations (6.3.9, items 2 and 3) for the different exposure categories according to the lengths of the average claim report lags.

Methodology for short-tailed exposure categories

As is generally true, the best methodologies to use are those which provide reasonable accuracy for least effort and cost. For short-tailed lines of business, such as most property coverage exposure, losses are reported and settled quickly, so loss liabilities are relatively small and run off very quickly. Thus, elaborate loss development estimation machinery is unnecessary.

Reinsurance categories of business which may usually be considered to be short-tailed (as with anything about reinsurance, be careful of exceptions) are listed in Table 6.3.12.

Table 6.3.12 Reinsurance Categories Which Are Usually Short-tailed (With Respect to Claim Reporting and Development)

Category	Comments*
Treaty Property Proportional	Beware of recent catastrophes
Treaty Property Catastrophe	Beware of recent catastrophes
Treaty Property Excess	Possibly exclude high layers
Facultative Property	Exclude construction risks
Fidelity Proportional	

* Exclude all international exposure, if possible, since there may be significant reporting delays.

Many reinsurers reserve property business by setting IBNR equal to some percentage of the latest-year earned premium. However, it is a good idea to separately consider major storms and other major catastrophes. A recent catastrophe may cause real IBNR liability to far exceed the normal reserve. Hurricane losses, even on proportional covers, may not be fully reported and finalized for a few years.

Another simple method used for short-tailed exposure is to reserve up to a selected loss ratio for new lines of business or for other situations where the reinsurer has few or no loss statistics. For short-tailed exposure, provided the selected loss ratio bears some reasonable relationship to past years' experience and provided it is larger than that computed from already-reported claims, this may be a reasonable method.

Another useful method for short-tailed lines of business is to use the standard American Chainladder (CL) Method of age-to-age factors on cumulative aggregate incurred loss triangles. If accident year data exist and the report lags are small, this is sufficiently good methodology. An advantage of this method is that it correlates future development with an overall lag pattern and very definitely correlates it with the claims reported for each accident year. A major disadvantage, at least for long-tailed lines, is simply that the IBNR is so heavily correlated with reported claims; so for recent, immature years, the reported, very random nose wags the extremely large tail estimate.

For some proportional treaties, summary loss reporting may assign claims by underwriting year, according to inception or renewal date of the reinsurance treaty, instead of by accident year; the reinsurer's claims accounting staff has no choice but to book the claims likewise. So the loss statistics for each false "accident" year may show great development because of future occurring accidents. To get a more accurate loss development picture and estimate IBNR properly, you can assign these "accident" year losses to approximate true accident year by percentage estimates based upon the underwriting year inception date and the general report lag for the type of exposure. Summary claims reported on a calendar (accounting) year basis can likewise be assigned to accident year by percentage estimates, if necessary. For short-tailed lines reserved by a percentage of premium or reserved up to a selected loss ratio, these re-assignments are unnecessary.

Methodology for medium-tailed exposure categories

Let us consider any exposure for which claims are almost completely settled within five years and with average aggregate report lag of one to two years to be medium-tailed for this discussion. Reinsurance categories of business one might consider here are listed in Table 6.3.13.

Even if a property claim is known almost immediately, its ultimate value may not be. Thus it may take longer to penetrate a higher per-risk excess attachment point. This happens more often if time element coverage is involved. The discovery period for construction risk covers may extend years beyond the contract (loss occurrence) period.

So for both these exposures, claim report lags may be significantly longer than normal for property business.

Table 6.3.13 Reinsurance Categories Which Are Usually Medium-tailed (With Respect to Claim Reporting and Development)

Category	Comments
Treaty Property Excess higher layers	If it is possible to separate these from working layers
Construction Risks	If it is possible to separate these from other property exposure
Surety	
Fidelity Excess	
Ocean Marine	
International Property	

For surety exposure, it is wise to consider losses gross of salvage and, separately, salvage recoveries. The gross losses are reported fairly quickly, but the salvage recoveries have a long tail. It is instructive to consider for mature years the ratio of salvage to gross loss; this ratio is fairly stable and may help explain predictions for recent coverage years as long as the underwriters can predict how the salvage ratio may have slowly changed over time.

For medium-tailed exposure, the CL Method using aggregate reported losses, with or without ACRs, will yield reasonably accurate answers. An alternative estimation method is the so-called Bornheuter-Ferguson (BF) Method (Bornheuter and Ferguson (1973)) which is discussed in the chapter on loss reserving. This method uses a selected loss ratio for each coverage year and an aggregate dollar report lag pattern specifying the percentage of ultimate aggregate loss expected to be reported as of any evaluation date. An advantage of this method is that it correlates future development for each year with an exposure measure equal to the reinsurance premium multiplied by a selected loss ratio.

A disadvantage is that the BF IBNR estimate is very dependent upon arbitrarily selected loss ratios; also, the estimate for each accident year does not reflect the particular to-date reported losses for that year, unless the selected loss ratio is chosen with this in mind. The to-date reported loss for a given accident year is strongly correlated with the place of that year in the reinsurance profitability cycle; it would seem to be desirable to use this fact in the IBNR estimate. As noted before, the reinsurance profitability cycles are more extreme than primary insurance cycles. Thus, when using the BF Method, one must select the accident year loss ratios carefully.

An estimation method which overcomes some of the problems with the CL and BF Methods was independently derived by James Stanard (described in Patrik (1978) and Weissner (1981)) and by Hans Bühlmann (internal Swiss Re publications). As with the CL and BF Methods, this method, let us call it the Stanard-Bühlmann (SB) Method, uses an aggregate known loss lag pattern which may be estimated via the CL Method. The key innovation is that the ultimate expected loss ratio for all years combined is estimated from the overall known loss experience, instead of being selected arbitrarily. The problem with the SB Method is that it does not tell the user how to adjust the overall loss ratio to an appropriate a priori loss ratio by accident year. It is left to the user to adjust each year's premium to reflect the profit cycle on a relative basis. A simple example will illustrate this.

Example 6.3.14

For a given exposure category with five years experience, assume that the yearly earned risk pure premiums (net of reinsurance commissions, brokerage fees and internal expenses) can be adjusted to remove any suspected rate differences by year, so that a single ELR can represent the expected loss ratio for each year. In primary insurance terms, assume that the premiums have been put on-level. This adjustment is difficult and uncertain, but must be done if you are to have reasonable exposure bases. Study primary business rate levels by considering industry-wide Schedule P line loss ratios by year, and work with your underwriters to adjust these for your reinsurance exposure categories. Let ELR represent the unknown expected loss ratio to adjusted earned risk pure premium. Suppose that Table 6.3.15 displays the current experience for this category:

Table 6.3.15 Example Data As Of 12/31/88 In 1,000's

(1) Cal/Acc Year	(2) Earned Risk Pure Premium	(3) Adjusted Earned Premium	(4) Aggregate Reported Loss	(5) Aggregate Reported Loss Lag
1984	$ 6,000	$ 8,000	$ 7,000	95%
1985	7,000	7,000	5,000	85
1986	8,000	6,000	3,000	70
1987	9,000	7,000	2,000	50
1988	10,000	10,000	4,000	30
Total	$40,000	$38,000	$21,000	

The IBNR estimate is given by 6.3.16:

6.3.16 *SB* IBNR est. $=$ Sum {year i IBNR est.}

$=$ Sum {*ELR* est. $\times$ [adj. earned premium i] $\times$ [1 $-$ lag(i)]}

$=$ *ELR* est. $\times$ Sum {[adj. earned premium i] $\times$ [1 $-$ lag(i)]}

$=$ *ELR* est. $\times$ {(8,000 $\times$ .05) + (7,000 $\times$ .15) + (6,000 $\times$ .3) + (7,000 $\times$ .5) + (10,000 $\times$ .7)}

$=$ *ELR* est. $\times$ 13,700

The *ELR* estimate may be written as in 6.3.17:

6.3.17 *SB ELR* est. $= \dfrac{\text{(Total reported losses)} + \text{(Total IBNR est.)}}{\text{Total adjusted earned premium}}$

$=$ (\$21,000 + IBNR est.)/ \$38,000

The trick is putting these two together:

6.3.18 *SB ELR* est. $\times$ 13,700 $=$ *SB* IBNR est.

$=$ (*SB ELR* est. $\times$ 38,000) $-$ 21,000

or

$$SB\ ELR \text{ est.} \times (38{,}000 - 13{,}700) = 21{,}000$$

or

$$SB\ ELR \text{ est.} = 21{,}000/24{,}300 = .864$$

Table 6.3.19 compares IBNR and estimated ultimate loss ratios for *CL* and *SB* Methods; the *BF* and *SB* Methods cannot be compared, since the BF loss ratios are not estimated by formula.

Table 6.3.19 Comparison of Chainladder and Stanard-Bühlmann Methods

(1) Cal/ Accident Year	(2) Earned Risk Pure Premium	(3) Chainladder Estimates IBNR	(4) Chainladder Estimates Loss Ratio	(5) Stanard-Buehlmann Estimates IBNR	(6) Stanard-Buehlmann Estimates Loss Ratio
1984	$ 6,000	$ 368	123%	$ 346	122%
1985	7,000	882	84%	907	84%
1986	8,000	1,386	54%	1,555	57%
1987	9,000	2,000	50%	3,024	56%
1988	10,000	9,333	133%	6,048	100%
Total	$40,000	$13,969	87%	$11,880	82%

As long as the rate relativity adjustments to yearly earned risk pure premium are reasonably accurate, the yearly and overall results are more accurate with the SB Method. It is easy to see that the above example would be more vivid if longer-tailed exposure were used.

Methodology for long-tailed exposure categories

Just as for pricing, the real problem in loss reserving is long-tailed exposure, especially excess casualty reinsurance. Reinsurance categories of business usually considered to be long- tailed are listed in Table 6.3.20.

Table 6.3.20 Reinsurance Categories Which Are Usually Long-Tailed (With Respect to Claim Reporting and Development)

Category	Comments
Treaty Casualty Excess	Includes the longest lags
Treaty Casualty Proportional	Some of this exposure may possibly be medium-tailed
Facultative Casualty	Some of this exposure may possibly be medium-tailed

The first step is to separate these exposures into finer categories. This is, of course, an iterative process. Depend upon your company's marketing, underwriting, claims, and accounting personnel for the first-stage categorization. Further refinements will then depend upon your hypothesis testing and upon your investigation of various comments from the marketing and under-writing people as they receive the estimated IBNR by major contract or category based upon the latest categorization. It may be desirable to treat claims-made exposure separately, if possible.

It may be necessary to separate out certain types of losses for special consideration; for example, claims arising from asbestosis, environmental, and other mass tort claims. Because of the catastrophic significance of these types of claims (nothing for many years, then suddenly, gigantic totals), they would drastically distort the development statistics if left in the normal loss data. Also, it is unlikely that normal actuarial loss development techniques, if used blindly, would yield reasonable answers for these types of losses. The question of which claims should be specially treated is difficult and should be discussed thoroughly with the company's claims staff. Also, it should be clear that losses from commuted contracts should be excluded, since their development is artificially cut off.

For long-tailed exposure, current methodology is usually the CL, BF or SB Methods. However, with the extreme lags encountered here, it may pay to consider the estimation of IBNER separately from the estimation of pure IBNR. For the estimation of pure IBNR, it is appropriate to consider the estimation of IBNR counts and amounts separately. These separate estimates can be input to standard risk theoretic models for aggregate losses so that the loss run-off can be viewed as a stochastic process.

An advantage of using a claim count/claim severity model is that we can contemplate intuitively satisfying models for various lag distributions, such as the time from loss event occurrence until first report and the lag from report until settlement. We can then connect these lags with appropriate models for the dollar reserving and payments on individual claims up through settlement. For surveys of some advanced methodologies, see van Eeghen (1981) and Taylor (1986) and many of the papers listed in the Bibliography.

Perhaps the best way to describe a simple modeling approach is through use of an example.

Example 6.3.21: Advanced Topic

Facts:

1. We want to estimate gross assumed IBNER and pure IBNR for our Treaty Casualty Excess working cover business assumed from large companies; these working covers would have fairly high attachment points.
2. We have the usual development triangles for reported and paid aggregate dollars and claim counts for the last 25 accident years; the claims are separated by major line: automobile liability, general liability, workers compensation.
3. We have earned risk pure premiums by year for the last 15 calendar years.
4. We have talked with the marketing people, underwriters, and claims people to see if there are any special contracts, exposures or types of claims which should be treated separately, or particularly large individual claims which should be censored so as not to have an undue random impact on the estimation.

As a result of our discussions(4), we decide to separate out only asbestosis-related claims. Also, we decide to censor (limit), to a value of $5,000,000 each, six large reported claims, in order to smooth their impact upon the claim severity estimates; the final claim severity estimates will be adjusted to account for potential severity excess of $5,000,000. An alternative is to use a lag estimation technique which trims developmental high and low outliers.

We shall pay particular attention to the estimation of the report lag distribution, the time from claim occurrence until first report. By first report we shall mean the month in which the claim first appears in the reinsurer's claims database with a significant (nonprecautionary) dollar value. If, in addition to the summary claim count development triangles, we also have individual claims data with accident date and first report date for each claim, then for various selected probabilistic models, we can obtain parameters via maximum likelihood estimation as discussed by Weissner (1978 and 1981) and John (1982).

Alternatively, suppose we have only the summary development triangles of reported claims. Also in this case, maximum likelihood estimates of model parameters may be made on these data by treating the increments for each development interval as grouped data, exactly as discussed by Hogg and Klugman (1984) for claims severity. The reported claim counts for each accident year can be considered to be a sample from a truncated model (unknown tail). A slight practical problem here may be negative increments. But for the estimation, the time intervals for the grouping of the data need not necessarily all be one-year periods, so the intervals can always be adjusted to avoid negative increments. Or, negative increments can be handled separately by estimating claim dropout rates (closed, no payment). To simplify this discussion, let us assume that claims closing without payment drop out of the count.

Various statistical and reasonableness tests can then help us decide which model best describes the data and which we believe will best predict future claims arrivals. This model with the fitted parameters can then be used to predict IBNR claim emergence.

Assume now that we have estimated claim report lag distributions for each line. Assume also that we don't trust the breakdown of reinsurance premiums by line, so they cannot serve as a by-line exposure base for IBNR estimation. Without a reasonable by-line exposure, the only achievable by-line IBNR estimates are via the CL Method, hardly credible for immature accident years. An alternative is to estimate the overall report lag distribution by weighing together the lags for each line. Technically, the weights could vary by accident year. Let us assume in this case that constant weights over all accident years are reasonable.

For simplicity, let us suppose that our combined all-lines report lag is estimated to be a lognormal with a mean of 6 years and coeffient of variation 1.311 ($\mu = 1.2918$, $\sigma = 1$), with time measured from the mid-point of the accident year. Suppose that Table 6.3.22 displays our claims situation:

Table 6.3.22 Treaty Casualty Excess Working Cover Example Claims Evaluated as of 12/31/88

(1) Accident Year	(2) Reported Claims	(3) Estimated Report Lag	(4) CL IBNR Est Claims
1964	39	96.89%	1.25
1965	27	96.58	0.96
:	:	:	:
1984	20	58.41	14.24
1985	11	48.45	11.70
1986	13	35.36	23.76
1987	5	18.77	21.64
1988	0	2.36	0
Total	473		231.42

Suppose that we can adjust the annual reinsurance risk pure premiums for rate relativities and relative excess frequency year by year with some, but not total, confidence. Then we can also estimate IBNR via the SB Method and a reasonable "credibility" method, such as shown in Table 6.3.23:

Table 6.3.23 Treaty Casualty Excess Working Cover Example IBNR Estimated as of 12/31/88

(1) Acc Year	(2) Adj.Earn Premium (1,000's)	(3) Reported Claims	(4) Report Lag	(5) CL IBNR Claims	(6) SB IBNR Claims	(7) Cred IBNR Claims	(8) Claim Freq (3 + 7)/2
1964	NA	39	96.89%	1.25	1.25	1.25	NA
1965	NA	27	96.58	0.96	0.96	0.96	NA
⋮	⋮	⋮	⋮	⋮	⋮	⋮	⋮
1984	$ 8,000	20	58.41	14.24	13.31	13.85	4.231
1985	8,000	11	48.45	11.70	16.50	14.17	3.146
1986	7,000	13	35.36	23.76	18.10	20.10	4.729
1987	8,000	5	18.77	21.64	25.99	25.17	3.771
1988	9,000	0	2.36	0.0	35.15	34.32	3.813
'74–'78	$100,000	166	6.00	205.93	234.02	231.21	3.972
Total	$100,000	473	Average Lag	231.42	259.54	256.66	

You can verify the following:

5. For those years with adjusted premium, the SB IBNR estimated claims in column 6 are computed with respect to a claim frequency of 4.0 per $1,000,000 (estimated via the SB Method for the most recent years for which we have adjusted earned premiums). The earlier years simply use the CL IBNR estimated claims.

6. The "credibility" IBNR estimated claims in column 7 is a weighing of the CL and SB estimated claims using the report lag as a weight for each CL estimate. Can you think of why using the report lags as experience credibility weights is not unreasonable? What properties does this procedure have?

Graph 6.3.24 is a picture of claim count and claim reporting lags for accident year 1984 from an actuarial point of view (using the total credibility claim count of 33.85 and the expected report lag distribution). Suppose that the commonly used Poisson distribution, with parameter n say, is a good model for the total claim count N. Then the number of claims reported *in* the ith run-off year, $N(i)$, will also be Poisson with parameter $np(i)$, where $p(i)$ is the lag probability for the ith run-off year; that is, $p(i)$ is the probability that a claim will be reported between i-1 and i years after its year of occurrence. This Poisson assumption allows us to make interconnected probability statements about claim reports from year to year. Under these assumptions, you can verify the following:

Graph 6.3.24 Claim Reporting Pattern
for Accident Year 1984

Evaluation Year-end

■ Actual reported ● Lognormal

Cumulative Claims Reported

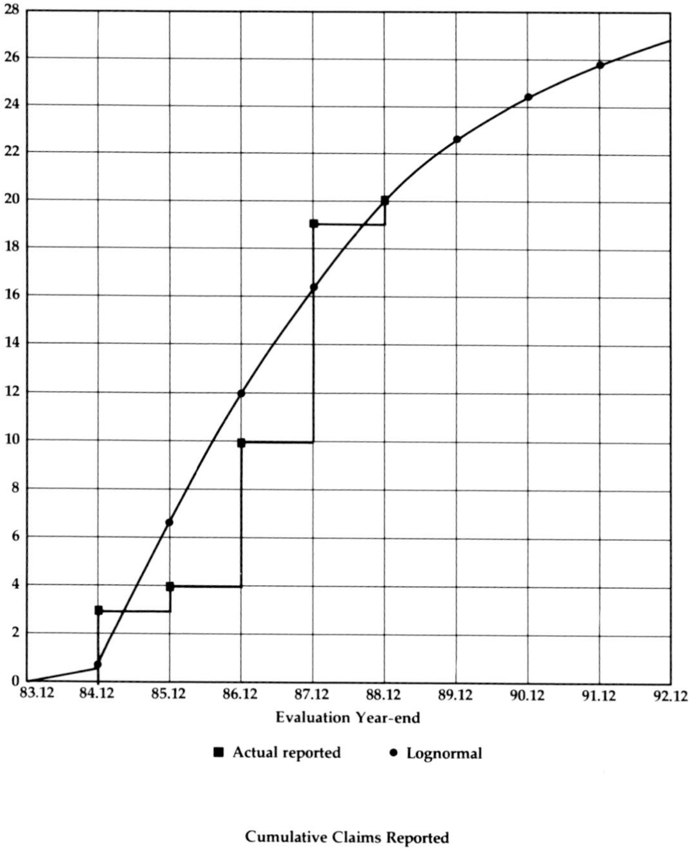

7. The standard deviation of the accident year 1984 Credibility IBNR is 3.72 claims.

8. Prob[225 $<$ Cred. IBNR total $<$ 288] $=$ .95 (approximate)

Please note that these estimates simplistically assume that we know the true parameter n for the Poisson. In reality, sample error with respect to the estimate of n should be considered, perhaps also simplistically inducing a negative binomial distribution.

In addition to estimating report lag distributions and estimating IBNR claim counts, we must also estimate IBNER and the IBNR claim severities. Various techniques from the chapter on loss reserving may be used. Or, if you have the information, an approach similar to that displayed by Table 6.2.20 might be used.

Once the various distributions for counts and amounts are estimated, the aggregate losses reported in year t of the run-off from a particular accident year can then be modeled via the standard risk theoretic model, under suitable assumptions for the claim sizes:

Formula 6.3.25

Aggregate Loss for Claims Reported in Year *t* Evaluated at Time *s*

$$L(t,s) = X(t,s,1) + X(t,s,2) + \ldots + X(t,s,N(t))$$

where $N(t) =$ number of claims reported in year t of run-off

and $X(t,s,i) =$ value at time s of the *ith* claim reported in year t

Let $L(t)$ be the final value of $L(t;s)$ as s gets large and all claims are settled. Then the sum of the $L(t')$'s, for $t' > t$, represents the pure IBNR for the particular accident year evaluated at time t. A parallel expression may be written for the pure IBNER at any time t. Given approximate models for N and X and suitable assumptions, we can approximate the probability distribution of these sums. Then we can ask various probability questions as we did in Section 6.2.

Given models like 6.3.25 for each part of IBNER and IBNR, the various L's can be added together and we can talk about the joint distribution of the sum.

We should note here that various authors have used very different approaches to estimate the distribution of aggregate IBNER and IBNR. You should refer to the Bibliography for advanced and/or different methodologies; especially see Taylor (1986), van Eegehn (1981) and various Advanced Techniques sessions in Casualty Loss Reserve Seminar transcripts.

A problem with increasingly sophisticated methodologies is that the answers may become less intuitive and may be much more difficult for the actuary to understand and explain to management and others. Here I recommend the use of an exhibit format like Exhibit 6.2.20; the few actual estimates (expected settlement average size for reported open and IBNR claims and the expected IBNR count) are cleanly separated from the known numbers, but are juxtaposed for comparison. Various probable future settlement scenarios can be displayed for comparison. These and the monitoring reports to be discussed in the next section are important for management (and actuarial) decision-making.

Monitoring and testing predictions

A loss reserve or an IBNR reserve is derived from a hypothesis about future claims settlements for past events. In order to validate your methodology, you must test your predictions against actual future experience. Monitoring and testing quarterly claims run-off against predictions may provide early warning of problems.

For short-tailed and medium-tailed lines, this can be fairly simple. As long as current accident year claims can be reasonably separated from past accident year run-off, the run-off can be compared with the previous year-end reported open and IBNR reserves.

For long-tailed lines, slightly more sophisticated comparisons are necessary. Table 6.3.26 is one possible format:

Table 6.3.26 Treaty Casualty Excess Working Cover Example

(1) Acc Year	(2) Reported Claims 12/31/88	(3) Cred IBNR Estimate 12/31/88	(4) Predicted Emergence 3/31/89	(5) Reported Claims 3/31/89	(6) Actual Emergence (5)-(2)	(7) Actual Less Predicted (6)-(4)	(8) Report Less Lag 3/31/89
1964	39	1.25	0.03	39	0	− 0.03	96.96%
1965	27	0.96	0.02	28	1	0.98	96.66
:	:	:	:	:	:	:	:
1984	20	13.85	0.70	20	0	− 0.70	60.50
1985	11	14.17	0.76	13	2	1.24	51.20
1986	13	20.10	1.12	12	− 1	− 2.12	38.97
1987	5	25.17	1.38	9	4	2.62	23.21
1988	0	34.32	1.18	2	2	0.82	5.71
Total	473	256.66	10.26	487	14	3.74	6.00
		Total(7)/Total(4) = 36%					Year Average lag

Columns 2 and 3 are from Table 6.3.23. Column 8 is the lognormal adjusted by one quarter. You can verify the following:

1. Column 4 is derived from Column 3 by using the lags at 12/31/88 and 3/31/89.
2. Assuming that the emergence is Poisson with mean = Total(4), then there is approximately a 12% probability that the actual emergence is 14 or more (use a Normal approximation to the Poisson).

Even though item 2 indicates a low probability for so many new claims, perhaps we wouldn't alter our opinion of the magnitude of the accuracy of the report lags and the estimated IBNR after only one quarter. However, we may want to pay close attention to the claim emergence over the next quarter. Note the negative emergence for 1986; most likely a claim was settled for less than the excess attachment point.

In addition to monitoring and testing claim count predictions, one should also review claim severities. Besides just report emergence, one can and should monitor and test claim settlements.

If you do not have the data to monitor counts and amounts separately, you can use your aggregate dollar IBNR estimates together with an appropriate lag distribution to monitor aggregate dollar emergence and settlement.

Conclusion of the reinsurance loss reserving section

We have seen some examples of how standard actuarial methods and some not-so-standard actuarial methods apply to reinsurance loss reserving. We must remember that there is no one right way to estimate reinsurance loss reserves. But there are many wrong ways. Common actuarial methods should be used only to the extent they make sense. To avoid major blunders, the actuary must always understand as well as possible the types of reinsurance exposure in the reinsurance company's portfolio. The differences from primary company loss reserving mainly involve much less specificity of information, longer report and settlement timing delays, and often much smaller claim frequency together with much larger severity, all inducing a distinctly higher risk situation. But with this goes a glorious opportunity for actuaries to fully use their theoretical mathematical and stochastic modeling abilities and their statistical data analytical abilities.

References

Included here are also works in addition to those cited in the text.

Introduction

Insurance Information Institute. 1983. *Reinsurance: fundamentals and current issues*. New York: Insurance Information Institute

Kiln, Robert. 1981. *Reinsurance in practice*. London: Witherby

Novik, Jay A. and Fisher, Gerald F. 1986. Launching a new tradition (nontraditional reinsurance). *Best's Review*. April

Swiss Reinsurance Company. 1982. *A reinsurance manual of the non-life branches*. Zurich: Swiss Reinsurance Company

Strain, Robert W. 1980. *Reinsurance*. New York: The College of Insurance

Webb, B. L., Launie, J.J., Rokes, W.P., Baglini, N.A., 1984. *Insurance company operations*. Vol. 1, Chapters 7, 8, Malvern, PA: American Institute for Property and Liability Underwriters

Reinsurance Pricing

Asch, Nolan E. 1986. Reinsurance pricing for the new transitional claims-made GL product. *CAS Discussion Paper Program*

Beard, R. E., Pentikainen, T. and Pesonen, E. 1984. *Risk theory*, 3rd ed. London: Chapman and Hall

Bühlmann, Hans. 1970. *Mathematical methods in risk theory*. New York: Springer-Verlag

Ferguson, Ronald. 1978. Actuarial note on loss rating and discussion by Gary Patrik. *PCAS*. Vol. 65

Gisler, Alois, Hofmann, Susanne and Schnieper, Rene. 1985. The calculation of the excess premium for unlimited cover in automobile third party liability insurance in switzerland. *18th ASTIN Colloquium*

Heckman, Philip E. and Meyers, Glenn G. 1983. The calculation of aggregate loss distributions from claim severity and claim count distributions. and discussion by Gary Venter. *PCAS,* 70. Exhibits omitted from paper in *PCAS* 71

Hogg, Robert V. and Klugman, Stuart A. 1984. *Loss distributions.* New York: Wiley

Insurance Institute of London. 1976. *Excess of loss methods of reinsurance: report by Advanced Study Group No. 201.* London: Insurance Institute of London

Jung, Jan. 1963. On the use of extreme values to estimate the premium for an excess of loss reinsurance. *The ASTIN Bulletin.* 3. part 2

Miccolis, Robert S. 1977. On the theory of increased limits and excess of loss pricing, with discussion by Sheldon Rosenberg. *PCAS* 64

Panjer, H. H. 1981. Recursive evaluation of a family of compound distributions. *ASTIN Bulletin.* 12, part 1

Patrik, Gary. 1980. Estimating casualty insurance loss amount distributions. *PCAS* 67

Patrik, Gary, and John, Russell. 1980. Pricing excess-of-loss casualty working cover reinsurance treaties. *CAS Discussion Paper Program*

Steeneck, Lee R. 1985. Loss portfolios: financial reinsurance. *PCAS* 72

Straub, Erwin. 1971. Estimation of the number of excess claims by means of the credibility theory. *ASTIN Bulletin.* 5, part 3

Venter, Gary G. 1983. Transformed beta and gamma distributions and aggregate losses. *PCAS* 70

Wiser, Ronald F. 1986. The cost of mixing reinsurance. *PCAS* 73

Reinsurance Loss Reserving

Berquist, James R., and Sherman, Richard E. 1977. Loss reserve adequacy testing: A comprehensive, systematic approach. *PCAS* 64

Bühlmann, Hans, Schnieper, Rene, and Straub, Erwin. 1980. Claims reserves in casualty insurance based upon a probabilistic model. *Bulletin, Association of Swiss Actuaries*

Bornheuter, Ronald L., and Ferguson, Ronald E. 1972. The actuary and IBNR. *PCAS* 59

Casualty Actuarial Society Committee on Loss Reserves. 1988. *Statement of principles regarding property and casualty loss and loss adjustment expense reserves*

Eeghen, J. van. 1981. *Loss reserving methods, surveys of actuarial studies No. 1*. Rotterdam: Nationale-Nederlanden N.V.

Hachemeister, Charles A. 1980. A stochastic model for loss reserving. *International Congress of Actuaries*

Jewell, William S. 1987. Predicting IBNYR events and delays. 20th ASTIN Colloquium

John, Russell T. 1982. Report lag distributions and IBNR. *Casualty Loss Reserve Seminar Transcript*

Patrik, Gary S. 1978. An actuarial procedure for estimating a reinsurance company's IBNR. *IASA*

Patrik, Gary S. 1982. Loss reserving problems for new or small reinsurers. *Casualty Loss Reserve Seminar Transcript*

Pinto, Emanuel, and Gogol, Daniel F. 1987. An analysis of excess loss development. *PCAS*. Vol. 74

Reinsurance Association of America. 1989. *Loss development study*

Robbin, Ira. 1986. A Bayesian credibility formula for IBNR counts. *PCAS*. Vol. 73

Taylor, G.C. 1986. *Claims reserving in non-life insurance*. Amsterdam: North-Holland

Weissner, Edward W. 1978. Estimation of report lags by the method of maximum likelihood. *PCAS* 65

Weissner, Edward W. 1981. Evaluation of IBNR on a low frequency book where the report development pattern is still incomplete. *Casualty Loss Reserve Seminar Transcript*

Appendices

Appendix 6.5A Pareto Distribution

1. Support: $X > 0$
2. Parameters: $b > 0, q > 0$
3. *C.d.f.*: $F(x) = 1 - [b/(b + x)]^q$
4. *P.d.f.*: $f(x) = qb^q/(b + x)^{q+1}$
5. Moments: $E[X^n] = b^n(n!)/[(q-1)(q-2)\ldots(q-n)]$ for $n < q$
6. Censored *c.d.f.*: (general definition) $F(X;c) = \begin{cases} F(X) & \text{if } X < c \\ 1 & \text{otherwise} \end{cases}$
7. Censored moments: If $q - n$ is not an integer, then

$$E[X^n;c] = [n!b^n]/[(q-1)(q-2)\ldots(q-n)] - q[b/(b+c)]^q \{(b+c)^n/(q-n) + \ldots + (-1)^i [(n!)/(i!)(n-i)!]\,[b^i (b+c)^{n-i}/(q-n+i)] + \ldots + (-1)^n b^n/q - c^n/q\}$$

8. Censored expectation: $E[X;c] = E[X]\{1 - [b/(b+c)]^{q-1}\}$ for $q > 1$
9. Conditional probability:

   $\text{Prob}[X > y \mid X > x] = [(b+x)/(b+y)]^q$

10. Truncated (conditional) distribution:

    Definition: $Xd = X - d$ for $X > d$

    Then Xd is Pareto with parameters $b + d$, q:

    $F(Xd) = 1 - \{(b+d)/[(b+d) + Xd]\}^q$

11. Trended distribution:

    Definition: $Y = tX$

    Then Y is Pareto with parameters tb, q:

    $F(Y) = 1 - [tb/(tb+Y)]^q$

Appendix 6.5B Lognormal Distribution

1. Support: $X > 0$
2. Parameters: $-\infty < \mu < \infty, \sigma > 0$
3. *C.d.f.*: $F(X) = \Phi[(lnX - \mu)/\sigma]$
4. *P.d.f.*: $f(X) = (1/\sigma X)\theta[(lnX - \mu)/\sigma]$
5. Moments: $E[X^n] = \exp(n\mu + n^2\sigma^2/2)$
6. Censored moments:

$$E[X^n;c] = E[X^n]\Phi[(ln(c) - \mu)/\sigma - n\sigma] + c^n\{1 - \Phi[(ln(c) - \mu)/\sigma]\}$$

7. Truncated (conditional) distribution: $(Xd = X - d)$
   a) $E[Xd][1 - F_x(d)] = E[X] - E[X;d]$
   b) $E[(Xd)^2][1 - F_x(d)] = E[X^2] - E[X^2;d] - 2dE[Xd]$
   c) $Var[Xd] = E[(Xd)^2] - E[Xd]^2$
8. Censored truncated distribution:
   a) $E[Xd;c-d][1 - F_x(d)] = E[X;c] - E[X;d]$
   b) $E[(Xd)^2;c-d][1 - F_x(d)]$
   $= E[X^2;c] - E[X^2;d] - 2dE[Xd;c-d]$
   c) $Var[Xd;c-d] = E[(Xd)^2;c-d] - E[Xd;c-d]^2$

Appendix 6.5C Aggregate Loss Model

1. Aggregate loss $L = X(1) + X(2) + \ldots + X(N)$

   where N = rv denoting number of claims

   $X(i)$ = rv denoting the value of the *ith* claim

Assume that N and the $X(i)$'s are mutually independent and the $X(i)$'s are identically distributed with *c.d.f.* $F_x(x)$. (Note: These are usually reasonable assumptions when the parameters for the distributions of N and X are assumed to be known.) Then the following statements are true:

2. *c.d.f.*: $F_L(x) = \sum_{n=0}^{n=\infty} \text{Prob}[N = n] F_x^{*n}(x)$

   where F_x^{*n} is the *nth* convolution

3. Moments:

$$E[L] = E[N]E[X]$$

$$\text{Var}(L) = E[N]E[X^2] + (Var(N) - E[N])E[X]^2$$

$$= E[N]\{\text{Var}(X) + (\text{Var}(N)/E[N])E[X]^2\}$$

$$E[(L - E[L])^3] = E[N]E[(X - E[X])^3] + E[(N - E[N])^3]E[X]^3 + 3\text{Var}(N)E[X]\text{Var}(X)$$

4. If N is Poisson, then

$$Var(L) = E[N]E[X^2]$$

$$E[(L - E[L])^3] = E[N]E[X^3]$$

5. Reinsurer's aggregate excess loss over aggregate deductible:

$$L^e d = \begin{cases} 0 & \text{if } L \le d \\ L - d & \text{if } L > d \end{cases}$$

6. Moments over deductible d:

   a) $E[L^e d] = E[L] - E[L;d]$

   b) $E[(L^e d)^2] = E[L^2] - E[L^2;d] - 2dE[L^e d]$

   c) $Var[L^e d] = E[(L^e d)^2] - E[L^e d]^2$

7. Moments over deductible d, censored at aggregate limit $c - d$:

   a) $E[L^e d;c - d] = E[L;c] - E[L;d]$

   b) $E[(L^e d)^2;c - d] = E[L^2;c] - E[L^2;d] - 2dE[L^e d;c - d]$

   c) $Var[L^e d;c - d] = E[(L^e d)^2;c - d] - E[L^e d;c - d]^2$

Appendix 6.5D Abbreviations

ACR: additional case reserve

AER: actual economic return

ALAE: allocated loss adjustment expense

BF: Bornheuter-Ferguson method of loss development

BF: reinsurance brokerage fee

CL: chainladder method of loss development

CR: reinsurance ceding commission rate

DF: loss discount factor

ELCF: excess loss cost factor

ELR: expected loss ratio

E[X;c]: expected loss cost up to censor c

IBNER: incurred but not enough reserved

IBNR: incurred but not reported

IXL: reinsurer's internal expense loading

L: random variable for aggregate loss

L(t,s): random variable for aggregate loss for claims reported in year t evaluated at time s

MPL: maximum possible loss

N: random variable for number of claims

Nd: random variable for number of claims in excess of d

PML: probable maximum loss

PP: primary company pure premium

PPLR: primary company permissible loss ratio

RCF: rate correction factor

REP: reinsurer earned premium

RER: required economic return

RIL: reinsurer incurred loss

RLC: reinsurance expected loss cost

RNd: random variable for reported number of claims in excess of attachment point d

RP: reinsurance premium

RR: reinsurance rate

SB: Stanard-Bühlmann method of loss development

TER: target economic return

UPRF: unearned premium reserve factor

X: random variable for the value of a claim

Yd: random variable designating the amount of the random variable Y in excess of truncation point d given that Y > d

Y^ed: random variable designating the unconditional amount of the random variable Y in excess of truncation point d

Chapter 7
CREDIBILITY
by Gary G. Venter

Prologue
by Charles C. Hewitt, Jr.

Setarcos: *What may we say about the basis for human decision and human action?*

Student: *I assume you mean conscious decision and action as opposed to instinct; all animals possess instinct to some degree. If so, we may say that human decisions (and actions) are based upon a set of beliefs—we may call this knowledge.*

Setarcos: *Of what does knowledge consist?*

Student: *Knowledge may consist of a set of suppositions or ideas, many of which exist in the absence of corroborating evidence. Also, knowledge consists of a set of facts accumulated throughout a lifetime.*

Setarcos: *How does a human being obtain knowledge?*

Student: *In the instance of ideas, these are obtained from many sources—parents, teachers, friends, and, importantly, from the creativity of the human mind. In the case of facts, these are obtained from personal observation and the reported observations of others.*

Setarcos: *What if there is a conflict between one's suppositions and the facts?*

Student: *Of course, we must first dispose of the situations where there are either no facts or no suppositions. Where there are no facts, the supposition prevails; where there is no basis for supposition, facts constitute the only knowledge.*

Sections beginning with an asterisk may be omitted in a first reading.

Setarcos: *Very well, but suppose a set of facts contradicts a set of ideas?*

Student: *The wise person must then weigh the ideas against the evidence and make a judgment. The judgment may be to alter the ideas to fit the facts or, alternatively, to question the facts themselves. Of course, one may compromise by giving partial weight to each.*

Setarcos: *But what weight do we assign to supposition and what weight do we assign to the evidence?*

Student: *That's the real question! Perhaps some day there will be a mathematical answer.*

Bayesian Analysis

In 1763 Thomas Bayes proposed that a priori probabilities could be assigned to the several hypotheses (suppositions). Next, calculate the probability of each outcome for each hypothesis. After making an observation, or a series of observations, the a posteriori probabilities of the hypotheses could be calculated. Hence, an improved knowledge of the underlying (but unknown) probabilities could be obtained. This approach is generally referred to as Bayesian analysis (sometimes as inverse or, where the judgment is mostly intuitive, subjective probability).

Credibility, an Answer to an Insurance Problem

The Casualty Actuarial Society (CAS) was formed in 1914—in part to deal with the problem of making rates for a new (to the United States) line of insurance, workmens' compensation. (Many of the charter members of the CAS were also members of the Actuarial Society of America.) Workmens' compensation had been available in Europe for some time but there were almost no data that might represent American experience, except for employer's liability insurance which workmen's compensation insurance was designed to replace.

As data became available for the new line of insurance, the question arose as to how to revise the hypothetical rates to admit this new evidence in ratemaking. A group of casualty actuaries, whose spokesperson was Albert Whitney, conceived the idea of assigning weights in the linear expression:

$$\textit{New Rate} = \textit{Credibility} \times \textit{Observed Rate} + (1 - \textit{Credibility}) \times \textit{Old Rate}$$

The underlying mathematics which determined the value of the term 'Credibility' was implicitly Bayesian but not generalized. Rather, it dealt with a specific a priori distribution and a specific random process. It produced the expression:

$$\textit{Credibility} = \frac{\textit{Number of Observations (Exposure)}}{\textit{Number of Observations (Exposure)} + \mathrm{K}}$$

where "K" was a positive constant to be determined from the underlying factors.

Classical Statistics — the Dark Ages for Credibility

As will be shown later, the development of "K" required a Bayesian approach. However, in the time of Whitney, and for many years to come, the theory underlying mathematical statistics refused to admit that element of Bayesian analysis which required a subjective approach to the assignment of a priori probabilities. In the Neyman-Pearson school of classical statistics, each hypothesis was something to be either accepted or rejected, but only after an examination of some data which admitted or denied the hypothesis. In Bayesian analysis the original set of hypotheses is not totally rejected, but, rather, the a priori probabilities of the hypotheses may be changed (a posteriori) to adjust to the new evidence!

Thus, it was to come to pass that casualty actuaries were to "sell their birthright for a mess of pottage". They "copped out" on calculating "K" on the basis required by Whitney's mathematics and settled for an arbitrary assignment of a value chosen by means most convenient. Having yielded to the demands of the then popular approach of statisticians, they capitulated even further by yielding to the demand by insurance buyers and insurance marketing people for "full" credibility.

The "Credibility Formula" as set forth above does not admit of "full" credibility being assigned to the observations—the expression may approach unity as the number of observations (or exposure) increases, but only asymptotically. Insurance buyers with better-than-average experience wanted full recognition in their rates. Since these buyers were, more often than not, the larger customers and also, a fortiori, the preferred risks, their wishes had to be respected. Once again an arbitrary assignment was made—the point at which exposures were sufficient to admit of "full" credibility—and, of course, on the basis of convenience.

The casualty actuarial literature during this period, which I will call the Dark Ages, was almost exclusively in the Proceedings of the Casualty Actuarial Society. It dealt with questions of determining standards for "full" credibility and with interesting, but rather baroque, approaches as to how to make the transition from the Whitney formula to "full" credibility as the size of the risks being rated increased.

There were, however, notable exceptions. A paper by Ralph Keffer (1929) in the Transactions of the Actuarial Society of America suggested a Bayesian approach in group life insurance. Keffer provides an interesting footnote (p. 135) identifying the Poisson Distribution as the "Bortkewitsch Law of Small Numbers". Readers familiar with the history of the use of the Poisson Distribution may readily infer the identity of (Oberst) Bortkewitsch. In 1940, Ove Lundberg in Sweden presented a classic paper, using a Bayesian approach to ratemaking for health insurance. And in 1950, Arthur Bailey rediscovered the original approach of Whitney and his colleagues, using subjective methods in probability theory rather than the classical approach (Bailey, 1950). In so doing Bailey reaffirmed the underlying strength of the Bayesian roots of Credibility Theory. Many persons regard Arthur Bailey as the "Father of Modern Credibility Theory".

Following this "Renaissance" of Bayesian Credibility, successive papers by Dropkin (1960), Robert Bailey (1961), son of Arthur Bailey, and Simon (1962) applied specialized Bayesian approaches to the experience rating of private passenger automobile insurance. The brief history in this paper omits reference to many works in this field. It is deliberately intended to highlight American actuarial efforts, with reference to foreign contributions where appropriate. A fairly complete, if not up-to-date, historical bibliography may be found on pp. 6–7 of the Simon paper.

It remained for two individuals in the 1960s to reawaken and restore interest in the true nature of the credibility concept. These were Hans Bühlmann in Switzerland and Allen Mayerson in the United States. The latter provided a paper on Bayesian Credibility (Mayerson 1964) using an approach which was not generalized, but, rather, used two specific cognate processes, the Beta-Binomial and the Gamma-Poisson.

Meanwhile in Europe, Hans Bühlmann (1967) took the more general approach to the problem. In a paper to ASTIN (1967), the non-life section of the International Actuarial Association, Bühlmann demonstrated that the "K" in the much earlier Whitney formula was:

$$K = \frac{\textit{Variance of the Processes}}{\textit{Variance of the Hypotheses}}$$

These "Renaissance" protagonists recognized that the straight line produced by the Credibility Formula represented a least-squares fit to the 'process means' generated by the differing hypotheses (with weight given to each point on the basis of the a priori probability of each hypothesis).

Current Developments

With the increased acceptance of subjective probabilities, see Savage of Yale (1954) Raiffa and Schlaifer of Harvard (1961), and Schlaifer (1959) the new/old approach to credibility has flowered —at least theoretically. Many latter-day members of the Casualty Actuarial Society have written on credibility.

Professor William Jewell at the University of California, Berkeley, has been prolific in his research and publication. In Switzerland, Bühlmann and his pupils, Hans Gerber and Erwin Straub, have contributed, and, in Belgium, DeVylder. In Australia, Gregory Taylor has published frequently on credibility.

Credibility may be thought of as a form of shorthand for the more descriptive Bayesian analysis. When Credibility Theory was first developed there were no modern high-speed computers; hence a simplified, two-dimensional linear substitute for the more complex Bayesian analysis was eminently desirable and acceptable.

Modern credibility theory has expanded to include non-linear and multi-dimensional approaches. Ultimately, with the advent of high-speed methods of calculation, credibility, as a form of shorthand, may yield to full Bayesian analysis. In the meantime, practical application of theoretical credibility has lagged far behind the state of the art. The Neyman-Pearson training of many mathematical statisticians seems to produce a revulsion for any subjective approach. However, the ideas are there!

Introduction

Credibility, simply put, is the weighting together of different estimates to come up with a combined estimate. For instance, an insured's own experience might suggest a different premium from that in the manual. These are two different estimates of the needed premium, which can be combined using credibility concepts to yield an adjusted premium.

Regression analysis is in some ways quite analogous to credibility, as will be seen in Section 5. An example, which would have been familiar to Sir Francis Galton, the father of correlation, in the late nineteenth century, is given by batting averages. Let B denote a player's average after 50 at-bats, A the average at the end of the season, and M the long term average of all batters in the league. One might find, for instance, that $A - M = .25(B - M)$, that is, that the batter's average is closer to the overall average at year-end. Further, if each batter is reviewed at year end to find the number Z such that $A - M = Z(B - M)$, the average of all those Z's might be .25. Since $Z < 1$, Galton would call this "regression toward the mean."

The analogy to credibility is that the year end average can then be estimated from the early season average by the formula $A = .25B + .75M$. This is a weighting of the player's own experience with the overall mean, and is a typical form that a credibility formula might take. As will be seen, credibility techniques, in contrast to regression, allow the weight Z to be estimated before the "dependent variable" A is observed. Doing the regression after the fact will be a useful check on the credibility estimate, however, and when credibility is used periodically to update a given estimate, as in annual rate reviews, the regression estimate of last year's Z might be used to provide an estimate of the credibility factor to use this year.

An even earlier example, which Carl Friedrich Gauss could have provided in the late eighteenth century, involves weighting together two samples from the same normally distributed population. If one sample, of size m, produces a mean of M, and the other, of size n, produces a mean of N, then the overall sample mean is $(mM + nN)/(m + n)$, which can be written as $ZM + (1 - Z)N$, with the "credibility weight" $Z = m/(m + n)$. Further, Gauss knew that the variances of the two sample means are inversely proportional to the sample sizes. That is, if σ^2 is the population variance, then the two sample means have variances $s^2 = \sigma^2/m$ and $t^2 = \sigma^2/n$, respectively. Thus dividing the numerator and denominator of Z by nm gives

$$Z = n^{-1}/\,(n^{-1} + m^{-1}) = t^2/\,(s^2 + t^2).$$

This formula for Z is similar to some credibility formulas that will be seen later in this chapter for more general problems.

A word about "data": it is assumed in this chapter that "data" is a singular English noun which derives from a Latin plural noun, as did "agenda". Moreover, it is a collective noun, like "snow". Thus, ideally, "snow is white" is true, and "data is reliable" is at least grammatical. In the words of Charles Kuralt, "However much purists may object, the fact is, 'datum' ain't an English word. 'Data', well, is."

An early actuarial application of credibility, dating from 1914, is experience rating for workers' compensation. An estimate for an insured's losses is available from class rates; the insured's own data is used to refine this estimate. Another example is ratemaking, in cases where the old rate is updated by weighting it with the new experience, rather than basing the new rate on the new data alone. In both these cases, the new rate might be calculated by:

$$\text{New Rate} = Z \text{ times Data} + (1 - Z) \text{ times Old Rate}$$

Credibility methods, then, combine existing estimates and new data to arrive at new estimates. These methods generally take the form of weighted averages between the old estimate and that from the data, with the weight to the data referred to as the *credibility weight*, or, more loosely, the *credibility of the data*.

The latter terminology is misleading if it implies that the credibility weight is an inherent property of the data. In addition to any features of the data itself, the context in which it will be used, including what it is to be weighted against, will explicitly or implicitly influence the credibility to be assigned. For instance, if different territories tend to have quite different results from each other, then the experience of a given territory should be given fairly high credibility, whereas the same amount of data might receive much less weight if all the territories tend to have similar results. In the second case, the statewide average should be a reasonable estimator for a given territory.

Credibility theory is the study of this weighting process, including development of the formulas for assigning the credibility weights, and estimation of the parameters or values that appear in these formulas.

Although pragmatically motivated, credibility weighting now has both theoretical and practical justification. Credibility formulas can be derived from statistical assumptions, and have proven useful in application. This chapter outlines the background and use of credibility, including the estimation of the parameters needed. Being an overview, the results are in many cases given without proof, or the proofs are just outlined, in order to present the type of reasoning involved without laying out every detail. The interested reader may wish to complete some of the proofs.

As with many disciplines, the real world is found to be more complex than the initial simple models assume, and so more intricate models are often needed in order to be truly practical. The more practical models are presented in the later sections, but their exposition will benefit from the simpler paradigms covered first. An asterisk will be used to identify sections or subsections which describe the more intricate models needed for real world applications. These sections can be omitted at first reading.

The general precepts of credibility theory can also be applied outside of insurance. An illustration is the baseball example mentioned above. In this case, giving weight to the averages of other players can improve the estimate. More typical insurance examples include estimation of claim frequency, severity, or total loss cost for an insured, a class, or a rating territory. If the most applicable data is not sufficient, it might be weighted with auxiliary data from a broader population. Experience for other insureds, classes, states, insurers, etc. may be the auxiliary data incorporated. These "broader base" credibility scenarios are probably the most typical applications of credibility theory.

A somewhat different application is the use of credibility for a time series. Rather than incorporating a wider population, earlier observations of the series itself may be used as the auxiliary estimate. For countrywide claim frequency, for example, the latest observation by itself might not be regarded as sufficient, e.g., if it is subject to significant random fluctuation. Then some weight may be given to prior years' frequencies, perhaps with the earlier weights decreasing toward zero.

Both time series and broader base credibility applications can be developed with two approaches to credibility theory: limited fluctuation and greatest accuracy. This terminology was introduced by Arthur Bailey in his far-reaching 1945 paper, although the essential features of both methods had already been established a quarter of a century earlier.

While discussed in greater detail later, the basic philosophical difference between these methods is as follows. The limited fluctuation approach aims to limit the effect that random fluctuations in the data can have on the estimate; the greatest accuracy approach attempts to make the estimation errors as small as possible. The most well developed approach to greatest accuracy credibility is *least squares credibility*, which seeks to minimize the expected value of the square of the estimation error. The term "classical credibility" has sometimes been used in North America to denote limited fluctuation credibility, and in Europe to denote least squares credibility. As both of these are classic, the term will not be used herein.

More recent statistical theory, Bayesian analysis for example, also addresses the use of data to update previous estimates, and this will be introduced later below. Credibility theory shares with Bayesian analysis the outlook toward data as strictly a source to update prior knowledge. Credibility, particularly least squares credibility, is sometimes labeled Bayesian or empirical Bayesian for this reason. It also gives the same result as Bayesian analysis in some circumstances, although credibility theory can be developed within the frequentist view of probability. A statistical approach known as Parametric Empirical Bayes, which will be discussed later, also incorporates a broader base into estimation, largely within the frequentist viewpoint.

Frequentist refers to an interpretation of probability as solely an expression of the relative frequency of events, in contrast to a subjectivist view which regards probability as a quantification of opinion. This latter view is a hallmark of Bayesian analysis, which uses it to justify the postulation of "prior" distributions before any data is observed. In the current chapter, the term "Bayesian" is reserved for methods that postulate priors without using data to do so. It will turn out that least squares credibility can benefit from Bayesian methods, even though most of the related theory does not require them.

Postulating a prior before observing any data does not necessarily imply a commitment to the subjective interpretation of probability, but it makes most sense in that context. Some analysts do in fact try to treat the prior as a purely formal device, not a reflection of their opinion about likely outcomes. This is especially prevalent among users of so called "diffuse priors," which are introduced in Section 2.

Historical Perspective

This section outlines the history of the methods to be developed in the later sections. The historical papers cannot be understood just from this section, and a rereading after completing the chapter may be helpful.

Credibility as known today is generally traced to Mowbray (1914), writing in Volume I of the *Proceedings of the Casualty Actuarial Society*. Decidedly in the limited fluctuation camp, this article approximates an assumed binomial claim count process by the normal distribution to derive a criterion for assigning full credibility to the data. The goal of the limited fluctuation approach is suggested by the title of Mowbray's article: "How extensive a payroll exposure is necessary to give a dependable pure premium?"

The greatest accuracy approach was introduced by Whitney (1918), writing in Volume IV of the CAS *Proceedings*. Whitney assumed that the number of claims for an employer with P employees is binomially distributed with parameters (P,M), and that M itself is normally distributed across all the employers in the class. This might be called the "normal-binomial model." Bayes' Theorem can be used to estimate the parameter M, given the experience of that employer. The resulting estimate for the next period's claims can be expressed as a credibility weighting between the employer's claims and the expected number of claims based on class experience. The credibility weight can be expressed as $Z = P/[P + K]$, with K a function of the binomial and normal variances.

Both Mowbray and Whitney were addressing workers' compensation experience rating. An application of limited fluctuation credibility to automobile classification ratemaking can be found in Stellwagen (1925). Group life insurance experience rating using greatest accuracy credibility was explored by Keffer (1929), who assumed a Poisson claim count distribution for each group, with the Poisson mean gamma distributed across the various groups insured. That is, each group has its own Poisson parameter, and the relative frequency of the appearance of these parameters follows a gamma distribution. This is then the gamma-Poisson model. Perryman (1932) addressed a number of then current issues, including the interpretation of limited fluctuation partial credibility, as described later, as equalizing the impact of random fluctuation on the credibility estimator among high and low credibility cases.

The least squares approach to greatest accuracy credibility was established in Bailey (1945), although the notation was cumbersome. Bühlmann and Straub (1970) formalized the least squares derivation of $Z = P/[P + K]$, where $K = s^2/t^2$, the ratio of the average risk variance to the variance between risks, and discussed a method of estimating s^2 and t^2.

Least squares credibility was recognized by Bailey (1950) to replicate the Bayesian predictive mean for the Bayesian normal-normal and beta-binomial models. Keffer's result shows this for the gamma-Poisson case, and it is also known for the gamma-gamma pair. For any distribution, the Bayesian predictive mean is the best least squares estimator, and least squares credibility provides the best **linear** least squares estimator. When the predictive mean is a linear function of the observations, then, it and the credibility estimator are the same. Ericson (1970) characterized a family of distributions (linear exponential family) for which this is the case. The models listed above are the main examples.

An apparent advantage of credibility over Bayesian analysis is that distributional assumptions are not needed for credibility. That is, credibility gives the best linear least squares answer for any distribution, whereas a Bayesian analysis will be different for different distributions. There are two problems with this conclusion, however. First, as will be illustrated in the concluding section of this chapter, when the Bayesian estimates are not linear, as in the case of most highly skewed distributions, credibility errors can be substantially greater than the Bayes' errors. Second, when Bayes' estimates are linear functions of the data, postulating normal or gamma distributions will give the same answer as credibility, because the Bayesian predictive means are linear in the observations for these distributions. Thus credibility analysis gives the same answer as assuming normal (or gamma) distributions and doing a Bayesian analysis, and it gives a useful answer only in those cases where normal or gamma distributions would be reasonable.

A useful alternative when working with highly skewed distributions, as discussed in the concluding section of this chapter, is to transform the data, e.g. by taking logs, before doing the analysis. The workers' compensation "multi-split" experience rating plan can be interpreted in this light. For small to medium sized risks, the experience modified rate is based on a credibility estimate which uses only the "primary value" of the risk's losses. The primary value is a transformation somewhat more complicated than the log, wherein each claim is multiplied by a primary factor. An example in recent use sets the primary factor for a claim of size L to 1 for claims with $L < 2000$ and to $10{,}000/(L + 8000)$ for larger claims. The purpose of this and other transformations is to get distributions which are closer to the normal or gamma, so that the credibility estimator is more nearly optimal.

Exercise 1.1

What is the maximum primary value a claim can have?

An advantage of Bayesian analysis is that it gives a distribution around the estimate, so that the degree of likely deviation from the estimate can be quantified. The principal advantage of credibility is ease of application and explanation.

Review of Probability

An understanding of some basic probability will be presumed in this chapter. A few of the topics most germane to credibility theory will be highlighted in this section, but reference to statistical texts may be helpful. The reader may want to briefly review this section, and refer to it in greater detail as needed. A word on notation: EX and $VarX$ are often used without parentheses to denote the expected value and variance of X. Thus $VarX = E(X - EX)^2 = EX^2 - (EX)^2$.

Covariance

For two random variables X and Y, the covariance of X and Y is defined as

$$Cov(X,Y) = E[(X - EX)(Y - EY)] \tag{2.1}$$

and often can be calculated more conveniently by

$$Cov(X,Y) = E(XY) - (EX)(EY) \tag{2.2}$$

Thus $Cov(X,X) = Var(X)$. The covariance of X and Y divided by the product of their standard deviations yields the correlation coefficient. The covariance is zero when X and Y are independent, but not necessarily vice versa.

Bayesian Estimation

Recall that if $f(x,y)$ is the joint density for X and Y, then the marginal density for X is defined as

$$f_X(x) = \int f(x,y)dy \tag{2.3}$$

The integral is taken over the entire support of Y, and the resulting marginal density is basically the probability density function for X. The same thing can be done for Y. The conditional density of Y given X is defined by

$$f(y|x) = f(x,y) \div f_X(x) \tag{2.4}$$

This is interpreted as the density function for Y given that X takes on the value x.

Substituting $f_Y(y)f(x|y)$ for $f(x,y)$ in (2.3), and substituting the result of that for $f_X(x)$ in (2.4) yields Bayes' rule

$$f(y|x) = f_Y(y)f(x|y) \int f_Y(y)f(x|y)dy \tag{2.5}$$

which is used to get from one conditional distribution to another. Note that the denominator of 2.5 is the integral with respect to y of the numerator, and thus provides the constant factor needed to make the entire right hand side a probability density for y, i.e., make it integrate to unity dy. In many applications it is easier to compute this constant as a separate step, and so Bayes' rule can be written

$$f(y|x) \propto f(x|y)f(y) \tag{2.6}$$

where "$\propto$" is read "is proportional to". The denominator of 2.5 is in fact the marginal density $f(x)$. To say this is a constant just means that it does not involve y. If all the factors containing y on the right side of 2.6 are maintained, any others can be dropped and the full density function can still be obtained later by this integration. (In 2.6 and hereafter, the subscript on the marginal density is dropped unless it is needed to avoid confusion.)

Conditional moments can be defined by using the conditional densities in the usual moment definitions. For instance

$$E(Y|X=x) = \int yf(y|x)dy \tag{2.7}$$

$$Var(Y|X=x) = \int (y - E(Y|X=x))^2 f(y|x)dy \tag{2.8}$$

Since $EY = \int\int yf(x,y)dydx = \int E(Y|X=x)f_X(x)dx$,

$$EY = E[E(Y|X)] \tag{2.9}$$

Similarly it can be shown that

$$VarY = EVar(Y|X) + VarE(Y|X) \tag{2.10a}$$

$$Cov(Y,Z) = ECov(Y,Z|X) + Cov(E(Y|X),E(Z|X)) \tag{2.10b}$$

Equation (2.10a) is the special case of (2.10b) given by $Y = Z$.

In applications of Bayes' rule, as given in 2.5, x is usually observed, and inferences are then made about y. To do this, a *prior* density $f(y)$ is needed for Y, as well as the *conditional* density $f(x|y)$. Then x is observed and the *posterior* density $f(y|x)$ is calculated. From the prior and the conditional densities, the marginal density of X can also be calculated, by integration, and this is sometimes known as the *mixture of the conditional by the prior*. The posterior distribution for Y represents an updated version of the prior, given the data x. The distribution of X can then be updated by mixing the conditional by the posterior to produce the *predictive* distribution. The predictive mean from this distribution can be used to predict the next observation of X, and in fact, this estimate is the least squares optimal estimate for that observation.

To illustrate this terminology and conditioning in general, examples are given below.

Example 2.1—Discrete Distributions

Walking out the door this morning you put 10 coins in your pocket(book), all of which are either quarters or Susan B. Anthony dollars. You are not sure how many of each you have, but after some reflection you decide that either 4, 5, or 6 coins are quarters, and you attach probabilities of .3, .4, and .3 respectively to these three possibilities. This is your prior distribution, i.e., Y is the number of quarters, and $f_Y(4) = f_Y(6) = .3$, and $f_Y(5) = .4$.

Original number of quarters:	4	5	6
Prior probability:	.3	.4	.3
Conditional probability of a quarter:	.4	.5	.6

X is the value, in cents, of the first coin you draw at random. The conditional distribution for X is given by

$$f(25|y) = y/10,\ f(100|y) = 1 - y/10,\ y = 4,5,6.$$

The probability distribution for X that takes into account both the conditional and prior distributions is the marginal, or mixed distribution

$$f_X(25) = \int f_Y(y) f(25|y)\,dy = (.4)(.3) + (.5)(.4) + (.6)(.3) = .5,$$

where, in the discrete case, the integral is interpreted as a sum. Thus, the overall or mixed probability of pulling out a quarter on the first draw is .5, and $E(X) = 62.5$ is the expected value of the first coin drawn. The first coin you pull out, which you give to a wandering minstrel, turns out to have been a quarter, so $x = 25$. How does this fact change your opinion about Y? By Bayes' rule,

$$f(y|25) = f(25|y)f(y)/f(25).$$

E.g.,

$$f(4|25) = f(25|4)f(4)/f(25) = (.4)(.3)/(.5) = .24$$

is the posterior probability for $y = 4$. By the same rule, $y = 5$ and $y = 6$ have posterior probabilities of .4 and .36, respectively.

Original number of quarters:	4	5	6
Posterior probability:	.24	.4	.36
Conditional probability of another quarter:	3/9	4/9	5/9

The value of the next coin to be drawn will be referred to as the random variable W. The probabilities for Y are given by the posterior distribution just calculated, but in reference to W, these are now the new prior probabilities. Since a coin is missing, there are new conditional probabilities as well. It is not hard to verify that

$$f(w = 25|y) = (y - 1)/9, \text{ for } y = 4,5,6.$$

The marginal probabilities for W are calculated again as the mixture of the prior and the conditional, and are referred to as the predictive distribution for W. Thus

$$f(25) = (3/9)(.24) + (4/9)(.4) + (5/9)(.36) = .452$$

is the predictive, or overall probability of a quarter on the next draw, and $f(100) = .548$ is the corresponding probability of a dollar, and so $E(W) = 66.1$ is the predictive mean. This is not much higher than the original expected value of X. Even though the number of quarters has gone down by one, the probabilities have shifted toward having had more to begin with.

Example 2.2—Claim Frequency Distributions

A population of drivers is insured by XYZ insurance company, and each driver has a Poisson distribution for the number of physical damage claims to be submitted each year. Different drivers may have different Poisson parameters, however. For a given driver, let N_i denote the claim count random variable for year i, and y the driver's Poisson parameter, which is assumed not to vary over time. Then, for any of the variables N_i, the conditional density, given y, is

$$f(n|y) = e^{-y}y^n/n!,$$

which has mean and variance both equal to y, and skewness of $y^{-1/2}$. In this example it is supposed that, before observing this driver's first year's claim count N_1, y is not known, but is a random variable having the gamma distribution with parameters r and b. This has the density

$$f(y) = y^{r-1}e^{-y/b}/\ b^r(r-1)!.$$

Here and throughout the chapter $a!$ will be used to denote $\Gamma(a+1)$, the gamma function at $a+1$, as these functions agree on integers, and the gamma function can be used to define $a!$ at other points. The gamma distribution could, for example, be interpreted as the distribution of the Poisson parameter across the population of insured drivers.

The gamma distribution is considered the prior distribution for Y, which is now capitalized to signify that it is a random variable. The gamma distribution in r,b has mean br and variance b^2r, and in general,

$$EY^j = b^jr(r+1)\cdots(r+j-1)$$

when j is a positive integer, and $EY^j = b^j(r+j-1)!/(r-1)!$

for any real $j > -r$. the shape of the distribution is determined by r; b is referred to as the *scale parameter.*

For simplicity, let N denote any one of the random variables N_i. The unconditional or mixed distribution for N is its marginal distribution with density

$$f_N(n) = \int f(n,y)dy = \int f(n|y)f(y)dy.$$

This is the distribution the insurer faces for the driver's claim counts, as it combines the conditional distribution for N given Y with the prior distribution for Y. This integral can be evaluated by use of the definition of the gamma function, after a change of variable. For the first year's claim count N_1, doing the integration finds the mixture to be a negative binomial distribution, with parameters r and $p = 1/(1 + b)$. The negative binomial density with parameters r and p is

$$f(n) = (r + n - 1)!\, p^r(1 - p)^n / n!(r - 1)!,$$

with mean $r(1 - p)/p$, variance $r(1 - p)/p^2$, and skewness $(2 - p)(r - rp)^{-1/2.}$

From the negative binomial distribution the unconditional expected value of the first year's number of claims for this driver can be found to be $EN_1 = rb$, since for $p = 1/(1 + b)$, $(1 - p)/p = b$. This could have been calculated using $EN_1 = EE(N_1|Y)$, because $E(N_1|Y) = Y$, from the Poisson distribution, and $EY = rb$ from the gamma distribution. Similarly, the negative binomial gives $VarN_1 = rb(b + 1)$. From (2.10) this should equal $EVar(N_1|Y) + VarE(N_1|Y)$, which it does: by the Poisson assumption these two terms become $EY + VarY = rb + rb^2$.

The two components of the total variance of N_1 have sometimes been referred to as "expected value of process variance" and "variance of hypothetical means", respectively. The latter terminology considers $E(N_1|Y)$ as hypothetical, since Y is not a known quantity. The term "conditional" could replace both "process" and "hypothetical". The first component in this case is the average driver variance, and indicates the degree to which individual driver frequency would display stability over time. The second is the variance of the individual driver means, and indicates how similar or dissimilar different drivers tend to be.

It should be noted that although individual risk Poisson distributions with Poisson parameters gamma distributed across risks produce an overall negative binomial distribution of risk claim counts, the converse is by no means the case. Thus a good fit of the claims to a negative binomial does not necessarily mean that there are Poissons and gammas producing it. In fact, a mixture of just two different Poisson populations can look a lot like a negative binomial.

Now suppose that the first year's claim count N_1 has been observed. The posterior distribution is the density for Y given N_1, as calculated by Bayes' rule, and can be used to update the prior distribution from the observation. By Bayes' rule, $f(y|n) \propto f(n|y)f(y)$. The proportionality means that any factors not involving y can be computed later, by the fact that the integral of $f(y|n)dy$ must equal 1. Thus

$$f(y|n) \propto e^{-y} y^n y^{r-1} e^{-y/b} = y^{n+r-1} e^{-y(1+1/b)}.$$

But from the gamma density above,the gamma distribution in parameters $b/(b+1)$ and $(n+r)$ is proportional to this same quantity, so that must be the posterior distribution of Y. The posterior distribution reflects the updated probabilities for Y yielded by the first year's claim count N_1. This distribution then can be used as the prior distribution for the second year's claim count N_2.

A measure of the dispersion of a random variable relative to its mean is the coefficient of variation, or CV, which is the ratio of the standard deviation to the mean. For the gamma in r,b this is given by $1/\sqrt{r}$, and so reduces to $1/\sqrt{n+r}$ for the posterior gamma after one observation.

Finally, the predictive distribution is the marginal distribution of N_2 resulting from the mixture of the Poisson model by the posterior gamma distribution for Y given N_1. Since a Poisson mixed by a gamma in r,b gives a negative binomial in $r, 1/(b+1)$, the Poisson mixed by the posterior gamma in $b/(b+1)$, $n+r$ can be seen to give negative binomial parameters $n+r$, $(b+1)/(2b+1)$. This is the distribution for N_2 the insurer faces for this driver after observing $N_1 = n$. It has mean $(n+r)b/(b+1)$, which can be written as $Zn + (1-Z)br$, with $Z = b/(b+1)$. This is a credibility weighting between the observation n and the previous mean br.

The usefulness of the predictive distribution goes beyond estimating the subsequent expected value. It gives the probabilities for $N_2 = j$ for all values of j, and thus quantifies the possible divergence of actual from expected results. It is important to clearly distinguish the posterior and predictive distributions. After some observations, the posterior distribution specifies refined probabilities of where the parameter Y might be; the predictive distribution specifies the refined probabilities for the next observation N_{i+1}, and is the mixture of the conditional by the posterior.

Exercise 2.1

a. Calculate $EE(N_2|Y)$, where the outer expected value uses the posterior gamma above.

b. Calculate $Var\ N_2$:

1. As $EVar(N_2|Y) + VarE(N_2|Y)$.
2. Directly from the predictive distribution.

When, as in this example, the posterior distribution is of the same type as the prior, just with different parameters, the prior and conditional distributions are said to be conjugate. Since the posterior of N_1 becomes the prior of N_2, etc., conjugate distributions allow for continued updating of the parameters of a single distribution type as subsequent data becomes available.

Thus the gamma-Poisson combination is a conjugate pair. Others are given in the attached Table of Distributions. The transformed gamma-inverse Weibull pair and the inverse gamma-gamma pair are illustrated in the next subsection.

***Bayesian Analysis with Continuous Distributions**

Distributions useful for severity and total losses are introduced in this section and used to further illustrate mixing and Bayesian updating.

Example 2.3 — Severity Distributions

The distributions in this example could be used for claim severity, but a different type of severity is used for illustration. The distributions used are given in the Table of Distributions, and the example in part illustrates the use of that table. The conditional distribution used is the inverse Weibull distribution. This is the distribution X follows if $1/X$ is Weibull distributed, and it is also the log transform of the extreme value distribution. It is a heavy tailed distribution like the Pareto, but, unlike the Pareto, it has negative moments of all orders. That is, $E(X^j)$ exists for all $j < 0$. This implies that the inverse Weibull will not have as many extremely small claims as the Pareto has, which makes it useful in some lines of insurance. (An indication of the heaviness of the tails is the number of moments existing [positive moments for the right tail, negative moments for the left]. Thus a distribution with infinite skewness will be heavier right tailed than a distribution with all positive moments, for example.)

You arrive at an airport near a major city, but your hotel is in a suburban location. Only the city cabs are permitted to serve the airport, and they do not know the suburbs that well. You have been informed before coming that the fare should be $20, but the drivers tend to go somewhat out of the way, and thus charge more. The extra charge, X, has a somewhat different distribution for each cab company. From your local contacts you have learned that each company can be considered to have a parameter y, with the probability of the extra charge given by the inverse Weibull distribution with parameters $2, y$.

The conditional distribution is thus given by $F(x|y) = exp[-(y/x)^2]$, with $E(X|y) = 1.77y$ (see Table of Distributions).

The parameter y is distributed across the cab companies by the transformed gamma distribution with parameters 3, 2, .17. This is not a particularly heavy tailed distribution. From the moment formulas in the Table of Distributions, it has mean .2825, and so the extra charge X has mean $(1.77)(.2825) = .5$. The transformed gamma is the conjugate prior of the inverse Weibull, as long as the "power" parameters (equal to 2 in this case) match.

With this prior distribution, the mixed distribution for X is given by the generalized loglogistic (GLL) distribution with parameters 3, 2, .17, and so $F(x) = [1 + (.17/x)^2]^{-3}$, with $E(X) = .5$. The GLL, also known as the inverse Burr, is a heavy tailed distribution similar to the Burr. The probability that X exceeds $1 is 8.2% for this distribution. You take a cab to the hotel, and the meter reads $21, so $x = 1$. From the Table of Distributions, you can calculate that the posterior distribution of Y for this company is transformed gamma in 4, 2, .1676, and the predictive distribution is generalized loglogistic in 4, 2, .1676. Thus the predictive expected value of the extra cost of another ride with this same company can be calculated from the generalized loglogistic distribution function, and turns out to be $.58. The probability of exceeding $1 is now 10.5%.

The information value of the observation is not great, because the conditional distribution is heavy tailed and the prior is not. The heavy tailed conditional implies that an unusually high value could come from a fairly ordinary company, and so observing a high value does not give much information about the company. This situation will often prevail in insurance situations as well. In fact, the most likely way a mixture of severity distributions could occur would be to have a heavy tailed conditional, like the inverse Weibull, mixed by a less heavy tailed prior, like the transformed gamma. This is because any risk could have a very large loss, and so the individual risk severity distribution should be heavy tailed. The differences among risks could be significant, but gamma-like distributions would normally be heavy tailed enough to capture them.

This example illustrated the use of the attached tables to calculate Bayesian values. The next example shows how those tables were calculated.

Example 2.4—Total Loss Distribution

In this example, the total workers' compensation losses X_i for a certain factory in year i are assumed to be gamma distributed with parameters y,r. Here, however the scale parameter y is not known, but is distributed across the various factories in the rating class by the prior distribution

$$f(y) = y^{-s-1}e^{-b/y}b^s/(s-1)! \qquad (2.11)$$

This is referred to as the inverse gamma distribution in s,b because Y^{-1} is gamma distributed in b^{-1},s. The moments are given by

$$E(Y^j) = b^j/(s-1)(s-2)\cdots(s-j)$$

for positive integers $j < s$ and

$$E(Y^j) = b^j(s-j-1)!/(s-1)!$$

for any real number $j < s$. If $j \geq s$, the jth moment does not exist. In particular $E(Y) = b/(s-1)$ for $s > 1$ and

$$VarY = b^2/(s-1)^2(s-2)$$

for $s > 2$. Note that this prior can be specified simply as $f(y) \propto y^{-s-1}e^{-b/y}$, and the conditional by $f(x|y) \propto e^{-x/y}x^{r-1}y^{-r}$. As opposed to the previous example, the prior here is heavy tailed, so there are significant differences among factories, but the conditional is not so heavy tailed, so risks are somewhat stable. As mentioned above, this is probably a less realistic model.

The posterior can be calculated as

$$f(y|x) \propto f(x|y)f(y) \propto e^{-x/y}y^{-r}y^{-s-1}e^{-b/y} \propto e^{-(x+b)/y}y^{-r-s-1}.$$

But this is the inverse gamma in $(r+s)$, $(x+b)$. This shows the conjugate nature of the pair.

The mixed distribution is $f(x) = \int f(x|y)f(y)dy$, and doing the integration (again a change of variable plus the definition of the gamma function) yields

$$f(x) = b^s x^{r-1}(r+s-1)!/(b+x)^{r+s}(r-1)!(s-1)! \qquad (2.12)$$

This is a generalization of both the F-distribution and the shifted pareto, and has been called different names. Here it will be referred to as the generalized pareto in r,s,b. The moments are given by

$$E(X^j) = b^j r(r+1)\cdots(r+j-1)/(s-1)(s-2)\cdots(s-j) \qquad (2.13a)$$

for positive integers $j < s$ and

$$E(X^j) = b^j(r+j-1)!(s-j-1)!/(r-1)!(s-1)! \qquad (2.13b)$$

for any real j, $s > j > -r$.

In particular

$$E(X_1) = rb/(s-1),$$

$s > 1$, and

$$Var(X_1) = b^2 r(r+s-1)/\ (s-1)^2(s-2),$$

$s > 2$. This is a heavy tailed distribution, which arose because of the heavy tailed prior.

Exercise 2.2

Calculate EX and $VarX$ via (2.9) and (2.10).

The predictive distribution for X_2 given $X_1 = x$ is the conditional gamma mixed by the posterior inverse gamma and is thus the generalized pareto in r, $(r+s)$, $(x+b)$. For $s > 1-r$, this has mean

$$E(X_2|X_1 = x) = (x+b)r/(r+s-1).$$

Letting $Z = r/(r+s-1)$, $1-Z = (s-1)/(r+s-1)$, the predictive mean can be expressed as

$$E(X_2|X_1 = x) = Zx + (1-Z)E(X_1).$$

It is also possible to write $Z = 1/(1+K)$, by letting $K = (s-1)/r$. Thus again a credibility formula arises for the predictive mean. As will be seen below, this does not always happen, but it does for an important class of distributions.

The generalized Pareto of this example and the generalized loglogistic of the previous one are similar three parameter heavy tailed distributions, and the Burr is also closely related. For all these distributions, the scale parameter determines the general location of the probability, and the other two parameters determine how heavy the right and left tails are. Here, the number of positive and negative moments that exist is taken as the measure of the heaviness of the right and left tails, respectively. As an example, the parameters of these three distributions are as follows for a mean of 1 and the yth moment existing for $-10 < y < 2$:

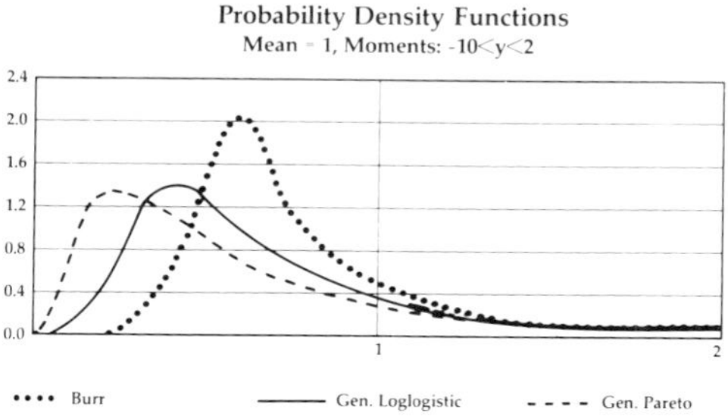

Generalized pareto: $r = 2$, $s = 10$, $b = .1$;

Generalized loglogistic: $r = 5$, $a = 2$, $b = .25869$;

Burr: $s = .2$, $a = 10$, $b = .50724$.

This can be verified by the moment formulas in the Table of Distributions. The three density functions are compared in the graph. A different shape is produced for each, especially in the middle portion of the distributions. Thus the parameters of each distribution determine the shape of the tails, and the choice of distributions can influence the center, giving a fair degree of flexibility overall. More flexibility can be obtained using the four parameter transformed beta, which is a generalization of all of these distributions.

**Diffuse Priors in Bayesian Analysis*

In the above example the prior distribution could have come from information about the distribution of risks within the class. Lacking such information, a prior could be developed by actuarial judgement. When information and judgement lack precision, it is often felt best to make the prior as nonspecific as possible. One method that has been developed to do this is the use of so-called *diffuse priors.* This class of prior distributions provides what some statisticians believe to be the most powerful estimation method available, and they have led to greatly improved credibility estimates in some cases. On the other hand, it is not always appropriate to use diffuse priors, especially when some more specific information or opinion is available. There is also a tendency to regard diffuse priors as a method of avoiding subjective judgement in Bayesian analysis, but this is probably not so.

In order to integrate to unity, probability density functions contain negligible area outside of some finite interval, which thus contains the bulk of the probability. Diffuse priors do not operate in this fashion, but rather use functions that do not contain finite area, such as $f(y) = 1$, or $f(y) = 1/y$. Because these do not integrate to unity, they are not proper density functions, but a mathematical device nonetheless allows calculation of posterior distributions. Diffuse priors get their name from the fact that non-negligible probability may be present outside any finite interval.

One class of diffuse priors for a positive parameter y is specified by $f(y) \propto y^p$. There is no value of p for which the integral of y^p over the positive reals is finite; thus no constant c can be calculated to make $f(y)/c$ a proper density function. Nonetheless, for a prior distribution proportional to y^p

and a conditional distribution $f(x|y)$, $f(x|y)y^p$ may have a finite integral, and if so, it gives the posterior distribution for $y|x$, up to a constant equal to that integral, by Bayes' rule. See Example 2.5 below. A more detailed discussion of diffuse priors may be found in Berger (1985).

The appeal of diffuse priors is essentially twofold. First, they may appear to mathematically express the state of no prior opinion, and which would bring "objectivity" into a Bayesian analysis. Secondly, they may have less impact on the posterior distribution than other priors would, thus tending to "let the data speak for themselves."

A case will be presented below that diffuse priors are no more objective than proper priors, and so the first appeal is illusory, but that judicious choice of the diffuse prior will have the pragmatic benefit of only weakly impacting the posterior distribution. This benefit could be a detriment, however, if it were to lead to the abandonment of relevant information or opinion that could be encoded as a proper prior.

As an example of the y^p prior, $p = 0$ specifies a uniform prior, on the positive reals. This distribution can be thought of as a limit of uniform distributions on $(0,M)$ as M goes to infinity. While a uniform prior on the positive reals may seem to reflect a state of no prior opinion for a positive parameter, it in fact tends to favor large values of y. For $p = 0$, the integral of y^p from 0 to M is finite, while that from M to infinity is not, for any number M, no matter how large, which in effect puts more weight on large values of y. This may make the choice of $p = 0$ inappropriate for a prior on the positive reals. For example, the likelihood of y being between 1 and 2 is the same as for it being between 1,000,000,000,001 and 1,000,000,000,002, which would not be reasonable in many contexts.

More generally, the infinite part of the integral of y^p is from M to infinity for $p > -1$, and from 0 to ε for $p < -1$. In the latter case the prior puts emphasis on values of y near zero. For $p = -1$ neither the interval 0 to ε nor the interval M to infinity has a finite integral. Thus for $p = -1$, even though the probability is concentrated in unlikely places (near zero and infinity), there is no clear cut pull by the prior to higher or lower values of y. This, then, may give reasonable results when used as a diffuse prior, even if it seems absurd as an opinion of the likely location of y. On the other hand, for $p = -1$, the first moment distribution $yf(y)$ is proportional to 1 on the interval 0 to infinity, and so by the above reasoning is weighted to larger values. This may indicate that $p = -2$ gives a more "opinion neutral" diffuse prior.

None of the priors in these examples, however, are really neutral as to where the probability is. Some diffuse priors concentrate the weight on large values of y, and some on very small values, but they all express prior opinion or belief. Rather than eliminating subjectivity from Bayesian analysis, they in fact appear to incorporate fairly strange opinions about where y is likely to be.

The impact of the choice of the prior on the posterior distribution may nevertheless be small. In order to see how much the posterior is affected by various priors, the table below shows the posterior mean for the parameter y of an exponential distribution under three diffuse priors ($p = 0, -1, -2$) and the inverse gamma prior proportional to $y^{-3}e^{-1}/y$, which is a proper prior with mean 1 but infinite variance. This is shown separately for samples of sizes 3 and 10, and for sample means of 0.5, 1, and 2.

Posterior Mean — Conditional Exponential Distribution

		$n = 3$			$n = 10$	
Prior	**Data:** 0.5	1.0	2.0	0.5	1.0	2.0
y^0	1.5	3.0	6.0	.63	1.3	2.5
y^{-1}	.75	1.5	3.0	.56	1.1	2.2
y^{-2}	.50	1.0	2.0	.50	1.0	2.0
$y^{-3}e^{-1}/y$	.63	1.0	1.8	.55	1.0	1.9

As anticipated, $p = 0$ leads to an upward pull on the posterior, as does $p = -1$ to a more limited extent. In this case, $p = -2$ returns the sample mean, and the inverse gamma gives shrinkage towards the prior mean of 1. To use a word processing term, $p = -2$ provides a WYSIWYG prior in this case (what you see is what you get).

Example 2.5

In Example 2.4, suppose the prior had been specified as $f(y) \propto y^p$. Then $f(y|x) \propto e^{-x}/yy^{p-r}$. As long as $p < -1$ this is an inverse gamma posterior, with parameters x and $r - p - 1$. The predictive distribution will thus be the generalized pareto, with parameters x, r, and $r-p-1$. Thus the predictive mean is $rx/(r-p-2)$. For $p=-2$ this is equal to the observation x, which is an appealing result in that it takes the observation at face value. For $p=-1$, the observation is increased by a factor of $r/(r-1)$, as long as $r>1$. This also has a heuristic interpretation, in that $r/(r-1)$ is the ratio of the conditional mean to conditional mode, which is the most likely observation. For $p=-1$, the posterior inverse gamma has parameters x_1,r and the predictive generalized pareto is in x_1,r,r. Repeated application after n observations yields a predictive generalized pareto in

$$(\Sigma_{i=1}^{n} x_i), r, nr.$$

If $r<1$, this will eventually have a finite predictive mean when $nr>1$.

Example 2.6

In Example 2.1, taking $f(y) \propto y^p$ yields the posterior $f(y|n) \propto e^{-y} y^{n+p}$. This is a gamma distribution in $1, n+p+1$ as long as $p>-n-1$. The predictive mean is $n+p+1$, which for $p=-1$ is the observation n.

Note that in both of these examples the posterior distributions are proper (not diffuse) and are conjugate to the conditional distributions. Thus they can then be used as priors to begin the Bayesian updating process as more observations become available.

Although the WYSIWYG aspect of diffuse priors is probably their most appealing feature, they can be used as intentional statements of probability, as in the following example.

Example 2.7

An astronomer, recognizing the possibility that certain objects may not presently be seen due to the fact that the light they emit has not yet had time to get here, postulates that the present time is an arbitrary point in history, and concludes that the greatest distance X at which we can now observe an object is uniformly distributed on $(0,M)$, where M is the most distant object there is. Reasoning that very large numbers for M only become very gradually less likely, the astronomer assigns a diffuse prior for M with $p=-1$. Thus $f(m) \propto 1/m$, and $f(x|m)=1/m$, $x<m$,

$f(x|m) = 0, x > m$. After finding out what x is, the posterior distribution can be calculated as $f(m|x) \propto f(x|m)f(m) \propto m^{-2}$ for $m > x$, and zero otherwise. The integral over the support of this posterior is $1/x$, so $f(m|x) = xm^{-2}$. The distribution function is $F(m|x) = 1 - x/m$, $m > x$. The posterior median for M, for example, is $2x$, and the 99th percentile is $100x$, although the posterior mean is not finite.

A WYSIWYG prior is not always appropriate, especially when there is important prior information. The following example has been attributed to Morris.

In a critical situation, a baseball manager would not be likely to replace a consistent .350 hitter with a new player who has had one hit for one at bat, and thus is batting 1.000. The manager's implicit prior for the new player would probably have a mean somewhere around .250, and the success so far would not be likely to alter that greatly.

This can be contrasted to a choice of two taxi drivers to go to the airport: a new driver has had one trip to the airport, and arrived there successfully; a certain experienced driver is very good around town, but tends to get lost going to the airport, and in fact over time has arrived there successfully on only 35% of his trips. The same baseball manager from above would probably prefer to take his chances with the new driver, although the data is just the same as the batting situation where he would make the opposite choice. The difference is in the implicit prior, which would be close to 1.0 for a successful drive to the airport. In this case a WYSIWYG prior would give the same result as the implicit prior, because the data with only a single observation is consistent with the implicit prior.

Aggregate Claims Distributions

The application of credibility to insurance problems often involves a decomposition of the total losses into frequency and severity components. This part of the statistical preliminaries will be the calculation of the moments and percentiles of aggregate claims from those for frequency and severity.

The definition of the aggregate claims T for a given period is:

$$T = X_1 + \cdots + X_N \tag{2.14}$$

where N is the number of claims in the period and X_i is the amount of the ith claim. It is usually assumed that the X_i are independent of each other and of N, and that all the claims follow a common severity distribution. Thus, the subscripts can be dropped when referring to the severity random variable X.

The moments of T are given by:

$$E(T) = E(N)E(X) \tag{2.15a}$$

$$Var(T) = E(N)Var(X) + E(X)^2 Var(N) \tag{2.15b}$$

$$Skw(T) = \frac{(Skw(X)CV^3 + 3n_2CV^2 + n_3)}{\sqrt{E(N)(CV^2 + n_2)^3}} \tag{2.15c}$$

Here CV denotes the severity coefficient of variation, and

$$n_i = E(N - EN)^i / EN.$$

"*Skw*" refers to the coefficient of skewness, e.g.,

$$Skw(X) = E((X - EX)^3)/Var(X)^{1.5}.$$

(2.15a) is obtained from (2.9) by noting $E(T) = EE(T|N) = E(NE(X)) = E(N)E(X)$. (2.15b) follows similarly from (2.10) since:

$$\begin{aligned} Var(T) &= EVar(T|N) + VarE(T|N) \\ &= E(NVar(X)) + Var(NE(X)) \\ &= E(N)Var(X) + E(X)^2 Var(N) \end{aligned}$$

This could alternatively be computed by evaluating $E(T^j|N)$ via (2.9), which is what is used to derive (2.15c).

Example 2.8

This example gives a method in which the variance of losses over time might be separated into two components—changes in the mean and random fluctuation around the mean. Essentially, any variance appearing which is greater than the conditional variance from model assumptions is attributed to fluctuation around the mean.

An automobile insurance coverage has been found to have an average claim size, when adjusted for inflation, of \$2000, with a claim size standard deviation of \$7000. Previous studies of the number of accidents per driver have found the individual driver accident frequency to be approximately negative binomial distributed, with a ratio of variance to mean of 1.25. The frequency mean is subject to change over time, however, with mean and variance to be estimated. The total losses, T, adjusted for inflation for a territory with 100,000 drivers is shown below:

Year:	**1**	**2**	**3**	**4**	**5**	**6**	**7**	**8**	**9**	**10**
Losses(000):	2,150	1,800	2,400	1,500	1,850	2,500	1,600	2,200	1,850	2,150

From this data, the sample mean and variance give the estimates $ET = 2{,}000{,}000$, and $VarT = 99{,}000{,}000{,}000$.

If the driver frequency mean is M, the territory frequency mean is $100{,}000M$, and the territory frequency variance is $125{,}000M$. (This assumes the drivers' losses are conditionally independent, given M.) Then by (2.15),

$$E(T|M) = 200{,}000{,}000M,$$

and

$$\begin{aligned} Var(T|M) &= 7000^2\,(100{,}000M) + 2000^2\,(125{,}000M) \\ &= 5{,}900{,}000{,}000{,}000M. \end{aligned}$$

Then by (2.9) and (2.10),

$$ET = 200{,}000{,}000EM, \text{ and } VarT = 5{,}900{,}000{,}000{,}000EM + 200{,}000{,}000^2 VarM.$$

The estimated values of ET and $VarT$ then lead to the estimates $EM = .01$, and $VarM = .001^2$. The average fluctuation around the mean is $EVar\,(T|M) =$ 59,000,000,000 and the portion of the variance of losses due to the fluctuation of the mean itself is $VarE(T|M) =$ 40,000,000,000.

Percentiles of T

One method of estimating the percentiles of T is to assume a particular distributional form, e.g., that T is normal or gamma distributed. If the moments of X and N are given, the distribution for T can then be estimated from its moments, which are computed via (2.15). The normal distributional assumption incorporates a skewness of zero. The gamma has a skewness of twice its coefficient of variation. This is probably more realistic for property-casualty lines, but neither distributional form is likely to be accurate enough in general.

Several approaches to improved estimation of percentiles of aggregate claims have been developed. One is to incorporate a third parameter so that the first three moments can be considered. For instance for the normal distribution the so-called normal power approximation (*NP*) incorporates a skewness correction as follows. Let σ_T denote the standard deviation of T, and t_p the pth percentile. Then the normal approximation estimates t_p by $ET + \sigma_T y_p$, where y_p is the pth percentile of the standard normal. The *NP* approximation for t_p is:

$$t_p = ET + \sigma_T y_p + \sigma_T Skw(T)(y_p{}^2 - 1)/6 \tag{2.16}$$

This *NP* formula is derived using a power series expansion for t_p. Pentikäinen (1977) recommends its use only for $Skw(T) < 1$, after which the *NP* tends to exaggerate the difference between the percentiles t_p and their normal approximation estimates. However, up to a skewness of 2, the results are generally reasonable.

Another approximation for aggregate claims is offered by Seal (1977), who adds a third parameter to the gamma that shifts the origin to the left or right. This can be accomplished by letting $-a + X/b$ be gamma distributed in $(r,1)$, so that the coefficient of skewness is still $2/r^{.5}$, and $VarX$ is b^2r. The mean is $a + br$. Thus the three parameters can be easily matched to the first three empirical moments. The percentiles are calculated by adding a to the percentiles of the gamma in (r,b). Pentikäinen (1977) finds the accuracy of this approximation comparable to that of the *NP*. A problem arises if a is negative, however, because negative losses are given positive probability.

Another way of adding a third parameter to the gamma is to use a power transform, i.e., to assume T is gamma distributed for some real number a, thus generating the transformed gamma distribution. If a is negative, this gives the inverse transformed gamma distribution. Applications of this method to aggregate loss distributions can be found in Venter (1983a).

It is also possible to compute the aggregate distribution function without making a distributional assumption for the aggregate claims. However this usually requires knowledge of the density functions for frequency and severity, not just their moments. One such method is simulation. A possible number of claims n is generated according to the frequency distribution, then n possible claim sizes are drawn from the severity distribution. This gives one possible realization of T. This process can be repeated many thousands of times to estimate the distribution function of T. While conceptually simple, this process is often expensive and time consuming.

Another method is to build up the aggregate distribution function recursively, i.e., the probability that $T < t$ is computed from the probabilities that T is less than $t - 1$, $t - 2$, etc. Panjer (1981) shows a fairly efficient way to do this for a discrete severity distribution and a Poisson, negative binomial, or binomial frequency. For the Poisson frequency, dePril (1986) finds an even more efficient algorithm for a piecewise linear severity distribution function.

Finally, a method of calculating aggregate claim probabilities by computing the characteristic function of that distribution is becoming widely used. The characteristic function is a complex analog of the moment generating function, and can be computed for aggregate claims from the moment generating function of frequency and the characteristic function of severity. The distribution function for aggregate claims can be recovered from its characteristic function via numerical integration. The calculation is thus somewhat intricate, but once programmed it is fairly efficient.

One difficulty is calculating the severity characteristic function, as this is not usually of closed form. An exception is the gamma severity, which was used in Mong (1980), the paper that introduced the characteristic function method to CAS literature. Heckman and Meyers (1983) extended the method to a step function probability density, and Venter (1983a) generalized this to a piecewise linear density. The latter two severity functions can be used to approximate other distributions, thus making this method of quite general application.

Limited Fluctuation Credibility

The initial idea of limited fluctuation credibility is that some insureds may be large enough to get a reasonable estimate of their future losses based entirely on their own past loss experience. In the words of Mowbray's original paper, "A dependable pure premium is one for which the probability is high, that it does not differ from the true pure premiums by more than an arbitrary limit."

For instance, if the past loss experience can be regarded as a sample from a normal distribution, an insured might be regarded as "dependable" if there is a 90% probability that the observed losses are within 5% of the mean of this normal distribution. Since the normal distribution is symmetric about its mean, the criterion will be satisfied if there is a 95% probability that losses are no more than 5% above the mean.

If all claims are of the same constant size, and claim occurrence follows a Poisson distribution (i.e., variance = mean for claim frequency), a normal approximation to total losses is reasonable, and from normal tables it can be found that an insured with 1082 expected claims will meet the above criterion. To verify this, note that a variance of 1082 implies a standard deviation of 32.89. For a normal variate, the 95th percentile is 1.645 standard deviations above the mean, which in this case is 54.1 claims, or 5% of the expected claims.

What if the insured is not large enough? It would seem reasonable to assign it the degree of credibility that would produce a loss estimate with the same degree of random fluctuation allowed for the large insured. For the above normal distribution and values, this will be seen to occur when the insured's own experience is given credibility derived from $Z^2 = n/1082$, where n is the expected number of claims for the insured.

To see this, the limited fluctuation credibility estimator can be expressed as:

$$C = (1 - Z)M + ZT \tag{3.1}$$

where T is the observation and M is a previous estimate. M is generally supposed to be the estimate one would use if the observation T were not available, and it could come from previous experience and/or related data. Typically T will be the loss ratio, pure premium, frequency, or severity for a class, state, or risk for a certain time period, and C estimates its value for another, usually future, period. Here, to be specific, T will be the aggregate losses for a one year period, thus $T = X_1 + \cdots + X_N$ as above, with the usual independence assumptions (i.e., see (2.14)).

For limited fluctuation theory, (3.1) can be rewritten as:

$$C = (1 - Z)M + ZET + Z(T - ET) \tag{3.2}$$

These three terms can be regarded as representing stability, truth, and random noise. Since truth and noise cannot be observed separately, the same factor Z applies to both. The highest possible factor Z is sought, so that truth will be emphasized, as long as noise can be kept within acceptable bounds. In this theory, acceptable bounds on the noise term are specified by requiring its absolute value to be below a selected small proportion of ET with high probability. The selected proportion of the mean is denoted by k. Thus we want a low probability that $|Z(T - ET)| > kET$.

For symmetric or even moderately right-skewed distributions, the probability that $|Z(T - ET)| > kET$ is no more than twice the probability that $Z(T - ET) > kET$, without the absolute value. Thus the credibility weight can be specified as the highest value of Z that will keep the random component $Z(T - ET)$ below kET (100k% of the expected value) with probability p. For distributions of interest, this then guarantees that $Pr(|Z(T - ET)| > kET) < 2(1 - p)$, that is, that there is a probability of less than $2(1 - p)$ that the random component exceeds k times the mean in absolute value.

For example, $p = .95$ and $k = .05$ are typical choices and result in requiring that the random component is less than 5% of the expected value ET with 95% probability. Thus for $p = .95$, $k = .05$, the credibility requirement provides that the random component has 90% probability of being less than 5% of ET in absolute value.

The criterion

$$Pr(Z(T - ET) < kET) = p$$

can be restated as

$$Pr(T < ET + kET/Z) = p,$$

or

$$t_p = ET + kET/Z,$$

where t_p is the pth percentile of T. To find Z, different methods of computing t_p can be invoked. Under the normal approximation,

$$t_p = ET + y_p\sqrt{VarT},$$

and so

$$Z = kET/y_p\sqrt{VarT}.$$

In terms of frequency and severity,

$$Z^2 = (k/y_p)^2(ENEX)^2/(EN(VarX) + (EX)^2VarN) \qquad (3.3a)$$

$$= (k/y_p)^2(EN)^2/(EN(CV^2) + VarN) \qquad (3.3b)$$

$$= (k/y_p)^2EN/(CV^2 + n_2) \qquad (3.3c)$$

where CV is the severity coefficient of variation and n_2 is the frequency ratio of variance to mean. The credibility Z for a given number of expected claims EN is computed via (3.3). The number of expected claims needed to yield a selected credibility level can be found by solving (3.3) for EN. Since the number of expected claims needed for credibility Z in this situation can be viewed as a function of Z, it will be denoted as n_Z. Solving (3.3) then gives

$$n_Z = Z^2(CV^2 + n_2)(y_p/k)^2.$$

Thus

$$n_1 = (CV^2 + n_2)(y_p/k)^2.$$

This value of EN is called the full credibility value, and is also denoted as n_F, for full. Then $n_Z = Z^2n_F$, or $Z = \sqrt{n_Z/n_F}$. (The reader will note that n with a subscript denotes a moment ratio for frequency if the subscript exceeds 1, and the number of expected claims needed for that much credibility if the subscript is 1 or less, or is an F.)

This "square root rule" holds only for the normal approximation. For the *NP*,

$$t_p = ET + \sqrt{VarT}(y_p + SkwT(y_p{}^2 - 1)/6) \qquad (3.4)$$

and so

$$kET/Z = \sqrt{VarT}\,(y_p + SkwT(y_p{}^2 - 1)/6).$$

This can be solved for z in terms of frequency and severity moments using (2.15) to yield:

$$Z = k/[y_p\sqrt{m_2/EN} + (m_3/m_2)(y_p{}^2 - 1)/6EN] \qquad (3.5)$$

where m_2 and m_3 are aggregate claim shape descriptors defined by:

$$m_2 = n_2 + CV^2$$

$$m_3 = CV^3SkwX + 3n_2CV^2 + n_3$$

The normal approximation formula (3.3c) can then be seen to be the special case $m_3 = 0$, i.e., $SkwT = 0$, which the normal approximation assumes, but which is unlikely in practice. The square root rule does not apply for the *NP* partial credibilities; rather they must be calculated from (3.5) directly. It is possible to solve (3.5) for *EN* by considering it a quadratic in $\sqrt{EN}$. This produces a formula for n_Z, the value of *EN* needed for credibility Z:

$$n_Z = (Z^2/4k^2)(y_p\sqrt{m_2} + \sqrt{y_p{}^2m_2 + 2(k/Z)(y_p{}^2 - 1)m_3/3m_2})^2 \qquad (3.6)$$

For comparison, the normal approximation formula can be written as:

$$n_Z = (Z^2/4k^2)(2y_p\sqrt{m_2})^2 = m_2(Zy_p/k)^2.$$

Exercise 3.1

Show that the square of the coefficient of variation of T is m_2/EN, and $(SkwT)^2 = m_3{}^2/m_2{}^3EN$.

A potential problem in these formulas for n_Z is that the expected number of claims also appears to be hidden on the right hand side of the equations within the n_2 and n_3 terms. It turns out, however, that n_2 and n_3 are somewhat fundamental measures of the claim count distribution, and are not necessarily affected by changes in the expected number. If EN increases due to the addition of independent, identically distributed exposure units, for example, then $VarN$ increases to the same degree, because the variance is also additive in this case, and so n_2 does not change. The situation is similar for n_3.

Also, CV and $SkwX$ are not changed by simple monetary inflation, because their numerators and denominators will be changed by the same factor. E.g., for the CV, multiplying each loss by a constant factor will increase the mean by that factor, the variance by the square of the factor, and thus the standard deviation will change by the same factor as the mean.

Thus m_2 and m_3 are invariant under both simple monetary inflation and the addition of independent identically distributed exposure units, and so the credibilities that derive from them are similarly invariant. Updates of the credibility values will thus be needed only when the shape of the underlying distributions change.

An example may help clarify these concepts.

Example 3.1

Commercial fire losses for a state are assumed to have a Poisson frequency distribution and a lognormal severity, with $CV = 7$. For the Poisson, n_2 and n_3 both equal 1, and so with this CV, $m_2 = 50$. The skewness of the lognormal is given by $SkwX = CV^3 + 3CV$, and so for this example $SkwX = 343 + 21 = 364$. Thus $m_3 = 364 \times 343 + 3 \times 49 + 1 = 125{,}000$. The credibility requirements are specified by $p = .95$ and $k = .05$, which gives $y_p = 1.645$ from a normal table.

The normal approximation n_F is given by $n_F = m_2(y_p/k)^2$, and thus in this case is $50(1.645/.05)^2 = 54{,}120$. For the NP, n_F can be calculated via (3.6) to be 80,030. Thus considering skewness has a substantial impact in this case, basically because the severity distribution is highly skewed. The assumption of a CV of 7 for commercial fire is consistent with the findings of Simon (1969). The skewness of aggregate claims may be calculated as $SkwT = m_3/m_2^{1.5}\sqrt{EN}$, which for 80,030 expected claims is 1.25. This is somewhat above Pentikäinen's recommendation for the boundary of the accuracy of the NP, and thus the NP n_F estimate may be somewhat too high. In fact, Nelson (1969) suggests that the main reason *NP* full credibility value estimates exceed those from the normal approximation is that a heavier left tail is imputed to the distribution by the *NP* derivation because the symmetry assumption is applied based on the heavy right tail. If so, this would imply that although the *NP* gives useful approximations of the higher percentiles, it may overstate the volume needed for full credibility relative to given standards.

Instead of the lognormal severity, it is interesting to consider a constant severity. This could arise, for example, in a group of life insurance policies all with the same death benefit. In this case, $CV = 0$, and $m_2 = m_3 = 1$. For the normal approximation, n_F then becomes 1082, which is a widely used credibility standard. For the *NP* approximation, n_F is 1094, via (3.6). Thus for the Poisson alone, the skewness correction is not substantial.

The negative binomial frequency could have been used instead of the Poisson. With parameters c and p, $n_2 = 1/p$ and $n_3 = (2-p)/p^2$. In a study of automobile claims, Dropkin (1959) found $n_2 = 1.184$. This implies $p = .8446$, and so $n_3 = 1.620$. For the constant severity case, $m_2 = n_2$ and $m_3 = n_3$; the normal approximation then yields $n_F = 1282$ and the *NP* gives $n_F = 1297$. For the lognormal above, n_F increases to 54,320 under the normal approximation, and to 80,150 with the *NP*. Thus the negative binomial assumption with these parameters seems to have some impact in the frequency only case, but little when a highly skewed severity has already been included.

Exercise 3.2

Verify the calculations in the paragraph above.

Meyers and Schenker (1983) discuss the possibility that the negative binomial n_2 may be substantially larger than 1 for individual large commercial risks. In their model, exposure units are not independent, so some of the above reasoning does not apply. However it is instructional to explore the implications of a large n_2. Thus suppose a negative binomial distribution is given with $n_2 = 51$. Then $p = 1/51$, and $n_3 = 5151$. For the above severity, $m_2 = 100$, and $m_3 = 137{,}500$. Then the normal and *NP* n_F's are 108,200 and 123,400 respectively.

Exercise 3.3

Verify these n_F's. What would they be for frequency only? How many claims would be needed for 50% credibility under the normal and *NP* approximations?

The limited fluctuation Z depends only on the distribution of T, and treats the previous estimate M as a constant. Thus Z does not depend on how good this estimate may be or where it comes from, although such matters could influence the selection of p and k, on which Z depends. If T is the aggregate losses for a state, M could be the previous year's estimate. If T represents only a single class or territory, M could be the statewide estimate for the same year. In general, M is supposed to be the best estimate available without the particular observation T, and in fact may be formed as a combination of other estimators. This criterion for the selection of M is not very specific, and leaves a good deal of room for actuarial judgment. The choice of the complement of credibility will be much more tightly specified in the least squares theory.

The choice of p and k is open, and has led to quite different criteria in different lines. For instance, $p = .95$ and $k = .05$ gives a full credibility standard of 1082.4 expected claims for frequency only. This is also used by some companies in auto insurance ratemaking for total claims, not just frequency, which is usually justified by the fact that for some choice of p and k this would be the result including frequency and severity. (Those companies may be losing market share, however.) In Canada, 4330 is used instead of 1082; in general liability, 683 is used, while in commercial fire a full credibility standard of 29,424 has been used, based on a calculation including severity. In workers' compensation class ratemaking, the pure premium for serious injuries is given full credibility based on 25 to 50 expected claims, depending on which rating bureau is doing the calculation.

This divergence has several historical sources. When general liability was a much smaller line, it was argued that it was so small that greater fluctuation must be expected, so a less stringent choice of p and k was appropriate. When severity is included, different distributions could have differing impacts by line of insurance. Another factor is that credibility estimation is a fairly robust procedure. Moderate differences in the credibility standard generally do not significantly change the final estimate, so a fairly arbitrary standard could work well over the years if it is somewhere in the right ballpark or even sporting complex.

In addition, the selection of a full credibility standard based on historical performance may implicitly take into account the relevance of the prior estimate M. The propensity for serious injuries varies widely by class for workers' compensation, so the overall mean is not as relevant for a given class, and thus high class credibilities are called for. This element is taken into account explicitly in least squares credibility, but it seems to have worked its way into limited fluctuation implicitly in some cases. As will be seen in the concluding section of this chapter, when the class differences are so great that the variance does not adequately reflect the extremes, least squares credibility also breaks down. Either Bayesian analysis or credibility with transformed data will then be appropriate, although ad hoc adjustments to the standards could continue to work reasonably well in many cases.

The openness of the limited fluctuation approach, such as the selection of p and k and the nondependence of Z on the properties of the previous estimator, is both a strength and a weakness. It provides flexibility and a simple algorithm for routine application, and does not require the estimation of additional parameters. However it may ignore or only judgmentally consider elements that can be quantified with additional research. The least squares methodology, to be reviewed next, takes such an approach.

Least Squares Credibility

Formulation

Since the previous estimator applied to the complement of credibility is specified in the least squares theory, more details of the estimation problem need to be modelled, which requires some notation. To have a particular problem to work with, it will be supposed that the losses for N risks are observed for a period of n years. The pure premium for the ith risk in year u is denoted as X_{iu}. Pure premium is loss divided by exposure; for now all risks are assumed to have the same number of exposure units, which is constant over time. In the section "Incorporating Risk Size," application of credibility theory to risks of different sizes will be made. The ith risk is assumed to follow some frequency and severity distributions, with parameters given in a vector (i.e., list) R_i. Conditional moments are denoted by $E(X_{iu}|R_i) = m_i$ and $Var(X_{iu}|R_i) = s_i^2$.

The pure premium for a future time period, time 0, is to be estimated for the gth risk. This will end up being estimated as a credibility weighting of the average observed pure premium for risk g over the n years, denoted as $X_{g.}$, with m, the expected pure premium for a risk drawn at random from these N risks; m in turn is estimated as the grand average of all the risks for those n years, which will be denoted as $X_{..}$. In formulas, $X_{g.} = \Sigma_u X_{gu}/n$, and $X_{..} = \Sigma_g X_{g.}/N$. The credibility estimate can then be expressed as $C_{g0} = ZX_{g.} + (1 - Z)X_{..}$.

Principal Results

The credibility given to the risk experience will depend in part on the stability of that experience, as in limited fluctuation theory, but it will also depend on the relevance of the grand mean to the individual risk, which is quantified by the variance across risks of the individual risk means. The greater this variance, the more diverse are the risks, and thus the grand mean provides less relevant information about an individual risk. This will in turn lead to greater credibility assigned to the risk's own experience, and less to the grand mean. The explicit consideration of the relevancy of the estimator applied against the complement of credibility is one of the distinctive features of least squares credibility.

There are two ways of deriving the value of Z to be used in the least squares credibility estimator: the easy derivation and the hard derivation. The easy derivation is to find the weight Z that minimizes $E[X_{g0} - (ZX_{g.} + (1 - Z)m)]^2$, and this approach will be developed in an exercise below.

The harder derivation reaches the same answer, but as the result of the following more general estimation problem. X_{g0} is estimated as *any* linear combination of all the observations X_{iu}, not just a weighted average of $X_{g.}$ with $X_{..}$, with the expected squared error to be minimized. The general linear combination of the observations can be expressed as $a_0 + \Sigma_{i,u}a_{iu}X_{iu}$, so the credibility criterion will be to find the weights (a's) that minimize:

$$E[X_{g0} - (a_0 + \Sigma_{i,u}a_{iu}X_{iu})]^2 \tag{4.1}$$

It will turn out that the resulting weights can be combined into a simple credibility formula, which gives further justification for such a formula.

Two quantities will turn out to be important in this estimation: s^2, the average variance of an individual risk over time, and t^2, the variance across the risks of the individual risk means. These are of course the two variance components mentioned earlier: the expected conditional (or process) variance and the variance of the conditional (or hypothetical) means. It will be possible to express the credibility weight as $Z = n/(n + K)$, where $K = s^2/t^2$.

The formula has some intuitive interpretations. From the definition of Z it can be seen that if t^2 is higher, so is the credibility given to the risk experience. Since t^2 measures the dispersion of individual risk conditional means around the grand mean m, it can be seen that greater dispersion leads to greater credibility; the more different a risk is likely to be from the average, the greater credence will be placed on a risk's own experience. On the other hand, Z decreases as s^2 increases; higher s^2 means that the risks are less stable over time, and thus less reliance can be placed on their individual results. Only this latter effect occurs explicitly in limited fluctuation credibility; in that approach, less stability gets less credibility, regardless of the dispersion of risks.

Example 4.1

Suppose severity is constant at one unit, frequency is Poisson in R_i, and exposure is one. Then the pure premium X_{iu} is the number of claims for risk i in time u; by the Poisson hypothesis, $m_i = R_i$, and $s_i^2 = R_i$ as well. If R_i is gamma distributed in r,b, then $t^2 = Varm_i = VarR_i = b^2r$, and $s^2 = Es_i^2 = ER_i = br$. Thus $K = s^2/t^2 = 1/b$, and

$Z = n/(n + K) = nb/(nb + 1)$. For $n = 1$, i.e., one time period, this gives the predictive mean computed in Example 2.2.

Example 4.2

X_{iu} is assumed to be gamma distributed in $R_i = Y_i, r$. Thus $m_i = Y_i r$, and $s_i^2 = Y_i^2 r$. Y_i is assumed inverse gamma in b,q; so

$$t^2 = Varm_i = r^2 VarY_i = r^2b^2/(q-1)^2(q-2),$$

and

$$s^2 = Es_i^2 = rEY_i^2 = rb^2/(q-1)(q-2);$$

then $K = s^2/t^2 = (q-1)/r$, and $Z = n/(n+K) = nr/(nr + q - 1)$. Thus the estimate of X_{g0} agrees with the predictive mean from Example 2.4.

Example 4.3

The risk Poisson means from Example 4.1 are now assumed to be gamma distributed in (r,b), with therefore a coefficient of variation of $r^{-.5}$. E.g., if $r = 5$, the CV is .45, so one standard deviation is 45% of the mean. Similarly, $r = 100$ gives $CV = .10$, and $r = 1111$ gives $CV = .03$.

In Example 4.1, $h = nbr$ is the expected number of claims in n years for a risk chosen at random, so $Z = h/(h + r)$. For r's of 5, 100, and 1111 this Z is compared to a typical limited fluctuation credibility $Z = \sqrt{h/1082}$ below.

Limited Fluctuation and Least Squares Credibility Comparison

Expected claims:	1000	500	100	50	10	5	1
$\sqrt{h/1082}$:	.96	.68	.30	.21	.10	.07	.03
$h/(h+5)$:	1.00	.99	.95	.91	.67	.50	.17
$h/(h+100)$:	.91	.83	.50	.33	.09	.05	.01
$h/(h+1111)$:	.47	.31	.08	.04	.01	0	0

In this example, when the standard deviation of risk (or territory, or class) means is about 10% of the overall mean ($r = 100$), the least squares and limited fluctuation credibilities are roughly comparable;

for a more diverse population ($r = 5$) the least squares credibilities are higher, ànd for a more tightly clustered group they are lower.

*Credibility Derivation

First the Z that minimizes $f(Z) = E[X_{g0} - (ZX_{g.} + (1 - Z)m)]^2$ will be derived as an exercise with detailed hints. The derivation from the general linear combination formulation will be done below. Both derivations will initially be based on the following pure premium model.

It will be assumed that the risk i pure premium for time u can be decomposed as follows:

$$X_{iu} = m + R_i + Q_{iu}$$

Here m is the overall average, R_i is the deviation of the ith risk from the overall average, and Q_{iu} is the random fluctuation for the ith risk at time u. The R's and Q's are treated as random variables, as their values are not known. The average over all risks of the R_i's is assumed zero, i.e., $ER_i = 0$. Also it is assumed that $EQ_{iu} = 0$, and so $EX_{iu} = m$. This is an overall expected value; $E(X_{iu}|R_i) = m + R_i$ is the conditional expected value for the ith risk. Finally, it is assumed that different Q's and R's are independent random variables with $VarR_i = t^2$ and $VarQ_{iu} = s^2$. Thus if t^2 is low, all risks are similar to the overall average, while if it is high, they are very different. If s^2 is low, each year each risk has a result near its mean, while if it is high, the annual risk results can be quite variable.

Models with such specific assumptions are needed in the credibility derivation only to get an expression for the covariance of two arbitrary observations, i.e., $Cov(X_{iu},X_{jv})$, which must be evaluated in a step of each derivation. To do this, recall from (2.10b) that

$$\begin{aligned} Cov(X_{iu},X_{jv}) = {} & ECov(X_{iu},X_{jv}| < R_i,R_j >) + \\ & Cov(E(X_{iu}| < R_i,R_j >),E(X_{jv}| < R_i,R_j >)), \end{aligned}$$

i.e., the expected value of the conditional covariance plus the covariance of the conditional means. Since all the Q's and R's are independent, and no two observations have a common Q, the observations are conditionally independent given the R's. This implies that the first term on the right hand side above is zero unless both $i = j$ and $u = v$, in which case it is $EVar(X_{iu}|R_i) = s^2$. The last equality follows because, given R_i, the only random component of X_{iu} is Q_{iu}. The second term is the covariance of the conditional (or hypothetical) means, which is the covariance of two R's, which is zero unless $i = j$, since the R's are independent. To sum up, the covariance in question is zero unless $i = j$, in which case it is $VarR_i = t^2$, unless also $u = v$, in which case it is $t^2 + s^2$.

Exercise 4.1

Derive $Z = n/(n + K)$ as follows:

Step 1. Show that $f'(Z) = 2E[(X_{g0} - m + (m - X_{g.})Z)(m - X_{g.})]$.

Step 2. Set this to zero and solve for Z to find $Z = Cov(X_{g.}, X_{g0})/VarX_{g.}$

Step 3. Verify that the numerator of Z is t^2.

Step 4. Show that the denominator of Z is $VarR_g + nVar(Q_{gu}/n) = t^2 + s^2/n$.

Step 5. Show that $Z = n/(n + K)$.

*General Linear Combination Derivation

This derivation will assume the same simple pure premium model, but it will find the a's from (4.1). In (4.1), there are $Nn + 1$ weights a_{iu} to find, which is approached by setting the partials of (4.1) with respect to these variables to zero. Doing this, with some algebraic manipulation, produces the following system of $Nn + 1$ equations:

$$EX_{g0} = a_0 + \Sigma_{i,u} a_{iu} EX_{iu} \tag{4.2a}$$

$$Cov(X_{g0}, X_{jv}) = \Sigma_{i,u} a_{iu} Cov(X_{iu}, X_{jv}) \tag{4.2b}$$

There are Nn equations expressed by (4.2b), one for each j,v combination.

Exercise 4.2

Derive (4.2). Hint: The partial of (4.1) with respect to a_0 will give (4.2a). Set the partial with respect to a_{jv} to zero and subtract (4.2a) multiplied by EX_{jv}.

To express $Cov(X_{iu}, X_{jv})$ in a single formula, it will be convenient to introduce the following notation:

$$\delta_{ij} = 1 \text{ if } i = j; \text{ otherwise } \delta_{ij} = 0. \tag{4.3}$$

With this in hand, note that $E(R_iR_j) = \delta_{ij}t^2$: since R_i and R_j are independent, if $i \neq j$, $E(R_iR_j) = ER_iER_j = 0$; also, $ER_i^2 = VarR_i + (ER_i)^2 = t^2$. Similarly, $E(Q_{iu}Q_{jv}) = \delta_{ij}\delta_{uv}s^2$.

With this notation,

$$Cov(X_{iu}, X_{jv}) = \delta_{ij}t^2 + \delta_{ij}\delta_{uv}s^2 \tag{4.4}$$

To repeat, this says the covariance is zero unless $i = j$, in which case it is t^2, unless also $u = v$, in which case it is $t^2 + s^2$. Substituting (4.4) back into (4.2b) will make many terms drop out, because so many of the covariances are zero, and in fact produces the equation:

$$\delta_{gj}t^2 = \Sigma_u a_{ju}t^2 + a_{jv}s^2 \tag{4.5}$$

There is still one such equation for every j,v combination; for fixed j summing all the v — equations (n of them) produces:

$$n\delta_{gj}t^2 = n\Sigma_u a_{ju}t^2 + \Sigma_u a_{ju}s^2 \tag{4.6}$$

and so,

$$\Sigma_u a_{ju} = n\delta_{gj}t^2/(s^2 + nt^2) \tag{4.7}$$

Substituting this into (4.5) will yield, after some algebra:

$$a_{jv} = \delta_{gj}t^2/(s^2 + nt^2) \tag{4.8}$$

This says the weight is zero unless $j = g$, and then it is:

$$a_{gv} = t^2/(s^2 + nt^2) \tag{4.9}$$

To find a_0, substitute

$$EX_{iu} = m \tag{4.10}$$

into (4.2a) to yield

$$m = a_0 + \Sigma_{i,u} a_{iu} m,$$

and so

$$a_0 = m(1 - \Sigma_{i,u}a_{iu}) = m(1 - \Sigma_u a_{gu}) = ms^2/(s^2 + nt^2).$$

Finally, since the estimator of X_{g0} is $C_{g0} = a_0 + \Sigma_{i,u}a_{iu}X_{iu}$, which simplifies to $C_{g0} = a_0 + \Sigma_u a_{gu}X_{gu}$, the credibility estimator can be written as:

$$X_{g0} \approx C_{g0} = ms^2/(s^2 + nt^2) + \Sigma_u X_{gu}t^2/(s^2 + nt^2) \qquad (4.11)$$

Now $\Sigma_u X_{gu}$ may be written as $nX_{g.}$; defining $Z = nt^2/(s^2 + nt^2)$ produces $C_{g0} = (1 - Z)m + ZX_{g.}$; here a natural estimate for m would be $X_{..}$, and in fact this is the minimum variance unbiased estimate of m (see ISO (1980)). Substituting this estimate gives:

$$C_{g0} = (1 - Z)X_{..} + ZX_{g.} \qquad (4.12)$$

Thus the best linear estimate of X_{g0} turns out to be a credibility formula. This formula can alternatively be derived as the least squares linear estimate having $a_0 = 0$ but constrained to be unbiased (see ISO, 1980).

By defining $K = s^2/t^2$, Z can be written as $Z = n/(n + K)$, which is basically Whitney's 1918 formula.

The credibility formulas illustrated by this simple model will be found to hold in more general situations. In fact, more general models satisfy (4.4) and (4.10), the mean and covariance formulas for arbitrary observations. For these models, the rest of the development will thus be the same, ending up with (4.12) with the same definition of Z.

This example is typical in another respect, which is in the division of the uncertainty about X_{iu} into two components: a time invariant risk specific component (here R_i), and a random fluctuation in each time period (Q_{iu}). Some observers may feel that this distinction is somewhat artificial, because neither component is ever observed in isolation; however it is an intuitively reasonable distinction, and leads to a model that seems to have practical value.

*A More General Model

In the simple model above, each risk has one parameter R_i which describes the risk, and then a random fluctuation. R_i is treated as a random variable because it is not a known quantity. More generally it is now assumed that each risk has a vector of (possibly unknown) parameters, denoted by R_i, that describe the risk, but the risk is still subject to random fluctuation. For example, risk j with a negative binomial frequency distribution and an inverse gamma severity would have four parameters specifying these distributions, and random fluctuation from year to year as provided by those distributions. R_j would be the list of these four parameters.

Letting R denote the vector $< R_1, R_2, \ldots, R_N >$, the list of all the parameters for all the risks, it is assumed that X_{iu} and X_{jv} are conditionally independent given R. Each risk has its own conditional mean and variance, which may be denoted by $E(X_{iu}|R) = E(X_{iu}|R_i) = m_i$ and $Var(X_{iu}|R) = Var(X_{iu}|R_i) = s_i^2$. As the notation implies, it is assumed that the conditional means and variances do not vary over time. It is possible that m_i and s_i will be functions of R_i, and so are themselves random variables.

It is assumed that for different i the R_i are independent, identically distributed random vectors with $E(m_i) = m$, $Var(m_i) = t^2$, and $Es_i^2 = s^2$. This implies that $EX_{iu} = m$ and $VarX_{iu} = s^2 + t^2$ (why?). Here again, s^2 is the expected process variance and t^2 is the variance of the hypothetical means. Thus, as far as the moments go, this model is very similar to the simpler one above. The only difference is that here the conditional variance varies from risk to risk, and s^2 is the average of these conditional variances. In the other model, s^2 was the conditional variance for every risk.

In order to apply (4.2), it is necessary to compute $Cov(X_{iu}, X_{jv})$ from these assumptions. By (2.10),

$$Cov(X_{iu}, X_{jv}) = ECov(X_{iu}, X_{jv}|R) + Cov[E(X_{iu}|R), E(X_{jv}|R)] \qquad (4.13)$$

Now by the conditional independence of the X's, the first term is zero unless $i = j$ and $u = v$, in which case it is $EVar(X_{iu}|R) = Es_i^2 = s^2$. Since knowing R means all its components are known, the second term is also $Cov[E(X_{iu}|R_i), E(X_{jv}|R_j)]$, which by the independence of R_i

and R_j is zero unless $i = j$, in which case it is $Var(m_{i)} = t^2$. E.g., see Example 4.1 above. Thus:

$$Cov(X_{iu}, X_{jv}) = \delta_{ij\delta uv} EVar(X_{iu}|R) + \delta_{ij} VarE(X_{iu}|R) \tag{4.14}$$

$= \delta_{ij}\delta_{uv}s^2 + \delta_{ij}t^2$, which is (4.4). Substituting this into (4.2) then yields (4.12) by the same reasoning used for the original simplified model above.

*Time Series Application

In some ratemaking applications, the data is not credibility weighted against a broader based estimate, but rather against an earlier estimate of the same series. For example, a company's indicated average rate for a state may be credibility weighted against the current average rate. Often limited fluctuation credibility is used for this, but Gerber and Jones (1975) have shown how to apply the least squares method to this problem. In the example below, the two methods are both applied with the same assumptions. Model assumptions for limited fluctuation are not usually made explicit in this area, but the assumptions in the example may be what its users may have in mind.

The series to be observed, denoted by N_i, could be anything of interest, e.g., state loss ratios, countrywide frequency, etc. N_i will denote the observation for year i, and C_i will denote the credibility estimate of N_i made based on the data through year $i - 1$. In the time series situation, both the limited fluctuation and least squares approaches to credibility use:

$$C_{i+1} = (1 - Z_i)C_i + Z_iN_i \tag{4.15}$$

The credibility weight, as has been seen above, has a different purpose and derivation in the two approaches.

Limited fluctuation credibility seeks to limit the fluctuations in the series of **estimates** C_j, at least insofar as those fluctuations are due to the randomness inherent in the series of observations N_j. The least squares approach, on the other hand, seeks to minimize the expected squared value of the estimation errors.

The assumptions to be made are as follows: N_i is hypothesized to be approximately normally distributed with mean M_i and constant variance v. (Constant in that it is the same for each year.) The mean M_i is hypothesized to change each year by the random amount D_i, that is, $M_{i+1} = M_i + D_i$. D_i is a random variable with mean zero and variance d. The D's are assumed to be independent of each other and of M_1. (This may be more valid for pure premium, say, if it is properly adjusted for inflation, than it would be for loss ratios, because of the underwriting cycle.) Because of the mean zero, each M_i has the same unconditional expected value, denoted by m, i.e., $E(M_i) = m$. (M_i is treated as a random variable because its value is not known, which in part is due to the random term D_i.) Because the M's change each year by the D's, the variance of M increases each year by d. E.g., $Var(M_{i+1}) = Var(M_i) + d$. Thus $Var(M_i) = w + (i-1)d$, with $w = Var(M_1)$.

The estimation process has to start somewhere, and so C_1 is the estimate of N_1 made before any of the observations N_i are available. This estimate could have been based on previous knowledge of similar processes, for example. C_1 can also be considered as an estimate of M_1. The variance w can be interpreted as an expression of the uncertainty about the value of M_1 before N_1 is observed; as such it may influence how willing we will be, when estimating N_2, to give up on C_1 in favor of N_1 once it becomes available. Given these model assumptions, the calculation of the credibility factor Z_i under the two approaches can be contrasted.

Limited Fluctuation

The limited fluctuation approach calculates Z_i based on the conditional distribution of N_i given M_i. It seeks to limit the impact on the credibility estimator (4.15) of random deviations of the observation N_i from its conditional expected value M_i. In other terms, it seeks to guarantee, at least to an acceptably high probability, that the random fluctuation component $|Z_i(N_i - M_i)|$ stays within certain bounds. As above, symmetry is invoked, so that this random component without the absolute value is what is to be limited. The criterion for doing so is established by first specifying a probability level p, e.g., $p = .95$, and then requiring, with a probability of at least p, that the deviation be no greater than some prespecified maximum. In this case that maximum will be taken to be km, where k is a selected small number, e.g., $k = .05$. Recall that m is the unconditional mean $E(M_i)$. In other words, Z_i is sought so that $Pr\{Z_i(N_i - M_i) < km\} = p$.

As in Section 3, the value of Z_i that meets the criterion is $Z_i = km/y\sqrt{v}$, *where* y is the 100pth percentile of the standard normal distribution. This is verified by showing that the Z_i so defined meets the criterion. By hypothesis, given M_i, $(N_i - M_i)/\sqrt{v}$ has the standard normal distribution, and so from the definition of y, we have

$$Pr[(N_i - M_i)/\sqrt{v} \; < \; y] = p.$$

Multiplying both sides of the inequality by $Z_i\sqrt{v} = km/y$ then gives

$$(Pr[Z_i(N_i - M_i) < km] = p,$$

as desired.

In many applications, the variance v is assumed to be proportional to m, e.g., $v = cm$. This yields $Z_i = (k/y)\sqrt{m/c}$. As in the general theory of limited fluctuation, the full credibility value is given by $m_F = c(y/k)^2$, and Z_i can be computed by the square root rule $Z_i = \sqrt{m/m_F}$.

In practice, actuaries may learn how much change such a series tends to exhibit over time, so that the limited fluctuation criterion can be chosen to produce reasonable accuracy as well as stability. Again, this is more explicitly handled in the least squares approach.

Least Squares

The least squares approach for determining Z_i does not start with formula (4.15), but derives it as the result of a more general estimation problem: N_{i+1} is to be estimated by $C_{i+1} = b_0 + \Sigma_{j=1}^{i} b_j N_j$, that is as a general linear combination of the available observations, in this case $N_1, \ldots N_i$, with the expected squared error to be minimized. That is, coefficients b_j are sought to minimize:

$$N_{i+1} - (b_0 + \Sigma_{j=1}^{i} b_j N_j)]^2 \qquad (4.16)$$

It turns out, after much algebra, that the solution to this estimation problem can be expressed in the form (4.15), that is, as the credibility formula $C_{i+1} = (1 - Z_i)C_i + Z_iN_i$. (Taking $b_i = Z_i$ and working backward through the b_j's recursively can show that the credibility formula is always a special case of (4.16), that is, is linear in the N_j's. See Exercise 4.3 below.)

The Z_i that when used in (4.15) give the best linear estimate (4.16) are computed recursively by:

$$Z_1 = 1/[1 + K] \tag{4.17a}$$

$$Z_{i+1} = 1/[1 + 1/(J + Z_i)] \tag{4.17b}$$

where $K = v/w$ and $J = d/v$. The details of the derivation, including more general conditions under which the best linear estimate can be put into the form of (4.15), are found in Gerber and Jones (1974). For the interested reader, a sketch of the proof is presented below.

The minimization of (4.16) is accomplished by first setting its partial derivatives with respect to the b_j to zero. This produces $i + 1$ equations, one for each b_j. For example the partial of (4.16) with respect to b_1 produces the equation:

$$E[N_1(N_{i+1} - b_0 - \Sigma_{j=1}^{i} b_jN_j)] = 0.$$

All these equations involve terms like $E(N_j)$ and $E(N_jN_k)$, which are then evaluated in order to solve for the b_j's.

To illustrate this procedure, evaluating the $E(N_jN_k)$ type term is outlined. Note that, given M_j, N_j and N_{j+h} are independent for $h > 0$, and the conditional expected value of each is M_j, i.e., $E(N_j|M_j) = M_j$ and $E(N_{j+h}|M_j) = M_j$. This is because $M_{j+h} = M_j + D_j + \ldots + D_{j+h-1}$, and the D_i's have mean zero. Then it follows that $E(N_jN_{j+h}|M_j) = M_j^2$, and eventually that $E(N_jN_{j+h}) = Var(M_j) + m^2 = w + (j - 1)d + m^2$. The "$v$" enters the formulation via $E(N_j^2) = v + w + (j - 1)d + m^2$. After evaluating all such terms and substituting for them in the equations from the partial derivatives gives a system of $i + 1$ equations for the $i + 1$ variables b_j in terms of v, w, and d. These can then be solved to produce (4.17).

Exercise 4.3

The repeated use of (4.15) with the Z's given by (4.17) expresses the estimates (C's) as linear functions of the observations (N's). Verify this for the case $i = 2$ by finding the b_j's from (4.16) in terms of C_1 and the Z's. (Answer: $b_2 = Z_2$, $b_1 = Z_1(1 - Z_2)$, $b_0 = C_1(1 - Z_1)(1 - Z_2)$.)

The least squares model above is an example of a more general estimation procedure known as the Kalman filter.

Example 4.4

In ratemaking, the ratio of the pure premium for a given territory to the statewide pure premium is often used as a step in developing the rate for the territory. Such territorial relativities are sometimes credibility weighted against the previous year's relativity for the same territory. Suppose that T_1 and T_2 are two (out of many) territories in a state, and they have the values given below, where the N_i's are the observed relativities to statewide for year i.

	T_1	T_2
d	.01	.01
w	.04	.04
v	.0025	.005
N_1	.80	1.25
N_2	.90	1.40
N_3	.95	1.35

The common value of d means that both territories are subject to the same potential for change over time. Also, before the above data (N's) are observed, there is equal uncertainty concerning their true value. This is reflected by the common value of w, the variance of M_1. It is supposed, however, that T_1 is a larger territory subject to less random fluctuation around its mean value, and so it has a smaller v than does T_2. It may be reasonable to suppose that T_1 has double the number of units of exposure of T_2, and thus half the random fluctuation. Both territories are assigned the initial relativity estimate $C_1 = 1$ before the observations are made.

The following values are computed using (4.17) then (4.15).

	T_1	T_2
K	.0625	.125
J	4.00	2.00
Z_1	.94	.89
Z_2	.83	.74
Z_3	.83	.73
C_2	.81	1.22
C_3	.88	1.35
C_4	.94	1.35

A heuristic interpretation of (4.17) can be made. Note that Z_1 is an increasing function of w and a decreasing function of v. The uncertainty concerning M_1 is measured by w; thus the greater this uncertainty, the greater is the weight given to the observation N_1. But the uncertainty concerning M_1 is not the only thing considered; the stability of N_1 is greater with lower v and this also leads to greater weight on N_1.

Z_{i+1} is an increasing function of Z_i and J. Greater stability (low v) continues to give greater credibility through a higher J; a higher d also increases the credibility which makes sense as follows: a high d indicates that the M's are greatly subject to change, so the older estimates should be given less weight, with more to the current observation, i.e., higher Z_j's.

(4.17b) can also be written as $Z_{i+1} = (J + Z_i)/(1 + J + Z_i)$. The special case $d = 0$ (constant conditional mean) gives $Z_{i+1} = Z_i/(1 + Z_i)$. The credibility of the latest observation gradually decreases as the accuracy of the previous estimate improves. In the general case Z decreases to a limit of $(\sqrt{J^2 + 4J} - J)/2$ (see Exercise below). Since the mean is subject to change over time, the latest observation has a certain degree of value that is not lost by having many previous observations. This limiting value, which involves only $J = d/v$, may be a reasonable Z to use in an ongoing estimation situation where C_1 and w are well in the past. Here d and v are components of the variance of the observations N_j over time. An approach to separating the observed variance to estimate such components was illustrated for a somewhat different model in Example 2.8 above.

Exercise 4.4

a. Prove that Z_i approaches $(\sqrt{J^2 + 4J} - J)/2$ as i goes to infinity. (Hint: Show by repeated substitution for Z_i that as i goes to infinity (4.17b) approaches the "continued fraction" $Z = 1/(1 + 1/(J + 1/(1 + 1/(J + \ldots \ldots$ But then Z can be substituted for everything past the second " + " sign in Z, giving $Z = 1/(1 + 1/(J + Z))$, which can be solved for Z in terms of J.)

b. Show that as J goes to infinity $(\sqrt{J^2 + 4J} - J)/2$ goes to 1. (Hint: try multiplying by 1 in the form of a fraction with numerator and denominator both $\sqrt{J^2 + 4J} + J$.)

Estimation of Credibility Parameters

Poisson Case

Up until now, s^2 and t^2 were treated as known constants, but in practice they usually have to be estimated. One approach is to estimate s^2 based on observed deviations of risk annual results from risk means, and t^2 from observed deviations of risk means from the grand mean. Sometimes it is more convenient to estimate the total variance $VarX_{iu} = s^2 + t^2$ from the deviations of individual risk observations from the grand mean, and then get s^2 or t^2 by subtraction. This is simplified when the conditional distribution is Poisson, because then the conditional mean and variance are equal, so $s^2 = EVar(X_{iu}|R_i) = ER_i = m$, the grand mean.

Example 5.1

In experience rating, the experience of individual risks is used to alter the risks' premium. This example explores how the credibility for a single vehicle could be estimated.

A group of 300 car owners in a high crime area submit the following number of theft claims in a one year period:

Number of Claims:	0	1	2	3	4	5
Number of Owners:	123	97	49	21	8	2

Each owner is assumed to have a Poisson distribution for X_{i1}, the number of thefts, but the mean number may vary from one owner to another. A credibility estimate is desired for X_{i0}, the number of claims for each driver for the next year.

The average number of claims per driver can be calculated to be 1.0. By the Poisson assumption, this is also s^2. The average value of X_{i1}^2 can be found to be 2.2, so $s^2 + t^2 = VarX_{i1}$ can be estimated to be $2.2 - 1.0^2 = 1.2$. This implies $t^2 = 0.2$, and so $K = 5$, and $Z = 1/6$. The credibility estimate for X_{i0} is thus $5/6 + X_{i1}/6$.•

This example can be generalized to other cases where t^2 is estimated by subtracting the estimated s^2 from the overall sample variance. One potential problem with this method is that the sample variance could come out less than the estimated s^2, so that the estimated t^2 would come out negative. It is customary to set $t^2 = 0$ in this case, and thus $Z = 0$. This is reasonable in that there is not enough observed variance to indicate any differences among risks.

Statistics to Estimate Variance Components

Without the Poisson or some similar assumption on the ratio of risk variance to mean, individual risk or class experience over time is generally needed to estimate s^2 and t^2. One approach to this estimation problem is to calculate the statistics:

$$S_i = \Sigma_u(X_{iu} - X_{i.})^2/(n-1), S = \Sigma_i S_i/N, \text{ and } T = \Sigma_i(X_{i.} - X_{..})^2/(N-1).$$

The expected value of these statistics can be calculated (laboriously) from (4.4) and (4.10). As a hint of how that might proceed, multiplying out the squares in S and T result in many terms of the form $X_{iu}X_{jv}$, whose expected values then need to be evaluated. This is done using (4.4) and (4.10), which together imply that $E(X_{iu}X_{jv}) = m^2 + \delta_{ij}(t^2 + \delta_{uv}s^2)$. The answers are:

$$E(S_i|R_i) = s_i^2; ES_i = EE(S_i|R_i) = Es_i^2 = s^2; ES = s^2; ET = t^2 + s^2/n.$$

The formula for S_i looks like a fairly usual statistical result. T looks like it should be something like t^2, but probably a little bit higher, because some extra fluctuation is added from the use of the estimated means rather than m_i and m. Thus the formula for T looks reasonable also. From these formulas, S is an unbiased estimator of s^2, nT is an unbiased estimator of $s^2 + nt^2$, and $T - S/n$ is an unbiased estimator of t^2. Since $1 - Z = s^2/(s^2 + nt^2)$, it could be estimated by S/nT, as both numerator and denominator are unbiased. Such an approach may be satisfactory in many cases, and is supported by the independence of S and T, as shown by Klugman (1985). In this method it is possible for the estimated $1 - Z$ to exceed 1, in which case it is capped at 1, and Z is assigned zero. Again, there is not enough observed variation among risks to indicate that there is really any difference among them.

Example 5.2

Table 5.1 displays the pure premium experience for 9 risks, all with the same constant number of exposure units, for a 6 year period. $X_{i.}$ and S_i are calculated from this experience, as shown, and $X_{..} = .563$, $S = .357$, and $T = .066$ can then be computed from the formulas above. These yield $S/nT = .899$, which can be used as the estimate of $1 - Z$, and so Z is estimated to be .101.

Table 5.1

Risk	Year1	Year2	Year3	Year4	Year5	Year6	*Xi.*	*Si*
1	.430	.375	2.341	.175	1.016	.466	.801	.649
2	.247	1.587	1.939	.712	.054	.261	.800	.615
3	.661	.237	.063	.250	.602	.700	.419	.072
4	.182	.351	.011	.022	.019	.252	.139	.021
5	.311	.664	1.002	.038	.370	2.502	.815	.792
6	.301	.253	.044	.109	2.105	.891	.617	.622
7	.219	1.186	.431	1.405	.241	.804	.714	.251
8	.002	.058	.235	.018	.713	.208	.206	.071
9	.796	.260	.932	.857	.129	.349	.554	.121
							.563	.357

Testing Estimation by Simulation

An important issue in credibility theory is the accuracy of this estimate of Z. This can be studied by simulating data from known distributions, estimating s^2 and t^2 from this data, and seeing how close this comes to the underlying assumed values. In fact, in the above example, Table 5.1 was generated by taking random draws from assumed gamma distributions for each risk. The parameters of these gamma distributions are shown below, along with the risk conditional means and variances.

Parameters Underlying Table 5.1

Risk	b	r	Mean	Variance
1.	.6159	1.0476	.6452	.3974
2	.8001	0.9063	.7251	.5802
3	.6098	0.9654	.5887	.3590
4	.2391	0.9219	.2204	.0527
5	.5206	1.0184	.5302	.2760
6	.6768	1.0937	.7402	.5010
7	.9575	1.1395	1.0911	1.0447
8	.1999	1.0153	.2030	.0406
9	.5083	0.9320	.4737	.2408
			.5797	.3880

Thus $m = .5797$, which is not too different from $X_{..} = .563$, and $s^2 = .388$, which again is fairly close to $S = .357$. The variance of the above conditional means can be found to be $t^2 = .0664$, and thus $t^2 + s^2/n =$ .1311, which is fairly different from $T = .066$. Thus the "population" value of $1 - Z$ of $s^2/(s^2 + nt^2) = .493$ and $Z = .507$ is quite a bit different from that estimated by the data.

This experiment was repeated twice more, that is, six years of data were simulated two more times, with the following results:

Experiment	S	T	$1-Z$	Z
1	.357	.066	.899	.101
2	.274	.103	.443	.557
3	.219	.172	.211	.789
Underlying	.388	.131	.493	.507

Note: Calculations based on unrounded values

Thus this method does not seem to be able to produce a close estimate of Z with this quantity of data when the process is this unstable. However the average of the three estimates, .482, is just slightly below the underlying value of Z, .507, which gives hope that with just somewhat more data good estimates are possible. Estimating the variance of the estimated Z would help provide an understanding of the accuracy of the calculation, and this is discussed further in Section 7.

For comparison, a limited fluctuation credibility using the normal approximation can be calculated by $Z = km/y_p S^{.5}$, which was used to derive (3.3). For $k = .05$ and $y_p = 1.645$, this gives $Z = .03$. The $(N-3)/(N-1)$ correction, to be discussed next, would apply a factor of .75 to each of the calculated values of $1 - Z$.

***Empirical Bayesian Approaches — the $(N-3)/(N-1)$ Correction**

Estimating $1 - Z$ by S/nT has a drawback in that while the numerator and denominator are both unbiased, $1 - Z$ is not. This is a typical problem for quotients of unbiased estimators. In this case it arises because $E(1/T) > 1/ET$ (see exercise below). This implies that $E(1/nT) > 1/(s^2 + nt^2)$, and thus $E(S/nT) > s^2/(s^2 + nt^2)$, i.e., S/nT overstates $1 - Z$, and thus understates Z, on the average.

Exercise 5.1

Show that $1/ET \leq \int E(1/T)$. Hint: Schwartz' inequality says that

$$[\int g(t)h(t)dt]^2 \leq \int g(t)^2 \int h(t)^2.$$

Take g^2 and h^2 to be $tf(t)$ and $f(t)/t$. Equality occurs only in degenerate cases.

The excess of $E(1/T)$ over $1/ET$ varies from one distribution to another, so it is not possible to find a general correction for the bias in Z. This excess is generally greater for heavy tailed distributions, however, so an approximate lower bound could be found by computing its value in the normal distribution case.

The calculation of $1 - Z$ when both the conditional and prior distributions are normal has been a focus of a field known as Parametric

Empirical Bayes. A classic article in this field is Efron and Morris (1977). Following Morris (1983), Klugman (1985) shows that if the prior and conditional distributions are normal, S and T are independent random variables, with S gamma distributed in $(N(n-1)/2,\ 2s^2/N(n-1))$ and T gamma in $((N-1)/2,\ 2(t^2+s^2/n)/(N-1))$. This result is related to the fact that the sample variance of a normal is chi-squared distributed. With these parameters, S and T follow the chi-squared distribution, which is a special case of the gamma. By the gamma moment formula, if Y is gamma in (r, b) then $E(1/Y) = 1/b(r-1)$ as long as $r > 1$, and is non $-$ existent otherwise. $E(1/Y)$ is greater than $1/EY$ by a factor of $r/(r-1)$. For T, the value of r is $(N-1)/2$, so

$$E(1/T) = (N-1)/(N-3)ET = (N-1)/(N-3)(s^2+nt^2),$$

as long as $N > 3$. Thus

$$E(S(N-3)/(N-1)nT) = s^2/(s^2+nt^2) = 1-Z,$$

and so $S(N-3)/(N-1)nT$ is an unbiased estimator of $1-Z$. This is the above credibility estimator of $1-Z$ adjusted by the factor $(N-3)/(N-1)$.

For $N \leq 3$, this school would recommend use of the individual class means without credibility weighting (i.e., taking $Z=1$), as then $E(S/nT)$ would not exist, and so no correction factor could make S/nT unbiased. Even with three risks or three classes, however, actuaries might want to use credibility, and it will be seen below that this is feasible. Using the group mean for all three classes (i.e., $Z=0$) may in fact in some cases be preferable to taking $Z=1$.

*Evaluating the $(N-3)/(N-1)$ Correction

For other conditional and prior distributions, the excess of $E(1/T)$ over $1/ET$ is likely to be greater than for the normal, so the $(N-3)/(N-1)$ factor is probably an upper bound.

However, even with the normal distribution, there is a potential problem with this correction factor which could cause it to actually overcorrect for bias, namely that it does not take into account the usual practice of capping $1-Z$ at 1. The true value of $1-Z$, $s^2/$

$(s^2 + nt^2)$, must be in the range [0,1]. In practice, however, the estimated value of nT may be less than that of S, which would make $S/nT > 1$. Typically $1 - Z$ would be capped at 1 in this case, giving $Z = 0$. However, by this practice, the estimator of $1 - Z$ has effectively become $min[1,S/nT]$, which has a lower expected value than S/nT. That is, the capped estimator has lower bias than S/nT, and may even be unbiased or be biased in the other direction.

To evaluate the effect of such capping, the table below shows the expected value of the capped estimator along with the factor needed to correct this estimator for bias, compared to the $(N\text{-}3)/(N\text{-}1)$ factor. This is shown for values of N of 3 and 18 in the normal-normal case with the simplifying assumption that s^2 is a known constant.

Effect of Capping on Parametric Empirical Bayes' Correction Factor

N	True $1 - Z$:	.800	.500	.200
3	$Emin[1,S/nT]$:	.799	.673	.426
	Factor needed:	1.001	.743	.469
	$(N - 3)/(N - 1)$ Factor:	0	0	0
18	$Emin[1,S/nT]$:	.809	.557	.227
	Factor needed:	.989	.898	.882
	$(N - 3)/(N - 1)$ Factor:	.882	.882	.882

Thus when $1 - Z$ is large, the capped estimator $min[1,S/nT]$ does not seem to be upwardly biased, although this is not true for smaller values of $1 - Z$. Even for $N = 3$, the upward bias in the capped estimator is always finite, and thus credibility weighting may be a useful possibility even with just 3 risks.

The above table was computed using the formula:

$$[((N-3)/2)]!Emin[1,s^2/nT] = \int_0 (N-1)(1-Z)/2y^{(N-3)/2}e^{-y}dy + .5(N-1)(1-Z)\int(N-1)(1-Z)/2\, y^{(N-5)/2}e^{-y}dy.$$

This is derived as follows. In the normal-normal case, $Emin[1,S/nT]$ can be calculated numerically by:

$$Emin[1,S/nT] = \int F_T(s/n) + (s/n)\int_{s/n} t^{-1} f_T(t)dt\} f_S(s)ds,$$

which can be derived by replacing s/nt by 1 in the region of the double integral of $(s/nt)f_S(s)f_T(t)$ in which s/nt exceeds 1. A practical problem with this expression is that the distribution functions of S and T depend on s^2 and t^2, and these cannot be brought out of the integral explicitly; however in the special case of this formula when s^2 is a known constant, $Emin[1,S/nT]$, the expected value of the uncorrected estimate of $1 - Z$, can be calculated as a function of $1 - Z$. This is because $Emin[1,s^2/nT]$ is given by

$$F_T(s^2/n) + (s^2/n)\int_{s/n} x^{-1} f_T(x)dx,$$

where f_T is the gamma described above (parameters $((N-1)/2$, $2(t^2 + s^2/n)/(N-1))$. The change of variables $y = (N-1)x/2(t^2 + s^2/n)$ in the integrals then gives the above formula, which for fixed N is a function of $1 - Z$.

Exercise 5.2

A population of risks with X_{iu} gamma in (r_i, b_i) is determined by independent draws of the b's from a uniform distribution on [0,1], and the r's from a uniform distribution on [.85,1.15]. What is K? (Hint: the uniform distribution with width a has variance $a^2/12$; use $E(b^2) = Var(b) + (Eb)^2$ and independence of b and r to find $E(b^2r)$; compute $Var(br)$ via $E(b^2r^2) - (EbEr)^2$.)

Example 5.3

The answer to the previous exercise is $K = 3.88$. As a test of the correction factor in a non-normal distribution case, 100 risks were drawn from such a population, and the average values of b_ic_i and $b_i^2c_i$ were found to be .500 and .330. These compare to the expected values from the uniform distribution of .500 and .333. The variance of the b_ic_i's (hypothetical means) was .085, compared to a theoretical value of .086. For each risk, 6 years of data were simulated, as in Example 5.2, and this process was repeated for five different experiments. For $n = 6$, $1 - Z$ should be .393 from the uniform prior, and $1 - Z$ was

.392 from the b's and c's actually drawn, so this is the target value to which the estimate values of $1 - Z$ can be compared. For the five experiments, $1 - Z$ was estimated using the $(N - 3)/(N - 1)$ factor:

Experiment	$X..$	S	T	$1-Z$
1	.504	.434	.164	.432
2	.482	.302	.109	.452
3	.455	.303	.122	.406
4	.510	.362	.141	.419
5	.471	.277	.102	.443

For comparison, the anticipated value of T is $.086 + .333/6 = .142$ from the uniform prior, and $.085 + .330/6 = .140$ from the 100 risks actually selected. The small but consistent overstatement of $1 - Z$ may be due to the excess of $E(1/T)$ over $1/ET$ being greater for these distributions than the normal-normal $(N - 3)/(N - 1)$ correction contemplates. This supports use of the correction factor, even in non-normal cases.

*Bayesian Estimates of Z

A case can be made that in actual experience rating and ratemaking applications, the most effective credibility approach developed so far involves Bayesian estimates of s^2 and t^2. This allows reflection of any prior sense, however faint, concerning where s^2 and t^2 are likely to be; it also produces an entire posterior distribution for these parameters, rather than just point estimates, and in some cases reduces the tendency to get negative or zero estimates of t^2. The Bayesian method is to use judgement to specify prior distributions of s^2 and t^2, then observe S and T, and use these to compute the posterior distributions of s^2 and t^2.

Klugman (1987) has found that the normal approximation is fairly reasonable for cases where least squares credibility is most applicable. As an example of how a practitioner might reason in a specific normal-normal case, S and T are both conditionally gamma distributed given s^2 and t^2, and so inverse gamma priors, as discussed in Example 2.4, could be postulated. In this example, s^2 will be taken to be inverse gamma distributed in (p, 2), and the quantity $t^2 + s^2/n$ is given an independent inverse gamma in (q, 2). While this approach ends up providing reasonable estimates, it does have a theoretical problem in that some possibility that t^2 is negative is allowed.

With the shape parameter 2, the inverse gamma has an infinite variance and mean equal to the scale parameter, so p and q are the prior means postulated for s^2 and $t^2 + s^2/n$. Because of the infinite variance, this approach does not tie down the possible values of s^2 and $t^2 + s^2/n$ too precisely, but it does specify an expected value for each.

Having assumed these priors for s^2 and $t^2 + s^2/n$, their posterior distributions can then be calculated from the observed values of S and T, and then $1 - Z$ can be estimated with the product of the posterior expected values as $E(s^2(t^2 + s^2/n)^{-1}|S,T)/n = E(s^2|S)$ $E[(t^2 + s^2/n)^{-1}|T]/n$. Following Example 2.2, the posterior distributions are:

$$s^2|S \sim \text{Inverse Gamma in } 2 + N(n-1)/2,\ p + N(n-1)S/2 \qquad (5.1a)$$

$$t^2 + s^2/n|T \sim \text{Inverse Gamma in } (N+3)/2,\ q + (N-1)T/2 \qquad (5.1b)$$

Thus

$$E(s^2|S) = [2p + N(n-1)S]/[2 + N(n-1)]$$

and

$$E[(t^2 + s^2/n)^{-1}|T] = (N+3)/(2q + (N-1)T),$$

from the inverse gamma moment formulas, and $1/n$ times their product is the posterior estimate of $1 - Z$.

Both of these posterior means can be interpreted as credibility weightings between the postulated prior means and the observations. For instance, S gets weight $(n-1)N/(2 + (n-1)N)$ and p gets the complementary weight $2/(2 + (n-1)N)$. The weight on S will usually be near one, as $(n-1)N$ is fairly large in most applications. For T, the inverse gamma jth moment formula with $j = -1$ shows that the prior expected value of $(t^2 + s^2/n)^{-1}$ is $2/q$. The reciprocal of the posterior expected value can be interpreted as a credibility weighting between T and $q/2$, with T getting weight $(N-1)/(N+3)$ and $q/2$ getting $4/(N+3)$. Thus T will generally not receive as much weight as S, making the choice of the prior more important for T.

Note also that the prior expected value of $1-Z$ is $2p/nq$. Thus a sense of reasonable values for Z may help select p and q. The parameters p and q chosen for the prior distributions are supposed to reflect the analyst's opinion of the most likely values for s^2 and t^2. If it is difficult to arrive at the selections, some analysts may feel comfortable establishing a prior value for Z. For instance, setting the prior expected value of $1-Z$, $2p/nq$, to .5 gives $q=4p/n$, which is a way of picking q once p has been selected. Alternatively, $p=nq/4$ could be used to set p after q has been selected. Since S gets greater weight than T, the selected q probably has more bearing on the resulting Z than does p.

This method will be illustrated for the three "experiments" of Example 5.2. First, suppose $q=.2$ is selected. This is in the general area of the true value of t^2+s^2/n of .1311, but not particularly close. Since n is 6, p can be taken as .3 using $p=nq/4$. Then by (5.1), this gives posterior expected values of $E(s^2|S)=\ (.6+45S)/47$ and $E[(t^2+s^2/n)^{-1}|T]=\ 12/(.4+8T)$. For the three experiments of Example 5.2, the following values are then produced, and the process is repeated for $p=.6$, $q=.4$:

Experiment	$E(s^2\|S)$	$E[(t^2+s^2/n)^{-1}\|T]$	$1-Z$	Z
$p=.3$, $q=.2$				
1	.355	12.93 $(=1/.077)$	.765	.235
2	.275	9.80 $(=1/.102)$	.449	.551
3	.222	6.76 $(=1/.148)$	.250	.750
$p=.6$, $q=.4$				
1	.367	9.04 $(=1/.111)$	.553	.447
2	.288	7.39 $(=1/.135)$	.355	.645
3	.235	5.51 $(=1/.181)$	.216	.784

Either selection of priors seems to improve the estimation over the use of S/nT shown in Example 5.2.

*Diffuse Priors

Instead of the inverse gamma prior, diffuse priors could be taken for s^2 and $t^2 + s^2/n$, as in Example 2.5. The posterior distributions will be inverse gamma, and Z can then be calculated by the posterior moments. With parameter p for the diffuse prior the posterior distributions are

$s^2|S \sim$ Inverse Gamma: $-p-1+N(n-1)/2,\ N(n-1)S/2$ (5.2a) -1

$t^2 + s^2/n|T \sim$ Inverse Gamma: $-p-1+(N-1)/2,\ (N-1)T/2$ (5.2b)

As discussed in Example 2.5, $p = -1$ or -2 may make the most sense for a diffuse prior.

	$E(s^2\|S)$	$E[(t^2+s^2/n)^{-1}\|T]$
$p=-1$	$N(n-1)S/(N(n-1)-2)$	$1/T$
$p=-2$	S	$(N+1)/(N-1)T$

$1-Z$
$S/nT[1-2/N(n-1)]$
$S(N+1)/n(N-1)T$

Both are somewhat greater than S/nT, which is the opposite of what $(N-3)/(N-1)$ would provide. Note that if diffuse priors are selected with $p = -2$ for S and $p = 0$ for T, then $1-Z$ is the unbiased estimator $(N-3)S/n(N-1)T$. None of these estimators take into account the possible capping of $1-Z$.

*Regression Interpretation of Credibility

Least squares credibility can be thought of as a least squares regression estimate in which the dependent variable has not yet been observed. The credibility estimate $X_{g0} \approx (1-Z)X_{..} + ZX_{g.}$ can be rewritten as $X_{g0} - X_{..} \approx Z(X_{g.} - X_{..})$. Since the expected squared error is minimized by Z, this is similar to a no constant regression for $X_{g0} - X_{..}$, with $X_{g.} - X_{..}$ as the independent variable, where there is an observation for each risk g. The regression estimate of Z is computed by minimizing the sum of the actual squared errors once X_{g0} is observed, whereas the credibility Z is derived by minimizing the expected squared error before the observations are available. A test of different methods of developing the credibility estimate then would be to compare Z to the regression estimate once the data is in.

Example 5.4

Efron and Morris (1975) computed the arcsin transforms of the batting averages for 18 players for their first 45 at bats in the 1970 season, as shown below, and used credibility methods to estimate each batting average for the rest of the season. The reason for the arcsin transform is that it results in an approximately normal distribution with $s^2 = 1$. Thus only t^2 need be estimated to get Z.

Player	First 45	Rest of Season
Alvarado	−3.26	−4.15
Alvis	−5.10	−4.32
Berry	−2.60	−3.17
Campaneris	−4.32	−2.98
Clemente	−1.35	−2.10
Howard	−1.97	−3.11
Johnstone	−2.28	−3.96
Kessinger	−2.92	−3.32
Munson	−4.70	−2.53
Petrocelli	−3.95	−3.30
Robinson	−1.66	−2.79
Rodriquez	−3.95	−3.89
Santo	−3.60	−3.23
Scott	−3.95	−2.71
Spencer	−2.60	−3.20
Swodoba	−3.60	−3.83
Unser	−3.95	−3.30
Williams	−3.95	−3.43

From the data, $X_{..} = -3.317$, and $T = 1.115$. Since $n = 1$, $S/nT = .897$, and as the $(N-3)/(N-1)$ factor is 15/17, an unbiased estimate of $1 - Z$ is .791, or $Z = .209$. The regression estimate of Z is .186, which appears reasonably close. Relying on capping alone to correct S/nT, i.e., not applying the factor 15/17, would give

$Z = 1 - .897 = .103$, which is not as close in this case. The inverse gamma prior for $t^2 + s^2/n$ with the prior Z of .5 gives $Z = .221$, as follows: since $s^2 = 1$, the choice of $q = 4$ as the inverse gamma scale parameter makes .5 the prior value of Z. Thus $1 - Z$ is estimated by $E[(t^2 + s^2/n)^{-1}|T] = (N + 3)/(2q + (N - 1)T) = 21/(8 + (17)1.115) = .779$. This is reasonably good in this case but not quite as close as the factor approach.

Looking at just 3 batters at a time gives a different picture. Without considering capping, the unbiased estimate would be $Z = 1$, as $N - 3 = 0$ and thus $1 - Z = 0$. For just 3 players, capping S/nT at 1 may in itself produce an unbiased estimate, however. Six different groups of 3 were selected from the above table, namely first 3, second 3, etc. For each of these 6 cases, the capped credibility estimate and the Z from the inverse gamma prior are calculated for comparison to the after the fact capped regression estimate of Z.

Estimates of Z

Case:	**1**	**2**	**3**	**4**	**5**	**6**
T:	1.679	2.455	3.072	1.748	.304	.041
$1 -$ Cap S/nT:	.404	.593	.675	.428	.000	.000
Inv Gamma:	.359	.535	.576	.478	.303	.257
Regression:	.378	.199	.000	.351	.000	.000

This table was computed as follows. Since $S = n = 1$, $S/nT = 1/T$. The inverse gamma estimate of $1 - Z$ is $6/(8 + 2T) = 3/(4 + T)$. There is not an unambiguous winner between these two estimators of Z; it is not even clear whether the goal should be the regression Z from the three points, or the estimate of .186 from the wider population. It is apparent, however, that the unbiased estimate which ignores capping, i.e., $Z = 1$, is not as close as the others. It should be noted that diffuse priors may also give reasonable estimates in this example.

Exercise 5.3

Find the square root rule credibility for a batter with 45 at bats if the expected batting average is .255 and the full credibility value is 1082.

The importance of the $(N-3)/(N-1)$ factor is not settled, but it appears to provide improved estimates of Z except when credibilities tend to be small (below .25, perhaps), and when N is small. If the factor is significant in a given application, testing along the above lines would be worthwhile.

Incorporating Risk Size

Introduction

Up to this point, each risk received the same credibility for a given exposure period, which implicitly assumes that the predictive value of the information for each risk is the same. In many applications (e.g., territory or class ratemaking, commercial lines experience rating), this is not a viable assumption. A large risk, class, or territory is more predictable than a small one. Credibility that varies according to size is addressed in this section.

In experience rating, the formulation $Z = P/(P+K)$ is often used to assign credibility to risks of different sizes, where P is expected losses. Larger risks will receive greater credibility, as their pure premiums, loss ratios, etc. will have lower variances than for smaller risks. The $P/(P+K)$ formula is based on a particular relationship between the variances of risks of different sizes, namely $Var(X_{iu}| R_i) = s^2/P_{iu}$. That is, the variance is inversely proportional to risk size. With this assumption, it can be shown that $K = s^2/t^2$, where again t^2 is the variance of the individual risk means. Note, however, that s^2 is not the expected process variance in this case (s^2/P_{iu} is), but is only the constant of proportionality in that variance. Also, s^2 can be interpreted as the expected process variance for a risk of unit size, i.e., with $P_{iu} = 1$. Naturally, larger risks will have lower expected variances.

It will be shown below that the inverse relationship of variance to exposure needed for $P/(P+K)$ is a reasonable assumption, but that in fact it does not appear to hold in practice. A few other relationships will be explored to see which best accord with observation. Each of these will lead to a different credibility formula, for example $P/(JP+K)$ or $(P+I)/(JP+K)$. In order to arrive at these formulas, a general credibility formula will be developed that will hold for any relationship of variance to risk size, then the particular relationship desired can be just plugged in.

For the sake of concreteness, let X_{iu} be the pure premium for risk i time u, with L_{iu} the losses, and P_{iu} the exposure. By changing the definitions of P and/or L, X could just as easily be frequency, severity, loss ratio, etc. E.g., taking P_{iu} as the expected losses gives the experience rating credibility formula above.

Time = Size

The somewhat relativistic title of this subsection refers to the special case in which a larger risk can be regarded as a longer observation of a smaller risk. An equivalent formulation is the famous sutra disproved by Hewitt (see below): "A large risk behaves as an independent combination of small risks." Even though we know now this is not the case, it is nonetheless the common point of departure for the more general cases.

From the section "Least Squares Credibility," a risk of unit size observed for P time periods receives credibility $P/(P+K)$. Thus if time = size, a risk of size P observed for one period would also have $Z = P/(P+K)$. The sample mean for a risk with one unit of exposure with expected process variance s^2 will, over P independent periods, have variance s^2/P. Similarly, a risk with P independent exposure units, each with variance s^2, will have a variance for one period of s^2/P. (Since the variance is additive in this case, the losses will have variance Ps^2, but the pure premium, losses/P, will have variance $Ps^2/P^2 = s^2/P$.) Thus this special case is equivalent to assuming that the variance for the ith risk at time u is s^2/P_{iu}. For this particular relationship between variance and risk size, the credibility formula is the same as in the section "Least Squares Credibility," $Z = P/(P+K)$, where $K = s^2/t^2$, s^2 is the expected variance for a single exposure unit, and t^2 is the variance between means for the various risks.

More General Credibility Formulas

Empirical findings on the relation of variance to size will be reviewed below. How to apply that to reach a credibility formula is covered here. Not only the expected process variance, but also the variance of the hypothetical means will be allowed to vary by size. The latter can occur if, for example, large risks are more like each other than are small risks. In one model to be discussed, all risks are composed of independent draws of exposure units from a common population, and so large risks are more likely to be close to the mean of this population. In that model it turns out that all risks should get the same credibility, irrespective of size! While this situation is unlikely, it illustrates that the degree of risk differences can depend on risk size.

First some notation. The variance of a risk's pure premium depends on the exposure, which can vary over time. For the gth risk, time u, denote the expected value of the individual risk variance as $EVar(X_{gu}|R) = s_{gu}^2$. For instance, there might be a constant s^2 such that $s_{gu}^2 = s^2/P_{gu}$, as discussed above. Let $P_{g.}$ denote $\Sigma_u P_{gu}$ and define $t_g^2 = VarE(X_{gu}|R)$, which is thus allowed to differ among risks.

Since t_g^2 is the between variance applicable to the gth risk, this allows different risks to have different between variances. The main application of this has been to risks of different sizes, where the large risks are sometimes found to be more uniform among themselves than are the small risks. If the large risks are random assortments of small risk components, for instance, then some of the differences among small risks could be expected to average out when looking at large risks. Or, if large risks are subject to more stringent regulation and scrutiny than small risks, the differences among them could again be less.

The general formula for the credibility to apply to the experience of the gth risk is $Z_g = P_{g.}/(P_{g.} + K_g)$, where credibility constant K_g is given by $P_{g.}/K_g = t_g^2 \Sigma_u s_{gu}^{-2}$. For instance, in the simple case $s_{gu}^2 = s^2/$

P_{gu}, $\Sigma_u s_{gu}{}^{-2} = P_{g.}s^{-2}$, and so, given constant t^2 across risks, $K = s^2/t^2$ and $Z = P/(P + K)$, as before.

For more complex relationships of variance and risk size, the formula for K_g does not simplify much unless there is only a single period of observation. In that case, the formula simplifies to $K_g = P_{g1}s_{g1}{}^2/t^2$.

If the accident propensity of a risk changes from year to year, it will be seen below that a portion of the variance will not be reduced for larger risks. (Namely, the portion that comes from shifts in accident propensity.) A formula expressing this is $s_{gu}{}^2 = y^2 + s^2/P_{gu}$. If there is only one time period u, and again assuming constant t^2, then $K_g = (P_{g1}y^2 + s^2)/t^2$. The formula for Z now becomes $Z = P/(JP + K)$, with $P = P_{g1}$, $J = 1 + y^2/t^2$, and $K = s^2/t^2$.

The credibility formula can be expressed as a weighted average between $X_{g.}$ and the overall expected pure premium $m = EX_{gu}$, as long as $X_{g.}$ is taken as $X_{g.} = \Sigma_u Z_{gu}X_{gu}/Z_g$. This is a weighted average of the observations, but where the credibility of each observation, rather than the exposure, is taken as its weight.

To summarize, then, the general credibility formula is:

$$X_{g0} \approx (1 - Z_g)m + Z_g X_{g.} \tag{6.1a}$$
$$Z_g = P_{g.}/(P_{g.} + K_g) \tag{6.1b}$$
$$K_g = P_{g.}/t_g{}^2 \Sigma_u s_{gu}{}^{-2} \tag{6.1c}$$
$$Z_{gu} = (1 - Z_g)t_g{}^2/s_{gu}{}^2 \tag{6.1d}$$

Here, $P_{g.} = \Sigma_u P_{gu}$, and $X_{g.} = \Sigma_u Z_{gu}X_{gu}/Z_g$. Note that (6.1d) is needed only to calculate $X_{g.}$.

An equivalent formula for Z_g is $Z_g = J_g/(1 + J_g)$, where $J_{gu} = t_g{}^2/s_{gu}{}^2$ and $J_g = \Sigma_u J_{gu}$. Then, $Z_{gu} = J_{gu}/(1 + J_g)$, which shows that $Z_g = \Sigma_u Z_{gu}$. In the case of only a single time period, $Z_{g1} = t_g{}^2/(t_g{}^2 + s_{g1}{}^2)$.

Since the experience of different years are weighted together by credibility, not by exposure, three one year periods cannot be considered equivalent to one three year period. The latter is an exposure weighting of the three individual years which, when variance decreases more slowly than the increase in exposure, gives too much weight to the years with more exposure. In practice, however, combining the years may work reasonably well.

*Development of Formulas

To illustrate the derivation of the above formulas in one case, the simple pure premium model of the section "Least Squares Credibility" is slightly generalized here. This model is $X_{iu} = m + R_i + Q_{iu}$, with $ER_i = EQ_{iu} = 0$, and $EX_{iu} = m$ with the different Q's and R's independent random variables with $VarR_i = t^2$ and $VarQ_{iu} = s^2/P_{iu}$. This last equation is the only change: before, the random fluctuation term had constant variance, but here it decreases inversely to risk size. By the same reasoning as before, (4.4) – (4.9) become:

$$Cov(X_{iu}, X_{jv}) = \delta_{ij}t^2 + \delta_{ij}\delta_{uv}s^2/P_{iu} \qquad (4.4')$$

$$\delta_{gj}t^2 = \Sigma_u a_{ju}t^2 + a_{jv}s^2/P_{jv} \qquad (4.5')$$

$$P_{j.}\delta_{gj}t^2 = P_{j.}\Sigma_u a_{ju}t^2 + \Sigma_u a_{ju}s^2 \qquad (4.6')$$

$$\Sigma_u a_{ju} = P_{j.}\delta_{gj}t^2/(s^2 + P_{j-.}t^2 \qquad (4.7')$$

$$a_{jv} = \delta_{gj}P_{jv}t^2/(s^2 + P_{j.}t^2) \qquad (4.8')$$

This says the weight is zero unless $j = g$, and then it is:

$$a_{gv} = P_{gv}t^2/(s^2 + P_{g.}t^2) \qquad (4.9')$$

Then, by the definition of $X_{g.}$, the weighted experience is $\Sigma_v a_{gv}X_{gv} = X_{g.}P_{g.}t^2/(s^2 + P_{g.}t^2) = X_{g.}P_{g.}/(P_{g.} + K)$. This leads to $Z = P_{g.}/(P_{g.} + K)$.

The derivation of (6.1) is by this same logic, just without the specific formula $s_{gu}^2 = s^2/P_{gu}$. The question of what assumption should be made about s_{gu}^2 is addressed next.

Relationship of Variance to Risk Size

Since $X_{iu} = L_{iu}/P_{iu}$, the dependence of $Var(X_{iu}|R)$ on risk size will be approached by seeing what the conditional variance of L_{iu} is under different assumptions. This conditional variance can then be divided by P_{iu}^2 to yield $Var(X_{iu}|R)$. L_{iu} is assumed to be the sum of the losses from P_{iu} exposure units. Let L_{iau} denote the losses from exposure unit a.

First, $Var(X_{iu}|R)$ is calculated under the assumption that for a given risk i, the units L_{iau} are independent and identically distributed. Since the exposure units are independent given R_i, $Var(L_{iu}|R) = \Sigma_a Var(L_{iau}|R)$. Since these units are also conditionally identically distributed given R_i, $Var(L_{iau}|R)$ does not depend on a or u, and so can be denoted as $s(R_i)^2$. Then $Var(L_{iu}|R) = P_{iu}s(R_i)^2$. Thus $Var(X_{iu}|R) = s(R_i)^2/P_{iu}$. Letting $s^2 = Es(R_i)^2$ gives $EVar(X_{iu}|R) = s^2/P_{iu}$. Hence, assuming that the risk is a collection of independent identically distributed exposure units yields that the expected conditional variance for a risk decreases in proportion to the exposure.

This assumption is commonly made, and, as seen above, it leads to the credibility formula $Z = P/(P + K)$. However, Hewitt (1967) estimated the variance for workers' compensation risks of different sizes, and found that the variance did not decrease as fast as this assumption would imply. Hewitt's estimated variance, along with fits to this variance based on various formulas for the variance as a function of risk size are shown below. Each risk size range in the table is specified by the average premium for the risks in the range.

Effect of Risk Size on Variance

Average Premium	Estimated Variance	13,150/Prem	.172 + 9900/Prem	1837 Prem$^{.773}$	12,230 + .133 Prem / 254 + Prem
296	26.3	44.4	33.6	22.7	22.3
628	12.3	20.9	15.9	12.7	14.0
869	10.4	15.1	11.6	9.80	11.0
1,223	7.58	10.7	8.27	7.58	8.39
1,924	5.35	6.83	5.32	5.32	5.73
3,481	3.07	3.78	3.02	3.36	3.40
6,050	2.18	2.17	1.81	2.19	2.07
8,652	1.59	1.52	1.32	1.66	1.50
12,265	1.15	1.07	.980	1.27	1.11
18,944	.749	.694	.695	.906	.769
33,455	.610	.393	.468	.585	.495
68,758	.345	.191	.316	.335	.310
220,786	.163	.060	.217	.136	.188

The variance in this case was not of the pure premium, but of the entry ratio, which is the loss ratio normalized to average to 1. The dollars are at 1958 levels. The other columns are fits of the variance by various functions of premium. The first of these functions specifies that the variance decreases by the inverse of premium. It can be seen that the actual variances are lower than this model would predict for small risks, and higher for large risks.

While this formula does not produce a good fit, it is based on specific assumptions about how exposure units are related. The difficulty for other functions of premium is finding models that explain them. Such models would have to incorporate exposure units that are not conditionally independent given the risk parameter R_i. There are various ways this can be done. For example, a workers' compensation risk with several units of exposure may have some units working in proximity to one another, which are then exposed to some of the same hazards. Also, even exposures that are not physically contiguous may be affected by similar economic conditions.

It is possible to model the situation of varying conditions affecting the risk, so that the loss probabilities are not the same in every year. For instance the risk parameters R_i could specify a distribution from which another parameter H_{iu} (the annual condition of the risk) is determined each year. If the exposure units are conditionally independent given H_{iu}, then given only R_i they are not independent; they have some correlation due to the common parameter H_{iu}. By the above reasoning, $Var(X_{iu}|H_{iu}) = s(H_{iu})^2/P_{iu}$. Then

$$Var(X_{iu}|R_i) = EVar(X_{iu}|H_{iu}) + VarE(X_{iu}|H_{iu}) = s^2(R_i)/P_{iu} + y^2(R_i).$$

Thus with the inclusion of varying conditions, the conditional variance becomes a linear function of $1/P$. The constant term essentially measures how much variance there is in risk conditions over time.

The second fit of the variance shown above uses this linear function, with $s^2(R_i)$ and $y^2(R_i)$ constant. A much better fit to the risk variances is produced, although the smallest and largest risks still do not fit very well. The final two columns represent (1) Hewitt's fit to this data based on $Var = s^2/P^C$, with $s^2 = 1837$ and $C = .773$, and (2) the function $Var = [y^2 + s^2/P]/[1 + C/P]$, with $y^2 = .133$, $s^2 = 12{,}230$, and $C = 254$.

Neither of these is based on a model decomposing L_{iu} into exposure units, but improved fits are provided. The latter formula approaches a linear function of $1/P$ for large risks, but is below that line for the small risks. For all the curves, the parameters were selected to minimize squared errors in the log of the estimated variance, so that percentage errors in that variance would be as small as possible.

To review, then, four formulas relating conditional variance to risk size have been considered. The first two are based on models of the risk process, and the second two are just curves providing better fits. Since the conditional, or "process", variance of X_{gu} is a function of the exposure P_{gu}, so is the expected value of this variance. That is, ${s_{gu}}^2 = EVar(X_{gu}|R)$, the expected process variance for the gth risk at time u, is a function of P_{gu}. For the four curves these functions are as follows:

1. ${s_{gu}}^2 = s^2/P_{gu}$
2. ${s_{gu}}^2 = y^2 + s^2/P_{gu}$
3. ${s_{gu}}^2 = s^2/{P_{gu}}^{.773}$
4. ${s_{gu}}^2 = [y^2 + s^2/P_{gu}]/[1 + C/P_{gu}]$

Each of these can be put into (6.1) to produce a credibility formula. This is done below, following two examples of negative binomial claim frequency distributions corresponding to the first two models. While the formulas based on models of the risk process have added justification over those selected for fit alone, the risk models implicitly assume that the exposure units in use really do measure the exposure to loss. In practice this is usually only approximately the case.

Example 6.1

In this example, L_{iu} will be the number of claims, so that X_{iu} is claim frequency. The parameter R_i is the ordered pair V_i, Q_i, and L_{iu} is assumed to be negative binomially distributed with parameters $P_{iu}V_i$, Q_i. (The sum of the claims for P_{iu} independent exposure units, each negative binomial in V_i, Q_i is itself negative binomial in $P_{iu}V_i$, Q_i.) These assumptions yield:

$$E(L_{iu}|R_i) = P_{iu}V_i(1 - Q_i)/Q_i$$
$$E(X_{iu}|R_i) = V_i(1 - Q_i)/Q_i$$
$$\text{Var}(L_{iu}|R_i) = P_{iu}V_i(1 - Q_i)/Q_i^2$$
$$\text{Var}(X_{iu}|R_i) = V_i(1 - Q_i)/P_{iu}Q_i^2$$

Thus the conditional variance of X_{iu} is inversely proportional to the exposure P_{iu}.

Example 6.2

The previous example illustrated the case where each exposure unit followed a negative binomial distribution with the same parameters. In this example, the exposure units are all Poisson with the same parameter, but that parameter is drawn at random each year. The claims for each exposure unit are assumed to be Poisson with parameter H_{iu}, so that L_{iu} is Poisson in $Y_{iu} = P_{iu}H_{iu}$. H_{iu} is in turn gamma distributed in $R_i = (C_i, B_i)$, and so Y_{iu} is gamma in $(C_i, P_{iu}B_i)$. Thus from Example 2.2, L_{iu} is negative binomial in $(C_i, 1/(1 + P_{iu}B_i))$. Thus:

$$
\begin{aligned}
E(L_{iu}|R_i) &= P_{iu}B_iC_i \\
E(X_{iu}|R_i) &= B_iC_i \\
\mathrm{Var}(L_{iu}|R_i) &= P_{iu}B_iC_i(1 + P_{iu}B_i) \\
\mathrm{Var}(X_{iu}|R_i) &= B_iC_i/P_{iu} + B_i^2C_i
\end{aligned}
$$

This is then an example of the second variance formula, a linear function of $1/P$.

It is also possible that t_g^2, the variance of the conditional mean, can be a function of risk size. For example, if a large risk is a collection of small independent units, randomly taken from the population of all such units, then it is unlikely that the mean for the large risk is too different from the overall mean. In fact, if every risk is the sum of equal sized small exposure units with losses L_{iau} and parameter R_{ia}, and for each risk the units are drawn at random, it is possible to have $t_g^2 = w^2/P_{g1}$, assuming one time period. This will be seen below to lead to every risk having the same credibility, because large risks are closer to the overall mean. A mixed model, where some portion of a risk has parameter R_i, and the remainder is made up of small units, each with independent parameter R_{ia}, can lead to $t_g^2 = t^2 + w^2/P_{g1}$, so that only a portion of the variance of the conditional mean decreases with risk size. This model, along with the varying conditions model for the process risk, leads to a specific credibility formula that appears to adequately capture size based differences in predictability of results.

Credibility Formulas Varying By Risk Size

Once an expression relating the variance for different risk sizes has been selected, (6.1) can be used to produce a credibility formula. If $s_{gu}^2 = s^2/P_{gu}$, as in the first model above, then $\Sigma_u s_{gu}^{-2} = P_{g\cdot}/s^2$, and so $K_g = s^2/t^2$. Thus K_g is a constant, as in the constant exposure case, and $Z_g = P_{g\cdot}/(P_{g\cdot} + K)$.

For the other models, K_g is more complex. However, a fairly simple expression is possible in the case of just one observed time period. In the second model, $s_{gu}^{-2} = P_{gu}/(P_{gu}y^2 + s^2)$ and $P_{gu} = P_{g\cdot}$, so $K_g = (P_{g\cdot}y^2 + s^2)/t^2$, which can be written $K_g = P_{g\cdot}A + B$, i.e., a linearly increasing function of the exposure. In this case $Z_g = P_{g\cdot}/((1 + A)P_{g\cdot} + B)$.

If $s_{gu}^2 = s^2/P_{gu}^{.773}$, in the case of one exposure period, s^2 is given by $s_{gu}^{-2} = P_{gu}^{.773}/s^2$, so $K_g = P_{g\cdot}^{.227}(s^2/t^2)$, or $K_g = BP_{g\cdot}^{.227}$, again an increasing function of $P_{g\cdot}$. The formula for Z becomes $Z = P_{g\cdot}^{.773}/(P_{g\cdot}^{.773} + B)$.

Finally, if $s_{gu}^2 = [y^2 + s^2/P_{gu}]/[1 + C/P_{gu}]$, and there is only one exposure period, $t_g^2 s_{gu}^{-2} = [1 + C/P_{g\cdot}]/[(y_g^2/t_g^2) + s_g^2/t_g^2 P_{gu}]$, so $K_g = [AP_{g\cdot} + B]/[1 + C/P_{g\cdot}]$. With this, $Z = P_{g\cdot}/(P_{g\cdot} + K_g)$ yields, after some algebra, $Z_g = [P_{g\cdot} + C]/[P_{g\cdot}(1 + A) + B + C]$. By redefining the constants, this can also be written as $Z_g = [P_{g\cdot} + C]/[AP_{g\cdot} + B]$.

As discussed above and in Mahler (1987), the variance between risks may be less for large risks, for example if large risks are made up, in part at least, of heterogeneous smaller risk units drawn from a common population of such units. If $t_g^2 = t^2 + w^2/P_{g1}$, and $s_{gu}^{-2} = P_{gu}/(P_{gu}y^2 + s^2)$, then, in the case of a single time period, the formula $Z_g = [P_{g1}t^2 + w^2]/[P_{g1}(y^2 + t^2) + s^2 + w^2] = [P_{g1} + C]/[AP_{g1} + B]$ again results. Thus this formula can be developed from reasonable assumptions of how individual units combine, and not just on the basis of a good fit of the fourth curve above to observed variances. Research at the National Council on Compensation Insurance (NCCI) has found this formula to provide an improved basis for experience rating credibility. As an interesting but unlikely special case, if $y^2 = t^2 = 0$, i.e., all risks are random collections of arbitrary risk units and parameters are stable, then this credibility can be seen to be constant for all risk sizes.

*Estimation from Data

A weighted average of the X_{iu}'s can be used to estimate m. However the usual exposure weighted average is not optimal. At least for the simplest model $s_{gu}{}^2 = s^2/P_{gu}$, it turns out that the minimum variance unbiased linear estimator of m, which will again be denoted $X_{..}$, is $X_{..} = \Sigma_i Z_i X_{i.}/Z_.$, where $Z_. = \Sigma_i Z_i$ (see ISO (1980)). This is sometimes referred to as the *credibility weighted average* of the $X_{i.}$'s. Standard statistical practice advocates weighting observations in inverse proportion to their variances. In this case $Var(X_{i.}) = t^2 + s^2/P_i = t^2/Z_i$, so the credibility is inversely proportional to the variance.

To estimate s^2, y^2, t^2, etc., extensions of the methods used for the equal exposure case in Section 5 can be used. First, the model with $s_{iu}{}^2 = s^2/P_{iu}$ (and so $Z_i = P_{i.}/(P_{i.} + K)$, $K = s^2/t^2$) will be addressed. Let $S_i = \Sigma_u P_{iu}(X_{iu} - X_{i.})^2/(n-1)$, where $X_{i.} = \Sigma_u P_{iu} X_{iu}/P_{i.}$ is the exposure weighted average of the X_{iu}, and let $S = \Sigma_i S_i/N$. The main difference between these statistics and the S and S_i of Section 5 is the weight P_{iu} in the definition of S_i. Again, S will be the estimator of s^2. The factor P_{iu} in the definition of S_i may make S seem too much by this factor to be the variance of X_{iu}, and this perception is in fact correct. In this model, the conditional variance of X_{iu} is s^2/P_{iu}, as opposed to s^2 in the constant exposure model, so the estimate of s^2 is higher to reflect this.

Enough algebra will show that the conditional expectation $E(S_i|R_i) = s^2(R_i)$. Since $Es^2(R_i) = s^2$, $ES_i = s^2$, and $ES = s^2$ as well, showing that S_i and S are both unbiased estimators of s^2. S is a lower variance unbiased estimator of s^2 than is S_i.

Bühlmann and Straub(1970) propose the following to estimate t^2. Let $W = \Sigma_{i,u} P_{iu}(X_{iu} - X)^2/(Nn - 1)$, where X is the usual exposure weighted average of the X_{iu}'s. W can be thought of as a measure of the total variation of the individual observations X_{iu} around the grand mean X, and thus it should be close to the sum of the expected process variance and the variance of the hypothetical means. It can be shown, in fact, that $EW = s^2 + qt^2$, where $q = \Sigma_g P_{g.}(1 - P_{g.}/P_{..})/\ (Nn - 1)$. Thus $(W - S)/q$ is an unbiased estimator of t^2. As Bühlmann and Straub point out, this can sometimes be negative, in which case they assign $t^2 = 0$, and so $Z = 0$.

Klugman (1985) gives an alternative approach, which appears to give a better estimate of t^2. Let $T = \sum_{i=1}^{N} Z_i(X_{i.} - X_{..})^2/(N - 1)$. (Recall that $X_{..}$ is the credibility weighted average of the $X_{i.}$'s, not the exposure weighted average.) It is possible to show that, given the Z_i, $ET = t^2$. T cannot be considered an estimator of t^2, however, because t^2 is needed to compute Z_i in the formulas for $X_{..}$ and T. However if the Z_i are initially set to 1, an iterative procedure can be used: compute $X_{..}$ and T, estimate t^2, compute new Z_i's, etc., until the estimate for t^2 stabilizes (usually quickly). DeVylder (1981) uses the term pseudo-estimator for such a T, and suggests another one. T can stabilize at zero, however, which leaves the same problem that faced Bühlmann and Straub.

Example 6.3

In this example, the percentage change in claims frequency is to be estimated using credibility for three territories, i, ii, and iii, where two years of data are available. Thus $N = 3$ and $n = 2$. The data is as follows:

	Car—years of Exposure (000)			**Freq % Change from Base Year**		
Terr: / **Year**	**i**	**ii**	**iii**	**i**	**ii**	**iii**
1	25	75	50	6.00	− 2.00	3.00
2	20	80	50	4.00	− 4.00	5.00
	45	155	100	5.11	− 3.03	4.00

First, the Bühlmann-Straub estimator will be computed. The overall average X can be calculated to be .53. Estimate s^2 by:

$$S = 1000[25x.89^2 + 20 \times 1.11^2 + 75x1.03^2 + 80 - x.97^2 + 100]/3$$
$$= 99{,}761. \text{ For } t^2 \text{ use:}$$

$$W = 1000[25 \times 5.47^2 + 20x3.47^2 + 75\ x\ 2.53^2 + 80\ x\ 4.53^2 + 50 \times 2.47^2 + 50x4.47^2]/5$$

$$= 882{,}934.$$

Also,

$$q = [45000x.850 + 155000 \times .483 + 100000 \times .667]/5$$
$$= 35{,}963.$$

Thus the estimates are $s^2 = 99{,}761$ and $t^2 = (W - S)/q = 21.777$, and so $K = s^2/t^2 = 4580$. The credibilities for the three territory averages are then $45/(45 + 4.58)$, $155/(155 + 4.58)$, and $100/(104.58)$, or .91, .97, and .96, respectively.

Next, these credibilities can be used as the first approximations of the Z's in Klugman's pseudo-estimator. The credibility weighted average observation is

$$X_{..} = [.91\,x\,5.11 - .97\,x\,3.03 + .96\,x\,4.00]/[.91 + .97 + .96] = 1.95.$$

Then T can be calculated by

$$2T = .91(5.11 - 1.95)^2 + .97(3.03 + 1.95)^2 + .96(4.00 - 1.95)^2,$$

or $T = 18.6$. Then K is estimated as $99{,}800/18.6 = 5370$. This gives credibilities of .89, .97, and .95, respectively. The next iteration gives $X_{..} = 1.92$, $T = 18.5$, and $K = 5390$, which gives the same Z's (to two decimals), so the iteration has stabilized.

It should be noted that for both of these methods, the complement of credibility goes to the credibility weighted average $X_{..}$, not to the overall mean X, and this differs somewhat for each method. The values of $X_{..}$ are 1.95 and 1.92, respectively, for the two sets of credibilities calculated.•

The methods of this example are probably applicable in practice to percentage changes in pure premium, which will probably not be too different from class to class (that is, the percentage changes could be normally distributed or gamma distributed across the classes). On the other hand, they may not be applicable to pure premium itself, which could have a much heavier tailed distribution for which special methods are required. This is explored further in the concluding section to this chapter.

*Bayesian Estimation of Credibilities

In part to deal with the problem of negative estimates of t^2, Klugman (1987) develops several Bayesian approaches to estimating s^2 and t^2, and shows that these give dramatically improved credibilities in some actual ratemaking cases. For instance, with large exposures, fairly high credibilities can result even with small t^2's. The above approaches often get negative estimates of t^2 in such situations, which gives credibility of zero, whereas the Bayesian methods avoid this.

One of these approaches generalizes the diffuse priors with $p = -1$, which in the constant exposure case lead to equations (5.2), by specifying that the joint prior density of s^2 and t^2 is proportional to $s^{-2}[\prod_i(s^2 + P_{i.}t^2)]^{-1/N}$. This particular prior is taken after Box and Tiao (1973, p. 426). Introducing the variable $r = t^2/s^2$ $(=1/K)$ gives $Z_i = rP_{i.}/(1 + rP_{i.})$ and we may define $Z = \Sigma Z_i$. Klugman calculates the posterior distribution for r given the observations X_{iu}. This turns out to be proportional to:

$$f_1(r) = (\prod_i Z_i)^{.5+1/N} r^{-(N+1)/2}[N(n-1)S + (N-1)T/r]^{-(Nn-1)/2} Z_{.}^{-.5}.$$

Once the data is available, everything in f_1 is known or is a known function of r. For instance, since $r = 1/K$, $Z_i = P_{i.}/(P_{i.} + K)$ is a known function of r, and can thus be written as $Z_i(r)$. S is a constant, but T is calculated from $X_{..}$, which in turn is calculated using the Z_i's, and so is a function of r. Once a routine is available to calculate $f_1(r)$ for any r, this function can be integrated numerically over $r > 0$ to produce the constant of proportionality needed to calculate the posterior density $f(r)$ for r.

With the posterior density for $r = 1/K$ available, posterior means and variances for many quantities of interest can be computed numerically, and several are explored in Klugman's paper. For instance, $E(r|$ *the* X_{iu}'s$) = \int rf(r)dr$, which gives an estimate for r, and K can then be estimated by $1/r$. This requires $N > 3$ for the integral to converge. If $E(1/r)$ could be calculated directly by numerical integration, this would produce the posterior expected value of K. Unfortunately, this integral never converges. However, once the numerical integration routine is set up, it is not difficult to compute the posterior expected value of Z_i for each i as $\int Z_i(r)f(r)dr$, and in fact these integrals converge rather quickly.

Inverse gamma priors are also investigated for s^2 and t^2. If the s parameter is taken as 2, the inverse gamma is an infinite variance distribution with mean equal to the scale parameter. Specifying prior means of m_s and m_t for s^2 and t^2, respectively, gives:

$$f_1(r) = (\prod_i Z_i)^{.5} Z_.^{-.5} r^{-(N+5)/2}[m_s + N(n-1)S + m_t/r + (N-1)T/r]^{-(Nn+7)/2}.$$

Example 6.4

The diffuse priors and the straight Bayesian inverse gamma priors can be used to estimate credibilities with the data from Example 6.3. With P in thousands, for the diffuse prior,

$$f_1(r) = (\prod_i Z_i)^{5/6} r^{-2}[299 + 2T/r]^{-2.5} Z_.^{-.5}.$$

Numerical integration of $f_1(r)$ from zero to infinity yields .000001798. Thus $f(r) = f_1(r)/.000001798$ is the posterior density for $r = 1/K$. For $N = 3$, neither $E(r)$ nor $E(1/r)$ exist. However the expected Z's can be found to be .77, .89, and .86, respectively. Consistent with no expected value of K existing, there is no single value of K that would give these results, and in fact an increasing K with risk size is implied.

For the inverse gamma prior, prior opinion on m_s and m_t is needed. It might be assumed that each territory is fairly stable, so a reasonable value for the standard deviation of a territory's annual results from its mean might be 1.5 points, and the variance would thus be 2.25. If a typical territory has exposure in a typical year of 50 or somewhat less (in 1,000's), a typical s^2 might be 100, which would then be the prior expected value for m_s. Judging that a 10 percentage point difference of a territory from the average might be large, e.g., 3 standard deviations = 10, m_t might be taken as 10, which is approximately 10/3 squared. Then

$$f_{1(r)} = (\prod_i Z_i)^{.5} Z_.^{-.5} r^{-4}[399 + 10/r + 2T/r]^{-6.5}.$$

Numerical integration of f_1 yields $1.11E-16$, so dividing f_1 by this yields $f(r)$. For this prior, the integral of $1/r$ converges, and $E(K) = E(1/r) = 17$, which gives credibilities of .73, .90, and .85.

For the diffuse and inverse gamma priors, the values of $X_{..}$ are 1.86 and 1.78, respectively.

Using some class ratemaking data, Klugman has found the pseudo-estimator to generally perform better than the Bühlmann-Straub estimator, and the Bayesian methods to improve on both. One of the main advantages of the Bayesian methods is that they avoid negative values of t^2. Interval estimates of the credibility estimates can also be calculated (see Klugman (1987)).

*Estimation for Other Models of Variance by Risk Size

So far, the estimates produced have assumed that variance is inversely proportional to risk size. However, the S_i defined above can also be used to estimate Z for the second model

$$s_{gu}^2 = y^2 + s^2/P_{gu}\ (Z_i = P_{i.}/((1+A)P_{i.} + B, A = y^2/t^2, B = s^2/t^2).$$

Some algebra will show $E(S_i) = s^2 + y^2(P_{i.}^2 - \Sigma_u P_{iu}^2)/\ (n-1)P_{i.}$. Thus if a linear regression is done for S_i against $(P_{i.}^2 - \Sigma_u P_{iu}^2)/(n-1)P_{i.}$ (there are N observations of each), the slope and intercept can be used as estimators of s^2 and y^2.

Estimation of t^2 for this model could perhaps be approached by generalizing Klugman's pseudo estimator for the simpler model above. Let $w_i = P_{i.}t^2/(P_{i.}t^2 + s^2 + \ y^2\Sigma_u P_{iu}^2/\ P_{i.})$ and $w = \Sigma_i w_i$. Define $X_{..} = \Sigma_i w_i X_{i.}/w$ and $T = \Sigma_i = {}^N{}_1 w_i(X_{i.} - X_{..})^2/(N-1)$, where again $X_{i.}$ is the exposure weighted average of the X_{iu}'s. In this case it can be shown that $ET = t^2$, and so T is an unbiased pseudo-estimator of t^2. However, for this and the two more complex models, the Bailey-Simon method is often used instead, as discussed below.

Bailey and Simon (1959) present the idea of estimating Z by seeing which values of Z would have worked best in the past. In their example, each risk has one unit of exposure, namely a single private passenger car. For the risks with no claims, the credibility estimate of X_{g0} is just $(1-Z)X_{...}$. This can be compared to the average experience for these risks in the next year to see what Z should have been. Since only a fixed number of years (usually 1 to 5) is used in automobile experience rating, this value of Z can then be used in the future.

Meyers (1985) uses a similar retrospective approach to estimate A and B in $Z_g = P_{g.}/((1 + A)P_{g.} + B)$ in commercial insurance experience rating. Rather than focusing on the zero loss risks, Meyers creates a test statistic for the overall performance of the plan, and optimizes the test statistic. NCCI adopted a similar procedure with a different test statistic to estimate A, B, and C in $Z_g = (P_{g.} + C)/(AP_{g.} + B)$ for workers' compensation experience rating.

The NCCI procedure is essentially as follows: each set of values for A, B, and C gives a different credibility formula, and thus a different estimate of losses for each risk. Risks were first segregated by size categories, then within each category they were put into five groups (quintiles) by the credibility estimated experience ratios. These ratios were credibility estimated losses divided by ratemaking expected losses. Each set of A, B, C values thus gave a different grouping of risks into quintiles.

The losses in the next period were then used to test these groupings, according to two criteria: (1) the ratio of actual losses to ratemaking expected losses should be quite different for the 5 different groups, which would indicate that the credibility formula succeeded in identifying risk differences; (2) the ratio of actual losses to credibility estimated losses should be quite similar for each group, which would indicate that the formula also succeeded in correcting for risk differences. The table below gives an example of the two ratios by quintile for one risk size group:

Ratio to manual rates:	.70	.78	.91	1.12	1.43
Ratio to experience modified rates:	.89	.96	1.06	1.09	.97

These two criteria were combined into a single test statistic by taking the ratio of the variance among the groups from (2) to the variance from (1), with lower values being preferred. The sum of the statistics over the different size categories was then minimized by appropriate selection of A, B, and C.

In practice, it was not quite this simple, in that there was another set of A, B, and *C* values estimated for excess losses simultaneously, and both sets of parameters were indexed for inflation and for state differences in loss severity. This can be accomplished by indexing *B* and *C* only, in that then the credibilities will not change if *P* increases according to the index.

The (extended) Bailey-Simon method thus obviates the need for estimating variances, and it also gives the credibility formula that would have worked best in the past. To the extent that subtle violations of the model assumptions are operating, the resulting formula could work better even than one with the actual variances, if they were known.

How Good Is Least Squares Credibility?

*Linearization Error

In Example 6.3, the percentage change in territory pure premium was estimated using least squares credibility. It is often felt appropriate to use this credibility for percentage changes in pure premium, and for loss ratios, but not for pure premiums themselves by territory or by class. One reason for this is that pure premium differences among territories and among classes may be greater, especially in the extremes, than would be accounted for in this theory. Since least squares credibility relies on the first two moments, it may not be well adapted for use with highly skewed distributions, for example. In this section it is shown that least squares credibility can perform quite poorly with highly skewed distributions. Taking the logs of the data before applying credibility is explored as an alternative.

As discussed earlier, the function of the X_{iu}'s that optimizes the expected squared error in X_{g0} is the predictive expected value $E(X_{g0}|$ the X_{iu}'s). The best *linear* function in this sense is the least squares credibility estimate.

Whenever the predictive expectation is a linear function of the observations, it is thus the same as the credibility estimator, and several examples of this were seen above. Jewell (1973) has shown that this occurs when the conditional density of *X* given the unknown parameter R is a member of the linear exponential family, i.e., when the density can be written in the form $f(x|R) = exp[xp(R) + b(-x) + q(R)]$ for functions b, p, and q, as long as R is distributed as the natural conjugate prior of f. The gamma-Poisson, inverse gamma-gamma, and normal-normal conjugate pairs are useful examples.

It is widely speculated that probability densities of the above form are the only cases where the credibility estimate is the same as the predictive expectation (e.g., see Goel (1982)). In all other cases, the difference between these two estimates can be described as linearization error, since it is the minimal additional error that can arise from using a linear estimator instead of the predictive expectation.

Many of the distributions that arise in casualty insurance practice, such as the lognormal, Weibull, Pareto, and inverse gamma are not in the linear exponential family, and in fact quite a bit of accuracy may be sacrificed by the use of linear estimators for variables having these distributions, as the following examples show. Taking logs before using credibility and then exponentiating the answer, as an alternative to standard credibility practice when estimating such variables, will be illustrated as well.

Example 7.1

The first example will consider the lognormal distribution with a lognormal prior in the constant exposure model. This might be a reasonable model for claim severity, for example. The predictive mean and credibility estimate will both be calculated and compared to each other to determine the extent of linearization error.

The lognormal distribution can be parameterized to have two parameters, b and c^2, such that $1/f(x) = cx\sqrt{\pi 2}exp([ln(x/b)]^2/2c^2)$ and $E(X^j) = b^j exp(j^2c^2/2)$. In this parameterization, b is the exponentiation of the usual parameter μ. In particular, $EX = bexp(c^2/2)$ and $VarX = b^2[exp(2c^2)exp(c^2)]$.

The following properties of the lognormal can be derived by the methods used in Example 2.4. If B is lognormal in (v, q^2) (the prior distribution), and $X|B$ is lognormal in (B, c^2) (the conditional distribution), then X is unconditionally lognormal in $(v, c^2 + q^2)$ (the mixed distribution). If n observations are made, denoted as $\{X_i\} = X_1, \ldots, X_n$, then the posterior distribution for $B|\{X_i\}$ is the lognormal in v' and $c^2q^2/(c^2 + nq^2)$, where $ln(v') = [c^2 ln(v) + q^2\Sigma_i lnX_i]/[c^2 + nq^2]$. The predictive distribution for $X|\{X_i\}$, being the mixture of the conditional by the posterior, is then lognormal in v' and $c^2 + c^2q^2/(c^2 + nq^2)$. The predictive mean is then $E(X|\{X_i\}) = v'exp([c^2/2 + c^2q^2/2(c^2 + nq^2)])$. Letting $z = nq^2/(c^2 + nq^2)$:

$$E(X|\{X_i\}) = exp(zlnX_{.} + (1 - z)ln(v))exp(.5[c^2 + (1 - z)q^2]) \qquad (7.1)$$

where $lnX_{.}$ denotes the average value of the log of the observations. Since $z = n/(n + k)$, where $k = c^2/q^2$, this predictive mean can be seen to be a constant factor M times the exponentiation of the credibility estimate of lnX, where the constant factor is $M = exp(.5[c^2 + (1 - z)q^2])$.

To find the credibility estimate of X given the X_i's, the lognormal moment formulas are applied to the conditional and prior distributions. The credibility is $Z = n/(n + K)$, where

$$\begin{aligned} K &= EVar(X|B)/VarE(X|B) \\ &= E(B^2[exp(2c^2) - exp(c^2)])/Var(Bexp(c^2/2)) \\ &= v^2exp(2q^2)[exp(2c^2) - exp(c^2)]/exp(c^2)v^2[exp(2q^2) - exp(q^2)]. \end{aligned}$$

This simplifies to:

$$K = [exp(q^2)][exp(c^2) - 1]/[exp(q^2) - 1] \qquad (7.2)$$

Table 7.1 illustrates a simulation test of the resulting credibility estimate vs. the predictive mean, in order to illustrate the potential linearization error for the lognormal. Parameter values of $c^2 = 4, v = 1$, and $q^2 = 2$ were used in this example. The c^2 value might correspond to the loss size distribution in a heavy tailed line. The q^2 value provides quite a large dispersion among classes or risks, perhaps more than would ordinarily be expected.

For the test, 10,000 risks were placed at each of the following percentiles of the prior distribution: 1, 10, 50, 75, 90, 99. Thus in this test, the b parameter value is known for each risk, and so the different ways of estimating it can be tested. For each risk, 50 claims were simulated from the lognormal severity arising from the B value at that percentile and the selected value $c^2 = 4$. Then the sample mean, the credibility estimator, and the predictive mean were computed from the 50 claims. Each of these was considered to be an estimator of the known conditional mean $E(X|B)$, and the absolute value and square of the estimation errors were recorded for each risk. The table gives the averages of these estimates and errors for the 10,000 risks at each percentile.

Table 7.1

Lognormal Linearization Error

Percentile of B:	1	10	50	75	90	99
B	.037	.163	1.00	2.60	6.13	26.8
E(X|B)	.275	1.21	7.39	19.2	45.3	198
			Average Estimate			
Sample	.276	1.21	7.41	19.0	45.3	200
Predictive Mean	.382	1.49	7.90	19.2	42.3	165
Credibility	11.2	11.7	14.4	19.6	31.3	100
			Average of Individual Risk Absolute Errors			
Sample	.131	.592	3.56	9.03	21.9	97.1
Predictive Mean	.114	.369	1.66	4.02	9.45	46.6
Credibility	11.0	10.5	7.04	3.88	18.6	113
			Average of Individual Risk Squared Errors			
Sample	.058	1.35	41.5	319	1,760	42,000
Predictive Mean	.021	.241	4.81	26.0	136	3,020
Credibility	120	110	57.8	63.8	544	18,000

To compute these estimates, $K = 62$ can be found using (7.2) with $c^2 = 4$, $q^2 = 2$, so $Z = 50/112 = .45$. Similarly, $z = .96$ resulted for the credibility estimate of lnX, with a K of $2 = c^2/q^2$. The constant $M = exp(.5[c^2 + (1 - z)q^2])$ from (7.1) is equal to 7.68; also, $EX = 20.1 = v exp([c^2 + q^2]/2)$, and $E(lnX) = ln(v) = 0$. With these values, $(1 - Z)EX = 11.1$, so this is a lower bound for the credibility estimate $(1 - Z)EX + ZX_{..}$.

The table shows that the average sample estimate is generally quite good, as the sample estimate is unbiased. The error of the sample mean can be large for any particular risk, however. The predictive mean shows up to be by far the best estimator in terms of either absolute or squared errors. Thus the linearization error is quite substantial in this case.

The sample mean is also linear in the observations, and it may appear more favorable than the credibility estimate overall in this example. By the expected squared error criterion, the credibility estimator is better: the sample squared errors at the upper percentiles are much larger, so the average squared error over the entire distribution is higher than that of the credibility estimator, even though the credibility errors are higher at the lower percentiles. The better performance of the credibility estimator by this criterion does not appear to carry over to absolute errors, or to percentage errors, however. This raises doubt about whether the overall expected squared error is really an appropriate criterion when heavy tailed distributions are involved.

A possible alternative is to use least squares credibility to estimate the logs of the observations. This will minimize percentage errors when converted back to full values, and thus may be more appropriate, even in cases when, unlike the lognormal, it does not give the predictive mean. The next example looks at such a case.

With the distributions in the above example, an ad hoc method, such as using limited fluctuation credibility with $n_F = 50$, would probably appear better than the least squares credibility estimate for most risks, even though such a low value for full credibility would appear strange by usual limited fluctuation standards. In some aspects of workers' compensation ratemaking, e.g., serious pure premiums, as a matter of fact, such low full credibility values have been selected over the years, based on performance of the ratemaking method. While this has given rise to actuarial suspicion, the above gives a theoretical context for its applicability.

Example 7.2

In this example, the conditional and prior from Example 2.4 are reversed. Now X is inverse gamma in (c, Y), and Y *is gamma in* (r, b). The unconditional or mixed distribution for X is the Beta2 or generalized Pareto, in (r, c, b).

With n observations $X_1, \ldots, X_n$, the posterior distribution is then also gamma, but now with parameters $(r + nc, a)$, where $a = [b^{-1} + \Sigma X_i^{-1}]^{-1}$. Thus the predictive distribution is Beta2 in $(r + nc, c, a)$, and the predictive mean is $a(r + nc)/(c - 1)$.

This is to be compared to the usual credibility estimate and credibility based on the log transform. The K value can be found to be $(r + 1)/(c - 2)$ by the usual approach. To do credibility in logs, $EVar(W|Y)$ and $VarE(W|Y)$ must be found, where $W = lnX$. These will rely on some lesser known facts about the gamma and inverse gamma distributions:

1. $E(W|y) = ln(y) - \Psi(c)$, where $\Psi(c)$ is the digamma function, the derivative of the log of the gamma function. This is a well tabulated function, e.g., see Abramowitz and Stegun (1965).

2. $Var(W|y) = \Psi'(c)$, the derivative of the digamma, which is called the trigamma function and is again well tabulated. Note that this does not depend on y.

3. $Eln(Y) = ln(b) + \Psi(r)$

4. $Var(lnY) = \Psi'(r)$

From these it follows that $EVar(W|Y) = \Psi'(c)$ and $VarE(W|Y) = \Psi'(r)$, and so for log credibility, $k = \Psi'(c)/\Psi'(r)$. Also, $ElnX = ln(b) + \Psi(r) - \Psi(c)$. Taking $z = n/(n + k)$, the log credibility estimate can be written as $Mexp[(1 - z)ElnX + (z/n)\Sigma lnX_i]$, where M is a constant needed to make the estimate unbiased. M can be determined by computing the expected value of this estimate without the M and then setting the estimate equal to EX. It can then be found that the log credibility estimator is:

$$nb^{1-z}(r-1)!(c-1)!^n exp[(z/n)\Sigma\, lnX_i]/$$
$$(c-1)(r+z-1)!(c-1-z/n)!^n.$$

For an example, 10,000 trials for each percentile shown were taken for a sample of $n = 25$, with parameters $b = 100$, $r = 0.5$, and $c = 4.0$. The results are given in Table 7.2.

Table 7.2

Inverse Gamma Linearization Error

Percentile of Y:	1	10	50	75	90	99
Y	.008	.789	22.7	66.2	135	332
E(X|Y)	.003	.263	7.58	22.1	45.1	111
			Average Estimate			
Sample	.003	.263	7.58	22.0	45.1	110
Predictive Mean	.003	.267	7.67	22.2	45.1	108
Credibility	.488	.741	7.84	21.9	44.2	108
Log Credibility	.003	.266	7.60	22.0	45.0	110
			Average of Individual Risk Absolute Errors			
Sample	.000	.028	.817	2.38	4.86	11.9
Predictive Mean	.000	.021	.608	1.75	3.54	8.63
Credibility	.485	.478	.797	2.33	4.85	12.0
Log Credibility	.000	.022	.639	1.86	3.79	9.30
			Average of Individual Risk Squared Errors			
Sample	.000	.001	1.13	9.59	40.1	241
Predictive Mean	.000	.000	.594	4.90	19.8	115
Credibility	.235	.230	1.13	9.07	38.5	235
Log Credibility	.000	.000	.652	5.49	22.9	137

In this example, $\Psi(4) = 1.25612$, $\Psi(.5) = -1.96351$, $ln100 = 4.60517$, and so $ElnX = 1.38554$. Also $\Psi'(4) = .283823$, $\Psi'(.5) = 4.93480$ so $k = .0575146$, and $z = 25/(25 + k) = .9977$. Since $K = .75$, $Z = .9709$, and $EX = br/(c-1) = 50/3$ can be computed.

For this sample, the log credibility performed almost as well as the predictive mean, and considerably better than linear credibility. In fact, due to lower absolute errors and percentage errors, the sample mean may be felt to be better than the linear credibility estimator, even though it can be shown to have a higher expected squared error overall. This again raises doubts about how appropriate the overall expected least squares criterion is for heavy tailed distributions.

To apply log credibility in practice, it is not necessary to use digamma and trigamma functions. At least in the constant exposure case, the empirical development of K can be applied to the logs of the observations, and the resulting credibility estimators exponentiated. This will not be in general unbiased, but a factor M can be developed so that the credibility estimators over all risks balance to the overall mean, simply by eliminating the off balance that would arise without this factor.

This procedure is applicable, for example, to loss severity, or to other instances of the equal exposure case. Before it could be applied in the more general situation, the relationship of $Var(lnX_{iu})$ to P_{iu} would have to be determined, and resulting credibility formulas worked out. For this it may be reasonable to use the simplest model $Var(lnX_{iu}|R_i) = s(R_i)^2/P_{iu}$, in fact. For a gamma distributed variable in (c,b), the sum of n independent observations is gamma in (nc, b), and the variance of the log of this sum is thus $\Psi'(nc)$. This is reasonably well approximated by $1/nc$, at least when nc is not too small. (Exercise. Prove this by twice differentiating Sterling's approximation for the log of the gamma function.) Thus assuming that the conditional variance of lnX is approximately inversely proportional to the exposure n makes sense at least in this case.

The principle of working with a transformed loss value, having a more manageable distribution, has been applied in casualty actuarial practice. An example, mentioned in the opening section to this chapter, is the multi-split experience rating plan, first introduced in 1940 in New York. For small and medium sized risks, credibility was applied only to losses transformed by a "primary value" function $p(X)$. An example in recent use is:

$$p(X) = X \qquad \text{if } X \leq \$2000$$

$$p(x) = 10{,}000X/(X + 8000) \text{ if } X > \$2000$$

The primary value is always less than \$10,000, which effectively limits the tail of the distribution.

Expected Squared Error of Credibility Estimate

Another approach to the question, "How good is least squares credibility?" is to compute the expected squared error of the estimate, either conditional on the parameters R_i or overall. First the conditional expected squared error is calculated. Through straightforward algebraic manipulation of probabilities, in the equal exposure case it is possible to show that, for any weight Z:

$$E\{[ZX_{i.} + (1-Z)m - E(X_{i0}|R_i)]^2|R_i\} =$$

$$Z^2 Var(X_{i0}|R_i)/n + (1-Z)^2[m - E(X_{i0}|R_i)]^2 \quad (7.3a)$$

and thus, taking the expected value of this, the overall expected squared error is:

$$E[ZX_{i.} + (1-Z)m - E(X_{i0}|R_i)]^2 =$$

$$Z^2 EVar(X_{i0}|R_i)/n + (1-Z)^2 VarE(X_{i0}|R_i) =$$

$$Z^2 s^2/n + (1-Z)^2 t^2 \quad (7.3b)$$

(Minimizing 7.3b with respect to Z gives $Z = n/(n+K)$, as it should.)

Taking $Z = 1$ gives the squared error for the sample mean. For any particular class, this may be greater or smaller than the credibility squared error, depending on how close that class really is to the overall mean, as (7.3a) shows. For Example 7.1, the conditional expected squared errors are given below for the credibility value $Z = .45$, the sample estimate $Z = 1$, and an arbitrary choice of $Z = .90$.

Conditional Expected Squared Errors

Percentile of B:	1	10	25	50	75	90	99
B	.037	.163	.385	1.00	2.60	6.13	26.8
E(X|B)	.275	1.21	2.85	7.39	19.2	45.3	198
Z = 1	.08	1.6	8.7	59	395	2,198	42,000
Z = .9	4	4.8	10	49	321	1,789	34,400
Z = .45	120	110	91	60	79	942	17,800

The overall expected squared errors from (7.3b) for these Z's are 3200, 2600, and 1400, respectively. This again illustrates that the expected squared error can be dominated by the large values of the parameter, which is not necessarily the way an estimation process should be evaluated. The last row can be compared to the simulated values from Table 7.1.

Even though the overall average squared error is lower for the credibility estimator, the individual (conditional) expected squared error can be much lower for the sample mean at some percentiles. This occurs even in the case of normal distributions, as Efron and Morris (1972) point out. An adaptation they discuss is placing a selected limit on how much the credibility estimator can differ from the sample value. This "limited translation estimator" effectively gives additional credibility to the observations furthest from the grand mean.

Since non-extreme risks can sometimes produce extreme observations, this procedure increases the overall expected squared error, but reduces the individual squared errors at the extremes, where they are often largest. Efron and Morris show how to compute the increase in overall expected squared error and the decrease in individual squared error when the limit is a constant difference from the sample value. This makes a lot of sense in their model, as all risks have the same conditional variance. For heavy tailed distributions, a percentage limit may be worthy of consideration, since the coefficient of variation is more likely to be constant across risks, as in the above examples.

For example, in a classification ratemaking context, workers' compensation class rates can range from 10 cents to $100 per $100 of payroll. Allowing a 10% error would seem more equitable than allowing a fixed $5 error in such a case.

Further Topics

A number of different extensions of the above methods have been worked out by various authors. A very limited selection of those with applications in casualty insurance is presented in this section, in the form of an annotated bibliography. In general, references noted in earlier sections are not included here.

Mahler, Howard C. 1986, An actuarial note on credibility parameters *PCAS* 73.

The least squares and limited fluctuation formulas for Z can be matched fairly closely with the right choice of parameters. Mahler shows that taking $n_F = 8K$ makes the credibilities close and the credibility estimators even closer.

Klugman, Stuart. 1987 Credibility for classification ratemaking via the hierarchical normal linear model, *PCAS* 74.

A Bayesian approach to estimating s^2 and t^2 in the normal-normal model is presented, using both diffuse and proper priors. The choice of prior turns out to have little effect on the outcome. In a test using live insurance data, improved results are obtained. Although numerical integration is needed, error estimates are provided which incorporate the uncertainty about s^2 and t^2.

Venter, Gary G. 1986, Classical partial credibility with application to trend *PCAS* 73.

The limited fluctuation paradigm is extended to trend estimates. A trend projection is given full credibility if the p-confidence interval around it has radius no greater than 100k% of the projected value. This radius is a function of the goodness of fit of the trend line.

Hachemeister, Charles A. 1975 Credibility for regression models with application to trend in *Credibility—Theory and Applications,* Kahn, ed. New York: Academic Press.

Least squares credibility is applied to regression models in a very general setting. In a particular application, trend lines for several states are credibility weighted against each other, with number of claims used as the basis of credibility.

Miller, Robert B., and Hickman, James C. 1975 Insurance credibility theory and Bayesian estimation in *Credibility—Theory and Applications,* Kahn, ed. New York: Academic Press.

Least squares credibility and Bayesian analysis are applied to the collective risk model for frequency, severity, and total claims.

Heckman, Philip. 1980 Credibility and solvency in *Pricing property and casualty insurance products*, New York: Casualty Actuarial Society.

A hierarchical least squares credibility scheme is presented in which risk means are weighted against class means, which in turn are weighted against the overall mean. The two levels of credibility are computed in an integrated manner, but these turn out to be separable steps.

DuMouchel, William H. 1983 The Massachusetts automobile insurance classification scheme *The Statistician*: 32.

Credibility is applied in a two dimensional setting. Class rate relativities by territory are initially modeled as a statewide class relativity plus the product of a territory relativity with a second statewide class relativity. The deviations of the individual cell relativities from this model are assumed normal, which leads to a credibility weighting between the sample cell relativity and the model expectation.

Venter, Gary G. 1985 Structured credibility in applications—hierarchical, multi-dimensional and multivariate models *ARCH*:2.

The hierarchical model described by Heckman is applied to calculating workers' compensation loss severity by class within hazard group, and two other models are described. A multivariate model is used to estimate several correlated quantities by class, e.g., frequency for different injury types. A two-dimensional model is developed to estimate class by state relativities by weighting the individual class-state cell simultaneously against the other classes and other states, without assuming any particular underlying additive or multiplicative structure between state and class.

de Jong, Piet and Zehnwirth, Ben 1983a Credibility and the Kalman filter," *Insurance Mathematics and Economics* 2.

The Kalman filter is a generalized model which is shown to include most of the known credibility models as special cases, while also allowing for changes in structural parameters over time.

de Jong, Piet and Zehnwirth, Ben 1983b Claims reserving, state-space models and the Kalman filter *Journal of the Institute of Actuaries*: 110.

Accident year loss payout timing can be modeled by various curves, such as exponential decay, generalizations of the inverse power curve, etc. Curve parameters are estimated based on payment triangles. Parameters are allowed to change from one accident year to another, but they are "credibility weighted" against the parameters for other years using the Kalman algorithm. Practical methods for how to use this algorithm are discussed. Standard errors for the resulting loss reserve estimates are provided by this method.

Robbin, Ira. 1986 A Bayesian credibility formula for IBNR counts *PCAS* 73.

For a given set of loss exposures, the claims emerging in each reporting period are postulated to arise from a process (Poisson for example) with a vector of parameters u (probably not precisely known). After some of these reporting periods, M claims have been observed and the number of claims yet to emerge is to be estimated. Credibility weights are specified for three estimators of this IBNR:

(a) the observed claims to date times a development factor

(b) the ultimate claims expected originally (prior to claims emergence), less the observed claims to date.

(c) the number of claims originally expected to emerge after this date.

To derive the credibility weights. the variance of M can be broken down into $EVar(M|u)$ and $VarE(M|u)$. The second component is further split out by defining n and q (independent functions of the parameters u) so that $E(M|u) = n(1-q)$. The interpretation is that *n is the conditional expected ultimate number of claims, and* q is the expected proportion of IBNR claims at this date, given u.

Since for independent X and Y, $Var(XY) = E(X^2)VarY + (EY)^2 VarX$, it follows that $VarE(M|u) = E(n^2)Var(1-q) + [E(1-q)]^2 Var(n)$.

Thus three components of $VarM$ are identified, and the three estimators above end up being weighted in proportion to these three components.

Estimator (a) has weight proportional to $Var(n)$. If the ultimate number of claims is not well known, $Var(n)$ is high and a large weight is given to the developed observed claims. The weight on (b) is proportional to $Var(1-q)$. If the development pattern is poorly known, (a) and (c) are less reliable. Finally, if M itself is highly random, little weight can be given to it. Thus if $EVar(M|u)$ is higher, the weight on (c) increases.

Conclusion

Credibility as a topic has been with the CAS since the first volume of the *Proceedings*, and it is by no means a finished one, as witnessed by the flurry of papers recently. The best form for credibility estimators has yet to be determined for many applications. It is not unreasonable to expect that the final volume of the *PCAS*, whenever it is published, will also contain a paper addressing credibility theory.

Postlogue

by Charles C. Hewitt, Jr.

Number of Observations

Sometime in the 1920s, Sinclair Lewis, the author, was to receive an award as a distinguished alumnus of Yale University. In accepting the award, Lewis took the occasion to assert his known atheism.

> *"I do not believe there is a God," said Lewis (in substance). "If, in fact, there is one, let him strike me down here and now!" And, of course, nothing happened. However, several days later the noted newspaper columist, Arthur Brisbane, took Lewis to task.*
>
> *"Lewis, you poor misguided fool," wrote Brisbane (in substance). "You remind me of the ants who lived along the right-of-way of the Atchison, Topeka, and Santa Fe Railroad. This colony of ants depended for its existence upon the crumbs thrown from the dining cars of the railroad trains as they passed by.*

> *"It came to pass that the ant colony fell upon hard times because, through chance, no crumbs were thrown out near its particular place along the right-of-way. The situation became desperate and the colony decided to hold a meeting. It was suggested that they all pray to the president of the Atchison, Topeka, and Santa Fe Railroad to send more dining cars so that crumbs would be thrown off in their area.*
>
> *"So they did pray and the following day they waited, but no crumbs were thrown off where they lived. So the ants concluded that there was no such person as the president of the Atchison, Topeka, and Santa Fe Railroad."*

Variance of the Processes

Four boys decided to play "hooky" from school, because they knew there was to be a test that morning. About 11 A.M. their consciences got the better of them and they decided to show up at school after all. Upon reaching their classroom, they explained to the teacher that they had been on their way to school in a car, but the car had a flat tire. This made them late because they had to have the flat tire fixed.

"No problem!", said the teacher. "Just come back here during the lunch hour and I'll give you a make-up test." At lunch time, when they reported back to the classroom, the teacher instructed the four boys to take seats in the four corners of the room.

"Now," said the teacher, "there's only one question on this make-up test. Which tire was flat?"

Variance of the Hypotheses

Television interviewer: *"Do you believe in miracles?"*

Guest: *"Of course!"*

Television interviewer: *"Have you ever seen a miracle?"*

Guest: "No."

Television interviewer: *"Do you know anyone who has actually seen a miracle?"*

Guest: *"No, but that doesn't prove anything!"*

References

Abromowitz, M. and Stegun, I. 1965. *Handbook of mathematical functions.* New York: Dover.

Bailey, A. 1945. A generalized theory of credibility, *PCAS* 32.

Bailey, A. 1950. Credibility procedures, *PCAS* 37.

Bailey, R. and Simon L. 1959. An actuarial note on the credibility of experience of a single private passenger car, *PCAS* 46.

Bailey, Robert. 1961. Experience Rating Reassessed. *PCAS* 48.

Berger, J. 1985. *Statistical decision theory and Bayesian analysis*, 2nd ed. New York: Springer Verlag.

Box, G. and Tiao, G. 1973. *Bayesian inference in statistical analysis,* Reading, MA: Addison-Wesley.

Bühlmann, Hans. 1967. Experience Rating and Credibility. 4 *ASTIN Bulletin.*

Bühlmann, H. and Straub E. 1970. Glaubwürdigeit für schadensätze (Credibility for loss ratios), English translation, *ARCH* 1972(2).

DePril, N. 1986. Improved recursions for some compound Poisson distributions, *Insurance Mathematics and Economics* 5.2.

DeVylder, F. 1981. Practical credibility theory with emphasis on optimal parameter estimation, *ASTIN Bulletin* 12.2.

Dropkin, L. 1959. Some considerations on automobile rating systems utilizing individual driving records, *PCAS* 46.
1960. Automobile Merit Rating and Inverse Probabilities. *PCAS* 47.

Efron, B. and Morris, C. 1972. Limiting the risk of Bayes and empirical Bayes estimators. Part II: The empirical Bayes case, *JASA* 67 (March).

—-. 1975. Data analysis using Stein's estimator and its generalizations, JASA 70 (June).

—-. 1977. Stein's paradox in statistics, *Scientific American* (May).

Ericson, W. 1970. On the posterior mean and variance of a population mean, *JASA* 65.

Gerber, H. and Jones, D. 1975. Credibility formulas of the updating type. In *Credibility: Theory and Applications,* New York: Academic Press.

Goel, P. 1982. On implications of credible means being exact Bayesian, *Scandanavian Actuarial Journal.*

Heckman, P. and Meyers G. 1983. The calculation of aggregate loss distributions from claim severity and claim count distributions, *PCAS* 70.

Hewitt, C. 1967. Loss ratio distributions a model, *PCAS* 54.

Hogg, R. and Klugman, S. 1984. *Loss distributions,* New York: Wiley.

Insurance Services Office. 1980. *Report of the credibility subcommittee: development and testing of empirical Bayes credibility procedures for classification ratemaking,* New York: ISO.

Jewell, W. 1973. Credible means are exact Bayesian for simple exponential families, *ORC*: 73-21, Operations Research Center, University of California, Berkeley, CA. (Also in *ASTIN Bulletin* 8:1, September 1974).

Keffer, R. 1929. An experience rating formula, *Transactions of the Society of Actuaries* 30.1.

Klugman, S. 1985. Distributional aspects and evaluation of some variance estimators in credibility models, *ARCH* 1985.1.

Klugman, S. 1987. Credibility for classification ratemaking via the hierarchical normal linear model, *PCAS* 74.

Lundberg, Ove. 1940. On Random Processes and Their Application to Sickness and Accident Statistics. Uppsala (Sweden): Harald Cramer Jubilee Volume.

Mahler, H. 1987. Review of "An analysis of experience rating", *PCAS* 74.

McDonald, James B. (1984). "Some Generalized Functions for the Size Distribution of Income," *Econometrica,* Vol. 52, pp. 647-663.

Mayerson, Allen L. 1964. A Bayesian View of Credibility. *PCAS* 51.

Meyers, G. 1985. An analysis of experience rating, *PCAS* 72.

Meyers, G. and Schenker N. 1983. Parameter uncertainty in the collective risk model, *PCAS* 70.

Mong, S. 1980. Estimating aggregate loss probability and increased limit factors in *Pricing Property and Casualty Insurance Products*, New York: Casualty Actuarial Society.

Morris, C. 1983. Parametric empirical Bayes inference: Theory and applications, *JASA* 78.

Mowbray, A. 1914. How extensive a payroll exposure is necessary to give a dependable pure premium? *PCAS* 1.

Nelson, D. 1969. Review of "The credibility of the pure premium", *PCAS* 56.

Panjer, H. 1981. Recursive evaluation of a family of compound distributions, *ASTIN Bulletin* 12:1.

Pentikäinen, T. 1977. On the approximation of the total amount of claims, *ASTIN Bulletin* 9.3.

Perryman, F. 1932. Some notes on credibility, *PCAS* 19.

Raiffa, Howard and Schlaifer, Robert. 1961. Applied Statistical Decision Theory. Cambridge: Harvard University Press.

Savage, Leonard J. 1954. The Foundations of Statistics. New York: John Wiley & Sons.

Schlaifer, Robert. 1959. Probability and Statistics for Business Decisions. New York: McGraw-Hill.

Simon, L. 1969. Review of "The credibility of the pure premium", *PCAS* 56.
1962. An Introduction to the Negative Binominal Distribution and Its Applications. *PCAS* 49.

Seal, H. 1977. Approximations to risk theory's F(X,T) by means of the gamma distribution, *ASTIN Bulletin* 9.C.

Stellwagen, H. 1925. Automobile rate making, *PCAS* 11.

Venter, G. 1983a. Review of "The calculation of aggregate loss distributions from claim severity and claim count distributions", *PCAS* 70.

—-. 1983b. Transformed beta and gamma distributions and aggregate losses, *PCAS* 70.

Whitney, A. 1918. The theory of experience rating, *PCAS* 4.

Table of Distributions

Preliminaries

Gamma function: $\Gamma(r) = \int_0^\infty y^{r-1}e^{-y}dy = (r-1)!$ The partial integral can be evaluated by a series:

Incomplete Gamma function: $\Gamma(r;x) = \int_0^x y^{r-1}e^{-y}dy \div \Gamma(r) = \frac{e^{-x}x^{r-1}}{(r-1)!}\sum_{i=0}^{\infty}\prod_{k=0}^{i}\frac{x}{r+k}$

Beta function: $\beta(r,s) = \frac{\Gamma(r)\Gamma(s)}{\Gamma(r+s)} = \int_0^\infty \frac{t^{r-1}dt}{(1+t)^{r+s}} = \int_0^1 u^{r-1}(u-1)^{s-1}du$, where $u = \frac{t}{1+t}$

Incomplete Beta function: $\beta(r,s;x) = \int_0^x u^{r-1}(u-1)^{s-1}du \div \beta(r,s) = \int_0^{x/(1-x)} \frac{t^{r-1}dt}{(1+t)^{r+s}} \div \beta(r,s) =$

$= \frac{x^r}{\beta(r,s)}\left[\frac{1}{r} + \sum_{i=1}^{\infty}\frac{x^i}{r+i}\prod_{k=1}^{i} 1 - \frac{s}{k}\right] = F(\frac{s}{r}\frac{x}{1-x})$, where F is the distribution function of the F distribution with $2r$ and $2s$ degrees of freedom. Thus either the series expansion or a package with the F-distribution can be used to compute the incomplete beta function. Note that the incomplete beta and gamma functions are both increasing functions, with range [0,1), and thus can be used as distributions.

When possible, the distributions below are parameterized with a multiplicative scale parameter b, so that $E(X^y) \propto b^y$. This is usually more convenient for applications, although the parameterizations given in Hogg and Klugman (1984) are easier to estimate by maximum likelihood. After estimation they can be readily translated to the forms below, however. In the following, F is the distribution function, and f the density.

1. Transformed Beta distribution (*r,s,a,b*)

$F(x) = \beta(r,s;\frac{x^a}{x^a+b^b});$ $\qquad f(x) = \frac{(a/b)(x/b)^{ar-1}}{\beta(r,s)(1+(x/b)^a)^{r+s}},$

$$E(X^y) = \frac{b^y\beta(r+\frac{y}{a}, s-\frac{y}{a})}{\beta(r,s)}, \quad -ar < y < as.$$

1a. Burr Distribution (*s,a,b,*) (*r* = 1)

$F(x) = 1 - (1 + (x/b)^a)^{-s};$ $f(x) = \dfrac{s(a/b)(x/b)^{a-1}}{(1 + (x/b)^a)^{1+s}},$

$$E(X^y) = \frac{b^y \frac{y}{a}!(s - 1 - \frac{y}{a})!}{(s-1)!}, \quad -a < y < as.$$

1a*i*. Loglogistic Distribution (*a,b*) (*r,s* = 1)

$F(x) = \dfrac{x^a}{x^a + b^a};$ $f(x) = \dfrac{(a/b)(x/b)^{a-1}}{(1 + (x/b)^a)^2},$

$$E(X^y) = b^y \frac{y}{a}!(-\frac{y}{a})!, -a < y < a.$$

1b. Generalized Pareto (*r,s,b*) (*a* = 1) (also called Generalized-*F*)

$F(x) = \boldsymbol{\beta}(r,s; \dfrac{x}{x+b});$ $f(x) = \dfrac{b^{-r}x^{r-1}}{\boldsymbol{\beta}(r,s)(1 + (x/b))^{r+s}};$

$$E(X^y) = \frac{b^y \boldsymbol{\beta}(r + y, s - y)}{\boldsymbol{\beta}(r,s)}, -r < y < s.$$

If y is an integer n, $E(X^n) = b^n \prod_{i=1}^{n} \dfrac{r + i - 1}{s - i}$.

The Pareto is given by $r = 1$, $F(x) = 1 - (1 + \frac{x}{b})^{-s}$.

1c. Generalized Loglogistic (*r,a,b*) (*s* = 1) (also called inverse Burr)

$F(x) = \left[\dfrac{x^a}{x^a + b^a}\right]^r;$ $f(x) = \dfrac{r(a/b)(x/b)^{ar-1}}{(1 + (x/b)^a)^{r+1}},$

$$E(X^y) = \frac{b^y(r - 1 + \frac{y}{a})!(-\frac{y}{a})!}{(r-1)!}, \quad -ar < y < a.$$

The special case $a = 1$ is the inverse Pareto, which only has moments $-r < y < 1$, and thus no mean!

2. Transformed Gamma (*r,a,b*)

$F(x) = \Gamma(r;(x/b)^a);$ $f(x) = \dfrac{a(x/b)^{ar-1}e^{-(x/b)^a}}{b\Gamma(r)};$

$$E(X^y) = \frac{b^y \Gamma(r + \frac{y}{a})}{\Gamma(r)}, y > -ar.$$

2a. Weibull (*a*,*b*) (*r* = 1)

$F(x) = 1 - e^{-(x/b)^a}$; $f(x) = (a/b)(x/b)^{a-1}e^{-(x/b)^a}$;

$E(X^y) = b^y \frac{y}{a}!, y > -a.$

2b. Gamma (*r*,*b*) (*a* = 1)

$F(x) = \Gamma(r; x/b)$; $f(x) = \frac{(x/b)^{r-1}e^{-(x/b)}}{b\Gamma(r)}$,

$E(X^y) = \frac{b^y \Gamma(r + y)}{\Gamma(r)}, y > -r.$ For an integer n, $E(X^n) = b^n \prod_{i=0}^{n-1} r + i.$

3. Inverse Transformed Gamma (*s*,*a*,*b*) (1/*X*) Transformed Gamma)

$F(x) = 1 - \Gamma(s;(x/b)^{-a})$; $f(x) = \frac{(a/b)e^{-(x/b)^{-a}}}{(x/b)^{as+1}\Gamma(s)}$;

$$E(X^y) = \frac{b^y \Gamma(s - \frac{y}{a})}{\Gamma(s)}, y < sa.$$

3a. Inverse Weibull (log-extreme-value) (*a*,*b*) (*s* = 1)

$F(x) = e^{-(x/b)^{-a}}$; $f(x) = (a/b)(x/b)^{-a-1}e^{-(x/b)^{-a}}$;

$E(X^y) = b^y(-\frac{y}{a})!, y < a.$

For $a = 1$, the inverse exponential has only moments $y < 1$.

3b. Inverse Gamma (*s*,*b*) (*a* = 1)

$F(x) = 1 - \Gamma(s; b/x)$; $f(x) = \frac{(1/b)e^{-b/x}}{(x/b)^{s+1}\Gamma(s)}$,

$E(X^y) = \frac{b^y \Gamma(s - y)}{\Gamma(s)}, y < s.$ For an integer n, $E(X^n) = b^n \prod_{i=1}^{n} s - i.$

4. Lognormal (*b*,*c*²)

$F(x) = N\left[\frac{ln(x/b)}{c}\right]$; $f(x) = \frac{e^{-[ln(x/b)]^2/2c^2}}{cx\sqrt{2\pi}}$; $E(X^y) = b^y e^{y^2c^2/2}.$

Note that all moments exist. McDonald (1984) shows that the lognormal is a limiting case of the transformed beta, transformed gamma, and inverse transformed gamma. (*N* is the standard normal distribution function.)

X, given Y, is distributed according to the conditional distribution. The distribution of Y is given by the prior distribution. The combination of these two gives the unconditional, or marginal, or mixed distribution of X. On taking n observations from this distribution, $x_1,\cdots,x_n$, the revised opinion on Y is given by the posterior distribution, and the new combined distribution for X is the predictive distribution. The distributions are conjugate when the posterior is of the same form as the prior.

Conditional	Prior	Mixed	Posterior	Predictive
TG (r,a,y)	ITG (s,a,b)	TB (r,s,a,b)	ITG $(s+nr,\ a,\ [b^a+\sum_1^n x_i^a]^{\frac{1}{a}})$	TB $(r,s+nr,a,[b^a+\sum_1^n x_i^a]^{\frac{1}{a}})$
ITG (s,a,y)	TG (r,a,b)	TB (r,s,a,b)	TG $(r+ns,\ a,\ [b^{-a}+\sum_1^n x_i^{-a}]^{-\frac{1}{a}})$	TB $(r+ns,s,\ a,\ [b^{-a}+\sum_1^n x_i^{-a}]^{-\frac{1}{a}})$
G (r,y)	IG (s,b)	GP (r,s,b)	IG $(s+nr,\ [b+\sum_1^n x_i])$	GP $(r,s+nr,\ [b+\sum_1^n x_i])$
IG (s,y)	G (r,b)	GP (r,s,b)	G $(r+ns,\ [b^{-1}+\sum_1^n x_i^{-1}]^{-1})$	GP $(r+ns,\ s,\ [b^{-1}+\sum_1^n x_i^{-1}]^{-1})$
Weib (a,y)	ITG (s,a,b)	Burr (s,a,b)	ITG $(s+n,\ a,\ [b^a+\sum_1^n x_i^a]^{\frac{1}{a}})$	Burr $(s+n,a,[b^a+\sum_1^n x_i^a]^{\frac{1}{a}})$
IW (a,y)	TG (r,a,b)	GLL (r,a,b)	TG $(r+n,\ a,\ [b^{-a}+\sum_1^n x_i^{-a}]^{-\frac{1}{a}})$	GLL $(r+n,\ a,\ [b^{-a}+\sum_1^n x_i^{-a}]^{-\frac{1}{a}})$
Expntl (y)	IG (s,b)	Pareto (s,b)	IG $(s+n,\ [b+\sum_1^n x_i])$	Pareto $(s+nr,\ a,\ [b^a+\sum_1^n x_i])$
IExpntl (y)	G (r,b)	IPareto (r,b)	G $(r+n,\ [b^{-1}+\sum_1^n x_i^{-1}]^{-1})$	IPareto $(r+n,\ [b^{-1}+\sum_1^n x_i^{-1}]^{-1})$
LN (y,c^2)	LN (b,q^2)	LN (b,c^2+q^2)	LN $\left(e^{\left[\frac{c^2 In(b)+q^2\sum_{i=1}^n In(x_i)}{c^2+nq^2}\right]},\ \frac{c^2q^2}{c^2+nq^2}\right)$	

(Predictive) LN $\left(e^{\left[\frac{c^2 In(b)+q^2\sum_{i=1}^n In(x_i)}{c^2+nq^2}\right]},\ c^2+\frac{c^2q^2}{c^2+nq^2}\right)$

Chapter 8

INVESTMENT ISSUES IN PROPERTY-LIABILITY INSURANCE

by Stephen P. D'Arcy

Investment Income

For the most part, the prior chapters in this text have focused on what is termed the underwriting side of insurance. This aspect of insurance involves estimating the value of losses to be paid, both for coverage that has already been provided and for policies to be written in the future, determining rate levels for various types of coverage, generating classification plans and establishing reinsurance contracts to share losses with other insurers. A more general view of an insurance company would regard the insurer as a financial intermediary, collecting and dispensing revenue. Premiums are collected from policyholders and the money is invested until needed for paying expenses, losses or taxes. The invested assets generate investment income that is either reinvested or used to satisfy obligations. Under this view of an insurer, the underwriting and investing aspects of an insurer are inextricably interwoven. In this chapter the investment side of insurance will be presented and its relationship with underwriting issues analyzed.

The property-liability insurance industry has traditionally segregated operating divisions and returns into the two components, underwriting and investments. The concentration of most insurance textbooks, allocation of personnel, and management attention have been on the underwriting side of operations. In many cases, this emphasis on underwriting has led to neglect of investment operations. Until recently, investment income was generally not explicitly considered in ratemaking. This neglect has produced an investment strategy for insurers that is often inefficient and uncoordinated with underwriting performance. In most insurance companies, investment departments tend to be isolated from the underwriting side of the business.

One reason for the relative neglect of the investment side of property-liability insurance operations was the comparative stability of underwriting profitability and net investment income, the value commonly used by insurers to describe investment performance. Figures 8-1 and 8-2 illustrate the underwriting profit or loss and net investment income for the period 1927 through 1967 and 1967 through 1987, respectively, for stock property-liability insurers. The net investment income is much less volatile than the underwriting profit or loss value.

FIGURE 8-1
Underwriting Profit & Net Investment Income

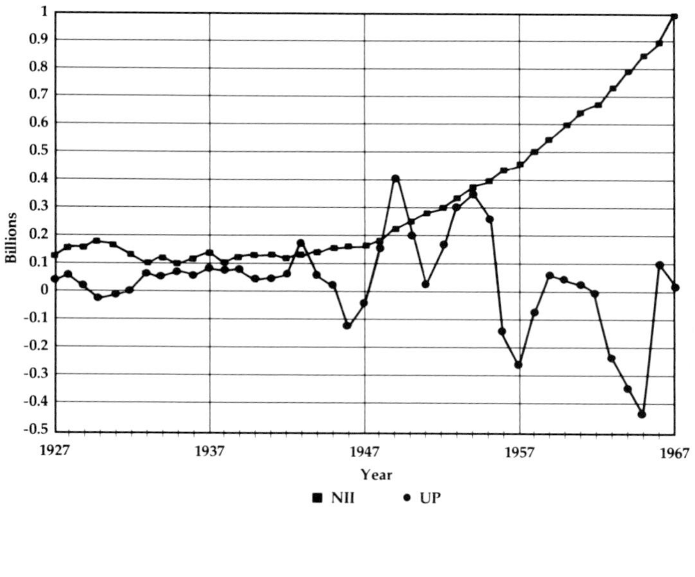

Source: Best's Aggregates & Averages (P/C) 1988, 1977, 1968

The variability of underwriting profitability led to an emphasis on this aspect of insurance operations as insurance managers concluded that close attention to the underwriting aspect of operations could minimize the adverse results and increase the likelihood of favorable results. The rapid growth of investment income during the 1970s, resulting from both higher rates of return and longer loss payout patterns, prevented the industry from neglecting investment income any longer. Concurrently with the rapid growth in investment income, some regulatory authorities mandated the inclusion of investment income in the ratemaking methodology. By the mid 1980s investment income had become recognized, by necessity, as an equally important component of insurance operating results as underwriting income.

FIGURE 8-2
Underwriting Profit & Net Investment Income

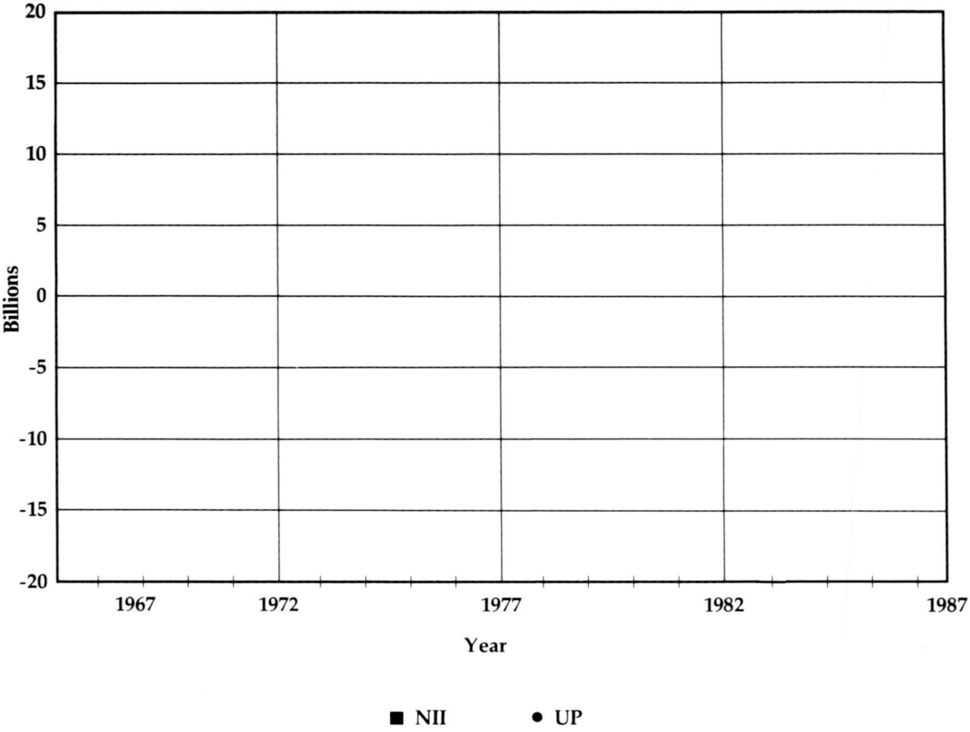

Source: Best's Aggregates & Averages (P/C) 1988, 1977, 1968

The purpose of this section is to describe the typical investments of property-liability insurers and define investment terminology. As of the end of 1987, the property-liability insurance industry had a total of $427 billion in admitted assets. Admitted assets are those recognized by statutory accounting conventions which tend to be conservative in valuing assets, with the notable exception being valuing bonds at amortized rather than market value. Invested assets at the end of 1987 comprised approximately $367 billion. The allocation of admitted assets among investment alternatives and other categories is displayed in Table 8-3.

TABLE 8-3
Distribution of Admitted Assets - 1987

Bonds	
U.S. Government	14.8%
State, Municipal, etc.	10.0
Special Revenue	22.0
Industrials	9.4
Other	3.1
Subtotal—Bonds	59.3
Stocks	
Industrials	6.7
Parents, Subs. & Affiliated Co.	4.1
Other	2.2
Preferred	2.3
Subtotal—Stocks	15.3
Real Estate	1.0
Cash	1.3
Short Term Investments	5.8
Premium Balances	7.8
Other Assets	9.5
Total	100.0

Source: *Best's Aggregates & Averages (Prop./Cas.) 1988,* A.M. Best Co. Inc. 1988, p.76.

Bonds

Bonds, including U.S. government, municipal (state and local government units), and corporate issues, represent the primary investment medium for the property-liability insurance industry. Bond investments have several characteristic attributes. Bonds typically consist of principal (the amount paid to the bondholder at the maturity date) and coupons (the periodic interest payments to the bondholder). However, bonds that have no maturity date (perpetuities) exist, as do bonds that pay no current interest (zero coupon bonds).

In most cases, the principal, maturity date, and coupon rate for bonds are fixed. However, some bonds are convertible, generally to the common stock of the issuing firm but occasionally to a commodity or a general price index. In addition, most corporate bonds have a call feature that allows the issuer to redeem them at a certain price prior to the maturity date. Frequently, the bonds cannot be called immediately, but only after a certain number of years. These bonds have what is termed a deferred call provision. The call feature works to the disadvantage of the purchaser. In the case of a decline in interest rates after bonds are issued, the issuer will redeem the bonds after the deferred period, forcing investors to reinvest the proceeds at the then current, lower interest rate. If interest rates rise, the issuer will not redeem the bonds early. Finally, variable interest rate bonds are available in which the coupon rate changes in line with current interest rates.

If an investor purchases a bond at issuance, the price is usually close to the principal value. The coupon rate produces an income stream that approximates the current interest rate on investments with similar risk and maturity. Any difference between the coupon rate and market interest rates is reflected in a price differential between the cost and principal. After issuance, changes in interest rates affect the market value of the bond. If interest rates were to rise, an investment yielding the prior, lower rate of interest would not be worth as much as it was previously. Thus, the market value of the bond would decline. Conversely, the market value of outstanding bonds rises as interest rates fall. The market value of any fixed income investment can be determined from the present value formula:

$$(1) \quad PV = \sum_t CF_t/(1+r)^t$$

where PV = present value
CF = cash flow from investment (coupon or principal)
r = current rate of return
t = time until cash flow is received

This formula, although commonly used, implicitly assumes a level term structure of interest rates in which the same interest rate applies no matter how long the funds are invested. This is an overly simplistic assumption, but the formula can be revised to reflect a more realistic interest rate pattern.

Insurance accounting uses an amortized value for fixed income investments rather than market value accounting. The amortized value is determined by equation (1) with the rate of return applicable at the time the asset was purchased instead of the current interest rate. Theoretically, equation (1) with the current rate of return as the interest rate would yield the current market value. The amortized value gradually adjusts the value of the bond from the purchase price to the principal over the maturity of the bond. The justification used for this treatment is that it prevents the value of insurers' assets, and therefore surplus, from fluctuating with changes in interest rates. The major drawback of the use of amortized values is that they do not reflect the current price in the market. If an insurer sold bonds, the market value would determine the proceeds. Although insurers frequently hold bonds until maturity, when an insolvency arises and bonds have to be sold, the market value reflects the proceeds that will be received. This distortion also frequently prevents even very solvent insurers from redeeming bonds early for tax considerations or other reallocation needs.

The interest received on corporate and U. S. government bonds is fully taxable under federal income tax regulations. Prior to the Tax

Reform Act of 1986 (TRA), interest received on municipal bonds was exempt from federal income taxation. The revised tax law subjects 15% of interest on municipal bonds purchased after August 7, 1986, to regular income taxation. The Alternative Minimum Tax (discussed later) increases the taxable portion of municipal bond interest, depending on the interaction of underwriting gains or losses, taxable investment income, tax preference items, and municipal bond interest. Traditionally, property-liability insurers invested heavily in tax-exempt securities because these issues generated a higher after-tax income for insurers. However, during the mid-1980s, insurers' investment portfolios shifted more heavily to taxable issues as statutory underwriting losses served as a tax shield for otherwise taxable investment income. The allocation of investable assets into fully taxable bonds and only partially taxable municipal bonds will also be affected by TRA.

In addition to interest income on bonds, investors may also incur gains or losses on the value of the bond itself. Realized gains or losses on fixed-income investments, which are the difference between the selling price and the purchase price, are fully taxable for all types of bonds in the year the bond is sold or redeemed. This provision provides for tax deferral on changes in the market values of bonds. The market value of bonds moves inversely to interest rate changes. Thus, depending on recent directions of interest rates, insurers may have a substantial amount of unrealized gains or losses that can be sold to maximize after-tax returns. These sales need to be coordinated with expected underwriting results to achieve this objective.

Investors in fixed-income securities are accepting investment risk and, as such, require a return commensurate with the level of risk. Investments in low-risk debtors, such as the U. S. government, generate lower yields than those in more risky debtors. Corporate bonds yield more than U. S. government bonds, and corporations with a low credit rating pay higher interest rates than more solvent firms. Similarly, the length of time until the debt will be redeemed also reflects different levels of risk. Thus, bonds of the same issuer with different maturities will provide different yields. The plot of yields versus time to maturity is known as the yield curve.

Normally, the yield curve is upward sloping, meaning that longer-term securities have higher yields than shorter-term ones. However, occasionally the yield curve is inverted, with shorter-term debt yielding more than longer-term securities. This inverted yield curve usually results from an upward spurt in the rate of inflation that investors expect to subside in the long run, from short-term capital shortages due to an expanding economy, or from the influence of the money supply.

In order to take advantage of the usual higher yields on longer-term issues, the property-liability insurance industry is normally heavily invested in long-term debt. The maturity distribution of bond investments for the industry is shown in Table 8-4. The advantage of a long-term investment portfolio is that it locks in current interest rates, making investment income less volatile and usually higher than short-term securities yield. The major disadvantages are that it locks insurers into historic rates of return when interest rates rise, and that the market values of long-term bonds are more volatile than shorter-term securities.

TABLE 8-4
Maturity Distribution of Bond Investments - 1986

Maturity	Allocation
1 Year or Less	4.3%
1 to 3 Years	10.7
3 to 5 Years	12.4
5 to 10 Years	25.4
10 to 15 Years	16.1
15 to 20 Years	13.5
Over 20 Years	17.6

Source: *Best's Insurance Management Reports: Online Reports,* (Prop./Cas.), No.21, Nov. 14, 1988, A.M. Best Co. Inc.

The long-term fixed-income investment strategy highlights one problem with the lack of coordination between underwriting and investments. An unexpected increase in inflation adversely affects underwriting performance by increasing loss costs above the levels anticipated when rates were set. The market values of long-term bonds are reduced by an unexpected increase in inflation, which tends to push interest rates up. Thus, both underwriting and investments are adversely affected by increases in inflation. Conversely, both areas are favorably affected by declines in inflation. An investment strategy that hedged the impact of inflation on underwriting could be implemented, which would reduce the total risk of the insurer. Consideration of such a coordinated strategy by increasing actuaries' awareness of investment operations is one objective of this chapter.

Equities

The second largest component of insurance company investments is in common and preferred stocks, commonly termed equities. Shares of stock represent ownership interests in the firms, as opposed to the debtor-creditor relationship generated by bonds. Common stock is the primary ownership interest in the firm; preferred stock is a hybrid between a direct ownership interest and a fixed-income investment. Preferred stock pays a predetermined dividend rate. The dividend can be omitted or reduced, but, generally, dividends to common stockholders cannot be paid until the preferred stockholders have been paid in full for any back dividends. Some preferred stock is convertible to common stock at a predetermined ratio. Without the convertibility feature, the prices of preferred stock fluctuate in line with bond prices rather than with stock prices. Preferred stock is an outgrowth of tax regulations that exempt a portion of dividends paid to stockholders from corporate income taxation. Prior to TRA this tax-exempt portion was 85%; TRA reduced this value to 80% and more recent legislation reduced it to 70%.

Dividends on common stocks are subject to more volatility than those of preferred stocks. These dividends can be raised or lowered, or omitted without any obligation to restore prior levels or pay omitted values. The total return on common stocks consists of the dividends, if any, and price changes. In general, the common-stock investor expects price appreciation to supplement the dividend income and thus produce a rate of return in excess of bond yields, as common stocks are more risky investments than fixed-income securities. The actual rate of return on common-stock investments has been higher and more volatile than on fixed-income securities. The average rates of return and standard deviations for common stocks and bonds by type are displayed in Table 8-5 for the period 1926 through 1986.

TABLE 8-5
Total Annual Rates of Return: 1926–1986

	Geometric Mean	Arithmetic Mean	Standard Deviation
Common Stocks	10.0	12.1	21.2
Long Term Corporate Bonds	5.0	5.3	8.5
Long Term Government Bonds	4.4	4.7	8.6
U. S. Treasury Bills	3.5	3.5	3.4

Source: *Stocks, Bonds, Bills, And Inflation 1987 Year Book*, Ibbotson Associates, Chicago, Illinois, 1987. p.25 Exhibit 3

Although bonds are stated at amortized value for statutory accounting purposes, stocks are stated at market value. Thus, changes in stock prices flow directly into statutory surplus. However, unrealized gains or losses have not been subjected to taxation. Thus, if an insurer were to sell appreciated stock and incur taxes, the actual surplus would be less than the statutory value just prior to the realization of the gains. Generally Accepted Accounting Principles (GAAP) does recognize this future tax liability.

Real Estate

Although insurance companies are allowed considerable leeway in real-estate investments, several statutory provisions limit the usefulness of this form of investment. Statutory requirements that vary by state establish upper limits on the amount of real-estate holdings that are allowed as admitted assets. Any excess real-estate investments are non-admitted, and thus are not included in surplus. Also, real-estate investments are valued at the lower of net book value (cost less depreciation) or market value. These restrictions explain the rather low level of real-estate investments by the property-liability insurance industry.

Real estate has traditionally been viewed as an inflation hedge for investors. As insurers are adversely impacted by inflation on underwriting operations, real-estate investments may serve to reduce overall corporate risk. However, the severe valuation and investment restrictions discourage such investments. Under current regulations, the potential benefits from real-estate investments must be weighed against the statutory drawbacks. Regulations that tend to reduce the desirability of holding a fully diversified portfolio reduce investment flexibility and may prevent the use of optimal portfolio choices. More enlightened regulation may be enacted in the future that allows full utilization of all investment possibilities for insurers to manage risk optimally.

Other Investments

A small portion of property-liability insurers' assets is invested in mortgage loans, collateral loans, cash, and miscellaneous assets, including oil and gas production payments, transportation equipment, timber deeds, mineral rights, and motor vehicle trust certificates. Insurers are now allowed to invest in options and futures under regulations in some states. An option represents the right, but not the obligation, to buy or sell a financial asset at a predetermined exercise price within a given time period. Financial futures are obligated transactions that will be consummated at a later date. Although the prices of options and futures are extremely volatile by themselves, investment strategies utilizing options and futures can reduce overall investment risk. Insurers are now beginning to adopt some of these approaches.

Investment Income

The total investment income of the insurance industry is segregated into several categories and reported separately in financial reports. Net investment income is reported in Part 1 of the Annual Statement. This value consists of all interest, dividend, and real-estate income earned during the year (adjusting for unpaid accruals), less all investment expenses incurred and less any depreciation on real-estate.

Net realized capital gains and losses consist of any difference between the net sale price and the net purchase price of bonds, stocks, or any other investment assets and are determined in Part 1A of the Annual Statement. These gains or losses can be realized as a result of a sale of an asset or upon the maturity of a bond. Net investment gain or loss is the sum of the net investment income and the net realized capital gains or losses. This total is displayed in the Annual Statement on line 9A of the Statement of Income.

Net unrealized capital gains and losses are also determined in Part 1A. These consist of adjustments in book value resulting from market value changes (for equities) or amortized value changes (for bonds) and any gain or loss from changes in the difference between book value and admitted value. Thus, this value is a combination of actual price changes on equities, amortization on bonds, and statutory accounting conventions. The entire net unrealized gain or loss flows directly into the surplus determination as listed on line 23 of the Statement of Income in the Annual Statement. The future tax consequences of the eventual realization of these gains or losses is not taken into account.

When investment income is considered in insurance ratemaking, either formally in the regulatory process or informally in company deliberations, the determination of the rate of return on investments must be established. Generally, one of two measures of investment income is used: the portfolio rate or the new-money rate. The portfolio rate of return is determined by dividing the net investment income earned by the statutory value of investable assets. This value is usually determined by averaging the beginning and ending values. This measure ignores capital gains, either realized or unrealized. As statutory, rather than market, values are used for investable assets, this becomes a weighted average of past fixed-income investments. If market values were used to determine the portfolio rate of return, the value of the investable assets would change in line with changes in interest rates, so the portfolio rate of return would approximate the new-money rate. The portfolio rate should be the net return to reflect the cost of investing.

New-money rates of return reflect the current rates of return available in the market. Frequently, a composite rate is applied that reflects a weighted average rate of different maturities and risk levels in line with the mix commonly followed by the insurer. This rate reflects current market conditions only, ignoring historic returns that the insurer may have locked in by past investments. The new-money rate reflects current market conditions and indicates the rate of return the insurer is likely to obtain on any funds generated for investment purposes by writing policies. This rate of return is for fixed-income securities, and does not apply to equity investments.

Investment and Tax Strategies

In a typical property-liability insurance company, the underwriting and investment operations are run separately. Each area attempts to maximize returns independently of the other. The underwriting area provides the cash flow for investment and generates the need for cash to pay expenses and claims. The investment area produces cash to reinvest from the sale and maturity of assets and generates investment income from the funds invested. Although the two areas are thus inextricably linked operationally, few insurers actively coordinated the two activities prior to the mid-1980s. In this section, several strategies that link underwriting and investment operations will be discussed.

Asset Liability Matching

The investment strategy behind asset-liability matching is to invest funds for exactly as long as they will be held. If a certain amount of funds will be needed in six years to pay claims, then investments would be made that would generate that amount in six years. If longer-term bonds were held, then the insurer might have to sell the bonds when the funds are needed, creating the possibility of a gain or loss on the sale depending on interest-rate fluctuations. A shorter-term investment would require that funds be reinvested upon the earlier maturity of the asset at the then available interest rates, exposing the insurer to interest-rate risk during the interim. By locking in the current rate of return for the applicable holding period, the insurer eliminates interest-rate risk.

Financial institutions such as banks and life insurers utilize asset-liability matching more heavily than property-liability insurers. By matching assets and liabilities, for example, banks avoid the problem of investing long term (fixed-rate mortgages), while borrowing short term (passbook savings accounts and short-term certificates of deposit). If assets and liabilities were not matched, banks would be exposed to interest-rate risk: a rise in interest rates would increase the cost of funds but would not increase the investment income.

If a property-liability insurer were to adopt asset-liability matching, the payout pattern on existing liabilities would be matched by an investment portfolio that produced the cash flow as needed. Changes in interest rates would not affect the availability of cash, as the desired flow would be locked in.

Three arguments are raised against the need for property-liability insurers to adopt asset-liability matching. First, in most situations the cash inflow in a given period from new and renewal policies is adequate to pay all losses and expenses. Even if premium receipts were not enough to pay all losses and expenses, they are predictable enough to avoid the need to generate all cash needs from investments. A small margin of liquid assets could prevent an insurer from incurring losses on premature sale of assets. However, paying claims on prior policies with the cash flow on new policies does not reduce the mismatch that is occurring in the pricing of policies; it merely obscures it by spreading it into the future.

The second argument against asset-liability matching revolves around the predictability of payout patterns for property-liability insurers. For banks, the values of liabilities are fixed and the maturity dates of savings accounts are known. For insurers, the loss costs and payout dates are not certain, but must be estimated. Future inflation rates could affect the value of losses. An investment strategy that generates a predetermined amount of cash at a set time may not match the need for cash as the loss payouts develop. A rise in the rate of inflation would most likely increase the cost of losses while, at the same time, increasing interest rates. Thus, a more appropriate hedging strategy for a property-liability insurer might be to invest in maturities shorter than the indicated need for cash in order to reinvest at interest rates that more closely approximate the underlying rate of inflation that affects loss costs.

A final objection raised to asset-liability matching involves its cost. Most liabilities for property-liability insurers have fairly short durations. Estimates of the duration (see below) of loss reserves for property lines run in the range of one half year for property lines, between one and one and a half years for automobile,and two to five years for general liability and medical malpractice. An investment strategy that matched the average durations of liabilities would, under normal yield curve situations, give up two to three percentage points in interest rates from long-term bonds.

Duration

The commonly used measure of maturity for fixed-income investments is inappropriate for analyses of interest-rate risk because it considers only the time when the principal will be repaid. However, during the time until maturity, the asset will be generating interest income which is either used by the asset holder or reinvested at the then current interest rates. The effective yields based on market valuation on two bonds with the same maturity dates but different coupon rates would be the same under stable interest rates but would differ if interest rates change.

The duration of a security is the weighted average of the length of time until payments will be received by the holder. Duration can be calculated as shown in equation (2) under the assumption of a flat term structure of interest (level yield curve):

$$(2) \qquad D = \sum_{t=1}^{n} \frac{C_t(t)/(1+r)^t}{C_t/(1+r)^t}$$

Where C_t = interest or principal payment at time t
t = length of time to payment
n = length of time until maturity
r = yield to maturity

The denominator of the equation is the present value of the fixed income investment. The numerator is the present value of the payments weighted by the length of time until they are paid. The higher the duration, the longer into the future the payments will, on average, be received.

To illustrate the concept of duration, two bonds of \$1000 face value, each with a remaining maturity of five years and annual coupon payments, will be used. The first bond has a coupon rate of 6% and the second 12%. Each has a yield to maturity of 9%, reflecting current interest rates on five year bonds. The duration of the first bond is calculated by:

$$D_1 = \frac{\frac{(60)(1)}{1.09} + \frac{(60)(2)}{(1.09)^2} + \frac{(60)(3)}{(1.09)^3} + \frac{(60)(4)}{(1.09)^4} + \frac{(1060)(5)}{(1.09)^5}}{\frac{60}{1.09} + \frac{60}{(1.09)^2} + \frac{60}{(1.09)^3} + \frac{60}{(1.09)^4} + \frac{1060}{(1.09)^5}}$$

$$D_1 = 3909.70/883.32 = 4.426$$

The duration of the second bond is calculated similarly, except the coupon is 12%, or 120 per year, rather than 60 per year.

$$D_2 = \frac{\dfrac{(120)(1)}{1.09} + \dfrac{(120)(2)}{(1.09)^2} + \dfrac{(120)(3)}{(1.09)^3} + \dfrac{(120)(4)}{(1.09)^4} + \dfrac{(1120)(5)}{(1.09)^5}}{\dfrac{120}{1.09} + \dfrac{120}{(1.09)^2} + \dfrac{120}{(1.09)^3} + \dfrac{120}{(1.09)^4} + \dfrac{1120}{(1.09)^5}}$$

$$D_2 = 4569.74/1116.68 = 4.092$$

The duration of the second bond is less than the duration of the first bond because the interim payments are larger. The weighted average of the date of the receipt of cash from the second bond is sooner than that of the first bond.

Duration is commonly calculated on fixed-income assets in which the coupon payments and principal are known. For property-liability insurers, the duration of liabilities, particularly loss reserves, can also be determined, although not with certainty. In this context the duration of liabilities would simply be the weighted average of the length of time until the payments will be made.

Immunization

Immunization of a portfolio is any strategy that eliminates price risk and coupon reinvestment risk on a fixed-income portfolio. Asset-liability matching is one method of immunization, but it requires an exact balancing of income from investments against cash needs. A less restrictive method of immunization is for the duration of the investment portfolio to equal the duration of the cash flow needs, or the duration of the assets to equal the duration of the liabilities.

On an immunized portfolio, interest-rate changes affect the two investment risks in offsetting ways. A rise in interest rates lowers the market price of outstanding bonds, but allows reinvestment of income to be made at a higher rate, preventing a change in eventual cash flow. A drop in interest rates raises the price of outstanding bonds but reduces the reinvestment rate. Thus, the predicted amount of cash can be available when needed.

The immunization strategy can be thwarted if the yield curve changes shape. If short-term interest rates fall proportionately more than long-term rates, the reinvestment rate will drop more than the price of outstanding issues will increase. Theoretically, the investment portfolio can be adjusted continually to minimize such distortions, but this increases the cost of this strategy. Also, the liabilities of property liability insurers can differ from the original forecast, making even an immunized portfolio inadequate to meet the new cash flow needs.

Taxation

The Tax Reform Act of 1986 (TRA) dramatically changed the income tax regulations for the property-liability insurance industry. The overall effect of this new law is still uncertain and many of the interpretations of statutory language are in the process of being clarified. The major provisions of TRA will be discussed here, but the reader is urged to refer to more complete and timely sources for a full explanation of this watershed tax legislation.

The stated goal of TRA was to raise significant tax revenue from the property-liability insurance industry starting in 1987. One provision of TRA is the delegation of a study to determine the amount of revenue being raised and to recommend any necessary changes in the tax law to achieve the intended target. One reason for the concentration on tax revenue is the federal budget deficit, currently running in the $150–200 billion level annually. The property-liability insurance industry was the target of such a significant change in tax regulations as a result of the failure of the prior tax code to produce any significant revenue from the industry. In fact, during the five-year period 1982-1986, the property liability insurance industry in aggregate recouped $6.2 billion in taxes previously paid. The sudden shift from recouping an average of $1.2 billion in taxes per year to paying $1–2 billion per year is bound to cause distortions and market tightening, as well as require price increases industry-wide.

In addition to the aggregate negative tax position of the property liability insurance industry, several other situations called attention to the industry during discussion about the 1986 tax legislation. Retroactive insurance was becoming a feasible product, fueled in part by tax subsidies and the differential tax treatment of property-liability insurers. After the MGM Grand Hotel suffered a major fire loss, it purchased additional coverage for less than the expected value of the losses that were incurred. The insurers expected that they could profit from this below cost pricing by immediately establishing loss reserves at the expected loss level and reporting an underwriting loss for tax purposes. This loss generated tax savings which, in addition to the net premium, could be invested until the losses were paid. Thus, the tax code was subsidizing insurers in pricing coverage to the extent that known losses could be covered by insurance more inexpensively than if the non-insurance corporation paid the loss itself. The tax regulations for non-insurance firms allow a tax deduction for losses only when the losses are paid, not when they are incurred. In addition to generating a market for retroactive insurance, this differential contributed to the growth in captive insurance companies as they attempted, unsuccessfully it turned out, to qualify for classification as insurers. This would have allowed the parent firm to utilize the more favorable rules of deducting losses when incurred rather than when paid.

Another aspect of the property-liability insurance industry that caught the tax reformers' attention was the growing practice of loss reserve transfers. Insurers were using this strategy to optimize the use of taxable income and tax loss carrybacks. Under this approach, an insurer with an excess of tax losses would sell loss reserves to another insurer in a tax-paying position through the use of reinsurance. The first insurer would transfer loss reserves to the second insurer and, at the same time, pay the second insurer a premium that was less than the statutory value of the losses, but more than the present value of those losses. The first insurer would immediately book an underwriting gain equal to the difference between the premium and the statutory loss reserve value. The second insurer would book an underwriting loss, which could be used to offset other taxable income.

The primary provision in insurance tax regulations that generated negative tax payments for the prior five years and promoted retroactive insurance, the growth of captives, and loss reserve transfers, was the ability of insurers to deduct the total future value of loss and loss adjustment expense payments on incurred losses as opposed to their economic worth, or present value. Discounting loss reserves at an appropriate rate would alleviate this problem. Although discounting of loss reserves was included in TRA, the mandated discount rate is not necessarily the appropriate rate, and several other, far more onerous, provisions were included in TRA.

For property-liability insurers, the primary provisions of TRA are to:

1. Tax previously tax-exempt interest and dividends
2. Include a portion of the unearned premium reserve as taxable income
3. Discount loss reserves for tax purposes
4. Eliminate the Protection Against Loss (PAL) account
5. Apply a strict Alternative Minimum Tax (AMT) to insurers as well as corporations in general

Tax Exempt Interest and Dividends

Municipal bonds have traditionally been exempt from federal income taxation as a subsidy to state and local government units in raising revenue. The property-liability insurance industry has been a heavy investor in such issues. A common investment strategy has been to invest in taxable bond issues to the extent of offsetting any underwriting losses, with the remainder of the investment portfolio invested in municipal bonds. This strategy led to the low effective tax rates on property-liability insurers during the past decade.

Common and preferred-stock dividends from domestic corporations have also received favorable tax treatment. In order to avoid double taxation of dividends for corporate investors, an income-tax deduction of 85% of the dividends received was allowed prior to TRA. Under TRA, this deduction was reduced to 80% of dividends received and subsequent legislation further reduced it to 70%. Thus, all municipal bond income and 70% of dividend income is exempt from taxation for corporate investors. However, TRA reduces the loss reserve deduction by 15% of this otherwise tax-free income on any investment acquired after August 7, 1986, in essence taxing 15% of this income.

Unearned Premium Reserve

The unearned premium reserve is the pro rata portion of premiums that reflect unexpired coverage. As expenses tend to be paid at the beginning of the exposure period and losses generated proportionally over the coverage period, the unearned premium reserve includes a well recognized redundancy to the extent that the reserve still includes a provision for previously paid expenses. This redundancy is commonly termed the "equity in the unearned premium reserve." This "equity" varies depending on the individual insurer's expense ratio and expected loss ratio. Accordingly, it would be highest for lines of business and insurers with high expense ratios and lowest for lines and insurers with low expense ratios. This distinction is not recognized under the revised tax regulations. Under TRA, 20% of the change in the unearned premium reserve will be included in taxable income. In addition, 20% of the unearned premium reserve as of December 31, 1986, will be included in taxable income ratably over the six-year period beginning in 1987. Thus, for 1987, taxable income included 20% of the change in unearned premium reserve from 12/31/86 to 12/31/87 plus 3.33% (one-sixth of 20%) of the 12/31/86 unearned premium reserve.

Loss Reserves

Prior to TRA, statutory loss and loss adjustment expense reserves were used to calculate taxable income. These statutory values are intended to be the total undiscounted value of all loss and loss adjustment expense payments to be made in the future for losses that have occurred prior to the evaluation date. By not adjusting for the present value of these payments, a payout to be made in ten years is valued equally with an imminent payout.

TRA requires discounting of loss and loss adjustment expense reserves for determining taxable income. The interest rate to be used for discounting is the five-year moving average of the Applicable Federal Rate on three- to nine-year securities, but months prior to August, 1986, are not included in the calculation. For accident year 1987 and prior, the average rate for the months of August, 1986, through December, 1986, is to be used. This rate is 7.20%. For accident year 1988, the average rate for August, 1986, through December, 1987, 7.77%, will be used.

The payment pattern for loss and loss adjustment expense reserves can be either the pattern promulgated by the Treasury Department, based on industry experience through 1985 as reported by A. M. Best, or a company's individual experience. Whichever choice an insurer makes for determining 1987 taxable income will be binding for five years. The payment pattern determined by the Treasury Department will not be updated during that five-year period. An insurer electing to use its own payout pattern must update the values each year, but only with respect to the new accident year. Payout patterns on prior years cannot be changed, even if the actual loss payment differs from the original projection.

A fresh-start approach is applied to discounting loss reserves. For 1987, the discounted loss and loss adjustment expense reserves for both beginning and ending reserves will be calculated and the difference included in the taxable income determination. Without the fresh start approach, ending reserves would have been discounted but not beginning reserves, which would have substantially increased taxable income for 1987.

Protection Against Loss (PAL) Account

Prior to the TRA, mutual property-liability insurers were allowed a tax deduction for contributions to a fund that could be drawn upon as needed in times of unprofitability. This fund, termed the Protection Against Loss (PAL) fund, was justified based on the inability of mutual insurers to raise capital by issuing equity, as stock insurers could do if additional funding were required. Maximum contributions were related to premiums written. The deduction for PAL accounts was repealed, starting in 1987. Amounts in existing PAL accounts can continue to be treated as provided by pre-TRA provisions: 1) the accounts are accumulated until offset by taxable losses, 2) amounts not absorbed by the fifth year are included in taxable income except for one-half of 25% of underwriting gains, 3) any continuing amount is included in taxable income when the insurer ceases to qualify as a mutual insurer.

Alternative Minimum Tax (AMT)

The more stringent provisions of the corporate Alternative Minimum Tax regulations will result in most property-liability insurers' calculating two indicated tax amounts and paying the higher. The regular tax is calculated on the regular taxable income; the AMT is calculated from the alternative minimum taxable income (AMTI). The AMTI is determined by adding tax-preference items to the regular taxable income. These preference items include:

1) book income versus regular taxable income
2) certain tax-exempt income
3) accelerated depreciation

Book income will normally be the statutory annual statement income after dividends to policyholders but before income taxes. However, if GAAP statements are filed with the Securities and Exchange Commission or audited financial statements used for other purposes, these income values take precedence over annual statement data. The tax-preference item for the years 1987 through 1989 is 50% of the difference between the book income and the AMTI excluding this item. After 1989 the preference item will be 75% of the difference between adjusted current earnings and AMTI before this adjustment. The definition of adjusted current earnings has not been finalized at the time this is being written (early 1989).

Tax-exempt interest on certain private activity bonds (e.g., industrial development bonds) issued after August 7, 1986, is included as a tax-preference item. Also, any depreciation taken in excess of the 150% declining balance method for tangible personal property or over 40-year straight-line depreciation for real property will be included as a preference item.

Tax and Investment Strategies

An entirely new operating strategy for property-liability insurers emerges as a result of TRA. Insurers will pay the larger of the regular tax or the AMT. Net after-tax income is generally maximized when the two taxes are equal. Thus, insurers should manage their investment portfolios by shifting assets between taxable and tax-exempt investments, depending on the relative yields and the company's tax calculations. Projected underwriting losses, based on discounted loss reserves and including part of the unearned premium reserve as income, will indicate the optimal investment mix. As the final tax liabilities will not be known until after the year is over, this strategy involves forecasting and rebalancing during the year to achieve the optimal after-tax income. In addition, the consequences of misestimation on either side are not equal. The penalty associated with the AMT is more severe in that, starting in 1990, no credit for AMT carryforward will be allowed, so the insurer should aim to err on the side of the regular tax calculation.

The need for coordination between underwriting and investment operations will be increased as a result of TRA. Actuaries will most likely be involved in developing this tax strategy because underwriting results must be forecast and loss reserves discounted. This new role for actuaries increases the need for actuaries to master investment and tax issues.

Rate of Return Measures

In order to quantify the profitability of the property-liability insurance industry, users of financial data have developed a number of measures that are relied upon to provide some insight into current and past operating results. Some of these measures are easy to calculate, and others are more complex. Some measures are widely used, whereas others are applied only in the more complex rate-regulatory hearings and in sophisticated company analyses. In this section we will describe several of these measures, discuss the meaning of the values, and analyze the strengths and weaknesses of the measures.

Combined Ratio

The combined ratio is determined in two different ways. It can be calculated as the sum of the loss ratio and the expense ratio, or as this sum plus the policyholders' dividends ratio. The loss ratio is determined by dividing the incurred losses, including all loss adjustment expenses, by the earned premium. The expense ratio is calculated by dividing expenses by the written premium. The policyholders' dividend ratio is determined by dividing dividends by earned premium. The combined ratio thus involves combining ratios with different denominators.

The combined ratio is calculated in the foregoing manner to make an approximate adjustment for the different rates at which losses and expenses tend to be incurred for property-liability insurers. Losses tend to be incurred evenly over the coverage period for most lines of business. If a policy is for an annual term, then, except for slight seasonal patterns, losses are likely to occur evenly over the year. One-twelfth of the losses are expected to occur in the first month the policy is in force, one-half by the middle of the exposure period, and so forth. Therefore, losses that have been incurred are divided by the earned premium to determine the portion of the premium incurred on losses to date.

Conversely, expenses for such items as commissions, premium taxes, policy coding costs, and overhead, tend to be incurred about the time the policy is written. Thus, the expenses are divided by the premium written to determine the portion of premiums that are used to cover expenses.

For an insurer that is writing a constant premium volume, eventually the written and earned premiums will be equal. In this case, the use of the different denominators in the combined ratio will not have any effect. However, most insurers do not write a constant level of premiums. During inflationary periods, even an insurer not writing any increase in exposures will be experiencing an increase in written premium. In general, the written premium exceeds the earned premium unless an insurer is scaling back operations. The combined ratio adjusts the expenditure pattern to reflect the different rates of payouts for losses and expenses for this normal difference, creating a better match between the numerators and the denominators and more accurately reflecting the true underlying experience which will eventually emerge.

The loss ratio included in the combined ratio is generally a calendar-year value. As any changes in reserve adequacy over the year distort calendar-year-loss ratios, the combined ratio will also be affected. An alternative approach is to use accident-year loss ratios, but other drawbacks exist for this measure. Accurate accident-year values would only be available for years long past, when the usefulness for the information is lessened. The accuracy of the accident-year loss ratios for current years depends on the accuracy of the loss reserve estimates and the combined ratios based on accident-year loss ratios for a given year can change over time.

The combined ratio is easy to calculate and widely used within companies and in public discussion of insurance profitability. Table 8-6 shows the combined ratio including dividends to policyholders for the period 1927 through 1987 for all stock property-liability insurers. This graph shows that the combined ratio fluctuates considerably and the levels during the mid-1980s were unusually high. Many industry publications concentrate on the combined ratio as a measure of financial health of the insurance industry. Levels below 100% indicate that an insurer, or the industry, is paying out less in losses, expenses, and dividends than it is taking in as premium, and therefore is profitable, even ignoring investment income. Levels in excess of 100% indicate that expenditures exceed premium income. Interpretation of the meaning of such values is difficult and often leads to erroneous statements. As the insurance industry receives both premium and investment income, the fact that losses and expenses exceed the premium income does not necessarily mean that the insurance industry is losing money or not achieving an adequate rate of return. Conversely, for coverages that are paid quickly, the fact that the combined ratio is below 100% does not mean that it is achieving an adequate profit.

FIGURE 8-6
Combined Ratio

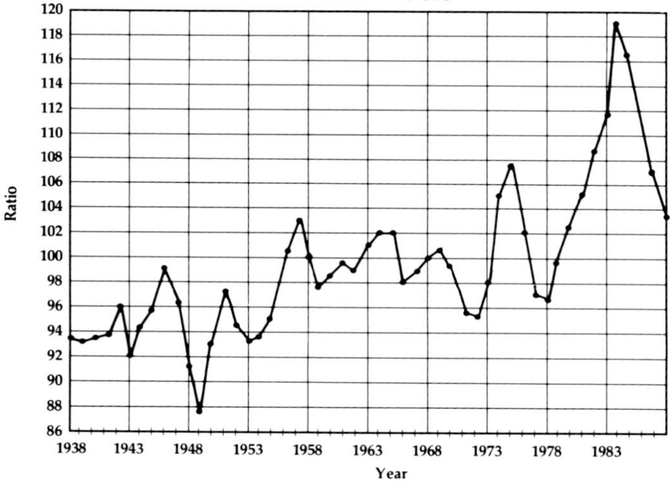

Source: Best's Aggregates & Average (P/C) 1988, 1977, 1968

The advantage of the combined ratio as a measure of insurance performance is its simplicity. However, this also leads to its major problem. The combined ratio does not include any provision for investment income. As insurers generally pay losses after premium is received, they earn investment income prior to payment of claims. If the delay between receipt of premium and payment of losses were stable among lines and over time, and the interest rate on invested funds were constant, then the contribution of investment income to insurer profitability would be consistent and an easy adjustment to the combined ratio could be made. Unfortunately, loss payout patterns vary among lines of business and over time, and interest rates have been volatile, especially over the past two decades. Thus, a combined ratio of 110%, for example, could be acceptable if the loss payout pattern is slow, as in liability lines, and interest rates high.

Conversely, if the loss payout pattern is rapid, as in a property line, and/or interest rates are at the low end of the cycle over the period, then the same 110% combined ratio could indicate a pricing problem.

An example of a combined ratio calculation is shown in Table 8-7, which represents an illustrative insurance company income statement. The combined ratio of 110.1% is determined by adding incurred losses and loss adjustment expenses divided by the net earned premium ((68 + 10)/95) to the other underwriting expenses divided by net written premium (28/100). This is a calendar-year combined ratio figure. The accident-year combined ratio is 112.2%, based on accident year losses and loss adjustment expenses of $80 million, as shown in the Discounting section of Table 8-7.

TABLE 8-7
Sample Income Statement

Competitive Insurance Company
(Dollar figures are in millions)

Underwriting Income	
Net Written Premium	$100
Net Earned Premium	95
Incurred Losses	68
Loss Adjustment Expense Incurred	10
Other Underwriting Expenses	28
Net Underwriting Gain or Loss	−11
Investment Income	
Net Investment Income Earned	14
Net Realized Capital Gains or Losses	2
Net Investment Gain or Loss	16
Net Income Determination	
Net Income Before Dividends to Policyholders and Income Taxes	5
Dividends to Policyholders	2.5
Federal and Foreign Income Taxes Incurred	−1.5
Net Income	4
Capital and Surplus Account	
Beginning Surplus	57

continued on next page

Table 8-7 (continued)

Gains and Losses in Surplus	
Net Income	4
Net Unrealized Capital Gains or Losses	1
Ending Surplus	62
Average Statutory Surplus	59.5
Rate Of Return Measures	
Combined Ratio	
Loss and Loss Adjustment Expense Ratio	82.1%
Expense Ratio	28.0
Combined Ratio	110.1
Underwriting Profit Margin	
Underwriting Profit Margin	—10.1
Operating Ratio	
A) Net Investment Income Earned/ Earned Premium	14.7
B) Net Investment Gain or Loss/ Earned Premium	16.8
C) Net Investment Gain or Loss Including UnrealizedCapital Gains or Losses/ Earned Premium	17.9
Operating Ratio Based on A	95.4
Operating Ratio Based on B	93.3
Operating Ratio Based on C	92.2
Discounting	
Accident Year Experience	
Paid Loss and Loss Adjustment Expenses	$35
Undiscounted Loss and LAE Reserves	45*
Discounted Loss and LAE Reserves	36
Loss and LAE Ratio — Undiscounted	84.2%
Accident Year Combined Ratio	112.2
Loss and LAE Ratio — Discounted	74.7
Accident Year Combined Ratio — Discounted	102.7
Return on Equity Measures	
Net Income/Average Statutory Surplus	6.7
Net Income plus Unrealized Capital Gains or Losses/Average Statutory Surplus	8.4

*Note that the calendar year incurred loss and loss adjustment expenses total $78 million but the accident year loss and LAE equal $80 million. This would result if favorable development were experienced on prior years' loss and LAE reserves.

Underwriting Profit Margin

The underwriting profit margin is calculated by subtracting the combined ratio from 100%. Conversely, the expected loss ratio is often determined by subtracting the sum of the target underwriting profit margin and the expense ratio from 100%. For the illustration on Table 8-2, the underwriting profit margin is −10.1%, based on this calculation. The underwriting profit margin suffers from the same basic problem as the combined ratio since the underwriting profit margin is calculated from the same data; investment income is not included. Thus, determining the appropriate underwriting profit margin is difficult.

Historically, the property-liability insurance industry sought to achieve standard underwriting profit margins. The industry standard was 2.5% for workers' compensation and 5% for all other lines. These standards were derived from the 1920 era of insurance regulation and had no mathematical or economic support. By achieving a 5% underwriting profit margin, an insurer was, in the long run, retaining 5% of sales, which was considered a reasonable proportion. This measure was not equated to a return-on-equity measure. As investment income was not included, it did not reflect total insurance profitability. Also, as different insurers operated at different premium-to-surplus ratios, total return on equity would vary among insurers with the same underwriting profit margins.

Fluctuations in the underwriting profit margin occur normally as a result of catastrophic losses and other unpredicted developments, as well as varying intensity of competition in the industry. The gradual increasing trend of the combined ratio shown in Table 8-1 (and therefore the decreasing trend of the underwriting profit margin) is the result of competitive pressures as longer payout patterns and higher interest rates developed. Negative underwriting profit margins occurred in almost each year since 1973, which some industry spokespersons claimed indicated inadequate rates. Although the statement about inadequate rates may have been true, negative underwriting profit margins do not, by themselves, lead to this conclusion.

Operating Ratio

The failure of the combined ratio and the underwriting profit margin to include the effect of investment income has led to the emphasis on the operating ratio as a profitability measure. The operating ratio is calculated by subtracting the ratio of investment income divided by the earned premium from the combined ratio. Thus, investment income is "included" in the profitability measure.

A number of problems still exist in the use of the operating ratio as a measure of profitability. The first problem is the definition of investment income. Some users of financial data include only net investment income earned which consists of interest and dividends received. Others use the net investment gain or loss value, which includes net realized capital gains and losses as well as investment income. A third possible definition of investment income includes net unrealized capital gains and losses in addition to the other components. Thus, three possible operating ratios can be calculated, leading to considerable confusion.

Regardless of which definition of the investment income is used, potential problems result. The most commonly used definition of investment income is net investment income earned. This is not a realistic measure of investment income for any investment other than very short-term debt instruments. Longer-term bonds pay interest and also experience fluctuations in value as interest rates and credit conditions change. Thus, the actual rate of return differs from simply the interest received. For investments in equities, the dividend income is generally only a small portion of the total investment income expected. Capital gains are expected to occur to provide the required rate of return commensurate with the investment risk accepted. Similarly, investments in real estate are also expected to produce capital gains.

An insurer could intentionally generate zero dollars of net investment income earned by investing in zero coupon bonds and common stock in firms that do not pay dividends. Such an investment strategy would produce a high operating ratio that would not reflect the investment income potential of the insurer. Thus, some reflection of capital gains is necessary to produce a reasonable measure of investment income. Therefore, the second operating ratio measure includes net realized capital gains and losses with net investment income, the total of which is termed the net investment gain or loss.

The problem with using realized gains and losses to measure investment income is the timing factor involved in this determination. Realized gains and losses occur when an asset is sold, and reflect all the change in value that has occurred since the asset was purchased. If an insurer does not sell any capital assets, then, regardless of the change in values of investments, no capital gains or losses would be recorded. When an asset is sold, though, all of the change in value is reflected in that year, even though all or most of the change may have occurred in prior years. Thus, unless an insurer is experiencing a constant portfolio turnover and consistent appreciation in asset values, the net realized capital gains and losses value will fluctuate considerably and will not necessarily reflect current investment earnings.

The third measure of investment income includes the change in unrealized capital gains and losses in addition to the net investment gain or loss. By including unrealized gains and losses, all investment performance is reflected in this profitability measure. By adding or subtracting the change in unrealized gains and losses to the net realized gains and losses, only the investment gains experienced during the current year are reflected. Changes in asset values that occurred in prior years would not distort the results.

Several problems still exist with this measure of the operating ratio. One problem is the degree of fluctuation that will occur as a result of changes in equity values. A rapidly rising stock market will inflate the investment income measure and reduce the operating ratio. A falling stock market will reduce the investment income value. This increased volatility is a cost of fully reflecting investment income in the operating results of insurance companies.

Another problem is that insurance accounting conventions value bonds at amortized values rather than market values. Thus, unrealized capital gains and losses for bonds are not representative of market values but are based on the values when the assets were purchased and the time left until maturity. In this regard, the investment income value based on reported unrealized capital gains and losses is not a true market measure.

Another major problem with all of the operating ratio measures is the mismatch in the asset base that generated the investment income and the earned premium that is used as the denominator in the calculation. To a large extent, the investable assets currently generating the investment income were produced by premium writings in prior years. The loss reserve outstanding comes from both current and prior years' writings. However, all the investment income is being credited against the current year's experience. This distortion will most significantly affect rapidly growing or declining insurers. However, even insurers with a stable premium volume may experience a change in loss payout patterns so that the operating ratio is distorted.

Calculations of the three different operating ratios are demonstrated in Table 8-7. To determine the first operating ratio, the ratio of net investment income to earned premium (14/95 = 14.7%) is subtracted from the combined ratio of 110.1% to yield 95.4%. For the second operating ratio, the net realized gains and losses are added to the net investment income and the sum divided by earned premium ((2 + 14)/95 = 16.8%). This ratio is then subtracted from the combined ratio to yield an operating ratio of 93.3%. The final operating ratio includes the unrealized gains and losses of $1 million in addition to the net investment income and realized gains and losses ((14 + 2 + 1)/95 = 17.9%). Subtracting this value from the combined ratio yields an operating ratio of 92.2%.

The operating ratios for the insurance industry for the period 1983 through 1987 (the only years that the necessary information is available), based on the net investment income earned, net investment gain or loss and the net investment gain or loss including unrealized capital gains or losses, are shown in Table 8-8. These values are calculated from the consolidated industry Annual Statement data published by A. M. Best Company.

Combined Ratio Based on Discounted Losses

The Tax Reform Act of 1986 instituted the discounting of property-liability loss reserves for tax purposes. Also in 1986, the National Association of Insurance Commissioners created a Working Group on Discounting Loss Reserves to consider changing statutory accounting provisions. The effect of discounting loss reserves is to reflect the time value of money in the reserving process, and hence net income. Undiscounted reserves value loss payments in future years equally with current loss payments. Statutory reserving requirements currently prohibit discounting loss reserves except those where the future payment stream is definite as to timing and amount. An example of such a claim would be a long-term workers' compensation indemnity case where predetermined benefits are paid at a periodic rate for a prescribed duration. A stated rationale

TABLE 8-8
Industry Operating Ratios

	1983	1984	1985	1986	1987
Combined Ratio After Dividends	112.0	118.0	116.5	108.0	104.6
Net Investment Income/EP	14.9	15.4	14.6	13.2	12.7
Operating Ratio I	97.1	102.6	101.7	94.8	91.9
Net Investment Gain/EP	16.9	18.0	18.7	17.3	14.4
Operating Ratio II	95.1	100.0	97.6	90.7	90.2
Net Investment Gain Including Unrealized Gains & Losses/EP	18.1	15.5	22.7	18.5	12.8
Operating Ratio III	93.9	102.5	93.6	89.5	91.8

Source: *Best's Aggregates & Averages (Prop./Cas.)*, 1984–1988, A.M. Best Co. Inc.

for using undiscounted loss reserves is to instill a level of conservatism into the reported financial position of insurers.

The level of conservatism included by not discounting property-liability loss reserves depends on the loss payout pattern of the line of business, on the general level of interest rates and on the amount of ad hoc discounting performed by insurers who realize the undiscounted loss reserves are excessive and therefore make unreasonably optimistic assumptions about future loss development. As the concentration of the industry moved from property to liability insurance, the loss payout patterns lengthened. Also, over the last several decades the general level of interest rates has increased. Thus, the degree of conservatism engendered by not discounting statutory loss reserves has increased, assuming no change in the reserve adequacy position of the industry. As taxable income was traditionally based on statutory accounting conventions, the federal government's tax receipts from the property-liability insurance industry eroded. Over the period 1976 through 1986, the industry as a whole did not pay any federal income taxes. The revenue needs of the federal government led to the adoption of discounting for tax purposes.

Discounting loss reserves at an appropriate rate of interest for the calculation of incurred losses would present the relevant economic value of losses instead of simply the sum of the stream of payments ignoring the time value of money. In addition, loss reserve discounting can be justified based on a desire to match revenues and expenses correctly, if premium rates have been lowered in recognition of the time value of money. Once the loss payout pattern is estimated, the primary problem is the determination of the appropriate discount rate. Rates that have been proposed include:

1) the current risk-free rate as measured by the return on short-term U. S. Treasury bonds

2) the rate of return earned by the industry over a particular recent time interval

3) the rate of return achieved by the specific insurer over a particular recent time interval or

4) a selected interest rate based on a specific index over a particular time interval.

No general consensus exists as to the proper discount rate. Basic finance theory suggests that the appropriate discount rate should reflect the relevant risk of the loss payment pattern. The Capital Asset Pricing Model (CAPM), a widely used model for analyzing security returns discussed in some detail in the next section, would determine this rate based on the systematic risk of loss payout patterns. Systematic risk is the covariance of returns for a given asset with the returns of the market as a whole scaled by the variance of the market returns. The Arbitrage Pricing Model (APM), a more recent and more general model for determining security returns, would base the discount rate on the results of a factor analysis of historical experience. Under the APM covariance of returns with factors in addition to, or in place of, the market as a whole would affect the relevant risk of an asset. The sparsity of market-value information on loss reserves makes the determination of a market-driven discount rate difficult. As insurance prices are affected by current, rather than historical, interest rates, the interest rate achievable by the insurer when the policies are written would be a better measure than the proposals to use moving averages of past interest rates, either general or company-specific. The most commonly used discount rate, for reasons of simplicity rather than technical accuracy, is the current risk-free interest rate.

Use of the current short-term U. S. Treasury bond interest rate to discount the loss payout pattern in the calculation of the incurred loss ratio would have the effect of including the time value of money in the combined ratio. Thus, investment income does not have to be factored in separately, as currently introduced in the operating ratio. The loss payout pattern expected to apply to the current book of business is used. Also, the current market conditions on risk free investments are applied. This measure avoids the distortions caused in the investment income measures when equity and other risky assets experience marked price movements in a given year.

Woll (1987) applies a similar technique in his paper "Insurance Profits: Keeping Score." The accident-year combined ratio based on discounted loss reserves is also illustrated in Table 8-7. The discounted accident-year combined ratio is the sum of paid losses and LAE and the discounted reserve for future loss and LAE payments divided by the earned premium [(35 + 36)/95 = 74.7%] plus the expense ratio (28/100 = 28.0%), which totals 102.7%. This compares with the undiscounted accident-year combined ratio of 112.2%.

Return on Equity

Corporate financial analysis commonly uses a value termed the return on equity (ROE) to measure profitability. This value is calculated by dividing the net profit after taxes available to common stockholders (after deducting preferred dividends) by the value of the common equity in the firm. The value of common equity is traditionally a book value either at the beginning of the year or the average of the beginning and ending values. The common equity values are not based on market value, although this may be a more appropriate measure.

Return on equity values can similarly be derived for property-liability insurers, but several adjustments are needed. Initially, a determination of net profit must be made. This value can be either on a statutory or GAAP basis. Neither profit figure includes unrealized capital gains or losses incurred during the period. For an insurer with significant values in this category, the ROE value would be distorted. However, if unrealized gains or losses were to be included, they cannot simply be added (or subtracted) from the net profit value. The present value of future taxes associated with realization of these gains or losses must be accounted for before an adjustment to the net profit figure is made.

The primary advantage of a return on equity measure is that it allows a comparison of insurance profitability with other industries.

All prior profitability measures discussed are specific to insurance companies. Return on equity measures for other industries are readily available for comparison purposes. However, the comparison of return on equity values must be done with care. Many industries have recognized distortions either in the net profit figure or the book values. For example, loan loss reserves for banks are often well below the level needed to absorb problem loans. Also, natural resource firms often carry assets at purchase price rather than market price. For the property-liability insurance industry, the distortions in net profits and book value must be recognized in order to interpret the ROE results meaningfully. Among the problems with statutory financial statements are:

1) the equity in the unearned premium reserve is not recognized
2) bonds are valued at amortized rather than market value
3) loss and loss adjustment expense reserves are carried at the sum of estimated future payments rather than the present value, and the estimates may be inadequate or redundant
4) anticipated salvage and subrogation is not recognized
5) some assets are not included in statutory surplus, such as nonadmitted reinsurance

Two return-on-equity values are illustrated in Table 8-7. The first divides the statutory net income by the average statutory surplus (average of beginning and ending values) during the year ($4/59.5 = 6.7\%$). The second includes the effect of unrealized capital gains and losses [$(4 + 1)/59.5 = 8.4\%$]. Neither of these values adjusts the surplus for the cited distortions.

Internal Rate of Return

The internal rate of return of an investment is the mathematically determined discount rate that sets the present value of the total cash flow equal to zero. When discounted at the internal rate of return, the present value of the cash inflows equals the present value of the cash outflows. For standard investment decisions, the initial investment outlay is the cash outflow and the subsequent receipts are the cash inflows. The situation is reversed when the internal rate of return is calculated from the insurer's point of view on an insurance policy. The standard treatment of this transaction is that the insurer receives a cash inflow when the policy is written, pays some expenses immediately and others in future periods, and pays losses in the future as well. In order for a positive internal rate of return to result, expenses and losses must exceed premium. (This would result in a combined ratio in excess of 100%.)

A more realistic description of the cash flows involved for insurance policies would have some expenses incurred prior to writing the policy. These prepaid expenses would include policy development costs and training expenditures. Other expenses would be paid when the policy is actually written. Premium income would be received several months after the policy is written, representing lags in collecting premiums from agents or insureds. Additional expenses and the losses would be paid subsequent to the receipt of premium. Following loss payments, salvage, subrogation, and reinsurance payments might be received.

This more representative cash flow model would thus entail cash outflows preceding and following the cash inflow, with the potential for more cash inflows at the end of the sequence. Solving the discount rate that sets the present value of the cash flows to zero may yield multiple values. Mathematically, the number of discount rates that solve the equation equals the number of sign reversals in the cash flow. Selecting the proper internal rate of return from competing values is occasionally a complex endeavor.

For example, assume that an insurer experiences the following cash flow pattern in writing a policy, based on incurring $10 of expenses associated with the policy 5 years prior to receiving premium income (training sales force, setting up computer system, etc.), receiving $45 on net premium (premiums less concurrent expenses such as commissions), and then pays a total of $35 in losses over the next four years as indicated:

Year	Cash Flow
0	−10
5	45
6	−10
7	−10
8	−10
9	−5

The two internal rates of return from this cash flow pattern, resulting from the two changes in sign of the cash flow, are 0% and 13%. The mathematically relevant internal rate of return is 13%. Thus, the insurer writing this business would be receiving a 13% rate of return on this business.

Impact of Investment Income on Pricing

Standard Profit Formula

From the promulgation of the 1921 standard profit formula until the mid-1960s, investment income was virtually ignored in insurance ratemaking. In establishing the 5% underwriting profit benchmark, the majority report of the 1921 Fire Insurance Committee of the National Convention of Insurance Commissioners concluded that "no part of the so-called banking profit (or loss) should be considered in arriving at the underwriting profit (or loss)." The model bill for state rate regulation approved by the National Association of Insurance Commissioners (NAIC) in 1946, in the wake of the McCarran-Ferguson Act's affirmation of the rights of states to regulate insurance, included the provision that "due consideration shall be given . . . to a reasonable margin for underwriting profit and contingencies . . ." All but eight states adopted the model bill including this provision. The other eight states excluded the word "underwriting." Despite the different statutory language, by the early 1960s a 5% underwriting profit margin was the normal loading for all lines except workers' compensation, where a 2.5% loading was accepted. This lower rate for workers' compensation was justified on the basis that the more stringent regulation applicable to this line of business would make it less risky (an arguable point), as well as on the basis that the longer payout pattern on losses would generate more investment income.

In addition to an established profit margin target, provision in insurance rates was made for a contingencies factor. The general concept of a contingencies factor was to provide a cushion in rate levels for events that could not be accurately forecast, such as severe economic conditions, unusual loss occurrences, or other "unpredictable" developments. Thus, the total factor included in the rate level was for a "profit and contingencies" factor. Lehmann (1985) discusses the contingencies factor in some detail. An in-depth discussion of the issues involved in including investment income in ratemaking is provided in the 1984 Investment Income Task Force Report to the NAIC.

New Jersey Remand Decision

During the 1960s, Florida, Maryland and Virginia began to require the consideration of investment income in ratemaking. A 1969 New Jersey Supreme Court decision ruled that investment income could not be ignored in setting insurance rates and remanded the case for reconsideration by the insurance commissioner. That ruling led to the New Jersey Remand Decision of 1972, which established a fair rate of return for an insurer and reduced that value by the policyholders' share of investment earnings. The policyholders' share of investment earnings is measured by multiplying the insurer's portfolio rate of return by the unearned premium and loss reserves less deductions for prepaid expenses. Considerable controversy has raged in New Jersey over both the determination of the fair rate of return for insurers and the application of the specific formula for arriving at the target underwriting profit provision.

Capital Asset Pricing Model

In 1975, rate regulators in Massachusetts began to require the inclusion of investment income. Protracted hearings led to the introduction of the Capital Asset Pricing Model (CAPM) into insurance ratemaking. The basic formula of the CAPM is:

$$E(r_A) = r_F + \beta\left[E(r_M) - r_F\right]$$

where r_A = return on an asset
r_F = risk free rate of return
r_M = return on the market portfolio
β = systematic risk of asset
E = expectation operator (expected value)

Applying the CAPM to insurance pricing leads to the following (for the specific derivation see the Fairley paper included in Cummins and Harrington 1987):

$$E\,(r_U) = -k(1-x)r_F + \beta\left[E(r_M) - r_F\right]$$

where r_U = underwriting profit margin
k = investable funds per dollar of written premium
x = expense ratio
β = systematic underwriting risk

For example, if claims are paid on average 9 months after the premium is received, the expense ratio is 30%, the systematic underwriting risk has been determined to be 25%, the yield on short-term government bills is 7% and the expected stock market return is 15%, then the indicated underwriting profit margin can be determined as follows:

$k = .75$
$x = .30$
$\beta = .25$
$r_F = .07$
$E(r_M) = .15$

$$E(r_U) = -(.75)(1 - .30)(.07) + (.25)(.15 - .07) = -.0168$$

The theory behind the CAPM is that the equity markets are controlled by well diversified investors that are not concerned about the total risk (volatility of price) of an individual asset any more than an insurer is concerned about the risk of an individual policy. The law of large numbers assures that independent volatility (unsystematic risk) will be of no consequence in the total risk of a portfolio of either individual investments or policies. The factor that does concern investors is the systematic risk, or that risk that cannot be diversified away. Based on the assumption that insurers are owned by diversified investors (which may not hold true for mutual insurers), this theory leads to the conclusion that only systematic underwriting risk needs to be considered in pricing insurance products. A more detailed discussion of this approach can be found in the papers by Heinz Muller (1987, 1988) and Andrew Turner (1987).

A number of problems arise in applying the CAPM to insurance pricing. Market values of beta cannot be determined for individual lines since no single line insurer is publicly traded. Instead, accounting data is used to generate an assumed beta by measuring the fluctuations in reported underwriting profitability in line with stock market movements. No known technique demonstrates that accounting data can be used to determine betas for use in the CAPM. In addition to this problem, the betas calculated from accounting data are not stable over time, so use of a beta determined from historical data is unlikely to be valid for the ratemaking horizon.

Total Rate of Return Model

Other methods for including investment income in ratemaking have also arisen as alternatives to the New Jersey Remand methodology and the CAPM. One method commonly used by insurers is termed the total rate of return model (see Ferrari 1968). The common application of this technique is to select a target rate of return for a given line of insurance, either after analyzing its volatility or by use of a company-wide standard. In some cases, the target rate is allowed to vary to reflect the underwriting cycle, with a lower target during very competitive conditions and a higher target during tight market conditions. The contribution of investment income toward this total return is then projected, usually by multiplying the portfolio rate of return by the expected holding period for premium income, and subtracted from the target total return. The remainder of the target rate needs to be obtained from underwriting, providing a target underwriting profit margin.

An example of the total rate of return model is as follows:

$$TRR = (IA/S)(IRR) + (P/S)(UPM)$$

where TRR = Total Rate of Return
IA = Investable Assets
S = Surplus
IRR = Investment Rate of Return
P = Premium
UPM = Underwriting Profit Margin

If an insurer with investable assets of two times surplus and a premium-to-surplus ratio of three to one wanted to achieve a 15% total rate of return at a time when the investment rate of return equaled nine percent, then the appropriate underwriting profit margin would be minus 1%, based on the following solution:

$$.15 = (2)(.09) + (3)(UPM)$$

$$UPM = -.01$$

The major weaknesses of the target rate of return approach are the difficulty in determining the proper target return and the frequent use of portfolio rates of return to determine the investment income contribution. The appropriate target should be adjusted to reflect such economic conditions as the inflation rate and alternative investment returns, and perhaps competitive conditions in insurance markets, as well. The portfolio rate of return does not necessarily reflect what the insurer can earn on the investable funds generated from selling insurance in the current period.

Discounted Cash Flow Analysis

Another approach that has been proposed in regulatory hearings is termed discounted cash flow analysis. Under this technique, all of the cash flows emanating from writing a policy are projected, period by period. The cash flows include premium income, expenses, taxes, and loss payments. All cash flows are discounted to the beginning of the policy term by the appropriate discount rate. The primary drawback of this technique is the difficulty of determining the appropriate discount rate. This drawback is avoided if the calculation is made as an internal rate of return determination. One advocate of this technique proposed discounting losses and expenses by the CAPM determined discount rate $[E(r_A)]$ and taxes by the risk-free rate.

Florida Investment Income Methodology

The Florida Insurance Department adopted a ratemaking methodology in 1987 that combines investment income in the determination of the allowable underwriting profit margin by discounting premium income and loss payment patterns. Under this procedure, an insurer calculates the investment income opportunities for all sublines and sets the target underwriting profit margin for the subline with the smallest value at a level no larger than 5%. The investment income opportunities are determined by multiplying the estimated portfolio rate of return for the insurer by the average length of time the funds will be held before losses are paid. The allowable underwriting profit margin for each subline other than the one with the smallest investment income opportunity is determined by subtracting the investment income differential from the initial target underwriting profit margin. In addition to the profit margin as determined above, the statute also allows for a contingencies margin, which is always positive, that is added to the profit margin for the total profit and contingencies margin.

Arguments Against Using a Specific Formula

The various methodologies for including investment income in the determination of an allowable underwriting profit margin have the advantage of producing specific indications which can be used to establish rates. However, each method is subject to criticism for ignoring certain circumstances or for requiring a value to be estimated that is difficult or impossible to obtain. An alternative school argues that investment income should be given indirect consideration, rather than be included directly in the ratemaking process. The arguments in favor of this position are:

1. no formula approach is recognized as producing the correct results in all situations

2. the effect of competition on insurance prices is ignored in ratemaking formulas, but is crucial to the ability of an insurer to charge a particular rate level

3. if rates in a particular market are producing an excessive rate of return for insurers in total, then new entrants will drive the price down to the proper level

4. if rate levels are inadequate to produce an acceptable rate of return in total, then insurers will exit from the market until price levels increase to the acceptable level, leading to temporary insurance availability problems

5. analysis of the difference in rate levels in prior approval and open competition states indicates that there are no significant differences in profitability over any extended time, although regulatory lag does tend to generate lower profits under prior approval during periods of volatile inflation rates

Value of a Generally Accepted Insurance Pricing Model

The conclusion of these observations is that financial and insurance markets will work to produce the proper total rate of return for insurers, without the need for complicated formula adjustments. Although this may be true in the long run, the well known underwriting cycle (the consistent pattern of fluctuation between profitability and losses for underwriting results as depicted in Figures 8-1 and 8-2) indicates that severe market distortions are caused as the market moves toward the proper level. Exits and entry take time to affect prices. Thus, the slowness of market adjustments needs to be weighed against the inaccuracies of any rigid formula approach to insurance pricing problems.

Having a generally accepted insurance pricing model is not necessary for the insurance industry to function, just as stocks were traded for a long time before the CAPM arose to explain security returns. Tests of the validity of the CAPM for pricing financial assets are based on how well it explains historical returns for securities. Similarly, the usefulness of any insurance pricing model depends on how well it explains the prices actually charged. Using the model to determine regulated prices should be redundant if competitive forces are at play. If the model is correct, then it would not be necessary to force insurers to charge the indicated price. This restriction would be similar to requiring investors to buy and sell securities at prices determined by a theoretical model and not allowing the market to establish prices independently. The model rests on being able to explain prices, and not on prices being set by the model.

However, having a generally accepted insurance pricing model would be a substantial benefit. Although prices should move toward the proper level in the long run, a usable model would assist insurers to price more accurately in the short run as well. This increase in pricing accuracy would not prevent insurers from periodically undercharging or overcharging the indicated price, and thus would not eliminate the underwriting cycle. Nevertheless, a generally accepted pricing model would allow insurers to determine the appropriate price level and might reduce the degree of fluctuations in results.

References

The references listed below expand on topics covered in this chapter. Not all of these references are cited in the text.

Best, A. M. Company. *Best's Aggregates and Averages.* Oldwick, NJ: A. M. Best Company, various years.

Cummins, J. David, and Chang, Lena. 1983. An analysis of the New Jersey formula for including investment income in property-liability insurance ratemaking. *Journal of Insurance Regulation* 1:555-573.

Cummins, J. David, and Harrington, Scott A., eds. 1987. *Fair rate of return in property-liability insurance.* Boston: Kluwer Nijhoff.

Cummins, J. David, and Harrington, Scott A., 1985. Property-liability insurance rate regulation: estimation of underwriting betas using quarterly profit data. *Journal of Risk and Insurance* 52:16-43.

D'Arcy, Stephen P. 1984. Duration-discussion. *PCAS* 71:8-25.

D'Arcy, Stephen P., and Doherty, Neil A. 1988. *The financial theory of pricing property-liability insurance contracts.* Homewood, IL: Richard D. Irwin.

Ferguson, Ronald E. 1983. Duration. *PCAS* 70:265-288.

Ferrari, J. Robert. 1968. The relationship on underwriting, investment, leverage, and exposure to total return on owners' equity. *PCAS* 55:295-302.

Gleeson, Owen, and Lenrow, Gerald I. An analysis of the impact of the Tax Reform Act on the property/casualty industry. DPP 1987, 119-190.

Harrington, Scott A. 1984. The impact of rate regulation on prices and underwriting results in the property-liability insurance industry: a survey. *Journal of Risk and Insurance* 51:577-623.

Ibbotson, Roger G., and Sinquefeld, Rex A. 1987. *Stocks, Bonds, Bills and Inflation* (SBBI) updated in *SBBI 1987 Yearbook.* Chicago: Ibbotson.

Lehmann, Steven G. Contingency margins in rate calculations. DPP 1985, 220-242.

Muller, Heinz H. 1987. Economic premium principles in insurance and the capital asset pricing model. *ASTIN Bulletin* 17:141-150.

Muller, Heinz H. 1988. Modern portfolio theory: some main results. *ASTIN Bulletin* 18:127-145.

National Association of Insurance Commissioners. 1970. Measurement of profitability and treatment of investment income in property and liability insurance. *Proceedings of the National Association of Insurance Commissioners* 2A:719-894.

National Association of Insurance Commissioners. 1984. Report of the investment income task force. *Proceedings of the National Association of Insurance Commissioners* 2:719-807.

Panning, William H. Asset/liability management: beyond interest rate risk. DPP 1987, 322-352.

Smith, Michael L., and Witt, Robert C. 1985. An economic analysis of retroactive liability insurance. *Journal of Risk and Insurance* 52:379-401.

Strain, Robert W. 1974. *Property-liability insurance accounting*. Santa Monica, CA: Merritt.

Turner, Andrew L. 1987. Insurance in an equilibrium asset-pricing model. Chapter 4 in Cummins and Harrington, 1987.

Van Horne, James C. 1978. *Financial market rates and flows.* Englewood Cliffs, N.J.: Prentice-Hall.

Webb, Bernard L. 1982. Investment income in insurance ratemaking. *Journal of Insurance Regulation* 1:46-76.

Woll, Richard G. Insurance profits: keeping score. DPP 1987, 446-533.

Chapter 9
SPECIAL ISSUES
by Stephen P. D'Arcy

The job of a casualty actuary goes beyond the confines of setting rates and reserves, establishing classification plans, developing reinsurance contracts, applying credibility theory, and analyzing investment returns. The casualty actuary is regarded as the resident mathematician in an industry that is dependent on numbers. As such, the casualty actuary becomes involved in a myriad of other projects and concerns within the insurance industry. A textbook on Casualty Actuarial Science would not be complete without mentioning some of these additional areas.

In this chapter, the topics of measurement, allocation, and uses of surplus; insurer solvency issues, risk theory, planning and forecasting, and data sources are covered. Inclusion of material on these topics, though, presents somewhat of a dilemma. Each of these topics is quite involved and could take an entire chapter, or even a book, to cover adequately. However, these topics are considered to be of secondary importance in an introduction to casualty actuarial science, compared to the material covered in prior chapters. Therefore, in view of space constraints, these topics must be covered concisely.

The purpose of these sections should be viewed as akin to a taste spoon at your favorite ice cream parlor. In no way should this material be considered adequate to satisfy the need for knowledge of a given topic. Instead, the intention is to whet your appetite for more information about these diverse and important areas, perhaps laying out a framework for these topics that can later be filled in by additional study.

Measurement, Allocation, and Uses of Surplus

The statutory surplus of an insurer is the difference between statutory assets and liabilities. Surplus represents the owners'(stockholders for a stock insurer, policyholders for a mutual or reciprocal) interest in the company and the cushion on which the insurer can rely in adverse situations. An insurer would be considered bankrupt if surplus were negative. Great reliance is placed on the surplus for regulatory purposes. Licensing requirements establish minimum levels of surplus for writing certain lines of business. Premium to surplus ratios are often monitored as an indication of insurer solvency. Regulatory tests establish a net written premium to surplus ratio of three to one as acceptable. These levels are applied on a company basis. Industry wide levels of premium to surplus ratios also fluctuate markedly as equity values and market conditions vary. Figure 9-1 illustrates the stock property liability insurance industry aggregate values of the premium to surplus ratio for the period 1927 through 1987. These values are not consolidated to eliminate double counting of some assets for corporate groups. Consolidated figures have been determined only recently.

FIGURE 9-1
Premium To Surplus Ratio

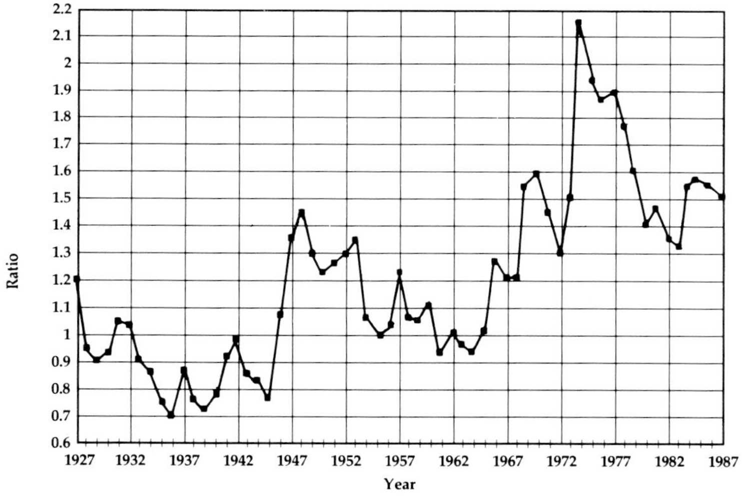

Source: Best's Aggregates & Averages (P/C) 1988, 1977, 1968.

Surplus serves as the margin of error for an insurer. Surplus is available to absorb losses generated by inadequate pricing, to offset inadequate loss reserving, or to cover investment losses. If an insurer did not have any surplus, then it would be bankrupt if anything went wrong in its financial statement. Because of the future financial commitments involved in insurance, surplus plays an important role in assuring customers that the commitments can be fulfilled.

The degree of reliance placed on the surplus measure is remarkable, given the widely recognized distortions in the statutory surplus value. The unearned premium reserve is universally recognized as being redundant as it is calculated based on the entire written premium and most expenses are incurred at the inception of the policy term. Loss reserves are supposed to be set at the undiscounted value of future payments, ignoring the time value of money. However, the Tax Reform Act of 1986, with its discounting of loss reserve provision, is contributing to an increasing awareness that the statutory loss and loss adjustment expense reserve may be excessive on a true economic valuation basis. The strongest argument in favor of overlooking these distortions is that statutory insurance accounting is meant to be conservative, and these conventions impart a safety margin to regulatory considerations. However, a safety margin could be included directly, if one were needed, without reliance on inaccurate and inconsistent measurements. The current procedure imposes a safety margin that changes from one valuation period to another as loss ratios and interest rates vary.

Two additional inaccuracies in the measurement of surplus do not necessarily have the redeeming value of being conservative. The tax liability of an insurer on unrealized gains in equities (as well as the tax benefit from unrealized losses) is ignored in the surplus measure. The market value of equities is included in surplus. However, any difference between the current market price and the purchase price of equities will be taxable when the gain (or loss) is realized. Although the tax liability is in exact, as prices may continue to fluctuate prior to the realization of the gain (or loss), and the timing of the tax liability is unknown, failure to consider this liability distorts the statutory surplus measure and, in rising equity markets, overstates surplus.

The final distortion in statutory surplus is ignoring differences between book value of certain assets and their actual market value, as discussed in Chapter 8. The largest impact is the treatment of bonds, which are valued at amortized value in the determination of statutory surplus. The amortized value of bonds is the initial purchase price plus or minus the amortization of any discount or premium at the time of the purchase. The amortization occurs over the period between the purchase date and the maturity date of the issue. A bond purchased at par value would continue to be listed at that value as long as the bond was held, regardless of fluctuations in interest rates. A bond purchased at a discount from the maturity value would increase in book value each year as the maturity date approached. Market values of bonds move inversely with interest rates. As interest rates rise, which was the common occurrence from the 1950s through the mid 1970s, outstanding bonds decline in value. These declines were not recognized by statutory accounting conventions as long as the insurer did not sell the bonds. This distortion led to the unintended situation that GEICO, in the early 1970s, could not sell municipal bonds to reinvest in taxable issues, despite the higher after tax income that this would have produced, because the use of overstated amortized values on its bonds was providing surplus that would have disappeared if the bonds were sold.

The use of amortized rather than market values for bonds can either increase or decrease surplus, depending on the movement of interest rates. Most other statutory book value conventions reduce statutory surplus. Reinsurance with nonadmitted reinsurers (reinsurers that have not been licensed to do business in a particular state or province) is excluded from book values. Real estate is valued at the original purchase price less depreciation, unless market value is lower. Agents' balances over three months due are not admitted as assets for statutory purposes. Equipment, furniture and supplies (other than computers) are also not admitted. Salvage and subrogation recoveries that are expected but not yet received are not included as an asset. Any asset that is not specifically allowed by regulatory authorities is considered a nonadmitted asset and, as such, excluded from the statutory book value determination.

In addition to the distortions in the value of surplus generated by statutory accounting, other anomalies exist with use of premium to surplus ratios as regulatory tools. A company with a lower expense ratio will have a lower premium to surplus ratio than a similar insurer with a higher expense ratio writing the same volume of expected losses supported by the same surplus. If an insurer raises rates and writes the same number of policies at the new rates, the premium to surplus ratio increases; this insurer is considered more risky even though rate levels are now higher. A potential solution to both of these problems is to substitute incurred losses for written premium when determining allowable levels of insurance writings. However, incurred losses are affected by loss reserve adequacy, which varies among insurers. As with the case of rate increases, reserve strengthening improves an insurer's true financial position, but causes the ratio of premiums to losses to appear less favorable. Another suggestion has been to monitor the premium to liabilities ratio, in a way similar to the approach for life insurance regulation. This ratio would have the same drawback as incurred losses, in regard to reserve strengthening.

Allocation of Surplus

The surplus calculation described above determines the total surplus for an insurer. Some ratemaking techniques require surplus to be allocated to individual lines or coverages, whereas other techniques require the investment income earned by an insurer to be allocated to individual lines of business and to the surplus. The primary reason for allocating surplus or investment income is to make accurate pricing decisions. No consensus exists about the proper allocation of either item.

The Insurance Expense Exhibit includes an allocation of investment income to each line of business and to surplus. Only the net investment income earned is allocated, and this value excludes capital gains, whether realized or not. The net investment income earned on all investments except equities is allocated to individual lines of business, based on the share of investable assets generated by the line of business. Investable assets are the funds the insurer has available to invest. In addition to policyholders' surplus, these funds include the cash that is charged, collected, and then available for investment until required to pay expenses, losses, or dividends. This continual cash flow process is frequently approximated by calculating the mean unearned premium reserves reduced by prepaid expenses and the mean loss and loss adjustment expense reserves. All net investment income earned not allocated to individual lines of business, including the dividend income from equities, is assigned to surplus.

Another reason for allocating surplus to individual lines of business is to enable an insurer to apply a discounted cash flow analysis to determine the rate of return on a given book of business. Discounted cash flow analysis includes surplus as a cash flow, first being invested by the insurer and later flowing back to the insurer. In order to accomplish this calculation, the surplus contribution must be determined and the length of time it must be invested must be calculated. The amount of surplus required can be determined by use of a rule of thumb about premium to surplus—ratios it can be a prorata allocation of the insurer's surplus to all lines of insurance equally or it can be based on a study of surplus needs by line, based on volatility. Surplus needs based on volatility or riskiness will be less for the company as a whole than the sum of the surplus needs for the individual lines of business, because aggregate volatility is lower than the sum of individual lines' volatility as long as the lines are not perfectly correlated.

The timing of the surplus flows back to the insurer also presents a choice. Traditional uses of the premium to surplus ratio imply that once the premium is written or the losses incurred, the surplus is no longer needed to be allocated to that line. However, if the surplus is viewed as a margin of safety for underpricing or under reserving, then some surplus should be allocated to the line of business until all losses are paid. One alternative discounted cash flow model maintains a constant loss reserve to surplus ratio until all losses are settled.

An alternative surplus allocation is proportional to the total marginal profit of a particular line of business. This allocation approach is based on classical micro economic theory. Another alternative allocation of surplus is determined by subjectively equating the riskiness of individual lines of business to each other by varying the premium to surplus ratios to equate the expected return on equity of the less volatile lines with that of the more volatile lines.

Paul Kneuer (1987) has analyzed the methods and considerations in allocating surplus to individual dimensions of insurer operations. The dimensions include type of risk or peril, branch office or producer, and geographic or temporal characteristics. Based on the practical considerations raised in an allocation of surplus, none of the current allocation methods completely achieves the goals of surplus allocation.

Insurer Solvency Issues

One of the primary objectives of insurance regulation is to assure the solvency of insurers. The future nature of the financial commitment made by the insurer in exchange for the policy premium creates a concern on the part of the insured that the insurer remain solvent in order to fulfill its part of the obligation. In this regard, insurers are similar to banks. Also, the knowledge that both banks and insurers are unlikely to become insolvent and that the consumer would be protected from financial loss in the case of an insolvency increases the likelihood of a consumer using the services of a bank or an insurer. Thus, regulation can increase the demand for insurance, just as banking regulation increases the demand for banking services. In this section, several approaches to monitoring insurance solvency are presented, with an additional section describing how consumers are protected when an insolvency does occur.

NAIC Early Warning Tests

In 1973 the National Association of Insurance Commissioners (NAIC) developed an Early Warning Test program designed to detect solvency problems soon enough to prevent insolvency or at least to mitigate the damages caused by insolvency. A series of eleven tests were performed on the annual statement data of insurers. Usual values for the results of each test were determined and companies whose results were outside the usual range were indicated as having unusual values for a particular test. Any insurer with unusual values for four or more tests was indicated to be a priority company and regulators were encouraged to give special attention to this insurer. The objective of the program was to assist regulators in selecting and rank ordering those insurers which require further analysis by drawing attention to the approximately 15% of insurers which have the greatest financial problems.

The eleven tests included in the program are listed in Table 9-2 along with the initial usual values for the results. Each year the usual values can be adjusted to reflect current conditions in the insurance and investment markets.

Table 9-2

NAIC Early Warning Tests

Number	Test	Usual Value
1	Premium To Surplus	Less than 300%
2	Change in Writings	Between + and − 33%
3	Surplus Aid to Surplus	Less than 25%
4	Two-Year Operating Ratio*	Less than 100%
5	Investment Yield	Greater than 5.0%
6	Change in Surplus	Between − 10 and + 50%
7	Liabilities to Liquid Assets	Less than 105%
8	Agents' Balances to Surplus	Less than 40%
9	One-Year Reserve Development To Surplus	Less than 25%
10	Two-Year Reserve Development to Surplus	Less than 25%
11	Estimated Current Reserve Deficiency to Surplus	Less than 25%

* This test has shifted from a five-year operating ratio to a two-year adjusted underwriting ratio (including dividends), and then to a two-year operating ratio.

The NAIC Early Warning Tests were first applied to the 1972 Annual Statement data. The results were provided to the state insurance commissioners approximately six months after the end of the year. In addition to the time lag in compiling results, several other problems exist. Except in a few states, participation in the program is voluntary. Insurers that do not submit their Annual Statements to the NAIC for analysis are not rated. Insurers that realize they will be classified as priority companies can avoid that position by failing to submit data. Also, the analysis is performed on unaudited figures. Unintentional errors in Annual Statement data, as well as intentional misrepresentations, distort the results of the tests. The most crucial problem with the system is the documented failure to provide a valid early warning of potential insolvencies. A study by Thornton and Meador (1977) of eleven insolvencies of Texas insurers, subsequent to the development of the NAIC Early Warning system, found that only 20% of the insolvent insurers would have been classified as priority companies five years prior to insolvency, as opposed to an expected early warning classification rate of 82%. Three years prior to insolvency, 55% of the companies would have been given priority ratings, as opposed to an expected 82%. The Annual Statement data of the year prior to the insolvency did classify 91% of the insolvent companies as priority companies, but this information would not have been provided to the state insurance commissioners until six months into the year of insolvency, providing little, if any, time for corrective actions.

After implementing the Early Warning system, the NAIC combined the statistical analysis with an analytical phase conducted by financial examiners and termed the approach Insurance Regulatory Information System (IRIS). This two phase system is considered more discriminating than the initial statistical only program. Financial examiners can quickly determine if the priority rating assigned by the statistical phase is unjustified because of special circumstances. This review helps focus regulatory attention on those insurers in more dire financial condition.

The NAIC tried to resist attempts to make the results of the IRIS system public. In particular, insurance agents have requested access to the priority ratings in order to avoid placing business with insurers most at risk for insolvency. The NAIC feared that public disclosure of priority companies would hamper any attempts to work out the financial difficulties of these insurers. Subsequent to adverse court decisions, the NAIC has agreed to provide raw statistical data to organizations, but to keep the results of the rating system confidential.

Discriminant Analysis

The statistical tests of the IRIS system are termed univariate as they focus on one variable at a time in classifying an insurer. An insurer is classified as either passing or failing each test. The degree with which an insurer passed or failed a given test is not considered. An alternative classification system, termed multiple discriminant analysis, has been found to perform much better at predicting insolvency than a univariate model based on similar data. Multiple discriminant analysis considers the results of financial ratio calculations in combination with each other so that a slightly excessive ratio for one variable can be offset by very favorable results for another ratio. In a sense, the difference between univariate analysis and multiple discriminant analysis is akin to the difference between essay and multiple choice examinations. Discriminant analysis allows for, in effect, partial credit, whereas univariate analysis is all or nothing. In two studies by Pinches and Trieschmann multiple discriminant analysis was used to predict insurer insolvency (Pinches and Trieschmann 1974, Trieschmann and Pinches 1973). The six variables found most useful in this type of analysis were:

1. Agents' Balances/Total Assets
2. Stocks Cost/Stocks Market Value
3. Bonds Cost/Bonds Market Value
4. Expenses Paid/Net Written Premium
5. Loss and LAE Incurred/Earned Premium
6. Direct Written Premium/Surplus

Results of this analysis were to classify 49 of 52 sample insurers, of which 26 were known to have become insolvent, correctly. A more recent discriminant analysis test by Cather and Harrington (1989) demonstrated the importance of the magnitude of reinsurance assumed and ceded in solvency testing, given the greater risk inherent in reinsurance. Although further tests of discriminant analysis would be necessary, current indications are that multiple discriminant analysis would be an improvement over the current IRIS system.

Other Rating Systems

Although the NAIC does not make its final IRIS ratings public, the insurance consumer does have access to several insurance rating systems. A. M. Best Company has reported on the financial condition of property liability insurers since 1900. Standard and Poor's, Moody's, Druff and Phelps, Conning and Company, and Consumers Union also provide ratings of insurers. Standard and Poor's and Moody's provide ratings of insurers similar to the ratings provided for firms in general, but with specific attention to the characteristics of insurers. Druff and Phelps provide a rating of insurance company claims paying ability, which focuses on the likelihood of an insurer making timely payments of policyholder and contractual obligations. This rating is based on both quantitative factors relating to profitability, operating efficiency, and leverage, as well as qualitative factors based on economic fundamentals, competitive position, management capability, relationships with affiliates, and asset/liability management practices. The Best's ratings are widely cited and will be discussed in some detail.

The objective of Best's rating system is to evaluate each insurer's financial position relative to the rest of the industry and to predict its ability to fulfill its financial obligations. The ratings are based on quantitative and qualitative factors. The quantitative factors, which are published with the individual company reports, include profitability, leverage, and liquidity tests. The eight quantitative tests are:

Profitability

1. Combined Ratio
2. Net Operating Income/Net Earned Premium
3. Return/Prior Year's Surplus
   (total return from underwriting and investments after tax over initial surplus)

Leverage

4. Net Written Premium/Surplus
5. Net Leverage
   Net Written Premium to Surplus plus Net Liabilities (total liabilities less conditional reserves) to Surplus
6. Gross Leverage
   Net Leverage plus Ceded Reinsurance Leverage (reinsurance premiums ceded plus net ceded reinsurance balances for unpaid losses and unearned premiums recoverable plus ceded reinsurance balances payable over surplus)

Liquidity

7. Current Liquidity
   (cash and securities other than in affiliated companies and encumbrances on other properties over net liabilities plus ceded reinsurance balances payable)
8. Investment Leverage
   (impact of a 20% decline in common stock values plus the effect of a two percentage point rise in interest rates on the value of bonds, preferred stock and mortgage loans as a percent of surplus)

In addition to the financial tests, Best's provides a set of adjusted results that reflect the equity in the unearned premium reserve, present value of loss reserves, market values of bonds, preferred stock and mortgages and a review of conditional reserves. These adjustments in total currently tend to produce an adjusted surplus in excess of the statutory surplus, reducing the return on surplus and leverage ratios.

In addition to the quantitative analysis, Best's also considers several qualitative factors in arriving at the final rating of an insurer. The qualitative analysis, which is not published, covers the extent of the insurance company's reliance on reinsurance and the soundness of the reinsurers, the adequacy of unearned premium and loss reserves, the spread of risk, and the competence, experience, and integrity of management. The ratings awarded to insurers after consideration of the above factors range from A + (Superior) to C (Uncertain). (Or, for any one of ten reasons, a rating is not assigned.)

The Best's ratings are a useful tool for insurance purchasers in evaluating the financial strength of a particular insurer. The public disclosure of these ratings and the significance attached to the ratings serves as a control on insurance management. However, the ratings do not provide information about some important aspects of an insurance operation for the insurance consumer. For example, the competitiveness of rate levels, the promptness of claim payments, and the willingness of the company to resolve customer disputes are all important to the insurance consumer but not included in the rating system. Thus, the Best's rating is only one element in selecting an appropriate insurer.

Loss Reserve Statement of Opinion

The largest liability of property-liability insurers is the loss and loss adjustment expense reserve. Numerous retrospective studies of these reserves on an industry-wide basis and for individual companies indicate the inaccuracies of these values. Although notable exceptions occur, cyclical patterns of over and under reserving tend to occur, and the general effect is to understate the degree of volatility in the underwriting cycle.

In 1980 the Fire and Casualty Annual Statement Blank was revised to allow insurance commissioners the option of requiring insurers to include a loss reserve statement of opinion by a qualified loss reserve specialist. For the 1986 Annual Statements, 17 states required at least some insurers to provide opinions on loss reserves. The range of insurers required to provide opinions varied by state from Ohio, which applied the regulation to medical malpractice insurers only, to Florida, Hawaii, New Jersey, North Carolina, and Texas, which required opinions from all licensed insurers.

The primary issues associated with loss reserve statements of opinion are the classes of individuals allowed to provide opinions and whether independence should be required. In general, states allow wide latitude in qualifying loss reserve specialists, including actuaries, accountants, and others with experience in this area. Independence of the provider is also not required, so company employees can, if qualified, provide the necessary opinions, although this practice has been criticized by some industry observers.

The goal of loss reserve statements of opinion is, by requiring an individual to put his or her professional reputation on the line, to reduce the likelihood of an insurer's significantly understating its liabilities. Although the requirement is too new to have provided any statistical tests of the effect of this procedure on insurer insolvency, anecdotal evidence suggests that it is having a beneficial effect in at least some cases.

State Guaranty Funds

In the foregoing discussion, we have described some of the efforts involved in preventing insurer insolvencies. However, despite the attention given to this aspect of insurance regulation, some insurers do become insolvent. When this happens, policyholders may avoid some of the financial consequences of the insolvency if a state guaranty fund has been enacted.

State guaranty funds exist to pay the claims of insolvent insurers so that policyholders do not suffer a financial loss when an insurer becomes insolvent. All states, except New York, have a post assessment funding provision under which all insurers are assessed a percentage of net direct premiums written in order to pay the claims of an insolvent insurer. New York has a pre-assessment plan under which funds are accumulated prior to any insolvencies by assessments on all insurers operating in the state. The pre-assessment plan works similarly to the post-assessment, except the added political problem of diversion of accumulated assets exists in New York. In 1982, $87 million of guaranty funds were appropriated for other purposes by the New York legislature. At the time, insurers filed suit to prevent such a diversion of guaranty funds, but the Court of Appeals, the state's highest court, ruled in 1985 that insurers were not being hurt by this diversion. No insolvency assessments were being made, the court noted, as the fund was above the $150 million level that triggered resumption of assessments. When the fund fell below this level in 1988, assessments were resumed and the suit was again brought by the industry. As of mid 1989, the issue had not been resolved.

Insurance guaranty funds operate on a state basis and are intended to cover residents of the particular state or property permanently located within the state. Numerous variations exist in the individual state statutes, but the general guidelines included in the NAIC Post-Assessment Property and Liability Insurance Guaranty Association Model Act of 1969 provide a measure of similarity among the state statutes. Under the Model Act, provision for the guaranty fund is dormant until an insolvency occurs and then a not-for-profit association is established to collect assessments from insurers in proportion to premium writings in the state and to pay the claims as they occur, subject to the availability of funds. The maximum allowable assessments on an insurer in a given year range from 1 to 2% of premium. Most states segregate workers' compensation and automobile insurance from other covered lines in determining assessments. The funds generally pay claims subject to a deductible and a maximum limit. Deductibles range from zero to $200 and limits range from $50,000 to $1,000,000. Most states include unearned premium as an allowable claim.

The effect of post-assessment guaranty funds is to force the surviving insurers to fulfill the obligations of an insolvent competitor. Concern about the domino effect of one insolvency on a marginal, but solvent, insurer has been raised, but not resolved. A current concern about insolvency funds is the inclusion of medical malpractice insurance. Most medical malpractice insurance is now written by health care provider controlled insurers. In many cases, physicians are determining the prices to be charged for this coverage with the knowledge that the state guaranty funds will pay claims if the organization becomes insolvent. The lengthy payout pattern on malpractice claims produces a potential major solvency problem. The danger exists that the premiums charged by a malpractice carrier could prove inadequate. In the short run, this would benefit the providers of medical care by allowing them lower insurance costs. If the insurer later becomes insolvent, however, then insurers in other lines of business will be assessed for any shortages, and these assessments will be passed on to their insureds. Thus, general insurance consumers could, in the future, pay more for insurance to subsidize lower insurance costs for medical providers now. This link through the guaranty fund system indicates the general concern over the pricing practices of provider-owned insurance carriers.

Risk Theory

Risk theory uses mathematical models to quantify uncertainty. A primary application of risk theory has been to the insurance industry, but developments in this area can be extended to any enterprise dealing with risk and uncertainty. Risk theory is part of the mathematical subject of stochastic processes that has been applied in the physical sciences and finance as well as in insurance.

Typical applications of risk theory assume that loss frequency and loss severity follow standard statistical distributions, allowing calculations of insurance prices, ruin probabilities, and credibilities. Such families of distributions as the binomial, Poisson, negative binomial, geometric, lognormal, Pareto, Burr, generalized Pareto, gamma, transformed gamma, loggamma, and Weibull have been used to model insurance losses and arrive at specific risk loadings. As the mean, variance, moment-generating functions, and derivatives of these distributions can generally be calculated, quantifiable results can be obtained.

The two main areas of application of risk theory have been in ratemaking and in assessing financial solvency. In ratemaking the use of risk theory allows mathematical determination of an appropriate risk loading. In solvency considerations, risk theory leads to measurement of ruin probability based on particular premium writings and surplus positions. Confidence intervals, which indicate the likelihood that actual outcomes will fall within specified limits, can be determined from the statistical properties of the distributions included in the model.

Insurance ratemaking historically has involved use of the expected value for losses, ignoring the variability around the mean value. Often, a selected underwriting profit margin is applied to all lines or coverages without consideration of the degree of volatility of a given coverage. In this situation, an insurer would include the same profit loading for lines that have very predictable loss patterns due to the high frequency, low severity nature of losses as it would for a much harder to predict line that has low frequency but high severity, if the expected losses for the two lines were equal. Use of risk theory to model these two lines would entail using a distribution with a higher variance for the more volatile line. In choosing a rate level that would be adequate to cover losses a specified percentage of the time (eg: 75 or 95%), the risk loading in the more volatile line would be higher, reflecting the greater variability of the distribution.

Typical applications of risk theory to ratemaking focus on the total variability of the aggregate loss distribution. The larger the variability, the higher the risk loading necessary in rates or the greater probability of ruin derived in solvency testing. A different view of risk is taken in the area of financial economics. Financial economic theories, including the Capital Asset Pricing Model and the Arbitrage Pricing Model, propose that only nondiversifiable risk should be priced in an insurance contract. Nondiversifiable risk is, in a sense, similar to the process risk described in actuarial literature. Process risk is the risk inherent in the model, as opposed to parameter risk, which is the risk or error in establishing parameter values. Diversifiable risk, although contributing to the total variability of losses (underwriting and investment income combined), is considered irrelevant for the owner of the insurance company, as this risk is offset by other investments in the owner's investment portfolio. Additional research that seeks to resolve these divergent views is required.

Another risk theory topic is utility theory. In utility theory, levels of satisfaction or utility are established to correspond with various possible outcomes. As individuals, and perhaps corporations as well, are not necessarily twice as satisfied with twice as much money, mathematical functions are assumed to describe the intangible satisfaction levels of the decision-maker. The shape of the describing function corresponds with the individual's or entity's attitude toward risk. A risk neutral decision-maker would have a utility function that is linear. A risk averse one would have a utility function that increased at progressively lower rates, or a negative second derivative. A decision-maker who favored risk would have a utility function that increased at progressively faster rates, or a positive second derivative. But many individuals both gamble, which is characteristic of a risk-seeker, and insure, which is characteristic of a risk averse entity. Therefore, actual utility functions are likely to be more complex than a simple curve with a consistently signed second derivative. Utility theory attempts to approximate the actual satisfaction levels of various outcomes to indicate the optimal strategies to follow in risky situations. This area of research has produced recommendations as to the optimal insurance policies to purchase, including deductibles and policy limits, and when to self-insure risks.

Another aspect of risk theory is termed the theory of games. Game theory contemplates the involvement of more than one player, each with a set of strategies. The payoffs of the game are dependent on the intersection of the strategies chosen by the players. Each player selects a strategy and the resulting payoff is determined by the selected strategy in combination with the strategies chosen by the other players. Each person attempts to maximize the utility of his or her own payoffs, but, since the player cannot mandate the choices of the remaining players, the optimal strategy often involves anticipating the choices of others, negotiating the individual selection of strategies, or randomly selecting a strategy to prevent opponents from correctly anticipating one's own selection.

Two branches of risk theory have evolved: individual and collective. Individual risk theory analyzes individual insurance policies to measure the likelihood that losses will exceed premium income. Total company operations are determined by summing the results on individual policies. Collective risk theory disregards individual policies and instead addresses the total gain or loss of the company on the entire book of business.

Illustration of Risk Theory

One illustration of risk theory is included in Chapter 6 of this text, where the Pareto distribution is used to describe reinsurance losses. Another example is illustrated here. An actuary has information about the loss frequency distribution for a book of business as follows:

Number of Claims During Year	Number of Policyholders
0	15,100
1	20,708
2	13,182
3	5,727
4	1,685
5	323
6 +	0

Based on this data, the 56,725 policyholders generated a total of 72,608 claims during the year. If the actuary wanted to know the likelihood of an individual policyholder having three claims in a year, then one method of determining an answer would be to divide the number of policyholders with three claims by the total number of policyholders, or 10.1% (5,727/56,725). Based on this approach, there would be no chance of a policyholder having six or more claims in a year. However, if the data could be fitted to a mathematical function under the assumption that the historical data represent a random sample drawn from a distribution, then perhaps more accurate answers to questions about the chance of a given number of claims could be determined.

One very common function used to fit loss frequency distributions is the Poisson distribution. This function is:

$$Pr(k) = e^{-y}(y^k)/k!$$

where Pr = probability
k = number of claims per year
y = expected loss frequency

One of the attractive features of the Poisson distribution is that one parameter describes both the mean and the variance of the distribution. The closeness of fit of the Poisson distribution to the historical data can be checked, generally using the mean of the data set as the expected value for the Poisson distribution. Based on this approach, the value of y in the above example would be 1.28 (72,608/56,725). Comparing the fitted values with the actual data shows:

Number of Claims In One Year	Actual Number of Policyholders	Fitted Number of Policyholders
0	15,100	15,772
1	20,708	20,188
2	13,182	12,920
3	5,727	5,513
4	1,685	1,764
5	323	451
6 +	0	117

Based on the Poisson distribution, the likelihood of a policyholder having three claims would be 9.7% (5,513/56,725), as opposed to 10.1%, and of having six or more claims in a year would be 0.2% (117/56,725), as opposed to zero. In this regard, risk theory leads to slightly different answers than reliance on historical data. As to which is more accurate, that depends on the accuracy of the model used describe claim frequency.

Examples of Risk Theory

Heckman and Meyers (1983) apply collective risk theory to describe an algorithm that calculates the cumulative probabilities and excess pure premiums for a book of insurance policies. This technique, although mathematically complex, can be used to determined the pure premium for a policy with an aggregate limit, the pure premium for an aggregate stop-loss policy and the risk loading for a multi-line retrospective rating plan.

Venezian (1981) develops a mathematical model of accident proneness that can be used to demonstrate that an upper bound of classification efficiency exists and is below 100% and that underwriting can serve to offset weaknesses in any classification system. In his model, two types of drivers exist with different accident propensities. Young drivers all initially have a higher loss likelihood, but randomly switch to the lower likelihood category over time. Drivers also can randomly shift from low loss likelihood to the higher category. The constant state of flux in classification, modeled to approximate empirical data, creates the classification problem and allows measurement of classification error.

Hayne (1985) applies risk theory to loss reserving by analyzing the variability of age-to-age and age-to-ultimate loss development patterns. The lognormal distribution is fitted to empirical data. Use of this model provides projections of loss development factors to aid in the standard loss reserving problems facing actuaries. In addition, this model allows the determination of estimates of statistical variability of loss reserves, which are difficult to determine using the current reliance on empirical data.

Dionne and Vanasse (1988) compare a Poisson distribution with a negative binomial distribution to see which provides the closer fit to a sample of automobile insurance experience from Quebec. The negative binomial is shown to be a better fit for this sample

Planning and Forecasting

Planning and forecasting are two separate but interrelated functions. Planning is a multi-step process involving establishing objectives, identifying alternative courses of action, establishing assumptions to evaluate the alternative courses of action, implementing a plan, and monitoring the outcome of the plan. Forecasting is the projection of the consequences of a particular course of action or the maintenance of the status quo. Actuarial involvement in the forecasting process is generally invited in order to determine the financial consequences of a set of contingencies. Planning relies on forecasting to evaluate the financial outcomes for potential courses of action. Forecasting of the likely results of the current course of action often inspires planning to avert the shoals sighted dead ahead.

The planning process can be subdivided into financial planning and operational planning. Lowe (1985) describes the centerpiece of financial planning as a financial forecast of operating results over the next one to five years and indicates that this process is currently done by most major property-liability insurers. He defines operational planning as that done by divisions within an insurance company that seek to accomplish area objectives.

Insurers, just like other business enterprises, need to use planning and forecasting in order to improve the decision making process. If operational changes are necessary, any enterprise has more alternatives and more leeway if the time horizon for implementing the decision is farther away. Finding out about problems too late provides for little choice in decision-making. If these situations are foreseen, then management has time to consider the alternatives and make the most appropriate choice. Thus, the first step in the planning and forecasting process is the financial forecast described by Lowe. The key elements of this forecast are generally direct and net premiums, both written and earned; underwriting expenses, incurred and paid losses and loss adjustment expenses, dividends, investment income and surplus on a total company basis, and often subdivisions of this information, where appropriate, based on lines of business and geographic areas.

The next step in the process is often to ask "What if?"questions. What would happen if we cut rates to write more business? What would happen if we pulled out of a particular market? What would happen if we changed our underwriting rules? Depending on the answers to these questions, a new course of action may be implemented.

Actuaries, as the recognized resource within the insurer for quantifying future financial contingencies, are usually involved in the planning and forecasting process. In some companies, the actuarial department has the on going responsibility for developing long-range forecasts. The actuary projects trends from available data, makes educated guesses about future developments, and calculates the resulting financial situation of the insurer.

A more comprehensive planning and forecasting process would include representatives from all affected divisions within an insurance company, including the actuarial department. Management would be responsible for establishing corporate objectives, which could range from maximizing profits over a certain period to attaining or retaining target market share values or achieving a particular rating from Best's. Marketing, underwriting, claims, accounting, data processing, and other operating divisions within the company would be included in developing and implementing the plan. The actuary would at the very least provide information about rate adequacy and reserve development, and may be the one responsible for quantifying the financial results of the alternative courses of action. Some insurers maintain corporate planning departments that regularly produce plans for various aspects of the company's operations. Alternatively, a resource person familiar with the planning process may be called upon to assist the individuals responsible for implementing the plan to devise the plan.

Common Problem Areas

The primary problem in planning and forecasting that appears consistently across firms is excessive reliance on the forecasted results and the effort expended in explaining why actual results differed from the forecast. A common defense against over reliance on forecasted results is to produce a number of forecasts illustrating potential outcomes. One notable application of this strategy is the set of four actuarial projections produced by the Social Security Administration: optimistic, intermediate, intermediate with optimistic economic assumptions, and pessimistic. In general the results can be expected to fall within the range of the various forecasts. A more mathematically valid procedure is to produce confidence intervals for the projected results based on the statistical properties of the distributions used in modeling the forecast. When producing such a forecast, the actuary should concentrate on the interval within which results should fall the selected percentage of the time and avoid use of the mathematical expression "expected value," which carries a different meaning for non-mathematicians. The problem of over reliance on forecasted results is generally only overcome when, after long experience with planning and forecasting, managers learn that the forecasted results are only estimates of future results and not inviolate goals.

Another common problem in planning and forecasting is to implement shifts in operations that were not contemplated by the plan. Such operational shifts could include negotiating a new reinsurance treaty, offering a new compensation package to producers, implementing a new claims payment procedure, expanding or curtailing operations in a given area or line, or any of a number of changes that could affect the company's financial position. The need for planning to be a continual process, constantly updated to include operational changes and revised assumptions, must be stressed to avoid this pitfall.

For actuaries, a major drawback of planning and forecasting is the tendency of forecasts to be "self-unfulfilling." This tendency expresses itself in the ratemaking process through input from the other divisions involved in establishing rate levels. If the forecasted results are favorable, then pressure to avoid or minimize rate increases develops. As the adequacy of the rate levels falls, the favorable results forecasted cannot be attained. Conversely, if the forecast is dire, then normal opposition to rate increases disappears and the rate levels adjust more quickly than would be expected. Thus, results are often better than the forecast. Projecting the psychological effects of a particular forecast on the internal operations of an insurer, and revising the forecast to reflect this feedback is rarely, if ever, done.

Forcasting Techniques

A large number of mathematical techniques are available for use in forecasting results. These techniques depend on the validity of past data to predict future results. Despite the apparent sophistication of these techniques, any change that affects the usefulness of historical data for predictive purposes negates the value of these techniques.

One common technique for fitting a time series model is termed simple linear regression. In this procedure, past data are used to fit the model:

1) $y_t = a + bx_t$

where y_t = observation of the dependent variable at time t

a = intercept

b = slope

x_t = observation of the independent variable at time t

The estimates of a and b are usually chosen to minimize the squared value of the difference between the actual and fitted data, which is called the least squares estimate.

Two special cases of simple linear regression are deserving of note. In some cases, the independent variable is simply the time period. In this case, $x_t = t$. Under the exponential trend model, the dependent variable is a function of an exponential expression:

2) $y_t = e^{a + bt}$

or $ln\, y_t = a + bt$

Multiple linear regression is similar to simple line regression, except that the dependent variable is assumed to be a function of more than one independent variable. A time series example of this model would be:

3) $y_t = a + bx_t + cw_t + dz_t$

where w, x and z are independent variables

b, c and d are unknown parameters

t is the time period

Again, the estimates of the parameters are generally chosen based on the least squares criteria. The validity of all regression models is dependent on the assumption that the observations of the independent variables are themselves independent of each other. For most time series, this assumption is violated. This technique also assumes that the errors from the model (the difference between actual and forecasted values) are normally distributed.

A time series could also be generated by a constant process that reflects a moving average. Such a model would be:

4) $x_t = a$

where a = mean of the last T observations

A moving average can also have a linear trend process such as:

5) $x_t = a + bt$

Under a process termed simple exponential smoothing, the dependent variable is assumed to be a function of one independent variable. The model could be similar to the moving average shown in equation (4), except that parameter is not chosen on the least squares basis but is selected to minimize the errors with a greater weight given to recent data. The weight assigned to each error term is k^{T-t} where T is the total number of observations used to project the dependent variable and k is a selected weighting factor between zero and one. The weights of the error terms decrease geometrically with the age of the data. Similar smoothing calculations can be made for linear trend processes and for multiple independent variables.

The most sophisticated class of forecasting models currently available is known as Box-Jenkins. Many computer statistical packages include this modeling process. The Box-Jenkins model is a three step iterative process in which a tentative model is identified through an analysis of the historical data, the unknown parameters are estimated, and then diagnostic tests are performed to determine the adequacy of the model. The class of models used in the Box-Jenkins procedure is termed autoregressive integrated moving average (ARIMA) and the process allows for any combination of these characteristics (autoregression and moving averages) to be included in the final model. Choice of the initial model is made after analyzing the autocorrelation and partial autocorrelation functions of the historical data.

The major drawbacks of the Box-Jenkins approach are the requirement of at least 50 historical observations, the need to completely refit the model periodically as no convenient way to update the parameters is available, and the time and expense involved in developing a Box-Jenkins model when the final forecast involves numerous individual time series variables.

Data Sources

Industry Data

The insurance industry generates massive volumes of information in the process of its operations. The entire business of insurance is dependent on the statistics generated by the insurance process. Although much of the data generated is kept confidential as it has proprietary value, the regulatory process requires the publication of a significant portion of insurance data. Much of this information is available for applications of actuarial problems. Also, other non-insurance information sources can be utilized by actuaries. The purpose of this section is to increase awareness of the available information that can be used to improve actuarial applications.

Annual Statement

The Annual Statement is the primary source of public information about insurers. This document is required to be filed with each state insurance department in which the insurer is licensed by March 1 of the subsequent year. The Annual Statement format is subject to periodic revision by the NAIC Blanks Committee, and thus the data included are subject to change. The exhibits included in the current Annual Statement are summarized in Table 9-3.

Table 9-3

Annual Statement Exhibits

Balance Sheet
- Assets by Type of Investment or Non-invested Category
- Liabilities, Surplus and Other Funds

Income Statement
- Underwriting and Investment Income Exhibit
- Analysis of Change in Capital and Surplus Account

Table 9-3 (continued)

Reconciliation of Funds Provided and Funds Applied
Investment Income by Type of Investment
Capital Gains and Losses by Type of Investment
Premiums Earned, In Force and Written by Line
Losses Paid and Incurred by Line
Unpaid Losses and Loss Adjustment Expense by Line
Expenses Paid by Category
Analysis of Admitted and Non-Admitted Assets by Type
Reconciliation of Ledger Assets
Premiums and Losses for the Particular State
Five-Year Historical Data on:
- Gross and Net Premium
- Underwriting, Investment and Net Income
- Selected Balance Sheet Items
- Allocation of Investments
- Gross and Net Paid Losses
- Operating Ratios
- One and Two Year Loss Development

Investments Owned, Acquired and Sold by Type
Investments Owned by Type and by Country
Maturity Distribution of Bond Investments
Ceded and Assumed Reinsurance
Analysis of Loss Development by Line
Premiums and Losses by State
Insurance Expense Exhibit
- Premiums, Losses, Expenses and Net Income by Line

Two very important Annual Statement exhibits for actuaries are Schedules O and P, which detail loss development for short and long-tailed lines, respectively. These schedules show the accuracy of prior years' loss and loss adjustment expense reserves and can be used to estimate current reserve adequacy.

A. M. Best, National Underwriter

A. M. Best collects and disseminates reams of statistical information on the insurance industry, with much of the data gleaned from Annual Statement data. Industry figures for premiums, expenses, losses, and investment income, including an aggregate Annual Statement, are contained in a publication titled *Best's Aggregates and Averages.* Experience in total, and by line, is shown for the industry and for stock, mutual, and reciprocal insurers. Each annual volume includes both the most recent data as well as historical data to facilitate long-term and trend analysis. This publication is generally the first source of analysis for comparative studies of industry performance.

Another A. M. Best publication is *Best's Insurance Reports,* which is a voluminous listing of detailed information on individual insurers. For each insurer, financial information is summarized, the history, management, operations, and reinsurance program are described, and the Best's Rating and comparative financial and operating exhibits displayed. The financial information shown for each insurer includes a summary of assets, liabilities, and surplus for the current and prior year and investment data.

In addition to published data, A. M. Best can provide databases in computer readable form on tape or diskette. This information is taken directly from the Annual Statement and provides the detail necessary to fully analyze each insurer. The user can obtain the data for the industry or for selected companies. The availability of this data enables the user to custom design any research.

The major competitor to A. M. Best in providing insurance information is the National Underwriter company, which publishes the *Argus FC&S Chart.* This more compact reference source provides information on the assets, liabilities, surplus, written and earned premiums, net income, investment income earned, underwriting gain or loss, premiums by line, and loss, expense and combined ratio, both for the current and prior year.

GAAP Financials

The Annual Statement, A. M. Best, and Argus data are all based on statutory financial data, except for the items displayed by Best's as adjusted in the rating analysis section. Statutory data does not necessarily represent the true financial position of the insurer. The use of amortized values for bonds and the lower of cost or market values for real estate, the unrecognized equity in the unearned premium reserve, the dismissal of non-admitted assets, and the failure to consider the present value of loss reserves all are among the distortions in statutory values. When financial statements are required to be produced by auditors for shareholders, adjustments to financial data are required by Generally Accepted Accounting Principles (GAAP). GAAP accounting recognizes the equity in the unearned premium reserve, the deferral of federal income taxes, salvage and subrogation recoverable, and some non-admitted assets.

Stockholder-owned insurers are required to file annual reports, Form 10Ks and other documents with the Securities and Exchange Commission (SEC), similarly to publicly held companies in other industries. These data are on a GAAP basis, as opposed to a statutory basis. In addition, companies with significant (as defined by the SEC) property-liability insurance operations are required to submit additional data and discussion.

SEC regulations require stockholder owned insurers to submit a Loss Reserve Disclosure report that displays historical loss development of the ten prior years' loss and loss adjustment expense reserves on a cumulative, rather than accident year, basis. Additional information required includes a three year reserve reconciliation and a historical summary of various balance sheet and income statement items, and discussions regarding the differences between GAAP and statutory loss reserves, loss reserve discounting, the effect of inflation on loss reserves, loss portfolio transfers and other significant reinsurance transactions, significant line of business mix changes, and significant adjustments to prior years'reserves.

Cooperative Industry Associations

The insurance industry has established a number of organizations that collect and disseminate information. Insurance Services Office, the primary statistical and advisory ratemaking organization of the industry, has been discussed in the earlier ratemaking chapters. In addition, organizations exist to combat insurance fraud by sharing information on suspicious claims and to promote automobile safety. For example, the Highway Loss Data Institute (HLDI) publishes crash statistics for each automobile model by year, for possible use in pricing automobile collision coverage. The Reinsurance Association of America (RAA) publishes reports of operating results for individual reinsurers and aggregate industry performance. The RAA also provides detailed size-of-loss reports to member companies for use in setting rate levels.

External Data

As the insurance industry shifts to a total rate of return pricing structure, investment data assume an increasingly important role in the actuarial functions of pricing, reserving, and forecasting. Current and projected rates of interest, inflation, and stock market returns are needed to incorporate into actuarial models.

Data on current interest rates are available from the Treasury Department, Moody's Investors Service, Standard & Poor's Corporation, and business publications such as the *Wall Street Journal.* Two useful compilations of aggregate data are Standard & Poor's *Trade and Security Statistics,* which is updated monthly, and the *Economic Report of the President,* published annually. Both references include historical as well as current values to facilitate trend analysis. Interest rate levels on short-, intermediate-, and long-term securities issued by the U.S. Government, states and municipalities, and corporations are included.

Government data may also be used for the underwriting, as opposed to investment income, component of insurance pricing. The Department of Labor and the Bureau of Labor Statistics also publish statistical information that may be useful in particular ratemaking situations.

Price level volatility has become an important aspect of insurance ratemaking, requiring consideration of general inflation rates in the pricing process. The Consumer Price Index, promulgated monthly by the Commerce Department, provides the most widely based inflation measure. Current and historical levels are published in Standard & Poor's *Trade and Security Statistics.* In recognition of the inadequacy of a general price index for insurance purposes, Norton Masterson developed a series of specific cost indices for insurance values, that was first published in 1968 in the *Proceedings of the Casualty Actuarial Society.* These indices are periodically updated in *Best's Insurance Management Reports.*

Investment results on stocks are both more variable than returns on bonds and more difficult to measure. The commonly reported barometer of the stock market, the Dow Jones Industrial Average (DJIA), is the arithmetic average of current prices of a portfolio of 30 individual issues. This is a price-weighted index, so changes in the levels of higher-priced stocks carry more weight than changes in lower-priced issues. The composition of the portfolio is also periodically revised to reflect shifts in the industrial sector. As a price index, it is not useful in measuring the total return on securities, which would include dividends.

A broader market index that is value- rather than price-weighted is the Standard & Poor's 500. This index includes 425 industrial stocks, 50 utilities, and 25 transportation securities. Although this index avoids some of the DJIA problems, it does not allow for a total rate of return measure. However, several publications compile dividend calculations for the securities included in the S&P 500 to allow such a calculation.

Numerous other market indices are available to reflect the investment performance of broader or more specialized issues. The Wilshire 5000 is the broadest based U.S. stock index, encompassing securities on the New York Stock Exchange, American Stock Exchange, and the OTC (which traditionally stood for Over The Counter) market. Stock indices for individual foreign countries are published, as is a composite world index, denominated both in local currencies and in dollars to account for currency fluctuations. Specialized indices including insurance, utilities, and banks are reported daily in business publications.

Commercial Forecasting Services

Current and historical values of financial and economic data are readily available, but actuarial calculations often require forecasted values of these items. Actuaries can either generate their own forecasts or utilize the services of an econometric service bureau. The business of selling economic data has developed over the last two decades, propelled by increasing computer power, enhanced mathematical tools, and increased economic volatility. The three basic services provided by econometric service bureaus are forecasts, data base access, and economic consultation. In this area, three firms dominate the industry—Chase Econometrics, Data Resources, Inc., and Wharton Econometrics—but numerous smaller and more specialized firms exist.

The specific econometric techniques used by the different service bureaus differ, but the overall operations are similar. All utilize government sources, supplemented by their own surveys, to compile the data base. The forecasting techniques all involve econometric models, judgement, time series analysis, and current data analysis. The number of equations used in the overall macro-economic model ranges from 455 to over 1000, and the number of variables forecasted ranges from 700 to 10,000. Each of the major firms provides monthly updates of the forecasts, which predict from two to ten years ahead. Each firm has made infamously inaccurate forecasts, but the overall track records of the forecasts are reasonably good. The specific costs of the forecasts depend on the extent of the services requested, but some major firms expend in excess of $100,000 per year for econometric forecasts.

References

The references listed below expand on topics covered in this chapter. Not all of these references are cited in the text.

Bass, Irene K, and Carr, Larry D, Corporate planning—an approach for an emerging company. DPP 1985, 5-24.

Beard, Robert E, Pentikainen, Teivo, and Pesonen, Erkki, 1984. *Risk theory: the stochastic basis of insurance.* London: Chapman and Hall.

Borch, Karl H, 1974. *The mathematical theory of insurance.* Lexington, Mass: Lexington Books.

Bühlmann, Hans, 1970. *Mathematical methods in risk theory.* New York: Springer-Verlag.

Cather, David, and Harrington, Scott, 1989. Incentive conflicts, excessive risk-taking, and default risk for property-liability insurance companies. Paper presented at the 1989 Risk Theory Seminar.

Dionne, Georges, and Vanasse, Charles., 1988. Automobile insurance ratemaking in the presence of asymmetrical information. University of Montreal, Center for Transportation Research, Publication Number 603.

Duncan, Michael P, 1984. An appraisal of property and casualty post-assessment guaranty funds. *Journal of Insurance Regulation* 2,289-303.

Gerber, Hans U, 1979. *An introduction to mathematical risk theory.* Homewood, Illinois: Richard D, Irwin.

Gillam, William R, 1985. Projections of surplus for underwriting strategy. DPP 1985, 140-171.

Hammond, J. D, 1968. *Essays in the theory of risk and insurance.* Glenview, Illinois: Scott Foresman.

Hayne, Roger M, 1985. An estimate of statistical variation in development factor methods. *PCAS* 72,25-43.

Heckman, Philip E, and Meyers, Glenn G, 1983. The calculation of aggregate loss distributions for claim severity and claim count distributions. *PCAS* 70,22-61.

Hogg, Robert V, and Klugman, Stuart A, 1984. *Loss distributions.* New York: John Wiley and Sons.

Jaeger, Richard M, and Wachter, Christopher J, An econometric model of private passenger liability underwriting results. DPP 1985, 195-219.

Kneuer, Paul J, Allocation of surplus for a multiline insurer. DPP 1987, 191-228.

Lowe, Stephen P, Pricing, planning and monitoring of results: an integrated view. DPP 1985, 268-286.

Masterson, Norton E, 1968. Economic factors in liability and property insurance claim costs. *PCAS* 55,61-89.

Migliaro, A, and Jain, C. L, editors. 1983. *An executive's guide to econometric forecasting.* Flushing, NY: Graceway Publishing Company.

Montgomery, Douglas C, and Johnson, Lynwood A, 1976. *Forecasting and time series analysis.* New York: McGraw-Hill.

O'Neil, Mary Lou, Applications of principles, philosophies and procedures of corporate planning to insurance companies. DPP 1985, 311-331.

On-Line Reports. 1986 property/casualty ratings completed. *Best's Review Property/Casualty Insurance Edition.* 87 (5),12, 117-118.

On-Line Reports. 1986. A compact view of 1985 property/casualty results. *Best's Review Property/Casualty Insurance Edition.* 87 (6),16, 142.

Pinches, George E, and Trieschmann, James S, 1974. The efficiency of alternative models for solvency surveillance in the insurance industry. *Journal of Risk and Insurance.* 41,563-578.

Seal, Hilary L, 1969. *Stochastic methods of a risk business.* New York: John Wiley and Sons.

Smith, Lee M, Actuarial aspects of financial reporting. DPP 1985, 343-424.

Snyder, Arthur, 1986. Best's ratings: a new look. *Best's Review Property/Casualty Insurance Edition.* 86 (12),14-16, 122-126.

Stewart, James D, Analysis of return on surplus under two approaches for including investment income in ratemaking. DPP 1979, 322-347.

Thornton, John H and Meador, Joseph W, 1977. Comments on the validity of the NAIC early warning system for predicting failures among property and liability insurance companies. *CPCU Annals* 30 (3),191-211.

Trieschmann, James S, and Pinches, George E, 1973. A multivariate model for predicting financially distressed property-liability insurers. *Journal of Risk and Insurance.* 40,327-338.

Venezian, Emilio, 1981. Good and bad drivers—a markov model of accident proneness. *PCAS* 68,65-85.

Index

Notes

Notes

Notes

Notes

Notes

Notes

Notes

Notes

Notes

Notes

Notes

Notes